The Tortured Soul Trilogy
Of Pain and Pleasure

The Edited Combined Works of Erotic Author C.J.Cassidy

Living La Vida Puta w/T. Oceanside
The Confessions of Jennifer X
A Tortured Soul – The Unauthorized Biography of Nicholas Anderson
And
The Seduction of C.J. Cassidy

"Everything below the line is fiction"

"Everything above the line is reality"

"Perception depends solely on what side of the line you happen to be focused on"
C.J. Cassidy

About The Author

C.J. Cassidy is a writer, poet and actor. He has written many screenplays, books and poems but none with any commercial success. His acting career was off to a flying halt. About ten years ago he interviewed a couple for a biography of their lives. That book was published as "*A Tortured Soul – The Unauthorized Biography of Nicholas Anderson*". The story introduced a femme fatale by the name of Jennifer X. Jones, who was reviled as being a cold conniving bitch. Further research into her life showed that she was more victim than villain. Those interviews called for a rebuttal biography to explain her involvement in their lives. The result was "*The Confessions of Jennifer X.*"

Both novels were met with rave reviews and now have a very devoted cult following. Some readers have even found the strength to free themselves from their own abusive relationships. The novels have found their way into the hands and hearts of a very diverse audience.

The following novel is based on actual events, as told to the writer, by the persons involved. However, all the names, dates, places and locations have been altered or changed to protect the privacy and anonymity of all the parties involved... especially Katherine.

Although this biography is the culmination of years of several interviews and private discussions, the writer has invoked using his poetic license in some of the story's transitions in certain chapters. Even with extensive interviews and research, there were some facts that were not easily obtained or verifiable. We tried to create a viable explanation to cover and bridge those gaps and make the story flow more smoothly. For the sake of brevity, some characters were merged into one person so as to eliminate any redundancy.

This biography is the combined edited works of my previous novels. The purpose was to give the first time reader of my work and my loyal fan base a chance to see the story from all persons involved in one novel.

As I wrote and re-edited this, I found myself constantly crying at my keyboard, sometimes for hours at a time. I understood and felt their heartache but I felt renewed and convicted by their ultimate triumph. The catharsis of writing the first two books helped me heal from my own wounds, and gave me the strength to publish my own memoirs, titled *"The Seduction of CJ Cassidy.* My final novel, *'Living La Vida Puta'* was written by Jennifer's friend Lady Latex. She wanted to tell her story in her own words and at Jennifer's insistence, I helped edit her notes; some of which where written on cocktail napkins. I just hope that by reading this novel, your demons can be exorcised as well.

These are our stories... in our own words... as told by author C.J. Cassidy.

Dedications

I, of course, dedicate this novel to Tobey, Katherine and Jennifer, but I must add a special dedication to Natalie, the Naughty Dancer. She has befriended me in a way very few women have. She opened up to me her own world of pain and heartache and she showed me that she is a survivor with a heart of gold. She put me to the task of being a better writer and rising to my true potential. I owe a lot to this amazing and beautiful young woman. I pray for her each and everyday. Mere words cannot express how much I love her!

This novel is also dedicated to the many amazing women that I have met on-line the past few years while promoting my novels. These are the women who have taken our experiences and learned from them and freed themselves from their own bonds of sexual abuse and domestic violence.

I consider them my daughters, my nieces, my sisters of survival... my greatest loves! Some of these women have now written their own novels of the tribulations that they have endured. Some of these women have garnered a voice to tell others that there is a way out and lead them to safety. These are women who have shown me love, in spite of all their personal pain and heartache. Some of these women opened their hearts to me and even had the courage to admonish me when I needed it the most. These are the women, who for their privacy and safety, I cannot name here, that have no idea how much I truly love them!

The Tortured Soul Trilogy
(Living La Vida Puta)
Chapter 1
(Homecoming Queen)

It was the day that everybody had marked on their calendars. It was the championship football game between the first and second ranked high school rivals. Two teams meeting on the gridiron. Two teams, two towns focused on one last game of the season. Legends would be made, hearts would be broken. That day was finally here. The stands were filled to capacity with parents, students and alumni. The bands played, the cheerleaders led the charge and the fans cheered as loud as they could for their side. Banners waved, faces were painted, mascots played and pandered to the crowd, it was without a doubt a day to go down in the annals of high school football history! This was a day, dreams were built on.

The game was as exciting as everyone expected it to be. The two teams fought for and defended every inch of the playing field. This was not going to be a runaway victory. Every touchdown was earned, hard! Each snap of the ball was a new adventure and a small victory on the field. Every hit was met with a spontaneous reaction. Every flag was met with boos from the crowd. It was as if, lives were on the line. It was if, the fate of the whole world was contingent on the outcome of this one game. The emotional level of the crowd was at an all time high and the players on the field gave all that they had to secure the win for their team.

It was the best game ever...

It all came down to the last quarter. The ball changed possession several times as the clock ticked away. Finally, the two minute warning sounded, the star quarterback quickly called a play and set up the offensive line. Only three points separated the two teams. This was to be the last play of the game. Go big or go home! Do... or die! Everything that they had trained for all season long was focused on one last play. The crowds in the stands got

6

louder and louder. The cheerleaders pulled out their best moves to motivate their team. The defensive line prepared like predators hungry for the game ball. The quarterback barked out the calls. The receivers were pumped full of adrenaline. The ball was snapped. The two teams collided with a loud resounding thud. Bodies hit the ground. The quarterback looked downfield for an open man. The quarterback scrambled around the defensive onslaught. The fullbacks held their ground and sacrificed their bodies to protect their quarterback. The quarterback reversed his direction. He was forced out of the pocket and his eyes quickly surveyed the playing field. There was an open man downfield. He threw just as a defensive tackle took him down hard. The crowd stood all at once to watch the ball in mid-flight. Half the crowd stood and prayed for the catch, the other half stood and prayed for the fumble. Both sides watched in awe as the football spiraled perfectly towards the wide receiver. They focused on the defensive end that was on him like white on rice. The ball came closer and closer. They had both passed the one yard line. They both leaped into the air at the same time. Twenty fingers clawed into the air, ten to catch, ten to block. Closer and closer the ball came down. Time seemed to slow down to a crawl as the crowd watched intently. An eerie hush formed and hovered over the stadium. No one dared breathe. Everything was now down to this last play. The referee fired the shot ending the game. The two men were now airborne in the end zone. This was it... the fate for two teams were in the hands of two lone players... literally! And then...

It doesn't matter what happened next. It doesn't matter who won the big game. I don't care which team was victorious and which went home in tears. I don't care which player was carried off on the teams' shoulders or which coach got a Gatorade shower. I don't care in which schools' trophy case the game ball resides. Or which player went to college on a full football scholarship. I don't care about what happened on the field that day at all... I only care about what happened under the football bleachers, later that night.

I was an average girl, in an average town, with average looks, making average grades. I wasn't good enough to make the cheerleading squad, or pretty enough to make the booster squad although I tried out for both. If you saw me in the hallway you would probably never notice me. Even my teachers had a hard time remembering who I was. I was virtually invisible and I kind of liked it that way. I drew no attention to myself and I quietly coasted through my young average life... My friends were few and far in between. As a matter of fact I wasn't invited to go anywhere, anytime. I was the girl who was an afterthought. The girl nobody knew existed. Until about two weeks ago...

He didn't play football; he wasn't a jock in any sense of the word. He just hung around the cool kids for no apparent reason. He was only slightly more popular than me. But he was kinda cute. I hadn't thought much of him and like I said, nobody ever thought much of me. So when he asked me out on a date. I was flattered... and amazed. He wanted to meet me under the football bleachers. He would meet me there on occasion and we would talk. We never went out to eat or a movie. I didn't mind, I liked his company. One day we kissed. It was nice. I liked it. He tried to touch me under my blouse and although I wanted him to, I wasn't ready. He would have to wait, so would I.

I didn't find it strange at all when he asked to meet me under the bleachers that night after the big game. The field was totally deserted. The grounds crew wouldn't clean up until tomorrow. The place was covered in confetti and cups and random trash. I got there and he was there, waiting for me. He had laid out a stadium blanket on the ground and he had a six pack of beer. Well, he had a six pack of beer left. He had obviously been drinking for a while. He patted the ground next to him and offered me a beer.

"No thanks! I don't drink..."

"Come on... don't be so stuck up... a beer will help loosen you up a bit... that's all."

He pulled one off the six-pack ring and opened it and pushed it at me as I sat down.

"I've had beer before... I just don't like the taste..."

He took a long drink of the beer and then he put it down. He kept offering me a drink. I took a sip to quiet him down. Okay... a sip... or two... After I had a few, he turned to me.

"Well... it's good for rinsing out your mouth after you had this...!" And he unzipped his pants and pulled out his dick. I had never seen a dick before. It kind of put me off. It looked so strange, kinda like a dead mouse...

"What? Don't tell me you're a virgin? You haven't touched one before?" he said in a near drunken stupor. He reached in my direction and took my hand. "Here... touch it!"

"I don't want to...!"

"Sure you do... all the girls want to touch it... they like it..."

He pulled my hand closer to his flaccid penis. "Stop! I don't want to! Stop it!" I begged. My meekness only served to egg him on. He held onto my wrist tighter and pulled my hand closer to him. I tried to close my hand but I couldn't. I didn't know why. I didn't want to make him angry at me. I touched his limp dick and it felt so strange. I can't explain it, but it felt weird in my hand but I wouldn't let it go.

"That's it... hold it and stroke it... just like that..." I did as I was told and it started to get bigger... not much bigger, but bigger and stiffer. I was fascinated by what I was doing. He continued to guide my hand up and down his shaft. I must say I kinda liked the feel of it now. He moaned and I let go. "Why did you stop?"

"I thought I was hurting you..." He shook his head and put my hand back on it. I continued to stroke him and watched the expression on his face. That's when he kissed me. I didn't like the smell of beer on him but I felt funny. My body was warm and... I don't know... fuzzy. I began to get into it. A feeling came over me I had never felt before... It didn't last long! He began to fondle and grope me. I tried to pull away. That's when I felt the sting of him slapping me. He hit me so hard he knocked my glasses off. I began to cry. It hurt, and it was insulting... not even my father slapped my face! Just when I thought I could muster up some courage, he slapped me again.

"Please don't hit me!" and I cried. That made him madder and he roughly grabbed me and slapped me again. He then grabbed the back of my head and pushed me down towards his penis. *"What did he want me to do...?"*

"Suck my dick... bitch!" And he pushed my head down on him.

"But...! Don't you pee out of that?" I said tearfully. That's when I felt him hitting me around my ears as he pulled my hair.

"I said suck my dick!" And he hit me again. "And don't try anything funny or I'll kick your fucking ass!" I cried because my ears were ringing from his slap and I put his dick in my mouth. I just wanted him to stop hitting me. I had no idea how to suck a dick so I made believe it was a blow pop and licked it. It was nasty. I don't think he washed. "Yeah! That's it you lying bitch! This aint your first time sucking a dick!" He pushed my head up and down on him. At one point I thought I was going to throw up. He heard me gag and slapped me again. I quickly learned what he wanted me to do. I did it... I hated it, but I did it. After a while he pulled me off him. I thought he was done. Little did I know; the party was just getting started! He held on to the back of my head and demanded I take off my panties. I refused. I tried to fight back, but I was scared. I didn't know what anyone would think if they found out what he made me do. He slapped me again and the tears rolled down my face. He pushed me down on the blanket. He reached under my skirt and ripped off my panties and stuffed them into my mouth. "That's to remind you to keep your mouth shut... or I'll tell everyone in school what a fucking cock sucking slut you are!" He held me by my throat and forcibly entered me. It hurt like hell. I was dry and scared but he didn't care. He just leaned back, spit on my vagina and tried again. Every time he pushed into me it hurt and burned. I was in so much pain but his weight held me down and my panties muffled my screams of pain and hurt. Then after seemed like an eternity he threw his head back and moaned.

10

"No! No! Dear GOD! NO!!!" I began to cry harder and the tears ran down my face. I felt an odd sensation and then I became sick to my stomach. He got off me a bit and I was able to roll over with my face to the ground. The ground smelled of beer and piss. I felt like I wanted to die, right there and then. Death would have been a relief... Just as I felt I was about to faint. I heard another man's voice from a short distance away.

"Hey, hey, hey! What do we have here?" Then I heard laughter come from a group coming towards us. Someone had stumbled upon this heinous crime upon my person. I didn't turn around. I didn't want anyone to see my face. *"A witness! Please! Please help me!"* I thought to myself...

"Hey guys! I was just getting a little victory pussy... you guys want a shot at it?" He said nonchalantly. There was a long silence.

"Sure! Why not...?" Someone in the group said. From behind, I felt a man's hand on my legs pulling my legs apart. I tried to keep my knees together. That's when I felt someone slap my naked ass... Mercifully, I passed out!

When I finally woke up, I felt totally numb except for a sharp pain in my privates that had just been made public. I was still on the ground in a fetal position, surrounded by empty beer cans and cigarette butts. I had no idea who else had raped me... or how many. I rolled over to see that the one who started this brutal invasion of my body, just sitting there, drinking a beer. I shivered and shook like a junkie. Did he want to rape me again? Was he going to kill me? Why was he still here? I looked up at him. He looked at me. He stood up, sipped his beer, reached into his pocket pulled out a couple of dollars and threw them at me. "For all your trouble..." He said. And he stumbled off into the night.

My blouse was open and my bra was gone. My skirt, panties and sweater was somewhere on the ground where they had been tossed. My breasts were cold and I shivered in the cool night air. My body felt... slimy and there was gobs of it all over me. On my chest, on my face, in my hair and it was between my legs. It was slimy and dirty and so was I. There was dirt and dead leaves in my hair and all over me. I had bite marks and hickies everywhere. There was a strange taste in my mouth. I tried to spit but I vomited violently. I saw half full beer can near me. I rinsed my mouth and spit again. He was wrong; it wasn't good for rinsing… afterwards. I felt and looked like hell. I got myself slowly together. I gathered up my clothes off the ground and I found my glasses about six feet away. Some one had stepped on them and broke them. I put them on as best as I could and I looked back at 'the scene of the crime'. All my young life I had dreamed of the night I would lose my virginity. Of the man who would sweep me off my feet and make me feel like a woman. The fairy tale wasn't supposed to look or feel any damn thing like this. I slowly made my way over to the girls' washroom on the other side of the field. The field lights were off but I felt like there was a spotlight on me. I imagined that the bleachers were filled to capacity as it was this afternoon and I was the focus of everyone's attention. I heard the laughing and jeering and cheering of the crowd. Then I heard a girl crying. That girl was me.

I walked in to the girls' bathroom and started to wash myself off. I took off whatever clothes I still had on except for my shoes and washed every inch of my body in that sink… I didn't want to see what I looked like in the mirror. I averted my eyes or closed them as I washed and washed. I rinsed out my mouth and threw up again. As I washed my vagina, I felt pain and when I pulled my hand away, I saw the blood. I almost fainted again. I continued to wash myself, over and over again. As hard as I tried, I just could not wash away what had happened to me. I could not wash away the vague yet painful memory. I must have looked like a sick, wet dog coming out of that bathroom. The night was chilly. I was wet, but I'm sure that wasn't the reason I was shaking uncontrollably as I walked back across the field to the exit. The two dollars he had left for me blew away with the leaves and the rest of the loose trash. The only evidence left was the dirty and beer stained stadium blanket which had flipped over in the breeze and was now wrapped around a pole under the bleachers. If was as if it too, was ashamed of what happened and wanted to hide. I turned around and took the long and lonely walk home, alone and ashamed. I don't know why, but I did not cry anymore… It didn't matter anymore! To this day, I don't remember that fuckers' name! And I never saw him ever again! He wasn't even from our town! He was a feral kid that roamed from town to town; everyone just thought he lived here!

The very next day, news of what happened the night before spread through the town like wildfire, just not my version of what happened. I got the education of a lifetime in that small town. Life is over for a 'whore' and a 'slut' in this town. Nobody wants to be your friend... nobody believes what you say happened or how you feel about it. Nobody believes the plain girl. The girl who tries too hard to fit in, the girl who was an outcast, the girl nobody remembers... oh fuck it! They just don't *want* to believe. The truth just gets in the way of a good story. Ha! Jennifer's friend Nicholas Anderson told me that some years later when we first met... But I'm getting ahead of myself.

So... there I am; a victim of a gang rape. I was disowned by my parents and the town, with no place to live, no place to go. No money for college... pregnant... Oh I'm sorry! Did I forget to mention that? Sometimes I forget myself... I didn't even know I was pregnant. I was living in a shelter, abandoned and I only had gotten my period a year or so ago, so I had no idea why it just went away. It just didn't concern me. I had other things on my mind. I found out the reason three or four months later. I didn't carry to term, one of those bastards gave me a STD... Without anyone to take me to a doctor, I never knew. I just hoped that it was my first one to give it to me, so the rest could share... By the time my counselor discovered my need to see a doctor and was able to find me a free clinic, it was too late for my child.

I don't like to think back about that day any more than the one that put me in this position in the first place. All I know is that there were too many adults talking at me, for me, around me but not with me. I didn't understand then what was the medical procedure the performed on me that day. All I knew is that afterwards... I wasn't pregnant anymore. Maybe I don't think about it on purpose. Not thinking about it works for me. The doctor said that the disease didn't affect my reproductive organs and I would able to have children normally. I don't fucking think so Doc! It'll be a cold day in hell before I let another man touch me ever again!

Oh, By the way, my name is Tobey Oceanside, but I now go by the name of Lady Latex, pleased to meet you!

The Tortured Soul Trilogy
(Living La Vida Puta)
Chapter 2
(Town Without Pity)

So? What kind of jobs are available for a 15 year old, high school drop out who's known in town as the Whore of Babylon? Not fucking much, I can tell you that. Not in this town anyway... I had no possessions, living in a shelter and no reason to stay here. So one day, I just started walking, anywhere had to be better than living here. I didn't even bother to pack a bag. I didn't want to bring anything with me that might remind me of this place or what happened to me here. I got to the edge of town and was about to travel down the nearest highway out of town. I guessed I could hitch a ride with someone, anyone, anywhere but here. As I got to the sign post that said "You are now leaving..." and the town's name, I took a rock, scratched out the name and scratched in the word 'HELL'. I dropped the rock and as I looked back, I saw someone I knew, standing there, with a suitcase on wheels. She had been following me since she saw me walk past her house. Somehow she knew I was leaving and never coming back to this shit hole!

"What do you want Cindy?" I said.

"I want to go with you..."

I shook my head. "Go back to your mommy and daddy..."

I started to walk down the road when I heard her say: "He raped me too!" No other words were said between us until we got into the next town. Funny, how 'family' comes together when you need them most!

God bless the 1970's, it was easy for two young girls to start a new life anywhere else. There were no terrorists, no heightened national alerts. It was a time in between the end of the hippie era and the birth of disco and you didn't need ten forms of ID to get work in a club or a bar. You just had to look like you belonged. Cindy and I looked like we belonged. Besides, young girls always showed up in the big city to make their fortune. It wasn't that uncommon. Fake ID's were easier to get than real ones and nobody questioned them. Cindy and I worked enough bars, one way or another, to get our own place to stay. She did the 'entertaining', I did the 'recruiting' and handled the financial arrangements. We were doing okay, until one day we decided to 'freelance' at a new club. The owner, Steven Callahan had us pegged the moment we walked in the door. He had his security team detain us in his office until after the club closed.

"You two can get me closed down... I don't want to see either of you in my club ever again..."

"Hey! I'm legal!" And I pulled out my fake driver's ID. He didn't even look at it.

"Open your mouth!" He said. The last time someone told me to open my mouth, they put something in there I didn't care for. "I said OPEN!" Cindy did as she was told relectantly and he looked in her mouth. He then turned to me.

"What am I? A horse...?" I said.

"I said open your mouth!" he repeated.

A woman came up behind me and said: "Do as he says... he's not going to hurt you!" I opened my mouth and he looked inside.

"You two are barely 17..." he surmised.

"How the hell do you know that?" I said.

"He can tell by your back teeth... your adult molars haven't come in yet!" she said. I stuck my finger in my mouth. Is she shitting me?

"Where are you two girls from?" he asked me.

"Nowhere... and we don't intend on going back!" I said.

He smiled at me. "You have quite an attitude... don't you?" I shrugged my shoulders. He turned to the woman behind me. "Ramona?"

"Yes Mr. Callahan?" the woman answered.

"See if there's any food in the kitchen and set up the back room for them to stay in...'

"We have a place to stay..." Cindy added.

"I'm sure it's no where near as nice as the back room... and a lot cheaper..." he answered back to her. He nodded at Ramona and she took us back there. He was right. What he called a back room was a palace compared to the shit hole we rented. The food wasn't bad either. Ramona pulled open a sofa bed and made our bed for us.

"So? How much rent is that guy gonna charge us?" I asked Ramona.

"I want to know what that guy is wanna take in trade!" Cindy said sarcastically.

"*Mr. Callahan*... isn't going to charge you anything to stay here..." She looked at us up and down and cut her eyes at Cindy. "You two young ladies have stumbled into an amazing opportunity..." As she closed the door behind us, she added. "Don't fuck it up!"

Damn! Just when I thought she was a real tight ass; she comes out all regular, but I got the hint. Respect Mr. Callahan and he would take care of us. Cindy wasn't too sure, but I had a good feeling about this. We hit the mother load, we just had to mind our manners and everything would be fine. The next morning, Ramona woke us up and had us straighten up the back room and then brought us breakfast. "If you're going to be staying here, this room must be kept clean at all times."

"Yes ma'am!" I said. Cindy was a bit put off with the way I kowtowed down to Ramona. She still didn't get it. Ramona sensed Cindy was eventually going to be a problem.

"After you've had breakfast, Mr. Callahan wishes to see you in his office..."

"Yes..." and I hesitated. "Um... What should I call you?"

"My name is Ramona Kirby, but you may call me Ramona... and your name?"

"My friends call me T.O."

"Doesn't that mean 'uncle'? Ramona asked.

"My name is Tobey... Tobey Oceanside, but I don't like to use that name so you can call me T.O. if you don't mind!"

"That's fine... Mr. Callahan will be in his office waiting... for you both..." And she left. She didn't even bother to ask Cindy her name; she really knew Cindy wasn't sticking around.

"Who does that bitch think she is?" Cindy asked after Ramona left.

"Obviously, she thinks, she's 'Ramona Kirby'... Why don't you show some respect?"

"What the fuck crawled up your ass? You getting all 'hoydie toydie' on me...? Why? Cause they gave you dinner, a place to stay and some pancakes?"

"Steak and potatoes, and a nice place to stay and besides when was the last time we even had breakfast?"

"Bitch please!" Cindy was not going to go with the program; at least I wanted to know what the program was! After we ate and I cleaned up, we went into Mr. Callahan's office and waited... and waited... and waited. Finally Cindy had enough. "I aint fucking waiting here any longer... I got shit to do! I'll meet you back at the room!" and she left. The moment the outer club door closed behind her, Mr. Callahan came in with a boy about my age.

"I'm so sorry for making you wait Ms. Oceanside... but I had to wait until your friend left... I think you understand..."

I nodded my head. "Yes Mr. Callahan... I do..."

He smiled at me. "This is my son Michael... he works here part time doing the clubs' books. I hope that someday he'll go to college and become a lawyer..."

"Pleased to meet you Michael..." and I shook his hand.

"I suppose that you and your friend wear the same size clothes?" Mr. Callahan asked.

"Yes... why?"

"I don't suppose that she can have your clothes?"

"I... guess!" and I shrugged my shoulders.

"Good... Miss Kirby is going to take you shopping today for new clothes... just make sure Michael here gets all the receipts..."

"Yes Mr. Callahan..." I answered.

"Tobey...?" and he hesitated. I got the feeling this wasn't a man who bit his tongue. He was trying to be... politically correct, I would guess.

"Yes sir?"

"No offense... but my son is off limits..."

"No offense taken Mr. Callahan... Cindy wasn't just my roommate... she was my lover!"

He nodded. "Then we have an understanding?" he said.

"Yes sir, we do..."

Ramona came in and then we went shopping for a whole brand new wardrobe for me. I still didn't know what was going on, but I knew I was going to be much better off than I am now. I wanted to get some sexy things but Ramona had a more conservative idea on how I should dress. I don't know why, but the fact she didn't let me dress like a whore made me feel like she had, I don't know... better plans for me? We returned to the club and I gave the receipts to Michael. He took them into the office never saying a word to me. *"I wonder what's up with him?"* I thought to myself. He was good looking and pretty handsome but I don't fall for that shit anymore. I'm pretty much a confirmed lipstick lesbian and I have no plans on switching sides now. I put him out of my mind. What I needed to know now, is what did his father want with me? I know he's taking good care of me, but I lay down for no man!

The Tortured Soul Trilogy
(Living La Vida Puta)
Chapter 3
(Tiny Dancer)

Cindy and I lost track of each other although she always knew where to find me. I went back to the room where we had lived once to visit her, but she and all our stuff was gone. I guess she had moved to another place or another city. Mr. Callahan had me take my G.E.D. and I was officially working for him in his club once I turned 17. Somehow he was able to get my records and knew everything about me. Well... almost everything! I was still too young to serve drinks so I helped out in the kitchen. The club had an all–you-can-eat buffet every Thursday and Sunday. I served food and soft drinks and I lived in the back room. Because he took care of my 'room and board' he didn't pay me but I could keep any tips I earned working in the club. On my nights off, it was okay with him if I partied with the regular crowd. It got to the point that I was known as the club hostess. I played nice with the regulars and I made a good living at it. Mr. Callahan even helped me open my own savings account. I had a decent life, good times, and money in my pocket... what else could a girl want?

I never saw Cindy again, but I did eventually read about her in the local paper. She had died of a drug overdose about two years later. I wish she wasn't so hard headed. She could have stayed with me, with Mr. Callahan. By the way, he paid for her funeral. He did it simply as a favor to me. He was classy like that. From that moment on, I thought of Steven Callahan like a father to me, better than a father really. Mr. Callahan never disowned me. Although I felt there were times he had good reason.

Some time in the late 80's or the early 90's... disco died! The crowds stopped coming, the regulars got older; and business slumped. Mr. Callahan had to try something very drastic to save his business. Okay! I'm not going to candy coat shit here... Mr. Callahan was *'connected'*. The club was really a front to launder money for his other... 'business ventures', but an empty club every night raised a lot of questions, questions that Mr. Callahan didn't want to have to answer. The 'senior partners' had a meeting and tried to find a way to increase attendance. They had no clue what to do to get it done.

"Mr. Callahan?" I whispered as not to interrupt.

"Yes Tobey?"

"With your permission... I have an idea..."

"Let's hear it..."

"I've gone to other clubs in town... and..." I hesitated.

"Spill it... We're listening..."

"Well... the hot clubs in town... added..."

"Added what? Come on... we won't laugh..."

"They added... dance cages..."

"What's a 'dance cage'...?"

"It's a cage above the dance floor where they have a go-go dancer..."

At first the partners looked at each other. Would that work?"

"Can you take me to one of these clubs?" Mr. Callahan asked.

"Sure... we can go to one right now if you like..."

Mr. Callahan nodded and adjourned the meeting. "I'm gonna see if her idea has any merit... and we'll see if it will work here..." he said to the others as they left the club. He smiled at me; he already knew what the other clubs were doing. He just wanted someone else to come up with the idea. "I'll call a contractor and we'll see if we can have the ceiling reinforced to hold the cages...."

"Okay!"

"I need you to do something for me..."

"Yes Mr. Callahan?"

"I would like you to be in charge of the dancers..."

"Me...? You want me to be in charge...?"

"You seem to know your way around this business... and it *was* your idea..."

"Thank you Mr. Callahan! I won't let you down!"

He smiled at me. "You can call me Steven... if you like..."

"Thank you... Steven..."

"Well? What are you still doing here? Go get me some hot 'cage' dancers..."

I left the club with a new purpose. I went outside and just got lost! Where should I start looking for dancers? I've never auditioned anyone before... Should I place an ad? I decided to hit a few clubs and just offer a shot to any girl who liked to dance and give them the same opportunity Steven had given me. Plus it would give me the opportunity to see how other clubs handled the talent and how they set up the décor.

Steven spoke with two contractors and hanging dance cages was out of the question. The ceiling would not hold the extra weight and the club could not carry the added insurance. I spoke with Steven and we decided to build six foot square columns rising from the floor and build the cage on top of them. It was the safest and most economical way to work it out. I hired and trained the girls and business picked up slowly but surely. We were now a hot dance club and popular with a younger crowd. The bar served top shelf and mixed drinks and the club actually made money all on its own. Steven was quite pleased. As times changed and tastes changed, the dancers in the cages went topless... Business only got better! I came in one day on my day off just to check if everything was going smoothly. It was that night one of the girls who was supposed to dance was high as a kite and paranoid. She refused to get in the cage so high up in the air and Steven couldn't take any chances that she would freak out up there. I fired the bitch on the spot, but now what? I just can't have an empty cage in the club. I tried a few numbers of other girls but none were available. "Shit! What I am going to do now?"

The club was getting full and even though you would think nobody would notice, it was just bad karma. You just can't have an empty dance cage. The other girls would slack off if they think they could take off whenever they felt like it. What can I do? What? That's when I decided to just get in the cage myself. I had changed my look over the years and I dressed as a butch biker on my days off. I took off my blouse and bra, put my leather vest back on and got in the cage. My sunglasses completed the look. That was the day 'The Leather Mistress' was born...

At first I didn't like dancing half nude in a cage, but I actually felt safe in there, above the crowds. I got into it and it was fun... Fun, until I saw Steven in the crowd looking up at me. He had a very disappointed look on his face. I knew that look. It was the same look my father gave me the morning after... the morning he threw me out of the house while my mother cried her eyes out. In one hastily made bad decision, I had ruined the plans Steven had for me. I was no longer the club hostess; I had become just a mascot. A mascot with a very big following and my fan base got bigger and bigger as time went by. Weeks past and I continued to dance in the cage and run the show. I wasn't fired, but my relationship with Steven changed. He wouldn't answer me if I called him Steven, he would only answer to 'Mr. Callahan'. I got the hint; we would never again be friends. I was just another employee. Eventually I moved out of the back room and got my own place. Steven... Mr. Callahan had Ramona put me on the club books.

I didn't like dancing in leather and denim and the look wasn't really working for me anymore. These were my street clothes; I wanted to wear something... special when I danced. Cat Woman was still popular from the Batman TV series, so I switched up to a latex and lace cat suit... sans the mask. Thus I became 'Lady Latex'... I liked that incarnation the best! It gave me a feeling of power... I like having power! I felt like a superhero! Instead of T.O. my friends now call me L.L.

The Tortured Soul Trilogy
(*Living La Vida Puta*)
Chapter 4
(*You're My Private Dancer*)

Again times changed and other dance clubs that didn't have a celebrity clientele closed shop. That wasn't an option for Mr. Callahan. Eventually, the columns came down and a runway with brass poles was added. Some of the dancers quit. Others, who got used to making good money and with the possibility of making great money, had no problem with going all nude. And that's how we became the hottest strip joint in town. It was all the theory of de-evolution, survival of the sexiest! Having already developed a huge following, I was now one of the top earning strippers in the club.

I'm going to get a little philosophical here. The idea of me standing on a stage, dancing and taking my clothes off while men threw money at me… empowered me. Every night I danced and the dollar bills flew at me, I relived the night that 'fucktard' threw money at me and said; "*Here… For all your trouble…*" For all your trouble, I danced, men threw money… but I was in charge… They got to watch, they got to desire me, they got to lust after me… and they were… *denied!* For all my trouble… you could look, but you could NEVER have. For all my trouble, you wanted and I teased. For all my trouble, you were left… broke and unsatisfied. I took back what was rightfully mine.

I was the HBIC on and off the dance floor. I ran the dancers like a military unit. It was like I was the head cheerleader. I was tough, but I was fair. Everybody made money as long as I ran the show and the girls knew it. One night some assholes who had booked a bachelor party were acting up a little, but it was nothing we couldn't handle. They were getting a little too grabby with one of the girls working the tables. I was at the bar talking with one of the regulars, when I heard the girl scream. The best man tried to goose her while she was giving him a lap dance. I saw the group surround my girl. I saw the look on her face. I got a feeling of déjà vu and I was over there in an instant. I snatched the girl away from them. "Hey! I don't care how much you bozos paid to be here, but you know the club rule is hands off..." The guys took umbrage that I was spoiling their fun. They laughed at me... until they saw the knife in my hand. "I think it's time you boys called it a night!"

"You're not gonna do shit! You do anything to us and the cops will shut this shit hole down!" the groom said. This guy reeked of too many beers. The smell gave me a flashback. I quickly held the knife tightly under his crotch. If touched me or if he pushed me away all I had to do was raise the blade upwards and this guy wasn't going to have a good wedding night, ever!

"And what are you going to do... without a dick?" The other guys saw the look on my face and realized that I was very serious and they were wrong for doing what they did. They figured that discretion was the better part of valor and grabbed his arms and started to lead his drunk ass out. He was just about to leave the pit, the area just under and around the runway; when he stopped suddenly, turned to me, reached into his pocket and took out his money and threw some dollars at me. At this point, he could have said anything and I wouldn't have cared as long as he said it on his way out. As luck would have it... he said the wrong fucking thing...

"Here...! For all your trouble..."

The Tortured Soul Trilogy
(Living La Vida Puta)
Chapter 5
(Pimping Aint Easy!)

Michael Callahan Esq. walked me out the front doors of the county court house six months later. "Thanks L.L....!"

"For what Michael?"

"For helping me 'cut my teeth' by being my first criminal trial case..."

"You're welcome!" I knew he was being facetious, but he really showed what he was made of by getting me off 'assault with a deadly weapon' charges with six months served and a small fine. Lucky for me, the guy only needed a few stitches and I didn't hit any 'vital' organs. Ha! It took a while for this guy to press charges. First, he was embarrassed to be taken down by a woman, and second, he didn't want his fiancée to know he was at a strip club when it happened. He told her it happened at a bar. (No lie there!) But she pushed the issue to have the 'barmaid' who assaulted him charged. I can't blame her. I kinda ruined her wedding night too! If he had called the cops that night, the club surely would have been closed for good. I really have to check my temper at the door... "You think that asshole will try to sue the club in a civil case?"

Michael smiled wryly. "Have you *met*... the men my father works with?"

"I guess it's safe to assume... he's dropping it..."

"Yeah... pretty much..."

I took another week off before going back to the club. I really didn't want to see Mr. Callahan, but it was time to face the music. I went in and walked right into his office. Miss Kirby was there and a stocky Spanish guy I had never seen before. "Mr. Callahan... I just want to say I'm so sorry for what happened..."

"You don't have to apologize... it was all my fault!" He hugged me and kissed my cheek. I didn't know what to think... was he fucking with my head? He wasn't there that night I gutted that guy. How was it his fault? Was it his fault for putting his faith in me? What? He brought me over to a chair and sat me down. "I should have beefed up security here the moment we switched to being a strip club. I want to apologize to you for putting you and the girls in danger. Damn my ego, I just knew nobody would dare start shit in my club. It's a mistake I won't make again." He pointed at the man sitting in the other chair. "L.L., I want you to meet Cisco Torres... he's going to be head of security from now on. He comes highly recommended from my associates in Florida. Cisco, this is L.L., the only woman in this club that probably won't be needing your protection..."

He stood up and took my hand and kissed the back of it. "Pleasure to meet you L.L."

"Oh please! Back the hell up! I'm a lesbian! Try that shit on a woman who gives a fuck!" I thought to myself.

"What does L.L. stand for?"

"Lady Latex..." I said. He smiled; I cut my eyes at him.

"You two will be working closely together from now on..." Steven said. My ears perked up a bit; at least I still have a job here.

"Why?" I asked.

"Cisco will be in charge of solely protecting the girls that work here, you'll still be in charge of hiring the girls and keeping a tight schedule... I have to tell you, shit fell apart here while you were gone!"

"He's going to protect all the girls... all by himself?"

"No... I'll be bringing in a full crew of bodyguards to cover the club, opening to closing. Mr. Callahan has made other arrangements for the other 'assets' of the club." I nodded. Steven asked Cisco to give us a moment to speak privately. He excused himself leaving Steven and Ramona and I alone in the office. Before he left Cisco said to me: "I hope to enjoy working *very* closely with you!"

(Let it go shit head! Your sister has a better shot than you do!)

"L.L., I am really sorry that you had to go what you went through, but it showed that you really care about the girls that work for you and me." Steven said. Steven paused. I waited to see what he would say next. He looked at Ramona, who nodded to him in agreement. "I have a special 'project' I want you to take over for me."

"Sure... what do you want me to do?"

"Before you agree to take on this task, I want you to know what you're getting into..."

I nodded again... I knew I needed to keep my mouth shut and listen.

"I have an outside venture that can never be linked to this club in any way..." I leaned forward to listen closely. "I have girls who provide a service to the community and I need someone like you to keep them in line and handle all the business end of things..." I knew what he meant, but you never said out loud what he meant... ever! Even if you didn't know what was being discussed, you never asked for clarification. If you couldn't figure it out, you had no business taking on the assignment.

"When do I start?" Steven looked at Ramona and they each had a slight look of disappointment on their faces. It was me who finally broke the silence. "I know you're not very happy with me right now, but you need me to be who and what I am right now... I'm sorry I'm not the 'little princess' you wanted, but I can never be her, but maybe someday she'll come along... I'm truly sorry that I disappointed both of you... Now that we got that all out in the open and out of the way... when do I start?"

Steven shook his head. "That's some attitude you got!"

I went over to Steven, threw my arms around him and hugged him and kissed his cheek. "That's what you said to me, when you first met me!" Steven asked Ramona to leave us and he ran down the particulars of how the business was being run. I didn't like it. I thought about it for a moment. The operating costs were too high and the girls were too spread out to keep and eye on them and control the cash flow. "I need a favor from you..." I said.

"What do you need?"

"I'm thinking of getting a mortgage and buying... I don't know... a rooming house? You know... a place that I can rent rooms out and collect the rent from the tenants. They would go to work, live there and pay a rent based on a percentage of, let's say... their income?"

Steven looked at me in awe. I had solved all his management problems in one felt swoop. "What do you need from me?" he asked.

"A loan to put a down payment on the property... It would be a proper loan of course... I would pay you back... with interest?"

Steven's jaw dropped. I just cleaned the paper trail! "How did you get so smart?"

"I learned from the best... Steven..." Steven, oh yeah, I get to call him Steven again, hooked me up with a real estate agent who got me a twelve room SRO building that was under foreclosure at a good price. Steven supplied the money, Michael supplied the legal advice. I became the landlord. Steven saw a great potential for me to run his call girl service. I took to the job like a fish takes to water. It wasn't all that different from when I was Cindy's 'agent'.

Running the place was simple. You got a room and the 'rent' was a pre-determined minimum that you had to earn at your 'job' to live there. Oh no, this wasn't going to be a rent by the hour, mop by the minute establishment. It was a rooming house first and foremost. No visitors are allowed, no phone, no pets! There was only one phone line for incoming calls only. If I needed to get in contact with a 'tenant' because a 'temp job' was available, I would call from my cell and who ever was willing to take the job would come in to 'work'. You paid extra if you wanted a specific employee. They would use our 'cab' service there and back. I collect the rent once a week, divide it in three; one for Steven to 'repay' my debt. One for me, cause I don't work for charity and if there was any money left, expenses, then the girls... Oh, I paid them well. I was tough but I was fair.

The girls had a decent place to live, safe and secure travel to and from 'work', good money and the legal services of one Michael Callahan Esq. I didn't even have to recruit for tenants... we actually had a waiting list! A year later, I had to get two more buildings to keep up with the demand! Did I mention I like having power?

The Tortured Soul Trilogy
(Living La Vida Puta)
Chapter 6
(You Can't Go Home Again)

I still worked the strip club, now called "The Kitty Bar", as an exotic dancer. I like to think the club was named after the Cat Woman character I had portrayed, but to tell the truth, Steven thought it was a cute twist on The Titty Bar... I told Steven never to tell that story to anyone! Ramona agreed. A few years passed and life for me is pretty routine now, work four nights at the club, one day collecting 'the rent' and two days to myself. To be honest, I began to hate my days off. I hadn't had a steady lover since Cindy and I really wasn't looking for her replacement. I didn't mess with the house girls and the club girls were out of the question. Those crazy bitches had way too much baggage in their lives. A third of the girls were college students trying to supplement their income to pay for books and tuition. Anybody with real potential wouldn't stay very long. The others were fucked up has-beens at 30! I'm not the pick of the litter but I didn't like the gene pool I was forced to swim in. My life was complicated enough, thank you!

I liked my life private. I didn't want anyone I knew to have too much insight into my business, personal or professional. I wound up taking a hiatus from dancing at the club for about a month. I had to take care of supervising repairs at one of the houses. The plumbing was shot and these were high priced call girls. I had to put them up in a hotel while the boiler, bathrooms and a busted pipe were being fixed. Steven didn't mind, business is business and this was the cost of doing business. Besides, it was just added to the 'loan' I had to 'repay'.

The best laid plans!

My one month hiatus became more than three months in hiding. After I got most of the problems at the house fixed and I thought everything would go back to normal, old business reared its ugly head. The asshole I cut; grew his balls back and decided to

29

sue the club and they wanted to subpoena me to testify! Steven had me go on unscheduled vacation and be incommunicado. I wound up taking having to take residence with the girls at the hotel, while things got sorted out. Michael did his lawyer thing to get the guy to back off. He threw a wrench into their lawsuit by telling them that the girl who the groom groped that night decided to file attempted rape and sexual assault charges against him. Which was a good trick considering that she dropped off the face of the Earth right after that night! Between the attack on her and the blood he spilled from a gaping wound I gave him, she had enough of the strip club scene. Funny thing about drunken strip club patrons... they can remember who stabbed them in their groin but they don't remember who gave them a lap dance in a dark club a few months ago! Hey! Girls gain weight, lose weight, change their hair color... they even change their ethnic background sometimes! Without my testimony and the threat of him being labeled as a sexual predator, his lawyer opted to drop the lawsuit. Even after the lawsuit was dropped, I still didn't go right back to work at the club. Just when I though all was well, I got a call from Steven. He was not sounding happy. I had no idea what was wrong. I listened as he told me to come and see him in his office. I refused. I wanted to hear the bad news now. He insisted he wanted to see me. I flatly refused. Tell me now! I held on to the receiver tightly as he informed me that my mother had passed away. I was stunned. Was it an accident? What? Steven honestly didn't know but Cisco was on his way to get me, so pack a bag and he would take me straight to the airport.

I didn't say a word to Cisco when he arrived an hour later and he understood. I didn't know what to pack. With all the clothes that I had, I had nothing for a funeral. Not even the dress I wore for Cindy's seemed appropriate. Cisco must have sensed my concern. "Mr. Callahan said it was okay for me to take you shopping... if you need a dress..." Cisco said quietly.

"Okay." I whispered. Cisco took me to a clothing store that had 'regular' dresses. God bless Ramona, she met us there and helped me pick out something... black, conservative and classy. Cisco put the dress in a suit bag and took me to the airport. My bags were already in the trunk. Ms. Kirby came with us. I hugged her so hard when I got to the airport. I never wanted to let her go. I kissed Cisco gently on the cheek. He was so very good about this. I got on the plane and flew home.

I arrived 'home' and the Callahan's had made hotel arrangements for me. Nothing fancy, I still didn't want to draw any undue attention to myself... not in this town. As I unpacked my bags in the hotel room I looked around the room. I went to the window and looked at downtown hell... "Fuck! This was the only way I would have ever come back to this shit hole ass backwards town!" I muttered. My mother's viewing was the next day and the funeral was that same afternoon.

L.L. got dressed for the viewing and went to the funeral hall where they were having the viewing. She got there just as everyone sat down. She quietly took a seat in the back while they had services for her mother. It was strange. She thought she would cry. She thought she would have more emotions. But she didn't. She was numb. After a while she noticed the random stares from different people that came to pay their respects. She could hear the whispers.

"Who is that?"

"Is she family?"

"Maybe she's the head of the cosmetics company Annabel worked for...?"

Nobody knew who I was, why should they? They didn't care who I was when I lived here. My god... it's been almost 15 years since I left here for greener pastures! I sat quietly in the back and that's when I saw my father sitting in the... oh, what do you call that chair? Does it even have a name? The chair for the bereaved... Whatever! Finally the pastor called for all mourners to pay their last respects to Annabel Oceanside. One by one they got up and paid their respect. They cried, they sobbed. They lost it at the casket. I sat there quietly and waited. As the last person made their way back to their seat, I slowly made my way down the aisle. The focus of attention was on me as I strutted down that aisle. Don't get me wrong, I didn't mean to walk like it was a cat walk. It's just that, that's the way I walk now. It took me a long time to develop that swagger and it's very hard to rein it back. I kneeled at the side of the casket, stood up, pulled back my black veil and gently kissed my mother's ice cold face. It was not how I remembered her, nor wanted to. I took the one white rose in my hand and laid in on her gently. I touched her hair and turned away. It was then I thought she had died of a broken heart. It was a shame my heart was as cold as ice. As I took one step to return to my seat, my father looked directly into my eyes. "How did you know my Annabel?" he sobbed.

I smiled. "Oh...? Annabel...?" I took two steps past my father and stopped and turned to him. He had turned and was focused on me as I was walking away. He looked at me up and down. He still had no idea who I was. "Annabel... was my mother!" I said plainly.

My father was in shock, but he didn't say a word, not to me, not to anyone. As I walked out of the funeral parlor, I saw Cindy's parents out of the corner of my eye and the look of disdain they had for me. Fuck them too! I went straight back to the hotel, grabbed my bags and went directly to the airport. To go to the burial would have been anti-climactic, besides. I didn't want to answer any of their questions. Let them guess where I've been all these years... and their guesses would be as good as mine!

I got back into town and Cisco picked me up at the airport. He knew not to ask how the funeral was. He took me straight home. I waited another day before I went back to work. I spent that day crying like a baby non-stop! A good cry, half a bottle of vodka, and a joint (okay two!) and I was as good as new. The only thing I really could have used was a good lay, but that was the one thing I denied myself. It was bad for business. I reached into my dresser and pulled out the "Purple Dominator", it would have to do until I found a lover I could trust... I looked at it. It looked like a purple pickle. I lit up a third joint and it was party time for mama! "Damn I could really use a woman right now!"

Lady Latex turned the Purple Dominator on and took a deep drag of her joint. She slipped out of her panties and exhaled as the Ganja Rush (or 'mellow' as it were) hit her. She lay back down on her bed and brought it to her swollen clit. The vibrations and hum relaxed her more than the joint did. She felt a wave of euphoria as she worked it up and down on her clit and across her moist labia. She took another puff and continued to work it back and forth. She never inserted it into her vagina. She only used it as a substitute for a woman's tongue. She didn't even like dildos and only owned a strap-on for her lover... ex lover Cindy. She had purchased the Purple Dominator for herself because it didn't look anything like a penis. L.L. cooed and played with her nipple rings. They were Cindy's gold earrings she had once bought for her. They were the only thing she had and kept as a memento of her first lover. Never again would anything intrude her body like that first night... but this is no time to dwell on that. Mama's nipples were getting hard and her clit was throbbing. Wave after wave of euphoria washed over her body. She took one more drag of her joint and then she reared her head back and moaned. Her eyes went to the back of her head and her jaw shuddered. She pinched her nipples. "Ummm... ohhh... nice...!" She moaned.

This would be a good time... for a flashback!

The Tortured Soul Trilogy
(Living La Vida Puta)
Chapter 7
(One on One)

You now know what happened to me when I was younger and you may think that it excuses my behavior or that I have a right to be the way I am, but what happened that day is only half the story.

I left home with my childhood friend Cindy, because we had something in common. We were both raped by the same drifter, a feral kid who preyed on young girls and then moved on to the next town and the next victim. Oh by the way, he was finally caught and he wasn't a kid at all. He was a 'man-child' who preyed on teenagers using his youthful appearance. That hillbilly pedophile was thrown in prison to rot.

We were young and not very 'worldly', but two young girls thrown recklessly into the real world, grow up really fast. Money was tight for two girls, on the open road with no education and all on their own. We weren't good enough to become thieves or grifters, but Cindy had one talent that men would pay through the nose for. Cindy could suck a golf ball through a garden hose, a talent she developed from over a year of sexual abuse by that kid. A talent she later perfected out on the road.

I, for the life of me, will never again have sexual relations with a man. That is the cross I bear from my experience. It is that reason, not wanting to be with a man, but still developing the sexual tension of a horny teenager that made me experiment with lesbianism. Cindy, of course was my first encounter. It was innocent at first. She had just turned a trick for a trucker and we used the money for one night at a motel. The manager there made it quite clear that there would be no 'visitors' allowed in our room. The room was near his office and he wasn't kidding about 'no visitors'. He watched our door like a hawk. All night long!

We settled into this one room roach motel. It was a little cold so we snuggled up together in the bed. Cindy began to cry softly. This is not how she wanted her life to turn out. She had plans, she had a future. It wasn't supposed to be this way. She got up, took a shower and then so did I. The TV didn't work so we went to bed. She couldn't sleep. This was really bothering her, and it was bothering me, that it was bothering her. She cried softly and I held her in my arms. I kissed her cheek to calm her. Then I kissed her cheek again... and again... and then she turned her lips into me and kissed me on the mouth. Our bodies shivered but it wasn't from the coldness of the room. We were both so very, very scared. This wasn't about sex. It was about needing each other. I needed to hold her. She needed to feel like somebody cared about her. We needed to be needed... Our bodies entwined and our lips searched out and probed each others mouths. Then the touching started. Nice and slow and sensual. *"Why couldn't my first time have been like this?"* I thought to myself. We slowly got undressed and were wearing only our panties. Our bodies touched and caressed each other. The kissing and touching became more intense. I don't know who touched who first but I remember a rush of adrenaline course through my veins. I fondled her, she stroked me. Then she tried to 'probe' me. I jumped up immediately and pushed her hand away.

"What's wrong?"

"I won't let nobody... anybody '*invade*' my personal space... ever again..."

She looked at me with sadness in her eyes. "I'm sorry... I... didn't realize... I'm so sorry...!" and she shed a tear. "I don't ever want to hurt you... like they hurt you..."

(Prophetic words... but I won't go there... just yet...) "It's just..." I said.

She looked at me with a little sadness in her eyes. "But you don't have a problem with me having my personal space invaded..."

I sat up on the bed. I knew she meant the tricks she had to do to make the rent. "You did that, because you wanted to. I never asked you to put out. I protect you and have your back... just in case... but *I*... have... *never*... invaded your personal space..." I said softly.

"And why do you protect me?"

"Cause a bitch has got a bitch's back..."

She rolled up behind me on the bed and whispered in my ear. "Would you *like*... to invade *my* personal space?"

I didn't answer. I just turned to her and pulled her panties away from her sweet young pussy and she spread her legs. I had played with mine before... in the shower, but I had never seen one before. I reached over and stroked her pussy fur and she cooed. I then remembered what I liked to do to myself and did it to her. She purred and cooed and began to pinch her nipples.

"Oh yeah... right there... do that... keep doing that..." She grinded her loins into my hand and she became very moist and wet. I rubbed her faster and faster, like I liked to do. She moaned and purred again. That's when I realized that what she did to pay our bills wasn't something she enjoyed. It was done out of necessity. No one cared about how she felt. No one cared what she wanted or needed out of the encounter. I pinched and fondled her clit and she arched her back and her eyes went to the back of her head. "Mmmmm, ha... muuuuuuuah! Oh baby! Don't stop!" She then reached over and grabbed my other hand and pulled me towards her. I had no idea what she wanted me to do. As she tried to maneuver my face towards her loins, I resisted... Bad flashback! Cindy would not be denied... she stuck her finger in her mouth and wet it and touched my clit over my panties again. I felt safe with my panties blocking her touch. My eyes fluttered and then I felt her ease me on my back. My head was hanging off the edge of the bed and I could see her reflection in the mirror hanging on the closet opposite the bed. She pulled my panties aside as she went down on me. I could see her pinch her nipples as she leaned down and put her mouth on my pussy and began to lick and suck me like it was nobody's business.

That 'skill' I told you about? Works just as well on a woman's clit and vagina as it does on a man's penis... I couldn't breathe... My head swung violently back and forth. My stomach muscles involuntarily contracted and I sat up. That gave her the opportunity to grab my breasts and massage them gently. I began to puff short breaths of air. The cold room suddenly became hot and stifling. I arched my back and a sound came out of me that I didn't think was possible. "Aaaaaaahhhhhh yiiiiiiiiiii yi yi yi! Hah!" It was that moment that the motel room door swung open and the motel manager burst into the room.

"I thought I told you girls..." and he stopped, shocked by what he saw. He expected to find a man in our room.

I quickly rolled off the bed grabbed my jeans to cover myself and opened my switchblade and held it out towards him. Cindy didn't even bother to cover up. "You... *told* us... no *visitors*... and that means you too... fuck face!" And I motioned for him to leave and shut the door behind him.

"I want you two heathens out of my motel!"

"Fuck you! We paid our money like any other guest and they can fuck in your rooms all night if they want to... We'll leave in the morning like our rental contract says we can... Now leave... with... *or* without your balls intact!" He closed the door behind him and mumbled incoherently while he walked back to his office. I turned to Cindy. "Damnit! That son of a bitch broke the mood!" Just another man to get in the way of my orgasm! Cindy held me and covered me in the blanket and spooned me. We went to sleep but not before I put the fucking chain on the door. The next morning when I woke up, Cindy and her clothes was gone. I jumped out of the bed and checked to see if any of my shit was missing. Everything I had was still here. What the fuck happened? Where's Cindy? About an hour later I heard the key in the lock. I grabbed my knife and got into position. The door opened and in came Cindy with breakfast from a local fast food restaurant.

"Wakey wakey... eggs and bakie..."

"Cindy... where did you go to?"

"To get breakfast silly..."

I knew Cindy didn't have any money and I still had all the cash I had. "Where did you get the money?" As if I had to ask.

"From the motel manager..."

Okay! I wasn't expecting *that* answer! "From the manager...? Really?"

"Yeah... it seems that his 'no visitors' rule... doesn't include his office..."

"You had sex... with the manager...?"

"I sucked his dick so good... he gave me an extra ten to stop!" and Cindy gave me the change. She always allowed me to handle all our finances.

I shook my head. "*Sure... he gets his rocks off...!*" I thought to myself. "Well let's eat and get out of here before check out time..."

Cindy tossed her jacket on the bed. "We don't have to leave..."

"Why not...?" Did I really have to ask?

"We can stay as long as he doesn't have to rent the room to someone else..."

"And what does he want in return?"

"What do you *think* he wants? But don't worry... I told him you were off limits. He's okay with that... considering you threatened to cut his balls off and I almost killed him..."

"You *what*???"

Cindy scoffed. "You know what I mean..." And she motioned pumping her hand into her mouth. I sat back down and had breakfast with Cindy. We were able to live at the motel for almost a month before it got busy and we had to leave. Although Cindy provided her 'services' for him and he paid for our meals, we let him know that we would never have 'guests or visitors' at his motel. We don't shit where we eat. He appreciated that. You know, for a sanctimonious, hypocritical, son of a bitch, he was pretty all right and treated us pretty good. He was almost sorry to see us leave... and I don't mean just Cindy and her 'skills'. He started to like us. He gave us sandwiches and coffee for the road when we left. He kissed Cindy and shook my hand.

"You two take care of yourselves..." he said. I actually began to like this guy. He treated us nice.

Oh... and if you were wondering... yeah Cindy was able to finish what we had started that first night... and I learned a trick or two myself!

The story doesn't end there... that explains how I became a lesbian... it doesn't explain the S&M fetish I developed...

Okay let's recap here; two pre-teen victims of sexual violence... check! One becomes a prostitute and the other becomes her pimp... check! One is bisexual and the other is a lesbian... check and check! All we need is a "Happily ever after!" and we have a New York Times best selling children's book!

Okay, I'm fucking around here... but there is a serious reason for the fetish I acquired. I was, until I got tossed out on my ass, raised Catholic. Yeah... nuns and all... So all that religious training instilled within me a need to be chastised for my 'sins'. I had to repent and redeem myself and I didn't know that Cindy felt the same way. We didn't get into flagellation until one day one of Cindy's 'tricks' took a belt to her. We had picked up this scrawny guy who paid top dollar and took him to a room we had rented for one night before we would move on. I was in the other room, when I heard the sound of a belt and Cindy cried out. This sick son of a bitch had tied her face down on the bed and was strapping her. I almost cut the bastard, when Cindy pleaded for him.

"What the fuck Cindy? He was beating you!"

"It's all right... I asked him to..."

He nodded and smiled at me. I so very fucking quickly advised him to get the fuck out and he did. I went to untie her and she refused. "You want to stay like that?"

"Yes... but I need a favor..." she said to me. It was more like she begged.

"What Cindy? What do you want?"

"Beat me..." she whispered.

"You *want* me to beat you...?"

"Yes... please... beat me... *mistress*!"

(*What the fuck did she just call me?*) She turned her head and wouldn't look at me. I picked up the strap. "Cindy?"

"Yes..."

"Did the nuns beat you?"

Cindy cried and nodded. "Yes mistress...! They did...!"

I stood there in shock holding the leather belt in my hand. I looked at it and I cried... "My father beat me too! Just before he threw me out!" I said. I just knew I was the only one who was punished by the people we trusted. And we both started to cry, we cried for almost five minutes; then I raised the belt and struck her...

"Thank you mistress..." Cindy cried out. "May I have another?"

My body filled with a feeling I had never felt before. I felt... relieved! It was a sensation and an experience I got used to... a lot! Cindy and I traveled the highways and byways of the country and whenever or wherever we bed down for the night, we chastised each other. It got to the point we couldn't sleep well without having a good beating first. We only had one rule; we never, ever beat each other if we were angry. We had to trust each other that the beating would stop once we had enough. That, with our love for each other was the only thing that kept us going. Love! Ha! We beat each other more than we made love, it got to the point a good beating was better than sex. She didn't always like to have sex with me because she did it all day sometimes, and I will never have sex with a man again. Punishment is all we had left; that... and a common background of abuse and rape.

So, that's my first experiences with lesbianism and S&M. Now let's talk about how that evolved me into the person I am today...

The Tortured Soul Trilogy
(Living La Vida Puta)
Chapter 8
(Back To the Future)

I kinda skipped over the years between the 1970's and the 1990's. Not because they were uneventful, but because I had to explain a few things to you about my life. Now that you know a little more about my past, let's go back to those days so I can explain a little more about myself... It was just after I met the Callahans and before I worked for them as a pimp!

Okay, so, before we begin, for those of you whose birthday is 1980 or later, you're gonna need a short history lesson so you can understand what I'm talking about.

Discotheque: A dance hall very popular in Europe, it became popular in the U.S. around 1970 and the big draw was actually making contact with your dance partner. DJ's became rock stars by showing their ability to mix different songs together live into a long dance set. Disco died when just about everybody had a 'disco' song released. Even radio DJ Rick Dees had a disco hit with a song that was supposed to make fun of the Disco overload. 'Disco Duck' was on top of the Billboard charts for a whole week in 1976. Google it!

The complex dance moves didn't work on a crowded dance floor, so the ballroom/acrobatic style of dancing gave way to just grinding into each other. The music didn't change much. We just called it 'Techno' in the 90's to shake the disco curse. I mention the evolution of disco dancing here because one; it was what the times were like back then and two; it kinda helps explain how I became a stripper and then a fetish diva.

Whenever I wasn't working at Steven's club, I could be found at a disco. I loved dancing and expressing myself through dance. It was somehow... empowering! I would go to a corner of the club and let my dance moves fly as it may. Needless to say, I was invited to dance on the floor by many men. Generally I refused. I don't like getting that close to men. I don't think I ever will. The really good thing was that it was okay for girls to touch dance and grind with each other. I would find a group that would be together and when the girls would get picked off one by one to the dance floor, I would go after the girl that was left. We would dance until a man came over to break up my good time. If I didn't accept his invitation to dance, she would and I would be left dancing alone again.

One night I met a group of girls who would only dance with each other and would not accept dance invitations from men. "*My kind of girls...*" I thought. The girls were mixed. Some were lesbian, some where bi-sexual and the straight ones hung out with them because we always knew where to have a good time. I worked my way into the group and they introduced me into the 'underground' dance scene. These were illegal dance clubs held in business lofts. The crowd was a little different and the house rules were a bit more 'relaxed'. They encouraged topless dancing by the guests, male and female alike and they would have a wet T shirt contest every Wednesday. It wasn't until my group danced topless that I got into it. We still only danced with and for each other, but I could see the reaction I would get from the men. One of the girls jested. "*You would make a great stripper...!*" I took it as an insult. Me? Take my clothes off for men? Not gonna fucking happen. As I became tighter with the girls they introduced me to cocaine. I didn't like it! I'll stick with my weed, thank you! Besides drugs killed my Cindy and I wasn't going down that road. I had a few flings with some of the girls, but they only had sex with other girls for the goof. They weren't serious about it. I was! One girl actually fell asleep while I was giving her head! What the Eff? The sheer boredom of what they called their lives made them escalate to stronger drugs (deal me out!) and fetish clubs. Now you're talking my language!

I took to the fetish scene like a fish takes to water. I loved going out in leather, latex and lace. I loved the shows they put on and I was even invited to go on stage once or twice. The slave/master, sadomasochistic lifestyle was just what the doctor ordered. I met many women who were into what I was into. There were some aspects I didn't like. I weeded out what I liked from what I didn't; like being involved with men. I derived no pleasure from beating and humiliating men. You would think I would, but I wanted *nothing* to do with men. Especially when I realized they liked that shit! Giving a man pleasure in any form; disgusted me! I was seen as a 'Dominatrix' so most didn't give me any shit. I didn't get to establish any long personal relationships with female fetishers, but they were a good diversion from my troubles. I pretty much kept that aspect of my life to myself. Steven and Ramona didn't have to know, and what they didn't know, wouldn't hurt them...

"Ohhhh... ohhhh.... Muuuuuuuuuuuahhh! Oh Yeah oh yeah! Mmmmmy iiiiiiah ggg... ggg... ggg... gawd! Hoooooooo yeah! That's what mama needed... right there!" I finger flicked my swollen clit and I relaxed as I took another hit from my joint...

(Oh... I'm so sorry! Did you forget that I was back at my house, on my bed, legs spread wide... diddling myself with the Purple Dominator? Tee-hee! Okay let's get back to where we we had left off... I'm back home from my mother's funeral, and the next day I went back to work at The Kitty Bar, a strip club owned by Steven Callahan... and SCENE...!)

The Tortured Soul Trilogy
(Living La Vida Puta)
Chapter 9
(So You Think You Can Strip?)

L.L. was back to work recruiting new girls to replace the ones that quit after the recent changeover to all nude dancing. There wasn't too much great talent out there. The ones with any skills or experience wanted more money, and the ones who needed to work on their floor routines wouldn't make the club any. And if you're wondering why I didn't just hire the clique girls I met in my club days. I told you. I don't like to mix my personal life with business...

The house kept the bar unless you were working a table then the club split any 'sets' that was ordered for the table while you worked it. Back in the day, a 'set' was a bottle of scotch, rum or vodka, sodas and a bucket of ice and went for $100 a table. Single drinks paid less in the long run unless you had a large group at your table. As time went on a set was just a bottle of overpriced champagne. The bill would have the girls' initials on it and it got paid out at the end of the night. Girls were required to settle up any dance tips with the house the moment you got off stage. Steven didn't want anyone 'shorting' the house. In the case of a dispute, the house kept the table tab. That would cut out the backstabbing bitches that would try to steal your tab.

I had about thirty girls show up to audition for three or four spots on the dance roster. Cisco eliminated about one third just by standing at the door and doing his doorman thing. The club advertised 'All Nude Girls', but it was up to the girls if they wanted to dance topless only, but we still needed a few girls that would show '*The Full Monty*'. Girls giving lap dances at the table were required to wear bottoms or 'Daisy Dukes'. Anything goes in the VIP lounge at the girls' sole discretion, but sex or prostitution on the premises was strictly forbidden.

The next girl to audition walked up to me on the catwalk was pretty but she was shaking like a leaf. I knew this chick may have taken her clothes off for her friends, but to a club full of horny strangers was a whole different thing. "M... mm... My name is Cindy..." She stuttered. Her name caught my undivided attention.

"You ever dance before?"

"Yeah... in clubs... all the time..."

"Not dance clubs... I meant in strip clubs... in front of thousands of drooling, leering perverts?" Our club only had a max occupancy of 175 but I wanted to scare her out of auditioning. I knew the deal with this wannabe. She still stood there on stage, she didn't run off. Okay! Let's turn up the heat a little. "Jackie... a little music please."

"What do you want to dance to Cindy...?" He asked trying to be polite.

I waved my hand to let him know to play anything and not to talk to her. The music kicked in. She stood there for a while and began to dance. She wasn't a bad club dancer, but she wasn't a stripper by any definition of the word. She was getting into it and was beginning to get more comfortable and expressive with her dancing. That's when I motioned for Jackie to cut the music. She stopped suddenly as if I had interrupted her good time.

"Is something wrong?" She asked quietly.

"Let's see the goods..."

"What?"

"The 'goods'... lose the blouse and the bra... let's see the goods!" She slowly put her hand on her top button but she shivered and hesitated a bit. "Come on honey! Time's a wasting... I have other people waiting to audition...show us your tits!" She trembled a bit and slowly began to unbutton her blouse. She looked like a trapped rabbit. I threw my hands in the air. "We getting naked *today* or *what*...?" I said sarcastically. She unbuttoned her blouse slowly and dropped it to the floor. "Let's go... lose the bra...!" She placed her hands on her shoulders to pull down the straps and slowly eased them off her shoulders. I stood up. "Do I have to *show* you what to do?" And I took my top and bra off and showed her my tits. There was a look of dismay on her face and she averted her eyes. I turned to the other girls waiting to audition. "It takes a lot of strength and courage to show your tits to total strangers and then have them throw money at you. If you bitches can't handle that, don't waste my time and get the fuck out! Now!" I pinched my nipples and worked my nipple rings. A few girls got their stuff and left quietly. I turned back to the stage and Cindy was still standing there, shivering. "And *you're* still here... *be... cause...*?"

"I could work here as a waitress..." She stammered

"Waitresses here work topless honey..." I said plainly. She started to cry. "What's your problem...?"

"I need the job and the money..."

"For what...?"

'Tuition... rent, books are so expensive... I had no idea how much it would cost!" She sobbed.

"What's your major?"

"English Lit... with... a minor in Political Science... I not sure what I want to do yet..."

I shook my head. (Okay the kid had brains but not too much common sense. Just another college girl who thought that they could supplement their income by stripping...) I thought. Don't get me wrong, three of my top girls who strip here are from the local college, two others work as hookers at the cat house, but this girl wouldn't be able to be either. "Put your shit back on and get your ass over here." I said as I went and got my top and put it back on. She got her blouse back on faster than it came off and she shuffled her sorry ass towards me.

"Yes Ms. Latex?" I shook my head again. (What fucking country ass farm did this southern fried bitch come from?) I took a page from my notebook and wrote a name and number and handed it to her. "Is this for another strip club?" She asked meekly.

Now I was getting angry! *"NO BITCH*! It's the name of someone in financial aide in your school... She'll hook you up with a job on campus... tutoring or something. She can even get you a scholarship to pay for your books if your grades are good enough..."

"They are... should I tell her you sent me?"

"You better fucking not!" And I shook my head. I didn't need anyone to know that '*my contact*' stripped at the club once or twice.

"Thank you so much..."

I cut her off. "If you call me 'Ms. Latex' again I *will* go over there and bitch slap you!"

She smiled guardedly and hugged me. "Thank you again!" she whispered.

"Get the fuck out of here!" I whispered back. She left but not without turning back one more time. "I said OUT!" I shouted. Two other girls left right behind her. There were only a few girls left to audition and I was still at least two girls short on the roster. *"Worse come to worse... I'll fill in this week until I can find a girl..."* I thought.

L.L. thought she had hit rock bottom when the next girl up actually had bullet and stab wounds on her body, and they were all keloid. No matter what, Lady Latex tried to run a classy club, Steven would accept no less. One by one she eliminated the applicants and still just needed two or three new girls because one usually dropped out anyway. On occasion the club would have a 'guest stripper', a popular porn star or a 'gypsy' to attract a bigger crowd. Cisco came over to her and gave her a list of potentials. She told the girls still waiting to go to the bar and have a drink while she checked on things. And just so you know, L.L. had told Jackie to eliminate any girl who liked to drink way too much at the bar. A drunken and rowdy stripper was bad for business and hard to manage and wasn't worth it in the long run. Also it gave him time to sort out any trouble makers. After a while Jackie gave L.L. the 'signal' that one girl was a bit of a 'player hater' and may be a problem. I nodded my head and acknowledged him.

I checked the list of 'guest stars' that were available to dance and would sign autographs for the clientele. "Hooker... hooker... nothing *but* trouble... prostitute... *She's* long in the tooth, what? Is my grandma gonna audition too?" I laughed and continued down the list. "Porn star... I thought she was dead...? Porn star... *undercover vice cop...*, way too much drama... hooker... When did she get out of jail...? Won't work with *her* ever again... I thought she quit the business...? Porn star... coke fiend... heroin addict..."

Don't get me wrong, I know about a third of my girls were users... I love my Ganja and I've had a little 'tootski' on rare occasions. I don't mind users... I don't hire abusers. Casual use by girls who understand the meaning of the word discretion and would never bring that shit into this club is a big stretch from some crazy bitch shooting up 'speed balls' up in the dressing room... I'm just saying!

I kept the porn stars in mind... They were the only celebrity guest stars that attracted a big crowd but they had to be paid a big 'stipend' to even show up and that didn't guarantee that they would show up and if they did show up, some felt that dancing on stage was beneath them. Ha! You have multiple men cum all over you, *in* you and in *your* mouth, they use you up like a fucking wind up toy... and *dancing* is beneath you? That thought brought a feeling of morose to L.L. She shook it off then looked down the list again. That's when she saw a name at the bottom that had no business being on this long list of losers.

"Natalie? *The Naughty Dancer*? She's available? Are you shitting me? Cisco where are you?" She called over to Cisco. "Cisco? Is this true or is there some other bitch trying to pass herself off as The Naughty Dancer?"

"I spoke to her myself... she's going to be passing through town and she gave me a call..."

"And you wasted my time with these other bitches on this list... *why*?"

"It's not sure that she can come to work here... I'd have to call her..."

"And there isn't a phone in your hand... *because...*?"

Cisco pulled out his cell phone. "All right! Alright! I'll call her... damn!"

"You *will be* damned if she doesn't come to work here!" L.L. didn't know Natalie personally but when she was checking out other clubs for research, she had caught her act once. This chick was amazing on stage. She would work as a gypsy in Vegas clubs. Cisco knew her from when he did freelance security at another club before he came to work here. Natalie doesn't warm up to just anyone but she liked that he had a respect for women and would call him if she was in town. This over the top bitch worked a stage like Wells Fargo bringing in the gold! It would be a real feather in her cap if she could get her to do just one night! It would be a real coo if she could get her to stay on as a regular...

"Okay ladies... back on the pole... Who's up next? She looked towards the bar and Jackie had asked two other girls to leave. Cisco escorted them out. Jackie just shook his head. L.L.

nodded. One of them was a girl she was going to hire. "Damn... I really wanted to work with her. That girl had skills..." Just as the next girl stepped up, Jackie gave her the signal that this was the problem child that 'was hating' while she and the others were drinking at the bar. L.L. wasn't about to hire a diva who was going to cause any trouble back stage. She had enough on her plate running this place but she would at least give the girl a chance.

"I'm Cecelia but you can call me CeeCee..."

"What have you got for me CeeCee?"

CeeCee hit the stage like an old pro. She had all the right moves, the attitude, the stage presence and she had no problem taking her top off. But something was a bit off. Would she have even noticed if Jackie hadn't pointed her out to her? She decided to see if she could push CeeCee's button's to see how much a problem she could be. "Do me a favor and wait there for a moment..." CeeCee stood there. L.L. wanted to see how long she would stand there without catching an attitude problem. It didn't take long!

"Well? Do I get the job or not... what are we waiting for?"

L.L. smiled. This was the same ploy Steven had used to weed Cindy out of his club when they first met. It worked every time. Also, when CeeCee became agitated her voice changed. That's when L.L. knew. "Just give me a moment... could you take your jeans down please?"

CeeCee got defensive. "Why?"

"I want to see your legs..."

"What about my legs do you want to see?"

"I want to see... if you have three of them..." L.L. said sarcastically. CeeCee cut her eyes and begrudgingly unzipped herself and pulled out her penis and let it hang out and put her hands on her hips.

"So?"

"So... your services aren't required here..."

"Bitch!" CeeCee shouted "I should have known this would happen. All you fucking prejudiced 'breeders' are nothing more that a bunch of..." and his voice got high. "Haters!"

L.L. just looked at her. "You wanna put that away now?"

She cut her eyes, crossed her arms and refused to tuck herself back in. "We're here, we're queer... get used to it!" And she snapped her fingers in the air and she stood there defiantly.

L.L. yelled out into the bar. "Cisco? Is Ms. Demeanor back there?"

"Yes she is..."

"Could you ask her to come out a moment please?"

Cisco nodded and came out of the back room with a tall, beautiful woman.

"Yes L.L.? Did you want to see me?" She said.

"Do you see what's happening here?"

"Yes... I heard it all too..."

"With your permission... would you mind?"

"Anything for you L.L..." CeeCee looked at this woman as if to say "*And what is this bitch going to do?*" CeeCee watched as she unzipped her jeans and took out her cock. "And mine is bigger than yours... bitch!" She looked at L.L. "Will that be all L.L.?"

"Yes, I think you proved my point..."

"Love you!"

"Love you more...!" And Ms. Demeanor tucked herself back in and strutted out of the room. L.L. turned her attention to CeeCee who was just zipping back up. "The reason I didn't hire you is not because you're gay... it's because I don't like your attitude... I don't hire bitches that throw shade!"

CeeCee looked at her. "What did you say?"

"You heard me!" And L.L. took her first and index finger, spread them, brought them to either side of her mouth and flicked her tongue wildly between them. "Bitch betta recognize!" CeeCee stormed off the stage and tried to strut his/her - he/she ass out. L.L. called out to her just as she got to the door. "And next time remember one thing! If it wasn't for two '*breeders*'... your gay ass wouldn't be here!"

L.L. would, if the 'girl' was talented, and could pass without detection, hire a cross dresser or a transgender dancer. They could dance and they could waitress topless. They were just not allowed to work the tables or give any lap dances. She used them as roster fillers so that the real girls could work the crowds on a busy night. There was no reason to upset a customer who might get something they didn't want to pay for. What the customer didn't know would not hurt them and it was 'a need to know' basis. She was checking out her options and was sorting out the roster and was making notes when the next girl to audition walked up to her.

"Hi... I'm Morgana Winston..."

"Hey..." L.L. said without looking up from her notes. "Why do you want to work here?" The girl began a slow and reserved answer which showed that she had very little confidence and maybe a low self-esteem. L.L. slowly looked up, starting with her feet and checked out the merchandise. Nice shoes, nice legs... Okay! She's got a little junk in the trunk. The clients will like that... small tight waist... nice... wow! Nice rack! Large and firm but not too 'over the top'... "Those tits real?"

"Yes ma'am..."

Okay! This might work and then L.L. focused on her face... Holy SHIT! It's a good thing the lights were dimmed, L.L. could have been blinded for life! This chick had a body that could stop traffic and a face that could stop a clock. No, really! I'm not over exaggerating. Her eyes were too far apart, her teeth were real short and she had a gap you could slide a dick into. She had an overbite that could cripple a man and misshapen lips. And the worse case of acne I had ever seen in my life! Did this bitch go bobbing for French fries? And her hair...? Looked like someone stuck a scouring pad on her head! She stuck her thumb in her mouth and began to suck on it, but not in a sensual way. It was a bit more obcene. L.L. knew this chick had to have been sexually abused as a child. L.L. tried not to stare but she could not help it. It was like looking at a terrible accident, you wanted to turn away but you couldn't. She turned to Cisco and raised her hands. *"Why didn't you eliminate this girl at the door?"* she mouthed. Cisco raised his shoulders and mouthed. *"I'm sorry... I thought she was here with a friend!"* After a moment L.L. turned to her and said... "Can you dance?" She asked, hoping she would crash and burn like Cindy did.

"Mmmm huh!" she mumbled with her thumb still in her mouth. She walked onto the runway and dropped her clothes faster than lightning. *"Hmm? Those clothes came off too damn fast... she must have been hooking too..."* L.L. thought. The girl began to dance and gyrate like it was nobody's business! She was graceful and very flexible but L.L. just could not get past how fucking ugly this bitch was! *"The only way this bitch was working here is if she put a paper bag over her head"* L.L. thought to herself. Then she was struck by an epiphany! L.L. took her scarf hanging around her chair and wrapped it around Mogana's face like a veil. "What are you doing?" she asked.

"You wanna work here?" L.L. asked her.

"Yeah...?"

"From now on... you go on stage as Princess Layah!" It was perfect, Star Wars was hot, and this chick was not; well not until she covered her face! It was a perfect fantasy...

"Why do I have to cover my face?"

"Does this bitch own a mirror?" I thought. "I'm sorry... did you want to work here... or *not*?" She nodded. "Then you're Princess Layah... and you don't dance here without the scarf around your face... to... give... the clients a little mystery... it really helps...!" (Yeah... helps them keep their lunch down!) "You have a problem with that?" L.L. asked her. She shook her head no. "Okay... put you clothes back on..." She took off the scarf and held it out to L.L. "Keep it... consider it your hiring bonus..." (I would have to burn it anyway!)

Okay...you think I'm being mean and cruel here... but I'm not. So let's make a long story short shall we? Princess Layah was one of our top earners in the club for about two months... she had become a club and fan favorite. There was a disco remix of the Star Wars theme that played for over twenty minutes and my girl worked 'it' like an Imperial Storm-trooper! All was fine, until one night that Layah was being coached and prodded by the crowd to 'take it off, take it off'... referring to the scarf covering her face (she was already naked!). Well... this totally oblivious bitch decided to make that her 'finale' that night... no truer words were ever spoken. Before I could snatch her ass off the stage she had un-wrapped the scarf off her face to the anticipation of the packed house. Then there was a hush in the room, then the groan of the startled clients all at once as they winced at the sight of her... then the laughing started!

"Fuck!" I exclaimed... She stood there in the bright lights of the stage and looked around the club. She actually could not figure out what they were laughing at! Then... reality slapped her in the face... literally. Some of the more rambunctious clients started throwing their drinks at her. They wanted her off the stage and they wanted her off NOW! They even threw beer bottles on the stage. They didn't really try to hit her but they wanted her off the stage pronto!

Two of the other girls, under the threat of bodily harm from flying debris, rushed up to get her off the stage. Security had their hands full trying to calm the rowdy customers and calm the other clients who were laughing hysterically. It took about five to ten minutes to get control back of the club floor. They had to remove two of them from the premises. I honestly considered turning on the house lights and calling it a night! But once they settled down I got another girl on the stage quickly and things got back to normal. By the time I was able to get back stage to check on her... she was gone! The two girls who had rescued her were softly crying in the back room. They liked her quiet and sweet demeanor. She was good people and didn't deserve to be humiliated like that. She had gotten dressed, packed her shit and she was gone and never coming back! But you know what really gets my goat? These two bitches blamed me for what happened! Are you shitting me? How is this... *my* fault?

"You never should have hired her in the first place..."

What? Are you fucking serious? These chicks are putting the blame on me because I gave her a job? I got her off the street and off her back and it's all *my* fault? I found a solution to a problem that this chick didn't even think she had... and *I'm* the bad guy? I just cut my eyes at them and promised myself never to put myself out there again! Speaking of putting out... now I have to put my naked ass back in rotation tonight! Damn!

Oh, in case you were wondering, Cindy is doing very well in school. Money is still tight but with her campus job, a book scholarship and her parents helping her out, she's doing okay. She sends me a letter or postcard every once and again, but I better NOT see that bitch in here ever again!

Now I have to break the story line here and the reason will make total sense to you in a future chapter. After this we'll go back to where we left off... promise!

53

A few years later, I was coming out of the club to take a break from doing the books and inventory with Jackie and waiting on liquor and linen deliveries. I stepped outside to light a cigarette when I saw a woman standing next to a car in the parking lot. She didn't seem familiar to me. She was conservatively dressed in a gray skirt suit. She looked like a librarian or a high school administrator. As I puffed on my cigarette she walked over to me. I didn't know who she was but then I recognized that stride coming towards me. "Can I help you?" I said as I exhaled out the smoke.

"You don't remember me do you…? I'm…"

"I don't remember you… because I don't know you! What do you want?" I crossed my arms and took another drag.

"I do believe we do know each other…"

"I *do* believe… we *don't*!" I said sarcastically as I flicked my ashes.

She smiled at me. "I just wanted to thank you…"

I took another puff and blew it out. "You're welcome… whoever you are!"

She nodded knowingly, smiled to me and said. "Take care of yourself…"

"I will…" and I flicked my ashes. "You take care of *yourself*…!" She headed back to her car and just as she opened the car door to get in, I called out to her. "Hey Cindy…!" She stopped and turned to me.

"Yes?"

"So what *did* you wind up majoring in… may I ask?"

"Political science…" was her reply.

"So…? You're gonna be the next governor or something…?"

She shrugged her shoulders. "I don't know… I guess we'll have to see how far I go…"

I took a long drag and exhaled. "How far do you think you *would* have gotten… if I *had* let you work for me?"

Cindy paused and shook her head. "Not as far as I *have* gotten… had I never met you… *Ms. Latex*…" and Cindy grinned. I smiled back. She got in her car and mouthed "Love you!"

I mouthed back. "Love you more!" "*Crazy country ass bitch*!" I thought as I took another drag of my cigarette. Cindy waved, put the car in gear and drove off. I put out my cigarette and just as I opened the door, Jackie was about to come out.

"Who was that?"

"I have no fucking idea! Maybe she was selling Mary Kay."

"Don't they drive pink cars?"

"Get your ass inside already!" I paused at the back door for a moment and for a split second I was in a parallel universe and the Cindy who had died of a drug overdose in a filthy back alley was replaced by the Cindy who was on her way to Washington… A tear came to my eye. I wondered what *my* 'equivalent' was up to, or was I the one who was better off?

The Tortured Soul Trilogy
(Living La Vida Puta)
Chapter 10
(Naughty Is A Dancer...)

L.L. and Cisco were getting ready to open the club for business L.L. was working on the night's roster in the back room when one of the girls walked up to her. "Who's the new girl...?"

"What... *new*... girl...? L.L. had no idea what she was talking about and Steven wouldn't hire a new girl without telling her about it. "Where is she?"

"At the bar with Cisco..."

L.L. walked out of the dressing room to see Cisco talking to the woman sitting at the bar. They were a little too 'chummy' for her taste. L.L. shook her head. What the fuck do I care who Cisco is being 'chummy' with?

The woman had her back to her, but she had a hot little body and a mane of hair to die for. It wasn't a weave because she loved running her hand through it and shaking it all about. She had an amazing tight ass in her jeans. L.L. felt funny that she was somehow 'flirting' with Cisco. Again, she didn't understand why she cared. She should have been more interested in her than him. Just as L.L. was about to walk up behind her Cisco spoke.

"L.L....? This is Natalie..."

And Natalie swiveled in her chair to L.L. and offered to shake her hand. "Hi... I'm Naughty..." she said with a smirk on her face.

L.L. shook her hand and smiled. "I'll bet you..." I started to say but then I noticed Cisco behind Natalie take his hand and make a cutting motion across his throat and shake his head no. Too many people thought it was funny and so original to say "*I'll bet you are!*" to the point that Natalie was pretty much sick and tired of hearing it. "...You're... anxious to check the place out..." L.L. finished.

Natalie looked at her and smiled. "Nice cover... I appreciate the effort that took..."

"So... would you like the nickel tour?"

"Sure..." L.L. showed her around. Natalie checked out the stage and walked it to gauge the width and length. She wanted to know how much room she had to work her magic. She did a spot turn on the stage to see how smooth the floor was and whether to dance in these heels or something else she had bought with her. She grabbed the brass pole to get a feel of its thickness. Different clubs had different size poles and if she was going to use it in her routine, she had to get used to its size and adjust her grip. She held onto the pole like it was an old friend. To some girls, dancing was a lot like sex. As a matter of fact I once heard that dancing was the vertical expression of a horizontal desire...

"Mind if I take the pole out for a spin?"

"Please do..." L.L. very was impressed with Natalie's professionalism. Natalie pushed and tugged on the pole to see if it had any give or sway and would take her weight. Natalie was a petite girl but her best dance moves required a strong pole. Satisfied that it would hold, she took a few steps back and launched herself at the pole. She then proceeded to do multiple spins on the pole that L.L. lost count of. She looked like a kid on a merry go round. Natalie didn't actually say it but she knew she was thinking, *"Wheeeeeeeeeeee!"* Despite that, Natalie was all business. She laid down certain ground rules before she would work in this club and those rules were *not* negotiable!

"No touching, no groping, no lap dances, and no bottomless under *any* circumstances..."

L.L. raised an eyebrow. "You're a tranny?" L.L. had to check her gaydar. It had never failed her before.

"No... I'm not a transsexual... I'm just very adamant about not showing my goodies to strangers... I like to make my money on the dance floor only... I'll work the bar, but not topless... I have issues with being groped... Is that a problem?"

"No problem at all... What about the V.I.P. room?"

"I'll work the room if the need arises, but I make the rules once I'm inside... Okay?" L.L. instinctively knew that '*making the rules*' didn't imply what *would* happen in the V.I.P. room as much as it meant what would *not* happen. L.L. nodded and agreed.

"If you don't mind... I want to go to the dressing room and get my station together for tonight, and I want to have a talk with the other girls..."

"Why?" L.L. was intrigued.

"I'm the 'new girl' here... I want to let them know I'm not gonna fuck with their 'sweethearts', but I'm here to make the rent money like anybody else. I don't need any shit jumping off!"

A 'sweetheart' was another name for a 'sugar daddy' or a girls' regular client, who would on any given night, would pay her bills. The girls each had a guy like that she would depend on. Stepping on a dancer's toes or fucking with her rent money... not cool! Most girls didn't trust the new girl or a gypsy to respect their territory and sometimes it would get ugly. Sometimes it would get violent. Natalie was determined to avoid conflict on or off stage. L.L. liked that.

"You're the boss!" she was very taken with Natalie at this point. L.L. knew Natalie was '*the shit*' and gave her a wide berth to work with and she did that for *no* girl!

All the girls were working it that night. Every girl was on top of her game and putting their best moves out there. Each one was a tough act to follow. That's when the DJ announced 'The Naughty Dancer' was coming on next. There was a lack luster reaction from the crowd. They only wanted to see a naked woman out there, and they wanted one now. These rubes had never heard of The Naughty Dancer and they were in for an unexpected treat. Jackie turned to L.L. sitting at the bar. "I hope this kid got the goods... It's a bad night to premiere an untested new girl..."

"Just wait... you'll see." L.L said and she sat back and sipped her bourbon.

Once the spotlight hit her, Natalie's mind went blank. She focused only on dancing, on the performance. She was like a veteran racecar driver and the green light was on. She was totally focused. Her bosom swelled as that first adrenalin rush hit her. Dance was her expression of her soul. It was her release. It was her gift. She stomped her right foot on stage and her steel-tipped stiletto heel hit the wooden stage and it sounded like a gunshot. That... was to get the crowds' undivided attention. She paused and took a deep breath; the crowd seemed to hold their breath in anticipation. The DJ hit her music. Natalie attacked the stage. She attacked it hard. Her routine was like a combination of exotic dancing, slam dancing and the Flamenco. She hit the pole and spun on it like it was on casters. She could spin four or five times without stopping. She was fluid and graceful, yet she hit all her floor moves hard and tight. The crowd didn't know what to expect from Natalie and Natalie wasn't about to disappoint them. She never disappointed the crowd; after all, she wasn't dancing for them. She was dancing for herself; the crowd was just being given the honor and privilege to be allowed to watch her.

Natalie blew the crowd away that night; she was in the zone and her amazing, toned, muscular body gave an aura of power and grace. When Natalie finished her set, her body was glistening with sweat and covered in bruises. Don't get it twisted... Natalie danced hard and sometimes her body took the brunt of her dance moves. Natalie gave 110% of herself when she hit the stage. She holds nothing back. That's just the way she rolls! As she exited the stage area, tips in hand, L.L. had gone back stage and was standing there with her mouth open.

"That was amazing! I have never seen dance moves like that in my life!" L.L. said. "*I wonder what in hell motivates her to dance that hard*?" she thought and then saw bruises and scars on Natalie that could not have come from her high intensity dance moves. She silently pondered over them, seriously considering the demons in her past. We all have them. L.L. would respect Natalie's privacy and not ask her about hers.

Natalie knew Lady Latex and Cisco didn't own the club, but they were in charge if the owner wasn't there. Natalie remained in the rotation for several weeks and Steven liked how she fit into the mix. The club was more popular with her in the new line up of dancers. Natalie liked working there. She made good money and she liked the people that worked there. She was also a favorite of the clientele. Unfortunately the life of a 'gypsy' is self-explanatory. You work at a club, you get paid, you move on... It was a lifestyle Natalie had gotten used to. Don't stay long enough to grow roots. '*Everybody leaves*' was her mantra, it was her code.

The day Natalie had to leave for greener pastures, she thanked L.L. and Cisco for the opportunity to work there and gave them a hug that most would consider 'insincere', but that wasn't the case. Natalie was a very private person and knew the nature of life on the road. True friendships were hard to come by and her aloofness was just her defense mechanism not to get too personally 'involved'.

L.L. watched as she got in her car and drove off. "Damn... I'm gonna miss that girl! How the hell am I gonna replace her?" Girls come and go... for different reasons, some good, some bad, and some very bad. L.L. tried to keep a core group of girls that she could count on, but the nature of this business required change. By the time Natalie left, there was a whole new group of girls working there than when she first started. She thought of that saying, *"People are in your life for a reason, a season or a lifetime..."* L.L. was the only veteran of the place and she thought the only reason she stayed so long is because she ran the place. It's like Natalie said. *"Everybody leaves!"* L.L. wondered when her day would come, but that day wasn't today.

The Tortured Soul Trilogy
(Living La Vida Puta)
Chapter 11
(Someone to Watch over Me)

Steven ran a square house and L.L. didn't play shit. This was their livelihood and they protected the club and the girls like a lioness protects her cubs. But even with due vigilance, sometimes trouble just… happens. L.L. smelled trouble in the ranks but she could not figure out where it was. One of the girls was pulling shit on club premises and she had to find out who it was. She didn't encourage the girls to rat each other out, cause then, how could she trust you? But whoever it was; was endangering all of them and the club rule was. "A bitch has got a bitch's back!" Another one of the club's rules was if you placed two fingers of your hand, one finger under each eye, it meant '*Watch me!*' One finger under an eye followed by a point meant '*Watch her or him!*' If a girl yelled '*Static*' it meant "*Get your ass over here now! The shit is going down!*"

One night Ebony was outside the back door having a cigarette break. Cisco was out there keeping an eye out like usual. Ebony put her cigarette out and was about to enter the club when she stepped back outside, placed a finger under her eye and pointed at the doors' threshold, that meant '*Keep an eye on the next person who walks through the door!*' Cisco nodded his head and Ebony went inside. A moment later, a gypsy named Tanya came out and put a cigarette in her mouth. Cisco lit it for her. "How you doing tonight Tanya?"

She puffed her cigarette. "Good Cisco… I'm good…" and she took another puff and put it out and began to walk towards the parking lot. Cisco found it strange that she put out a fresh cigarette and she didn't go back inside.

"Where you going?"

"To my car… I want to make a call on my cell… it's too noisy in there…"

"You want me to walk you?"

"You're sweet... but I'm good... my car is just across the street... and I have my cell if I get into any trouble..." and Tanya sashayed over to her car.

Nothing happened that night, but for the next two weeks Tanya needed to go her car to make a call a lot. L.L. knew she was doing something shady but she didn't know what and as long she did her dirt off club premises... it really wasn't her business. "You think she's a snitch?" Cisco asked.

"Nothing to snitch about! Steven runs a square club, but I'm gonna keep a close eye on her..." L.L. responded. L.L. could not catch this chick doing anything wrong, she wasn't doing heavy drugs, but the hairs on the back of her neck would tingle whenever she walked past her or if she was in the room. L.L. didn't need any more reasons to call out the big dog. She called Michael and told him the deal, he said he would *Make a call and take care of it...*" Two days later Tanya went to the parking lot to *'make a call...'* Ten minutes later there were sirens and two cop cars were in the parking lot down the block. Cisco called L.L. over, L.L. went into the back room and any girl who was 'dressed' but not working the floor was told to come outside. They all stood there as Tanya was cuffed and placed in a squad car. She was arrested for prostitution. She had been propositioning clients in the club to meet her at her car and her *'side business'* was bringing in over $500 a night. Michael had an undercover cop sent to the club and she propositioned him. Once they were off club property, he busted her. The cop was 'on the payroll' so to speak. "Ladies? Anyone else with any secrets that you're keeping from me?" L.L. said loudly. They shook their heads and went back inside. L.L. knew the news would spread like wildfire in the club and any other girl with any bright *'ideas'* of being an independent contractor would think better of it. L.L. took a drag from her cigarette, put it out and sighed. "Stupid bitch should have come to me... she would have easily made twice as much working at my brothel and Michael would have protected her instead of throwing her ass under the bus..."

The Tortured Soul Trilogy
(Living La Vida Puta)
Chapter 12
(Don't Stand So Close To Me)

L.L. saw that the next girl set to dance, Lady Hendricks, was nervous and antsy by the back curtain. She seemed worried and upset about something and kept peeking through the curtains at the crowd. L.L. didn't care but she had to know if there was a problem in her club that she needed to know about. "What's the problem...? Since when do you have stage fright?"

"L.L.... I can't go on tonight..."

"Why the fuck not?"

"It's embarrassing..."

"Bitch... you've been shaking your naked ass on that stage for over a year... *now* you're embarrassed?"

"You don't understand..."

"En... light... ten... me..." L.L. enunciated.

"There's a guy out there I don't want to see... or more important, I don't want him to see me!"

"What now? Don't tell me you have a stalker? Or worse, a boyfriend that doesn't know you're a stripper?"

"Worse than that...!"

"What could possibly be worse than that...? Your father...?"

"No! My college professor... who doesn't know I strip to pay my tuition..."

L.L. peeked out of the rear stage curtain. "Where is he?" Lady Hendricks carefully peeked and saw him sitting way the in the back drinking a shot and smiling as if he was the cat that ate the canary.

"That's him in the back with the dark rimmed glasses..."

"Where?"

"Wearing the Oxford jacket..."

"The *what*...?"

"The jacket with the leather patches on the elbows... guy who *looks* like a college professor..."

L.L. looked at him. "That geek...?"

"Yeah that's him... what am I going to do? I can't go out there tonight...cover for me tonight! Please?"

L.L. looked at her like she was crazy. "Bitch please... I'm *not* dancing tonight, and we don't have enough girls in the rotation as it is...

"But I thought a bitch has got a bitch's back?" she said softly.

I looked at her. She was right. "Even if you didn't go out there tonight, you still got big problems kid."

"Why do you say that?"

"That chucklehead asked Jackie if you were dancing tonight... and he specifically asked for you by name... he already knows you're a stripper!"

"Damn it! I've been putting off his sexual advances for most of the semester. I know he's going to use this to blackmail me into having sex with him..."

"You're shitting me...!"

"No I'm not... he would do anything to get me in bed... or give him head in his office..." L.L. thought for a moment. She looked at Lady Hendricks in the eye. (*Was that a problem*?) "I am NOT giving him head... I'll rather fail the course first!" Lady Hendricks said.

"Does this guy have a weakness? Something that we could use against him?"

"Not that I know of... He has no family and he came here, so he doesn't care who knows he's here..."

"What if we had pictures of him with a prostitute?"

Lady Hendricks sighed. "Knowing him, he would probably send them out as Christmas cards..."

"Okay then... subtleties are wasted on this guy... We're gonna have to go *old school*..."

"What?"

"Stay here... Don't take your turn on stage until I say so..."

"Why?"

"Don't ask questions... do as I tell you..." L.L. changed the rotation and put Jessie, 'The Cajun Queen' on first and then left the back stage. Lady Hendricks waited and then L.L. came back about five minutes later. "Okay kid... you can go out there after Jessie finishes her set..."

"But what about...?"

"A bitch has got a bitch's back! It's all taken care of... you'll never have to worry about him ever again!"

"What did you do?"

L.L. cut her eyes at her. "You don't need to know... now get out there... you're on next!"

Lady Hendricks came out to "*Foxy Lady*" and danced a bit apprehensive until she noticed that the professor was gone. She finished her set to "*Purple Haze*" without any incident. After that she went to the back room. Cisco was there washing up in the sink. From her viewpoint it looked like he was cleaning blood from his rings. "Cisco! Are you alright? Did you cut yourself?"

"No sweetie... this isn't my blood!"

"It's not?" Cisco shook his head no as he dried his rings with a paper towel. "Whose blood is it?"

Cisco smiled. "You don't need to know..." Lady Hendricks was a bit put off by that response. Cisco put his rings back on and kissed her on the cheek. "You don't have to worry, everything will be alright... I promise!"

The next day Heather, Lady Hendricks real name, went to class and her professor was there. He didn't seem harmed in any way but he was extremely respectful and mindful of her. It was if something or someone put the fear of God in him. Neither he nor Heather ever spoke about that night and she passed her class honestly and was never harassed by him again. That night, Cisco had poured some fake blood on his knuckles and convinced the professor that he didn't take kindly to people blackmailing or harassing his girls... The professor got the hint!

The Tortured Soul Trilogy
(Living La Vida Puta)
Chapter 13
(Cuckoo for Cocoa Puffs)

Now I told you that the girls that worked for me at the strip club had issues and carried a lot of personal baggage. They suffered from broken homes, drugs, alcoholism, financial problems, abuse (child and domestic), low self-esteem, mental disorders, being a single parent, criminal records and any combination of these problems. The girls who worked in my cathouses were no better. We were the dregs of humanity; a sub-culture of women who society had turned their backs on and generally ignored... unless we were dancing naked - vertically or horizontally. They came from all walks of life, different ethnicities, social classes and different levels of education. Oh yeah, I've had school teachers with degrees working for me in one capacity or another! One girl was a concert pianist! It was for this reason that I did not get involved with their lives and I did not want them involved in my personal life. I have way too much to deal with my own shit; I sure don't need to deal with yours. I have a business to run here. Come to work on time, do your job and keep your nose clean and we were square. Bring drama into my life or the job and your days were numbered bitch!

Having said that, there was one girl who got me involved in her life and drama; her name was Chanel Decker but went by the name of Cocoa Chanel because of her smooth mocha skin. Cocoa was a lesbian... I'm sorry... Did I forget to list that under these bitches' issues? Hmmm? Maybe cause I don't see that as an issue! Well she was a girl who had a different personality flaw. She liked to take in strays. No, not dogs or cats, stray... people. This chick thought that she was personally responsible for fixing the troubles of every hard luck story that came her way. All you needed was a sob story, puppy dog eyes and a need to be taken care of and Cocoa was 'Johnny on the spot'. I guess it was a reaction to her parents not giving her enough love and attention while she was growing up.

Personally I don't care what you do on your own time as long as it doesn't interfere with my business. Cocoa had a revolving door of loser lesbian lovers in her life but the worse one of them all was Traci. This bitch wasn't the bottom of the barrel, you had to turn the barrel over and scrape this bitch up. Traci had no job, no skills and wasn't even that good looking; as a woman or a man! Cocoa could do much better than her... just by being all by herself! Cocoa paid for everything for her, her rent, her bills, bought her clothes (expensive men's clothing). She paid when they went out together and paid for Traci if she went out without Cocoa. Traci would even show up some nights and just take Cocoa's take that night and then put her drinks on Cocoa's tab! Traci was nothing more than a low life pimp! (And I say that present company accepted!) How stupid is this bitch? I mean really...?

Like I said, I don't get involved, but Cocoa started taking days off without any advance warning. She started to stiff the staff at tip out even when she pulled in serious cash. Oh, Steven doesn't like it when you short the house! That's a huge no-no! The other girls started to avoid her because she kept bumming off them. She would bum cigarettes, food, loose change, or gas money, whatever. She would borrow your shoes, body oil and make-up. The other girls were really getting tired of her. Don't get me wrong, every girl has a bad day once in a while. Cocoa's bad day lasted for months! Her work ethics was slipping and her act on and off stage was getting a little tiresome. One night she was supposed to be working the pole but she was M.I.A. The girl on stage extended her set to two more songs but she needed a break. "Where the *FUCK* is Cocoa?" I said. One of the girls pointed towards the dressing room. "Tell her to get her ass out here... NOW!" The girl went in the back but came out a moment later... no Cocoa...! "What the hell is going on back there...?" The girl just shook her head without saying a word; she wasn't going to rat out another girl. But the stage was now empty and the paying customers were cooling off. This is a bad day to piss me off! Technically, any day is a bad day to piss me off... but I digress... "You... get on stage right now!" I said to the girl. She nodded and went and did her set to cover for Cocoa. I went into the dressing room to see what was holding her up. "This bitch better *not* be dead... because it would really interfere with me killing her!" I went to the back only to see

Cocoa at her dressing station... still in her street clothes... on a cell phone arguing with who I knew had to Traci!

"I don't want to talk to you... (Pause) I don't want to talk to you... (Pause) I don't want to talk to you..."

She kept repeating that over and over. "*If you don't want to talk to her... then hang up the fucking phone, bitch!*" I thought! "Cocoa! Hang up the phone and get your ass on that stage... you got five minutes to get naked and shake something... *move it!*" And then Cocoa did something I didn't expect her to do... she held up her index finger up to me and... *shushed* me! "*OH NO... THIS BITCH DIDN'T!!!*" I ran up on her, snatched the phone out of her hand and turned it off. "My office... NOW!" I had to pull her out on the carpet to try to save her from herself. Cocoa just kept saying "*But my man, cause my man, when my man... blah, blah, blah!*" to defend (s)him and herself. Every lover she had, it was the same excuses. I have had enough of this shit!

"Cut the shit Cocoa... They're not MEN! Even if this bulldyke bitch *had* balls, she'd be no man! Your lover is supposed to complete you, not *deplete* you! They're *using* you, taking your money and stepping on your heart and what do they have to offer you? They lick your pussy? Is that *it*? Traci is a low life 'Nogrow'...! That's right, she aint shit, she aint about shit and the only thing she does is take and take and take until you have nothing left and then they always leave your ass broke and crying, and then another one comes along... and the shit starts all over again!"

"It's not like that!" she sobbed.

"It's not? Okay Cocoa... Tell you what... you tell me just one fucking thing this he-she shim bitch has ever done for you? Prove me wrong...!" Cocoa just kept crying but she didn't answer my question. She couldn't. She knew I was right.

"He..." she sobbed.

"*SHE! SHE! SHE!* I just told you... even if Traci had balls... she'd be a low life bitch!" Cocoa cried out loud and wiped her tears. "Why don't you for once in your life get yourself a *real* man?" I said.

Cocoa cut her eyes at me. "Why don't you get *yourself* a real man?" She snapped back. She must have been really feeling her 'Wheaties' right then... (It's an expression we used in the 80's meaning she was full of piss and vinegar!) Cocoa really overstepped her bounds with me right then. I meant she should have someone who would support her, not drain her, emotionally and financially. I was trying to help. I nodded to her, tossed her phone to her, turned my back and began to walk away from her.

"Pack your shit... and get the fuck out... *you're* fired!" I said calmly.

"What???"

"You heard me... your services aren't required here anymore... Pack your shit and get to stepping..."

"B... bu... but what am I going to do?"

"You should have thought of that before you pissed in my cornflakes!" Cocoa pleaded her case crying for over ten minutes, but it was too little, too late. I spent too much time on her problems as it is and now she's back talking me? I told you, I have enough drama in my own life to deal with, and this shit was quickly getting old! Cocoa finally left but not without having the last word. She called me everything but 'collect' on the way out the door. Oh yeah... she could read *me* the riot act, but to the bitch that was using her... it was all '*I don't want to talk to you...*!' with them. Fine, say your piece, get that off your chest. Just say it on your way out!

Cocoa couldn't find work for about a month or so because business was slow everywhere and nobody wanted her drama in their club anyway. Sure enough, once Cocoa was broke Traci left her for greener pastures, but not before emptying her bank account and running up her cell phone bill and charge cards and spending it all on some other woman. This bitch had even paid for another strippers boob job with Cocoa's money! Cocoa lost her apartment and wound up living in a shelter... none of the bitches she bent over backwards to bail out in the past came to help her. Not one!

I was through with putting myself out there any more... No, I really mean it this time.

Okay... I gave her a few bucks to get by on... but that was it!

The Tortured Soul Trilogy
(Living La Vida Puta)
Chapter 14
(Fast Food & Furious)

Cisco and I were out taking care of company business and I was a little hungry. We pulled into a fast food restaurant where I really liked the fries they served. We didn't use the drive in because the line was too long. We parked the car and went inside instead; besides, Cisco didn't allow eating in his car. Well, considering the last woman he dated, not *food* anyway! Ha!

"I got this…" Cisco said to me as he took out his money.

"Thanks, but no thanks…" I replied. Cisco and I were business partners and sort of friends, but I don't like men to buy me anything. I don't like the idea of being 'obligated', and *no*, I didn't think that Cisco would try to trade sex for a small order of fries! Ha! We stood on the short line for a moment when there was a commotion at the counter. Some asshole was reaming the counter girl for fucking up his order. "*It's just a burger, asshole! Move it along…*" I thought to myself. I looked at Cisco and I could see this was starting to agitate him. "We could go somewhere else…" I suggested. It wasn't the wait that bothered him; it was this sanctimonious jerk that was pushing '*the customer is always right*' crap way too far. The 16 year old manager was too slow in getting involved so Cisco stepped up.

"Excuse me a moment L.L.… I'll be right back!" He walked over to the guy and smiled at him. "May I be of assistance?" he said.

He looked at Cisco up and down for a moment. "Yeah you can!" and he was about to give Cisco an earful.

Cisco interrupted him. "Oh…? I wasn't talking to you… I was talking to the young lady…" The guy looked at Cisco as if he were crazy. "Allow me to explain something to you, *asshole*… I don't *work* here… *and…* I have a serious problem with the way you've been treating this young lady… and I have absolutely *no* problem whatsoever with kicking the living shit out of you, dragging your limp, broken body out into the parking lot and leaving you there for dead…" The guys jaw dropped and he finally shut up. "Now..." Cisco continued. "That you have that *very* important piece of information, do you wish to continue with your little tirade?" and he leaned his ear towards the man. He shook his head no. Cisco took him by the elbow and led him to the front door. "And we're walking...we're walking..."

"I... I... I..." he stuttered.

And Cisco showed him the door. "And *you*... were just leaving..." The guy left stunned. Several patrons actually clapped. We got to the counter and placed our order.

The girl smiled at us and said. "Your order... is on me!"

I knew Cisco protected the girls at the club like a lioness protects her cubs, but I thought that was just 'business'... a job he was paid to do. I just learned that Cisco has a very profound respect for women, and he don't play that shit! I now had a newfound respect for Cisco...Oh? He wasn't getting any pussy from me, only respect! Let's not get it twisted sister!

The Tortured Soul Trilogy
(Living La Vida Puta)
Chapter 15
(A Moment of Silence Please...)

Just before her 22nd birthday Jessie Journeay, known to everyone here as '*The Cajun Queen*', died. Her live-in boyfriend beat her to death after a huge fight while he was high on crystal meth. She died, trying to protect her son. That next night after her funeral, all the girls danced with a white armband on that had a broken heart logo on it. What should have been a birthday celebration became a wake... Everybody danced for a fallen sister that night. All the proceeds from that night's take was donated to help Jessie's six year old son. Steven matched whatever the club took in. I told you... Steven was classy like that...

"Hey Billy?"

"Yeah Fred?"

"What's with the armbands?"

"Fuck if I care..." And Billy put a dollar in the dancers' G string.

Her murder was in all the local papers and on the local news for a week and these bastards had no idea who she was or why we were honoring her... How quickly we forget! But not Cisco, he was moody and withdrawn for almost a month after she died. She didn't deserve that. No woman does...

Well, that's all water under the bridge. I have to hire a new girl fast. I couldn't find any replacements through the usual channels. Steven said he would place an ad in the local malls near the college to get some new talent. The ad was up for about a week but no hits. Steven gave me a few weeks off as a working vacation. I'm going to hit the Vegas clubs as a gypsy and in the meantime see if I can recruit some real talent.

The Tortured Soul Trilogy
(The Confessions of Jennifer X)
Chapter 16
(The X Files)

Jackie came in early to restock the bar for tonight. He went into the back room and pulled a full box of assorted liquors. As he set the box on the bar the phone rang. It was some girl from out of town who wanted to audition for the open spot on the roster. He gave her directions to the club and went back to working behind the bar. He looked around the club and sighed. He usually helped L.L. pick out the girls. Today he would have a one on one. "I hope this chick is good looking..." He said. He really hoped that she was good looking and easy. Steven didn't like employees dating the girls, but at least if this girl didn't make the cut, maybe he could get her phone number. It had been a while since... well.

He continued stocking the bar for about an hour before she finally showed up. He didn't even bother to turn around when she came in. He didn't want to look anxious or desperate.

Jennifer went inside and walked over to the man behind the bar stocking it. "I'm here for..."

He didn't bother to look up at her. "Get on the stage honey..." Jennifer got up on the stage and the guy turned on the stage spotlights. "Take off your top and let's see what you got!" Jennifer jumped on the stage, took off her coat and dropped it off stage. "Let's go honey... I have things to do..." She took off her blouse and stood there waiting for some music. "The bra too! Let's go..."

Jennifer cut his eyes at him, was he kidding? "The ad said *'no nudity'*..." She could tell this guy just wanted to check out her nipples.

"That's the only way they'd let us post the ad... it don't say nothing about no topless...! You want the job or not?" She reached behind her and undid her bra and shimmied out of it. The guy's jaw dropped. "Impressive... Those things real?"

Jennifer grabbed them and bounced them. "What do you think?" she said.

The man behind the bar licked his lips. "I think... I'm gonna need... a little more convincing..." And he started to come from behind the bar. Jennifer reached into her back pocket and pulled out a gravity blade and snapped it open. Living on the street, toughened her up a lot. He wasn't the first guy who wanted to take a shot at her, she was sure as hell he wouldn't be the last. She wasn't gonna '*up the nani*' without a fight. "Or... I can take your word for it..." He said; Jennifer nodded. "You can start tonight... be here exactly at 9PM to get ready to go on stage. You're on from 10 to 10:30 to start..."

"You haven't even seen me dance..."

The guy laughed. "Nobody gives a flying fuck if you can dance honey... and from what I've just seen so far... you'll have no problem breaking the house tip record..." Jennifer jumped down from the stage and walked over to him at the bar. The man looked at her a little nervous.

"So... what do you say we get started on that record... right now...?" I said.

The guy smiled. "How much...?"

"Twenty should do it..." The man smiled and pulled out two tens from his wallet and handed it to Jennifer. Jenny put it in her pocket and walked back to the stage to get her clothes and put them back on.

"What the hell are you doing...?"

Jennifer smiled and started to walk out. "You didn't *really* think you were gonna see my tits for *free* did you...? You got off cheap!"

The guy smiled as Jennifer exited. Then he yelled out to her. "Hey honey...! Do yourself a favor! Leave the pig sticker home! We got security to take care of any problems..."

"I will see you at 9..."

"Oh yeah... and don't forget to bring valid ID or you don't go on!"

"No problem...!"

"By way what's your name?"

"Jennifer Jones..."

"No... I mean your 'stage' name..."

"Jennifer X... with a body like this... you don't need another fantasy! By the way, I didn't catch your name..."

"Jackie... Jackie Butler... I'm the head bartender and house manager..."

"Pleased to meet you..." And Jennifer left.

Jackie smiled. "I hope she comes back! I wanna see what she can do with that body! Damn! I should have let her at least dance for me for the twenty I paid her..." And he went back to doing inventory. Jenny spent the rest of the day looking for a place to stay. She found a one room flat near a college in a nice house within her budget... cheap! She told the landlord she went to the school. She paid two month's rent in advance. They never checked her references.

The Tortured Soul Trilogy
(Living La Vida Puta)
Chapter 17
(The Devil & Miss Jones)

While I took a short 'working' vacation in Vegas to take some time off, Cisco collected the rent from the cat house girls and the club girls pretty much policed themselves. I was checking out what the 'big boys' offered in their clubs as entertainment. I was there for about three weeks and on occasion I would hit the pole as a gypsy. That gave me a chance to check out a clubs' operation from the inside. Steven put an ad around town and the outlying counties for a new girl to fill in my rotation at the club after Jessie died. I didn't like the idea of a girl being hired without me checking her out first. I didn't want any divas in my club that thought they were the alpha bitch. That was my spot, and I certainly did not want a girl that needed too much supervision. The girl that would work in our club would have to fit in the mix. Imagine my surprise when Steven called to tell me Jackie the bartender hired the first girl he saw that answered the ad.

"Fuck me! Knowing Jackie, this bitch is either his girlfriend or she blew him to get the job!"

I got no complaints about the new girl from the other girls, but I still had to check her out for myself. Our schedules clashed and I didn't see the new girl at all the first week I got back. There was a rumor that the girls were starting to get upset that she was out earning them every other night. They decided to have a 'strip off' to decide who should be the headliner of the club. Nothing wrong with a little healthy competition, I thought. I didn't interfere, besides it would give me a chance to see what this girl was really capable of. To see if she was good as they said she was. I got to the club that night just as the competition was being announced by the DJ. He announced the 'combatants' and when he called out the name Jennifer X... the place went nuts! "Who *is* this bitch?" This I have got to see. Jackie handed me a drink and I settled back. I stirred my drink and took a sip. Jackie knows how I like my drinks... right after I get my pussy licked. Ha!

All the other girls pulled out all the stops, to the point that it made Jackie nervous. He was afraid the girls would go too far and get the place raided. Good ole Jackie, as long as the patrons drank and enjoyed the show, he was okay with it. Besides if things ever got out of control he could always hit the panic buttons, the house sprinklers would go off and the bodyguards would clear the stage. Sometimes we would set up a Plexiglas cage and he would hit a button if a girl asked him to so she could do a 'shower scene' on stage. One of the girls that went by the name of Lilac, who was a cheerleader at the college trying to supplement her tuition costs, actually climbed one pole, did a monkey flip off the top and landed on another pole. Even *I* gave her a standing ovation for that one. Tasha and Sterling Piasano were identical twins and were always a crowd favorite. They loved to dance together, face-to-face and back-to-back. Tonight they got into the true Gemini position and danced in a 69. One stood and held the other upside down and then they would cartwheel changing positions. I have to admit, it was hot! The crowd agreed and showered money like crazy.

These girls were determined to beat this Jennifer X, whoever she was. I didn't see her on stage anywhere. Then the crowd started to point on stage. A tall, amazingly beautiful Hispanic woman with long dark hair calmly walked out on stage. She was wearing skinny jeans, stiletto heels and a simple blouse. "What the fuck is she wearing? What kind of stripper outfit *is* that? She looks like she just walked in off the street for crying out loud!" I turned to Jackie and he was focused on the stage as was every person in the club. I watched her as she walked up and down the stage. That was it! She walked up and down the stage like she was the queen 'B' in here. She applauded the other girls as they worked the pole and even got the crowd involved to clap and tip for them. "What the fuck is she doing? I have to stop this shit…" I got up to walk to the stage when all of a sudden the girls cleared a way for her. I was amazed. Why did they do that for? That's when the crowd began to chant: *"Show your tits! Show your tits!"* Like a conductor, she motioned for them to yell louder and they did. *"Show your tits! Show your tits!"* It got to where you couldn't hear yourself think in there. I sat back down. Then she signaled for the crowd to quiet down and they did! She then rubbed her first fingers and thumbs to the crowd. A guy ran up and threw a dollar on the stage. She picked it up, crumpled it up and threw it back at him. *"Okay? What is this? A joke?"* I thought to myself.

She yelled into the crowd and pointed at herself. "You wanna see these?"

The crowd responded with; "Show your tits, show your tits…!"

"I can't hear you! You wanna see these?" she said.

Louder they chanted; "Show your tits, show your tits…!"

She yelled back… "Then show me… *THE MONEY!*"

"Are you fucking kidding me?" L.L. thought. Then the crowd rushed the stage and made it rain? No, these horny bastards made it thunderstorm! And she didn't even take her top off yet! I was flabbergasted, especially when I realized that the DJ wasn't playing any music! Then I saw Steven walk up to her and throw his money clip on stage. I thought Steven hadn't met her yet. I found out later he had the same idea I had to check out the new girl tonight… but more on that later…

"Okay bitches!" She shouted. "The show starts NOW! Mr. DJ… Play my fucking music!"

The sound system cranked up and a heavy techno beat filled the club and this bitch ripped her top off and danced like it was a cross between Kung-fu fighting and an apache dance! The place went ballistic. I had only seen a crowd reaction like that once before in my life! *"Holy shit!"* I said to myself. *"Does Natalie have a sister?"* This hard driven crazy bitch actually shut the place down! I literally sat there never lifting my drink to my mouth as she danced. The only thought that crossed my mind was 'What was this chick like in bed?' When she finished she was covered in bills stuck to her sweaty body. The club sighed as if every man and woman in the joint had an orgasm all at once! The club noise died down, everyone settled down and everyone started buying drinks like they were buy-one-get-one-free! I looked down at my hand, it was shaking. "Oh! I have got to meet this bitch right now!" I walked to the back through an exhausted club crowd. The girls working the tables were making stupid money with lap dances. I caught the new girl just as she got back stage. She was still topless and a waitress had scooped up the rest of her money in an empty beer pitcher and brought to her. I could tell by the wad she carried that she must have had over $500 in her hand! Not even counting

Steven's money clip. Damn! On my best night I only barely cleared that and she did it on one pass! I walked up to her and said; "I can't believe you did *all that*... and you never once took off your pants..." I reached into the front of her jeans above her belt, pulled it slightly away from her body and stuck in a hundred dollar bill. "If you *ever* want to make some serious money... you let me know!"

She had no idea who I was and looked me up and down. "Thanks... but no thanks!"

"It's just a job offer...! Keep the change..."

"Oh! I was *keeping* the tip!" She replied. "By the way, who are you, anyway?"

"My name is Lady Latex, I run this club..."

"Funny, I've never seen you here before... I thought Jackie runs the club...?"

"When I'm not here he does... I was on vacation for a few weeks."

"Okay...! I have to change... if you don't mind... boss!" I nodded and she strutted her hot little ass back into the dressing room. I laughed to myself... *"That's some attitude you have."* I thought to myself and smiled. *"That's what Steven said about me when I first got here!"* I wanted to talk to Steven about her but he already left the club. I went back to the bar and my drink.

The Tortured Soul Trilogy
(The Confessions of Jennifer X)
Chapter 18
(Who's The Boss?)

That was the night I broke the club's tip record... for the second time. Nobody gave me shit ever again. After the club closed, most of the girls carpooled home, I had my own car. It was a piece of shit, but it got me from point 'A' to point 'B' and all I could really afford right now. I was just coming out from the back door when I heard someone in the parking lot, clapping. I turned to see a man about 60 years old, leaning on a limo. "Something I can help you with mister? And when I say that, what I really mean is... *'Get in your car and get the fuck outta here'...!*"

"I believe you have something that belongs to me..." He said. I pulled my knife out of my back pocket. "I thought Jackie told you to leave that pig sticker home... Cisco takes care of all the problems here." He said.

"That fine... inside the club... but we're in the parking lot bitch!" He smiled. Jennifer raised an eyebrow. "Wait...! How did *you* know what Jackie said to me?"

"As the owner of this club... I know everything that goes on around here..." I wasn't buying it. If he's the owner, how come I've never seen him before either? "But there's still a matter of my property..." he said.

"And that is?"

"A gold money clip..."

"I thought that was for me...!"

"No... It was just to get your attention... may I have it back?"

I reached into my pocket and tossed it to him. I kept the money... I'm not stupid, thank you...! "You know... if you're *really* the owner of this club and you wanted to get my attention..." It was right then that Jackie and security were coming out from closing the club.

"You okay, mi negrita?" Cisco Torres, one of the guards that became my personal body guard said.

"I'm good... this old player tried to convince me he owns this club... that's all..."

"He does own this club Jenny!" Jackie said. I turned to him and all the guards nodded in agreement.

"But if you have a problem with him... I will drop him like first period algebra..." Cisco said. "You just say the word!"

"But... Isn't he your... boss?" I asked.

"Oh... I'd quit... *first!*" Jackie nodded to assure me Cisco would.

"Make sure Jennifer gets home safe Jackie..." The man said.

"Yes sir..."

"And Cisco..."

"Yes sir...?"

"Keep up the good work..." He turned then turned back. "But in the future... make sure someone walks all the girls' to their cars at the end of their shift."

"Yes Mr. Callahan..." Cisco answered.

And he got in his car and drove off. I put my knife away. "What the fuck was all that shit about? What the hell *was* that...?" I said to Jackie.

"It's no shit Jenny... Mr. Callahan specifically told the bodyguards when he hires them, they don't work for him; they don't work for the club. They work only to protect the girls. Nobody but nobody fucks with Callahan's girls... not even Callahan." Cisco nodded.

"I'm not one of his *girls*...!" I said.

"As long as you work *here*... yeah... you are...!" Jackie said.

"And that's a good thing... especially now that it looks like he's taken a personal interest in you..." Cisco said.

"Nobody gets *personal* with me without *my* permission...!"

"You better head on home Mami... It's been a long night..." Cisco said.

I kissed Cisco then Jackie. "We *will* talk more about this..." Jackie nodded in agreement.

"Get home safe Jenny... we'll see you tomorrow night..." Cisco said.

"Yeah and don't be late... you know the show don't start until you get here..."

I got in my car and drove home. '*What the fuck just happened*?'

The Tortured Soul Trilogy
(Living La Vida Puta)
Chapter 19
(Who's That Girl?)

I got outside after the club closed only to see Steven drive off in his limo and Jennifer kissed Cisco then Jackie, then Cisco walked her over to her car. Jennifer drove off. "Oh I get it now... She's fucking Cisco, not Jackie... I got this girls' number..." I thought to myself. Funny... why didn't I think she was fucking both of them? Why was I so fucking focused on Cisco? The guys walked back to the club, said good night to me one by one and went inside. Cisco stopped and turned to me.

"Do you want me to walk you to your car L.L.?" Cisco said. "Mr. Callahan asked us to walk everybody to their cars whenever a girl left or if the club was closed..."

I scrunched up my face. "Get the fuck out of my face..." He turned and headed towards the back door but he waited until I got in my car before he went back in. Why did I snap at him? He was just looking out for me for crying out loud...

I went to Steven's office the next morning; we had a lot to talk about concerning this new girl. Steven straightened me out. Jennifer wasn't like that at all. She got her job honestly, I couldn't argue. This bitch had skills. I wondered why I never heard of her before. I wonder what her story is.

The Tortured Soul Trilogy
(The Confessions of Jennifer X)
Chapter 20
(Rehab)

The night nurse was doing her rounds in the pediatric ward of the state mental hospital. She was a little concerned about the new patient that had just been admitted a short while ago. She would just there, staring into space, she had not spoken since she had arrived and now she was just sitting there, motionless holding a rag doll she found in the children's ward toy chest. She finished her rounds and walked over to the doctor on call for the evening. "Doctor Imani...?"

"Yes Crystal?"

"I need you to take a look at Jennifer, the new girl..."

"Is she in pain...? Or acting up...?"

"No... but I would like you to look at her..."

"If there's nothing wrong with her... I have other patients to tend to..."

Crystal cut her eyes at Dr. Imani. She was a little tired of these doctors acting like they have better things to do. You're here to care for the patients. '*Do your fucking job... damn it!*' she thought to herself. "I didn't *say*... there wasn't anything thing wrong with her... I *said*; I need you to take a look at her..."

Normally Dr. Imani would just ignore the staff, they had a tendency of getting too close and personally involved with the patients, but Crystal was not one to be put off by anyone. Crystal was considered a 'problematic' employee. He followed her to the new girl's room. Dr. Imani saw Jennifer just sitting there, on the edge of her bed, holding a rag doll, quietly, motionless. He took her chart from Crystal and read it over. He checked her pulse and heartbeat. Jennifer sat there seemingly unaware. The doctor quickly noted her chart.

"So...? What seems to be the problem... young lady...?"

"Her name is Jennifer..." Dr. Imani ignored Crystal. Crystal was quickly losing her patience with Dr. Imani. Jennifer did not answer him, nor did she react as the doctor continued to examine her. She had been here for almost a month and had not spoken a word to anyone since she was admitted. The doctor continued to fill out her chart and handed Crystal the chart after prescribing meds for her and calmly left the room.

"Try to get some sleep..." he said to her on his way out. Crystal touched Jennifer's face gently and followed Dr. Imani out.

"What the hell is that...? You check her temperature and then prescribe a sedative for her...?"

"Look! Miss Joseph... The girl has undergone a very traumatic emotional experience... it's normal for her to be a little moody and withdrawn..."

"A little *'moody and withdrawn'*...?" She said. "She doesn't interact with anybody on any level... She's practically comatose!" Dr. Imani cut his eyes and walked away. "At least recommend that she see the psychiatrist...!" She said.

"Are you a doctor now, Miss Joseph? Is that your 'professional' opinion?" Crystal crossed her arms defiantly. "She is getting the best care this facility has to offer, what do you want me to do...?" Dr. Imani said. He then continued on his tirade with that condescending tone he always had. And then he walked away. Dr. Imani had just leaned on Ms. Joseph's last nerve ending.

"How about you just do your fucking job?" She blurted out.

Dr. Imani was waiting for that. He knew if he pushed her buttons, Crystal would become defiant and confrontational. He turned on his heels. "Need I tell you Miss Joseph? That you are already on report for insubordination? You don't want me to file this incident as well... do you...?"

"No... Doctor Imani..." Crystal said softly.

"Good...!" And Dr. Imani whispered to her. "Now do *your* fucking job... medicate her and put her to sleep... I have other patients who need attending to..." With that Dr. Imani walked right into the break room, poured himself a cup of coffee and sat down to read the paper. Crystal could feel her blood pressure rise, but she had to do what she was told. She was just one more incident away from a suspension. Crystal went to the pharmacy to pick up Jennifer's prescription. She slowly walked back to her room with the shot. When she opened the door, Jennifer didn't look up at her. She just raised her arm in preparation for the shot. Crystal paused and sobbed a bit. She prepared the shot and Jennifer's arm. She jabbed her with the needle and pulled it out again. She dressed the wound and then emptied the needle into the sink. Jennifer needed love... not a sedative...

- - -

It was now almost a year since Jennifer had been admitted to the childrens hospital by a court order. She was a victim of child abuse. She wasn't sexually abused. Her father 'orchestrated' her mother to beat her at his whim. Even at her tender young age, Jennifer knew that either her mother would obey her father or fall victim to his abuse herself. The beatings started when she was about six years old. Her mother would beat her while her father 'supervised'. It got to she point she expected a beating on a regular basis. She knew her mother held back, only giving her enough of a beating to satisfy her father's blood lust. One day, when she was about twelve or thirteen, all hell broke loose. Mom was out shopping and her dad came home early from work. She was in her room doing her homework when her father barged into her room.

"Where is your mother?" He demanded.

"Grocery shopping..." She replied *"Asshole!"* she whispered; and she went back to doing her homework. Jennifer was not afraid of her father. He had never actually touched her and with mom out of the house, she oddly felt safe.

"What did you say?" he said incredulously.

"You heard me... She's grocery shopping... why don't you clean your ears...?"

His eyes widened. "How *dare you* speak to *me* like that...!"?

"Mom's not here... and you don't have the balls to hit me...!" she said, never looking up from her homework. Her father was flabbergasted. He couldn't speak. He couldn't believe this little bitch had the nerve to... Jennifer's bravado became more intense. "Maybe you should go sit down in front of the TV, have a beer and relax until your *bitch* gets home..."

He turned and left the room stunned. '*I knew it....*' He said to himself. He knew this would happen the moment she hit puberty. She was going out of control. Well... he wasn't having any of that. It was time he took control around here. He knew his wife was way too lenient with the beatings. He knew it. Well, the party was over. If she was old enough to bleed, she was old enough to butcher. He didn't want her to just get a beating this time. He wanted to hear bones break. It was time she learned, once and for all, who was the boss around here. He went to his closet and took out a sawed off pool cue. He smacked it into the palm of his hand and felt the sting. "Yeah... this otta do it!" He calmly walked back to Jennifer's room and opened her door.

Jennifer looked up at him, looked at the pool cue in his hand and crossed her arms. "And what to you think you're gonna do with that... you *pussy*...?" she calmly said.

Her father saw red, raised the cue stick over his head and said. "Heeeerrree's Johnny!"

When the police and coroner finally arrived, Jennifer was covered in blood, brain matter and bits of skull and bone. The coroner placed the body in a body bag and put it in the van. The police tried to interrogate her mother who was crying hysterically... Or was she laughing? Mom had come home from shopping. She saw what was about to happen and had had enough. She quickly and quietly retrieved the gun that her husband had used to threaten her with for so many years, and when her husband raised the bat over his head to beat her daughter, she calmly stood behind him and blew his brains out... all over Jennifer. Jennifer just stood there, in shock, watching the events unfold around her as if she was watching a made for TV movie. One of the paramedics was checking her to see if she was alright. She licked her lips and tasted her father's blood, and spit it out.

"No sweetie...! Don't do that...!" the paramedic said to her. And he began to wipe her face with a towel and some water.

"Hey... that's evidence...!" A cop on the scene said to him.

"Take a fucking picture..." he whispered to him. *"Can't you see the kid's been through enough?"* and he continued to clean her face. Jennifer was unmoved. She just continued to watch silently as they arrested her mother for murder. Jennifer slowly took her hand and blew her mother a kiss and waved goodbye. Strangely, her mother returned the gesture and they took her away in handcuffs.

"Momma loves you baby!" was the last thing she heard her mother say to her.

The Tortured Soul Trilogy
(The Confessions of Jennifer X)
Chapter 21
(Back to the Future)

Crystal had been in the middle of giving Jennifer a sponge bath and was washing her face, when Jennifer stood there looking into space, blew a kiss and waved. "Who are you waving to Jennifer?" She asked as she continued to wash her. She didn't expect an answer.

"To my mother... she's going away and I'm never going to see her again."

Crystal dropped the sponge. This was the first time Jennifer had spoken a word in almost a year since she was first admitted to the clinic. A tear came to Crystal's eye and she hugged Jennifer. "You're back...! You finally came back!" Jennifer hugged Crystal back.

Jennifer was released from the clinic once she turned 18. She wasn't necessarily cured, but the courts couldn't legally keep her any longer as a ward of the court. Dr. Imani was in charge of her exit interview. "Well Miss Jones... I see you're to be released today?" Dr. Imani said.

"No thanks to you..." she replied. Dr. Imani looked at Crystal and cut his eyes. "Don't look at her... I said it! What are you going to do about it bitch?"

Dr. Imani cut his eyes at Jennifer. "You *know* I have the power to keep you here...?"

"*Faa-uuck you!* You aint keeping nobody you don't get *paid* to keep...! And you better get that bass out your voice... the last man that threatened me, got his brains blown out!"

"Yes..." Dr. Imani said smugly, "But your mother isn't here... *is she?*"

A voice from the hallway replied. "There *are* other people around here who know how to fire a gun!" Dr. Imani didn't recognize the voice, but he was shaken by the thought.

Jennifer smiled. "I believe you have a release form to sign... *bitch!*"

Dr. Imani signed the form and handed it to her. "No skin off my ass... you're someone else's problem now...!"

Jennifer took the form and wiped her ass with it as she left. She was free. Free of this mental prison that she had been in for over five years. She walked up to Nurse Joseph. "You gonna be okay?"

"I'll be fine... I should be alright, but shouldn't I be asking *you* how you're gonna be?" Crystal answered.

"Me...? This bitch knows how to take care of herself!" and she rocked her shoulders in defiance.

"Really? Well just be careful you don't get into any trouble with all that piss and vinegar you're full of..."

"Please... I got this!" And Jennifer pursed her lips as she let out a sigh. And Jennifer walked away, took three steps and ran back to Ms. Crystal, threw her arms around her and hugged her and cried. "I'm gonna miss you Ms. Crystal..."

"I'm gonna miss you to Jenny... If you need me you know how to reach me..."

"I wish I could come live with you Ms. Crystal..."

"I told you before... I have one crazy bitch living with me already, I don't need another!"

Jennifer laughed. "Tell your daughter Emily I said hi..."

"I will... take care of you!"

"Take care of you... Ms. Crystal..." Jenny reached under her jacket. "Here... I won't be needing this anymore..." Jennifer handed Crystal the rag doll. Crystal smiled a bit and Jennifer left the clinic to go out into the cold, cruel world.

Jennifer's mother had been tried and convicted of murder; the court appointed lawyer couldn't make a case of self-defense stick. After all, he never touched any of them, mom was 'in charge' of all of her beatings. And because she was standing behind him when she shot him, she was quickly convicted and sentenced to life in prison without the hope of parole. I couldn't even testify in her behalf because I hadn't said a word for more than a year after my mother killed my father. Did you know that there's a law that says the penalty is worse if you shoot a man in the back? What the fuck? Mom's in jail for life and my fucking dad gets a hero's funeral from the V.A.! If I didn't say it before...

What the fuck? John Jeremiah Jones was no fucking hero in my book!

The Tortured Soul Trilogy
(The Confessions of Jennifer X)
Chapter 22
(Janie's Got a Gun)

Jenny was now living in the projects. She was on a waiting list for almost a year before she got in. It was all she could afford right now and it didn't look like tomorrow was gonna be any better. Before she was committed, she was an 'A' student. She was a gawky, nerdy teenager. She was too tall, too smart and she kept pretty much to herself. She had never developed any real social skills because she had trust issues, and who could blame her. But once she hit 18, her body underwent a dramatic change; she blossomed into a beautiful sexy woman. Over time, her body had streamlined, she had lost all her baby fat and her body matured. She now had a body that could stop traffic but she had never learned how to take full advantage of it. She wore baggy clothes to hide it and never showed any confidence in herself. It was a sign of most women who are abused. They would become introverted. She had earned her G.E.D. while in the hospital and as soon as she was released, she got herself a menial waitress job to pay her bills. She had no idea of the potential she had in her. It was pretty certain she would be just an average girl in a below average life.

It was a little after 2am and Jenny couldn't get any sleep. The noises from the one of the other apartments were getting louder and louder. Banging on the wall wouldn't help any, because the sounds were from a lower floor, across from the building airshaft. She wasn't going to put up with it any longer. She just worked a double shift and she needed her sleep, she had four hours before having to go back to her crappy waitress job. She had to cover the breakfast shift to make this month's rent. 19 and a G.E.D. didn't open up many opportunities for her. She opened her bedroom window and yelled into the airshaft. "Hey! Cut the shit out! Some people have to go to work in the morning!" The noises didn't stop. Just as she was about to close the window, she heard the faintest sound. It sounded like... a child... whimpering. Then she vaguely heard.

"I want my mommy!"

Jennifer calmly walked over to her closet, put on her jeans, sneakers and a leather jacket and got out an aluminum baseball bat she had by her bed and walked out into the hallway of the building. She stopped at each and every door listening for the sound of the child that was in such distress. Door after door she checked, she heard many different things coming out of the apartments, but not what she was looking for. She prayed that she would find the apartment before it was too late. It wasn't long before she found the source of the noises. She was about to bang on the door, when she heard the faint sound of an old lady's voice through another apartment door.

"He's not gonna open it... He beats that little girl like an animal..."

Jennifer never remembered how she got into that apartment that night. All she remembered was standing in a bedroom doorway, seeing a naked little girl, tied face down to a bed while a grown man was beating her with a leather barber strap. She focused on the fresh welts and bruises on the child's back and legs. She was instantly engulfed by a rage that hell itself could not have generated. She stood there focused on the girl. That is until she heard the man, cowering in the corner of the room, say to her.

"Who the fuck are you...?" he stammered.

She slowly turned to him, raised the bat over her head and very calmly replied. "I'm you're worst fucking nightmare... *you bitch ass punk!*" Jennifer's blood boiled. What happened next was just a fuzzy blur.

- - -

"Mister Foreman... Has the jury reached a unanimous decision?"

"Yes we have your honor..."

"Will the defendant please rise?" Jennifer and her court appointed lawyer stood up. "In the case of the state verses Jennifer X. Jones on the count of murder in the second degree... how does the jury find the defendant?"

"In the count of murder in the second degree, the jury finds Ms. Jones... Not guilty...!" There was a hush in the courtroom. The judge continued to read the charges against

Jennifer; the foreman continued to read off verdict after verdict. "We find the defendant... Not guilty...!"

"And in the count of involuntary manslaughter... How does the jury find the defendant?"

"We find the defendant... Not guilty...!" There was still no reaction from the courtroom. They couldn't charge her with murder in the first degree, because the act was not pre-meditated. If the prosecuting attorney could have charged her with spitting on the sidewalk, he would have. He wanted her put away for life... just like her mother.

"I want to thank the jury for their service.... Ms. Jones... You are free to go..." The judge banged his gavel and the courtroom began to empty. Because of the nature and the circumstances of the crime, the court had been cleared of all press, more to protect the victim, Ashley, than Jennifer. Jennifer slowly exited the courtroom as the few spectators emptied the room. Her public defender shook her hand and quietly exited the room. He knew the verdicts were out of sympathy. No one, except for the prosecuting attorney, had a problem with the verdicts. "Ms. Jones...?" Jennifer stopped and turned around. The judge motioned her to come to the bench. Jennifer walked over to him. "You literally got away with murder today... If it weren't for the fact that Ashley was a kidnap victim and was being physically abused, you would be doing hard time young lady. Don't let me find you before me in my courtroom ever again...!"

Jennifer remained silent; she knew the judge was looking for any reason to find her in contempt of court. As she exited the room, the judge stood up, she paused at the door; she just couldn't let it go. She turned to him. "I can't make that promise... you and I both know that..."

The judge raised his gavel menacingly, and then dropped his hand by his side. "Yes I do... now get out... before I change my mind!"

"Yes sir..." She stepped outside into the hallway where the prosecuting attorney had waited for her.

"I think it would be a good idea for you to move to another state... start over fresh...!"

"Fuck you...!" Jennifer replied.

The district attorney shook his head. "Was it worth it...? Killing a man?" He demanded.

Jennifer looked over at Ashley who was reunited with her mother. Ashley's mother mouthed '*thank you*'. Ashley pulled away from her mother and ran to Jennifer and hugged her and said: "Thank you auntie Jennifer..."

"You're welcome sweetie..." And as Ashley ran back to her mother Jennifer turned to the attorney and said: "Yeah! It *was* worth it...!"

The district attorney dropped his head and walked away. '*Damn it...*' he muttered. '*It was worth it...!*'

Jennifer stood there. She was vindicated of murdering a kidnapper and child abuser, but she had no job, no money, no place to stay and no place to go. Jennifer laughed to herself. If only she *had been* convicted, she would have at least three hots and a cot right now, and having bashed a pedophile's brains in with a baseball bat; would have put her at the top of the 'food chain' in the joint. Jennifer walked out into the cold afternoon air. Everything she now owned was on her back. She had no place to go and all the time in the world to get there. She stood there wondering what her next move would be when a strange man walked up to her and reached into his jacket pocket. Jennifer balled up her fist. "You better be reaching for a candy bar... cause I'm gonna make you eat the motherfucker!"

The man paused, looked at her. "*Oh...!* No...! This is for you..."And he held out an envelope.

"If you're a process server trying to sue me for wrongful death..."

"No Ms. Jones... it isn't that... Ashley's family found out about your 'predicament' and took up a collection and they wanted you to have this..."

Jennifer took the envelope and opened it. Inside was a bank check for $17,352.27. Jennifer looked at the man. "I can't take this..."

"Please... It was the reward we had offered for any information on Ashley's whereabouts... we only wished it could have been more. Getting Ashley back home safe is more than we could ever have hoped for..."

Jennifer hugged the man. "Good! Cause I was bullshitting about not being able to take it..." Just as the man turned to walk away, Jennifer spoke. "$17,352 dollars and twenty seven cents...?"

The man turned back and shrugged his shoulders. "With bank interest..." The man smiled and then walked over to a waiting car. Inside the car were Ashley and her mom, who blew a kiss to Jennifer and they drove off. Jennifer waved as they drove off and then began to cry. Ashley was reunited with her mom; Jenny would never see hers ever again, her mom died in prison while she was waiting for parole. They didn't even let her go to the funeral.

Jennifer went straight to the bus depot after depositing the check. She walked over to the ticket counter and took out a map of the U.S. and placed it on the floor. She then took a coin out of her pocket and threw it into the air and it landed on the map. She looked at the ticket agent. "One one-way ticket to... Scranton, Pennsylvania please!" Jennifer got off the bus in Scranton a few hours later and looked around. "Hole *lee* SHIT! This place is the only place in the world that can be described as a hole *above* ground!" Other than the map and the bus ticket and lunch, Jennifer didn't spend any of the 17 grand plus that was given to her, but she knew, even here, that wouldn't last her long. She needed a job, and she needed it now. She now had some money saved, but she wasn't about to spend it. She had no place to stay, so she alternated between homeless shelters and the street. For a while she called an abandoned car home. One day she lucked out and found a house that was shut down for the winter and lived there for a short while, but the owners came back at the end of the season. Back out on the street, she checked a bulletin board at the mall for any rooms to rent. She saw a notice that might be better than a place to stay. It was a sign that would change her life forever...

Exotic Female Dancers Needed!
No Nudity – Top Pay!

And there was an address and phone number in Philly but no specific time. She figured anytime she showed up she could audition. Jenny had never danced as a stripper before but she had since 'discovered' that she was gifted with a great body. She figured it was time to use it to make some real money. She took the next bus out and arrived in town about four hours later. She called to make sure someone would be there. She showed up to the club named "*The Kitty Bar*" about an hour after that because she didn't know the town. She went inside and walked over to the man behind the bar stocking it.

Well, you already know what happened next. Jennifer continued to work at the club four to five nights a week. The money was good but inconsistent. Some nights she could clear a couple of hundred dollars but some nights she worked for spare change. She needed a change in her life and she needed it soon. Jenny and LL became buddies in the club, but she wasn't sure of how their relationship would faire. She just wasn't sure about L.L. Although L.L. was technically her boss, she was also a fellow dancer. L.L. would, when needed, do a set to fill in for a girl if the club was short. Last night was one of those nights. Every girl had to do double duty. Jennifer was exhausted and couldn't wait to go home and get some sleep.

The Tortured Soul Trilogy
(Living La Vida Puta)
Chapter 23
(It's a Hard Knock Life)

I was on my way home from working the pole one night at the club. Normally I would change to my regular clothes there first but I was all sweaty and sticky. The AC in the club was on the fritz and I didn't want to use the shower at the club. I was tired and cranky and I just wanted to straight home, get out of this outfit, get in the tub and soak until tomorrow morning. Oh yeah and drink a bottle of vodka... you know, so I don't dehydrate. I lit a cigarette, got in my car and started my long drive home. The car had been acting up for a while and I meant to take it to the shop, but when do I have the time? "Come on Betsy... Give mama one more night!" The car made a new noise and I took it to her saying "*I'll try*!" I had to take an alternate route home tonight because of a detour and I really didn't know this neighborhood. It didn't matter; I would be home ten, maybe fifteen minutes later than usual. It wasn't like the bottle of vodka in my freezer wasn't gonna wait till I got home. I was half way home when this Ford P.O.S. I drive, conked out at a stop sign. It sounded like she gave out a death scream before she finally conked out. I tried to get her to start again but she wasn't having it. I pumped the gas, turned the key... nothing. I got out of the car and kicked her. "Great! I'm nowhere near my house! *And* I'm lost..."

I picked up my cell phone and the battery was dead! Fuck me! I forgot to put it in the charger again! And I didn't have my lighter adaptor, so I couldn't use the cigarette lighter to power it. I couldn't call "Triple A" to come get me. I opened the hood and turned on my hazards. Maybe someone would come by and I could use their cell. No way, I was hitching a ride in this get-up, not in this neighborhood! I waited for almost an hour and not a single car drove by. I figured at least one more car would have to take that detour. But nothing came by at this hour! I decided to walk for a while and maybe find a gas station or a payphone or an all night diner... I walked for about four or five blocks before my feet gave out. These shoes are tough enough to dance in and much less easy to walk around in. I stopped at the next corner and slipped out of my shoes. Ahhhh! It felt so good to take these evil fuckers off! Even, if it was just for a moment. About ten minutes later I put my shoes back on so I could continue on. As I was bent over, zipping up my shoes, a car slowly pulled up. "Hey baby! You need a ride tonight?" I looked up at the joker that was driving. He was focused on looking down my blouse. Not that he had to; the top I had on was sheer and my high beams were on from the cool night air. Only my open leather vest covered them a bit. I straightened up and shook my head no. "No thanks... I'm good!"

"How good?"

I looked at this asshole... and shook my head. "You couldn't afford me!" And before I could tell this guy to get lost, I was being handcuffed and being put in the back of a squad car! This asshole was an undercover cop and I was arrested for solicitation! To make matters worse, I had over two hundred dollars in small bills in my clutch purse! Dressed like this, loose cash and with no ID, off to jail I went. The matron at the station had a ball searching me at my booking. I decided not to joke with her and say something stupid like 'There's a charge for touching the merchandise.' Or; 'If you break it you bought it.' I could tell this closet lesbo didn't like me, I didn't like her either. I was about to break bad with her when she found my switchblade. I was also charged with possession of a concealed weapon. I was put into the general population and wasn't interrogated until about 8 am. I demanded to see my lawyer, Michael Callahan and get my one phone call. I didn't have my wallet and the only number I could remember was Jennifer's. For some reason, I didn't think to call Steven, Jackie or even Cisco. The phone rang about ten times.

Jennifer received the call on her home phone at 9am, not a good time to wake her after working the pole all night. She tried to ignore it but they wouldn't hang up.

"Damn! I should have bought an answering machine...!" Needless to say, she was a bit put out having to get up to answer it. She decided to just pick it up and leave it off the hook so they wouldn't call back. She rolled over and went back to bed when she heard a voice from the receiver.

"Bitch! Pick up! I know your ass is there... pick up the fucking phone"

She recognized the voice. It was Lady Latex. Jennifer picked up the phone. "The fuck you want this early in the morning? I'm trying to sleep!"

"I don't care... I'm at the police station... come get me!"

Jennifer had concern in her voice. "Oh my god! What happened?"

"I got arrested... what the fuck do you think happened?"

"Arrested...? Why were you arrested?"

"I don't have time to play twenty questions, bitch... come get me!"

"Excuse me...? You need a *favor*...? From me...? And you're giving me *attitude*...? Tell you what... I'm gonna put you on hold for a moment... its gonna *sound* like I hung up... but you wait right there...!"

"*No!* Don't hang up...!" Jennifer held the phone silently. L.L. paused and changed her tone. "I'm sorry... could you *please* come pick me up from the police station... I would really appreciate the help...!"

"That's better... where are you?" Lady Latex gave her the address and directions.

As L.L. hung up the phone, the matron was a little too grabby escorting me back to my cell. I had a real problem with that but I wasn't going to start any shit. I didn't want to add to my problems right now. Being in the cell with the general population didn't bother me at all. I had been arrested before and besides I was used to dancing in a cage. I wasn't back in there for more than fifteen minutes when some bull dagger butch bitch wanted to play.

"Hey baby? Who do we have here?" She stepped up to me and licked her lips.

I cut my eyes at her and held my ground. "If you don't know... maybe you should ask around..." She smirked and glanced around the cell to get the crowds reaction to my statement. The girls there didn't work for me, but my reputation had preceded me. Some of the girls backed away from us, giving us room to fight. Girlfriend then glanced to her back-up and instead of moving in on me, they backed the fuck up! "You know that's right!" I said as I stared her down. She then realized this wasn't a good idea. She looked me in the eye and thought she might as well try it anyway. I didn't back down. I got up all in this bitch's face. "If you're feeling a little froggy... jump!"

I knew not to make the first move. Even though I had all the room I needed and I could take this bitch down, I didn't have any back up here. Everyone in here could jump in and even though they knew who I was... this wasn't my turf. I was the 'outsider' here. We stood there for a moment when we heard another girl whisper. "Even if you get her now Nena... she can have you taken out on the outside...!" That was referring to me... But her rep was at stake here; to back down now would take her down in the eyes of the other girls. Not a good place to be in the joint. She started this shit; there was no graceful way for her to back down. But luck was on her side.

"Hey! New girl! I'm getting a little sick of you right now!"

Out of the corner of my eye I saw the matron, who was making her rounds. I was not taking my eyes of my opponent. It would be too easy for her to cheap shot me if I did. "Why don't you take a number and get on line? This bitch is ahead of you!" I said out loud. I stayed focused on Nena. If she breathed wrong she was going down!

"Knock it off...! Now!" The matron barked. "Back it up the two of you!"

Nena's crew stepped up and pulled her back. Her rep was saved and now that I think of it, so was my ass, but I still had the matron to deal with. She opened the cell door and stepped up to me.

"Now serving number two..." I announced.

"Your lawyer is here... and posted your bail, let's go..." I followed her out of the cage but not before giving the girls the evil eye. I never knew when I would ever be back here and I needed them to remember me. As I was escorted down the hall the matron whispered to me. "Were you really going to take Nena and her crew on?" I nodded. The matron looked at me with a new found respect. She put me in a holding cell to keep me away from the others until my paperwork was ready. I sat there alone for about another hour. This shit takes time.

Jennifer got dressed and gathered her tips from the night before, in case she had to bail the bitch out. The club rule was that the dancers were family and if they needed you, '*a bitch has got a bitch's back*'. "All I know, is I better not get *my* ass arrested doing this crazy bitch a favor...!" Jennifer got her coat and car keys and went to the station to get her. She wondered what she could have done to get herself arrested. "If this has *anything* to do with drugs, I'm leaving the bitch in there! Sorry... I don't play that shit!" Jennifer arrived at the station and after a quick search at the metal detector; she went over to the duty desk. Thank goodness I rushed out of the house... I forgot to bring my 'pig sticker' with me... and I really think that bull dyke cop would have had a ball strip-searching me!

"What can I do for you young lady?" the desk sergeant asked.

"I'm here to pick up a friend of mine..."

The officer opened a journal. "What was she arrested for...?"

Jennifer paused. "I don't know... she forgot to tell me..."

"Okay... what's your friends name...?"

Jennifer realized that she never knew L.L.'s real name. "Lady... *Lay*... *tex*...!" she stammered.

"*Lady Latex*...? I can *guess* what *she* was arrested for..."

Jennifer cut her eyes at the officer as he checked the night's bookings. "Sorry Miss... we don't have a '*Lady Latex*' in lock up..."

"But she called me from here...! I came right over."

"Best I can do for you is to get the matron to walk you through and see if you recognize your friend... Have a seat and she'll be out in a few..."

"Thank you...!" And Jennifer sat down on the bench. The officer called for the matron on the phone.

"It's gonna be a while... she's occupied with an inmate right now..."

"Thank you..." ...'*occupied with an inmate*'...?' Jenny thought to herself. '*I'll bet you that's L.L.!*' Jennifer also thought that it was a good thing the desk sergeant didn't know who L.L. was; it meant that maybe she was picked up for something minor. Jennifer sat and waited patiently for the matron to come get her. At one point she fell asleep on the bench. She got up to ask the desk sergeant what was taking so long, when the outer door opened and in walked in a man. He was gorgeous! Jennifer watched him as he walked over to them at the desk. He reminded her of that actor in 'The English Patient'. Jennifer was almost 5'10", this guy was 6'2", dressed to the nines and his cologne 'matched' his look. He walked past her and spoke to the sergeant. He mesmerized her and Jennifer has never been awestruck over a man like that before.

"I'm here to get my client released..." He said.

(Ohh! I even like his voice!) Jennifer leaned a bit in to catch another whiff of his cologne.

"What's her name counselor?"

"Tobey Oceanside... I believe all the paperwork is in order."

Jennifer came out of her trance. "Excuse me... but I believe I was here first!"

"When the matron comes out with Ms. Oceanside, we'll see if we can find your friend Miss..."

"Jennifer... Jennifer X. Jones...!" She turned to see if the man caught her name, but he had already sat down on the bench. She walked over and sat down on the bench, but left space between them. She wasn't about to let him know she was 'interested'. He made it quite clear... he wasn't. She was about to try to start some 'small talk' when the matron came out with Lady Latex in tow. Jennifer stood up.

"It's about time you got here!" L.L. said.

"I've been here for over an hour... I didn't know your real name..." Jennifer said.

"Not you... him!"

Jennifer turned to see the lawyer standing behind her. She turned back to Lady Latex. "Your real name is 'Tobey Oceanside'...? Pffftt!" Jenny scoffed.

"Don't start bitch! I'm in no mood!"

The lawyer signed Tobey out with the desk sergeant and said to L.L. "I see your ride is here so I guess you won't be needing me anymore...!"

"Yeah Michael, Jennifer got me... Thanks..."

(Michael... huh...? When are you gonna introduce me Tobey?) Jenny thought to herself. And Michael left without even acknowledging my presence. (Well fuck you too! Michael!)

"Let's go... I need to stop off my place and take care of some shit..."

"Oh... so now I'm your fucking chauffeur?"

"Bitch please... come on... before they change their minds..." And L.L. started walking out.

"Hey *Tobe*y... who's the hot lawyer?"

Jennifer was yanking her chain. "Keep playing...! And stay away from Michael Callahan..." (Steven told L.L. that Micheal was off limits, she knew full well that would also mean anyone else that worked in the club.)

"Callahan! You mean...?"

"Yeah that's Steven Callahan's son... and his personal attorney..."

"If you knew he was coming to bail your sorry ass out... why am I here?"

"Because he had to stop by on his way to court... *You* on the other hand didn't have any other plans!"

"I'm sorry... I didn't know you were gonna *walk* home from here..."

"Stop playing I said! Walking around dressed like this is what got me arrested in the first place!"

"You were arrested for streetwalking?" Jennifer laughed.

"Yeah... my damn car broke down so I walked a bit and then I tried to hitch a ride to a gas station... I guess he thought I said *police station*... cause I was brought straight here..."

"Damn! They really thought you were a hooker?"

"Yeah! I aint no hooker... I'm a pimp!" Jennifer laughed. "Why are you laughing? I'm serious..."

Jennifer's jaw dropped. "*You are serious!*"

"Of course I'm serious... I run my own brothel... when I told you, you could make serious money that night at the club... what did you think I was talking about?"

"I thought you meant dancing at another strip club!"

L.L. shook her head. "What you made that night in tips, you would make in an hour being my top girl..."

Jennifer shook her head no. "No thanks... I'm still not interested..."

"I know... we established that, that night..." L.L. and Jenny got in her car.

"Well… it's a good thing the Callahans don't know about your side gig…" L.L. ran her fingers through Jenny's hair. Jenny flinched. "What are you doing?"

"Checking to see if there's still a green banana in there from when you jumped off the boat to get into this country…"

"*What*…?"

"*Sister*… I work *for* the Callahans… you didn't think *I* could afford a lawyer like Michael? He's one of the fringe benefits of being Callahan's girl…"

"You mean the Callahan's are…" L.L. used one hand to bend her ear, the other to bend her nose. "Oh!" Jennifer sighed. She couldn't believe she was so naïve.

"Come on… I gotta go to the house and check on my girls…" L.L. gave Jennifer the directions and drove her there. When they arrived at the house it was just a simple unattached home with very simple front and a small yard.

"So this is a…"

"No… this is where the girls live when they're not working. They're strictly outcall. I don't let them shit where they eat. I don't allow any men on the premises."

"It looks pretty… plain…"

"What did you expect? Neon lights?"

Jenny shook her head. "And *you* live here too…?"

"Hell to the no…!" L.L. escorted Jenny into the house. "Don't tell them your name, they don't need to know who you are, I just want them to see that you're with me…"

"And am I *with* you…?"

"We're BFF, bitch… nothing more…"

Jennifer nodded. "BFF bitches it is!"

"Daddy's home!" L.L. announced as she entered. One by one, girls came out of the woodwork placing the nights take on the kitchen table. Jennifer whispered to L.L.

"Why didn't you have one of *them* pick you up?"

Tobey whispered in Jenny's ear. "The last thing I want, is to be seen with these girls by the police… as far as anyone knows I'm just the landlord here… and I don't need *these chicks* to know my personal business…."

"But you don't have a problem being seen with *me* by the police…?"

L.L. shook her head no, and smiled. That's when Jennifer realized that L.L. respected and trusted her. As the girls walked away they checked out Jennifer but none spoke a word to her... except for Brownee.

"Who are you? A new girl...?"

Jenny didn't reply.

"This is Brownee Androse..." L.L. said. "Brownee... this is *Nunya Biz!*"

Brownee walked off and mumbled in Jenny's direction. "*Puta!*"

To which Jennifer replied out loud. "*Lambeculo!*" Brownee cut her eyes at Jennifer.

"Is there a *problem*?" L.L. asked Brownee.

"No ma'am..." She answered sheepishly and walked away.

"Don't make me have to remind any of you who the HBIC is around here." L.L. announced. Lady Latex sat down at the table and bid Jennifer to sit. She then started to count the money and separate the take into three piles, one for L.L., one for the house and one for Callahan. "Hey!" She said into the next room. "Where's Phishy's envelope? Phishy! Phishy Dezi-Siete... get your ass in here!" A beautiful young blonde came into the room. She didn't look to be more than 17. She was topless and stood there rubbing and fondling her breasts and nipples. "Where's your envelope Phishy?"

A voice came out of her that sounded like a ten year old but not that intelligent. "Gee Lady Latex... I *didn't* work last week... It was *my* turn to do all the house chores... remember?"

"Sorry sweetie... I forgot... but I expect you to bring in twice as much next week..."

"Okay!" She said in that sweet bubbly voice while she continuously rubbed and fondled herself. Jennifer had to ask her.

"Why are you doing that?"

"Oh! I just got these and the doctor said I have to keep rubbing them so they'll stay supple and won't harden up... How long did you have to keep rubbing yours?"

Jennifer cut her eyes at her. "These are real!"

"Wow... they're real nice... can I touch them?"

"No!" Jennifer looked at this chick like she was crazy.

106

"Okay!" And Phishy went back into the other room.

"Hard to believe that chick is 32 years old!"

Jennifer looked at L.L. in amazement. "Are you shitting me?"

"Nope... started with me when she was 19 and she's been with us for twelve years now... She attracts a 'special' clientele..." Jennifer shuddered. "Yeah I know... but I look at it this way... when they're with Phishy, some little girl is safe somewhere. Besides if I ever hear of her clients pulling any of that '*short eyes*' shit... well... let's not go there..."

Jenny thought to herself "*Yeah... let's **not** go there...*"

I didn't need to tell Jennifer what happened to me when *I* was 15. It was 'need to know' only and Jennifer didn't need to know. I took a deep breath and thought of Cindy... I hate revisiting the past. I finished dividing up the envelopes. L.L. got all the money separated and said to Jenny. "Lets' go..." They exited the house back to Jenny's car.

"Where we headed to now?"

"I have to hit two more houses and then I have to pick up my car from the garage Michael had it towed to, and then I'm going over to hand in the take..."

"I'm going with you?"

I looked at her and thought about it. I wanted to spend the day with her... maybe we could go back to my place and... no... I better not... I really shouldn't try to get involved with the girls I work with. Even if they are as hot as Jennifer is! L.L. looked at her. "No... Once you drop me off to get my car, you can go ahead and get some sleep... you gotta work tonight!"

"Yeah... I forgot!"

"Besides... I only brought you here cause I had to... I don't want you mixed up in any of this..."

"You don't have to worry about me!"

"But I do worry about you..." L.L. gave Jenny $20 from her envelope.

"What's this?"

"Ass, gas or grass... nobody rides for free... That's gas money!"

"Thanks!" And they got in Jenny's car and drove off.

"Say L.L., I wanted to ask you..." Jenny paused.

"What?"

"While you where in the 'joint'… did you have a problem with the matron?"

"*Yeah*…! Why?"

"No reason…" then Jenny chuckled to herself.

"*What the hell was that about*?" L.L. thought. We drove for a bit and curiosity got the better of me just as we got to the mechanics garage. "Jenny?"

"Yeah L.L.?"

"What is a '*Land Bee Kullo*'?"

Jenny smiled. "*Lam-bay-cool-oh*…" she enunciated. I focused on her mouth as she said it. "Is Spanish for someone who sticks her tongue way up someone else's ass…" and she grinned with a naughty smile and bit her lip slightly. I shuddered while the visual thought of having my face buried in Jennifer's ass came to me. I got moist right there. Jenny saw my reaction. "Yeah! It's not a good thing…" She said and chuckled.

That's what you think honey! That's what you think! She totally misread me! She drove me to two more of my places to pick up 'the rent' and then she dropped me off at the mechanic's. I kissed Jennifer on the cheek and she drove off. I would see her later tonight at the club. The mechanic walked up to me while wiping his greasy hands into a greasy towel.

"May I help you?"

"Yeah… light blue Ford… they brought it here this morning…"

"A Ford? Yeah… that's the perfect name for it…"

"What the hell does that mean?"

"F. O. R. D.? **F**ound **O**n **R**oad, **D**ead!" and he smiled.

"That's not funny… where's my fucking car?" The mechanic shook his head. He wasn't even gonna bullshit me about repairing her… the transmission had seized up, she was gone! I leaned my head way back and took a deep breath. Now what? Jennifer already left. "How am I getting home?" I sighed out loud.

"Oh… your boyfriend is sitting in my office. He got here to pick you up about ten minutes ago…"

I looked at the mechanic like he was out of his mind. "What fucking 'boyfriend'…?" He turned to point at his office and when I turned around, Cisco was walking towards me.

"He's not my fucking boyfriend!"

The mechanic looked at me with a look of disbelief on his face. "Whatever you say honey... what *ever* you say!" and he walked away.

"Why are you here?" I asked Cisco as he came up to me.

"Michael called me after the mechanic called to tell him your car was unrepairable... and here I am!"

"I appreciate the lift but I'm still gonna need a new car..." *Ass, gas or grass...*! I thought to myself and I knew which Cisco would choose! Cisco held out the car keys in his hand towards me.

"You wanna drive or shall I?"

"You're shitting me right?"

"The Callahans take care of their own... but you knew that already! Besides... "A bitch has got a bitch's back..." Cisco walked me over to my new car and opened the door for me. It was a beautiful, rebuilt Chevy 'muscle car'. It wasn't fancy or brand new. Steven said 'flashy' draws too much attention. I found that out for myself last night when I got busted. "I took all your stuff out of your old car and put it in the trunk..."

"Michael and Steven... picked *this* car out... for *me*?"

"They paid for it... but I picked it out... you like?" And he handed me the keys. I got in the drivers seat and I swore it hugged and held onto my ass like she was an old friend. The radio was even already set to my favorite station. I fondled the steering wheel and caressed the dashboard. I put the key in the ignition and the engine roared! I felt a rush of adrenaline sweep through my body as I revved up the engine. I grabbed the stick shift tightly. My mouth opened, my eyes closed and I sighed. "Would you two ladies care for some privacy?" Cisco chided. I cut my eyes at him but I could not be mad, this car was built just for me. I liked her, I liked her a lot. I think I'm gonna name her Trixie... no... Roxie... yeah, Roxie... I like that name! I patted the passengers' seat.

"Get in... or get left behind!" I purred.

"Yes ma'am!" and Cisco jumped in on the passengers' side.

"Make sure your seatbelt is securely fastened... cause the ride may get a little rough!"

"Baby! You know what I like!" I ignored him and his feeble attempt to 'play'. Right now I wanted to know what my new baby could do. I put her in gear and I must have left an inch of tread in the garages' driveway as I peeled out!

Oh by the way… Cisco screamed like a little girl! Ha!

The Tortured Soul Trilogy
(The Confessions of Jennifer X)
Chapter 24
(Behind Blue Eyes)

Jennifer met Tobey a.k.a. Lady Latex at a private dance club a little after ten o'clock on night they were off. LL worked the schedule so they could party together. She was in the VIP section with some heavy hitters drinking champagne like it was water. The moment Jennifer sat down a waiter brought her a bottle. "No thank you..." Jennifer said.

"Don't worry about it... *you're* not paying for it... it's all on my dime..." Tobey said.

"No offense... Lady Latex, but I know these bottles come with a price..."

"Not for you... they don't Jennifer... and frankly, I'm a little hurt that you would think that of me... when it comes to you..."

The waiter poured Jennifer a glass; Jennifer picked it up and tipped it to Lady Latex.

"Alright then... as long as you and I have an understanding..." Jenny said.

LL tipped her glass to Jennifer. "As long as you know... you're the only person I extend that courtesy to..." They sat and drank and danced for about an hour. While LL was speaking to one of the men, Brownee Androse, the girl Jenny met at L.L.'s cathouse, stepped out of the crowd. She walked over to the velvet rope separating their table from the crowd, and dropped a wad of money on the table and walked away. Tobey picked up the cash, thumbed through it without counting it, and handed it to Jennifer.

"What is this for...?"

"Come with me... I need to use the ladies room..." And Lady Latex stood up, as did Jennifer and they walked out. L.L. found Brownee waiting in the ladies room when she got there. She announced to the half full bathroom. "Ladies! I'm gonna need some privacy here!" The bathroom quickly emptied out, leaving only the three of them. Jenny checked the stalls. She knew a bum's rush was coming. It happened a lot in lockup whenever a new girl was arrested while she was waiting for her trial. Lady Latex walked over to Brownee and backhanded her with her studded glove. Her head spun back. The studs from the glove scratched her face. Blood from her mouth trickled down her lip. Normally, Jennifer would be enraged seeing a woman being abused like that, but this time she had a reaction she didn't quite expect. Her nipples got hard and she was wet. "See... this is why pimps get such a bad reputation... A bitch don't know her place...!" Brownee trembled; she had no idea what she had done wrong. "First of all, don't you *ever* disrespect me like that ever again... you don't *throw* money at me..." Jennifer kept a straight face, she knew very well that men threw money at her all the time in the strip club, but this was business. Then she heard the click of a switchblade in Lady Latex' hand. The knife was under Brownee's chin in an instant. "Secondly... I said; '*HAVE my money, not HALF my money*'... bitch!"

"I'll get the rest of it... I promise... don't cut me... please..."

"You'll have *all of it*... before this night is over..."

"But I gave you..." And Lady Latex held the knife tighter against her throat. Brownee's eyes widened. She didn't want to fuck with LL. "Yes Lady Latex... I'll have *all* your money before the night is over..." Lady Latex pulled the knife away and pointed to her own cheek with her other hand. Jennifer expected Brownee to slap her back; instead, she leaned over and gently kissed it.

"Clean yourself up and get to stepping... bitch!"

Brownie then went to the sink and tended to her wounds. Jennifer held the wad of cash out to LL. "No... you keep it... it's yours..." Jennifer put the wad of cash in her purse. Brownee looked at Jennifer in anger and disgust. Lady Latex said to her. "You got a problem...?" Brownee dropped her eyes and left. "That bitch and her attitude are starting to get on my last nerve..."

"You know... there was almost a full 'yard' in that wad?" Jenny asked. Strippers quickly develop the ability to sight count cash. It was never a good idea to count your money out. It could get you robbed. It was like that song; "*You never count your money when you're sitting at the table...*"

Tobey nodded. "You and I... still... have an understanding... right?" Jennifer said.

"You and I both know, I would never try this on you... and I know you would never go for that shit!"

"Good!" Jennifer said. But deep down inside the thought of it excited her. Jennifer paused. "If she doesn't get you your money by morning... I want you to cut her a break..."

"You know you're pushing our friendship... right?" L.L. replied.

"I could always just give her this money back, but that would only disrespect you and undermine your authority..."

L.L. smiled. "Okay! Only for you... and only because you understand the business... besides, I *still* owe you one." Tobey held out her switchblade. "Just... don't get it twisted, sister..."

Jennifer reached into her back pocket and opened her gravity knife. "Don't start none... and there won't be none..."

L.L. closed her knife and put it away. "You have no idea how much I love you right now!" Tobey said.

Jennifer closed her knife and put it away. "I *believe* we were at a *party*?"

"Yes, yes we were..." L.L. replied. This established a level of respect between them. L.L. put her arm around Jennifer and they went back to the dance floor. Brownee did in fact come up with all of Tobey's money by the end of the night. It was a bittersweet victory for her. Now that Tobey knew what she was capable of, with the right motivation, Tobey upped her 'vig' to two thousand a week.

A month or so later, Jennifer was to meet Tobey at a private house. Tobey had made a deal to direct a film for the men they partied with that night at the club. They specifically requested that Jennifer be there. "Why am I here... Lady Latex? You know I'm *not* gonna do a fuck film...! Besides I thought you said you didn't want me involved with this... *business*..."

"You're a big girl... you don't want to do this... you don't have to... I won't take any offense..."

Jennifer nodded "Okay then..."

"Don't worry... you won't be in front of the cameras... I just need you here to be a 'fluffer'..."

"And what does that pay...?"

Tobey looked at Jennifer. "I believe... you've already been paid for this job..." Jennifer didn't flinch, didn't blink.

"Okay... I gave it a shot... can you blame me?" Tobey smiled and took three hundred dollars out of her pocket. Jennifer didn't count it and put it in her pocket.

"What do you want me to do?"

Jennifer had no idea what a fluffer did. Tobey smiled again. "I need you to make sure the men are 'happy' so they're ready, willing and able to 'perform'... when I need them..."

"You're gonna be in the film?"

"No... I'm just directing today... Besides, if you haven't figured it out yet... I don't do 'dick'... If I did, I wouldn't need a fluffer..."

"Why not use one of your regular girls..."

LL cut her eyes at Jenny. "You want the money or not! Besides, these guys asked for you... specifically." L.L. shifted her eyes toward the direction of the men they had partied with before. "I got this gig cause *they* wanted *you* here..."

Jenny nodded again. She realized L.L. was *using* her, or testing her, but she was a big girl... it's time she grew up. She would have to treat this as if it was just another job. Besides she could always use the money. "Stupid question... why do porn stars need a fluffer?"

"Simple... these men have been jaded from working the business too long... they need encouragement on the side lines...!"

"So why doesn't the girl *in* the film..."

"Takes too long... and it tires the girl out. We need her 'fresh as a daisy', besides the producers don't want flaccid penis in the shot, so they have to be ready when I say action..."

"So... where should I start?" L.L. pointed at a man sitting, having coffee wearing only a robe. Jennifer walked over and introduced herself. "Hi... My name is Jennifer, and I'll be your fluffer today..."

"Honey... I don't care what your name is..." And he opened his robe and calmly exposed himself. Jennifer focused on his eyes, slowly unbuttoned her blouse and unhooked her bra from the front.

"After I'm finished with you... you *will* care..."

The porn star sat there... mesmerized by Jennifer's hard body. "I've been in this business for over ten years and I've never seen *anyone* as beautiful as you!"

"Shhh! You talk too fucking much..." In between 'fluffing' the stars of the film, Jennifer had the opportunity to watch how a porn film was produced. It wasn't what she thought it would be. It wasn't erotic or sensual at all. In fact, it kinda grossed her out. It actually made her angry, very angry, but she was here to do a job, not change the industry. The men were treated like kings; the women were treated like bitches in heat that needed to be mounted. Each scene only served to remind her of when she was growing up, beaten and abused, while her father was treated is if the sun rose and set at his command. Don't get me wrong, some of the girl's enjoyed what they were doing... a lot... and you could tell... they weren't doing this for fame *or* money. But, there was one girl, who went by the name Domaina Luquer. Her eyes were dead inside; *she* was dead inside; She only 'came alive' while on camera. Once L.L. said *'action'*, she was a volcano of lust and passion, once she said *'cut'*... coma...! It was if she became horny on command. Jenny walked over to her in between takes. "Hi... I'm Jenny..."

"Hi." She said with a deadpan expression.

"You've been doing this long?"

"Too long..." she replied.

"Why?"

"It pays the bills..."

"Why don't you do something else?"

"Why don't... *you*... do something else...?" And she walked away. Jennifer realized she hadn't been compassionate with her at all; she had been rude and condescending. L.L. called her to do the next scene; Domaina got into 'character'; Jenny went back to her fluffing. The next scene was a girl on girl scene, Jennifer's 'services' were not required so she sat and watched the scene unfold. Lady Latex was now in her element – hot lesbian sex, with all the accoutrements. The stagehands brought out a large six-foot wooden "X" that had many leather restraints on it and stood it up mid stage. Jenny's eyes widened at the sight of it. This was going to be a bondage and discipline scene. A woman was gonna get her ass beat right before her. Domiana came out dressed in full leather regalia and a leather mask. It looked so very uncomfortable. The second woman came out dressed as a high-school cheerleader.

115

"*Holy shit*! *It's Phishy*!" Jennifer's hands trembled. She wanted to stop this. This was too damn close to home for her, but she was frozen, she couldn't move. She kept saying to herself. "*It's only a movie... it's only a movie... it's only a movie...*!"

"Just don't hit me in the tits... they're still healing..." Phishy said.

"No problem sweetie..." And Domiana kissed Phishy deeply."

"Hey! Save it for when I say action!" L.L. said. The girls giggled.

"Where do you want me?" Phishy said. L.L. directed Domaina to tie Phishy to the open sided "X". The cameras shot everything they did. It would all be fixed and remixed in editing later. Domaina took a leather whip from her side and took a few practice swings to make sure nothing was in the way. Every time the whip sung around and around, Jennifer held the armrests of her chair tighter and tighter. She was wet in anticipation. But she was very conflicted. Part of her wanted to stop it; another wanted to feel the sting of leather. Her nipples were hard and tight, she began to pant in short breaths. Then Domaina struck Phishy and Phishy let out a yelp.

Jennifer cried out. "Ohhhhh!"

Everybody turned to Jennifer. Phishy said to her. "It's okay Nunya... It doesn't hurt that bad... it's called '*acting*'..."

Jenny raised her eyebrow. (Why did she just call me '*Nunya*'...? Ohh...! This *bitch* is just stupid...!) The laughter of the crew helped alleviate some of the tension Jennifer felt.

"I didn't say cut... people! Let's shoot this bitch!" L.L. said. And Domaina started on Phishy again. With every lick of the whip, Jennifer became more and more aroused. Phishy was covered in pink and red welts; Domaina was sweating profusely. Jennifer was all hot and bothered. L.L. glanced in Jenny's direction... she knew the scent Jennifer was giving out. No one else noticed, after all, it was a porn shoot, the whole place smelled of pussy. But L.L. knew the smell of *new* pussy, and Jennifer was brand new pussy! L.L. saw Jennifer in a whole new light. L.L. would protect her at all costs from now on.

"My tits hurt... could you rub them for me, please?" Phishy said to Domaina.

Domaina glanced at L.L. "Go ahead... we'll work it into the script..." L.L. said. Domaina dropped the whip on the floor and roughly opened Phishy's top and ripped off her bra. She began to rub and knead her breasts and nipples.

"Oh... that's nice... you do that better than I ever could..." Phishy cooed.

"If you ever need massaging in private... I'm open for it...."

Phishy giggled. "Okay!" But then the massage made her horny. Domaina began to suck and lick and stroke her nipples.

"Oh...Oh...Ohhhhhh!" Phishy swooned. "How much would you charge...?"

"Honey... I'd do you for free...!" And Domaina kissed Phishy deeply. Phishy was now really into it.

"Ohh... My! I'm all moist and horny!"

"Really?" And Domaina dropped it like it was hot and lifted Phishy's skirt and dove into her hot wet hungry pussy with her thumb and tongued her. Phishy screamed in pleasure. L.L. made sure the cameraman caught it all.

"Right there... right there... oh don't stop... you hit the spot! You hit the spot." Phishy's voice changed... dramatically. "Oh you fucking bitch... lick my clit... suck it you mother fff.... fff... fucccckkkkeerrr!" Phishy screamed in the throngs of orgasm. L.L.'s head turned to the side. (Damn! This bitch is a better actress that I thought she was! She was only *playing* stupid...! Oh I'm gonna keep my eye on this one from now on!) After the scene, L.L. called cut and the camera crew relaxed.

"Lunch! Let's take five everybody..." The producer said.

"That's okay... I'll just hang out here." Phishy said. L.L. looked at her, she wasn't gonna fall for the dumb chick routine anymore. She had this bitch's number. Jennifer left the room to 'freshen' up. She didn't want to soak through her jeans and she needed to put some cold water on her face. Domaina picked up her whip but held it backwards with the handle towards Phishy and began to pant harder and heavier.

"Wait a minute..." She said to the cameraman. "Leave the camera on..."

"You got it... film's rolling..." And he left.

L.L. stood behind Domaina and whispered in her ear. "Whatever it is... you have on your mind... go right ahead..."

L.L. focused on Phishy, Phishy looked at Damiana and nodded.

"Bring it bitch!" Phishy said, again out of character. Domaina held the handle like a dildo and spat on the end of it and began to rub Phishy's clit with it. Phishy was all wet and bothered again. Domaina continued to rub her clit with the whip and lick her nipples. Then she turned around to face L.L., Domaina began to grind her ass on Phishy and reached over her head and grabbed Phishy's nipples and squeezed them.

"Would you like a better view?" Domaina asked.

L.L. whispered. "Yes..." It had been awhile since she had gotten her freak on. Domaina went behind Phishy and placed her hand with the whip handle between Phishy's legs. First she used her fingers to warm her up then she used the handle. She pushed and pulled it back and forth and Phishy squirmed with delight.

"Fuck me you bitch! Stick that leather dick in me! Fuck meeeee!"

Domaina complied and eased the handle deep into Phishy. She pulled and pushed in into her slowly at first but then faster and faster. Phishy threw her head back and came again. L.L. wanted so bad to get involved right here. But then she realized... this was a trick... Phishy worked for her, she was subservient to her. To get involved would give her something over her, and since when is she getting so chummy with a chick she doesn't know? L.L. slowly walked up to Phishy and licked her lips. "Would you like me to get *up close and personal* with you... right now?" Phishy panted and nodded yes. Domaina pulled the leather handle out of Phishy and held it between Phishy's legs like an erect penis. They wanted L.L. to ride it. L.L. looked down at it. (So...? You wanna fuck me...? *Fuck you*!) And she reared back and slapped Phishy unconscious. Domaina jumped back and whimpered. "How's that for 'up close and personal'...?" L.L. said and turned to Domaina. "Untie your bitch... and get the fuck out... neither one of you is gonna work in this town ever again." Domaina turned the whip around and began to puff up to L.L. L.L. opened her switchblade. "Go ahead...! You're not the first bitch to whip me... and you aint gonna be the last bitch I cut into little pieces... Tell you what... I'll *give* you the *first* shot… for free! Cause I'm really into that shit!" L.L. opened her stance in anticipation; Domaina thought better of it and dropped the whip. She slowly reached up from behind Phishy and untied her as she began to revive.

"What the fuck happened?" Phishy moaned.

"Shhh! She's on to us… we have to go…" Domaina whispered. Domaina dragged Phishy out just as Jennifer and the crew came back from their break.

"What the hell just happened?" Jenny asked in bewilderment.

"Oh that…? Artistic differences…!"

Jennifer watched as they left and raised her eyebrow.

"*That*… was artistic differences?"

"Yeah… I had to paint the bitch's face!"

Jennifer just shrugged her shoulders. Business is business. At the end of the film shoot, the men from the club spoke to Lady Latex in private. L.L. just continued to look at Jennifer and shaking her head no. Afterwards L.L. went over to Jennifer and handed her another three hundred dollars. "What's this for?"

"They were so very impressed with your 'skills'… They thought you deserved a bonus!"

"Bullshit! What do they want from me?"

"I already told them… the answer was no…"

"No to '*what*'…?"

"Do you really *want* to know?"

"No… it doesn't matter… Thanks!" And Jennifer held the money out to Lady Latex. She wanted to make sure that there was still an understanding between them.

"No… you keep that! They were really impressed with your skills… They have never seen a fluffer do what you did today!"

"What…? I kept the men 'happy' and ready to perform… just like you asked…"

"Yeah you did…" And Lady Latex laughed.

"What's so fucking funny?" Jennifer asked.

"You were… *supposed*… to give them blow jobs…!" Jennifer's jaw dropped. L.L. laughed. "Too late for that now… close your mouth honey!" L.L. chuckled. "You actually kept all those men erect by simply dancing for them… and not one of those

119

man-bitches complained… as a matter of fact, they were so horny that they did their best work in front of the camera ever. The producers loved it!"

Jennifer now realized the bullet she dodged. "I'm never doing anything like this ever again… you okay with that?" Jenny said.

"I kinda figured that out for myself… thanks… I'm cool with it!" L.L. held out her hand to shake Jenny's. Jenny threw her arms around L.L. and hugged her. L.L. began to well up. (Protect her… no matter *what* the cost…) "Let's go… there are poles that need some serious polishing tonight… and I have a girl I need to replace… Let's get some sleep…" L.L. said.

"Can we get something to eat first…? I'm starved…!"

"I know… you haven't eaten 'dick' all day!" Jennifer hit L.L. on the arm and laughed. L.L. put her arm around Jennifer and they walked to the car together. Jennifer now knew that she had the power to incite the animal instincts in any man. She could exude a powerful sexual energy no matter what she was doing. When her 'Jenny Mojo' was on… no man could resist her wiles. She just hadn't learned the true extent of what she was capable of. For now… that was a good thing. Later, her 'super' powers would be put to the test.

In actuality, Jennifer did work as a fluffer on four more porn films. Money was getting tight, and stripping wasn't paying what it used to. On two of the films her 'Jenny Mojo' didn't work at all on some of the more jaded porn stars. Try as she could to avoid personal contact, she had to get more physically involved. At first, she tried to just masturbate them, when that didn't work; she had to perform fellatio on them. It was not a pleasurable experience for her. They forcibly made her do it and they treated her like dirt during and afterwards. She abhorred doing it and she began to drink on set in order to get into the mood to 'fulfill' her duties. Although Jennifer learned all the tricks of giving great head, she never liked the 'position' it put her in. Being paid to do it only made her hate doing it more and more.

On the last film she worked, the producers saw her excessive drinking as an opportunity to get her to 'perform' on camera. They maneuvered her onto the 'set' and tried to convince her to fluff the star. Fortunately, Jennifer had enough sense to have pre-arranged to have Lady Latex pick her up because the last time she was too drunk to drive herself home. Lady Latex arrived early and got Jennifer out of there before they were able to take advantage of her. Jennifer never worked on a porn movie ever again. Lady Latex was blackballed and never directed another X rated film again.

Chapter 25
(And The Runner Up Is...)

Steven called me into the law offices of his son Michael one afternoon. I wasn't worried. Business was good at the club and the cat houses. I could only guess he had another project in mind for me. I was up for it. Ramona wasn't there when I arrived so I tried to interrogate the receptionist Susan to see if she would give me a 'heads up'.

"I'm sorry Ms. Oceanside... but Mr. Callahan specifically told me that only he was supposed to speak to you about this matter... sorry..."

"Which 'Mr. Callahan'..."

"Steven..."

"It's okay Susan... I just wanted to know if there was a problem..."

"I can tell you that he was kind of 'happy' when he discussed the matter with Michael... more than that..."

It was then that Steven came out of his office. "Tobey! I'm glad you could make it... come on in..." He closed the door behind us. "Would you like a drink?"

"Two fingers... if it's no bother..."

"Anything for you..." Steven poured us both a drink and sat down. I took a sip. Steven doesn't serve anything as smooth as this in his club; but most of those rubes wouldn't know the difference.

"So... Why did you ask to see me...? Is everything okay...?"

Steven took a sip. "I want to talk to you about one of the girls..."

"Is there a problem?"

"I'm not sure... I'm hoping you could enlighten me..."

I knew that was a crock of shit... Steven was never unsure of anything. He knew before he asked you. Michael learned his lawyer skills from Steven. Michael learned that you never ask a question you don't already have the answer to. "The new girl... Jennifer..."

"What do you need to know?"

"What's your impression of her?"

I sipped my drink. "I like her... she's trustworthy... she's a great dancer... I can count on her in a pinch! Yeah... I like her... why?"

"Is there... anything you think you need to tell me about her...?"

He already knows... so there's no reason to lie. "She worked as a fluffer in a couple of porn films for me and some of my associates..."

"Anything else?" Steven took a sip of his scotch.

"She had developed a drinking problem from working that job, but she straightened up the moment she stopped..."

"You mean she straightened up when 'you' stopped her..."

"They tried to get her to perform on camera... I got her into that business... she wanted no part of it... I got her out..."

"Is there anything on film with her in it...?"

"No... I got there in time..." Steven refreshed my drink. "Why all the interest in Jennifer all of a sudden, Steven? Is she in some kind of trouble?"

"I know you and Jennifer are best friends, and I just wanted to talk to you about her..."

"Again... why?"

"Times are changing and the company is going to have to expand into more... legitimate endeavors..."

"And?"

"We're looking for the new face of Callahan Enterprises and we're looking into grooming... Jennifer..."

"Oh!"

Steven put his drink down. "I wanted you to know that we wanted..."

"Someone who wouldn't be an embarrassment to the company... I get it..." I interrupted.

Steven stood up and came around his desk and hugged me. "You have never been an embarrassment to me or the company..."

"I love you Steven... but you and I both know the look you had on your face that day I danced in the cage... and the day I took on new 'responsibilities' with the company..."

"That look wasn't embarrassment, but I will admit, I was a little disappointed that you chose the path you did..."

"I did what I had to do... I have no regrets..."

"I do... I always wonder if you would have made that choice if I told you what I had planned for you... and that this wasn't it..."

"Thinking back... if I hadn't made it then... I would have made it sooner or later... I am what I am... I like me... its okay!"

"So you don't have a problem with us grooming Jennifer...?"

"Nope!" and I drained my glass; that was my way of 'ending' the meeting. "Anything else you need Steven?"

"No... I think that just about covers it..."

"Always a pleasure..." And I left. Ramona was just coming in the door.

"Are you okay Tobey?" She's the only person on this planet other than Steven that I allow to call me Tobey.

"Yeah I'm okay..."

"With what Steven spoke to you about?"

"Yeah... I think he's making a good choice... If it was up to me... I'd pick Jenny first too!"

"She's going to need you as a friend... now more than ever...!"

"She'll be just fine... If she ever needs me... I got her back."

"Thank you Tobey..."

"Anything for you and Steven, Ramona... I owe you two more than you'll ever know..."

Ramona kissed and hugged her. In spite of what happened just now L.L. still considered them to be the parents she never had. But even with her promise to Ramona, L.L. treated Jenny a little differently, almost as if she was 'hating on' her for taking advantage of an opportunity she had screwed up years before. It was just a subtle change in attitude... or so she thought!

The Tortured Soul Trilogy
(Living La Vida Puta)
Chapter 26
(The Twilight Zone)

The club had been getting a string of tickets and all kinds of inspectors kept coming by the check out the club. Michael and Steven knew that there was a 'shakedown' coming. It wasn't until the fire dept did a third safety inspection that one of the firemen who was a club regular pulled him aside and told him that somebody had lit a fire under the community board to get the place shut down. Some pain in the ass neighbor was upset that a patron of the club parked in front of his house. On the street! That's public parking! It didn't matter, but the complaint put the strip club in the cross hairs of some assemblyman wannabe. Sure enough, Micheal found out that the city was going to try to re-zone the area and it would not allow a bar/strip club in the building they owned.

Michael came out of the local community board meeting feeling defeated. They were determined to change the zoning law in order to shut down the club. They tried everything from harassing them with frivolous fines to putting undercover cops in the mix of the clientele every night, but Steven ran a square house and L.L. didn't play that shit. They pushed but they didn't have a leg to stand on. Sure they found little violations but nothing that they couldn't handle. This was their last desperate attempt to shut them down for good.

The company had real estate agents hunting down new locations but the chances of finding one they could use was near impossible. If word got out that someone was opening a strip club in the area... they would change the zoning law and bam... shut out again! One of Cisco's friends tried to open a tattoo parlor, he had all the licenses, permits; everything was in perfect order. He spent over 20 grand to fix the place up. It was going to be a high class place. No bikers, no freaks, only people who wanted serious ink at top prices. He had two top tat artists coming from the east coast and one from Hawaii for the grand opening. Every thing was running like clock work and... BAM! They changed the zone on the building and he was out 20 G's and out on his ass! He couldn't afford to fight the ruling because he was already hocked up to his eyeballs!

"No!" Michael said to himself. "We have to stay put; right there... if we back down and pull out, we'll never be able to open a new club... anywhere!"

They had considered opening up a 'legit' establishment, but that would take more money than they wanted to invest and the returns would be significantly less. Besides, those new clubs were now owned and operated by celebrities and they and their famous friends were the clubs' main draw. Steven was connected, but not in those circles. Michael had to find a way to save The Kitty Bar for now. Callahan Enterprises still needed that 'front' until more money could be funneled to other more lucrative legitimate business endeavors. He was about to get in his car when the assemblywoman who was on the board walked up to him.

"Mr. Callahan?" Michael put his briefcase on the passengers' seat. "I thought you should know that we took a vote and I thought you should have the results before you leave..."

"You know I'm going to fight the boards' decision to my last breath?"

"I don't think that you will..."

"You have no idea how tenacious I can be...!" Michael said.

"And you have absolutely no idea with whom you are dealing with...!"

Michael shook his head. He had to figure out a way to take this woman down.

She took a deep breath. "You can keep your establishment open... the board vote was in your favor by three votes..." She said.

"And I take it you are going to do everything you can to reverse that decision...?" and he leaned on his car door.

She stepped back away from the car and paused. "I voted... *not* to change the zone on your strip club..."

"Why would you do that?" Michael asked quizzically.

"I would have voted to shut you down, but all investigations into your business dealings came up clean... I suggest you keep it that way."

"Thank you! I don't know what to say... except, does this mean you're calling off the dogs?"

"The 'harassment' will stop... A letter has been sent to your 'neighbor' that the street is public and he can't stop anybody from parking in front of his house. He kicked, but he backed down. Especially when he started getting tickets from the sanitation dept for leaving his trash cans out on the street." She shook her head. "But I'm still going to be keeping my eye on you and your club... just to keep you honest, I have a constituency to protect!"

"I'm okay with that... Thank you again..." And he shook her hand.

She smiled. "Just tell L.L.... that 'Cindy' said hi..."

"You and L.L. know each other?" Michael said, very confused.

"No... we don't know each other... and you can tell her that *I said* that..." Michael did not take that as a 'shot'. It was more of an inside joke. She took a step and stopped and turned around and smiled. "And tell her... that I *still* love her..." And Cindy walked over to her car and drove off leaving a very perplexed Michael standing there. Michael was very confused. He knew the type of women L.L. got *involved* with, and she was certainly not that *type* of woman, business or personal, not even in L.L.'s wildest dreams. Michael got in his car and drove off. He would ask L.L. about what had just happened when he saw her later in his office.

Plans that were made to legitimize Callahan Enterprizes would have to be acclerated. He called Ramon and asked her to set up a meeting with their key player to see if everything was in place. They had a five year plan but in order for it have a chance to succeed, it would have to be implemented immediately. They could not take another chance that the club could be closed and ruin everything.

All Michael thought as he drove to the office was. "*Good thing we bribed those other two members!*"

The Tortured Soul Trilogy
(The Confessions of Jennifer X)
Chapter 27
(Don't You Want Me?)

Jennifer was called into Steven Callahan's office on a Tuesday afternoon. She had no idea why she was being called in, but he was the boss and didn't have to explain himself to her. She would do as she was told. The offices were very nice, kind of like a law office with lots of mahogany and marble. She sat down and was very intimidated by her surroundings. The receptionist was very nice to her, even though she was dressed a little out of place to be there. Jennifer was dressed nicely, just too casual for the surroundings. She kept fidgeting with her hair.

"Mr. Callahan will be with you in just a few moments... would you care for a cup of tea while you wait?"

"No... thank you..."

"You can call me Susan..."

Jennifer smiled. "Thank you Susan... I'm fine thank you!"

The office intercom buzzed. "Mr. Callahan will see you now." And Susan walked her to the door.

"Susan...?" Jenny asked nervously.

"Yes?"

"Um... never mind..."

Susan smiled. "It's okay... Jennifer... relax... you'll be just fine..." And Susan held the door for her as she entered the office. Mr. Callahan was putting golf balls on the carpet. He offered her a seat. Jennifer sat demurely and crossed her ankles.

"Sorry to keep you waiting Ms. Jones... May I call you Jennifer...?"

"Sure Mr. Callahan..."

"Jennifer... you're probably wondering why I asked you to come here today..."

"It did concern me a little bit..."

Callahan smiled. He knew then he had made the right decision. Jennifer was perfect for the task at hand.

"Good! I have a project that I think you would be perfect for..."

"What type of 'project'...?" She was a little anxious. She didn't want to work in the porn industry in any capacity any more and she had absolutely no idea what Callahan had in mind.

"I'll let my son explain the details..." With that, a young man entered the room. Jennifer had seen him before. It was Michael, the lawyer that bailed out Lady Latex when she was busted for solicitation. She was very 'glad' to see him again

"I believe we've met... unofficially." And Jennifer stood up and held out her hand.

"Michael Callahan..." He shook her hand. "I see why father is so impressed with you..."

"Oh? Do tell..." Jenny asked.

"At first you give the impression of being crude... but you have great potential... I like that!"

"Great potential for 'what'...?" She was about to say something about that remark about being '*crude*' when Steven interrupted them.

"I'll let you two kids talk it all out... I have other 'business' to attend to..." And Steven hugged Michael.

"Will I see you later, dad?"

"I should be home in time for dinner... but... *you* might be late..." And Steven shook Jennifer's hand. "Take good care of my son..." And he kissed her cheek and left.

Jennifer raised her eyebrow at Michael. "Exactly... *how* am I supposed to *take good care of you*...?"

"Don't worry... As much as my father likes to toss around innuendo... I don't get 'personally involved' with..." He paused.

"Girls like me...?"

"...Anybody I have 'business' dealings with... including... 'girls' like you..."

Jennifer didn't know whether to be insulted or not. She would reserve her judgment for later. Michael explained that she was going into a pilot program to hone her for a management position in another branch of Callahan's company. He jokingly referred to it as '*Operation; My Fair Lady*'.

"Why hasn't L.L., I mean... Tobey... been picked for this project?"

"Ms. Oceanside best serves the company in the capacity she now has... besides... she's damaged goods..."

"... *Damaged goods*...?" Jennifer raised her eyebrow again. This was her best friend he was talking about. She was starting to have a problem with his attitude but she would hear him out before she would blow up his spot. Besides he *was* the boss' son.

"Ms. Oceanside has acquired too many bad habits and her reputation has been made public and preceeds her wherever she goes... not the sort of image we want to be the face of Callahan Enterprises."

"And what about me...?"

"You have been very fortunate enough to have stayed under the radar... Your 'misadventures' are manageable... in spite of your checkered past..."

"So you don't have a problem with me being a stripper in your father's club...?"

"No... we have that information 'under control'... but what I was referring to was your parents..." Jennifer's jaw dropped. "We know all about your mother and your father... and your five year stay in a mental institution..."

"Those records were supposed to be sealed!"

"Ms. Jones... there is sealed... and there is 'sealed', anything that is left in the dark is always revealed in the light..."

"You're going to try to blackmail me... aren't you...?"

Michael walked over and sat at the edge of his desk nearest Jennifer. "Blackmail you for what...? Everything you have... everything you own... is because *we* gave it to you..."

"I'm where I am because I earned it... nobody *gave* me anything!" Jenny was about to read this guy the riot act.

Michael smiled and went to sit back down in his chair. "You know what? I'm really beginning to like you... a whole lot! You have brains, beauty and ambition... and you don't take shit from anybody! When I'm finished with you, you're going to be quite the formidable young woman!"

That comment appeased her, for now... "I like the sound of that... when do we start?"

"Right now…!" Michael buzzed his secretary on the intercom. "Ramona… may I see you in my father's office Please?"

"Yes, Mr. Callahan…" She answered over the intercom. Ramona, a sixty-ish woman, entered the office a moment later.

"Jennifer Jones… this is my personal secretary, Ms. Ramona Kirby…"

"A pleasure to meet you Ms. Kirby…"

"The pleasure is mine Ms. Jones…" Ramona smiled. She took an immediate liking to Jennifer.

"As of right now, Ms. Kirby is *your* personal secretary and mentor… She will do for you whatever it is you need her to do…and… you will do whatever it is she tells you to do… Do I make myself clear?"

"Yes Mr. Callahan…" Jennifer answered.

"Jennifer dear, would you mind waiting for me in my office? Susan will show you the way… "

"Yes Ma'am…" And Jennifer excused herself and left to go to Ramona's office and closed the door behind her.

"So… what is your first impression of her, Ramona?"

"I like her… She learns quickly… even now… she's not even the same as when she first walked in here…!"

Michael took a credit card out of his wallet and handed it to Ramona. "Here… I want the works for her; clothes, manicure, pedicure, hair, the whole nine yards and I want her enrolled in etiquette classes… and whatever else you can think of… spare no expense…"

"What about a formal education…?"

"We'll cross that bridge when we get to it…"

"Very good sir…" And Ramona began to exit his office. As she got to the door, Michael called her.

"Ramona…"

"Yes Mr. Callahan…?" she said as she turned to him.

"Don't forget to get yourself something nice too… Just make sure I get the bill…"

"Yes… Mr. Callahan… Thank you!"

"Oh… by the way, Ramona?"

"Yes, Mr. Callahan?"

"You know I love you!"

"I love you too… Mr. Callahan… now behave yourself!"

Ramona exited; Michael smiled. Ramona had been working with the company since he was born. She should have retired long ago, but she was more like family than an employee. Jennifer was in the best possible hands, she better damn well appreciate it.

For the next few months, Jennifer and Ramona were inseparable. Jennifer liked all the attention she got and she really liked shopping, although Ramona was very strict with her fashion choices. Jennifer didn't complain, after all, Michael was footing the bill and she had promised to do whatever Ramona told her to do. Jennifer could get very used to being pampered like this. The salons, the spa treatments, the physical trainer, yeah, she could really get used be being pampered like this. And she didn't have to work the pole anymore. The Callahan's took care of all her expenses. Although she was always under Ramona's supervision, she was allowed to let her hair down and go out clubbing on the weekends. She would meet with Lady Latex on occasion and party with her, but she was very careful not to get into any trouble. Tobey knew all about what Jennifer was into with the Callahans, and she was totally okay with it. Instinctively, Tobey knew that Jennifer was meant for better things and she was not going to give her any shit about it. She also wasn't gonna do anything to fuck it up for her.

The Tortured Soul Trilogy
(Living La Vida Puta)
Chapter 28
(The Cruiserweight Division)

Jenny was very busy with her special project and they saw very little of each other lately. Jenny had stopped working at the strip club all together. The extra time that L.L. had, was filled up with working the pole until she could a suitable replacement. L.L. was lonely without her best friend so she started fetish club hopping for dates again. She hated doing it but she desperately needed a diversion from her everyday life. Between the club and the cat houses, she had no time for herself. She couldn't maintain a relationship with her crazy hours so, a cunting we will go...! She was a regular at this spot so she knew the bartender Ritchie B. real well. He would hook up her drinks and he knew she was a good tipper. She looked around and acknowledged some of her previous lovers in the room but she would only take one of them home if no one else was looking good. She considered them a 'fallback' good time. Ritchie had a waitress bring L.L. her 'usual', two fingers of whiskey, on the rocks. The waitress was cute, but she never tried to fuck the hired help. It was bad karma, bad for business and it would wreck your social life at this club. There would be no more cruising here! L.L. sipped her drink and was about to set it back down when she heard a familiar voice.

"Well... look who we have here...!"

L.L. turned to see her '*old friend*' Nena.

"It's 'Nena'... right?" and L.L. sipped her drink. Nena nodded. "We're not starting any shit tonight... are we?" I asked.

Nena threw her hands up in the 'I surrender' pose. "Don't start none... there won't be none..."

L.L. smiled. "Then have a seat..."

"Actually, I'm here with my woman, I just thought I'd swing by to say hi..."

"Call her over... The first round is on me..." Nena nodded and called over her bitch. They sat down and L.L. bought the first round.

"So? What brings you here?" Nena asked.

"Looking for a sweet young thing to take home with me..."

"Well, let me give you a heads up..." Nena started telling me all about the men in the club. I shook my head.

"I don't do... *dick*... what do you know about the ladies here tonight...?" Nena smiled and proceeded to give me a rundown of the talent in the room. I knew Nena wasn't bullshitting me because she confirmed what I already knew about the ones I had already dated. "Thanks for the intel... That frees up most of my night..."

"Well if you don't find yourself a hook-up, you can always come home with us tonight..."

"I appreciate the offer... but I don't like to... do *groups*... No offense!"

L.L. instinctively knew Nena was a 'poker', not a 'liquor', and L.L. don't play that shit but there was no reason to ruin a developing friendship by bringing it up now.

"None taken..." Nena got up with her girlfriend and paid for the next round. "Say... was there anyone you saw 'that' day... that interested you?"

L.L. thought for a moment. "There was a girl... I wouldn't mind getting to know better..." L.L. described her, Nena knew who she meant, but she didn't approve of her choice.

"That one is too much head case and not enough 'head'..." L.L. smiled. "I'll tell you what... let me make a few calls... I think I know someone you'd like..."

"Why would you do that for me...?"

"Remember when you told me if I didn't know who you were, to '*ask around*'?"

"Yeah...?"

Nena shrugged her shoulders. "I asked around..." L.L. smiled, nodded and sipped her drink. About an hour later a young beautiful blonde came by her table.

"I understand that you're a friend of Nena's?" she asked.

"And you are...?" I said.

"A 'gift'... would you like to take me home and unwrap me?"

"Sit... Have a drink with me and we'll see what the night brings..."

L.L. actually spent the rest of the night dancing and drinking with her 'gift'. The girl wasn't really into the rough stuff but L.L. didn't mind too much. She took her home and had some quality time with her, but it wasn't just a good time she was looking for. She was looking for a more substantial relationship. She made sure that the girl thanked Nena for the present of her company but that she would find her future diversions on her own. Her 'services' would no longer be required. Come on… L.L. was a pimp, and she didn't need the services of one!

The Tortured Soul Trilogy
(Living La Vida Puta)
Chapter 29
(Looking For Mrs. Goodbar)

L.L. finally had a night and the next day all to herself. She wasn't going to work at the club and the cat house was straight for now. She tried to get involved with 'independent' film projects but she was shut out by 'the boys'. She didn't have the time or the inclination to shoot a film without proper funding and without a distributor Steven would lose any investment he put into the project. It was all a moot point. She didn't have any spare time as it was, so starting a new venture from scratch was out of the question. Besides, what L.L. really needed... was to get laid!

L.L. didn't want to go out cruising for a date. She was getting a little tired of the fetish club scene. No more one night stands that went nowhere. She needed to develop a relationship, not get just a slap and tickle. She decided to take the night off from hunting pussy and just walked into the nearest neighborhood bar and found an empty barstool and sat down. She tossed her clutch purse and her pack of cigarettes on the bar. The bartender came over and she ordered a whiskey on the rocks. The bartender served her drink and she dropped two twenties on the bar. That meant to keep the drinks coming. He went to serve other guests as L.L. stirred her drink and took a sip. She then took out a cigarette and put it in her mouth. She had to turn it around because it was filter end out. She checked her clutch for her lighter but it wasn't there. The bartender walked over, to light her cigarette or so she thought... when he said. "There's no smoking allowed at the bar Miss."

"Since when?"

"New law..."

L.L. let the cigarette hang from her mouth. "You're shitting me?"

He shook his head no. "If you want to smoke... it is allowed in the smoking lounge..." L.L. hadn't been in a legit bar in a while and had no idea of the new law! There was never any smoking in The Kitty Bar only because Steven didn't allow it!

Who knew Steven was ahead of his time? Some restaurants and bars added a room where you could smoke away from non-smokers to circumvent the new law. L.L. looked in to the room. It was a bunch of old guys smoking smelly cigars. No way, she wanted to hang out in there. She shook her head no and put the cigarette back in the pack. She nursed her drink for a while and a few men came over and tried to start a conversation with her. Needless to say, she wasn't interested. One guy did not want to take no for an answer. He became persistent. L.L. politely told him to get the fuck out of her face. He snidely remarked. *"You must be a lesbian...?"* To which L.L. replied. *"I wasn't until you sat next to me...!"* and the guy just walked away. L.L. ordered another scotch and listened to the guy playing the piano. He didn't suck, but he wasn't that great either. She walked over and put a ten in his tip glass.

"What would you like to hear?" he said smiling at her.

"Silence... for about ten or fifteen minutes... no offense..."

"None taken..." It was the only tip he had gotten all night and he could use a break anyway. He bowed to L.L., took his tip and walked away. L.L. was about to go back to her seat when she saw her. She was sitting in a corner booth all by herself, nursing a mimosa. She was about 28, wearing a nice cocktail dress, blonde, hair done, lips done, nails, the works. She wore glasses and looked like a librarian or a school teacher who had a hot date... that didn't show up! She too had been spending most of the evening fending off the wolves in the bar. L.L. motioned to the bartender that she was switching seats to the booth. He nodded. He brought over her drink just as she walked up to the booth.

"Is this seat taken?"

The woman looked up at her with sad eyes. "No... it's not... I *guess*..."

L.L. sat down next to her but not so close to make her feel uncomfortable. "My name is L.L."

"Angie... What does L.L. stand for?"

"Maybe I'll tell you later..." Angie smiled. "He stood you up...?" L.L. asked. She didn't answer. "I didn't mean to pry..." The woman sobbed softly and pulled out a hankie and wiped her eyes. L.L. slid over and leaned into her. "You wanna talk about it?" After about an hour, three shots of whiskey and several mimosas, Angie was sobbing softly on L.L.'s shoulder and felt like the weight of the world was lifted from her shoulders. Angie wiped her tears and finally said to L.L.

"I have half a mind to just give up men, once and for all…"

L.L. motioned to the bartender. "Check please!"

The next morning L.L. came out of the bathroom after washing up. She turned to see Angie still tied face down on her bed. She still had a red ball gag in her mouth and moaned sensually as she began to awaken. L.L. went over and kissed her buttocks up to her shoulders and carefully removed the gag from her mouth and kissed her gently.

"You okay baby?" L.L. asked her as she loosened her wrist restraints.

"Ahhhhh huh! That… was fucking amazing… where do you learn to do that?"

"I've been around…"

"And around… and around… and… around…" Angie began to giggle sensually and sighed. L.L. untied her hands and was about to untie her ankles. "Leave those on… if you don't mind…" Angie moaned.

"Hey… they're *your* ankle cuffs… enjoy!" L.L. sat on the side of the bed as Angie reached under herself and began to finger herself softly then a little faster. She then took her other hand and began to slap her own ass. L.L. shook her head with quiet amazement. She had found the one chick at that bar, who was a bigger freak than she was. What luck! "I can't believe your date didn't show up last night… I bet he's kicking himself in the ass right now…"

Angie moaned and giggled again. "What '*date*'…?"

L.L. stopped and looked at Angie who had a wicked smile on her face as she probed herself deeper. "Why you dirty little…" L.L. began.

"Fucking whore?" Angie finished. L.L. shook her head. Angie had set her up with the old 'damsel in distress' routine! "Come on… call me a dirty little fucking whore… I really need a good spanking…" She cooed and she spanked herself.

"What you *need* is a good chewing out…" L.L. replied as she spread Angie's ass cheeks, smacked them hard and buried her face between her legs and did all the nasty little things to her that she had done the night before.

Angie had the same idea L.L. had, to cruise a regular bar for her next date, I guess great minds *do* think alike!

Chapter 30
(Aint No Woman Like the One I Got)

L.L. and Angie saw each other regularly for the next three months or so. L.L. really liked Angie. She was sweet and gentle and so very... co-operative. Angie was a salesclerk in a department store. Angie didn't know what L.L. did... outside the bedroom; and she didn't ask. It was still all new and exciting between the two of them. L.L. felt like she hadn't felt in a very long time. After another amazing night of sex and discipline, Angie confessed to L.L. how she felt. "You make me feel like I'm the most important person in the world... No man has ever done that for me... I always wished I could meet a man that would make me feel the way I feel when I'm with you..."

"Why do you feel that way?" L.L. asked Angie.

"Men only groped me... men fucked me... men... *beat...* me... but *you*...? You... '*touch*' me...! You touch my very soul!"

"You don't need a man... you have me...!" L.L. whispered and she held Angie so gently in her arms.

Weeks had past after that special moment Angie had with L.L. There was so much more Angie wanted to tell her, but the time wasn't right. Angie walked into her apartment tired of a long day dealing with customers at the store. If she had to hear one more person piss and moan about customer service and how '*The customer is always right!*' she was going to lose it. Fortunately, tomorrow was her day off and she could sleep in late. She stepped into her apartment and was met with the wonderful smell of pot roast and garlic potatoes and was instantly envious... "Someone in the building is getting a nice home cooked meal... I sure wish it was me..." she muttered. She didn't even bother to check the fridge, there was nothing in it except and old container of Moo Goo Gai Pan which probably would have looked more like '*Ugh Lee Guy Spam*'...! She saw that there were no messages on her machine. "*I sure could use a long hot soak in the tub...*" She thought to herself, but to soak in the tub would require washing it first and she didn't have the strength or the inclination. Angie kicked off her shoes, picked them up and walked barefoot towards her bedroom and opened the door. She stopped and stood there in total amazement.

Angie surveyed the room that had been decorated to look like the most romantic place on earth! There were scented candles *everywhere*! A path of red, white and yellow rose petals led to the bed and it was also covered with them. Angie walked over and there was a naughty little negligee draped on the bed. There was champagne on ice and a tray of chocolate covered strawberries on the night stand. Strands of silk and satin were hung on the walls to her bedposts. Angie put her hand on her heart and a tear came to her eye. This… was the most wonderful thing her lover had ever done for her. Just then she felt someone come up behind her. "Baby this is…" and she hesitated when L.L. came up behind her and hugged her tight. She turned to L.L. "The most beautiful thing you could have ever done for me…" and a tear came to her eye.

L.L. kissed her. "Surprised?"

Angie looked around the room. "You have no idea…"

L.L. kissed Angie so very gently. "You in the mood to soak in the tub, filled with bath oils and lavender?"

"You cleaned my tub…?"

L.L. whispered in her ear. "It's so clean… we can… eat in it!" Angie almost swooned right there. It was if a genie heard her deepest wishes and they were all being granted. Angie kissed L.L. so passionately and L.L. held her in her arms and then L.L. pulled away from her. "We have all night… let's not rush things… I want to take my precious time with you…" A tear came to Angie's eye as L.L. led her to the bathroom. L.L. gave Angie privacy as she got naked to take her bath. L.L. entered the bathroom with a soft sponge and a towel and Angie was wearing a soft terrycloth robe.

"What are you going to do with that?"

L.L. motioned for Angie to sit on a small bench Angie had in her bathroom that she used whenever she wanted to lotion her body after a quick shower. "I'm going to give you a sponge bath…" Angie sat and sighed as L.L. gently sat her down and then started filling the tub with water. She then took a body wash, poured some into the sponge and wet it in the sink. L.L. slowly, softly and meticulously hand washed her lover. Angie cooed and purred and felt like a princess as L.L. washed every inch of her, paying particular attention to her hands and feet. She was aroused but so relaxed. L.L. washed away every care she had in the world... and she hadn't even gotten in the tub yet! By the time she was ready to soak; her body was clean and covered by goose bumps. L.L. had kicked up the thermostat in the apartment so that she could truly enjoy her experience. L.L. escorted her to the tub and helped her get in. L.L. then added the bath oils and some more rose petals. The scent of lavender quickly filled the room. She then turned the hot water on as to raise the water temperature slowly. She then continued to wash her in the tub, but now she paid close attention to her erect nipples and her clitoris. A lone flickering candle was the only witness to this sensuous act of love and affection. Angie spread her legs as L.L. stroked and fondled her and just when she felt like she was floating on air. L.L. dropped her robe and got in with her. "You didn't think you were going to have all this fun... all by yourself... did you?" Angie giggled as L.L. got into the tub with her. They lay in the hot, steamy water as they touched and caressed and probed each other, with their hands and tongues. After about five more minutes of underwater foreplay, the girls lovingly toweled each other off and began to lotion each others bodies. They took their sweet time taking baby oil and rubbing each other down in the steamy bathroom. Angie used her hands to oil and caress L.L. and she used her whole body to oil her. L.L. used her tits to rub oil on her. She used her ass to grind the oil on her. It wasn't until they sat on the bench and got into the 'boxing' position, where they were vulva to vulva did things get truly heated up.

"Take me to bed..." Angie moaned.

"I thought you would never ask." L.L. answered. L.L. escorted Angie to the bed where she lay down and spread her legs and began to pinch and squeeze her nipples. L.L. went down on her gently licking and sucking her labia and clit. Her tongue flicked in and out of her juicy pussy. Angie moaned and thrashed her head from side to side. She really needed this... right here... right now...

"Oh... mmmuuuuuuuu! Muaaaaaaaaah! Ha-ha haaaaa! Oh yeah! Oh yeah! Ohhhhhhh! Muuuuuah!" Angie's body shivered and shook, her nipples became hard and tight. Angie took her fingertip and kissed and licked it. Then she started pumping her finger in and out of her mouth. That was the signal for L.L. to probe her. L.L. eased her fingers into Angie while her thumb stroked her clit. L.L. bent her fingers upward and stoked Angie's "G" spot while she licked her clit. Angie began to wail and moan. "More! More! Ohhhhhh! Right Therrrrrre! Oh! Faster... faster... Fff... fff... fffuck meeeeeeee!" L.L. stood up from her kneeling position between Angie's knees and continued to pump her fingers in and out, in and out, faster and faster. She could feel Angie's pussy contract and tighten around her fingers and she pulled out, rubbed her clit and entered her again. Angie arched her back and moaned and cooed and threw her head back and forth violently. Angie threw her head side to side and her hair whipped around. Angie's voice rose in pitch and got louder.

"Oooohhhhhhhhhaaaaaaaaaaaaah!" Then her jaw trembled. "That's so ggg... ggg... ggg... good bay...bee! That's nice!" Then Angie began to cough. Every time she did, her vagina got tighter around L.L. fingers. "Ohhhh Fuck me baby! Fuck meeeeeee!" Angie was only a closet lesbian, she still liked the feel of a man inside her, and L.L. was prepared. She had picked up a present for Angie from the Callahan's sex shop, 'The Warehouse'. It was a ten-inch, latex, oil filled, strap-on which L.L. had under the bed in a pot of hot water. It had gone down to almost room temperature while they bathed. It was still warm and was the closest thing to feeling like a real cock. L.L. put it on and was about enter her when Angie stopped her. "No wait..." L.L. thought that she didn't want her to use it on her. She was wrong. Angie sat up and began to perform fellatio on it. Angie was really getting into it, but it didn't do a thing for L.L.... until Angie reached under it and began to fondle L.L.'s clit with her thumb. L.L's eyes fluttered as Angie rubbed and stroked her clit faster and faster, left to right. Angie knew never to try to 'invade' L.L.'s personal space, so she had learned to use her thumb as well as she used her tongue. She could tease her vagina but would never ever try to probe her. L.L. loved the fact that Angie respected her wishes. It was one of the things about her she loved about her so much. Other than Cindy... Angie was the only other woman she allowed anywhere near her pussy. Other women could not be trusted playing around down there without trying to probe her. That was always a deal breaker with her. Angie continued to suck the strap-on and fondle L.L. Finally

143

Angie could wait no longer and she rolled over on her knees and spread her cheeks. L.L. eased up behind her and slid the dildo slowly into her. "Ohhhhhhh yeah! Do that again!" L.L. eased out and slid back in again. Angie started to slam her hands on the bed. "Ohhhhhh That's it... right there!" L.L. continued to pump Angie with long deep strokes. Angie was very appreciative. After some long strokes, Angie grabbed her ass cheeks and held them apart for better access. L.L. pulled out and placed the tip near Angie's anus.

"Baby...? Do you want me to...?"

Angie immediately covered her anus with her hand. "No... *don't*...! You have your boundaries... and I have mine..." She panted and moaned.

"I understand..." L.L. understood respecting boundaries and she eased the dildo back into her hot, moist, wet pussy. Angie cooed. L.L. continued to ease in and out with long slow strokes until Angie started bucking and pushing back, faster and faster, harder and harder. L.L. grabbed her hips and started to pump her pussy in earnest.

"Oh! Oh! Right there... right there you mmmother... fff...fff... fucker! Shiiiiiiiiiiit! Yeah baby right there... don't sss...sss. Stop! You *bitch*! Fuck meeee youuuuuuu biiiiiiiiitttttttch! Oh! Shhhhhiii... oh shhhiiii... ahhhhhhhhhhhhhhhh ha!" Angie dropped her face into the pillow and screamed at the top of her lungs.

L.L. continued to pump her hard and fast. Just at the right moment L.L. yelled out. "I'm gonna cum!"

Angie turned her head to L.L. "What the fuck you mean *'you're gonna cum'*...?" She whispered all confused.

"Roll over!" L.L. barked, and Angie did as she was told. L.L. grabbed Angie by the back of her head and pulled her closer to the dildo.

"Blow me bitch!" Angie did as she was told and began to suck on the dildo again and then after a moment, L.L. pulled her off, and began to stroke the dildo faster and faster in Angie's face. Angie had no idea what L.L. was doing... until... L.L. grabbed the latex ball sack on the strap-on and squeezed it hard. A stream of vanilla-creme flavored oil shot out from the tip of the strap-on into Angie's face. Angie shuddered from the shock and her nipples throbbed. Angie immediately placed the tip in her mouth and sucked the rest of the sweet liquid out. Angie fell back on the bed satiated and totally amazed.

"Where the fuck did you get that amazing toy?"

"I have a friend who owns a sex shop; sometimes I take a sample... for research and testing purposes..." She didn't want to tell Angie that it was from her employers' sex shop.

"Well... you tell them that inspector number nine gives it two thumbs up!" Angie laughed.

"A thumbs up... where?"

"Right here... smart ass!" And Angie started in on L.L's clit with her thumb again. L.L. jaw quivered. "You have me at a disadvantage you know..."

"How so...?" L.L. said in a trembling voice.

"You... have your little 'devices' to help you... I have to do you without any help...!"

"Oh... I'm... sure... you are not without your own... 'devices'..." LL said. Angie flicked her tongue in and out of her mouth quickly as she pulled the strap-on down off L.L. and maneuvered her onto the bed.

"I think... I can come up with... something you might like..." And she dove down on L.L. swollen clit.

The next morning, L.L. and Angie were laid in bed, totally spent, basking in the glow of an amazing night of love making and intense sex. Both of them lost count of how many times they had orgasms last night. After that session, they had a wonderful dinner of pot roast and potatoes L.L. had brought from their favorite restaurant and it re-fueled them for an all night triathlon of passion. They even took a few moments to just slow dance with each other. Both their bodies were covered with rose petals. L.L. looked at Angie and got a flashback of the first time she saw Jenny covered in ten dollar bills. She shook that image from her mind. She had to remember who she was here with. L.L. rolled over and picked up the naughty nightie she had purchased for Angie.

"You never even got a chance to wear this for me..."

Angie took the nightie and tossed it on the floor. "Trust me... That's where you would have seen it... as if it really mattered..."

They both laughed and kissed, that's when the doorbell rang and L.L. moaned as Angie jumped out of bed, put on her robe and went to get it. When Angie came back into the bedroom, she sat on the edge of the bed and kissed L.L.'s back and very gently and then lay on top of her. Angie kissed L.L. between her shoulders to her neck. "Who was at the door baby?" L.L. moaned, still half asleep. Angie didn't answer. L.L. closed her eyes and moaned as she kissed and caressed her back and shoulders.

"L.L.?"

"Yeah baby?"

"Do you love me?"

"Of course I love you!"

"I mean... do you really, really love me?"

L.L. turned her head. "You know I do..." and they kissed. Angie paused.

"Tie me down... and beat me..." Angie whispered. L.L. rolled over and looked at her. She didn't want to punish her, this night was about love and passion and not pain and chastisement, but if this is what she wanted, L.L. would accommodate her... L.L. tied her face down on the bed and took out Angie's favorite rubber paddle and laid into her ass... L.L. pinched her nipples and felt her nipple rings. She had a flashback to Cindy, but she still remembered who she had before her all tied down. L.L. was a little concerned with her lover. Angie always slept well after a good discipline session. I don't know how to explain it... it was if she was relieved and could finally relax... but not this time. Angie was antsy and fidgeted a lot. She shivered and shook like a junkie going through withdrawal. Tears welled in Angie's eyes and it wasn't from the beating she took. L.L. got a joint from her purse and lit it, took a puff and passed it to Angie. Angie took a drag but it didn't help.

"Angie? What's wrong? What's the matter?"

"I... I..." She stuttered.

L.L. knew that it had to have something to do with whoever had come by before. It didn't concern her then, but now... "Angie? Who *was* that at the door earlier?"

"I have a confession... to make..."

"What is it baby...?"

"The man who rang the door earlier..."

146

"Yes...?"

"Was my..." Angie's eyes and voice dropped.

"Was your what? Your father? Your brother? Who...? Who was he?"

"That was... my fiancé... the man I'm going to marry in two weeks...!" There was a deafening silence in the room... for about ten minutes... or an eternity... it's hard to say. Neither one said a word to each other. Angie just stared at L.L., L.L. just stared into space. L.L. took the joint from Angie, took a deep drag and held her breath until she coughed...

"Does he know about me?" L.L. asked quietly, wondering why he didn't enter the apartment.

Angie just nodded her head and sobbed. "Yes..." she sighed and paused for a moment. "He said it was okay for me to get it out of my system before we got married..."

A million obsenities crossed L.L.'s mind. "*I can't belive this bitch just used me*!!!" she thought. "*And she KNEW there was never going to be a future for us!*" then she calmly got dressed... took her key to Angie's apartment and left it in the bowl of half chewed and eaten strawberry bits next to the empty bottle of champagne on the end table... and quietly left.

L.L. realized that Angie knew L.L. would never forgive her for betraying her like this. That was what the chastising was all about. It was supposed to have made Angie feel better about herself. It didn't work and didn't do a damn thing for L.L. because at the time, L.L. didn't know *why* Angie wanted to be punished. Had she known, Angie surely would have gotten her money's worth! As the apartment door closed behind her, she heard Angie cry hysterically from inside the house. "*That... is your punishment... you lying, treacherous bitch!*" L.L. whispered as she walked out of the building.

L.L. didn't remember getting into her car and driving to the club that afternoon. It had taken her four hours to get to the club that was only twenty minutes away. It was as if she had traveled in an alternate universe to get there. Through an unknown dimension and she was on autopilot. She entered the club and she was the only one there. The club was deserted. She went straight to the bar and poured herself a double, no ice. Normally she nursed one drink all night if she was working. She had to keep her wits about her to run the place. *"Fuck it!"* She poured herself another. She walked over to the sound system and put on some music, not the heavy beat driven hard rock music that usually filled the place. She put on some smooth jazz from a cassette tape* nobody ever played.

For those of you that don't know what a cassette tape is... in the 80's, it's what a CD was, before there were CD's!

The club took on a whole new atmosphere, a different persona as it were. It became more... can I say... comforting? She looked around the club and thought back. She had been here almost twenty years now. She saw this club grow and change over the years. Just as she did since the day she first arrived here... She thought of the life she had lived... of the life she had left behind... She took another sip of her drink and wished that somebody... anybody... would just hold her right now! That's when Cisco walked in, put his coat on a chair, walked up behind her and said. "L.L....? Are you alright?" L.L. turned to him, put her drink down and threw her arms around his waist and hugged him tightly and would not let him go. L.L. buried her face into his strong chest and she could not see the totally surprised look on his face. Cisco put his arms around her and she cried... Jackie the bartender entered right behind Cisco and had seen the entire thing unfold before his eyes. He shook his head.

"Damn it!" he thought to himself. *"If only I had gotten here ten minutes earlier!"* Jackie cursed the double latte he picked up on the way here and made his way to the back storage room so that they could have some privacy. Cisco rocked L.L. in his arms as she sobbed quietly. He kissed her forehead and held her tightly in his arms. L.L. did not mind one bit. She needed his strength right now. Cisco was the first man, she truly trusted to fall completely apart in front of. Cisco thought of the first thing Steven told him when he met L.L. *"This is probably the only woman that doesn't need your protection..."* Boy! Was he ever wrong! L.L. wept softly on his broad shoulder as they danced slowly in place.

L.L. softly whispered. "This doesn't change shit between us..."

Cisco kissed L.L. on her forehead. "Oh course it doesn't…"

Chapter 31
(It's A Thin Line - Between Love & Hate)

Jennifer was supposed to meet Ramona at the mall to do some more clothes shopping and maybe get pedicures. Jennifer looked at her watch. It wasn't like Ms. Kirby to be late. '*I hope she's okay...*' Jennifer wanted to call her but she would wait another five minutes. She might just be stuck in traffic. Jennifer was a little hungry so she went to the food court to get a breakfast sandwich or something. As she ordered her breakfast, she turned to see a kiosk in the center of the mall. She didn't know why it caught her attention. It was very plain and unattractive. There weren't any signs; nobody knew why it was there or what they were selling. Actually there wasn't any merchandise in the kiosk at all. People walked by, but the woman in charge seemingly ignored them and only randomly handed out brochures without saying a word. Whoever was in charge of marketing for this company should be fired. Jennifer sat down to eat her breakfast. She spent most of the time rejecting men's advances instead of eating. '*Don't they get the hint? Fuck off... I'm not interested... and stop staring at me! Damn! Let me eat in peace!*' Jennifer's cell phone rang. "Hello?" It was Ms. Kirby; she *was* stuck in traffic and would be there in about ten minutes. "No problem... I'll meet you in front of the spa... Do you want me to get you some breakfast?"

Ramona thanked her but declined, she would get some coffee when she got there. Jennifer took her tray to the waste receptacle and walked towards the spa. It was past the kiosk where the woman was working handing out brochures. Jennifer walked right passed it, but then she stopped and turned to look at it one more time. She saw only a large black & white photograph of a middle-aged woman standing, all alone. She was wearing an ethnic peasant dress. She reminded her a bit of her Grandma, Xiomara, if she were in her thirties. But it wasn't the dress or the resemblance to her grandmother that caught her eye. It was the strip of duct tape on the glass frame, right over the mouth of the woman in the picture. Jennifer was intrigued by the photograph and stepped closer to get a better look. She stared at it. She stared into the woman's eyes. There was a great pain there, behind her eyes. Then she focused on the piece of duct tape over her mouth. She couldn't take her eyes off it. Why was it there? She slowly reached out for the duct tape while keeping eye-to-eye contact with the woman in the photo. Just as she was about to touch it, the woman who worked there had gently put her hand on top of Jennifer's. This broke her concentration.

"Her name was Maria Suarez…"

"What?" Jennifer was a bit startled as if she was brought suddenly out of a trance.

"The woman in the photo…? Her name was Maria Suarez…"

Jennifer turned to the woman that was speaking to her. "Huh?"

The woman held Jennifer's hand gently in both of hers. "Her name was Maria Suarez… she was a victim of spousal abuse for many, many years…"

"He killed her?"

"No… she tried to get help, but no one would listen… finally, when she couldn't take it anymore… she… *mutilated* him…"

"Good for her!" Jennifer looked back at the duct tape covering her mouth. "But why…?" She began to ask.

"Nobody ever listened to her when she cried out for help… so she never spoke again… not even at her trial… She died having never said another word ever again. "

Jennifer looked at the photo again. "She *never* spoke again?"

The woman shook her head. "Why should she? Nobody loved her… nobody cared…. Nobody wanted to hear her cries…"

"I find that very hard to believe…" Jennifer said.

"Me too…!" Jennifer was a bit flabbergasted that the woman who worked there didn't believe the 'hype'. "*You* cared… You *felt* her pain… You *wanted* to hear her cries… you are one of the very few people that tried to take the gag off her mouth!" The woman began to tear up. Jennifer felt herself start to well up as well. The woman held out a brochure. "Here… this is for you… if you really want to know more… about *us*… and if you need to *talk…* If you ever need someone to hear *your* cries… I'll be here till the end of the month…"

Jennifer took the brochure and puffed herself up a bit. "Yeah… whatever…!" and she turned to walk away.

"My name is Marisa…" she said.

Jennifer paused and turned to her. "Jennifer…"

"I hope to speak with you soon… Jennifer…"

Jennifer threw her hand up. "Whatever!" and walked away. She glanced at the plain beige brochure. The cover said; *"La Sociedad De La Mujer Muda"*. She didn't speak much Spanish but her grandmother spoke it all the time. '*The Society of the Silent Woman*' she said to herself. She folded the brochure, put it in her purse and wiped the tears from her eyes. She walked a little faster to get to the spa; she didn't want to have Ramona wait on her. She stopped for a moment and thought of her mother. She hadn't thought of her for over ten years. Jennifer shook it off. She had a spa treatment with her name on it, and she needed it now more than ever. Some guy walked up on her.

"Hey Mami… why so sad? Maybe I could cheer you up?"

(Geez… don't these *assholes* ever quit?)

The Tortured Soul Trilogy
(Living La Vida Puta)
Chapter 32
(Cock Blocking Bitch)

Cisco and I were working the club, him as security and I was running the floor show. Jackie had the bar. After the club closed we started closing shop and getting ready for the next night. It only usually took a half an hour so we let Jackie take off early. Steven was letting us run the club while he was taking care of personal business. Michael, Ramona and Jennifer were still busy with their little 'special' project. Jenny would call me every once in a while but I didn't take her calls anymore. Fuck her! She moved on, so did I! Steven spent less and less time at the club, leaving Cisco and I to run things. He said it was good for us to learn the ins and outs, just in case. Cisco was a little put off today. I didn't know who put a hair up his ass and to be honest with you, I didn't much care. We played the 'there's nothing wrong game' back and forth for a while. Then Cisco couldn't take any more.

"You're a selfish bitch sometimes! You know that L.L.?"

I looked at him like he had lost his fucking mind. Who the hell did he think he was talking to? "What the hell is your problem?"

"You know what my problem is... Why are you pissing all over Jennifer's big chance?"

"Oh... so this is about your 'girlfriend' Jennifer? I knew there was something going on between you two..." Cisco and I were now toying with the idea of 'dating' for a while but I still didn't trust men. We were still playing 'footsies' so to speak.

"Don't change the subject... this is not about Jennifer... this is about what you're doing to Jennifer and you know it!"

"And exactly 'what' am I doing to Jennifer?"

"You now damn well what you're doing... you're cock blocking her!"

"I'm WHAT? What are you talking about...? Jenny can get laid anytime she wants to..."

"Now you're just fucking trying to make jokes..." I looked at him and made a face. "You've been giving her attitude and the cold shoulder ever since Steven decided to groom her... the way they wanted to groom you... until you decided to go another way...

"How did you know about that?"

"Mr. Callahan and I talked... about lots of things..."

"I have not been giving her the cold shoulder..."

"Yeah you are. It's like you're mad that she has all the attention from the Callahans that you used to get and you're jealous..!"

"Fuck you! I am not jealous...!"

"Ever since she stopped dancing here, you don't call her, you don't hang out with her... you basically wrote her off..."

"So?" I shrugged my shoulders. "She has new friends now... I don't have any influence in her life anymore..."

"You know damn well Jenny is not going to take advantage of the Callahans' offer to put her through college until you say its okay..."

"They're sending her to college...?" L.L. had no idea of the extent of 'grooming' they were going to put Jennifer through. If she wasn't 'hating on' her before... this news put her over the top!

"Not yet... but it's a just matter of time..."

"How do you know?"

"Ms. Kirby said she's made huge improvements in her personal life and she's very impressed with her... and you know Ramona don't impress easy!"

"She didn't need my permission for them to take her under their wings. She doesn't need my permission to do anything else..."

"No, she doesn't... but Jennifer respects you... and she doesn't ever want to feel that she took away something that she feels you should have..."

"I don't know what you're talking about..."

Cisco went into the office fridge and pulled out a sandwich still in the paper bag it came in. He put it on the table in front of me. "You know what this is?"

I picked it up and put it back down. "Yeah...? It's the sandwich you bought me..."

"It's the sandwich I bought you...a week ago!"

"So? What's your point?" He opened the bag, turned it over and the dry and hard turkey sandwich fell on the table. It was nasty, the mayo was biege and curdled and the lettuce was brown and wilted and the tomatoes were all dried out. "What the fuck does this have to do with anything?"

"I got you this sandwich because you asked for it, but you didn't eat it... fine. The next day, when the sandwich was still good, I asked if I could have it. You said no. You wanted it, but you still didn't eat it. Now it's a week later. The sandwich is shit, but it's still sitting in the fridge. It's useless to anybody... even you!"

"What's your point Cisco? Throw the sandwich out then!"

"It's not the sandwich... it's your fucking attitude that when you want or don't want something, everybody else has to wait on you... Then time passes and nobody gets a chance to take advantage of the situation... and that's why you're a selfish bitch!"

"Then eat the fucking sandwich..." I said dryly.

Cisco slammed his hand and crushed the sandwich. I wasn't afraid Cisco would hit me, but I knew he was really pissed at me right now. "No... NO... **NO**! It's not about the fucking sandwich... it's about *you*, always having to have your way... you stop everybody else from getting their shot while they wait on you! And then; after it's too late for them... You didn't use it... you threw the opportunity away and that fucking sucks!"

"Maybe you would rather be with Jennifer then..."

Cisco eyes became clear and he calmed down, but not a calm that was relaxed. It was a scary calm... like he didn't care anymore. "Say that to me... one more time... I dare you..." he said with a quiet tone that shook me to my core. I looked at Cisco. I was scared. Again, not that he would hit me, but that he was... somehow very disappointed with me. I truly didn't understand why I cared. "Jenny's not the first girl who had a chance to leave the business... She wasn't the first girl who waited on you... Remember Mary?"

I lowered my eyes... I didn't want to remember that. Not now. "That wasn't my fault..."

"Of course not... all she wanted was some time off... to go home... to visit her family... to see her mother in the hospital... maybe a week... I forget... what *did* you say to her?"

"I told her I needed her to work…" I said quietly.

"That's right… you needed her to work… but you promised to clear the schedule as soon as you could so she can take some time off…"

I started to cry. "Please stop…"

"Did you *ever* clear the schedule for her?"

"No…" I sobbed.

"Yes you did… *Yes you did*… I remember… it was about a month or so later… you let her go home for her mother's… funeral…"

I was crying openly now. "You son of a bitch…" I sobbed.

He whispered to me; "No… *not* you '*son of a bitch*'… it's you *selfish bitch*…! When Steven needed you to work, he let you go to your mom's funeral… He didn't hold you back; he put himself and the business out for you… And now… instead of paying it forward… you're screwing up Jennifer's chance… maybe her only chance…"

"I… I…" I couldn't speak I was so upset.

"You what…? Spit it out…"

"I… I don't want her to go… I don't want her to leave…"

"I know… but this isn't about you anymore is it?"

I shook my head no. "No… it's not…" And I sobbed.

Cisco gently put his hand on my shoulder. "So? What are you going to do about it?" I looked at Cisco. I knew he was right. I was 'cock blocking'. This was a great opportunity for her, and I was all in her fucking way.

"I'll let her know its okay to go… to take the shot…"

"When?" I looked at Cisco, he was right again. If I didn't do this now, I would never tell her and fuck up her chances for sure.

"I'll take her out dancing tomorrow night… we'll have some drinks, some laughs… and then I'll tell her… She'll be okay with that…!" I looked at Cisco. "Come with us?"

He looked at me. "You *want* me there?"

I nodded. "Yeah… To keep me honest…!"

"I'll tell you what… You let me know where you two will be… and I'll be there if you need me for moral support…Okay?"

"Okay!" Cisco tried to hug me but I gave him the butt out, shoulders only hug. I still had a problem with men touching me, even if he was a very close friend. He then reached for the phone and handed me the receiver. I dialed the number.

"Hey Jennifer... It's L.L.... what are you doing tomorrow night...? How about you and I paint the town red? Okay... I'll pick up at about eight? Okay... nine!" I laughed and hung up the phone. Cisco nodded. I felt better already.

The Tortured Soul Trilogy
(Living La Vida Puta)
Chapter 33
(Please Don't Go)

L.L. picked up Cisco first and drove him to the club. She didn't want Jenny to see him just yet. She needed some alone time with her first, to ease into telling her that it was all right to take full advantage of the Callahan's offer. That it was fine with her. About twenty minutes later she went to pick up Jenny. It was about ten to nine when she arrived. Jennifer buzzed her into her building. Jenny's door was open. L.L. looked around at the place Steven and Michael had set her up in. *"What the fuck?"* She thought as she looked around the apartment. *"This bitch was living large and if she took full advantage of Callahan's offer, she would be living even larger."*

"L.L. is that you?" Jenny called out.

"Yeah bitch!"

"Give me a minute while I put my face on... I'll be out in a minute..."

"Okay!" L.L. checked the apartment out. *"Oh I know this bitch is fucking and sucking somebody to be living like this!"* she mumbled to herself.

"Okay... I'm ready..." Jenny said as she sauntered in. L.L. turned and she was thunderstruck! Who the hell was *this* woman standing in front of her? I mean it kinda *looked* a lot like Jennifer... but the woman standing in front of her getting her clutch bag and fixing her lipstick was not the Jennifer X. Jones she knew. Just like the day she first saw Jennifer that day on stage, she was mesmerized. This woman was a cross between a Playboy bunny and a Victoria Secret model... L.L. did what she could not to let her jaw drop... but she was... moist! Jenny saw L.L.'s stunned expression and turned her head and looked around. "What? What? Is something wrong? Is my lipstick smeared? What?" Jenny took out her mirror and checked her face again. If L.L. wasn't 'hating on' Jennifer before, this bitch was livid now! She looked at Jennifer and realized the severity of her bad decision to burn the bridge that Jenny had the good fortune to cross now.

158

Jenny looked at her friend with great concern. She sensed that she wasn't very happy. L.L. tried to defuse this awkward moment with a joke.

"Don't tell me you're going out... looking like *that*... are you?"

Jenny shook her hair and laughed. "Bitch please! Come on... let's go... I haven't been out dancing in months..." Jenny put her mirror away and took the crook of L.L.'s arm and walked out with her. They arrived at the club and Jennifer was the center of attention; that was something L.L. was used to. Anytime Jenny hit a stage all eyes focused on her. You just couldn't help it. She was hot then, now... with her looks all amped up, she was totally irresistible. They danced a bit and found an empty table in the back to sit a spell. L.L. couldn't keep her eyes off Jennifer. The waitress bought them their drinks. Jennifer was watching the crowd dance, bobbing her head to the music and without turning her head she very plainly said: "No..."

"No... 'what'...?" L.L. responded wondering what she was referring to.

"No... I didn't blow anybody to get where I am..." And Jennifer picked up her drink and sipped on the straw.

"I know that..."

"Yeah... sure you do...! But I know you thought it!" Jenny said plainly.

"Can you give me one good reason why I wouldn't think that?" Without looking at her, Jenny gently shook her head no. "Well then... I'm just going to have to take your word for it... as my best friend!" Jennifer smiled. Put her drink down and hugged L.L. The wall L.L. had built between them, melted away.

That night while they were clubbing and dancing, one of Lady Latex' 'regulars' recognized her and decided to make an *offer* for Jennifer's services. Lady Latex explained that Jennifer was not a call girl but a friend. The man would not take 'no' for an answer. He continued to bid higher and higher to have Jennifer have sex with him. Tobey was at a distinct disadvantage, normally she would have cut the motherfucker, but she wanted to stay low-key for Jennifer's sake. Tobey decided that discretion was the better part of valor and opted to just get Jennifer out of the club and call it a night. As they made their way out of the club, the man came out of nowhere and grabbed Jennifer by her arm.

"Look bitch! I don't give a flying fuck what your pimp says... you and I are going to party... And it looks like tonight, I aint paying for pussy!"

Jennifer reached for her back pocket, forgetting that she didn't carry her knife on her anymore, and Lady Latex was trapped behind the crowd unable to get to her. The man began to pull her away when Jenny heard a familiar voice behind her.

"I wouldn't do that if I were you..." Jennifer turned to see Cisco... at the bar, sipping on a drink.

"Mind your fucking business pal!" The man answered.

"I'm just saying... that's a dangerous woman you have hold of there..."

"*What...?*" And the man held onto Jennifer's arm tightly.

"I'm just saying..." Cisco sipped his drink. "That is one *dangerous* woman..."

The man looked at Jennifer then looked at Cisco. "Oh yeah...?"

Cisco walked up to the man. "Yeah...! All she has to do... is point her finger at me... then point her finger at you... and you wake up three days later in a hospital with tubes up your nose and connected to all kinds of machines making all kinds of scary sounds." And Cisco scratched his face with his right hand showing he was sporting a gold and diamond studded set of 'brass' knuckles. The man slowly let go of Jennifer and stepped away and disappeared into the crowd. Jennifer watched him go. "Did he hurt you mami...?"

Jennifer shook her head no and hugged him. "Cisco...! What are you doing here?"

"Just because you don't dance at the club anymore, doesn't mean I'm not your personal bodyguard anymore..."

"Callahan put you up to this?"

"No... I just happened to be here tonight... I got here just as you two were leaving..."

Lady Latex came up to them. "Thank god you were here Cisco...!" She looked around and winked at Cisco when Jenny wasn't looking. She was glad she asked Cisco to be here tonight. She looked around. "We better go before something else jumps off or that asshole finds some courage and comes back...!" They nod and exit the club together. Once outside Lady Latex pulls Jennifer aside. This was the perfect moment to break ties with her. "We can't do his anymore..."

"What are you talking about L.L.?"

"We can't hang out together anymore..."

"Why the hell not?"

"Look... we got lucky tonight... The next time anything might happen..."

"But..."

"But nothing... I attract trouble wherever I go... I don't have a problem with that, but tonight you almost got jacked because I held back and it could have gotten us both in serious trouble or worse..." Jennifer looked down. "I can't afford to be 'careful'... it gets you killed in my profession... I have to be able to let fly as the spirit moves me... I can't afford to be seen as weak! Besides, the Callahans have bigger and better plans for you..."

Jennifer nodded quietly; she knew L.L. was right, protecting her only made Tobey vulnerable to her enemies. "Does this mean..."

"Bitch please...! You aint getting rid of me that easy! This just means we won't be going clubbing anymore... we're still B.F.F. bitch!"

Jennifer smiled. "What makes you think I want to be 'best friends forever' with a lowlife bitch like you?"

L.L.'s jaw dropped. "Oh... I know this bitch just didn't..." L.L. said.

Jenny did the head move, snapped her fingers and replied. "This bitch just *did*...! They all laughed and Jennifer threw her arms around L.L. and hugged her. "If you ever need me..."

L.L. pushed Jennifer away. "What? We doing a scene from '*The Color Purple*' now?" L.L. and Jennifer laughed and hugged each other. Then Jennifer hugged Cisco. Cisco then hugged L.L. "Get the fuck off me... I aint going nowhere...! Dang! Always trying to cop a free feel...! Grab ass!" LL exclaimed.

"Hey... I give it a shot...!" Cisco said.

"And don't think I don't know how you 'watch' me when I'm working the pole... Don't be getting any ideas about you getting any...!"

Cisco smiled. "Come on... I'll take you two crazy bitches home." They got in L.L.'s car and she let Cisco drive. L.L. and Jenny got in the back.

"Cisco?"

"Yeah Jenny?"

"What about your car?"

Cisco looked at L.L. in the rear view from the corner of his eye. "I'll pick it up in the morning... L.L. will drop me off..." Jenny didn't need to know L.L. dropped him off at the club before picking Jenny up for their 'date' tonight.

"Can we get something to eat first? I'm starved!" Jenny said. Cisco smiled and took them to a nice restaurant. It would be her 'moving on' party, just the three of them. About a month later, the Callahans would send Jennifer off to college on a full company sponsored scholarship. Jennifer and Michael also began a torrid love affair. L.L. wanted to be upset, but they looked so good together, she couldn't be anything but happy for them. She just wished she was in a committed relationship too. She and Cisco got closer and closer as friends although there was no chance in hell they could ever be lovers.

The Tortured Soul Trilogy
(The Confessions of Jennifer X)
Chapter 34
(She Blinded Me with Science)

As the months went by, Jennifer kept in contact with L.L. but they didn't see each other as much as they'd like. Jennifer justified it by thinking that they could always get together after she finished her 'training'. Ms. Kirby called Jennifer to the office one day. Jennifer went right over. She wondered what she was in store for her next.

Ramona stepped into Michael's office. He was surprised that she didn't buzz him first. "Mr. Callahan... there's a young lady here to see you...!"

Michael checked his appointment book. He didn't have any appointments this morning. It must have been a referral. "Have her wait in the lobby, I'll be right with her in a moment... and let me know the moment Jennifer gets here."

"Jennifer *is* the young lady waiting to see you!" Jennifer said as she entered his office behind Ramona. Michael looked up at the sound of her voice. His jaw dropped and he was mesmerized by her presence. She was wearing a black Chanel suit with a slight slit in the skirt. Her hair and make-up was perfect. She had a smart clutch purse under her arm. She had on stylish black pumps and had on black leather gloves. The air now had the subtle scent of Coco-Chanel. Michael stared at her. This could *not* be the same woman that walked into his office three months ago. It was like a scene from '*Pretty Woman*' when Richard Gere saw Julia Roberts for the first time after her shopping spree.

"Michael?" Ramona asked. No response. "Michael...?" Still no answer from him. "*MR. CALLAHAN!*"

Michael blinked. "Yes... Ms. Kirby...?"

"Miss Jones is here to see you..."

"Yes...Yes... I can see that...!"

"Would you like me to close the door...?"

"Yes... No...! Leave it open please..."

"As you wish..." Ramona leaned into Jennifer and whispered. "You look fabulous! I think you made a very good impression! Congratulations!"

"Thank you Ramona... I couldn't have done it without you!"

"You're *damn right* you couldn't... good luck Jenny!"

Jennifer smiled. Ramona left the room. "You wanted to see me Mr. Callahan?"

"Ah... yes I did..."

Jennifer took three steps towards him, paused, did a models turn for him and turned back. "So...? What do you think? You like?"

"You look..." Michael was at a loss for words. As far as he could tell, 'Operation; My Fair Lady' was a huge success.

"Thank you...!" she replied.

"You're welcome Jennifer..." Michael just sat there.

"Was there anything else? Mr. Callahan?"

"*Yes...!*" he hissed. He caught himself staring. "*Yes...* yes there was..." Jennifer shrugged her shoulders. "I've decided it's time to... go to the next level in your development..."

"And when did you make *that* decision...?"

"The moment you walked in the door..." Jennifer smiled. Michael took a folder from his drawer and placed it on his desk. "This is for you..."

"What is it?"

"Only one way to find out..." Jennifer smiled again, walked over to his desk and leaned dangerously over to take the folder from his desk. Michael wiped the sweat off his brow. He had a full unobstructed view of her ample cleavage. She then sat on the edge on his desk to read it. She knew full well her ass was in his direct view. Micheal fidgeted with his tie. Jennifer smiled but her smile turned into a look of bewilderment when she read the papers inside the folder.

"This is an enrollment application... for college..."

"For one of the finest colleges in this state... your tuition will be paid in full... all your courses have been picked... you start the first week in September..."

Jennifer stood up and placed the folder on his desk. "I can't accept this..."

"Why not?"

"It's one thing to pay for some spa sessions and new clothes... but college...?"

"I have faith in you... I know you can handle the curriculum..."

"It's not that..."

"Then what is it...?"

"When we started this, you said you wanted me to be the face of Callahan Enterprises..."

"That's right! And based on the improvement I'm seeing... We've made the right decision..."

"You also said that my 'misadventures' were just under the radar..."

"That's right!"

"There's one thing you *don't* know about me..." and Jennifer paused.

"We know all about you working as a fluffer for Tobey's porn film... Thanks to Tobey, there's nothing of you on film... we have that under control too!" Michael said.

"It's not that..."

"What then?"

Jennifer took a deep breath and exhaled. Michael was very focused on her chest when she did that. "I... bludgeoned a man to death with a baseball bat...!"

There was deafening silence in the room; Jennifer saw that as a sign to leave. She turned to walk out. It was Michael who broke the silence as she got to the door. "He kidnapped his step-daughter and was beating her... the bastard got what he deserved!" Jennifer paused at the door and turned to look at Michael in amazement. He came from behind the desk and sat on the edge of his desk. "I'm a lawyer with connections Jennifer... I told you... There's nothing in the dark that doesn't come out in the light!" He picked up the folder off his desk and held out the enrollment papers for her. Jennifer closed the door to his office and locked it. "What are you doing...?"

"There's something I want to give *you* first..."

"And what would that be...?" Jennifer removed her jacket and slowly unbuttoned her blouse. Michael held up his hand. "I told you... I don't get involved with..." Jennifer unhooked her bra.

Michael inhaled. "I told you... I won't...." he couldn't speak as Jennifer slipped out of her blouse and bra. He was mesmerized by her amazing fit body.

"I'm a virgin...!" Jenny whispered.

Michael took a deep breath. "I don't believe you!"

"What purpose would it serve to lie about that?" And she walked closer to him. Michael was frozen in time. "No man or woman has ever touched me in the way you're about to touch me..." She walked slowly towards his outstretched hand and it touched her breast. Jennifer inhaled deeply and breathed out slowly.

"My god... These are real!" And Michael fondled her breasts. Jennifer cooed and purred. Jennifer unzipped his pants and reached in and felt his throbbing cock. Michael pinched her nipples. Jennifer felt faint. Her jaw trembled. She only knew how to give head and she hated doing that.

"I... I... don't know... what I should do...!" she stammered.

He still didn't believe her, but that didn't concern him right now. Michael stood up and picked her up in his arms; she touched his face gently as he carried her and placed her gently on the couch. He then went over the office intercom. "Ms. Kirby...?"

"Yes Mr. Callahan?"

"I'm going to be in a conference call on my cell for about an hour or two. Hold all my calls and reschedule any appointments I may have until later this afternoon."

"Yes Mr. Callahan... could you please pick up line one first?" Michael picked up line one on his desk phone. "Please... be gentile with her Michael..." Ramona whispered.

"I promise...." And he hung up. Michael turned to Jennifer lying down on the couch and began to loosen his tie. Jennifer lay there shivering and panting slowly. She was covered with goose pimples. He went over to the thermostat in his office and turned the heat up a bit to make it more comfortable for her. He then walked towards her taking off his shirt. Michael had the body of a boxer. He was very fit and trim. He slowly lay on top of her without pinning her down. She kissed him deeply.

"You don't have to do this...!" He said softly.

Jennifer put her finger on his lips. "Shhhh! You talk too fucking much!" And she kissed Michael deeply. Michael gently fondled and massaged her body. Jennifer began to pant heavily and spread her legs for him. She was very wet, very wet indeed. Michael placed his hand gently between her legs and stroked her clit. Jennifer's eyes went to the back of her head and she moaned. Michael kissed her nipples and bit them gently. Jennifer felt that she would surely faint now. Her head was swooning. She felt as if she was on a roller coaster and she didn't want the ride to stop. She kissed him more passionately. She hungered for him. Michael worked his hand under her panties and began to probe her with his finger. "Owwww!" Jennifer sighed softly. Michael stopped. "Don't stop... Please! Don't stop!" Michael again tried to probe her and Jennifer's eyes began to fill with tears. She didn't think it would be this painful. Michael stopped again. Jennifer was now crying. She felt... embarrassed and ashamed... Michael kissed her gently. He realized this wasn't a ploy; she really *was* a virgin. There *was* something he didn't know about her. "I'm sorry!" and she cried.

"Don't be sorry Jenny... We're just gonna have to go very, very slowly... Do you still want to do this...?" Jennifer put the back of her hand on her mouth, cried and nodded yes. "I'm gonna try something... I promise I will not hurt you at all... do you trust me?"

Jenny sobbed and nodded. "Of course I trust you..."

Michael eased up and slid down her body until his head was between her legs. As he did so, he had eased her out of her panties. Jenny closed her eyes hard. She didn't know what to expect now. Michael began to lick her labia and clit. Jennifer had never felt anything like that in her life. She was back on the roller coaster ride she had just learned to love so much. Her jaw trembled, her thighs quivered, her eyes went to the back of her head and she covered her mouth to stifle her screams of pleasure. "My office is soundproof... no one can hear anything that goes on in here... The clients demand it..." He whispered. He didn't want to startle her. And he dove right back into her wet and hungry pussy. Then he sucked on her clitoris and nibbled on it so very gently. Jennifer screamed in ecstasy. She came so hard she didn't even realize that Michael's fingers were deep inside her pussy stroking her 'G' spot. He continued to lick and stroke her until she was so hot and horny that she no longer felt any pain. Jennifer grabbed her nipples and squeezed them. Her leather gloves felt so good as she pinched her nipples. It couldn't possibly get any better than this. All of a sudden, Jennifer felt naked. She looked up at him. Michael had gotten off her. '*What was he doing*?' She said to herself. She saw him pull a condom from his wallet and put it on. Now, Jenny relaxed. He came back to her and positioned her on her knees on the couch, bent over the back of it. Her ass was up in the air. He stared at her. "Is there any part of your body that isn't magnificent?"

"You're talking again!" As much as she loved to hear his voice, she didn't want to take the chance that he would say something stupid and kill the mood. Michael slapped her on her ass. Jennifer's lip quivered. "Ohhhhh! My!" And she spread her knees on the couch. Michael didn't catch the subtle hint that she wanted to be spanked but no matter. He got behind her and entered her very, very slowly. His hard throbbing cock reached farther and farther into her. Jennifer began to beat her fist into the back of the couch as his cock probed her deeper and deeper and deeper.

(My GOD...! Is he using his fucking fist?)

He wasn't, because his hands were on her waist pulling her closer and closer to him. Michael was so deep inside her that she felt she was going to choke. And just when she thought she couldn't take any more, he began to pump his cock into her. In, out, in, out, long, deep, slow strokes. Jennifer's nipples got so hard she felt they were going to explode. That would have been fine, until Michael got into the zone and began to pound her like a jackhammer. She could barely breathe. Her taught nipples kept hitting the leather couch with every thrust of Michael's cock. His loins were now smacking her on the ass harder and harder and louder and louder. It was more than she could take. The wicked sensations occurring on both ends of her body and deep inside her were sending chills and shivers up and down her spine. "Holy Sh... sh... shhhiiiiit! You mu... mother fuc...ccc... kkk... kkkerrrrrr!" She moaned. Her mouth opened wide and she grabbed her throat. "Ohhhhhh! Ahhhhh!" she screamed. Jennifer didn't remember passing out. She only remembered waking up on the couch and finding Michael fast asleep in the chair in his office. He was totally exhausted. Jennifer got up, used his private bathroom to freshen up, got dressed and began to leave.

That's when she heard Michael's voice softly say; "Ramona has the limo waiting for you to take you home... and don't forget your enrollment papers..."

Jennifer took the papers from his desk. "Thank you Michael..."

"No... Thank you Jennifer... twelve years of celibacy shot to hell... but it was damn well worth it!"

Jenny paused. "If you've been celibate all this time... When did you buy that condom?"

"Yesterday..."

"So you knew?"

"No... But I was hoping...!"

Jennifer walked over to the office door and unlocked it but didn't open it. "What... made you hope...?" She asked with her back to Michael. "And why... did you pick me... for this project...?"

"You're not gonna believe me..." Michael moaned. He was still feeling the effects of the full and undiluted 'Jenny Mojo'.

"Try me..." she whispered, not knowing what he would say.

Michael paused; Jennifer turned the doorknob. "Every year... no matter what... you send Ashley a birthday present and a Christmas present..."

Jennifer froze. Her heart beat just a little bit faster. Jennifer held her breath; she didn't want Michael to hear her... She didn't know what it was she didn't want him to hear. She felt her face flush; she didn't want Michael to see. A tear came to her eye. "Thank you Michael!" And she left quietly. She didn't admit it to herself then but she admitted it to me when I interviewed her for this book; that was the very moment she fell in love with Michael Callahan.

The Tortured Soul Trilogy
(The Confessions of Jennifer X)
Chapter 35
(In Your Eyes)

For the next three years Jennifer went to school, studied hard and got excellent grades, well, there was a rough patch when she had to adjust. But adjust she did and she surpassed all of the Callahan's expectations. She always came 'home' for the holidays and was a frequent guest at the Callahan's estate. On occasion she even spent the weekends there *wink, wink!* Jennifer and Michael were inseparable. They did everything together whenever they could. They dined, they danced, (Jennifer and Michael were amazing touch dancers to the point people thought they were professional ballroom dancers) and they went to the theatre and on family vacations together. Jennifer was at home in D&G as she was in dungarees and sneakers. Steven and Ramona were quite taken with this young lady and Michael was falling deeply in love with her. Nobody had a problem with that, especially not Jennifer.

One Saturday morning, Michael and Jenny were lying naked in bed after an amazing evening together. Michael pulled the covers back to see her amazing body sleep all cuddled next to him. "Stop checking out my ass... it's chilly in here..." She whispered.

"I think I know a way to warm that ass up...!"

"Yeah...? Me too..." And Jennifer kissed him deeply. "Put the covers back on my ass!" She laughed.

"Oh! I have something to cover that ass with..." They rolled over with Jenny face down and Michael on top. She spread her legs. She liked this position; it gave him total access and the deepest penetration. Jenny didn't feel pinned down, she felt, protected. Suddenly there was a knock on the bedroom door.

"Are you two coming down for breakfast... or are you staying in bed all day?" Steven said through the locked door.

"We're staying in bed!" They said in unison. Then they laughed.

"Kids!" Steven muttered as he walked away to give them privacy. "I'd be doing the same thing if I were their age... and had a woman with a hot ass body like hers!"

"I heard that!" Ramona said.

"I don't give a damn! This is my house and you're *my* employee... I don't answer to you..." He mumbled.

As they heard Steven's footsteps go downstairs and Ramona's follow, Michael's throbbing cock slowly entered Jenny's soft, moist pussy. She moaned and grabbed the pillow tightly in anticipation and placed it between her head and the headboard.

(Do I *really* have to tell you *why*...? I didn't think so!)

He didn't even want to pump her. He just wanted to be inside her. It felt like home. Jenny cooed. "I love you Michael!"

"I love you too Jenny!"

Author's Note

*Oh well...! So much for not pumping her... Why don't we leave these two kids alone to have some privacy? You don't really need to know everything that happened. Let them enjoy some quality time... alone. Now back to our story... The next morning... **oh yeah...! The **next** morning!*

Doesn't it just piss you off that I know everything that happened in vivid detail... and I'm not telling? Pffftt!

P.S.

*And if you think, **I** tell this story well, you should hear Jennifer tell it personally... She is one HELL of a visual aide!*

Let me put it to you this way, my wife Mandy was very 'thrilled' when I came home after each one of our interviews! Man, if I could only just bottle the 'Jenny Mojo'...

But I digress... back to the story.

The next day Jennifer had to head back to school. This was her last year and she really needed to concentrate on her studies, even though the Callahan's told her she didn't have to do this anymore. She wanted to do this. She wanted her degree more than anything else. She did not want anyone to think she was a kept woman. When she came back, she could truly be proud of what she had accomplished and so would Michael. Michael held Jennifer tightly as she kissed him and said goodbye. "When will I see you again?" He asked.

"Silly, you know when…! But if you really miss me… you have my cell number…!" Jenny said.

Michael whispered in her ear. "Phone sex?"

"Hmmmm… okay!"

"You know I'm still worried about you being around all those hormonal college students… What if you get *lonely* on campus…?"

"You say that to me every semester…"

"Cause every semester there's a new crop of horny college kids…"

"Don't worry about me… I'll be just fine till I get back to you baby!"

"I know she will be… I packed like a dozen "D" cell batteries for her!" Ramona whispered.

Jenny's jaw dropped. "*Ramona*…! That's for my tape recorder…!"

"Tape recorders don't… 'buzz' dear…!" Michael laughed. Jenny cut her eyes at her.

"Then what buzzes in *your* room, Ramona?"

"The '*Dominator*'…! But it doesn't use batteries, it plugs in…"

Michael stuck his fingers in his ears. "TMI! Lalala… lala Lalala… lala…! I can't hear you!" Ramona and Jenny laughed. Michael pulled his hands away. "You two set this up?" They both nodded.

"Got you!" They both laughed. Ramona hugged Jenny and whispered in her ear. "You think he bought that?"

"I sure hope so…" Jenny whispered back. Jennifer got in the limo and the chauffer drove her to school. They watched and waved as the car went up the driveway.

"God… I miss her already…"

"Maybe you should do something about that!" Ramona said.

"Maybe I should…"

They walked arm in arm back to the house. "Say Ramona…?

"Yes Michael?"

"What *is that* that buzzes in your room at night?" Ramona let go of Michael's arm and walked towards the house and fidgeted with her hair. "That's it… I'm calling the carpenters to sound proof all the bedrooms." Michael said.

"Thank you… sometimes you two keep me up all night with all that noise you two make…!"

Michael put his hands over his ears again. "La lala lala…"

"Please…! That girlfriend of yours is *not* a quiet woman… I can understand… but damn! Put a sock in her mouth or something!"

"Wait… what do you mean…? '*You can understand*'…?"

"Well… there was one time your father and I…"

"La lala lala…"

Ramona laughed. "All I can say is the 'banana' didn't fall far from the tree…"

"La lala lala…"

The Tortured Soul Trilogy
(The Confessions of Jennifer X)
Chapter 36
(Aint No Sunshine)

Michael hung up the phone in his office. He was on the phone with Jennifer for over an hour. He couldn't wait to see Jennifer again. He realized that this woman had captured his heart. He couldn't eat, he couldn't sleep and he couldn't concentrate on his job without thinking of her. Just hearing her voice brightened his day. He missed her terribly and he knew she felt the same way about him. He threw his head back while sitting in his chair. "My God... what has this woman done to me...? I like it!" And he let out a deep breath, and that's when he decided... he was not going to let her get away. He wanted this feeling to last forever. He leaned forward on his desk and began to pray. He wanted to make the right choice... he didn't want this relationship to become stale as the years went by. It was the reason he took a vow of celibacy in the first place. He looked up and saw the picture of his mother and father on his wall. It was the sign he needed. Theirs wasn't the perfect marriage... there was no such thing, his father said, but that's no reason not to be happy with the woman you love...! Michael hit the intercom button to Ramona's office

"Ramona..."

"Yes Mr. Callahan?"

"Get your coat please..."

"Where am I going Mr. Callahan?"

"*We*... are going jewelry shopping...!"

Ramona squealed on the other side, Michael had to lean away from the speaker. "And what *type* of jewelry are *we* buying today...?" She asked.

"*You know*... what I'm shopping for... don't play dumb with me!"

"I want to *hear* you say it...!" she demanded.

Michael paused and laughed. "It's an engage..." He didn't even get a chance to finish before Ramona squealed again. "I'm so glad you approve Ms. Kirby!"

"I guess I can live with your decision... Mr. Callahan...!" she said nonchalantly.

"I trust this information will remain between the two of us Ms. Kirby?"

"Sir! I beg your pardon... I am your personal secretary... secrets are my job description..."

"Good!" Five minutes later Ms. Kirby entered with her coat on and Steven in tow.

"Congratulations son...!" And Steven hugged Michael.

"What happened to 'secrets are my job description'...?"

"*What*...? I'm *his* personal secretary too...!"

"Just remember... you're *not* Jennifer's personal secretary anymore...!" Ramona nodded in agreement. Michael escorted Ramona out and as he closed the door he said. "After we buy this ring... there's going to be a little extra something for you in your paycheck..."

"Really?"

"Yes...! Your pink slip!" Ramona hit Michael on the arm, Michael laughed.

"So what size diamond are you getting...?"

"I don't know...!"

"What's her favorite cut...?"

"Um... I don't know..."

"Gold or Platinum setting...?"

"Um..."

"Okay let's start with the basics... What size *ring* does she wear...?" Michael stood there, dumbfounded. Ramona reached into her purse and took out a sheet of paper with all of Jennifer's personal information from when they used to go shopping together. "Pink slip *my* ass!" And Ramona led Michael out to the car. Michael laughed.

The Tortured Soul Trilogy
(The Confessions of Jennifer X)
Chapter 37
(Hot For Teacher)

Jennifer walked across the quad on campus. She felt as if all eyes were on her, and they were. A new student walked up to her. "Excuse me Ms.... but what class do you teach? Because I *really* want to sign up for it!"

"Sorry...! You couldn't possibly handle the curriculum...!" And I continued to walk down to the dorm rooms. I had gotten used to young college boys and some teachers hitting on me but *damn*...! Now the girls too? It was a very different world out there now. Don't get me wrong; I was hit on by females during my stay at the clinic almost every day, and once or twice in the joint, but Jenny don't play that shit. I just learned about men and I wasn't about to switch sides now. Hell! I didn't even want to be traded. I headed to the dorm, checked the room assignments and went to my room. I opened the door to find two horny teenagers at it hot and heavy on one of the beds. Both were naked from the waist up. Both jumped up when I entered. Both were girls.

"Are you the floor matron?" One asked me.

I put my hand on my hip. *"Do I look like a fucking floor 'matron'...?"* she thought to herself. "No! I'm your roommate bitch! Now put your damn clothes on!" They both awkwardly put their tops on.

"You're my new roomie?" the other one said amazed.

"Yes I am, and by the way... that *is your* bed... right?"

She nodded. I started to put my stuff away when I felt 'heat' on my ass. I turned to them; they were staring at me. "And don't get any fucking ideas that you two little bitches are gonna gang bang me!" (Ooops... I channeled my 'hard time' past.)

"No... it's not that... aren't you a little..."

"Oh hell no...! If you ask me if I'm a little 'old' to be in college I *will* bitch slap you and have your *girlfriend* hold my jacket while I do it!" They held each other totally scared of me...

Good...! They needed to know who the HBIC is here. "You... the one that actually lives here, what's your name?"

"Princess Tika Greenleaf..."

"*Princess Tika...?*"

"Greenleaf... I'm from Hawaii..."

"And you..."

"Brittany Brown..." And she held out her hand.

"No...! I don't need your name honey... don't you have someplace to be... an hour ago?" Her countenance fell and she walked out sheepishly.

"I'll see you later Tika!" And she kissed her and left, closing the door behind her.

"Hey! That's *my* girlfriend and she can come visit me *anytime* she likes! This is my room *too* you know!" I cut my eyes at her. "Please?" she asked.

I nodded. "Okay... but we're going to have to devise a system... there are gonna be times I'm gonna need some 'privacy' too!"

We decided on the old sock on the doorknob sign. If there was a sock on the doorknob, find another hangout for about an hour then you could knock and enter.

The rest of the semester was quite uneventful. Jennifer went to class; her roommate hung out the sock. On more than several occasions Jennifer walked in on them in mid debauchery. She got the impression they liked to be watched or the thrill of being caught was their high. Whatever it was... those two weren't very good at what they were doing, and they never took their pants off. They were only bi-curious but yellow.

Jennifer was doing quite well in school and Michael called her almost every other day. She was still approached for 'private tutoring' by almost everybody on campus, but she very politely declined... she wasn't here for that kind of 'education'... to give or get! Most dealt with rejection very well.

One professor decided that he wouldn't take no for an answer and tried to give Jennifer a 'pass/fail' test. Jennifer knew she could handle the class, but the teacher was not having it unless he was getting it. Jennifer struggled with her dilemma. She didn't want to get Michael or Steven involved. She considered dropping the class and taking it over with another instructor, but he was the only professor who taught the class and she needed it to complete her requirements and he knew it. She called Ms. Crystal for her advice. Ms. Crystal was very proud of her and knew she would make the right decision and she would pray for her. Jenny thought for a moment; let me call L.L. and see what she says...

L.L. was just getting home from shopping and Cisco had made and left dinner for her. They had become very good friends. She was just about to sit down and eat when the phone rang. It was Jennifer. "Hey bitch! How's my favorite academic scholar? Did you get your PhD yet?"

"*I'm not getting a PhD...*!" Jenny said strangely.

"Are you sure? Cause I heard you were getting a *Pretty Hard Dick* a lot lately..."

Jennifer and L.L. laughed their asses off! "Bitch you're so crazy!" Jenny snickered.

"So? What's going on? To what do I own the honor and privilege of this phone call?"

L.L. hung up the phone after speaking to Jennifer for about an hour. Some teacher was pissing on her cornflakes at the school... L.L. knew just what to do... L.L. called Cisco's house where he was home watching the ballgame.

"Cisco?"

"Yeah L.L.?"

"Remember that '*thing*' you did for Lady Hendricks a while back...?"

"Yeah... why?"

"Jenny needs your help..." L.L. explained the problem, Cisco put on his jacket.

"I'm on it..."

Two days later at the club, after he had gotten back from his field trip, LL. asked Cisco how things went with Jenny's little 'problem'.

"Good..."

"Was he any problem?"

"Nope... It was actually the *same* asshole professor... He... *remembered* me!"

L.L. laughed. "But what about the next girl he pulls this shit on?"

"I left him my business card... I told him that the next time he gets an 'urge' to fuck with somebody's future... to not waste any time and just call me directly..."

"Do you have any idea how much I love you?" LL said.

"No... but I'll let you show me later!"

Wait! Did I just tell Cisco... that I *loved* him? L.L. paused to see Cisco's reaction. She knew he heard her because he had responded so quickly. L.L. glanced in his direction again. No overt facial response from him. Maybe he took it as just a friendly statement.

"L.L.... is everything okay?" He asked.

"Yeah... why do you ask?"

"You look a little pale... like something just scared you..."

"Oh... really? Maybe I should put some cold water on my face..."

"Okay..." Cisco said nonchalantly and L.L. headed to the bathroom. The moment she went inside Cisco had a huge grin on his face. He started singing. *"You said you looooove me...! You wanna kiss me...! You wanna hug me...!"* Just then Jackie walked up on him.

"What the hell is wrong with you?" Jackie asked.

"Huh?" Cisco said startled. "Oh... it's from that movie *"Armed and Fabulous"*... with Renee Russo..."

"It's from *"Miss Congeniality"*... with Sandra Bullock... but that doesn't explain why you you were singing that song..."

"Are you sure it was Sandra Bullock?"

"Yeah... I'm gonna marry Sandra Bullock someday... I'm sure..."

"Maybe I should look it up..." And Cisco walked towards the office to check the internet.

Jackie just shook his head. "Lucky son of a bitch!"

The Tortured Soul Trilogy
(Living La Vida Puta)
Chapter 38
(What the Fuck Were You Thinking...?)

One night things were going pretty regular. It was a good night, the place was jumping and everyone was having a good time. Things change! A guy entered the club that night. He wasn't any different than anyone else that frequented a strip club on any given Friday night. He sat near the stage, ordered drinks and enjoyed the show like anyone else. He sat there for over an hour and didn't do anything to warrant any undue attention until... A girl that was giving him a lap dance jumped up and yelled 'Static!' The club code for the shit is going down. It's seems that this chucklehead tried to pull her thong over and goose her. And although that may be okay in the privacy of the champagne room, touching was not allowed on the main dance floor. When L.L. made her way over the guy was being very condescending with the girl. In the case of a dispute between a client and a girl, L.L. would always take the girls side. "*A bitch has got a bitch's back*!"

"*Static*? What the fuck is that supposed to mean? What? Is that some kind of code...? Bitch?" he said with a snide tone as he sat there and sipped his beer.

"Okay buddy... play time is over... you're leaving..." L.L. said as she walked up on him.

He looked at her and smiled a crooked smile as if to say. "*And who the fuck are you*?" and then... he said it. "And who the *fuck* are you?"

"I'm the club manager and you have to go..."

This biker – poser asshole had the nerve to shake his head no. "I don't think so... *honey*..."

L.L. cut his eyes at him and he cut his eyes right back at her. This is a guy that had no respect for women and had no problem with letting you know. He had no respect for her authority in her own place.

"I said: *You're leaving...*" L.L. enunciated.

Now, this is a time when it would have been a good thing if he had read this biography... then he might not have stood up and said what he said next...

"Suck my dick... bitch!" What happened next; happened in the blink of an eye. It happened so fast that I don't even think that to this day this chucklehead knows what happened. L.L. rushed at the guy, switchblade in hand and took a broad swing at the guys' neck. He didn't even have time to duck. That would have been all she wrote except two of Cisco's bouncers were able to stop her in mid lunge. As they tried to subdue L.L., the guy smiled, ran his fingers through his hair and sat back down. This chucklehead actually thought it was over. As he sat back down, Cisco walked up beside him and stood slightly behind him and to his right. Cisco kept his arms behind him. The guy turned to Cisco and said. "Hey buddy... get me another beer..."

Cisco just stood there, he didn't look at him; he just kept his eyes on the club. "I'm not a bartender... I'm the head of security here..." Cisco said cool and calmly.

The guy looked at Cisco and Cisco still did not acknowledge him and kept his eyes on the club floor. The other two body guards had removed L.L. back to her office. She was okay with letting Cisco handle this... his own way... The guy motioned for a topless waitress to come serve him. Cisco waved her away. He looked at Cisco; Cisco again did not acknowledge him.

"Hey! I got money to spend... I got business here..."

Cisco leaned into him and whispered. "Your *business...* in here is done... and when you step *outside... you* and *I* have personal business to attend to..." And Cisco straightened up again and adjusted his tie. The guy looked around the club. None of the other bouncers stepped forward and kept to their stations. He caught the eye of one bouncer across the room. The bouncer just shook his head and smiled and went about his business. It was just him and Cisco. This chucklehead was starting to get nervous. He sat there. Cisco just stood there watching the club.

The guy looked around the club to where L.L. had exited and said to Cisco. "Was that your old lady?"

Cisco looked him dead in his eye... and smiled. The guy hesitated and reached for his cell phone. "Even if your boys are standing right outside the club... they won't get here in time..." Cisco said calmly, without looking at him.

"I'll call the cops...!" he said defiantly.

Cisco tightened his lips, shook his head, smacked his lips and said. "They won't get here in time...!" The guy just sat there twisting in the wind. I'm sure he contemplated sucker punching Cisco, but Cisco was still positioned to the right and behind him. From that position the guy did not have a good shot at Cisco and one shot is all he would have. Cisco had his left foot against the chairs' back leg. There was no way this guy could stand and turn in time. Cisco knew his craft well. And then there were the other bouncers in the club to consider. He didn't know how many bouncers it would take to kick his ass, but he knew how many would get involved. A bead of sweat formed on his brow. Cisco still kept his eyes on the club. After what felt like an eternity, the biggest bouncer in the club, Jinx, walked up to the guy. He looked at Jinx and he shivered a bit. He had no idea what was going to happen next.

"The owner asked me to come get you and escort you out of the club." Jinx said. The guy just sat there shaking. Jinx smiled. "Come with me, if you want to live..." Jinx then positioned himself between the guy and Cisco. Cisco was now behind Jinx. The guy tried to peek around Jinx but he couldn't see him. He looked Jinx in the eyes. "It's okay... he's not going to touch you..."

"You sure...?"

Jinx got very serious and put some bass in his voice. "You wanna ask me that again?" The guy shook his head no and slowly got up. Jinx escorted him to the door. Cisco did not move from his spot. If Steven didn't want this guy hurt near his property, Cisco would have to respect that. As the guy walked out the door he said to Jinx.

"You're a real gentleman... thanks!"

Jinx did not acknowledge the compliment.

"I take it you won't be coming back here? *Ever*!" The guy shook his head no. "And tell all your friends..." and Jinx closed the club door behind him. The guy took two steps away and threw up.

The Tortured Soul Trilogy
(The Confessions of Jennifer X)
Chapter 39
(Teach Me How To Love)

Jennifer went back to her dorm room after class. The 'sock' wasn't tied to the doorknob. She entered the room slowly. "Anybody home?" No answer. Her roommate and her girlfriend weren't there. Hours passed and it was getting late. Tika didn't come home; I guess they were spending the night in Brittany's room. I swear, I've worked with strippers and porn stars and whores (Oh my!) but those two are the horniest little bitches I've ever seen. There wasn't a day the sock wasn't on the doorknob. It didn't bother me; I just spent the hour or two in the library or the student hall studying. I think their sexcapades actually helped my grades. Good! They're out for the night; maybe I can finally get a full night's sleep. I got undressed and was in my panties when the phone rang. It was Michael... I got moist at the very sound of his voice. I lay down on my bed to take the call. We spoke for almost two hours. I was so wet and horny and so was he. We spoke for so long that my cell battery was dying out.

"I gotta go baby! I have an exam in the morning!"

"Me too... I have court at 9am!"

"Love you!"

"I love you more!" Then Michael paused.

"You okay...?" I asked.

"I just wanted to say... I'm *so very* proud of you..."

"Aw... thank you baby!"

"When you graduate... I'm gonna have a big surprise for you..."

"What kind of a surprise...?" I cooed.

"What kind of a surprise would it be...? If I told you now?"

Jenny laughed. But then it dawned on her what the surprise might be. "*Oh...!* Baby!" she purred.

"Say my name baby!"

Jennifer moaned deeply, "Michael!"

"Ohhhhh! Haaaah hah!"

"Was it good for you?" Jennifer asked seductively.

"When I see you again… it'll be *much* better!"

I hung up the phone and I was so horny and excited and I couldn't fight it. That's when I noticed that the entire time I was on the phone with Michael; my left hand was on my pussy. Without realizing it, I had been gently stroking myself. Damn, I thought only men did that! I really should stop doing that, but *not* tonight. I spread my leg over the outside of my twin bed and started to finger my clit. I rubbed myself slowly at first but then I started flicking it with my fingertips. The finger flicking became slapping and I swooned with every pat. I peeled off my panties and took my first and index fingers and parted my labia. I licked my other index finger to make it wet and began to stroke and rub my swollen clit. I alternated rubbing and flicking it. I began to smack it, all the while thinking of Michael's balls hitting me on the ass. "Ohhhh! My! Ah ah ah huh! Yea ahh! Yea ahh!" I stuck my middle finger deep inside me while the palm of my hand rubbed my clit. I used my other hand to caress and pinch my nipples. I wanted Michael here so bad! I used two fingers and then three inside me. I reached deeper and deeper but I couldn't reach the spot I wanted to hit. I rolled over on my knees and reached into my purse hanging off the bedpost and took out my 'travel buddy'. I was so hot and wet I didn't need a lubricant. I got back on my knees and buried my head in the pillow. It was *our* favorite position with my ass in the sky. I took my left hand and spread my labia and with my right, I buried my friend deep inside me. My jaw trembled and shook. My eyes went to the back of my head. I worked that dildo like I was digging for gold. And honey…! I done hit the mother lode! "Oh yeah, oh yeah ah! Ah! Oh yeah, yeah!" I began to pant and moan but I had to keep it quiet, the walls in the dorm rooms were so thin, if some one on the first floor sneezed, you heard gesundheit from the third floor. I buried my head deeper into the pillow to muffle my screams of pleasure. I pushed and pulled and twisted and turned it until I…. "Ommmmfffff! Ammmmmm! Muuuuuuah!" I screamed into the pillow. I was glistening with perspiration and my pussy was contracting in waves with wild abandon. I pulled my 'friend' out slowly and my pussy made a popping sound and I laughed sensually. I turned my head to get some air. I cleared my hair away from my face and I saw that I was not alone.

"You didn't put a sock on the doorknob!" I heard a voice say softly behind me.

I didn't hear them come in with my head in the pillow and they sure as hell weren't going to interrupt the show I just put on! I rolled over covering myself with the sheets. After two years stripping you'd think I'd be used to a live audience. They were both standing there trembling, mouths wide open, totally amazed by what they had just seen. "And how long have you two bitches been standing there?" I asked my roommate and her girlfriend.

"Long enough to learn that we're just fucking amateurs...!" Brittany said. Tika just nodded.

"If you'll excuse me... I'm gonna go take a shower and get some sleep... I have an exam in the morning." I wrapped myself in the sheet and went to the communal shower. It took a little longer for me to shower than usual, that massaging spray head... Well, I'm just gonna have to buy me one when I get home... When I got back to the room there was a sock on the doorknob! "Fuck'em! I've seen them at it before and now we're even!" I entered the room without knocking. "Damn! They finally got it right!" I grabbed my jeans and a top and went to sleep on the couch in the student hall. I see the 'Jenny Mojo' works on women too!

The Tortured Soul Trilogy
(The Confessions of Jennifer X)
Chapter 40
(Pomp and Circumstances)

Jennifer sat there at the graduation ceremony waiting for her name to be called, but she couldn't keep still. She kept looking into the crowd to see if Michael was in the viewing stands. She didn't see him anywhere. She didn't even see Steven or Ramona... *'I hope they didn't get struck in traffic... I don't want Michael to miss my big moment.'* It was her graduation day and she wanted so bad to hear the surprise Michael had in store for her. She felt like a schoolgirl waiting to be taken to the senior prom.

"And graduating with honors... Ms. Jennifer Jones..."

Jennifer stood and got her diploma to an ovation... The Callahans were nowhere to be found. But that was okay... she did this for her. She was proud of herself. She took her tassle and ribbons and held onto them dearly. She had worked so very hard for this moment. She only wished... Oh well... Jennifer walked slowly back to the parking lot. She was about to throw her cap and gown into the trashcan when she heard her name called. She looked up and it was Steven Callahan. She ran to him. "Mr. Callahan... you made it! I thought you weren't here... where were you sitting? I didn't see you anywhere!"

Steven hugged Jennifer. It was a strange hug, but Jenny was so excited to see him she didn't notice. "You have no idea how proud I am of you Jenny!" he said. And he hugged her tighter.

Jennifer looked around and saw Ramona. "Ms. Kirby! I'm so glad you're here!" And she hugged her. Jenny looked around for Michael. "Where's Michael?" Jenny asked. And that was it. Ramona started crying hysterically and couldn't stop. "What is wrong with Ramona...?" Jenny exclaimed. Jennifer turned to Steven. His eyes were red and were welling up. "Mr. Callahan...? *Steven...?* What is going on...? Where is Michael? What happened to...?" Ramona walked over to Steven and cried on his chest as he hugged her. Steven just shook his head. "Somebody SAY something!" Jenny was livid. Steven sobbed. "*WHERE the fuck is MICHAEL...!*" I yelled. Tears started to well in Jennifer's eyes. No one would answer her. Finally after what seemed like an eternity, Steven spoke.

"It was... so sudden...!" Steven sobbed.

Jennifer shook her head slowly. She kept saying '*no...! no...! no...!*' over and over again. She couldn't hear a word Steven said after that. All she remembered next is that Cisco slapped her. "Come out of it Jenny!" he said.

"You slapped me!" And Jenny went after him but she felt someone grab her from behind, holding her back. It was Tobey.

"Calm down bitch! He had to do it...!" Jenny struggled but Tobey had her in a rear naked choke and she couldn't get loose. "Calm down I said! I aint letting go of you until you relax... or I'm gonna have to 'relax' you!" And Tobey tightened her grip. She knew how to handle a crazy bitch when she needed to. Jennifer eventually calmed down. Tobey let her go. Jennifer then slapped Cisco, hard. He didn't flinch, he didn't respond. He just held his arms open and Jenny hugged him and she started crying.

"Why did you hit me?"

"I had to do it Mami... you were staring into space for almost ten minutes, I had to bring you back!"

"Where is everybody?"

"Steven and Ramona are in the car waiting for us... let's go..." L.L. said.

She knew not to ask about Michael. "Where are we going?" I asked L.L.

"We're going home... mami, we're going home...!" Cisco replied. Cisco and Tobey helped her get into the Callahan's limo, Steven was still consoling Ramona, who was still very distraught. Michael was like a son to her. Jennifer sat with a stoic expression on her face. She was responsive but she was totally emotionless.

Steven poured her a double shot of bourbon from the limo bar. "Here... drink this!"

Jennifer threw the drink back in one gulp and handed Steven the glass. "No thank you... I don't drink..." On the ride home Steven explained to Jennifer what had happened to Michael.

- - -

L.L. thought back to when she first heard the news. Cisco called L.L. at about 9am to meet her. L.L. was not happy about it.

"I just did a full shift dancing last night and I just got home about two hours ago, can't it wait?"

"I'm coming to get you. It's an emergency; we have to shut the club down…" Cisco arrived a few moments later. "Aren't you dressed yet…?"

"What the fuck is going on? Is there going to be a raid on the place? Is there going to be a mob hit? What?" L.L. was confused and a little concerned. "*Cisco… talk* to me… what the fuck is going on?"

"Get dressed and grab your coat, Jackie is gonna take care of shutting the club down… we have to go…"

"Go where?" L.L. was getting visibly upset. "What *the fuck* is going on Cisco?" There was a quiet calm in his voice that was eerie… I will never, ever forget what he said to me that day…

"Ramona just called me… Michael is dead…!"

The blood rushed from my face, I felt faint. Cisco grabbed my arm to keep me from falling over. "Michael was murdered?" I asked.

"No baby… it was a heart attack…"

"Wha… wha… what? A heart attack? When?"

"This morning during his daily run…"

"Oh my god… poor Steven! That boy was his reason for living!"

"We have to go… right now!"

L.L. quickly threw on some jeans and a top. "Where are we going?"

"First to the Callahan's house and when everything is settled there… then we have to go get Jennifer and tell her…"

A look of shock and dismay flashed across L.L.'s face. "Oh my god *Cisco*…! Jennifer *doesn't* know yet…?"

Cisco shook his head no. L.L. grabbed his hand. L.L. had only recently found out from Steven that Michael was going to propose to Jennifer when she graduated. They got to the Callahan's house and it was like an emergency room. People, friends and associates are coming in and out constantly, crying and losing it.

No one expected Michael to die. The family had no history of heart disease. It was totally unexpected. The best any one knew by what the emergency room doctor said and what the autopsy showed was that it was an embolism. A blood clot that had formed years ago from a virus infection he had gotten, broke off and blocked a major artery in his heart while he was out on his mid-morning run. It was twenty minutes before another runner came across his body. Michael was pronounced dead on arrival at the hospital. Funeral arrangements were made and then changed.

"We can't bury Michael... without Jennifer being there..." Steven said quietly.

"I'll pick her up from the school in the morning..." Cisco said.

"No... She still has a few more days before she graduates... She worked hard for her diploma... I won't take that from her... We wait... we'll pick her up after the graduation ceremony... not a word until after she gets her degree..."

Cisco quietly nodded in agreement. Nothing would be said to her, not a word... L.L. touched Steven's hand gently. "Does she know that Michael was going to...?" L.L asked

Steven shook his head no. "It was supposed to be a surprise... He was going to propose the moment she came home." They didn't have a chance to put the decorations up.

L.L. hugged Steven tightly and sobbed. Steven just looked at Cisco and nodded. They arrived at the college on graduation day and saw Jennifer in the general area but they ducked from her view. They didn't want her to see them, come over and find out what happened before her name was called. They waited for her in the parking lot until after the ceremony.

- - -

L.L. looked at Jennifer after Steven explained what happened. She was totally unmoved. Lady Latex leaned into her and whispered. "Do I have to make Cisco slap you again?"

"No L.L., that won't be necessary..." Jennifer said totally emotionless. Tobey leaned back, she was now scared of Jennifer... and *nobody* scared Tobey. She was not all there, and what was left behind was in a bad place, a very bad place. Jennifer did not speak again until they arrived at the Callahan estate. They arrived and Jennifer got out of the car. Steven and Cisco escorted her inside.

"Cisco will show you to your new room…" Steven said.

"I can't stay here…"

"Of course you can… and you will… Just because Michael's gone, doesn't mean you're not family. You're *still* going to be the daughter I never had…" Jennifer almost showed emotion then. Steven had just verified that Michael *was* going to ask her to marry him. At the funeral, Jennifer was cold and emotionless and didn't cry. Ramona was very concerned about her well being; but Steven said that's just the way she was grieving, people handle emotional pain differently. Months later she found out that Michael and Ramona took almost three months to pick out the right engagement ring. He was going to propose to her the moment she came back from school. Steven had already put a down payment on their new house as a wedding present. Steven and Ramona became the parents she never had. Although she appreciated it, it was such a shame she just couldn't truly enjoy it. It was a very bittersweet time in her life.

The Tortured Soul Trilogy
(The Confessions of Jennifer X)
Chapter 41
(Working Girl)

Jennifer took over Ramona's duties at the company. With Michael gone and Ramona's advanced age, Steven needed all the help he could get with running the company and Jennifer needed to occupy her time. Going back to work the pole, wasn't an option. Second only to Ramona, she had become the best personal assistant Steven ever had. Jennifer was in charge of making sure that Steven was up-to-date with all his appointments, and took care of all the office duties. She was able to save a lot of money because she lived with Steven and Ramona. Jennifer learned a lot about the 'business' Steven was in, and if it wasn't for the fact that he thought of her like a daughter, some of the information she knew could get a person killed. Steven trusted Jennifer with all aspects of his life, business and personal.

One day while working on some filing for Steven in his office, Cisco and Jinx escorted a young man into the office. Cisco did not acknowledge her presence. That's how she knew; this was business, bad business. She turned to leave; Steven motioned her to stay. Jennifer sat quietly in the corner, working on the file at hand. Steven on occasion would let her watch him 'work'. Steven walked over and sat down on the edge on the mahogany coffee table in the middle of the room. Cisco and Jinx brought the man closer and stood just slightly behind him on either side. The man was nervous but confident. Jinx took a thick envelope out of his own jacket pocket and handed it to Steven and whispered in his ear. Steven dropped the envelope on the table and lit a cigarette.

"It has been brought to my attention that you owe me a sizable amount of money... it has also been brought to my attention, that you just made a substantial payment against that debt..." Steven took a long drag from the cigarette and blew the smoke out. He pointed to the man with the cigarette in hand. "I like you... you're a gentleman... you didn't cry or bitch and moan about the unfortunate situation you're in… you came straight to me, with a payment, three days early…" The man loosened his tie. "I'm gonna do something for you I don't do for anybody… I'm gonna cut you a break…" Steven took another drag from the cigarette. "I'm gonna give you till the end of the month to come up with the rest of my money…" Steven stood up and walked up to the man, the cigarette still in his mouth very close to the man's face. Steven fixed the man's tie and adjusted the collar of his jacket. He then collared the man and held the back of his neck tightly and leaned into his ear and whispered. "I'm putting a lot of faith in you… don't disappoint me… If you disappoint me… I'll fill your lungs with water…" The man now had beads of sweat on his brow. Steven dropped the cigarette between the man's legs and stepped on it. "Do we have an understanding?" The man nodded quietly and Jinx escorted him out. They stopped at the office door when Steven spoke. "I take it that you won't find yourself in this position ever again?"

"Yes sir! Mr. Callahan…" the man answered. The man turned, and Jinx escorted him out, Cisco was about to exit when Steven called Cisco over.

"If he doesn't come up with the rest of my money by the end of the month… Take whatever he gives you and tell him we're square…!"

"Yes Mr. Callahan…"

"One more thing…" Cisco paused. "Now that I have you and Jenny here… That night in the parking lot…"

Cisco answered without waiting for Steven to complete the question. He knew what Steven was referring to. "You're like a father to me Mr. Callahan… but if Jenny had given me the word, you were going down… It would have broken my heart, but you would've gone down…"

"Thank you Cisco…"

"No… Thank you Mr. Callahan…" As Cisco closed the door behind him, he winked at Jennifer. Jenny waved slightly to him.

"That's why I keep him… Not only does he do his job well. He has a good heart; he would do the right thing no matter what! That young man would lay his life down for you, not because I pay him, but because he wants to… you remember that

Jenny!" Jenny nodded. Steven picked up the envelope and handed it to Jennifer. "Take care of this for me please Jennifer…"

"Yes Mr. Callahan…" Jennifer took the envelope and took it over to the office safe and placed it inside and locked it.

"Jenny…?"

"Yes… Mr. Callahan…?"

"I wanted you to see… for yourself… what it is… I do…"

"I don't have a problem with what you do… Mr. Callahan, you were tough… but you were fair…" Jennifer looked at the cigarette butt on the floor.

"…But since when do *you* smoke…?"

"Visual aide…" Steven replied. Steven hugged Jennifer tightly, it was then he knew… this wasn't the life he wanted for her.

- - -

About a year later, Steven called her into his office with a special project. "Jennifer… I need you to do something for me."

"Anything for you Mr. Callahan…" Jennifer only called him Steven when they were home. This was business.

"I have stock in a company called Faber Data Co. and I'm not getting the return on my investment I was hoping for…"

"You want me make the arrangements to 'sell' your interests for you…?" Jennifer knew full well there was no 'stock', Steven had the 'bite' on someone there and they weren't paying their 'vig'. Selling his interest meant trading the 'vig' to someone else or… you really don't want to know!

"No… I need you to take a job there, to work for them, undercover for me, and find out who's holding the company back, and take over their position…"

"You want me to work for another company?"

"I want you to take it over and, do whatever is needed to make it profitable again…"

"What about Callahan Enterprises…?"

"With Michael gone… and once I'm gone… there is no 'Callahan Enterprises'… And this is no business for an intelligent young lady as yourself… you need to establish yourself in a legitimate endeavor…"

"But what about you and Ramona…?"

"Don't worry about us… we'll be just fine… there's no future here for you. You're young and beautiful and you should be married and having my grand kids…"

Jennifer hugged Steven. "I'm gonna miss you…"

"What are you talking about? You're still coming over holidays and weekends… you're not getting rid of us that easy!"

Jennifer smiled. "But still… who's going to…?"

"Don't worry… L.L. and Cisco are going to run the operation from now on… they have the 'proper' skills and demeanor to handle just about anything…"

"When I do leave…?"

"Two-weeks… that'll give you enough time to get packed. You'll be meeting with Charles Hagen and Costas Theo… theopoop… ah! I can't pronounce his name… but they're aware that you're coming and are going to train you in all the aspects of the business. I know you can handle this for me. I have a lot of faith in you…"

Jennifer got suddenly serious. "You're not gonna… fill my lungs with water… are you?" and she smiled.

Steven laughed and hugged her. "Silly rabbit!"

Jennifer nodded and smiled, and just before she was going to leave the office she turned to Steven. "Steven… I need to ask you a big favor…" Steven knew this was personal; she called him 'Steven' in the office.

"Anything you want Jenny… Just ask…"

"With your permission…" Jenny hesitated.

"What is it honey…? What can I do for you? You know I will do anything for you if it's within my power…"

"With your permission, I would like to purchase the plot next to Michael, so when the time comes…"

Steven's eyes welled up and he hugged Jennifer. Jennifer hugged Steven back. "Sweetie you *can't* buy the plot next to Michael…"

"I… understand…!" Jennifer looked down and away.

"No honey… you *don't* understand… I bought that plot for you already… in case you ever wanted it…!"

Jennifer cried tears of joy. "Thank you Steven…"

"Call me Dad!"

Jennifer turned her head away and shook her head no. "I can't do that!"

"I'm sorry... I forgot... Steven is just fine with me sweetie!" They hugged and rocked each other in their arms and cried. "Are you sure you want to be next to Michael...?"

Jenny leaned back and looked at Steven incredulously. "Of *course* I do!"

"You sure...? Cause I would have thought you would have preferred him on *top* of you...! I know that's where *he* liked to be...!"

"Pfffftt...! *Steven*...!" Jenny laughed embarrassed and she hit Steven's chest with her open hand.

"Hey... the walls in my house are fucking thin!" Steven joked. Jenny and Steven hugged and laughed and cried together.

"I miss Michael..."

"Me too sweetie... me too..."

"Sometimes I spray his cologne on my pillow and dream of him."

Steven kissed Jenny on her forehead. "I still do that with his mother's perfume..." Steven felt so good in Jenny's arms. Why couldn't her father have been more like this? "How about we visit Michael before you go...?"

"I would love that Steven!" Jenny said. And Jenny kissed Steven on the lips.

"Oh...! If only I were 40 years younger...!"

"I wasn't *born* yet Steven!"

"Pfffttt!" Steven and Jenny laughed.

L.L. heard the news the next day. Although L.L. was happy for her that she was moving on to bigger and better things, she was still more concerned with herself right now. L.L.'s position in Callahan Enterprises was safe... for now!

The Tortured Soul Trilogy
(The Confessions of Jennifer X)
Chapter 42
(Genie in A Bottle)

Two weeks later, Jenny was all packed and ready. She had already said her goodbyes to Tobey and Cisco at her going away party the night before. They didn't want to be there today to see her off. It would be too painful for them. A limo was at the house waiting to take her to the airport and to a new adventure in a new city. She kissed Ramona goodbye, and then she kissed and hugged Steven. It was at that precise moment that Déjà vu hit her. This was the same as when she went away to college. She knew... right then... without a doubt in her mind, she was never going to see Steven ever again. The epiphany stabbed her right in the heart. She grabbed him and hugged him tight. She didn't want to let him go of him. She couldn't stop kissing him. "I love you Steven!" She whispered in his ear.

That's when Steven knew, she knew. "I love you too sweetie..."

She turned to Ramona. "You make sure you call me!"

"You know I will Jenny... You know I will..." Tears welled in her eyes.

Jenny kissed Ramona and got in the limo and rolled down the window and as the car pulled away, she blew a kiss and said. "Goodbye... *dad*!"

As the limo pulled down the drive way, Steven cried uncontrollably. "Little bitch is too smart for her own damn good...!" He sobbed.

"I know..." Ramona said as she waved to her. "I love her too!"

The limo made the turn outside the gate and there was L.L. and Cisco, standing by the Callahan limo with a banner.

Good Luck Jennifer X!

And they waved to each other as she drove by. Cisco looked at L.L. with tears in his eyes.

"What? What's wrong with you... are you *crying*? Geez what a *pussy* you are. Man up you little *bitch*!" And she shook her head. L.L. kept watching the car drive off and turning back to Cisco. She shook her head again. Finally she raised her arms and said. "Okay, okay... come get some... but keep your hands off my ass!" Cisco and L.L. hugged each other and... they... lingered. "Oh my...! This is nice..." L.L. said. "... Real nice...!" L.L. began to grind her hips into Cisco. Cisco reciprocated by leaning into it. "Oh *damn*...! That feels..." L.L. whispered. And L.L. began to breathe heavy. Cisco's strength comforted her. His emotional state reassured her. She only became a lesbian to avoid what she was feeling right now. But this was different; this wasn't under the bleachers. It wasn't against her will, she *wanted* this and it felt damn good. L.L. began to kiss Cisco softy at first, then long and hard. L.L. and Cisco grinded their hips together in a slow dance. Cisco led her lead; L.L. liked that.

The night before when they had their special farewell for Jenny, she had leaned into L.L. and whispered in her ear. "I know you said you '*don't do dick*'..."

L.L.'s eyes had sparkled a bit and she smiled. "*Could Jenny finally be willing to take a walk on the wild side?*" Technically, she wasn't an employee anymore but then Jenny glanced in Cisco's direction...

"I lost Michael because we waited for the time to be right... Things did not work out for us... Please, you have a chance at happiness... take it! Don't go to sleep on Cisco... he's a good man!" L.L. had looked at Jenny like she was crazy! "Please... don't go to sleep on Cisco... I mean it!" Jenny begged.

L.L. stroked his crotch and moaned. "May I have this...?" Cisco picked her up and put her in the back seat of the limo. "Be gentile with me...!" she said.

Cisco smiled. "Who's being a pussy now?"

"I guess *I am* baby!" she cooed. L.L. unbuttoned her blouse and rubbed and stroked her nipples. Cisco did not need any more encouragement. He looked around to see if anyone was coming and unzipped his pants. She pulled him closer to the car and he stood outside the open car door. Cisco wasn't very big, but he was very 'playful'. He felt smooth and strong in L.L.'s mouth. She licked him and stroked him for a moment and whispered '*Okay*!' She undid her belt and pulled her jeans and panties down to her ankles. She then rolled over on her knees and fondled her clit. She was very wet and horny. She couldn't believe what she was about to do for a man. Cisco climbed in and closed the door behind him. Cisco did not disappoint her... then or ever again.

The Tortured Soul Trilogy
(The Confessions of Jennifer X)
Chapter 43
(This Is a Man's World)

Jennifer arrived a little after six at the apartment that Steven had set up or her. It was nice and cozy but it needed a woman's touch. '*I guess Ramona wasn't in charge of the decorating.*' All her stuff was here but still in all the boxes right were the movers left it. Jennifer would worry about unpacking and redecorating later. Right now she needed to get some sleep. Tomorrow she had a 9:30 meeting with Charles Hagen at Faber's main office. She had trouble sleeping in a strange bed, so she sprayed Michael's cologne on her pillow and drifted off.

Jenny arrived at the main office of Faber Data Co. at 9:15 the next morning. She was received with a lukewarm reception at best. Not anything like the first time she came to Callahan's office. This was a large company that took up several floors in two buildings with hundreds of employees. Callahan Enterprises had less than 50. Nevertheless, she was here to do a job for Steven, and do it she would. She went up to the receptionist. "Excuse me but I have an appointment…"

"Please take a seat… some one will be with you in just a moment…" Jennifer was a bit 'put off' by being dismissed so bluntly, but she would bide her time before she blew this bitch up. She sat quietly on the couch and waited, and waited. Other men came in and were greeted immediately and offered coffee or tea while they waited or they were shown directly into Hagen's office after a very brief wait. Jennifer was being treated like a fair-haired stepchild. Jennifer read the magazines and sat patiently. As more and more men were escorted in, Jennifer was left in the waiting room to cool her heels. At about a quarter to twelve Hagen came out of his office.

"Ms. Delafield… when Ms. Jones finally arrives; send her home! We had a meeting at 9:30 this morning and I don't like people who miss appointments and don't call to cancel."

"Yes Mr. Hagen… I'll tell her the moment she arrives…"

Hagen was about to walk back to his office. Jennifer spoke from where she was seated. "Ms. Jones *was here* at 9:30..." she said nonchalantly without looking up from her magazine.

Hagen turned around. "I beg your pardon?"

"I said... Ms. Jones was *here* at 9:30 this morning!"

"Ms. Delafield... If Ms. Jones was here at 9:30 this morning... why didn't you show her in?"

"I don't know what she's talking about... Ms. Jones never came in Mr. Hagen..."

"She most certainly did... come in at 9:15 and she saw Mr. Hagen arrive to work at 9:50 and take his first meeting at 10:15!"

"Excuse me... are you calling me a liar?" Ms. Delafield said.

Jenny looked up from the magazine. "Right to your face... YES!"

"Well... *I... never...!*" she said insulted.

And Hagen and Ms. Delafield began to discuss what had just occurred between them, again ignoring Jennifer. She put the magazine down, stood up, grabbed her briefcase and walked over to them. "If you two are finished circle jerking each other... your office Mr. Hagen...!"

Hagen had a look of anger on his face. Ms. Delafield smiled. "I don't know who you think you are young lady..." He said.

"I'm the *young lady* that was sitting right here since 9:15, and... when you first came in... at 9:50 this morning. I know you remember me, because you kept staring at my legs and almost tripped over the wastebasket and told Ms. Delafield to move it. Oh and Ms. Delafield... he *did* look down your blouse when you bent over to move it!"

"Why I never...!" Hagen said as he looked Jennifer up and down in anger.

Jennifer snapped her fingers and pointed at her face. "I'm up here...! The sound of my voice is *not* coming from *my* blouse!"

"Why of all the insolence! Who the hell do you think you are...?"

"I'm Jennifer X. Jones... Steven *Callahan* sent me..."

Hagen froze. Jenny finally got his attention. *"You're* Jennifer Jones...?"

Jennifer nodded. "Your office...!" And she took a step past Hagen.

"Actually I was going to take an early lunch today..."

"You've wasted enough of my precious time... you're *skipping* lunch today..." Hagen stood there, emasculated while Jennifer took out her cell and called her limo driver and asked him to bring her some lunch from any local restaurant. A cheeseburger would be fine she told him.

"You're ordering lunch in?" Hagen asked.

"Is there a *reason* why *I shouldn't have lunch...?"*

"No...! It' just that I..."

"Good!" She turned to Ms. Delafield. "When my driver arrives with my lunch... send him *directly* in... You think you can handle that?"

Ms. Delafield had no idea what to say, but to see Hagen being bossed around by this woman intimidated her. "Yes...!" she answered quickly.

"Yes... 'what'...?"

"Yes Ms. Jones!"

Jennifer led Hagen towards his office. "You're *damn right...* Yes, Ms. Jones!"

Ms. Delafield looked at Hagen and shook her head. Hagen had set that whole scenario up to intimidate and humiliate Jennifer and it backfired in his face. He had no idea that 'Jennifer Jones' was Hispanic. He thought she was here to interview for the typing pool. Now he had to contend with Callahan's girl that he pissed off.

"Oh Ms. Delafield...? Get some new magazines for the waiting room; those are older than *he* is..."

Jennifer made sure she led Hagen to his office and opened his door. She made sure she was the first to enter; giving him the impression the he was following her in. She wanted him to know, she was the lead dog. Hagen entered his office and Jennifer sat in the guest chair.

"Ms. Jones... I wish to apologize for Ms. Delafield..."

"Why...? She did exactly what you told her to do!" Hagen's jaw dropped again. "That little scenario you tried to pull out there was cute… don't you ever try to pull that shit on me again… Do I make myself clear?"

"Yes… Jenny." Hagen said curtly. Jennifer cut her eyes at him. "Oh! Callahan might have some things on me… But I'm *still* the boss around *here*… and I will address you as I please…"

Jennifer knew Hagen was posturing. It was his company after all and Jennifer was only a 'hired gun'. He had to try to regain control of the situation. "Okay… I'll let you have that one… for now! We'll start the meeting the moment Theo gets here… he should be wondering by now why you haven't met him for lunch yet and be here in about… *five minutes*…" Theo barged into Hagen's office. "Oh good… he's early! We can begin."

"How did you know that he…?" Hagen stammered.

"I'm always going to be two steps ahead of the both of you…! And although the view from back there *is* quite spectacular… try to keep up…" Jennifer was bluffing. She was scared and totally out of her element, but she had learned so much watching Steven conduct an 'interview' that she knew how to keep these two men in the palm of her hand. She was not going to give them any chance to undermine her. Besides if she couldn't handle the situation in a business-like manner… there was always Cisco and Jinx… '*You can take the girl out of the hood…*' Jennifer made Charles and Theo give her a complete rundown of the company, what they do, who their clientele is, the whole nine yards. The only interruption was Ms. Delafield bringing in her lunch twenty minutes into the meeting.

"Here's your lunch Ms. Jones… your driver didn't bring you a beverage… Is a ginger ale acceptable to you?"

Jennifer nodded and Ms. Delafield placed the can of soda on the table with a glass of ice for her.

"Thank you Ms. Delafield… please hold all calls and reschedule all of Mr. Hagen's and Mr. Theopolous' appointments for another day… we'll be in a meeting for the rest of the day."

"Yes Ms. Jones…"

"And Ms. Delafield, please order them some lunch too… I can't concentrate with their stomachs growling!"

"Yes Ms. Jones… right away!" And Ms. Delafield closed the door behind her never acknowledging either man in the room. *"You know, I've changed my mind about Ms. Delafield… I'm beginning to like her...*" Jenny said to herself as she bit into her burger. It was empowering to be eating and they had to wait on her to eat.

For the next few weeks Jennifer did reconnaissance. Not only did she find out everything she could about the company that Hagen and Theo would tell her, she also found out the things they wouldn't tell her. Faber Data Co. was no different than the porn films she had worked on. The men were treated like kings and the women were an after-thought, an adornment, only there to satisfy their needs. You had your *porn stars*, the men who thought the world revolved around their dicks but they were jaded, and the *fluffers*, the women whose sole purpose was to stroke their egos so they could perform. The *hookers*, professional women who thought that by doing whatever was asked of them, would 'make it' in this business, and the *producer/directors*, the two slime bags who made all their money off this circus of pain and humiliation. (Oh yeah, I'm talking about Hagen and Theo here!)

The one thing Jennifer didn't expect to see was the number of women with 'dead eyes' like Domiana Luquer. So many women, whose passion was gone; they did the job to pay the bills. No more, no less. They got into 'character' when the director said 'action', and went back into a coma when they heard 'cut'. So many, many women that were brow beaten down, humiliated and intimidated into submission, drained physically, mentally and emotionally. They all had the look on their faces like sheep waiting for the slaughter; with one major difference, they prayed for the slaughter to come!

Jennifer walked through the offices with confidence and pride. The women looked at her as if she were the first primate to walk upright. They were in awe of her. They acted as if they wished they too could be able hold their heads up high; Not all women felt that way, but Jennifer would encourage the ones who did. She would not make the same mistake she did on the porn set that day.

"Good morning Ms. Delafield!"

"Good morning Ms. Jones!"

"I brought you some coffee... Light, two sugars?" Jenny said to Ms. Delafield.

"*What...?*" She said unbelievingly.

"Your coffee... you take light, two sugars... right?"

"Why that's right...! You brought me *coffee*...?"

"Yes..."

"Thank you...!"

"Nooo problem... oh...! I love your shoes... where did you get them?"

"A catalogue... You *like* my shoes...?"

"Uh huh! Can I see that catalogue later... if you don't mind?"

"Sure... I'll bring it right over to you...!"

"Thanks... you're a doll!" And Jennifer waved to her and walked away. Jennifer wanted Ms. Delafield to trust her. She was Hagen's personal secretary and if she knew half about Hagen that Ramona knew about Steven, she would be a valued asset. Jennifer spent the next few weeks working side by side with all the women in the office one-by-one. Learning their jobs, not just *what* they did, but *how* they did it. She would take over a project from them to see if she could do it on her own. They didn't mind, less work for them. Jennifer wanted to know how things were done because she did not want to rely on someone else to be in control of a situation that she couldn't handle. She didn't learn that from Steven, she learned that from Oprah...

The women slowly warmed up to her. They used her; she used them. They complimented each other. The women walked around with a new vim and vigor. They felt as if... they mattered! Office moral was at an all time high... but the profit margins didn't get any better. There was still a leak that Jenny had to plug up. She needed inside info and she needed it fast. She knew exactly what to do.

The Tortured Soul Trilogy
(The Confessions of Jennifer X)
Chapter 44
(I'm Just Jenny From The Block)

Jennifer walked past Ms. Delafield in the hall. "Ms. Delafield?"

"Yes Ms. Jones…?"

"Are you losing weight?"

Ms. Delafield gushed. "No…"

"New outfit?"

"Yes! You like it?"

"It looks fabulous on you…"

"Thank you!"

Jennifer turned away and turned back. "Would you like to have lunch with me today?"

"Lunch? With *you*…?" Jennifer nodded. "Okay… but my lunch isn't until 1:30 today…"

"I'll pick you up at twelve…"

"But… I…"

Jennifer smiled. "I'll pick you up at twelve… Don't worry… I'll take care of it!" Ms. Delafield gushed again. "Oh Ms. Delafield?"

"Yes Ms. Jones?"

"May I ask you a personal question?"

Ms. Delafield became a little leery. "Okay!"

"What is your first name?"

She relaxed. "It's Bonnie…"

"I'll see you at noon… Bonnie!" Bonnie walked away excited as if she was going to have an audience with the Queen. Jennifer did not take Bonnie to some big fancy restaurant. She didn't want to impress her or intimidate her. She wanted her to feel comfortable and safe. She did not want to alienate her; she needed to be her *girlfriend*. She was still working as a fluffer, just with a different clientele and with different methods.

"*You*… eat here?" Bonnie said.

"All the time… I love the cheeseburgers here! But if you'd like to go somewhere *special*… I know of fancier places…"

Jennifer also wanted Bonnie to know she didn't think of her as a 'cheap date'. Bonnie was so taken by Jennifer at this point.

"No! This is fine... *Thank you*" And Bonnie gushed again. (Dang! If she keeps this up, I wouldn't be surprised if she went *down* on me after lunch!) They began to eat and JACKPOT! Bonnie was an all-you-can-eat buffet of information, and she dished it *all* out! By the end of lunch, Jennifer knew everything about Hagen, Theo and the company at large. Now, Jennifer did have to weed out fact from opinion, but she had more than enough info to get a handle on the situation. She got a lot of intelligence for a cheeseburger, fries and a diet coke, but still no idea why profits were down. She needed more time to find the leak.

"This was fun! Would you like to do this again tomorrow Bonnie?"

"No I can't... but I would *love* to do this again...! *Jennifer*..."

(Good! She called me by my first name and she turned *me* down... now it's not on me... it was on her *and* she trusts me.)

"Let me know whenever you're free!" I said. And Jennifer took Bonnie back to the office. Hagen was at standing at her desk waiting impatiently.

"Where were you all this time...?" He demanded from Bonnie.

Bonnie hesitated. "She was having lunch with me... is there a *problem*... Hagen?"

"No... no problem...!" And Hagen left in a huff.

"He's upset!" Bonnie said to me.

"Not upset enough to tell us what it is he wanted so badly... It wasn't that important. Besides he knew full well we were having lunch together... he didn't have anything to say to *me* about it!" Bonnie looked at me as if I were her guardian angel. I kissed her cheek. "I'll talk with you later." And I went on with my business. Bonnie was *my* bitch now... I owned her, but that didn't mean I was going to take unfair advantage of her. L.L. was good for that... that wasn't my style. As time passed, Bonnie blossomed. She was more confident, more outgoing, and although Hagen was still her boss, she didn't take as much shit from him as she used to.

"Good morning Ms. Jones..."

"Good morning Bonnie..." And I paused and looked at her. She was... content and... glowing. "Uh Uhh! Let *me* find out you're 'getting some'...!" I said.

Bonnie put her hand on her bosom and blushed. "*Jennifer!*" Bonnie had never though of herself as a sexual being... but now... the seed was sown. An impish grin came across her face. "I got you coffee... Light and sweet right?" She said to Jenny.

"Thank you sweetie! Thank you so much... But ah... we still have to *talk...*!" I circled my finger in her direction. "...About what's going on here!" Bonnie smiled and I took the coffee and waved to her as I left. Hagen came out of his office.

"Ms. Delafield, coffee!" he barked.

"Get it yourself... I'm busy right now!"

I almost tripped and fell when I heard that shit. '*Damn! This bitch is just gotten bold!*' I hope I didn't amp her up too much... I didn't want her to get fired for crying out loud! I went to the ladies room and poured out the coffee she gave me. I take my coffee black, but I wasn't about to break Bonnie's heart. I would just drop a hint as time goes on that I changed the way I take it. I spent the rest of the week with the girls learning the last of the company protocols. The men were more than willing to 'take me under their wings' so to speak. But I knew why they were so interested in 'mentoring' me. No thanks, besides most of these men were as useless as the chest hair on a playboy bunny. In fact, I got used to calling them 'Chester'. I was just about done with my 'training' and I went to see Hagen to get the last codes I needed.

"Is Mr. Hagen available Ms. Delafield?"

"No Ms. Jones... he's in a conference with Mr. Theopolous..." Bonnie leaned in to me and whispered. "They left the building about an hour ago, I have no idea where they are or what they're doing...!"

"Love you!" Jenny said.

"Love you back!" she said.

Okay... what are these two trying to cook up? I was going to have to wait to find out. My *inside man* was oblivious... and that's not good!

Chapter 45
(Where The Boys Are)

Theo and Hagen were having cigars at an exclusive 'men's club'... Okay... It's a titty bar... but that's not the point here. They went there to plot and plan a way to get rid of Jennifer. She was messing up the delicate 'balance', the status quo of the office.

"Damn it Hagen! Why do I have to put up her meddling? She's *your* problem, not mine!"

"Do you think I'm having a picnic here? All the women in the office are acting up... My secretary won't get me coffee... and that hot blonde in the typing pool won't give me head in my office anymore...!"

"Which one?"

"The flatchested one..."

"I thought that was a guy? I like my girls a little more... endowed!"

"Never mind that now... What are we going to do about this bitch? She's nothing more than a PMSing brain cell!" Hagen said.

"Yeah... she's a real cunt... but I wouldn't mind having *her* down on her knees in my office...!"

"Maybe we should have this meeting at the sports bar instead... you can't seem to concentrate here."

"Look... she's still your problem... handle it... I have problems of my own to deal with..."

"What problem do you have?"

"There's a woman filing sexual misconduct charges on one of our accountants in the downtown office..."

"Who?"

"Maggie..."

"Maggie? I thought she retired?"

"That's what she was doing in accounting when she caught this putz reading a porno mag..."

"Can't we make it go away...?"

"No… she's gonna make a federal case out of it…"

Charles was hit by an epiphany. "Why don't we kill to birds with one bitch!"

"*What…?*"

"Transfer Maggie to our office and send Ms. Jones to our downtown office!"

"How does that help us?"

"It gives us a chance to calm Maggie down. Well, in least until she retires. We'll set up some kind of 'political correctness' seminar at the downtown office… You know, make her think we're sensitive and empathetic to her needs; by law we were supposed to do one every year anyway, and we'll sick our pit bull in a push-up bra on our *problem child* in our downtown office…"

"The *accountant…?* I'm making him take an 'early retirement'… he'll be gone before the end of the month…"

"No not *him*…" Hagen grinned.

Theo sat up in his chair. "*Nicholas… Anderson!*" Theo exclaimed.

"*Bingo…!* She gets rid of him for us, takes his job and she's out of our office and out of our hair! Everybody's happy!"

"You really think she can take him down? Remember how you tried that with Katherine… Look how well that worked out!"

"Have you *met…* Ms. Jones?" Theo nodded and sipped his brandy and dipped the end of his cigar in it to flavor the mouthpiece. "I hate when you do that…!"

"How do we sic Jennifer on Nick?"

"She's looking to plug the hole that's killing the company's bottom line… and Nick is it!"

"And you think she'll take *our* word for that…?"

"No… but she'll listen to marketing…!"

"Oh… they *hate* Nick in marketing! It's perfect!"

Hagen leaned back and puffed his cigar. "And our hands are clean!"

"I like the way you think Charles…"

"Thank you Costas! Care for a lap dance before we go back?"

"How about two?"

"Done!"

Charles called two of the girls over and they began to dance for them.

"It's a shame women just don't know their place! Aint that right honey?" Costas said. The girls giggled. "Hey...! Are you two twins?"

The girls nodded, Charles and Theo laughed. Then Tasha and Sterling smiled at each other as they grinded their asses in the men's laps.

- - -

Jennifer was called into a meeting with Hagen and Theo the very next morning. They were early. Jennifer knew they were anxious to implement their plans to get her out of their hair. It was a shame that although Tasha and Sterling knew they were up to something, they never found out what their plans were.

"Ms. Jones... we have a *special project* for you..."

"*Here it comes... The unveiling of the master plan!*" Jenny thought to herself.

"Ms. Jones for the next six to eight weeks you're going to be training with marketing at their offices..."

"*Six to eight weeks! What the fuck! I thought I was almost done with this shit!*" This was going to put a huge dent in her time schedule.

"... You must understand that in order to truly know what we do here... you need to know *all* the marketing protocols... but if you feel you're not up to it...!"

"*Damn it! I know what you do here... and I know what you're doing now, but there aint a damn thing I can do about it right now!*" Jennifer shook her head. "When do I start?"

"Right away... Ms. Delafield will give you all the details..." Jennifer stood up and began to exit. "I think that working with marketing is going to be very educational for you Ms. Jones... listen to what they have to say... very carefully!" Hagen said.

"Gentlemen...?" They nodded. "...This aint over!" And she left.

"The hell it's not...!" Hagen said. And Hagen gave Theo a high five.

Jennifer got in her car and headed to the offices of the marketing company that was hired to handle all the customer protocols. They were happy to see her, they were also very happy to dish out information about their thoughts on how Faber Data would benefit from a minor personnel change. They had a problem in the Faber downtown office. There was an employee that wouldn't embrace the marketing protocols. It wasn't a difficult program to learn, the only problem was it wasn't being implemented properly... The source of the problem was a man named Nicholas Anderson. Nicholas worked in the downtown office as a data processor. He was adamant not to use the marketing protocols and had butted heads with marketing for several years. Their marketing plans were quite simple; just give the customer what they want using a basic common denominator. Why did this guy have a problem with that? Marketing said he was just a disgruntled employee. At one point, marketing arranged to have him suspended for two weeks without pay. It straightened him out... for a while, but the performance levels dropped dramatically afterwards. Nick was definitely sabotaging the company from within.

Katherine Stark was hired almost five years ago to convince him to go with the program. That failed miserably, now Jennifer was swinging the big bat, and would be sent downtown to 'eliminate' him... Nicholas was in her way... she would have no problem taking him down... With Nicholas gone, the profit margins would soar! But that wasn't enough for Jennifer; Steven said to her; *'take over the company...'* and to do that, she realized she would have to take over Katherine's job to get into the proper positioning, but first things first, Nick, and then Katherine and *then* the company. Her goals were just within her sight, she just had to reach out and take it by force.

Jennifer got right to work. This may take another month or two to learn the marketing protocols, but maybe a month or two more to learn the computer program language also. She would deal with the problem child once she got to the downtown office. She had no leverage on anyone there so she just needed a cover. She heard that an executive secretary was being transferred to the main office. She would use that job opening to get her foot in the back door.

Steven's prostrate cancer was making him sicker and weaker and he probably would not make it to the end of the year. As long as Steven Callahan was alive she had a hold on Hagen. Once Steven dies and the 'stock' is 'traded' she would have no leverage... Hagen and Theo could just fire her... done! This was a race against time... success or failure. It was all in her hands now! She did not come this far to go back to working the pole... too damn far! Nick was going down, and he was going down hard!

I wasn't worried about what was happening at the main office. I had Bonnie there as my eyes and ears and Tasha and Sterling as backup at the strip club. Yeah... Steven owned that place too and that's how he acquired the 'stock' on Hagen in the first place. Hagen and Theo, fortunately, had no idea.

(About Six Years Ago...At The Downtown Offices of Faber Data...)

212

The Tortured Soul Trilogy
(A Tortured Soul)
Chapter 46
(Welcome to the Jungle)

In a small business community, just outside of a quiet suburban neighborhood called 'Indy Park', is the office building where I work. The neighborhood is called Indy Park because it used to be an industrial park that was surrounded by brownstones. These were warehouses and business lofts before they were turned into condos and co-ops, much like Soho in New York City. There were still some businesses that called this place home, mostly law firms, production companies, financial offices and one data entry corporation. Our building, looks just like any other office building in the area. Twenty floors of office space made of brick, steel and glass. Depending on the time of day, there are people mulling around having coffee, people rushing to get somewhere else, people sneaking a cigarette, people coming to work, and people going home to their families. It's just an ordinary office building. It could be the one you work in, or your friend, or your relative... there's nothing special about this building, except that in this building, occupying about six floors, is Faber Data Corp. F.D.C. is a not a huge corporation. It only boasts a few hundred employees, not big by today's standards. Here, men and women go about their daily lives, working on computers, inputting data and processing information for other companies around the world. We also programmed the codes for web-based businesses. Not the kind of company that could be considered essential by any means. But with the DotCom revolution there was a lot of money to be made. Our biggest competitors are the companies who do their own data entry in house. We cater to those companies who 'farm' out their work. The entire firm is housed in two buildings, this one and the one downtown, which is considered to be corporate headquarters. What the company does is not really germane to this story, only the diverse group of people who happen to work here. Specifically, the people work on the third to ninth floors of this building. The people I work with...

My name is Nicholas Anderson.

I have been working for Faber Data Corp. for over twenty years. I started out here when I was 25 in data processing and never left. Some people think that I have no ambition... that I have no drive. It's not that... I like it here, I like what I do, and I'm comfortable where I am in life and in business. I don't ever want anything to ever happen to change that. The best laid plans of mice and men...

Today shouldn't have been different than any other day. I didn't expect it to be, I didn't want it to be... I got up about six thirty in the morning like I always do. I put on a kettle to boil, jumped in the shower and by the time I got out the hot water was ready for my morning tea. I opened my tea box and sifted through the many favors of tea I had assembled. This morning, I decided on a mix chamomile and green tea with a hint of ginger. I placed the bags in my mug, filled it with hot water and placed the saucer on top of the mug to let it steep while I went back to the bathroom to shave. I had to shave with two razors, an electric one to clean my face and a disposable to tighten up the edges around my beard. I grabbed a light brown mascara to touch up the stray gray hairs in my moustache. It's not that the gray hair bothered me it's just that for some reason they seemed to accumulate under my nostrils and it kinda looked like I always needed to wipe my nose. Not a good look... I've thought of just shaving it off and I have at times, but although it made me look younger, I've learned that the ladies like the beard. My ex-wife used to say that she liked the fact that it tickled the inside of her thighs... I kept it, just for that reason.

I sat at the breakfast nook, sipped my tea, while watching the morning news. The weatherman said it was going to be a dank and dreary morning. The traffic report said that there were major tie-ups on almost all the major highways. Only the weather report concerned me, I live ten blocks from work. It would take a major disaster for me to be late or miss work, that's not to say I won't use traffic as an excuse to show up late whenever I wanted to, just that it wasn't really a factor...

I went to work and it looked like the sun was coming out. Today might be a good day after all. I got in five minutes early, checked my in-box, and hung out with the guys at the water cooler talking about the events of the weekend. That's when Charles Hagen, co-owner of the company, entered with a young woman, about twenty years old. Hernandez, the manager of floor nine greeted him. "Mr. Hagen... what brings you to our office this morning?"

"I just wanted to stop by to introduce you to the new office floor manager..."

"So they finally found a replacement for old man Connors, I guess Hernandez will be glad he doesn't have to handle two floors anymore!" Bob said.

"Wow... It's the new guy's first day and he gets himself a hot new secretary..." Hernandez said aside to Hagen.

"Actually, Ms. Stark *is* the new office floor manager...." Hagen said.

"You can call me Katherine..." And she held out her hand to shake Hernandez's.

"You can call me 'embarrassed as all hell', but my real name is... Juan Hernandez... I'm in charge of nine"

"Hi, Ms Stark... I'm Nicholas but everyone calls me Nick... I'm not in charge of anything..."

"A pleasure to meet you... Nick..." She shook my hand, she had a very nice handshake, just not the type of a handshake of someone in charge; it was... friendlier.

"If you ever need help with anything... just ask..." Hernandez said.

"Actually, I'm here to help you..." Katherine replied. Katherine must have sensed my apprehension. "You don't think I can help... Nick? Or is it that I'm too young to know what I'm doing?"

"With all due respect Ms. Stark, I have a daughter about your age, but I have no problem whatsoever taking constructive criticism..." Nick said.

"I'll try not to be too critical..."

"I'll try to be more open minded..." I replied.

Mr. Hagen then took Ms. Stark to meet the other employees. As they walked off Hagen leaned over and whispered in Katherine's ear. "Do yourself a favor and avoid Bob at all costs!" Katherine nodded and Hagen continued to give her the nickel tour.

John cornered us later at the water cooler... "What do you think of her?"

"I like her; she seems to have a good heart…"

"…Yeah! But would you bang her?"

"If I were 20 years younger… I'd tap that ass!" Bob said and laughed.

"So Nick… what's your opinion on the new girl?"

"You mean our new *boss*…? I just met her like you did, but she seems nice enough…"

"Please, we all know that she only got this job because she's built like a hot cheerleader gone wild; I'm surprised she didn't wear her knee-pads to work today."

"You know… my daughter had to put up with that same shit when she got promoted at her job, are you saying my daughter had to give head to get ahead?"

"Ah come on Nick… we're not talking about your daughter here… man!" John answered.

"Yeah, but Katherine is somebody's daughter… how about giving her a chance before you start ruining her reputation…"

"Okay… okay… we'll cut her a break for now, but what if she did bang the boss to get this position?"

"Then she won't last very long… because if being on your back got you anywhere in this company… *you* would be the chairman of the board by now!" John laughed an '*I'm gonna get you for that*!' laugh.

"Okay Nick… now that you've banged the drum for women's rights… what do you really think of her?"

"She's hot, but women like her don't give guys like me a shot… besides at my age, *any* woman under 30… is jailbait to me…."

I didn't know it at the time that the number 30 would be so very prophetic in my life. I tossed my empty water cup in the trash when I heard Katherine's voice behind me.

"Nick… May I speak to you for a moment?"

The water cooler club dispersed. "Absolutely Ms. Stark… what can I do for you… or should I say; 'What would you like to do for me?' After all, you did say you were here to help…"

Katherine smiled. "May I see you in my office…? I want to go over the new marketing plan with you, so I can get your opinions…"

216

"Oh, you can have my opinion now if you wish…"

"Really…?"

"Sure… the new marketing plan stinks!"

"You've already *seen* the new marketing plan?"

"No… but I know our marketing department… and they couldn't come up with a good idea if it bit them on the ass…"

"You *did* say you would be more open-minded didn't you?"

"To *you*, yes; to marketing… *no*…"

"What makes you so sure their plan won't work?"

"Our marketing department tries too hard to make 'one size fit all' and real life doesn't work that way… our clientele doesn't fall for catch phrases only results… And results must be tailor fit to the needs of the individual client…

"Okay… I'll tell you what… step into my office and let me go over the new plans with you… try to be open minded… and we'll see what we can do to 'make it fit'…"

"Sure, but is it okay if we leave your office door open?"

"Why?"

"Because the guys who work here are a bunch of perverted, male chauvinistic pigs… and the last thing you need right now… is a lot of idle office gossip…"

"…And what about *your* reputation…?"

"Are you kidding…? Me? Locked in an office with a beautiful young woman…? *Hell*… I'd start *that* rumor myself!"

"Wow! That was brutally honest of you…"

"That's who I am… you'll never have to worry about what I'll say behind your back, because I have no problem saying it to your face!" I followed Katherine back to Connors old office.

"I want to thank you Nick…"

"For what…?"

"For what you said about me at the water cooler…"

"You *heard* that?"

"Yes… But it's okay… I'm not afraid of what's said behind my back…"

"You heard *all* of what I said?"

Katherine shook her head no; Nick breathed a sigh of relief. Katherine led Nick into her new office. "…But I do find it very hard to believe that women like me don't give guys like you a shot!"

"Oh dear... I'm gonna have to learn to use my inside voice!"

"If you ever need 'privacy'... check to see my door is closed... my office is virtually soundproof!"

We stepped inside and Katherine spent the rest of the day trying to 'sell' me the new marketing protocols. I wasn't buying. I've been here too long to go along with any of the new protocols and the new computer programming required to implement those protocols. I was getting a little tired of explaining myself to Katherine, and she became frustrated that I wouldn't just go along with the program. We were at an impasse. She had a job to do and I knew you couldn't get there from here. I like Katherine; she has a youthful exuberance I haven't seen around here in a long while. She was ready to conquer the world and it didn't hurt that she was really easy on the eyes.

Although she wasn't the only woman her age working here, she wasn't very popular with the other girls. She tried to be friendly and outgoing with them but they more tolerated her than liked her. Sure, they would have lunch with her or have a 'girl's night out' on occasion but actually, deep down, they despised her... I noticed that women tend to hate the head bitch in charge; it wasn't any fault of Katherine's. It's just the way some women are. My office was no exception. Even the women who didn't work with her directly had a problem with her. They were nice to her to her face but only because she was a boss, but when her back was turned that's when the claws came out. Katherine wasn't stupid, she knew the deal but opted to keep the peace rather than call anyone out, unless it was absolutely necessary. Katherine was fair, but you did *not* want to get on her bad side. Katherine did exactly what I expected she was gonna do... She was a bull in a china shop... Full of vim and vigor... piss and vinegar... she thought that she could single handedly save the company... and why shouldn't she? After all, she was 'the golden child' hired to do just that! Don't get me wrong... she wasn't unorganized or head strong or pushy... she had just what the company needed, a fresh outlook... It was my opinion that she was just pointed in the wrong direction. It wasn't my job to pull her reins... that's way too much work... I would just let her do whatever she wanted to do and eventually she would just burn herself out. Sooner or later she would settle down and resign herself to a life of drudgery and apathy, just like the rest of us... That didn't work out at all... Every time we thought she was about to run out of steam... go with the program... corporate or marketing would light a new fire under her ass and she was off to the races again... It would be later that I would realize that her need to please others would come back to bite her on the ass... Working for and with Katherine was a cross between a rollercoaster and a bucking bronco... You would line up for hours to get on, but then you would get thrown off after about 7 seconds. I tried hard not to imagine what she would be like in bed... That failed miserably also... This kid was at least 20 years my junior... I had a daughter her age for crying out loud! But it wasn't easy not to think of her in *that* way. She was 25 when she started here; I was 44... an intimate relationship would have to be just a fantasy only. There is a line that I just don't cross. But then one day, something happened, something I hadn't counted on...

Katherine wasn't the only woman working for Faber Data Corp, but at 25 she was the youngest female executive the company ever had. At 26, she was still the youngest executive, by the time she was 28, she was just another employee. There was no longer anything particularly special about her. It wasn't until the time she reached 30 and had five years with the company, that I took notice of her. In my opinion, she was no longer a child star... she was a young adult, and I could comfortably think of her as a desirable young woman and not just a young girl... When Katherine turned 30... It was if someone turned on a light, I no longer saw her as a child... she became a young vivacious woman. She had become desirable to me... Oh... I've had sex with other women before and since she arrived, but for some reason, Katherine affected me differently. I wanted her, more than any other woman I knew or had known. At first I thought at 55, I was going through male menopause... my *mid-life crisis*, but then I decided, what the hell, if she gave me a shot I was gonna take it!

Over the last five years at Faber Data Corp, Katherine's weight fluctuated, at times she would gain 25 – 30 lbs and then she would diet back down to a size 2. There was a time that everyone thought she was pregnant but she wasn't... as far as anyone knew... I started to notice a pattern to her weight gain. If she was happy and content in her life, she would lose weight and keep it off. If she was stressed for an extended period of time, the pounds added on. She carried the weight of the entire floor on her shoulders. It's what eventually gave old man Connors a heart attack and he had to take an early retirement. Katherine's stress manifested itself by her gaining weight, but I must admit; whether she was thin or heavy, she was one hot looking woman. I would have bet the rent that it was the stress of fighting to accomplish the needs of this job was causing her weight problem. I discovered later, it was only a minor contributor...

Bob called me over. "Nick, Katherine would like to see you in her office..."

"Okay... tell her I'll be there in a moment..." I finished handing out the days files and entered Katherine's office. "Hey Ms. Stark... what can I do for you?"

"I just need your help while I rearrange my office equipment, can you to hand me that printer cable so I can plug it into my computer?"

"So you're finally getting yourself settled in to your office?"

"I just can't function properly with this layout... and you know how much women just *love* to redecorate!"

Nick laughed. She pulled out her chair and began to kneel down. "Hey! Let me do that for you..."

"It's okay... I've got it..." And she shimmied under the desk and stuck her hand out from under the desk. "Hand me the cable..." As I stepped toward the desk to grab the cable, I noticed the compromising situation Katherine was in. Because of her weight fluctuations, sometimes her clothes didn't fit quite right. Her ass was up in the air and her belt less pants had slid down, revealing the top of her pale blue thong and her voluptuous ass was half out. But it wasn't that that caught my attention as much as the black and blue bruise on her alabaster hips. They looked like belt strap marks. It was obvious to me she had been beaten. "Umm hello...? Hand me the cable..." I passed the cable to her. "Is it in?" She asked.

If I had a nickel...! "Yes... the printer is on..." She shimmied out from under the desk and then turned to the fax machine behind her. Surely she must know her ass was half exposed to me. She pulled up her pants and when she turned around I had already turned my back away from her...

"I'm so sorry! Did I just 'moon' you?"

"Huh?" I turned back to her. "Ah...No... was there anything else you needed?"

"Yes... I want to go over the new download protocols with you and I need to print them out when we're finished..."

"I'm on it!"

That night I thought of Katherine and spanked off like a teenager... although the bruises she had concerned me a bit.

The Tortured Soul Trilogy
(A Tortured Soul)
Chapter 47
(Owner of A Lonely Heart)

The next afternoon at work, Nick is rewriting the marketing codes to fit company protocols as he's done in the past to get his work finished for the next day. Katherine walked past Nick's desk to speak with Wilson and as she leans forward to speak to him; her ass is in Nick's direct view. Nick tries not to stare until he looks over and notices that she is fondling her ass gently and slowly. Nick thinks that she he is probably rubbing the area where her bruises are healing. As Anderson wipes the sweat of his brow, Katherine turns and came over to him.

"Hi Nick…"

"Hi Katherine…"

"You can call me Kitty, all my friends do…"

"I… ah… don't think I should, at least not at work… so what's going on?'

"Same old, same old… Listen, I'm gonna need the 'M' Tech files on my desk as soon as you're done with them… I really need it…"

Nick begins to explain how the files have to be prepared for coding but Katherine isn't listening; she's fantasizing making sweet passionate love to Nick on top of his desk. "*Give me! Right there… give it to me hard! I want it*!" she moaned in her fantasy.

"…I know you do… I'll make sure you get it…" Nick said.

"*What…?*" Katherine replied with a stunned tone in her voice as if she was caught unaware.

"I said... know how much you need it and I'll make sure you get it… Is something wrong?'

"Oh… No… just make sure I get it on my desk…as soon as possible…" Katherine again fantasizes being bent over Nick's desk with her skirt above her waist as he tears off her panties and then he holds her wrists behind her while making rough love to her.

"I'm all over it…" I said.

"Huh... *What*?" Katherine was getting hot and bothered.

"Katherine...? Are you sure everything is alright?"

"Oh... yes... it's just that... I'm a little distracted today... that's all!"

"Okay! I'll get this file to you as soon as I'm finished with it..."

Katherine walked away but she tripped slightly and caught herself. Okay... I knew the signs, the look, the expressions the stolen glances. I was like a shark that smelled blood in the water. I could tell Katherine was getting 'in' to me... All I had to do was encourage her a bit and I was sure I was going to get this lady in bed, and there is nothing that is gonna stop me... that is, until I came to work one Monday morning.... There are lines that I still don't cross. Katherine was at her desk one day and all the office hens were surrounding her desk, except the one or two girls who couldn't stand her.

"Hey Wilson... what's all the commotion about? Did Katherine get a promotion or something?"

"Sort of... Her fiancé proposed..."

"I didn't know she had a fiancé..."

"Nobody knew..."

"I wonder why she kept it a secret."

"Beats the hell outta me..."

"Do you know who the guy is?"

"Nope... but whoever is tapping that ass... is one lucky son of bitch! Too bad he's gonna marry her..."

"Why would you say that Bob...?" I quickly realized that I was gonna be sorry I asked.

"*Please*... you know the moment you put that ring on a woman's finger, you can't put your dick in her mouth anymore..."

"Bob... can I ask you a question?"

"Sure Nick..."

"Why the fuck do I even talk to you?"

"Yeah right! 'Mister Politically Correct'... like you never thought about tea bagging her..."

I walked away from Bob. (Yeah, I have but I wouldn't say it out loud... *especially* if her office door is open!) I walked right into the midst of the cackle club meeting. "Congratulations Katherine..." And I kissed her cheek.

"Thanks Nick!"

She showed me the ring; the stone was almost two carats. "Wow… that's some piece of the rock you got there… so when are you two tying the knot?"

Katherine looked surprised by my question. "*What…?*"

"You know… getting *married…?*"

"*Oh…!* Well we haven't decided on a date yet… we're waiting until his career takes off…"

"Really? What does he do?"

"He's a rapper…" Anna-Marie chimed in

"He wraps gifts?" I asked.

"No silly he's a *Hip Hop* Rapper!"

"Oh yeah! That's my favorite kind of music… I have all the CD's… Snoopy Diggetty Dog… Extreme Breakfast Biscuit… Boogaloo Shrimp and the Cool Em-Effer's…"

"Not funny Nick…" Katherine said dryly.

"Sorry Katherine… So what's your fiancé's 'handle'?"

"*The Plain White Rapper*" said Anna-Marie jokingly.

"His *name* is Johnny 'Precious'…"

I raised my eyebrow and snapped my fingers like a gay man and lisped. "His name is *Johnny Precious…?*"

"All *right…!* Isn't it time everyone got back to work?"

They all cleared out of her office. I lagged behind… "Sorry Katherine… but I'm really happy for you…"

"…Really?"

"*Word to your mother!*"

"Get out!"

After work I stopped by the bar to get a drink before walking home. I was halfway through my '7&7' when a young lady approached me. She wasn't a regular. I had never seen her there before. She smiled and leaned a little too close to whisper to me.

"Hey honey… you need a date for tonight?"

"How old are you?"

"I'm 22!"

"*Please…!* I have gray hairs in my moustache older than you." I shook my head no.

"I can make you feel good… real good"

(This chick don't take no for an answer.) "Yeah... for about a five minutes... look little girl, my wife has been making me feel good since *before* you were born. At my age, I don't need a woman who puts out; I need a woman who puts *up*... *Now*... what have you got...?" This chick looked at me, turned and left to wait at the bar for the next man to walk in. "Yeah... that's what I thought...!"

"Anderson...?" I turned to see Katherine had just walked in the bar.

"Hey Katherine...? What are you doing in here?"

"I just came in to hang out for a while, have a few before going on home..."

"Please... sit with me... give the lady whatever she wants, Jimmy." I said to the bartender.

"No it's okay..." she replied and she looked around for a place to sit.

"Come on... we work all day together... we can spend a little time together... just as long as we don't talk about work..."

"Okay... I guess I can sit with you..."

"I feel so special!"

"No! I didn't mean it that way..." Katherine laughed.

"It's okay... relax... I'd ask you how your day was but, I already know; so what else is going on in your own little corner of the world?" We talked and drank for a while and we really enjoyed our time together. After a while I stopped to check my watch. "Oh look at the time! I gotta go home and get some rest. I can't be late for work tomorrow... My boss will get pissed!"

"She sounds like a real bitch!"

"Actually, she's a sweetheart! I will *see you* in the morning..." I leaned in to kiss her on the cheek, but she turned into it and kissed me on the lips. She pulled back but not so quickly.

"I'm sorry...! I didn't mean to..." Katherine averted her eyes.

"Don't be... That was nice! I'll see you in the morning!" I said. I kissed her on the cheek, paid the bar tab, and exited. The bar chick walked over to Katherine.

"You're *good* honey... he didn't even give me the time of day!"

"*I'm his boss*!" She said in a commanding tone.

"You sure are honey...! You sure are...!" Katherine finished her drink and left. The bar chick sipped her drink and thought to herself; "Girl...! If I wasn't straight, *I would* be *your* bitch any day!"

The Tortured Soul Trilogy
(A Tortured Soul)
Chapter 48
(Message In A Bottle)

Katherine and her fiancé, Johnny, relationship was a roller coaster at best. When he was in town, her weight was up; when he was 'on tour' she would drop back down to a size two. I don't know about anybody else, but I preferred Katherine thin and happy than fat and miserable.

"I see you're your fiancé is back in town..."

"How can you tell?"

"You gained some weight..."

Katherine crossed her arms in front of her to hide her girth. "What? What are you talking about?"

"When your fiancé is in town you get stressed when you stress... you overeat... when you overeat...."

"Excuse me? You don't know me like that!"

"I know you better than you think! But you are right; my comment was totally out of line and uncalled for... I'm sorry..."

"Get out of my office..."

I came in to work the next day and I was called into Katherine's office again. "Katherine... if this is about yesterday, I just wanna apologize..."

"No... this isn't about yesterday, consider it forgotten..."

"Okay..."

"I need you and Bob to take a conference call with L.A. this afternoon, it's about the new program protocols for the Bensen account... I need you two to go over them with a fine tooth comb and work out any glitches in the system before we present it..."

"What time this afternoon?"

"I'm not sure, but I need you two in the office when the call comes in, so if you don't mind, I'll need you to order lunch in today..."

"No problem... you want me to order in for you too?"

"No thank you... I'm gonna skip lunch today..."

"Okay... I'll let Bob know..." I began to exit her office.

"Please close the door behind you... I don't want to be disturbed today..." She said.

"As you wish..." I closed the door behind me and placed her "*Do not disturb – On a conference call*" sign on her door. I had heard her quietly sob as I closed the door. Normally when Katherine spoke to me, she would look me straight in the eye, she was all business. Today she couldn't make eye contact. Her eyes darted around the room as if she couldn't focus on one place. She would avert her eyes if she did look at me and noticed that I was looking at her. That's when I realized... her fiancé wasn't just beating her; he was abusing her...

Katherine started missing work for a week or two at a time. Being in upper management, she had a more lenient absentee policy than the rest of us. The excuse was either it was "that time of the month" or she was out of town with her boyfriends' tour. When she came back to work, she was skittish and jumpy. I also noticed that her style of dressing changed. She wore more pants, long sleeves and high collars after Johnny returned from one of his 'tours'. Normally she would show more skin when she was thin. I knew she was dressing to hide the bruises. She was overeating to hide her shame. Johnny's beatings were escalating. Katherine and Johnny had been together for almost three years. It was obvious to me that he didn't have the sense or maturity to handle a relationship with an older woman. So, the only way he knew how to control her was to abuse her. He probably started out by verbally abusing her and when he saw she didn't listen or if she stood up for herself, he turned to physical abuse. He wasn't working a regular job and she was paying all his bills... She was footing all his expenses and she did for him by depriving herself. This probably made him feel like less of a man so he justified 'pimp slapping' her to make himself feel like a 'thug', when he was really just only a punk. I know he was just taking advantage of her, but that's just my opinion and nobody asked me. One day Johnny came by the job to pick her up, and when I say he came to pick her up, I mean he waited outside so she could drive him to a gig in New Jersey. He was already in her car when she came out. I could see that when she got into the car, he raised his hand to her and she cowered behind the wheel. I had never seen Katherine cower... I didn't like it. I really wish I could get my hands on that little son of a bitch... but it really wasn't my place. Katherine had to decide for herself how much she would put up with and when she should put a stop to it... Katherine drove off with him.

- - -

One day I just came into her office with a cup of tea. "What do you want Nick?" She avoided any eye contact.

"I brought you some chamomile tea..."

"I don't want any tea... thank you..."

"Okay... I'll just leave it here in case you change your mind... it will help soothe your nerves..."

"What makes you think I need to have my nerves soothed?"

"Are you kidding? Your shoulders are hunched over your ears!" I walked behind her and put my hands on her shoulders.

"What are you doing?"

"Trust me..." I began to rub her shoulders, she resisted and squirmed at first but then she gave in to my strong hands and gentile touch. She cooed and moaned gently.

"Oh... I'm getting goose bumps..."

"Have a sip of tea while it's still hot..." She reached for the tea I had left on the opposite edge on the desk. This gave me the opportunity to slide my hands onto her back and work her shoulder blades around her bra strap. He cooed and moaned again. Katherine was almost lying face down on her desk by now. It was hard not to fantasize about her in this position. Her ass was so... perfect! She was now totally receptive to my touch. I kneaded her back like bread dough. I was a little worried that I might aggravate any bruising she might have but she was wearing a sleeveless top so I knew that the bruising was minimal.

"Ohh... that feels so good..."

Okay... no bruises or tenderness here, so I concentrated more on her neck and shoulders.

"Would you like me to close the door so you two can have some privacy?"

"No Bob, leave it open... thank you..." I said.

Katherine ignored him and purred. After I was finished, Katherine was fully relaxed. I left her office. "Thank you Nick... for the tea... and the back rub..."

"Anytime Katherine..." And I closed the door behind me to give her some privacy... Lisa walked up to me.

"So... Nick, are those back rubs for Katherine only or can anyone get one?"

"Your desk...? Or mine...? Oh... Wait...!" I looked over to Bob's at his desk, he was hunched over his keyboard, rubbing his neck and shoulders and typing. "We *are* talking about *you* right?" Lisa laughed and led me back to her desk while all the men in the office watched in quiet amazement, but I knew what they were all thinking.

- - -

Nick was working on the rewrites of the company codes at his desk as Katherine was watching him work while standing behind his chair. One set of codes began to crash and he had a big problem getting it to flow into the system. He tried a few times but the codes wouldn't enter properly and the computer kept highlighting 'error – error". He tried two more times and 'fatal error' popped up. Nick threw his hands up, and was totally frustrated by now.

"Here... Let me..." Katherine placed her left hand on Nick's back and leaned over his right shoulder to reach the mouse. She was now halfway leaning on his back and reaching over him as she innocently cut and pasted the codes to correct the problem. Her left breast was full on his back and her right would on occasion touch his ear as she maneuvered the mouse on the pad... He could smell the scent of baby powder on her breasts... she leaned a little forward. He closed his eyes, for he dared not to glance. The same weight loss that made her skirts a little loose also made her blouses ill-fitting at times. Her blouse had drifted away from her right breast and her exposed nipple was in full view just under her bra. It was all he could do... not to turn his eyes to his right to get a better look. It felt like an eternity before she leaned back to be standing behind him again. "That should do it!"

"Thank you Katherine... I believe that did it..." (It sure did it for me...)

"Anytime Nick..." And she turned to return to her office. Nick took out his handkerchief and wiped the sweat off his brow. Bob came by and dropped a file on Nick's desk.

"Please tell me you saw the 'promised land'...!"

"Bob? What the hell are you taking about?" I didn't need to feed into his fantasies.

Bob sipped his coffee and walked away. "I would have given a month's salary..."

(A Tortured Soul)
Chapter 49
(Sharp Dressed Man)

One day Katherine invited everyone to come after work to hear her boyfriend do a gig at a local club. By this time everybody knew what was going on and really weren't interested in supporting Johnny. I decided to go... to support Katherine. I came to work dressed in a nice suit, I had never been to one of these things, but I do remember that most clubs have a dress code. I didn't want to embarrass Katherine.

"Hey Nick... nice suit...! Do you have a hot date tonight...? Or a funeral...?"

"Fuck you Tommy!"

Katherine stepped out of her office. "Hey Nick... *Nice suit*!"

"Why thank you Katherine... but don't be so impressed... under all this high fashion, I'm wearing torn underwear!" Katherine laughed and put her hand on my chest... and lingered a bit. Not enough to be inappropriate... but long enough to get my attention and make me a little... anxious... After work, Katherine asked me how I was getting to the club. I told her I was gonna take a cab. She offered to drive me there. "Don't you have to pick up Johnny *'The Plain White Rapper'*...?"

She laughed and put her hand on my chest again... and again she lingered a bit. "He's already at the club doing a sound check... and don't you dare call him that to his face when I introduce you to him!" We got in her car and drove off. This otta be interesting... We arrived at what was nothing more than a sports bar with a small stage complete with stripper a pole. The place was already packed with kids half my age. There was barely enough room to breathe in there.

"Wow... this is a great turn out..."

"Yeah!" Katherine said as she checked out the crowd.

"So... you come here often?"

"This is the first time I've ever been here..."

"Are you sure? I mean doesn't that stripper pole look a little familiar to you?"

"What? I can't hear you..."

I leaned into her ear. I rethought my prior statement as too racy to repeat. "So you have no idea why everyone is staring at me?"

"Oh... it's probably because they think you're the owner... or a vice cop!"

"*Funny*! Don't quit your day job!" The place was too loud, too smoky and we were packed in like sardines. I was over dressed and I wasn't having a good time. That is, until I realized that Katherine was pressed tight against me. This time both her hands were on my chest but she was focused on the stage. She was very anxious. "Don't worry! I'm sure your boyfriend will rock the house!"

"What?" she asked never taking her eyes off the stage.

I leaned in again. I could smell the delicate fragrance of her hair even in that smoke filled room. I inhaled her scent deeply. "I said..." Then the music stopped and the DJ announced Katherine's boyfriend onto the stage... the crowd was at best, apathetic. Then this kid came out to the stage to a jeering crowd. "Is that him?"

"Yes...! That's Johnny."

"How old is this kid? Is he old enough to even be in a bar?"

Katherine tapped my chest with her open hand. "Don't be so mean... he's gonna be twenty four next June..."

"He's ...*gonna*... be twenty four...?" Katherine was almost ten years older than him. I never thought of her being a cougar.

"Shhh... the show's gonna start." The lights went on and the kid started his set. All I heard was a string of profanities, and *then* he got raunchy. The music was too loud and the words were unintelligible and off beat. The crowd reacted to the DJ's mix more than his rap... then suddenly he just stopped rapping. I don't know why... it wasn't like anyone could understand what he said anyway. That's when I realized he got flustered and forgot his words... The crowd began to boo and jeer him... he left the stage under a hail of flying beer bottles. I don't know rap music but I know what I like and it was obvious I wasn't the only one that didn't like this shit. I turned to look at Katherine. She was very dismayed.

"I take it you never heard him perform before?" No response. "Katherine?" ...Still no response; by now she had a look of fear on her face... "Katherine? Are you okay?" She looked at me as if she had forgotten I was there.

"I have to leave... now!" She turned and began to push her way out of the angry mob in the club. The DJ began to spin again and the crowd slowly settled back into party mode. I followed Katherine out. Katherine went straight to her car, again forgetting I was still with her.

"Katherine... what's wrong?"

"I'm gonna drop you off at the job okay?"

"Okay...?" I barely got into the car before she peeled out of the parking lot. We didn't speak a word the entire time back. I got out of the car and said goodbye.

"Oh yeah... goodbye... I'll see you tomorrow..." And she peeled off. I guess I'll find out what that was about tomorrow.

Katherine called in sick the next morning and was out for almost two weeks. Whenever Katherine was gone M.I.A. nobody knew where she was or what had happened to her... Okay... nobody said out loud where they thought she was or what happened to her. When she finally showed up to work, she was at least 10lbs heavier than when we saw her last. She was nervous and squirrelly and couldn't look anyone in the eye. All the men just knew she was ashamed about her weight gain, all the women knew she was having problems trying to keep up in the corporate world. Although, they're both kinda right, I knew exactly what all this shit was all about... I decided not to push it. I knew that little shit took his frustrations out on her. A month after the big fiasco, conversation between Katherine and I was limited to office banter only... she was still skittish and evasive.

I walked by her office and she was on the phone, leaning on her hand on her desk. I noticed that the engagement ring on her finger had a smaller diamond than before. She was busy with the Lincoln-Hanna files and I knew she wasn't coming out of that office for a few days. Another symptom of her problems was she would become introverted and immerse herself into her work,

234

which made her bosses happy; and her co-workers were happy that she was so busy with her own problems that she would basically leave them alone. I was gonna let her have her space. Now is not the time or place to question her about it. It took about two weeks for Katherine to act more like herself although she would still avert her eyes from time to time. She didn't realize that quirk made people nervous. People just don't trust anybody that won't look you square in the eye when they talk to you. They think you're lying to them or hiding something.

"Nick?"

"Yes Katherine?"

"Could you please go over the new codec's to see if they're correct and get them back to me ASAP?"

"You got it..." As she handed me the files, her hand entered mine. I looked at her ring and she looked at me then focused on her hand. She pulled her hand away and put it on her hip. "Are you all right?"

"I'm fine... just get these codec's back to me as soon as you can... I need to call the corrected codes in to marketing..."

"I'm all over it..." Katherine went back into her office and I went to get Lisa to help me go over the HTML codes line by line... We had the corrected codes back on Katherine's desk before lunch. Katherine came to my desk with the file in hand. "Is everything okay with the corrections...?" I asked her.

"The codes are fine... Thank you... but I don't remember me telling you to get Lisa to help you with these..."

"Lisa is the best person in this office when it comes to HTML codes... without her help it would have taken two or three days to check all those codes..."

"Then you should have taken two or three days... not spend the whole morning with Lisa..."

"Excuse me? Aren't we getting a little possessive about the employees?"

"*What*?" Katherine was a bit put off by my remark.

"Lisa works here just like anyone else and I can use her skills and expertise just like anyone else to get the job done... she is not *your* personal assistant..." I looked into Katherine's eyes. She stared at me. Then it hit me. "Wait a minute... this *isn't* about

Lisa..." Katherine averted her eyes. "This is about *me*...? Are you getting possessive over *me*?"

Katherine cut her eyes back at me. "What...? I don't know what you're talking about..."

"You know 'what'...! You're engaged... and Lisa is a happily married woman... there is no need for you to be jealous..."

"I am *not* jealous! And yes I am engaged..."

"...Speaking of which... what the hell happened to your engagement ring? Did it shrink in the wash?"

"That's none of your damn business!" It was at this point that we were nose to nose when we realized that this conversation was in center stage, although everyone went about their business and acted as if they didn't notice... Katherine crossed her arms, dropped her head and went back into her office and closed her door behind her.

(Oh hell no... I did my best to avoid this confrontation... but she brought it to me... and I'm still hot and bothered about it!) I went into her office and closed the door behind me.

"Get out!" she barked at me.

"Blow it out your *ass* Katherine..."

Her jaw dropped. "How *dare* you!" She looked at the open blinds. She was totally shocked and embarrassed by my comment.

"They can see us but we both know no one can hear us in here... Now! I've known you now for almost seven years... something is wrong... talk to me... talk to somebody... but talk about it!

"GET... *OUT*!"

I closed the blinds, sat down in the chair across from her and crossed my legs. Katherine just looked at me. I threw my hands up. "I'm waiting...and I finished all of my corrections so *I* have *all* day!"

Katherine settled into her chair and fondled the ring. "I gave Johnny the ring back because he needed money for his demo... and this is the replacement until I get mine back..." I knew Johnny didn't pay for a replacement ring. She must have bought it to avoid being embarrassed and I called her out on it. Tears started to well in her eyes. I uncrossed my legs and got up.

Katherine jumped out of her chair. "I can't believe this... you got me to open up and you're just gonna walk out on me? Where do you think you're going?"

"To lunch... join me..."

"What?"

I stepped behind her and took her jacket off the back of her chair; put it over her shoulders and I escorted her out the door. "This is not the place to talk about this..." As we exited the building I asked Katherine. "So...? Pepperoni pizza...? Extra cheese...?" Katherine began to cry on Nick's shoulder. "O... *kay*... we don't *have* to have pizza..." Katherine cried and laughed. I hugged her. "Come on... I know of a nice out of the way place... that no one who works here knows about... we can talk there... privately." I put my arm around Katherine and she nestled into my chest. I walked with her to small hole-in-the-wall bistro a few blocks away.

"Wow! This is nice... what is this place?"

"It's a neighborhood coffee house... they have poetry readings and jazz sessions in the afternoon... and some really nice biscotti... it's a real bohemian, hippy dippy kind of a place..."

"What's it called?"

"The "C" Cup..."

Katherine looked at me, glanced down at herself, and crossed her arms nervously. "Nice... but how do you know about it?"

"Duh! I live in the neighborhood!" I sat down at table and Katherine sat across from me.

"If you live so close to the job, how come you've never invited me over to your place?"

"Double Duh! We work together! People are gonna talk about us too much on the job as it is..."

"Why would they talk about us?"

"*Deet di di*! We just had a lover's quarrel on the floor and walked out together..."

"It wasn't a *lover's* quarrel..."

"I know that... and you know that..."

The waitress came over with a large cup of chamomile sat it in front of me and turned to Katherine.

"...And what would you like Luv?"

"I'll have the same thank you…"

"Coming right up…"

"I guess I don't have to ask you if you come here often…" Katherine said while checking the place out.

"Good, cause that pick-up line doesn't work on me… unless I'm drunk…" The waitress returned with Katherine's tea and a plate of biscotti… I reached for one.

"She seems to know what you like…"

"You know you *really* need to work on your jealousy issues."

"I don't *have* jealousy issues…"

"*Right*! You were jealous of me working with Lisa and you even had that look on your face when I worked with Maggie last week, and she's a grandmother!"

"I didn't like the way that old cougar undressed you with her eyes." She said; I almost choked; Katherine laughed and took some biscotti. "I know Maggie would have no problem whatsoever taking her teeth out for you and giving you a 'gummy bear'…!"

"Oh no! You didn't go there!" Nick said.

Katherine sampled the biscotti. "Hey these are quite good…

"Thanks!'

"Why are you saying 'thanks'? You didn't make them!" and Katherine sipped her tea. "Say… doesn't this tea come with a back rub?"

"No… here they only come with biscotti…" Katherine and I spoke for over two hours… It was nice. I like Katherine. I don't like it when she's unhappy. I just wish there was more I could do to help her. "Well… we better get back to work…you still have to call in those corrections…"

"The corrections aren't due until next week…"

"That's why you wanted me to take a couple of days… you needed to stall…" Katherine nodded yes. "Well, we should still go back to keep the gossip down to a minimum, besides I think my boss would be upset if I came back late from lunch…"

"The 'boss' doesn't mind… but…"

"…But what?"

"Just don't let me catch you pulling this shit with Lisa... or Maggie... or even Mandy here... I can see why they call this place The "C" cup..."

"Oh yeah... no jealousy issues here! Nope, not a one...! And by the way the 'C' stands for coffee..."

"*Sure* it does...! But I don't see any flat-chested women in here serving any..."

"It's no 'Hooter's'... but it'll do in a pinch..."

Katherine closed her jacket and crossed her arms. "Don't get any ideas about pinching these 'hooters'..."

I laughed. We sipped tea... ordered dinner and checked out a few of the spoken word poets. We left out of there a little after seven. "I'll walk you back to your car."

"How about I walk you home instead? I would love to see your place..." She said.

"I don't think that's a good idea..."

"You still worried about what everyone might say?

"Not really... Not anymore!"

"Oh I'm sorry; I should have realized... you mentioned you have a daughter... You're married..." she said with a touch of disappointment.

"Divorced from my first wife, my second wife passed away about two years before you came to work for F.D.C."

"I'm sorry, I didn't know..." she said apologetically.

"Yeah... there's a lot we don't know about each other... you would think that after seven years... oh well, water under the bridge Katherine..."

"Nick... when we're not at work, you can call me Kitty..."

I laughed. "No... I don't think I can..."

Katherine purred. "Try!" I learned a lot about Katherine during our time at the 'C' cup. She was very open and straightforward and honest. She had no problem telling me about herself and what she was going through. This chick really needs a girlfriend, I said to myself, but I was happy to be there for her. Katherine was in a bad relationship with her fiancée, she was paying all his bills and financing his doubtful rap career. I found out she even paid for her own engagement ring! She would do without, while pouring all her hard earned money into this idiot's dreams. Plus the guy was at least ten years her junior! '*Poor kid*!' I thought, this guy is using her for all she's got... *and* he gets to have crazy sex with her! Damn! Some guys have all the luck! Don't get me wrong, Katherine isn't drop dead gorgeous, actually she's kind of plain, but you could tell she had an athletic build from when she was younger. She probably played tennis or beach volleyball in college. She had amazing legs and a tight round ass. She had nice perky breasts, not big, but they looked great in a sweater. For me, she looked her sexiest when she wore her eyeglasses and wore her hair in a ponytail or a tight bun. I have a 'thing' for authoritative women.

Author's Note

When Nick was about nine years old, he was sexually molested by an 17 year old co-ed who was hired to baby sit him and his four year old sister while his single mom worked two jobs. He was sleeping and had a 'wet dream'. She gave him a bath and was amazed by his size and girth. The abuse continued for almost three years. One day, she just disappeared. Nick only remembers that she happened to wear glasses and had a ponytail.

- - -

I was sitting at my desk going over the new computer codes, when I heard Katherine say my name. I looked up and she was standing over me. She was wearing a tight white knit sweater and a sports bra. The air conditioning was on and her nipples were hard. They were hard and tight like raisins. I could just barely see her areola through the fabric of her bra; they were *just* the right size. I averted my eyes. "What can I do for you Ms. Stark?"

Katherine looked around the office. "Will you at least call me Katherine?

"Okay... Katherine..."

"Can I see you in my office for a moment?"

"Sure, give me a minute and I'll be right with you..."

"I'll wait... I want you to walk with me..."

"Okay... would you like to borrow my jacket?"

"Why?"

I averted my eyes down and away. "You... *look... cold...*"

Katherine looked down and noticed that she was fully protruding; she crossed her arms and spoke to me curtly... "I'll see you in my office in five minutes..." She walked away slowly with her arms crossed; I needed the five minutes to adjust my crotch before I followed her into her office, I didn't want the whole office to see she gave me a hard-on. "Close the door behind you..." She had put her jacket on.

"I'd rather leave it open..."

"Close it! I don't want the office to hear what I'm about to say to you..." I closed the door as she requested and sat down, but I checked that the blinds were open. "How dare you!" she said.

"I beg your pardon? What did I do?"

"How dare you embarrass me like that?"

"I beg your pardon? I offered you my jacket..."

"Because I 'looked cold'...?"

"...Because your nipples were popping right through your blouse!" Her jaw dropped. "Hey...! You know I don't bite my tongue...!"

"You know, just because you and I hung out a few times doesn't give you the right..."

"Look, I warned you that the men here are sick, perverted, male chauvinistic pigs and I told you the last thing you need, is a lot of idle office gossip... but if you want to walk around here with your high beams on... I'm *okay* with that..."

"Oh, so you... *like* my nipples?"

"I don't... *hate* them..." I said nonchalantly, "...If that's what you're getting at..."

"You know, I can file sexual misconduct charges against you!"

"I'll call the human resources director..."

"*What?*"

"You said; you wanted to file sexual harassment charges against me, I said; I'll call the human resources director for you..."

"You think I won't do it?"

"What I *think*... is that, what you do, is entirely up to you... and you get to decide... when you have had enough..."

"What are you talking about?"

"You... decide... when *you* have had enough! Nobody gets to draw that line... except you! All you have to say is "when".

"Get out! Out of my office..."

"...*When* it is..." I opened the door and exited her office, closing the door behind me. Two minutes later she followed me back to my desk, still wearing her jacket.

"You made me almost forget... I still need to see you in my office... and bring the new computer codes with you." I got the codebooks and followed her back to her office. She held the door as I entered and she closed it behind her. I sat in the chair; she sat on the edge of her desk and crossed her legs. "What the hell was that all about Nick?"

"It's about you understanding what control is and who really has it..."

"And... *who...* has the control?"

"*You do*...! You just haven't learned it yet!"

I dropped the computer code files on her desk and I turned to leave her office when I heard her whisper... "Will you be willing to teach me...?"

I stopped at the doorway and as I closed the door behind me I said: "Yes madam..."

The Tortured Soul Trilogy
(A Tortured Soul)
Chapter 50
(Smooth Operator)

Katherine went out shopping at the mall, one Saturday afternoon, not really buying anything. She just really wanted to get out of the house. Get some fresh air. She saw a kiosk where there were some massage tables. The hawker kept telling her how wonderful and soothing it was. Hard to believe, considering that her voice was like gravel, she sounded like she needed it more than I did. Oh what the hell, I'll let her feel me up for ten bucks. Katherine laid face down on the chair and this woman began to knead and massage her back. Katherine didn't like it. It was uncomfortable and actually began to make her feel more tense than when she first laid down. She tried to get up but then a hand held her down, and the other began to massage the back of her neck. "Oh! That's more like it... *right... there...*" I guess she just needed to warm up a bit. Her hands were stronger, more confident and hit all the right spots. The hands started at the scruff of my neck and worked their way down to my shoulders. I could feel the weight of the world just melt off me. Her hands hit a tight spot between the shoulder blades and Katherine jumped a bit but then, she felt thumbs hit the spot. It hurt a bit, but it was a good hurt. Slowly and methodically the rubbing and kneading worked out the muscle spasm. Katherine settled back into it. She heard her bones pop like it did at the chiropractors. "Hmmm! *Yes!*" The hands molded and kneaded all of her back and she felt refreshed and renewed. Katherine let out a low and deep moan. (*If this is what is feels like to be a lesbian... sign my ass up! I would soooo be your bitch!*)

"Would Madam care for a 'happy ending'...?"

Katherine recognized the voice, opened her eyes and quickly turned over. Standing over her was Nick. His hands were now hovering over her breasts. The girl was standing by and had allowed Nick to take over the massage. "I... I... I..."

"Okay...? Is that a 'yes' or a 'no' to the happy ending? Cause I have to re-adjust the chair!"

Katherine giggled and Nick helped her up out of the chair. "What are you doing here Nick?"

"Shopping... like the rest of the free world... May I join you?" Katherine nodded. Katherine and Nick walked across the mall side by side. "I hate to bring this up... Katherine..."

"What is it Nick?"

"But I *believe* you owe me ten bucks for the massage..."

Katherine reached into her purse and handed Nick a ten. Nick took it and put it in his pocket. They continued to walk. "Chump... I would have paid *twenty*..." she said.

"Sucker... I *would* have paid you!" Nick replied. Katherine hit Nick and latched onto his arm and they walked the mall together. They toured up and down the aisles but only really just window-shopped.

"I thought you said you needed to do some shopping Nick?"

"I have everything I need... I just came here hoping to pick up a little something that catches my eye."

"And nothing caught your eye yet?"

"*You* did...!" Katherine let out a hushed sigh and blushed. "Hungry?" Nick asked.

Katherine licked her lips. "I could eat a little something..." They walked over to the food court. "Are you sure we should be doing this?"

"Eating?"

"...Being seen in public together!"

"What? Can't two co-workers go out for a bite to eat? Silly girl!"

"What will everyone think?"

"Well... they are either going to think, That old man is banging his hot boss while she's wearing leather and latex, or they're having lunch...what do *you* think they'll think?"

"You're sick!"

"*I'm* sick? I'm not the one who's gonna be banging some old fart while wearing latex and leather later!" Katherine laughed nerviously. "Come on... have the Rueben sandwich... you'll love it..."

"Isn't that a little heavy?"

"Trust me... you'll gonna burn off those calories later!"

Nick ordered and brought the food to the table where Katherine was waiting. Katherine took a bite. "Wow... this is a nice sandwich..."

"Told you..." Nick handed her a soda. "I've eaten here before... I've never gotten a sandwich like this before!"

"Well Sanjit always hooks me up if he's here working..."

"You know the counter guy...?"

"...Only from eating here..."

"You know the counterman's name...? In the food court...?"

"I've learned that you always should know the people that serve you... In all things in life..."

A 40ish woman walked up behind Nick. "Hello 'Professor'..."

Katherine raised an eyebrow. (*Professor...?*)

Nick turned to the voice. "Michelle! It's good to see you again!"

"Good to see you too..." And she kissed him.

"How is John... and the kids?"

"He's good... but the kids are driving me to drink! They're tearing up The Gap as we speak... I have to go... but it was so good to see you again Professor..."

Katherine wasn't about to let that go one more time. "...*Professor...?*"

Michelle looked at me as if she didn't realize I was there. She turned to Nick. "I'm sorry! I didn't realize you were in the middle of a session..." She turned to me. "Do whatever he says honey... Nick is the BEST!" And she left, but not soon enough for Nick's liking.

"So... *Professor*... what kind of a 'session' are we having?" I chided Nick.

"We... are not having a *session*, we... are having lunch... or at least we *were*... having lunch..."

"So... tell me about this little side job you seem to have... As your boss, I should be made aware if any of my employees is moonlighting..."

"It's not a side job... it's just... *something* I do..."

"Something you... 'do'...? That you just *happen* to have a doctorate in?"

245

"I... I don't have a doctorate..."

"Oh no...? *Pro*... fessor...?"

"That is just... a... name... Michelle gave me... that made her feel more comfortable..."

Katherine raised an eyebrow. This was getting interesting. "Comfortable...?"

Nick was a little nervous. "It's... at best... difficult to explain..."

An epiphany struck Katherine... "Are you... a '*man-whore*'...? ...A gigolo?"

Nick busted out laughing, and coughed. "No...! I am... *not*... a gigolo..."

"So you *don't* have sex for money?"

"Damn...!" Nick paused. "...I hadn't though of that... I guess I *am* a man-whore!"

"*Really*...? Cause I still got that twenty in my purse! And you *did* offer me a 'happy ending'...!" Nick and Katherine laughed and finished their lunch together. Nick tried to be as vague as humanly possible to explain what it is he 'did'. Katherine was puzzled but still intrigued by Nick and his evasiveness. She never knew Nick to dance around a subject: he was always straightforward with her. Nick later walked Katherine back to her car. Katherine rolled down her window and waved to Nick. "I wanna hear more about these sessions you do... it sounds interesting!" I waved to Katherine as she drove off...

I can't let her into my world... Not yet... there's no way she's ready... she has no idea what she would be getting herself into... And I'm really not sure of what I'm getting myself into...

- - -

Today is the most dreaded day of the year on the Data Corp. calendar... it was the day that each employee had a one on one sit down with middle management to discuss the company performance levels... They jokingly referred it as '*Judgment Day*"... I personally didn't give a shit... my performance levels were always 8-11% higher than the company standards. Not enough to brag about and nothing for management to complain about, but it was right where I wanted it to be... just below the company radar... The only thing that concerned me was; who would my interview be with?

"Nick?"

"Yes Katherine?"

"You ready for a little one on one action?"

Nick stood up and fixed his tie. "With *you*...? Anytime Katherine...!"

"My office, please... and don't forget your key book!" I grabbed my key book and followed Katherine to her office. She held the door for me. "Age before beauty..."

I entered and replied. "Man before beast." She closed the door behind me. I sat down opposite her desk; she sat in her desk chair. Over the past few weeks, Katherine and I had developed a very comfortable relationship where we had no problem speaking fluent 'double entendre' to each other without her feeling threatened... it was cute... not sexual... we knew where to draw the line and when it wasn't appropriate... We kept it professional when it needed be... but I still won't call her 'Kitty'. I respected Katherine and her position over me... um... above me...I mean... oh! Never mind...! Going over the performance levels amounted to cross checking the company standards against the marketing protocols against your productivity level for the year... Most people spent the meeting trying to defend their actions over the past year. I didn't find that necessary. Other than that, it was pretty boring shit and the process lent itself to you acting silly.

It wasn't long before Katherine and I weren't going over the figures as much as just having fun, laughing and joking around... She laughed, sat back and stretched her legs so her foot was past the edge of her desk and I noticed her shoes. She was wearing a cute black leather ankle high boot with 4" stiletto heels... but what caught my attention was the thick leather strap around the ankle with a 1½" steel ring attached to it.

"Cute shoes...!" I commented.

"Oh these...?" And Katherine raised her right foot straight in front of her higher than her head and grabbed the ring with her index finger... She then raised her left foot above the right and crossed her ankles in mid air, and held them both there hands free. Nick focused his gaze on her long muscular legs. "I saw them in the '*Foot Fetish Shoe Catalogue*' and I just had to have them..."

"They're hot!" I imagined what they would look like on my shoulders.

"Yeah... I like them a lot... and they're a lot more comfortable than they look..." And she put her feet back on the floor. Katherine turned to the other side of her desk and grabbed the company codec files and opened them and began to read the codes to me. I followed with my key book highlighting any codes I felt I should upgrade. Innocently, while reading the codec's to me, Katherine reached into her purse pulled out a scrunchie and put her hair into a ponytail. I watched her intently as she raised her arms over her head and twirled her fingers around the newly formed tail. She seemed not to notice my gaze... then she tossed her hair back and continued to recite codes. "Oh wait a minute... let me just..." And she reached into her bag again, taking out her eyeglass case and put her glasses on. They were simple black rims. "That's better..."

(Yes! Much better... thank you!) Every time Katherine turned her head from book to book, I would watch her ponytail swing from left to right, right to left.... It drove me crazy... But I tried hard to concentrate on the task at hand... This went on for over five minutes, when suddenly she tossed her pen and her glasses on the open book, and rubbed her eyes... She leaned back in her chair, put her feet on the top edge of her desk and crossed her ankles. She let out a sigh and placed her hands over her head and crossed her arms behind her. She let out another deep sigh. I looked at her and she looked as if she was laying on a lounge chair on a beach in Hawaii. I pictured her in a two-piece bikini, the sweat glistening on her rock hard abs. I imagined the soft breeze move the sarong around her hips... In my mind, she was just laying there tanning herself in the hot summer sun... A pina colada on the table beside her... soft jazz music was in the air... suddenly... her bikini was gone... "Katherine?" I whispered.

"Ummmm?"

"Katherine...?"

"Hmmmm... what?" She mumbled, half-awake.

"Katherine!"

"Uh... What?" Katherine sat up suddenly. "Oh my... did I just fall asleep?'

"Yes you did!"

"How long was I out?"

Nick checked his watch. "About ten minutes…"

"Why didn't you wake me?"

(Because I was very busy daydreaming of you naked… *Duh!*) "You looked so peaceful… I didn't want to disturb you." (If I haven't said it before now; there is *nothing* sexier than a woman at peace.) Katherine had a look of embarrassment on her face.

"Was I snoring?"

Nick laughed. "No!"

She touched her hand to the corner of her mouth. "I wasn't drooling was I?"

(No… but I was…!) Katherine tried to get herself together. "Let me get you a cup of coffee…"

"Okay!"

"You want it the way you sleep?"

"Huh?"

"…Light and sweet?" Katherine laughed. I returned with her coffee and gave it to her. She took two sips.

"Perfect!" And she put the cup down and reached for the manuals.

"Okay… let's play a game, shall we?" I said.

"What kind of game?"

"Well we don't have enough room for 'naked twister' in here so let's play… 'What's wrong with this picture?'…"

"O… kay?" she said hesitantly.

"Do you have your code book handy?"

"Yes!" Katherine pulled out the Data Corp. 'bible'.

"Now, we agree that the QMT-PMT codec's are the lifeblood of Data Corp.?"

"Agreed…!"

"… And to circumvent those codes is a disaster in the making?"

"Agreed…"

"Good! Now turn to page 5…"

"Got it…!"

"Now grab your marketing protocol manual…" Katherine grabbed the file. "Now go to pages 15 to 20…"

"Got it!"

"Okay... now let's play..."*What's wrong with this picture?*"... Give us 60 seconds on the clock... and... GO!"

"What am I looking for...?"

"You tell *me*... 45 seconds left..."

Katherine skimmed the codes and compared them. "Well... here are the company codec's... and these are the new marketing protocols and... *What the hell?*" Katherine eyebrows furrowed at what she saw.

"Ding, ding, ding! I believe we have a winner!"

"...But this doesn't make any sense... If we use these marketing protocols the way they're written..."

"The company's codec's would crash!"

"But I don't understand! That would make the data entries take weeks... maybe months to download!

"Exact-a-mundo!"

"But why aren't these programs properly coordinated?"

"Simple... the highly paid marketing programmers don't 'speak' our company data protocols..."

"Like a 'Mac' and a PC?"

"Bingo! But it's more like trying to play a CD in an 8-track player..."

"So why not use a common computer language? I mean why hasn't anyone figured this out before?"

"Well... the geeks in programming for marketing don't want to use our outdated programs and the company doesn't want to spend millions of dollars to upgrade our systems..."

"How were you able to overcome this problem?"

"Well... I was here when they introduced the original protocols so I know the actual programming language by heart... I also knew what the marketing program was 'supposed' to accomplish... so I 'translated' the codes and merged the concepts to our programs to accommodate the purpose of the marketing plans."

Katherine nodded. "That would work..."

"Yes, but a temporary fix at best... the codes have to be 'Frankensteined' in with each new protocol marketing comes up with..."

"And that's how the office performance rating went up..."

"Uh huh!" And Nick settled back into his chair. "...After you helped me 'fix' those codes the other day... I realized you would understand the problem I deal with everyday..."

Katherine took off her glasses and put them on her desk and rubbed her eyes. I could tell she was very tired. "Nick... I really need your help here..."

"What do you want me to do...?"

"I need your help to get the office performance levels back to at least 30% above standards..."

"This office...? The *whole* office...? 30%...? Its not gonna happen!"

Katherine stood up and leaned over her desk to me. "Nick... my job is on the line here..."

I tried so very hard not to stare at her ample cleavage. "*Please*...! They are *not* gonna fire the child prodigy..."

"What can I do...? To help you...? Nick... I'm desperate here...! I will do anything...!"

"...*Any*... Thing...?" I said seductively, my gaze focused on her breasts.

Katherine leaned back and crossed her arms. "Nick... I'm serious here..." She pleaded to me with her eyes. "I know you can do this for me! Just tell me what I can do to help!"

Nick paused. "You really wanna help me?"

"Yes Nick... I do...!"

Nick leaned back into his chair. "Get marketing off my ass...!"

Katherine dropped back into her chair and scrunched up her face. "...Anything... but that!" Nick threw his hands in the air, Katherine pouted. "Nick... You're acting like there's someone out to get you...!"

"It aint paranoia, if someone *is* out to get you!"

"What makes you think I'm out to get you?"

"Not *you* Katherine... Marketing...!"

"What makes you think that...?"

"Look... My grandmother once told me... Nicky, if you have a hand on your back and you feel something up your ass, you have to stop and think... but if you have two hands on your back and you feel something up your ass... You don't have to think about it... you know you're being fucked!"

"And you think marketing is trying to fuck you…?"

"They have *one* hand on my back and they're using *you* to get me to hold still…"

"Nick… I really need your help here…"

"Sorry kiddo… I can't be nailed to that cross again… You call off the dogs… you take charge of what goes on around here… you free up my hands and I will do… anything and… everything to make you happy!"

"I don't have the stroke to pull that off…!"

Nick threw up his hands and placed them behind his head. "Then my hands are tied…"

"Nick… I'm asking you… *begging you*… for your help here!"

Nick leaned forward in his chair. "Help me… help you…! Help ME… help YOU!"

"Damn it Nick! Enough with the movie references…! Do this for me!" Katherine stomped her feet. "Nick! I need your *help*!"

"Now you're acting like a spoiled brat…"

"I… am… not… acting like a spoiled brat!" Katherine was getting a little upset with Nick not being cooperative.

Nick went back to reading his codebook. "Yes you are… and if you continue with this little 'hissy fit' of yours young lady… I'm gonna put you over my knee and give you a good spanking…!" I waited for Katherine's witty reply… it didn't come… I paused. (Oh shit! I just overstepped my boundaries with her… again!) I waited a moment to see if she would say something… anything… *Nothing…*! Damn! I thought quickly of a way to apologize for my rude comment. I looked up slowly at her… I saw the expression on her face… She wasn't mad… or angry… or shocked… or disappointed… She was… *aroused*! I looked at her face… her face was turning pink… She parted her lips and let out a soft sigh… She placed her hand on her slowly heaving bosom and focused on me and she gently bit her lower lip… I *knew* that look! And then she blinked.

"I'll… I'll tell you what… I'm gonna try to run interference for you… I'll… take the hit from marketing… you go in for the touchdown…!" Nick nodded, stood up and he felt this would be a good time to excuse himself and leave. "Nick?"

"Yes Katherine?"

"Anybody gives you any shit... You let me handle it... deal?"

Nick lowered his eyes. "You're the boss!" And with that I turned and closed the door behind me, stopped and loosened my tie. I took my handkerchief and wiped the beads of sweat off my brow. Bob was sitting at his desk... staring at me... his jelly donut seemed to be frozen in mid air inches from his gaping mouth. "Bob... breathe!" Bob blinked twice, shook his head and mumbled something incoherently. Then he stuffed the donut in his mouth. I walked back to my desk. Someone in that room just sold their soul... I just wasn't so sure who!

Later, I checked my watch and it was a little after five, I shut down my computer, and got my jacket. On my way out I passed Katherine's office just as she just stepped out and closed her door. "So, Nick... It's been an interesting day...! Have a good weekend... I'll see you Monday morning..."

"Have a good one kiddo..."

"Hey Nick... why don't you stop by the bar and have a few drinks with me... everyone else from the office is going to be there..."

"Sure... why not? I've got no place to go and all weekend to get there..." We walked out the door and Katherine placed her hand into the crook of my arm and walked close to me.

"I'm sorry... I hope you don't mind?"

"Not at all... it's so very European..." Katherine laughed as I escorted her to the bar where everyone went on Friday nights to drink the edge off... Almost half the office was there. A few eyebrows were raised when we entered arm in arm. We sat down and talked and drank and mingled... switching cliques as the night went on. It was almost ten o'clock before Katherine and I noticed that we were the only two from the office still in the bar. "Oh my... look at the time... I should be getting home..."

"What happened to *'No place to go, and all weekend to get there'*...?"

"A man's gotta sleep..."

"Okay party pooper... I'll take you home..." Katherine stood up, but was very unsteady on her feet. "Oh! I'm a little drunk..." She lost her footing and put her hand on my chest to steady herself, and her touch lingered... again.

"Why don't I just drive you home instead?"

"I'm not as 'think' as you 'drunk' I am…! Haha! I'm kidding, but you're right, I shouldn't be driving… are you sure *you're* good to drive?"

"I only had one drink when I got here; I've been drinking ginger ale all night…"

She put her head on my chest. "Yeah… take me home…" She looked up at me. "If it doesn't put you out…" She laughed nervously. "…And don't think that just because you're taking me home that I'm gonna put out…"

"Don't worry about it… I would never take advantage of you while you were drunk…"

"Really…?"

"Yeah…! I would at least wait until you had totally lost consciousness…"

She laughed and hit me on my arm. "You set this up… didn't you? Mr. *'I only had one drink'*…?"

"If I remember correctly… you… invited me… to have drinks with you!"

"Oh… Yeah… I forgot! Pfffftt!" And she laughed. I walked her over to her car and she handed me the keys. Just as I sat her into the passengers' side and buckled her in, her eyes began to glaze over. She *was* as think as I drunk she was. She had become relaxed and the alcohol was now taking over. She was able to tell me her address just before she passed out. She slumped over and I tightened her seat belt to secure her. I had to reach over to do it and my face was in her sweet and perky bosom. Although she reeked a little of alcohol, her breasts still smelled like baby powder. It was right then that I kinda wished I were the kind of guy who would do what I was thinking about doing. But I'm not. *Damn!* As I drove her home I noticed that her blouse was dangerously close to popping open… it was becoming more and more difficult to concentrate on the road knowing every time she moved, her breasts might pop out. I kept an eye on her and one on the road until I kept repeating to myself; *'I have daughter her age… I have daughter her age…'* I pulled over so I could adjust her blouse so she wouldn't have a wardrobe malfunction. She moaned a bit and I pulled my hand back. She mumbled *'What are you doing?'* then she passed out again.

We arrived at her place and she was a little bit more conscious and was able to walk with a little help from me. She opened the door, went inside kicking off her shoes and leaving the front door wide open. She hobbled over to the couch and slumped down. I entered and closed the door. "Katherine... where is your bathroom?" She barely pointed to a door to the right. I went in, looked around and raised the toilet seat. I came out leaving the bathroom door open and walked over to Katherine on the couch. I took the scrunchie she had on her wrist and used it to tie her hair into a ponytail.

"What the hell are you doing?"

"Putting your hair into a bun..." I continued to put her hair into a tight bun.

"Why...?"

"Because in about thirty seconds you're gonna hurl your guts out and trust me, you don't want your hair in the way..."

"I am *not*... gonna... er... ulp!" She didn't get to finish her sentence. She ran right into the open bathroom and stuck her head in the toilet. Ladies, just so you know, there is an advantage to leaving the toilet seat up! From her prone position, her skirt was pulled tight over her smooth round ass. It would have been a huge turn on... if it wasn't for that projectile vomiting thing...! I don't know which is worse, the smell or the sound...! I looked back at her when I thought she was done. It was then that I saw that her blouse had risen a bit above her waist. I could barely see she had bruises from a recent beating on her back and hips. That son of a bitch! But, it still wasn't my place to say anything... She lifted her head out of the toilet, flushed and fixed herself up a bit. She went to the sink to rinse her mouth out. She undid her skirt. She then stumbled out of the bathroom stepping out of her skirt. I could now see the welts on her thighs and buttocks clearly. She passed by me as if she didn't realize I was still there and sat down on the couch... well, more slumped than sat... then she laid face down and pulled off her blouse. Her back was covered in black and blue bruises. My fist balled up and a tear came from my left eye. I would give anything to have ten minutes alone with this guy. There was this beautiful young woman wearing nothing but a pink thong laying on a couch and all I could think about was what I would do to the guy who would do that to her... it sucks to be me! I turned off the lights and closed the door behind me. A cab I called on my cell had arrived to take me home. I would not ever bring this up to her… ever.

Chapter 51
(Sexual Healing)

I was sitting at the "C" cup sipping my tea when Mandy sat down next to me. "Something's bothering you Nick... I can tell..."

"You always sit with the customers and get all in their personal business?"

"No... but I do sit with close personal friends when they're hurting... even if they are my boss..."

"You know me too well Mandy...."

"So...? What's going on with Katherine?"

"What makes you think this has anything to do with Katherine?" Mandy just cut a 'surely you jest?' look at me. "Okay then... I just don't get it... What's the attraction? Why does she put up with all this abuse from this young punk?"

"You of all people should know what's going on...!"

"No... I just don't get it..."

"Oh my God... you've got it bad for Katherine don't you?"

"Pfffttt! *No!*"

"You *bitch!*"

"I don't know what you're talking about...!"

"...Bullocks!"

"Huh?"

Mandy walked over to get a tray of biscotti for me. "Well that's neither here nor there now!" And she sat back down. "A pox on both your houses..."

"Don't you go all 'Shakespeare' on *me* young lady!"

"Okay... let me run it down for you, because you're too close to see what's going on here..."

"I can't see the forest for all the trees?"

"Exactly! Now here's the skinny..." I sipped my tea and listened intently to Mandy's explanation. "Katherine is a borderline nymphomaniac... She loves sex, but she's not a slut or a whore. She won't have sex with just anybody. Her fiancé... is too young for her. He doesn't know how to handle a woman of her maturity and sexuality. He has a low self-esteem, probably the result of an abusive father. His father might have abused him and his mother. So his abuse toward Katherine results in him feeling better about himself and also it's all about 'control'... he couldn't control his own father's abusive behavior and couldn't protect his Mum because he was only a lad, so now that he's an adult, he feels he needs to have control of Katherine... it makes him feel like more of a man..."

"So... in a perverted twist of fate, Johnny, in trying to avoid his father's legacy of abuse, has become just like his father!"

"Pretty much..."

"Okay...? But why does Katherine put up with it?"

"Duh...! For the sex...! In order to have sex on his terms, Johnny feels he has to 'control' her and the situation, just as his father did. So he beats her into submission. Katherine puts up with it because she wants the sex... so..."

"She lets him beat her, gives him what he wants..."

"...So she can get what she needs...!"

"...And in the process..."

"...She's become a Masochist... or at least, she thinks she has..."

"...And it's that emotional conflict that is causing her weight fluctuations..."

"She seeks refuge in food..."

"And when Johnny goes away... on 'tour'..."

"So does the conflict and her weight goes back to normal..."

"But now there's another problem..."

"And what's that?" Mandy asked.

"Katherine has probably become addicted to pain... she likes it now... maybe as much as sex... and with Johnny holding the reins..."

"And with her *not* being the one in control... he might hurt her bad..." Mandy said, completing my thought.

"He might kill her...!" I said.

"Do you know what to do?" Mandy asked.

"I think so..." We stood up. "Thanks Mandy..." Mandy suddenly kissed me. "What the hell was that for?"

"Don't get your knickers all in twist about it... that was for me..."

"For you...?"

"Yeah... I just wanted to thank you!" Mandy turned and began to walk away, then turned back. "And don't forget to tip your waitress Luv... the pay here sucks!"

"Really? You would think with that type of service you just gave me, your tips would be off the hook!"

"You'll do right to keep your mind off my 'tips'..." Nick dropped a five-dollar bill on the table. Mandy stuck out her pierced tongue at him. "Shame, you dropped only a fiver... you could have found out what I do for twenty quid!"

"You know... I do remember when you used to do that for a ten!" Nick then left the shop.

"Bugger... just had to have the last word!"

Nick stuck his head back in the shop. "Yep! I sure do!" Mandy laughed as he left. Nick now knew what he should do... the only problem was... how to get Katherine to ask him for his help?

- - -

Monday morning, I made my rounds saying good morning to everyone in the office. Katherine was at the printer getting Monday mornings' reports and last weeks' figures for processing. "Good morning Nick..."

"Good morning Katherine..."

"My office, please..."

"Let me grab a cup of coffee and I'll be right in... would you like a cup?"

"No... thank you..." I walked into Katherine's office with my coffee. "Close the door please..." I put down the cup on her desk and closed the door. I picked up the cup and took a sip. "I thought you only drank tea?"

"There's a lot of things you don't know about me... What's going on?"

"How did I get home Friday night?"

"I drove you home from the bar..."

"And how did I get undressed?"

"I would assume you undressed yourself... *after* I left..."

259

"And you didn't see me naked? On the couch…?"

"If I saw you naked… I would think I would *not* have left your house that night…"

"So you didn't try to take advantage of me?"

"Define… 'take advantage'…" I sipped my coffee.

She crossed her arms. "You never tried to kiss me?"

"*After* you *hurled*…? Ah Nooo…! I don't think so…!"

"You didn't try to feel me up?" She cut her eyes at me. "…In the car?"

I knew she only had a vague memory. I threw up my hands "I plead the fifth…!"

She uncrossed her arms and smiled. "Okay then…" I got up and turned to leave. "We *will* talk more about this later…"

I turned back. "How about over dinner this Friday?"

"What…?" She was a little thrown aback by my sudden dinner invitation.

"We can talk over dinner… Is Friday after work convenient for you?"

"I don't think that would be appropriate…" she said.

I started to pull the door closed behind me. "Please…! How inappropriate could it possibly be…? After all…I've *already* seen you naked!" I closed the door behind me not waiting for her reaction.

- - -

We made our dinner 'appointment' to meet at the bar across the street at about nine pm. Anybody from work would usually have left there before eight so there was little chance of being spotted. She walked in sheepishly about a quarter after nine. I walked up behind her. She was a bit jumpy. "Are you okay?"

"I'm fine… it's just…" and she looked around bar.

"Its okay, nobody's here… and don't worry, there's nothing wrong with two co-workers having dinner together…"

"You've done this before… haven't you?"

"Eaten? Yes, once or twice…"

"…Have 'dinner' with co-workers…"

"...Male and female... plenty of times... Sometimes..." Nick whispered "Even in... *groups!*" Katherine smiled. "So... how long has your fiancé been away?"

"How did you know he was away?" and she turned her head in an odd angle.

"Your toilet seat was down in your bathroom, and he doesn't seem like the type that would care... and you met me here instead of going straight home after work on a Friday like you usually do when he's in town..." I wasn't going to mention that she had lost some weight. I knew that her weight was a sore subject with her. She nodded in agreement.

"He's on tour with a hip hop showcase trying to get some sponsors for his demo, and he's been gone a week now... but he should be back in a few weeks..."

She may have believed that's where he was, but I knew that was a load of bullshit. Nobody was gonna let him tour with them unless he was driving the bus, but I wasn't about to call her out on it. "Well, okay then... shall we go?"

"Maybe I should have a drink first..." She raised her hand to signal a waitress.

I took her hand in mine. "Maybe you shouldn't..." I walked her out to her car.

"Should we take yours or mine...?" as she pulled her car keys out of her clutch bag.

"Let's take yours, that way if I have to take you home, your car won't be stuck at the bar's parking lot all weekend... you wanna drive... or shall I?" She handed me the keys. I saw this simple gesture as her giving me control. She focused her eyes at me as I opened the door for her. "Relax... its just dinner." She got in. I got in. She turned to me.

"Okay I guess... besides... What do I have to worry about...? You've already seen me naked...!" and she smiled a broad smile.

"Truth be told... I've only seen you in your underwear... but the night is still young!" Katherine laughed nervously as we drove off.

We arrived at the restaurant about twenty minutes later. The maitre'd checked for our reservations. "Mr. Anderson? We have a lovely table for you and your daughter..." Katherine covered her mouth and laughed nervously.

"Thanks... please let me know if you're ever going on an awkward date so I can embarrass the living shit out of you..." Nick said to the maitre'd. Katherine chuckled. The maitre'd cleared his throat and quietly escorted us to our table. The waiter came by and gave us our menus.

"So... we're on 'an awkward date'...?" Katherine asked.

I ignored her. "Waiter... I'd like a seven and seven to start please..."

"I thought we weren't drinking tonight?"

"I said *you* shouldn't drink... that never applied to me..."

Katherine turned to the waiter. "I'll have an *'Electric Lemonade'* please..."

"I'll need to see some I.D. please..." Katherine giggled and pulled out her drivers' license.

"...And the night just keeps getting better and better!" Katherine began to laugh and tried to cover it up.

"...Waiter... please make that 7&7 a double..."

"Very good sir..." And he left to get our drinks.

"An *'Electric Lemonade'*...?" I asked.

"Uh huh... all us *kids* are drinking it..." Katherine smiled.

"Maybe you should have ordered an Enfamil on the rocks..." I said.

Katherine giggled. "...And you should have ordered a Metamucil cocktail..."

Nick tried to do his best Sean Connery. "I like my Metamucil shaken, not stirred..."

Katherine busted out laughing. "That was the worse Jim Carrey I've ever heard!"

"Waiter! *Where the hell* are those drinks?" I called out jokingly. The waiter came right away with our drinks. Katherine giggled and laughed. I liked Katherine when she laughed. She lit up the whole room when she was happy. I liked making her happy. By the time we were ready to order dinner we were both giddy and laughing and the liquor had very little to do with it.

The waiter returned. "Are you ready to order?"

"Yes thank you..."

"...And what would you like sir?"

"Please, take the young lady's order first…"

Katherine picked up the menu and glanced at it quickly.

"Gee… I don't know… can you give me a few more moments?"

"Very good… would you care to order now sir?"

"Yes… I'll have the filet mignon…"

"And how would you like it prepared sir?"

"…Medium rare… and could you please add a lobster tail to that?"

"Very good sir… baked potato or mashed?"

"Is that 'garlic mashed'…?

"Yes sir…"

"Garlic mashed it is…"

"…And would madam care to order now?"

"I'm still not sure what I want…"

I watched Katherine's face. "Do you mind if I order for you?" A relieved look came across her face. I hadn't realized she'd never been to a fancy restaurant before and was feeling a little intimidated. I should have known better, her *fiancé* probably only took her to fast food restaurants… and made her pay for it!

"Yes… please do…" She paused and tried to cover herself. "I'd like to see what you think I would like to eat…"

"How do you feel about seafood?"

"I love seafood, but I'll try anything new… one time…"

I pointed to three items on the menu. "Please bring us this, this and… this… and could you add two lobster tails to my dinner?"

"Very good sir… and I'll be right back with fresh drinks for you…"

"That won't be necessary…" I said. I wanted Katherine to stay sober tonight.

"Its okay sir… the maitre'd has graciously offered to take care of your bar tab." Katherine and I held our glasses up to the maitre'd, who bowed. "I'll have your entrée's momentarily." And the waiter left.

"Wow! What great service!"

"Well, it does help when you threaten the owner…"

The waiter returned shortly with our meals and fresh drinks.

"Wow! This all looks so good... what is all this?"

"Some pasta, some seafood, some appetizers... a little bit of *this*... and a little bit of *that*..."

"Where should I start?"

"Allow me madam..." I rose out of my seat and pulled an empty chair from the next table and sat next to Katherine, I put her napkin in her lap and took a little of the pasta on a fork and brought it to her mouth... She waved it off.

"I'm a big girl... I can feed myself..."

"I know you can... but *please*, allow me..."

"What if I don't like it?"

"You're still young, try it, if you don't like it you never have to try it again... but if you like it you'll be willing to experience it again..."

"But what if I really, really like it?"

"Then the world becomes your oyster... opening its treasures to your every whim..." I held out the fork, Katherine hesitated then opened her mouth. I saw this gesture as her again giving me control. I gently placed the fork in her mouth and she took it in.

"Mmmmm! That is delicious!" I sampled another dish for her. She opened her mouth again and allowed me to feed her. "Mmmmm!" She pointed to another dish. "That looks interesting... I wanna try that next..." I smiled; she was being more adventurous now.

"Yes madam...!" I reached over and picked up the morsel and placed it in her mouth with my fingers and she bit into it and ate it. She was beginning to trust me.

"Oh my! That is marvelous! You *have* to tell me what that was..."

I whispered in her ear. "Escargot in a garlic sauce..."

"Why does that sound familiar...? What is that?"

I took another and put it into her mouth, this time she licked my finger and rolled her eyes back. I whispered into her ear. "They're 'escargot'... that's French... for *snails*..." I didn't expect her reaction. She didn't flinch.

"May I have another?"

"Yes madam..." And I held the escargot up to make her lean her head back and I placed it on her eager tongue.

"Mmmmm! That is *so* good!"

"You have a little sauce on your chin..." I took the napkin and dabbed her chin, she placed her hand on my face... it was then that another couple that had just finished their dinner walked past us. The woman hissed at us.

"Shame on you... a man your age! Such a disgusting display... Why don't you two get a room?" Her companion escorted her out by putting his hand on her back, as they walked away he made a 'thumbs up' sign behind her back. "I know what you just did!" She grunted. And they left. Katherine giggled.

"Well at least *he* gets it..."

"Yes, but not from her, I would have to assume..."

Katherine choked and almost spit up the food in her mouth. She covered her mouth with her hand. "You are sooo bad!"

"Well, if you'll excuse me madam, I believe I have a filet mignon waiting on me." I got up, returned the chair from whence I got it and went back to sit down to eat my meal. Katherine seemed a little bit disappointed. I placed my napkin in my lap and I cut my steak and raised the fork to my mouth.

"You're not gonna put any steak sauce on that?"

I looked up at her without raising my head. "Noooo!" I mouthed. ...And I put the steak in my mouth. It was tender and juicy and melted in my mouth. My eyes rolled back in my head. When I opened my eyes, Katherine was staring at me intently. "What?"

"If I didn't know any better... I could swear you just had an orgasm..."

I smiled. "Well... watch closely my dear, because you're about to see a man have a multiple orgasm..." I cut the steak and put the fork in my mouth, and can you believe it? Katherine watched me! I placed my napkin to cover my mouth. "Okay... now you're making me feel dirty!" Katherine smiled and placed a forkful of food in her mouth, licked the tines and looked directly at me and moaned seductively. I placed my hand over my mouth to stifle my laugh. We finished our entrees and we just sat there talking and having a little wine to top off the meal.

"So... how about some dessert...?" Nick said.

"What do you have in mind?" Katherine cooed.

"I'm in the mood for a little '*pick me up*'...!"

Katherine raised her eyebrow. "Oh... *really*...?"

"Oh *yeah*... definitely!" Katherine slipped her foot out of her shoe and played footsies with me. I called the waiter over.

"Yes sir?"

"Two tiramisu... with some whipped cream on the side if you please..."

"Yes sir...!" And the waiter left.

Katherine tried to pronounce the desert "Terra...?"

"Tea-Rah-Me-Sue!"

"Tear a miss you?"

"Tea... rah... *me*... sue..."

"Tiramisu!"

"By George... I think she's got it!"

"Tiramisu!" Katherine purred. "Okay... now that I know how to say it... what the hell is it?"

"It's Italian... for a *pick me up*..." Katherine raised her eyebrow again. Nick explained. "It's very delicate sponge cake soaked in espresso coffee, Marsala, mascarpone cheese, and chocolate..." Nick explained.

"Ohhh! That sounds fantastic!" And the waiter returned and served the tiramisu and held out the bowl of whipped cream and put a dollop on Nick's and then went to Katherine who waived it off. "No thank you... but leave the bowl please..."

"Yes ma'am..." And the waiter nodded, put the bowl down and left. Nick took a forkful of tiramisu and put it in his mouth.

"Mmmmmm!" Nick moaned. Then he looked at Katherine who hadn't touched hers. "Is there something wrong?" Katherine picked up her fork and held it out with the handle towards him and licked her lips.

"I see...! Would madam like me to show her how to *enjoy* her tiramisu?"

Katherine bit her lower lip. "Yes please..." Nick nodded and stood up and again pulled over a free chair from the next table. He sat down to the right of Katherine and picked up the plate with his left hand.

"May I...?"

"Please do...!" Nick took the fork from her hand and then wrapped his left arm behind Katherine's neck, holding the plate in his left just in front of Katherine's face. Katherine's face was now just inches from Nick's. He cut a piece of the tiramisu and held the fork in front of her.

"Open...please..." Katherine opened her mouth slightly and Nick gently fed her the dessert. Katherine put her hand on his chest.

"Mmmmm! That is so good!" And she licked her lips seductively.

"...More?" Katherine nodded. He took another forkful and fed it to Katherine.

"Um Mmmmmm!"

"Would madam care for some whipped cream?" Katherine nodded and Nick took his pinky and dipped it in the whipped cream and held it to her. She licked his finger and sucked off the cream. Nick took turns feeding her the tiramisu and then the whipped cream from his finger. When she finished hers, Nick fed her his tiramisu.

"Aren't *you* having any?"

"Don't mind if I do..." And Nick kissed Katherine deeply. Katherine held his face softly with her hand.

After dinner, I walked Katherine to her car and opened the drivers' door for her. "Aren't you gonna take me home?"

"Actually, you're gonna drive yourself home... you'll be fine."

"You're staying?" Nick nodded. Katherine was a bit disappointed. Are you sure...?" Nick nodded again. She didn't want this night to end, at least not this way. "Can I drop *you* off then?"

"It's okay... I just live a few blocks away... the fresh air will do me good, besides I need to walk off that dinner..." Katherine kissed me deeply.

"There are other ways to burn off those calories..."

"I know... Which is the main reason why I won't take you home tonight..."

Katherine looked disappointed again. "Are you *sure*?"

"*Hell no...* I'm not sure! Now get out of here before I do something that I will cherish for the rest of my life..." Katherine got in the car and rolled down the window.

"Thank you for dinner... and the company..."

"No, *thank you* for such a lovely evening…" And I leaned into the car and kissed her again. "I'll see you Monday morning…"

"See you… oh by the way Nick?"

"Yes Katherine?"

"…Just so that you know…" I leaned into her open window. "I'm going straight home, taking off all my clothes, getting in my tub… get nice and clean and then I'm going to bed and I'm gonna masturbate all night long…"

Nick shook his head. "Why would you say that to me?"

"I just wanna make sure that tonight, when you jack off, you'll be only thinking of me… and not Lisa…"

"*Damn!*" I said to myself "…*she's not even gonna let me cheat on her in my fantasies!*" And she drove off… I called a cab on my cell to take me home. Our waiter came outside to smoke a cigarette. He saw me, and his jaw dropped.

"You gotta be kidding me? She *left* you here? I would have bet the farm you had that all sewn up…! Oh… I'm sorry… I didn't realize I said that out loud! Sorry! But what the hell happened?"

"Nothing…"

"Well *yeah*… I know nothing happened… but *why* did nothing happen? I mean… what *happened* to make 'nothing' happen?"

"Why are you so interested in my love life?"

"Aw come on…! I've dreamt all my life of a date like that, knowing how it should end… and now to see it didn't 'end' like that… I wanna know what went wrong!"

"Nothing went wrong…"

"Dude…! You're in a parking lot with the waiter that served you and your date the hottest food related foreplay session in history!"

"It wasn't *that* hot…"

"…'*Nine and a Half Weeks*' wasn't that hot compared to what happened in there tonight…"

"You're joking!"

"Are you kidding? The owner is putting your order on the menu as the '*Getting Lucky Special*'…!"

"*Really?*"

"Well… it sounds a lot better in Italian… So…? What the hell happened?"

"Umm…" I needed a moment to think. "…It actually went according to plan…"

"*It did*?" The waiter said facetiously.

"Yeah… it did…"

"Yeah *right*…!"

"No seriously, it all went according to plan…"

"…And the plan was for you to be left in the parking lot?"

"No… the plan was for her to go home, get in the tub, and 'prepare' for my arrival…"

"…'Prepare'…?"

"PRE-Pare…!"

"Oh…? Ohhhh!" And the waiter made a shaving motion near his crotch. "*Prepare*…! I get it… when will you know she's ready?"

"A cab will come get me…" And with that my cab arrived… I got in and it drove off… I guess I can never take Katherine to *that* restaurant ever again…

We never did speak about the topic that brought us together that night. We were having way too much fun to bring up such an uneasy subject. Besides, the night served to quash any anxieties that may have existed about our age difference, as of tonight, it was a moot point. If she ever dumps Johnny, our personal relationship would be able to move forward.

The Tortured Soul Trilogy
(A Tortured Soul)
Chapter 52
(Stacy's Mom)

I came to work the next Monday morning and there was an e-mail that Katherine would be at an impromptu seminar at company headquarters for the next two or three weeks. Bob waved to me

"Hey Nick... so now that your girlfriend is away for two weeks, what are you gonna do?"

"Drop dead Bob!" I answered curtly. Bob was only yanking my chain. He had no idea what was going on. Nobody in the office did. I walked over to my desk in my cubicle and I noticed that Lisa was leaning over it with her back to me going over some file on my desk. She took her finger, licked it and turned the page on the file one by one. She was wearing that 'little black dress' that I had complimented her on once or twice. She was also wearing her hot red 'do me' pumps. Lisa was what we called in computer lingo a SM-U-W2F, '*Soccer Mom You Wanted 2 Fuck*', and even after two kids, she still had the hard body of a playboy centerfold. This chick had a rocking ass! Speaking of which, as she stood, bent over my desk, she began to shift her weight from her right to her left, her left to her right, I watched as she rocked back and forth, like a subject being hypnotized. She then bent way over my desk to put the file back in my desk drawer. Lisa never wore panties when she wore that dress, she didn't like the panty lines. The dress was just sheer enough that I could see she was wearing a black thong underneath. Does *she know* that I'm standing behind her? "Hey Lisa... what's up...?" (Besides me, that is?)

She turned around and sat down on the edge of my desk and crossed her legs. "Oh...! Hi Nicky." Lisa had just enough of a smoky Russian accent to make her sound sexy. She always reminded me of a woman that was born to be a Bond girl. I couldn't think of some childish name to give her, but every time I fantasized about her, her name would be 'Svetlana'... My eyes were focused on her ample bosom... She didn't wear a bra today...

"I just wanted to know if those codes corrections I helped you with the other day were okay."

I didn't sit down, because to do so would give me a direct view up her short skirt. Don't get me wrong... I wanted to... I just don't do things without a proper 'invitation'... It's just the way I am.

"Katherine didn't turn them in yet... they're not due until next week..."

"Oh? If I had known..." She leaned into me. "I would have taken more time...!"

"Do you two need a room?" Bob asked. He was in rare form today. Bob was standing there, for no apparent reason. I walked around Lisa and sat down in my chair opposite her.

"No Bob... we don't need a room..." Lisa answered.

I motioned around my cubicle. "We have a semi-private room... what we needed was some more privacy... what do you want?"

"Yes Bob... what was so important, that you felt the need to interrupt our intercourse?" Bob stared at Lisa. He couldn't believe what he just heard her say.

"Bob...? Intercourse also means a 'conversation'...!" I said. Bob froze... tried to smile, but you could tell he was uncomfortable that his 'little joke' had backfired.

"Um... ah... I wanted to know if you had the progress reports on the Collins account so I can cross reference them with the PMT-QMT account settings." Everyone in the office knew that I don't work on the Collins account... Bob just wanted to be nosey. I just watched Lisa sit there while she watched Bob talk... Except for a birthmark on her neck and shoulder, Lisa's skin was flawless... Although she was now facing in my direction, I knew her back was lean and muscular. Through her dress I could see her nipples were well defined and fully erect... I pictured her bent over my desk with her tits on my desk and her dress over her hips in crotch less panties wearing a studded belt around her thin waist I was holding on to. She would call me a *'filthy Cossack'* as I grabbed her by her long blonde hair and... "Nick...? Did you hear me?" Bob asked.

I turned to look at Bob. "Bob... I have a beautiful blonde Russian Amazon of a woman, sitting cross-legged on my desk;

barely wearing a hot little black dress and stiletto heels..." I turned back to Lisa who was watching my lips as I spoke. I turned back to Bob as if I had forgotten he was there. "I'm sorry Bob... what was the question again?" Bob excused himself and walked sheepishly away... Lisa smiled at me and slid the back of her hand on my face..."

"I'll see you later... Yes?" She stood up... smoothed out her dress... adjusted her dress straps, turned on her heel and began to seductively walk back to her desk.

"Lisa, I honestly don't know if you look better walking towards me or away from me..."

Lisa stopped and turned to me. "That's easy... walking towards you... cause then you know you'll be watching me walking away... by the way... does Katherine know yet?"

I looked Lisa right in the eye. "Does Katherine know... *what*... yet?" Lisa took her right hand and ran her fingers through her hair and brought it down between her breasts... and she sighed... heavily... her face had turned a bright red... she paused and quickly turned and nervously walked back to her desk. In all the years I've known Lisa, I've never known her to blush... that was a very powerful turn on to me...very powerful... There are two things stopping me from taking a shot at Lisa... One, the fact that's she's married and two, I know she's just a tease and a flirt... if I ever did respond to her advances, she would run and hide, and I didn't want that... A man my age likes to flirt with hot young women. Katherine returned to the office after her seminar, wearing a plain high-buttoned blouse, jacket and long skirt... She had her hair in a tight bun, and was wearing her eyeglasses. She was all business. This had nothing to do with hiding bruises. It looked as if she was trying to 'tone down' her look... she had no idea that to me, she couldn't have looked more sexy and alluring. She called an office meeting in the coffee room.

"Starting today, everyone in this office working for Faber Data Corp. and its subsidiaries will be required to attend a seminar on sexual harassment in the workplace." Everyone groaned. "Attendance is mandatory..." And that was that...

"Why is everyone looking at me for?" I asked. All the men laughed. Bob shook his head, knowingly. But I knew he didn't know shit.

"This is serious!" Katherine snapped. Katherine was back, large and in charge. "The company will NOT tolerate, nor condone this type of behavior. If you have a problem with that, don't tell me about it; take it up with corporate headquarters." Katherine looked at me. "That goes for *everybody*...! The schedule will be on the bulletin board." With that, Katherine went back to her office.

"The company is trying to cover their ass..." Bob whispered. "I wondered who fucked up...and who snitched?"

I looked around the room to see who averted their eyes or turned away. No woman in the coffee room turned her eyes away from me... not even Lisa... I walked back to my desk and looked into Katherine's office. She looked up at me and looked down and away... Oh NO...! She couldn't have...? Could she? What did I do to her to throw me under the bus?

- - -

Sensitivity Training Seminars are supposed to be a good thing but it actually has a very diverse effect on some people... Some become withdrawn... the water cooler conversations changed to safer topics. The 'unofficial' dress code is now being enforced and casual Friday was more conservative. Rumors and gossip don't stop, but they are no longer spoken boldly. They went back to being whispers in the shadows. The number one whisper is '*who snitched*?' I had an idea, but I wasn't gonna be one of the gossipers. Besides, I could be wrong. The opposite effect is an increased sexual tension in the office place. Knowledge of there being a 'sexual predator' in the office, only served to peak the interest of some women. Some women who you wouldn't think of that way, would blossom... they would now take their time to get dressed for work. Manicures and pedicures, getting their hair 'did', posturing and strutting, new shoes, new clothes and new attitudes. Lisa was in her element now and as for me... I couldn't give a flying fuck one way or another. I am what I am. If you don't like it, please notice as I exit that I have mistletoe hanging from my coattail. But not Katherine, she retreated into her ivory tower, dressed down, and stayed away from the general population. The one thing I had noticed is that Katherine no longer had a weight problem, or an engagement ring. I knocked on Katherine's office door.

"Come in."

I entered. "May I speak with you Katherine?"

"Sure Nick... just leave the door open..."

"It's about the sexual harassment seminars..."

"Close the door..."

"In...? Or out?"

She motioned for me to enter. "...In."

I shut the door and sat down. "Almost everyone here is on pins and needles, and the work is suffering..."

"Tell me about it... I've been on three conference calls with Mr. Hagen this week alone..."

"Okay... as long as you know that there's a problem... I just wanted you to know that if there's anything I can do to help out, let me know..." I stood up and reached for the doorknob.

"Nick... it wasn't me..." I paused; she paused. "It was Maggie..." My jaw dropped! "No! Not against you! Against Tim in accounting..." She said.

"I knew it wasn't against me; otherwise I would have been called into the main office by now, but Tim in accounting? ...And *our* Maggie...? What the *hell*...?" I sat back down. "So...? Dish sister...!"

"Maggie went to accounting to take care of a problem with her 401k and found Tim enjoying a 'questionable magazine' in his office and reported him to human resourses."

"Ohhh...! Okay, I know what to do..."

"Wait! You *can't tell* anyone what I've just told you..."

"Don't worry I've got this..."

"But what are you gonna do? If it backfires, it's gonna be all on me..."

"Don't worry... I know just what to do... I'll handle this... and you'll be in the clear..." I turned to leave and hesitated at the door. "Oh... by the way Katherine..."

"Yes Nick?"

"...*Love the suit*." Katherine blushed... I exited her office. I loved knowing I could do that to her. Okay, I know I stole that line from "*Silence of the Lambs*" but I felt it served the purpose better than "*It puts the lotion in the basket*..." I was trying to seduce Katherine not make a dress out of her... Wow, I think that's the first time I've admitted to my self that I wanted to seduce Katherine...!

If anyone knows me; they know that I never let the truth get in the way of a good story. In the weeks to come, a rumor started around the office that the reason Faber Data Corp. was having these 'sensitivity training' sessions was because of a multi-million dollar sexual discrimination lawsuit against some local retail store, and Faber Data was only covering their assets. Once the 'reason' became public, things around the office went back to normal... well, normal, IS a relative term. The story may have stopped the tension in the office, but not the sessions. We were still required to have small group meetings with trainers, counselors and someone who called herself a 'political correctness coordinator'. These sessions were more useless and embarrassing than a high school sex education class, and high school Sex Ed classes had better graphics. The only classes I enjoyed were the role-play sessions, not because they were any good, because it gave me the opportunity to see if I could make the facilitator, Ms. Ramirez, blush. Today, because of scheduling conflicts only Lisa and I were in role-play class. This is gonna be fun... I can feel it!

"Okay... seeing that it is going to be only Lisa and Nick today... we're going to try to do as much as we can with just the three of us..." Lisa looked at me, I looked at Lisa, and we turned to look at Ms. Ramirez, leaned forward and grinned and nodded our heads at her. Ms. Ramirez looked at us and her cheeks turned red... this was gonna be easier than I thought! Ms. Ramirez tried to compose herself and pulled out a deck of flash cards from her bag. "These... are... role playing cards. They each have a scenario, which the two of you will enact, and then we will discuss the ramifications and repercussions of the situation. Nick why don't you take the first card..."

"Can I shuffle the desk?"

"Sure... they aren't in any particular order..."

I cut the deck and pulled out a card and acted like I was reading it.

"Do you want me to read it, or are you supposed to guess what the situation is?"

"No... read it out loud... we will re-enact the scene and then we'll discuss it..."

"Okay..." I turned the card over and made up my own story. "I'm a college political science teacher and Lisa is an exchange student who just has entered my office and is desperate to get an 'A' in my class... I'm desperate to get some 'A' in my office..." Ms. Ramirez did a double take... I looked at her. "...And *you* are a film student, preserving the encounter on high definition DVD for an Internet porn site..." Lisa leaned back in her chair and smiled. Ms. Ramirez looked at Lisa and then me. I stood up and took off my jacket and began to loosen my tie. I commented to Ms. Ramirez. "You're supposed to say 'Action'..." Ms. Ramirez grabbed her flash cards, got her things and stormed out of the room. I looked over at Lisa who was laughing into her hand. "I guess today's class is officially cancelled..." I looked at my watch. "We still have the room for another hour, got any ideas on how we could spend some quality time together?" Lisa smiled and unbuttoned the top button of her blouse and bit the tip of her index finger.

"What do you have in mind? Nicholas?"

"Oh... I think I know what you want...!

(Twenty minutes later... in the same room.)

"I know you want this... Don't you?" I asked Lisa.

"Yes Nicky... Put it in my mouth...Please?" And Lisa opened her mouth and closed her eyes.

"Yes ma'am..." and I complied with her request.

"Mmmm Nick, this is absolutely the best idea you've ever had!"

"I know... sometimes I even amaze myself..."

"*Yes*! Ordering sushi appetizers for lunch from 'Okahama Mama' was pure genius!"

"I aim to please... More wasabi?"

"Oh yes! You know I like it hot baby!"

"Take it easy with that stuff... you're gonna sweat right through your blouse..."

"You say that like it's a problem?" I fed Lisa another California roll.

276

"I don't have a problem seeing you in a wet T shirt, but I don't need any more 'sensitivity training' *thank you...*"

"I know! What idiot named it '*sensitivity training*', I mean, it sounds dirty..." Lisa said. I muffled a laugh. "No *really!* Doesn't it sound to you like we're all in a dimly lit room feeling each other up?" She asked.

I laughed and pointed at her with my chopsticks. "Now... *that* class, I would have no problem attending!"

"...Even if Bob was in the room?"

"Damn Lisa, you just killed that fantasy forever!" Lisa laughed. "Oh look at the time... We better get back to work before somebody catches on." We began to clean up the room and walked out. "I'll walk you back to the office. Lisa...? You know I always meant to ask you something..."

"Yes Nicky darling..."

"You're Russian, right?"

"Second generation... yes... why?"

"How did you get the name Lisa?"

"Oh that... It's my middle name; I just use it to give me a more 'American' sounding name..."

"Oh... so what's your given name?"

Lisa walked past me and put her hand on my face and hissed seductively. "It's Svetlana..." And she blew me a kiss... and exited the room,

(One fantasy dead... another one supercharged!)

- - -

Tim took an "early retirement package' a few weeks after Maggie was transferred to Mr. Hagen's office as a 'special liaison' with a minimal pay raise. No one in the office put two and two together. The story I started was good enough to satisfy the office gossipers and the rumormongers. The sessions continued, but Lisa and I were never gonna have sushi alone together again. We were only allowed in a full room or in separate classes. Damn! Given enough time alone together with her, I might have had a chance to break her, although there still is the 'she's married' thing. The office topic of discussion changed from '*Who snitched*?' to '*Who is gonna replace Maggie*?'

Chapter 53
(The New Guy)

All the bigwigs in corporate and marketing decided to have their meetings in our offices about the new marketing plans. It was failing miserably, corporate wanted to know why, marketing wanted to know how they could blame us... their presence in the building didn't help morale... Katherine was totally stressed for those weeks, running around like a chicken with her head cut off. The good news was... she didn't gain any weight. She was constantly in her office trying to get the protocols to match. What I had taught her about the old codes plus her own understanding only got her so far. Unless the company loosened the purse strings and come up with a new and updated computer program, this would always be a problem. I popped my head into her office. She was figuratively sweating bullets. "You okay?"

"Yes..." She continued to work.

"Stressed?"

"Yes..."

"Johnny?"

"No..."

"...Marketing?"

"No..."

"Not... *corporate*...?"

Katherine looked up at me. "Newbie..." I paused because I knew what that was... A "newbie" wasn't just a new hire... a "newbie" was a new hire brought in to replace someone... some one the company needed to get rid of.

"So, when does the newbie start?"

"They have him in training right now and should start to work here in about two or three months"

"Why so long?"

"They have him learning all the marketing protocols and computer programming..."

Nick knew this was bad news; usually a newbie was trained 'on site' by one of the floor managers. To have him trained

278

in the marketing offices meant the company was up to something big. This was no ordinary newbie.

"So... tell me about the 'newbie' they hired to try to replace me..."

"You mean; to replace Maggie..."

"Kiddo... I've been here longer than you... Whether Maggie retired or what just happened to get her transferred... her position was never gonna be filled... Her leaving was just the perfect smoke screen... to sneak the newbie in."

"How do you know the newbie isn't gonna replace me?"

"Ahhhh! No...! Thank you for playing our game... Tell her what she could have won Roddy!"

"How can you be so sure?"

"Collateral damage... I'm more disliked in corporate and marketing then you could ever be..."

"Nothing ever gets past you does it?" she said to me.

"Not much..." Nick said. Katherine sighed. "Need a back rub?" I asked.

"Yes...! But I don't have the time thanks..." I went behind her and began to rub her shoulders. Katherine purred. "Oh yeah... you hit the right spot!"

Katherine calmed down and relaxed. All the tension in her body melted away. But even with that, once I stopped she went right back to work.

"See? This is why they'll never replace you..."

"Do tell... I'm intrigued..."

"You react favorably to having smoke blown up your ass!"

"*What?*"

I started to massage her again. She gave herself to my whim. I worked her back around her bra strap. Katherine cooed. "Right now you are more determined than ever to make sure that their marketing plan is implemented properly. You're running around here like you have a new purpose in life, when all they really got you doing is chasing your own tail..."

"Excuse me... but I don't seem to remember you expressing your disdain to marketing and corporate about the new plans... like you did to me the first day I arrived... I should have known you were all talk and no action..."

279

"Okay…! Only because you weren't here many years ago when I first confronted marketing about their plans… allow me to bring you up to speed…" I stopped rubbing her back and sat down and began to tell my story… "Because of my background in marketing and my extensive experience in public relations… to be honest… since before you were born… I felt that I knew more about running this company than our marketing department ever could… so I did 'my own thing' as they say. I ignored marketing protocols while getting the job done… and I was correct… the offices' productivity levels jumped to 150% above the minimum requirements for three years straight… But then marketing found out that if I was able to circumvent their programming, the company might realize that they didn't need them so…"

"…They tried to get you to come around and use their programming protocols instead…"

"Righty 'O'…" I said. "Marketing then tried to recruit me to utilize their protocols and let them take the all credit… I *flatly refused…*"

"You *'flatly refused'*…?"

"…I told them to go fuck themselves… let's move on…" Katherine stopped working to listen. "Marketing wanted to know how steadfast I was to my opinion, so they tried a little experiment. They gave me two weeks off, without pay, to reconsider my opinion as to who should run this company, me or them… and do you know what my decision was?"

"…That they should run the company…"

"No… that *I* should run the company, but because they had the ability to indiscriminately restrict my income and possibly bankrupt me financially, and not visa versa… I said fuck them… I'm gonna do the job they *pay* me to do… and if they ever wanted my opinion… they would gladly tell me what it is…"

"…And the productivity levels…?"

"After a huge drop… have not exceeded 12% since…"

"…And marketing and corporate are okay with that?"

"…Are you kidding me? They circle jerk each other…!"

Katherine leaned back in her chair. "Well… that explains a lot…"

"What do you mean?"

"It explains why the productivity level dropped so dramatically after you had your 'Two weeks unpaid vacation'…"

"They told you I was sabotaging the company… didn't they?"

"…They did…"

"…And you were hired specifically to find out how I was doing it…"

"…I was…"

"…And you finally figured it out…?"

"Yes… you're fucking the company by doing exactly what it is marketing tells you to do…"

"No more… no less… and now you're afraid the newbie is here to replace you because you didn't do the job, you were hired to do…"

"What am I gonna do?"

"The devil is in the details and this place is hell!"

Katherine turned her computer off and put on her jacket.

"Where are you going?"

"It's after five o'clock and I don't get paid overtime…"

I looked at my watch. "Shall I walk you to your car Katherine?"

"Sure… thanks…" Katherine grabbed her purse and I walked her out.

"So… what are your plans for the weekend?"

"I wanna get drunk… would you like to join me so you can hold my hair if I puke?"

I've had better invitations, but I had nothing better to do. "Why not? I've got no place to go and all weekend to get there…" I escorted her to the bar across the street from the job.

"Are you drinking tonight… or are you just having ginger ale…?" She asked.

"We'll see where the night takes us…"

"Okay!"

Author's Note

We have now returned to the point where Jennifer Jones has started her 'internship' at the main office of Faber Co. And Theo and Hagen plan to transfer her to Katherine's office after she learns the marketing protocols.

The Tortured Soul Trilogy
(A Tortured Soul)
Chapter 54
(Take Me Home Tonight)

Katherine didn't know anything about the newbie... except that he was currently in an extensive training program and we would meet him sometime in the next few weeks or so. Besides I didn't really want to talk shop... I just wanted Katherine to get drunk so I could take her home... and this time, if she put on a show for me... I would do a puppet show for her...oh yeah I'm packing and I'm staying for the curtain call this time! Katherine didn't get too drunk that night... she got nice... and 'friendly'... she couldn't keep her hands off me and I was dying to get my hands all over her. I took her to her car. "I... ah... don't wanna go home right now... can we just stop off at your place for a while?"

"What about Johnny?" I asked. Not that I really cared.

"*Fuck 'im!*" she said. I pointed to myself. "You *know* what I mean..." she replied.

"Why can't we just go to your place...?" I asked. A woman is more comfortable in her own home and more willing to allow things to just happen. And she looked at me and bit her lip. "Oh... he's staying at your place isn't he?"

"No, but he might drop by... unexpectedly... for a booty call... and I'd rather not have him find us there together... Just in case... you know... You understand..."

"Totally... okay... my place it is... but ah..."

"What?"

"Well... I wasn't expecting to have company tonight so my place is a little messy..."

"Oh... I don't mind messy... it's *dirty* I have a problem with..."

"...Well still... I'd like to freshen the place up a bit... you know... bachelor and all..."

"Oh... you wanna hide all your dirty magazines and pornos..."

"...Among other things..."

"Well... maybe I'm okay with dirty after all..."

282

"Behave yourself…"

"Why…? Is Poppa gonna spank?"

My ears were red hot and my pants became tight around the crotch. "Behave… I said…"

"Okay… I'll be good…" Katherine kissed me. "Real good…"

I walked Katherine to my house. I lived only six blocks away from the bar. It was just past the bistro I had taken Katherine to. Mandy waved to me from the window. Katherine saw it, waved to her and stopped and kissed me again. I guess Katherine was just marking her territory, Mandy laughed. We continued to walk in the fresh evening air. By the time we got to my place Katherine wasn't as drunk as when we left the bar. The walk, the night air… or just the realization of what was about to happen, sobered her up. She hesitated at the steps to my building.

"Katherine? Are you okay?"

"Yes… I… just…"

I turned to her. "You don't have to come in… it's okay… we can walk back to the bar and I'll drive you home…"

"But I want to…"

"Yes… I know, but you don't *have* to…"

Katherine pulled me closer to her and kissed me deeply; she held my face with her hands and kissed me more passionately… "But I really, really want to… give a guy like you… a shot!" I kissed Katherine softly and held her hand and led her to my door. I kissed her again before I opened it and took her inside. "Wow… this is nice… and it's not so messy… for a bachelor…"

"Thanks… but I do want to put a few things away… will you excuse me?"

"Sure… where's your bathroom, I'd like to freshen up…"

I pointed to it. "Hey…? You're not gonna…?"

"*No…*! I'm okay…! I just want to freshen up a bit…"

"The light is on the left. And the seat is up!"

"Thanks for the warning!" She went in and when she closed the door I grabbed a few things and some 'catalogues' I had left out and put them into the second bedroom and when I came out, I locked the door. I sat down on the couch waiting for Katherine to come out of the bathroom.

"Would you like to hear some music?" No answer. "Katherine?" Still no answer. "Oh god… I hope she hasn't passed out in my bathroom…" I went to the door but it was wide open and she wasn't there. "Katherine?" I went back to the living room. She wasn't there either. "Katherine…?" (Did she chicken out and leave? Funny, I didn't hear the front door, where could have she have gone to?) Then I heard a sound in my bedroom. I opened the door and there she was, in my bed. She had propped up my pillows on the headboard and was just sitting there with her legs crossed and her arms across the headboard. She was only wearing my white silk shirt, my blue silk necktie and her pumps. "You *do* know… that's *not* a proper Windsor knot you tied…?" Katherine smiled. I don't really know if she got the joke or not, but I really didn't care. I just loved her smile. I couldn't wait to see her wearing nothing else. Or I could use my tie as a leash…

"What took you so long to find me?" She cooed.

"I had no clue where you were…" I said. Katherine slowly unbuttoned my shirt she was wearing, only the tie held it over her breasts. I could see she had a rock hard six-pack, just like I knew she would. I took out my wallet. She gave me a look of concern. I opened my wallet and took out a condom I always carried. I held it up for her to see. She smiled and nodded approvingly.

"Marco…" She whispered.

"Polo…" I answered.

She rolled over on her knees on my bed and she rotated her hips. "Marco…"

"Polo…"

She spread her knees and placed her face in the pillows. Her ass was in the sky. "Marco…"

"Polo…" I walked to the edge of my bed. She reached behind her and pulled my shirt up over her ass… Good Lord… her ass… was… magnificent!

"Marco…" And she gyrated her ass in a circle… I kneeled up on the bed behind her.

"Polo…" I unzipped my pants and put the condom on and when I looked up at her again that's when I saw it… Katherine was wearing a pale blue lace thong with a pink heart on the back patch. I was a little puzzled. "Where did you get that thong?"

"I found it in a gift bag in your closet when I got your shirt and tie... you like?"

"Take it off!" I barked.

"Yes daddy..." She purred and she slowly reached for the patch and began to pull it down.

"No! No...stop!" I closed my eyes and turned my head. "Take it off now!"

She turned to me and saw that I was very dismayed and upset. "What? *Why*...? I thought you would like to see me in these... I saw the gift bag in your closet and I thought you bought them for me...!" I got off the edge of the bed and turned my back to Katherine. I stifled a cough... "Are you crying?"

"*No*..."

"Are... you... *laughing*...?"

"Yes!" came out muffled through my hand covering my mouth.

"Why are you laughing?" I couldn't answer and Katherine threw a pillow at me. "Why *are you* laughing?" Now I could hear it in her voice that she was totally pissed at me.

"Because..."

"*Because*... why?" And another pillow flew by my head. I was hysterically laughing by now. I turned to Katherine and she had my nightstand lamp in her hand and she was about to throw it at me.

"I'm laughing...because... you're wearing... *my daughter's panties*!" By now I was now laughing uncontrollably. Katherine had a look of horror and disgust. I ran out the bedroom. I was laughing so hard I couldn't breathe. I closed the door and tried to speak to Katherine through the door. "I'm not laughing *at you*... it's just..." I couldn't breathe. I was hyperventilating. My daughter had purchased those panties the last time she visited me and had left them here by mistake. Although my daughter never wore them, just the idea of them *being* my daughters... threw me off! I went to the kitchen and put a paper bag over my mouth. I was still breathing into the bag when Katherine came out my room, fully dressed and totally embarrassed. She refused to make eye contact with me. "You have to understand... seeing you wearing my daughters' panties..."

Katherine kept her eyes down and whispered. "Take me home... please!" Katherine never spoke to me on the walk back to her car, and she never even looked up. She didn't even see the surprised look on Mandy's face as we walked past the 'C' cup. Katherine handed me the keys and got in. I got in and started the car. That's when she spoke to me. "I...have...never...been...so... *embarrassed* in all my life...!"

"Neither have I..." And I drove off. "Well, except for that one time when I was in high school and my mother caught me having sex with a cheerleader on her couch!" Katherine busted out laughing and hit me with her purse. By the time we got to her house. We were both laughing and telling each other our most embarrassing stories... trying to play '*Can you top this*?' We arrived at her place and I got out of the car and came around and opened Katherine's door. We were both laughing. "Well... I guess you can't beat *that* story..." I said.

"Sure I can..."

"...Really...?"

"Sure...! Did I ever tell you the time my co-worker caught me in his bed wearing his daughter's panties?" I coughed and laughed. I hugged Katherine and kissed her on the forehead. We both laughed in each other's arms. I handed her, her car keys. "Are you gonna get home alright Nick?"

"I'll be fine... and you?"

"I'm good..." and she kissed me gently. We both were a little more relaxed. "You wanna come in for a night cap?"

"No... it's getting late... I better get on home."

"You sure...? I can assure you that the underwear I can model for you are mine...!"

"*I... don't... have another...*"

Katherine smiled and nodded. "It's okay... I love the fact that you care enough about me not to want to ride bareback..." We both knew that the moment had passed and we would have to wait until the planets aligned before the opportunity would present itself again. I watched her as she opened her door, pause, blow me a kiss and go inside. I turned and walked back to my place. Had I walked Katherine inside or called a cab and waited, maybe, just maybe I would have noticed that her bedroom light turned on... before she got all the way inside...

I'm starting to think that if it wasn't for bad luck, I wouldn't have any luck at all. Not only did I not get to have sex with Katherine, but when I got home, there was a voice message from Lisa. She had finally decided to get separated from her husband and was bored as hell and wanted to go out and party. She and her playmate, Valerie wanted to spend the weekend in Vegas. Valerie could always get comp rooms in Vegas, because she was an exotic dancer in one of the casinos. Lisa specifically said on the message; *'You bought me sushi and sashimi... would you like me and Valerie to make you a sandwich?'* This time I knew Lisa wasn't being coy... Now she had an excuse to cut loose and I no longer had an excuse not to... *you know*! The message concluded with *'Call me back before nine and we'll pick you up.'* I had partied with them once before and if Lisa and Valerie were spending the weekend in Vegas, Vegas was in big trouble. I looked at my watch. 11:15pm it said. I would have no problem catching a redeye and flying out there tonight... *if*... I knew where they were staying tonight. Damn it Janet!

I got ready for bed and took out a porno I liked, but I wasn't in the mood and it would only remind me of what I had missed and what I was missing and that would have been much better than any porno... Oh please... who am I kidding? I played the tape and spanked it like a high school geek who found his sister's Victoria Secrets catalogue... I woke up the next morning, still erect from last night's fist fest. "Well, good morning to you too... but I'm so sorry that you're all dressed up cause there's no place to go..." I turned on my computer to check my MySpace site... and catch up on what all the total strangers on my friends list were doing. That's when my computer chimed; *"Good Morning Nick!"*

"Good morning *bitch*!"

"You have... *two*... *new*... messages!" The first message was from someone I didn't recognize. Normally I delete those, but the subject was '*We need Male!*' and it was from a Vegas hotel... maybe it was from Lisa and Valerie. It was, and it was a series of the most provocative pictures I had ever seen. Actually to say they were provocative was like saying the Grand Canyon was a crack in the sidewalk. Lisa finally let it ALL hang out, and I missed it. I looked at all the pictures one by one. How did they do that? I wondered. I unzipped my pants, took out my stiff cock... and looked down at it...

"Well what do you know? It's for you!" I don't know what turned me on more... the high def pictures or the fact that I personally knew these two crazy bitches in the photos... As I polished the ole bayonet, I realized I wasn't thinking of Lisa or Valerie... my thoughts were focused on Katherine's tight ass in the air from the night before... without my daughter's panties of course! After I was done surfing the net, I made myself some tea and went back to the computer to download the photos into a new file titled "Svetlana". That's when I remembered that I had two messages. I opened the second message; it was from the job... it was from Katherine. I guess she E-mailed me from work, but why didn't she just come over? I read the message and it asked me to meet her at the 'C' cup at 11am. I looked at my watch. Damn it, it was way past twelve already! I quickly got dressed and ran down there. I got to the bistro and Mandy ran up to me and hugged me.

"Thank God you're okay..."

"Of course I'm okay... why would you think I wouldn't be...?"

"I'm sorry... but after I saw your friend..."

"You mean Katherine?"

"Yes... after I saw her... I thought you two had gotten into a terrible accident..."

"What are you talking about Mandy...?"

"Oh my God...! You don't know? Here... she left a note for you..." Mandy went and took a note off the register and handed it to me. I didn't open it.

"Mandy... why would you think that Katherine and I were in an accident?"

"Oh Nicky..." Mandy started to cry. "Her face was all bruised up, she had a black eye and her lips were all swollen... I didn't even realize it was her until you didn't show up and she left the note for you." Mandy looked down. "I think she was mugged...!" She whispered.

I lifted Mandy's chin to look at me. "You know damn well, this wasn't an accident... and she wasn't mugged..." Tears formed in her eyes. I needed her to deal with this. I didn't want her to rationalize what happened to Katherine. "Why didn't you call me?" I asked.

"I tried... but your line was busy..." (Damn... I was on the Internet...) "I tried to get her to wait but she just left out of here..."

"Was she alone...?"

"She was... but then some young kid came and got her... they left together..." I crumbled the note in my hand. Mandy then realized who that was with her. "I'm so glad you're okay... We were so worried... I tried to call you again but then you didn't answer..."

"I was probably already on my way here..."

Mandy hugged me and sobbed. She dabbed her tears with her apron. "Is she gonna be alright?"

"I don't know Mandy... I don't know...."

"Fix it...Nicky... Fix it like you did for me... please?"

I hugged Mandy. "I'll see what I can do..." I kissed her on the forehead and began to leave when Mandy called to me.

"Nicky...!"

"Yes Mandy?"

"The note...!"

I looked at the crumbled paper in my hand and put it in my pocket. I didn't open it until I got home. I needed a moment to calm down before I did anything rash.

Dear Nicholas;

I'm going to be out of the office for about a month or so traveling with Johnny on his tour. I need you to contact Mr. Hagen and let him know, also go to personnel and clear it with payroll, I still have vacation time coming... whatever my vacation time doesn't cover I'll use my comp time. I'll straighten it all out when I get back. Also, while I'm gone I'm gonna leave the office in your hands, you have carte blanche, do what ever you feel is right, I'll take the heat with marketing when I get back...

Love You
Katherine

289

The note was stained with Katherine's' tears... and a smudge of blood. "Son of a BITCH! I wish I had that punk right here, right now!" I went by her place. No one was home. I called her house, several times... no answer. I even went back in the middle of the night. No lights were on. She didn't answer her door. She didn't even answer her cell phone. Her voice mail was off. I even called the local hospitals, no Katherine... I don't know if that calmed my nerves or scared me even more... I went home and there was another e-mail from her. It simply said.

"I'm okay! Please don't worry about me and don't come by my house... I know you understand why!"
                                                              Love, Katherine.

I took a deep breath and a tear came to me eye... She was alive! She was hurting... but she was alive... It wasn't long before I was crying like a punk... Lord! What has this woman done to me?

- - -

It got to the point that Katherine not coming into work on a Monday was no longer a surprise to anyone. Maggie was floated back to our office to help out wherever she could. I was handing out the day's codes for entry when I stopped by to drop of a file at Lisa's desk. "Morning Lisa... I see you're finally back from your 'Vegas Vacation'..."

"Good morning Nick... Val and I really missed 'having' you last weekend... did you happen to get my e-mail?"

"Yes, yes I did..."

"And did you get a chance to look at it?"

"Yes... I did... thank you."

"So... aren't you gonna ask me about the rest of my weekend?"

"I don't really have to ask... do I?"

"Maybe I *want* to tell you all about it... over lunch perhaps?"

"Perhaps… and speaking of 'lunch' I did happen to notice that you two enjoyed the… uh… 'all-you-can-eat-buffet' in Vegas…"

"Yes we did… but it needed a little *something* more…"

"Oh yeah…? What?"

"We really wanted a little 'kielbasa' to top off the meal…"

"Well… maybe next time… you'll put in your meat order a little earlier and you won't have delivery problems…"

"Oh… Absolutely…"

The Tortured Soul Trilogy
(A Tortured Soul)
Chapter 55
(Where Have All The Cowboys Gone?)

It was almost two months before Katherine was able to come back to work. It was at least two weeks later that she was able to come out of her office and mingle with the rest of us. I went into Katherine's office late one afternoon; I felt I needed to speak with her. "Katherine?"

"Yes Nick?"

"May I have a moment of your time?"

"Sure come on in..." Nick closed the door and sat down in the chair across from her desk. "What can I help you with Nick?"

"You remember the sexual harassment seminars we had to go to?"

"Of course..."

"I want to make an appointment with Ms. Ramirez..."

Katherine laughed out loud. "Ms. Ramirez...? You *do* know that woman doesn't *ever* want to see *you* again?"

"The appointment isn't for me..."

Katherine was puzzled. "Who's it for...?"

"For you..."

"But I'm not being sexually harassed at work..."

"She also counsels victims of domestic violence..."

"*What?*" Katherine didn't get what I was saying.

"I've checked her credentials... she's actually quite good at what she does..."

"And *yet* you ridiculed her!"

"I don't *need* sexual harassment counseling Katherine."

"...And I don't *need* counseling for domestic violence... *Thank you!*"

"I used to think that too..."

"I don't give a *shit* what you *think!*" She was getting a little pissed I was in her business.

"I was talking about me..."

Katherine's face was in shock. "*You*...? A victim of..."

"Yes... *me*..."

Katherine now looked at Nick with a quiet disbelief. "But I don't want to... I mean..."

"If necessary, I will go with you and hold your hand... if that what it takes..."

"I broke up with Johnny..."

"... Cause he's a low down dirty mother fucker..."

"That's right!"

"...Until the next time... when he's a *sweet ass* motherfucker... and then he hurts you again..."

"Mind your damn business... I don't need your fucking help here Nick!" Nick sat there. "Get the fuck out of my office!" Nick just sat there. Katherine became more and more defensive and aggravated. "Did you hear me? Get out... I don't need your help... or your pity...! You don't know anything about me... You went through something like *this*? *Did you*? So *fucking* what? What are you? Some kind of expert...? Huh? You're just gonna come here and fix all my problems? Who do you think you are...? Superman? Are *you* Superman, Nick? Do you have a big red 'S' on your chest? Do *you*...?" Then she calmed down; she spoke very calmly and sarcastically. Nick knew she was about to blow. "So? Tell me... Do you happen to have the answers to *all* the problems I have? ...In your *pants*, maybe? Are the secrets to the universe to be found in your dick? Hmmm...? Is that where it's been hiding all this time...?" Katherine laughed. "If I rub it... will a genie appear and grant me three wishes...? Nick didn't answer. The room became dead silent... for a moment... "Get *the* FUCK out of my office! NOW!" Nick still just sat there. He patiently waited for her to vent all her venom and to break down... it didn't take her much longer. Katherine stood up and slammed her file on her desk and screamed at the top of her lungs. "Did you hear me? I *said* get the *fuck* out of my office!" Nick just sat there. He knew what she was doing, and he was prepared for it. Katherine looked at him silently and broke down into tears. "You... would... come with me...?" She sobbed. Nick nodded his head. "You would... hold my hand...?" Nick nodded his head again and he stood up. Katherine walked over to Nick. Nick held her in his arms and rocked her gently as she cried.

"Shall I make the appointment for us?" Katherine nodded and cried. Nick took out his cell phone and dialed Ms. Ramirez as he held Katherine close to him. "Hello Mercedes…? Its Nick… we'll be there in about an hour… is that good for you?"

Katherine began to cry uncontrollably. Katherine did *not* cry pretty… if you know what I mean. "We're on our way… Thank you Mercedes! I owe you one…" Nick opened the door and Maggie was standing there waiting for them. She looked around and signaled that the coast was clear. "Maggie is gonna walk you to the parking lot, I'll bring your car around."

Katherine gave him the car keys. Maggie hugged Katherine. "There, there Kathy… It's gonna be alright… Nicky is gonna take good care of you… I *promise!*"

"I don't know how this happened! How did this happen to me? How did I get here?" Katherine sobbed.

"It's a dark and lonely road we've all walked at one time or another… and it's easy to lose your way… and although we walk it alone… we're not the only ones who have passed through here… If you look closely, you'll see the road is covered with our footprints… and our tears…" Katherine looked at Maggie in amazement. "Yes dear… No one is immune… or safe… not even me!" Katherine hugged Maggie tightly and they cried in each other's arms. Maggie dried their tears with her hankie. "Come on Kathy… let's go… Nicky is waiting for you… and if you're smart… you *won't* keep *that* man waiting…" Maggie walked her out and helped her get in the car and the two of them drove off. Maggie waved and blew a kiss to them. Maggie said a prayer for them.

Chapter 56
(I Touch Myself)

A few weeks into her therapy sessions with Ms. Ramirez, Katherine was feeling a little better about herself. She was working out and watching her diet. She wasn't all right but she felt things were getting better. She dealt with her problems one day at a time. Things at work were a little better and Nick was so very helpful to her. He helped relieve a lot of the stress of the job off her. He instinctively knew when to help her and when to let her do it herself, but he was always around to lend a hand if she needed him. He would take over a difficult job, rub her back, tell her jokes and bring her tea to brighten her day, but never let her think she was being patronized in any way. She was so very grateful for Nick's kindness and friendship.

After work one day, Katherine settled into bed to get some rest and she grabbed the TV remote to catch up on some of her favorite shows she had taped. That's when the phone rang... She let the machine take it... It was Johnny. He was all; '*Baby I'm sorry... Baby it won't happen again... Baby I need you... Baby, you know how I get sometimes...*!" Just like Mercedes said he would. Then the next call from Johnny came about ten minutes later... It was a lot of cursing and swearing and threats... Yeah, Mercedes warned her about that too! She checked the caller ID. He was calling from California so she wasn't afraid he would stop by. Then phone rang again... it was Johnny... again. She took the phone off the hook. Katherine was very shaken by hearing Johnny's voice. He was *not*... just gonna go away... Katherine began to shake and shiver like a junkie going through withdrawal. Katherine sat on the middle of the bed holding her knees to her chest and rocking and crying to herself. "I'm not falling for that shit! I'm better than that!" She said and she began to cry harder. That's when she remembered Mercedes told her that if she found herself getting weak... to find safety in a private place. Katherine got out of the bed and went to her closet and took out a gift bag and placed it on her end table. Inside was a present she had purchased for herself on the Internet but she didn't have the nerve to open it... until now.

"*Find safety in a private place...*" she remembered Mercedes say to her. Katherine took a scissor and cut open the package. She then opened a pack of "D" batteries and put them in. She turned it on and it buzzed in her hand. She liked the feeling and the texture of it. The vibrator was the latest thing in latex sex toys. It felt almost real. She stroked it and fondled it. In her hands the vibrations relaxed her nerves. She brought it to her lips and kissed it. The sensation was very strange but she liked that too. She found herself licking it and kissing it. It tasted a little funny, that's when she remembered that it came with a flavored lubricant. She took the tube and squeezed a bit into her hand and rubbed it down. That felt even better in her hands. It tasted even better in her mouth, between the vibrations and the cinnamon in the lubricant her lips and mouth tingled and got warm. Katherine sat back on her bed and licked and sucked her new best friend. Her nipples were hard and her pussy was wet. She pinched her nipples and purred and cooed. "You'll never hurt me... will you?" She took her feet and spread them over the bedposts to hold her legs open. "Would you like to see your new home?" Katherine giggled because she knew she was being silly. She took the dildo and slowly brought it down to her wet and hungry pussy. "You're so bad... Yes you are! Yes you are... You are soooo bad! Yes you are..." It touched her clit and her eyes went to the back of her head. "*Holy... SHIT!*" Her mouth was open wide and her tongue came out and wiggled like a snake. "Kitty *like!*" And then she took her fingers and held open her labia and slid the dildo deep inside her... Katherine sat up and her mouth was wide open and she was breathing heavily and her jaw trembled. "Where in the *HELL* have *you* been all my life?" She lay back down and began to push and pull and twist and turn it. "Why... didn't.... any... body... tell... me... about... *THIS*?" she stammered. Katherine let out screams she didn't know she had in her. "Yes! Yes! Oh yeah! Oh Yeah! Oh YEAH! Ohhhh... *You... Mother...* fuckerrrrrrrrrr!" Her jaw trembled and eyes went in back of her head again and she began to pant like a caged animal. She unhooked her legs from the bedposts and slapped her ass and began to suck her thumb. "Oh! Ohh! Ohhh...! NICK...eeeeeee!!!!! And she orgasmed and squealed like a banshee. She pulled it out, dropped it on the bed and began to cry like a baby. "It's not fair...! It's not fucking fair! And she rolled up into a ball slammed her hands on her bed again and again. "It's *not fucking* fair!" Katherine fell asleep crying and sucking her thumb.

The Tortured Soul Trilogy
(A Tortured Soul)
Chapter 57
(White Rabbit)

At the end of the workday, Nick is sitting at his desk getting ready to go home. The office is just about emptied out and George, the janitor has started to clean up so he can get an early start to his weekend. "Nick...?" Nick turns to see Katherine standing behind him.

"Hey Katherine..."

Nick looks around. "How long have you been standing there...?"

"Just a moment... or two..."

"Is there... something you wanted to speak to me about?"

"Yes... may I have a moment of your time?"

"Of course... anything for you..." Nick sat on the edge of his desk. "What's up...?"

"Nick... I..." Katherine hesitated.

"Are *you* alright?" Nick asked.

"Yes... I... Just don't know how to ask this..."

"You know you can ask me... *anything*!"

"Remember when you said; that is was all about control and who had it...?

"Of course I remember..." Nick looked at her with concern.

"You said; I was in control but I didn't know it..."

"That's right..."

"Well... after that time we spent at the mall together and that woman..."

"Michelle..."

"Michelle... said that I should do whatever you said... because you were the best... I got the impression... you helped her alot... with a problem..."

"I did... but I can't discuss her problem with you..."

"I know... I get that... what I want is... I mean... could you..."

"Help you with your problem...?"

"Yes...! Would you be willing to take me on as a client...? I'll pay you whatever you want..."

Nick stood up. "I don't charge for my *services*..."

"Oh...! I didn't mean to..."

"It's okay... it's okay... no offense taken..."

Katherine leaned into Nick and put her hand on his chest. "You said once; you would 'teach me'..." Katherine bit her lower lip. "Would you be willing to... *help me*...?"

Nick took Katherine's hand and kissed it gently. "What about Mercedes...? Do you feel like she's not helping any more...?"

"Oh...! She's great... and I've learned a lot from her in the last two months and I will continue to see her, but... I need something... *else*... that I can't get from her... Do you understand...?"

"I think I do..."

"Will you help me Nick... Please...?"

"My methods are pretty radical and it's not for everybody... Are you *absolutely* sure you want to do this?"

"*No*...! But I feel that you're the only one with the solution to my problem...!"

"I have no guarantees that I can help you..."

"I don't know why... but I have a very strong feeling in my gut that you can..."

"What are your plans for this evening?"

"My dance card is free and clear all weekend..."

"Do you remember my address...?"

"Of course... why...?"

"I want you to meet me there tonight at eight o'clock sharp..."

"Why can't I just come with you now...?"

Nick quickly changed his tone. "Because... I *said* so! My place... Eight o'clock..."

Katherine blinked and acquiesced to his authority. "Do you need me to bring anything... or wear anything...? 'Special'...?"

"No... just go home and freshen up a bit and meet me at my place at eight... I'll leave the door open."

"Okay...! I'll be there with bells on!"

Nick paused and thought for a moment. "Hmmm… *bells…*"

"What?"

"Nothing… just a thought…" Katherine turned to leave. "Katherine…" Katherine stopped and turned back. "…Are you *sure* you want to do this?" Katherine nodded with a desperate look on her face. "Do you prefer red or white wine…?" I asked her.

"White… but anything you have is fine…"

"Okay!"

"Okay…" Katherine nodded. She turned and left but mumbled to herself; "Okay… *okay…*"

Nick put his hands in his pockets and watched Katherine leave. He took a deep breath and let it out slowly. "Okay *Alice…* tonight… we go down the rabbit hole… and find out what's really on the other side…" Nick breathed in and let it out slowly. "I just hope we *both* know what we're doing…!"

The Tortured Soul Trilogy
(A Tortured Soul)
Chapter 58
(Hanky Panky)

That night Nick is waiting for Katherine to arrive and is making a peanut butter and jelly sandwich in the eat-in kitchen. Katherine knocked twice and entered. It was five to eight. "Nick?"

"Come on in Katherine... You're five minutes early... Make yourself at home... would you like a sandwich?"

Katherine folded her jacket over the living room chair. "Maybe later.... You know the last time I was here I never really got a chance to see the place..."

"Yes... you ah... did want to leave quite abruptly..."

Katherine giggled. "So... you wanna give me the nickel tour now?"

"Sure... let me show you around..." Nick began to lead Katherine around the house. He started to show his things as if he were Vanna White on a game show. He stopped at the bedroom door and hesitated. "Well I believe you've *seen* the bedroom..."

Katherine shielded her eyes and giggled and walked past it to the next bedroom door. "So... what's in here?"

"*This*? This is my private... um... 'Game room'..."

"Game room...? So what kind of games do you play in there?"

"I don't think you're ready to find out that out yet..."

"Really...? I know you think I'm just a kid... but I'm a grown woman and I'm not so easily shocked or surprised!"

"Is that so...?"

"Yep... I've pretty much seen it all, except what you have in your game room of course! So...? What's in there? A pool table...? Foosball...? An *iron maiden*...?"

"Okay... but you can't say I didn't warn you..."

Nick slowly opens the door. Katherine looks inside. "*Holy SHIT...!*"

"So much for not being easily surprised..."

Katherine walked right in; Anderson is pleasantly surprised by her boldness. "I wasn't expecting anything like this…" In the middle of the room was a large six and a half foot in diameter steel ring bolted to the floor, ceiling and walls. Behind it was a seven-foot tall, freestanding mahogany door with leather restraints and steel rings built into it. The opposite wall was covered with different, whips, chains, paddles and martial arts weapons. Katherine stepped into the middle of the ring and instinctively grabbed the top of it. "Where did you get the door?"

"A salvage yard…"

"Is it from a church?"

"I don't know, but I do believe some people have found *religion* strapped to it…."

Above the door was a hand carved plaque with Latin written on it. "And what does that say?"

"It's Latin for; *'That which does not kill us, only serves to make us stronger.'*"

Katherine looked at the wheel and the many leather restraints attached. "And what is this thing?"

"It used to be a German gym wheel, people would work out on it, but I modified it a bit and now I call it the *'Portal of Pain'.*"

"And you use it to…" She queried.

"Work other 'things' out on it…."

"You punish people…?"

"Not *people*… I only have female clients…"

"*Clients*…?" She asked wondering why he would use that word.

"I should have said acquaintances… what I do… is a 'mutual' relationship… They get what they need; I get what I need… no money ever changes hands."

Katherine turned around to Nick, but never let go of the wheel. "And do you have a lot of 'acquaintances'… that you get what you need from?"

"Not as many as you might think… and not anyone you know!"

"So… no one from work has been in this room?"

"You're the first woman that I've ever worked with, that has been in this room…"

"I feel so *special*…!"

"You... should feel 'privileged'..." Katherine bit her lower lip. "You'll feel 'special' when you're tied to the portal."

"So how does this 'work'...?"

"There are two safety protocols in here... First; is this remote..."

"What is that?"

"It's exactly what it is... a control... you press the button and everything stops... press it again and it continues..."

"What continues?"

"Whatever was happening to you before you pressed the control. The second safety protocol; is the safety word..."

"What's a safety word?"

"It's a word that when you say it... the pain stops..."

"What kinda word is it?"

"I like the word 'when'..."

"...When...?"

"Yes... like 'say when?'...!"

Kitten held onto the ring and began to breathe heavy. "When do we get started?"

"Little girl...! We already have!" Katherine held onto the ring tighter. She arched her back and stood there, waiting. Nick stepped up to her, reached up and grabbed her by the wrists. Katherine sighed and shivered a bit. He breathed softly on her neck, Katherine purred. Nick pulled her hands off the ring. By now Katherine was out of breath and panting. "Relax... not today..." Nick escorted Katherine out of the room, and sat her in the living room. He poured her a glass of red wine. Katherine sipped it twice. It helped calm her nerves.

"So... you're really into that Sadomasochistic kinky sex stuff?"

Nick poured himself a glass and sat next to Katherine. "No... I'm into slave/master relationships..."

"What's the difference?"

"To those who are not in the lifestyle, it's very difficult to explain... and very easy to confuse."

"You do this a lot?"

"No not really... a slave/master relationship is very tricky... you have to absolutely trust your partner."

"Is that what *happened* to you... you know...?"

"No... *this* has absolutely nothing to do with the woman who abused me..."

"I'm sorry... I didn't mean to pry..."

"It's okay... one of my sex partners was very much like Johnny... she liked to hurt people, it took a while before I had enough..."

"Enough to say 'when'...?" Nick nodded. "What was it like for you to endure that kind of pain?" she asked. She really needed to know what Nick thought.

"I didn't like it..."

"What ever happened to her?"

Nick took a sip of wine. "I don't know... and I pretty much don't give a shit..."

Katherine paused. "So you *don't* like to be punished?"

"No... *I don't*...!"

"Why not...?" It felt strange to ask that.

"It doesn't *do* it for me... besides... the executioner *never* offers to stick his head on the chopping block..."

"And you'll *never*..."

Nick took a deep breath. "It's a level of trust I've yet to achieve with any woman... I would much rather be the submissive...."

"Huh...? But I thought it was the submissive that gets abused..."

"Like I said it's very difficult to explain... you know very little about the lifestyle... When done properly, *no one* gets abused, and with the right partner, it is really a very controlled environment... You might even like it..."

"You think I like being abused?" Katherine was a bit put off by that statement.

"I never said you like to be abused... you enjoy *pain*, you're problem is; you gave up your control and it became abuse..."

"That's a load of bullshit!"

"I'll prove it to you..."

"How...?" He took the glass of wine from her and put it on the table and grabbed her neck and started to choke her. Gently at first but then he began to squeeze tighter, Katherine fidgeted a bit but didn't move; Nick continued to squeeze harder and tighter.

Katherine's' eyes widened and she was feeling like she was about to lose consciousness. "Please don't kill me... STOP!" Nick abruptly stopped and walked away. Katherine felt her throat. She coughed and choked a bit.

"See what I mean?"

"You tried to kill me!"

"You didn't try to stop me!"

"I said *stop*!"

"Eventually...! But you never pulled away from me... even when you thought your life was in danger! You almost allowed *me* to decide 'when' it was enough!" Katherine rubbed her throat. "Now answer me a question..." he asked. Nick handed her back her glass of wine.

"What?"

"Are you madder that I choked you... *or* that I stopped when you told me to?"

"I... I don't know!"

"Well... If you are going to have and keep control, you'd better know for sure!" Katherine rubbed her throat again. Nicholas got up and went into the kitchen, to the fridge and handed her an ice pack. Katherine placed the cold pack on and around her neck and he sat down across from her. Nick freshened up her drink. "Relinquishing your control of the situation will cause you to lash out to regain it, and that's when people really get hurt... physically and emotionally..."

"But why do you have to hurt me?"

"Because it's what you want me to do..."

"I don't understand..."

"As your slave I would do... anything for you... If you asked to... *cook* my dinner, I would allow you to do so... If you asked me to... do the dishes, I would do so... because it pleases you. If you ask me to inflict pain on you... I would do so... as long as it pleases you. I would do whatever you asked me to do, simply because it pleases me, to please you... If you want me to hurt you... I will hurt you to your pleasure, until you say when..."

"You would do anything I tell you to do?"

"Yes Madam..."

"Would you make love to me?"

"Until *I* was finished... or until *you* were finished?"

"Until I was finished…"

"Yes Madam…"

"I'm scared…!" And Katherine trembled a bit, but it was more from anticipation than fear.

"You should be… but you're not scared enough…" Nick said but Katherine didn't understand his reply.

"When can we start our sessions…?" Katherine held her neck. She was now anxious for more.

"Right now… if you like…"

"Okay…"

"Do you trust me?"

"Yes…"

"Well you *shouldn't*…" Katherine was confused by his reply, but before she could question him about it, Nick cut her off. "First, before we begin, we have to lay down some ground rules. These are NOT negotiable."

"Okay…"

"I will do anything for you, or to you… that pleases you…"

"I get that…"

"However, there are lines that I have drawn, that I will not go beyond. Any attempt to make me cross those lines, severs our personal relationship *permanently*. Understood…?"

"Ah huh…"

"First and foremost; I will never strike you with a closed fist or kick you. I'm into giving *pain*, not *brutality*. Nothing that I do or use will ever break your bones, incapacitate you or leave any permanent scar tissue, physically or mentally. That also means that I will not disrespect or humiliate you by calling you any derogatory names, unless you're okay with it."

"I don't like the 'c' word… other than that… you can call me anything you want!"

"…Very well then…" And Nick continued. "I will never use any sharp or jagged objects to cut you or draw blood. I will never use a flame or a chemical that will leave a burn mark on your body." Katherine sighed a sigh of relief. She was deathly afraid of needles. She wouldn't even get her ears pierced and only had one pair that her mother did when she was very young.

"What about hot wax…?"

"Because you brought it up... I will be willing to discuss the possibility with you..." Katherine nodded. Nick continued. "I will never leave any bruise on you that can be seen in public. These sessions are between us and us alone. What I do for you is not for public amusement or discussion; I consider these sessions to be more private than sex. I have no intention of being held to public ridicule, nor will I ever put you in that position. Other than the occasional drink, I do not condone any drug use..."

"I understand..." Katherine took another sip of wine.

"Now, because you are new at this... there will be times when I alone will choose a situation to place you in, I will do this at my sole discretion. I will not put it to you to decide, however, if the scenario is unpleasant or distasteful to you, we will not re-enact it. It always stops when you say when."

"...And if I do find it pleasurable?"

"Then it will be added to our repertoire and you can request it any time you desire..."

"Okay..."

"...And one more very, very important thing... the most important..."

"And that is?"

"I will pleasure you with pain... I will make love to you... I will *not* have sex with you..."

"*What*?" She didn't understand. What was this leading to, if it wasn't sex?

"Don't be so disappointed... I don't want you to equate what we do with sex... I will show you that I love you... but I will not intermix our sessions with intercourse... What I do to you and for you must be done in a controlled environment... and sex is something that I feel should have no boundaries... and when the time comes, it won't!"

"I don't understand... about us not having sex..."

"Okay... Have you ever heard of 'Pavlov's Dog'...?"

"I think so..."

"*No*... it's not a rock band..."

"Oh...! Then no..."

"Pavlov was a behavioral scientist. One day he began an experiment. Every time he fed his dog, he rang a bell first. As time passed the dog got used to hearing a bell before he got fed."

"So…?"

"So… whenever Pavlov rang the bell, the dog would salivate, whether he intended to fed him or not!"

"That seems cruel!"

"True, but the experiment showed that when two events coincide on a regular basis the expectation is that when the first event happens the second event must follow…"

"The bell and *then* the food…!" Katherine was beginning to understand.

"Exactly…! What I do *not* want to happen is for you to equate our private sessions with intercourse. I don't want you to be conditioned to have sex during or after a session, and I don't want you to feel that the only way you can have sex with me is through pain. I will pleasure you in any way you want but I will not have sexual intercourse with you during or after a session…"

"What about before a session?"

"Trust me… if we *have* sex… you won't have the strength for a session afterwards…!"

"Oh! You *got it* like that?"

"*Yes I do*… moving right along…"

"So… let me get this straight… we aren't *ever* gonna have sex?"

"*Oh*… you're *gonna* put out… and I *will* put it to you… just never in conjunction with a session. Also… a condom is to be used whenever and wherever we have sexual intercourse. I will be carrying and you'll be expected to carry as well. If nether one of us is packing… there will be no penetration!"

Katherine crossed her arms. "*Damn*! You're just bold aren't you?"

"We're both adults here… when I fuck you, I don't wanna hold back and when you fuck me, I want you to give me all you got… I will teach you how and when to let yourself completely go. I don't have the time for any childish games… do you?"

Katherine uncrossed her arms. "I guess I don't…"

"One more thing…"

"…Just '*one*' more?"

"For now yes… I need to concentrate on you and you alone during our sessions; there will be no guests, surrogates, visitors or audience members. These sessions are just for you and me..."

"Wait... you say... *for now*... and in the future...?"

"We'll move forward one step at a time..."

"I don't know if I can get into all that kinky shit..."

"When I am finished with you... you will know exactly what kind of kinky shit you'll want to get into... and be able to decide for yourself to get into only the kinky shit you'll be okay with!"

"So for now... we're in an exclusive relationship?"

"...When the two of us are alone together... yes!"

"And nobody is ever gonna know about any of this?"

"Nobody has to know anything *you* don't want them to know..."

"You're not gonna brag to your friends? There isn't gonna be any compromising pictures or video of me on the Internet?" Nick shook his head no. "You're... *not* gonna use anything that happens here against me at work...?"

"You haven't figured it out yet have you...? *You're* the boss... *here* and at Faber..."

"So... this is only going to be between the two of us?" Nick nodded. "You said there'll be no penetration... what about... oral...?"

"You or me...?"

"Both!" and Katherine licked and bit her lower lip.

"As much as you want... however you want... Whenever you want..." Katherine smiled. "So... do you have any other questions?"

"Just one..." Katherine hesitated. "ummm..." Nick looked at her and waited patiently. "I... just need to ask you... I mean... I really should have asked this before... when we *almost*... but when I saw you take out the condom... I kinda..."

"What is it that you want to know Katherine?"

"I don't... I mean... this is embarrassing but I *have* to know..."

"Katherine... *Just ask...!*"

"I need to know... if... you've... taken..."

"...An AIDS test?"

Katherine breathed a sigh of relief and averted her eyes. "Yes... have you?" She asked.

"Yes I have..." Nick replied.

"And...?"

"It was negative... and I *will* show you my recent test results..."

Katherine was relieved. "Aren't you gonna ask me?"

"It's not necessary..."

"...Why not?"

"Nobody would ask about an AIDS test unless they've taken theirs and passed..."

"Mine was negative too... I'll show you my results too..."

"Good... are there any other questions...?"

"No... I think that just about covers it!"

"I want to thank you Katherine..."

"For what...?"

"For asking... If everyone would just *ask* and then... *wait* for an answer..." Nick then reached for Katherine's glass and she took it and finished it before giving it to him. Nick took it into the eat-in kitchen and turned back to Katherine and leaned on the table. "...Very well then... Do you understand the rules as I have explained them?"

"Yes!"

"...And you're going to abide by these rules?"

"Yes."

"Yes 'what'...?"

"Yes Nicky..."

Nick stood up and unbuckled his belt. "Yes '*what*'...?"

Katherine eyes widened. "Yes... Nick...?" Nick slowly slid his belt off by the buckle and held it in his hand and let it swing slowly as it dangled. Katherine watched the belt. She had no idea what he wanted her to say. Her heart pounded. Nick folded the belt in half and snapped it until it made a very loud pop. Katherine was startled. "Yes... *daddy*?" Katherine stammered. Nick pulled out the chair away from his dinning room table and sat down.

"Now... come here..." And he motioned for her to come to the side where he held the folded belt. Katherine stood up and hesitated. Nick snapped the belt on his thigh. "NOW!"

"Yes daddy!" Katherine sheepishly walked to him and stood where he pointed to and she stood there with her back to him. Her ass was close to his face and the belt in his hand. She smoothed out her pants. Nick reached over and fondled and squeezed her ass. Katherine moaned.

"Turn around and kneel down please..."

"Yes daddy..." And she did as she was told. Katherine started to shake. Nick took her arm with his left and laid her across his lap. Katherine whimpered.

"Pull down your pants please..."

"Yes daddy..." Slowly she grabbed the waistline of her pants from behind her and shimmied out of them, revealing her soft, round bottom. Katherine was wearing white silk panties with a lace trim. Katherine's ass twitched in anticipation. Nick paused and waited a moment to let Katherine consider what was about to happen. As she shivered in Nick's lap, Nick hiked up her panties to reveal more of her tender flesh. Katherine cooed as the panties tightened on her crotch.

"Do I have your undivided attention, young lady?"

"Yes daddy..."

"I don't believe that I do..." And Nick raised the belt and it made a sharp smack on her buttocks. Katherine inhaled deeply from the sting of the belt. She bit her lip and sighed.

"Ohhh...! My...!" Katherine then arched her back raising her ass just a little higher. Katherine purred. Nick hesitated and Katherine became a little impatient. "May I have another... daddy?"

"Yes you may..." And pulled on the waist of her panties giving her a tighter wedgie and Nicholas hit her with the belt again. Katherine cooed and purred.

"Ohh... may I *please*... have another... daddy?" And Nicholas struck her again and again. Katherine writhed and gyrated with every stroke. In between some strokes he would stop to fondle her ass until she would relax and coo a bit, then he would suddenly strike her again. Katherine felt as if she was on a rollercoaster with no idea when the next thrill would come. She had never experienced anything like this in her life. From where they where positioned Nick was able to reach the kitchen table and he stuck his left thumb into the open jar of jelly and placed his sweetened thumb into Katherine's open mouth. Katherine sucked his thumb voraciously, licking and sucking the jelly off his thumb with every stroke of the belt.

"Bad girl... bad, bad girl!" Suddenly Katherine pulled his thumb out of his mouth and shuddered violently. She began to breathe in short quick breaths. And then she let out a high-pitched squeal. By the time Katherine came, her ass was a bright red. "That's gonna leave a mark..." Nick said; Katherine giggled. Nick grabbed her by the scruff of her neck and stood her up. He stood up and while still controlling her he bent her over the back of the chair. "Take your pants off and then put your hands on the back of the chair..." Katherine complied. Nick went and got the ice pack, now mostly melted and gently massaged Katherine's exposed ass with it. Katherine jumped a bit when the cold bag touched her, but it began to soothe her. The water that had formed outside the bag trickled down her legs. Nick reached between her legs and fondled her clit.

"Ahhhh ha..." Katherine cooed.

"You're all wet... let me get you a towel." Nick left, Katherine stayed in that position until he returned with a towel. Nick took her panties down to her ankles and Katherine stepped out of them and then he gently wiped her ass and pussy with the towel.

"Owww!" Katherine moaned. "That hurts!"

"It's supposed to hurt..."

"Kitty likes it!" And she purred again. When he was finished he helped her put her panties back on and helped her put her pants back on. "Ouch!"

"That's gonna sting for a while... good news is... where I spanked you won't interfere too much with you sitting down."

"Thank you daddy..."

"...My pleasure!"

Katherine paused and licked her lips. "Speaking of which... what about... *your* pleasure?"

"I took care if it when I got you the towel..." Katherine sighed and bit her lip. Nick got her jacket. "Let's go..."

"Where are we going?"

"Out to dinner..."

"Out to dinner?"

"Yes aren't you hungry? 'Cause I'm starved..."

Katherine put on her coat and they left to go to a nearby restaurant. As they walked down the street Katherine remarked. "Can't we take my car?"

"You think you can sit in your car to drive anywhere right now?"

Katherine felt her ass and cooed. "You're right, maybe I should stand."

"Don't worry... the place we're going to doesn't require you to sit."

"Okay..." Katherine grabbed Nicks arm and walked with her head on his shoulder. "Nick..."

"Yes Katherine?"

"How long do you think it's gonna take... before..."

"It takes as long as it takes... Katherine..."

"I meant... until we can use the game room...?"

"All in due time Katherine... all in due time..." Katherine hugged Nick tighter. "We have to develop a trust between each other first."

"Okay... But I trust you now, Nick..."

"I know you do... but we have to have a deeper trust that we haven't developed just yet..."

"I don't understand..."

"Exactly! I need you to trust me with your life to the point where you know I will *never* let anything hurt you..."

"...Even while you're inflicting pain on me?"

"*Especially*... when I'm inflicting pain on you...! You have to trust me to stop when you say so... and to stop when *I* think it's going too far...!"

"I think I get it... I need to understand my boundaries..."

"*You got it!*"

"And once I understand the boundaries I set... I have to trust you to bring me there..."

"And back!"

"And just how do I set those boundaries?"

"I will take you to places you've never been before, I will show you the wonders of the universe. And I will hold your hand and make sure you don't fall... You'll decide where to draw the line and *when* to cross it..." A tear formed in Nick's eye.

"Nick? Are you all right? What's wrong?"

Nick stopped to wipe his eye. "Oh... it's uh... my allergies... I'll be alright..." Just then, the lights went on a private club up the block called *'Dante's Dance Emporium'*. There were several people waiting on line to get in. The crowd looked like a modern Goth version of *"The Rocky Horror Picture Show"*

"Hey... can we go into that club?"

"No... that place isn't for you..."

"What do you mean? I always see a lot of interesting people coming in and out of there..."

"You're nowhere ready to deal with anybody that goes in or comes out of there, promise me you'll stay away from there... promise!"

"Okay... I promise I'll never go in there..."

"Come on... the pizza place is this way..." Katherine held on tight to follow Nick's lead. But she looked back towards the club when they turned the corner.

- - -

For the next few months Katherine and Nick worked closely together to get the office performance levels above 30% and keep it there. That wasn't as easy as it sounds. The new marketing protocols would have to be translated and Frankensteined into the old codes without crashing them. Even if you did successfully merge the codes together the fix was temporary at best and had to be individualized for each and every client. Every time you thought you were done, marketing came up with a new plan and you had to start literally from scratch all over again. Nick was actually working his ass off to protect Katherine, and Katherine was right there in the thick of things. But even with Nick's tutelage and her experience, Katherine could not translate the codes on her own. It was kind of like shorthand, even though the basic mechanics were standard, every stenographer has their own personal take on translations and another stenographer can't necessarily decipher someone else's writing. Nick was the only one who had the experience and know-how to program in the protocols. Katherine would have to trust Nick on and off the job. This undertaking was no easy task for Nick. It was hard enough for him to keep his own levels up. To do it for the whole floor was a monumental task. Katherine was sick and tired of trying to make this work; she was going to have to find a way to get the old programming updated once and for all.

Katherine made very sure that Nick knew that she appreciated all his efforts; she would fuck him every which way but loose. There was nothing that she wouldn't do for him. All he had to do was ask and she would do it for him even if he didn't ask.

Now, all this talk company protocols and computer programming is fine and all, and talking about company politics and corporate treachery makes good 'made for TV' movies... but it's fucking boring as hell... Let's get to the real story, shall we? Nick had his S/M sessions with Katherine on a regular basis; he would switch from straight sex to B&D at his whim. Katherine never knew what to expect unless she initiated the sex and then there would be no torture or pain. Nick would always keep his promise not to initiate sex during or after a session. Sometimes she would just fuck him; sometimes she would ask to be 'punished'. Nick complied with her every whim. It was Nick's sole purpose to please her and to find new and exciting ways to arouse her. Oh yeah, they also went out to dinner or dancing or to the movies or a show every now and then. They aren't fucking animals... just so you know!

* *Author's Note* *

The following chapters describe some of the more important sessions that they had in the months to come; that helped them to define and perfect their slave/master relationship. Although they are listed in chronological order, there may have been several weeks in between these sessions. Not all the sessions they had are described here. Let's be honest here; not all their sessions were all that great and some sessions were... let's face it... just a little too sick and twisted to be included here... And I really couldn't figure out a way to even try to begin to describe their 'duct tape' sessions. You literally had to be there!

(Hey! You really want to know...? Look up duct tape on the Internet! But for now let's move on shall we?)

Just a reminder: Jennifer was at the Faber Data main office raising hell and is being 'transferred' to marketing to learn the marking computer protocols...

The Tortured Soul Trilogy
(A Tortured Soul)
Chapter 59
(You Can Ring My Bell!)

Nick popped his head into Katherine's office. "Katherine… is your cell on vibrate?"

"No…"

"Put it on vibrate please!"

"Why?"

Nick took out his cell and flipped it open. "I'm gonna be out of the office today and I may want to be able to reach you…'

"But…why does my phone have to be on vibrate?"

"Just do it!" Katherine took her phone out of her purse and set it to vibrate and began to put it back in her purse. "No…" Katherine put the phone on her desk. "No…!" He said. Katherine had a puzzled look on her face. Nick dialed her number… the phone vibrated and danced on the desk. Katherine watched it and then the realization of what he wanted her to do came to her. Katherine's face turned red. Nick hung up. "Do it!'

"Okay…"

"Do *it* now!" He said with authority. Katherine reached slowly for her phone and paused and watched Nick's eyes. Nick leaned back into the hallway to see if anyone was coming. He looked back to Katherine and nodded. Katherine took the phone, still in its leather case and placed it on her lap. "No…" Nick said. Katherine began to breathe heavily. Surely he didn't *mean*… "Open!" Katherine spread her knees and placed the phone under her skirt between her thighs. "Higher!" Katherine began to breathe faster and placed the phone where she knew he wanted it. "Clip it to your panties so it… doesn't move…" Again she did as she was told. "Close…" Katherine closed her legs and the phone fit… perfectly… just the feel of the leather between her legs excited her. Nick closed his phone and put it away. "Wait for my call…" And Nick put Katherine's '*Do Not Disturb*' sign on her door and closed it and left. Katherine stayed at her desk. She was very nervous and anxious; she had no idea when Nick would 'call'… Time passed and still no call. Then her office phone rang. She jumped; she answered it… It was Hagen… he wanted to go over the new company program codes with her.

"Are you at your terminal Katherine?"

"Yes Mr. Hagen…"

"Okay… I just sent you an e-mail of the new marketing protocols and I want to cross reference them with the company codes…"

"Yes Mr. Hagen…" Katherine opened the e-mail and began to go over the codes line by line with Mr. Hagen. As he read the code lines to her, Katherine entered the corrections from the Data 'bible'. Hagen began to read off a long line of codes when Katherine's cell phone rang. (Not now! Oh no…! *Not now!*)

"Katherine? Are you there?"

"Yes Mr. Hagen!"

"Did you get that?'

(Hell *yeah* I got that!) "Yes Mr. Hagen… I got it!" Her phone rang again.

"Katherine… Is that your cell phone ringing?"

"Yes Mr. Hagen…"

"Do you want to get that?"

"No sir… I'll let it go to voice mail…" Katherine's nipples became hard and raw. The phone rang again. Katherine was conflicted. She wanted to ride out Nick's call but she had to stay in control while she was on the phone with her boss. Mr. Hagen continued to read off codes, Katherine continued to correct the codes, and Nick kept calling…

"Katherine?"

"Yes Mr. Hagen?"

"Are you laughing?'

"*No*…! Mr. Hagen…"

"…Because you sound like you're out of breath!"

"I'm okay… it's just an allergy…"

"Well you should take something…"

"I will take care of it just as soon as I'm off this call…" (I sure as hell will! Now get off the phone you old goat!) Katherine was all hot and bothered and in total agony.

"Katherine… we're gonna have to finish this call some other time… I can't concentrate with all that noise you're making…"

(Then get off the fucking phone... you old fart!) "Yes sir... I'll call you back tomorrow morning...?"

"Fine... just wait a moment... Nick wants to talk to you..."

"*What?*"

"Nick... Nick Anderson...? He works in your office? He wants to speak with you... Hold on, I'll put him on..."

"Hello Katherine?" Nick said.

"You son of a *bitch*...!" Katherine whispered. She had no idea he was in Hagen's office today.

"Yes... I'm so very sorry about that Katherine...

Katherine began to breathe heavily. "You *will* be very sorry when I get my hands on you!"

"Hagen left to go back to his office... let me make it up to you..."

"And just *how* are you gonna make this up to me?" Katherine's cell phone rang again. She threw her head back. She could now enjoy the call.

"Katherine? Are you there?"

"Almost!" She whispered.

"...Are the blinds in your office still closed?'

"Yes!"

"Will you unbutton your blouse for me please...?"

"Yes..."

"Yes... what?"

"Yes daddy..." Katherine squeezed her knees together and unbuttoned her blouse.

"Does your bra unhook from the front or the back?'

"The front..."

"Undo your bra for me please..."

"Yes daddy..." She undid her bra and the phone rang again.

"...Are your nipples hard?"

"Yes daddy... and I'm all wet!"

"Very good... would you please pinch your nipples for me?"

"Anything you want daddy..." Katherine did as she was told and cooed and purred and worked her nipples.

"Katherine?"

319

"Yes daddy?"

"Are you there?"

Katherine sighed. "Just about…"   And her phone rang again. Katherine threw her head back and put her hand over her mouth to stifle her screams of pleasure… her office isn't *that* soundproof…the last thing she needed was the entire office rushing into her office breaking down her door and finding her in this compromising 'position'… a tear came to her eye. Katherine shuddered and cooed softly.

"Katherine?"

Katherine moaned. "Yes Nick?"

"I'm going straight to your house from here… would you like me to bring a bottle of wine?"

"Yes… Please…"

"And Katherine…?"

"Yeah baby?"

"You're welcome!" Katherine took a few moments to compose herself before she stepped out of the office. One of the employees walked past her.

"Are you okay Katherine?"

"What?"

"Are you okay?"

"Oh I'm fine… why?"

"You looked all flushed…"

"Oh… it's just an allergy…"

"You should go home, take something and go straight to bed!"

"I think I'm gonna take that advice… Thanks!"

"Well… I guess I'll see you tomorrow… have a good evening!"

"You too…!"

As Katherine exited the office, the employee bumped into another in front of Katherine's office "Allergy my *ass*… She's all worked up from that call she was just on from the head office…"

"…Really?"

"It must have been torture for her…"

"Yeah… It sucks to be her!"

Nick arrived at Katherine's house with a bottle of white wine. He opened it and transferred it to a carafe to let it breathe a while. They had a little wine before and during dinner. Katherine had cooked a fine homemade meal of meatloaf and mashed potatoes with mixed vegetables. After dinner they sat in the couch and had a little more wine.

"So... How was your meeting with Hagen?"

"A total waste of time... He knows the computer languages don't jive... He's known it for years... but his position is; '*If it aint broke, don't fix it*!'..."

"But it *is* broke!"

"Yeah... *I* know that and *you* know that and even *he* knows that, but it's not bad enough to budget ten million dollars or more to upgrade the system... Not to mention that the turn around down time would cost the company millions more..."

"You've had this meeting with Hagen before... Haven't you?"

"Yep... about fifteen years ago... and the problem hasn't gotten better in all that time..."

"But why won't they budget the upgrades?"

"Can you say; 'Executive Bonuses'...?"

"So it's all about the money?"

"It's all about Hagen's money... but thank you for setting up the meeting for me... you gave it a try... at least it shows you have your head in the right place..."

"...Speaking of having my 'head' in the right place..."

And Katherine unbuttoned her blouse, undid her bra and slid her hand onto Nick's crotch, unzipped him and began to voraciously devour him.

Chapter 60
(My Hips Don't Lie)

Katherine arrived at Nick's and knocked on the door. "Its open... come on in..." Katherine was hit by the strong smell of curry and exotic spices.

"Hmmm that smells wonderful... what is it?"

"Just some Middle Eastern food I prepared... I hope you like it hot and spicy!"

"You *know* I do... I'll eat anything you serve me!"

"Behave!"

"Why? Are you gonna..." Nick held up his index finger. Katherine caught herself. "So... you're a chef too!"

"Well... I dabble a bit in exotic cuisines..."

"I know... I still remember when you served me peanut butter and jelly..."

Nick laughed. "I said; *exotic* not erotic...!

"Whatever! When do we eat?"

"Not for a while, go ahead and wait for me in the living room."

"We're not gonna use the game room tonight?" She couldn't wait to take their relationship to the next level, but she would be patient.

"Not tonight... I have other plans you might enjoy..."

Katherine smiled, cause she knew, no game room meant 'hot monkey love'. Katherine entered the living to see that the furniture was moved and there was a brand new Persian rug on the floor. "This is so beautiful! When did you get it?"

"It arrived today..."

"It's very nice... but it doesn't match the décor of the rest of the room... you're thinking of redecorating the apartment?"

"No it's just for whenever I want to bring it out..."

Katherine bent down and felt the carpet. Nick stared at Katherine's ass. "I just love the feel of new carpet... and... I caught you checking out my ass!"

"Whoops!"

Nick took a box from the table and handed it to Katherine. "What's this? A gift...? For me...?"

"A little something for tonight..."

"A new 'toy'...?"

"No... but I think you'll like it...

"Oh... I can't wait to open it..." Katherine opened it and pulled out several silk scarves. "Oh my...! These are beautiful... thank you Nick!" And she kissed him.

"Go try them on..."

"This is a dress?"

"Well, when wrapped properly... yes! The instructions are in the box."

Katherine took the box into the bedroom and came back out wearing the dress. She did a little model turn for him. "This feels so wonderful on my skin... hey! You *know* with the right pair of shoes I could go out dancing in this!"

"I'm glad you said that..."

"Why? What do you have in mind?" Nick took out another box. "What's in there?"

"Just a few accessories for the dress..."

"What kind of 'accessories'?"

"Remember when you once said you would meet me 'with bells on'?"

Katherine shook her head; she had no idea what he was talking about. "No..."

"Well trust me... you did..." Nick shook the box and it jingled.

"What is that? What's in there?" Nick opened the box and pulled out several delicate gold chains with little bells and coin like charms on them. "Oh Nick... these are absolutely fabulous!"

"Let me help you put these on..." And Nick helped her get the strands of gold on her wrists, ankles, waist and neck.

"And of course let's not forget the earrings!" And he put them in for her.

"What...? No nose ring?" Nick held up his finger and motioned her to wait. "You gotta be joking!"

Nick pulled out a gold nose ring from a box in his pocket. "It's only a clip on..." And her put it on for her, and pulled a scarf across her face.

"I feel like the Queen of Sheba!" Katherine pinched her nipples. "You don't happen to have any other clip-ons you want me to wear?"

"Damn...! I hadn't thought of that...! Maybe next time... Kick off your shoes..."

Katherine took them off and Nick escorted her onto the carpet. "Ohhh! That feels so nice." Katherine wiggled her toes on the carpet.

"I'm glad you like." Nick went over to the stereo and turned it on. East Indian music played. Nick pulled out a pair of bongos.

"Wow, you have a real theme going on here..." Nick sat crossed legged on the edge of the carpet and began to play the bongos to the beat of the music. "Wow! A musician too! Is there anything you can't do?"

"Do you think you remember how you put that dress on?"

"I think so..."

"Think you can get out of that dress without taking off any of the gold chains?"

She looked at herself. "Yeah... I think I can... why?"

"Try..."

"You want me to strip for you?"

"*No*... I want you to *dance* for me..."

"I've never danced to this kind of music before..."

"Give it a shot..." Nick closed his eyes and began to play more intensely to the music.

"You're not gonna watch me?"

"Make me!" And Nick got into the rhythm of the music with his playing. Katherine slowly began to gyrate to the music. She was awkward at first but she got into the mood and began to move a bit more fluidly. "...If you want me to look at you... I need to hear the bells..." Katherine paused and shook her wrists. "*All*... the bells..." She tapped her feet. "...Two out of three!" She rotated her hips. "Don't think hula-hoop, think the bump..." She thrust her hips forward and backwards. "Don't think stripper... think belly dancer..."

Katherine thought; '*How the hell does he know what I'm doing with his eyes closed*?' She put her right foot forward and popped her hip.

"Better..." She did it again on the other side. "Good...
now think hula dancer but stay on the beat!"

(Oh no, he didn't... What? Now he's a choreographer?)
Katherine began to pop her hips and stomp her feet and shake her
wrists. The music, the smell of the curry, and the movement of her
body... she really got into it... Nick was now watching her
intensely. "*There* it is!" Nick and Katherine were really into the
music now. "I thought you said you never danced to this music
before?" Katherine shook her hips and turned with her back to
Nick and moved her hips at a rapid pace.

"Seven years of jazz and ballet and two years of African
ballet... did you really think I got this tight, rocking ass bowling?"
And she stopped, dropped it like it was hot and smacked her ass.
Nick's bongos and heart skipped a beat at the same time.

"Okay...! I underestimated you... but here comes the
hard part... Take off the scarves..." Katherine reached for the scarf
over her face. "No... save that one for last!" Katherine danced,
Nick played. Every once in a while a scarf would drop to the
carpet. On occasion a chain would get caught but she was able to
regroup and continue without skipping a beat. She danced until the
only scarf left was the one on her face. Her body was totally naked
but still wrapped in all the gold chains. Katherine continued to
dance, Nick continued to play. The music stopped, Katherine
switched gears and began to dance an African solo. Nick kept up
with an Afro-Cuban beat. Katherine's body was glistening with
sweat. The smell of curry was intoxicating. The air in the room
was stifling. Katherine took a wide African stance facing Nick and
stomped towards him while shaking every part of her body. Just as
she stood right in front of him she dropped to her knees and laid
back on her shins with the back of her head on the carpet. She
continued to shake her shoulders and wrists. Her glistening and
hungry pussy was right in front of him. The bongos stopped
abruptly.

- - -

Katherine stepped out of Nick's apartment freshly
showered and fully dressed. She was wearing one of her new

scarves around her neck and the gold chains around her wrists. "Are you sure you don't want me to take you home Katherine?"

"I'm sure... I want to thank you so much for such a wonderful evening... and my lovely gifts." And Katherine felt her scarf.

"No... thank *you*...! I've never eaten Middle Eastern food off a naked body on a carpet before..."

"Sorry about that! Was the carpet expensive?"

"Oh no... just a few... thousand... dollars...!"

"Oh my... I am so sorry! I will try to pay you back for it..."

"Don't worry about it... I'll just take it out on your ass!"

Katherine bit her lower lip. Then she looked down the hallway. "Do you think... the neighbors heard us?"

"There are no neighbors... I own this building outright and I live alone."

"Oh? Excuse me! You got it like that?"

Nick nodded. "Good night Katherine." And Nick kissed her.

"There are *no* neighbors?" She asked.

"No...! I have the building all to myself. Why?"

Katherine pulled her blouse open in the hallway and exposed her nipples and pushed her right shoulder forward. "Kiss it!" Nick kissed her nipple. And she pushed the left one forward. "Kiss it!" He did and then she turned around and hunched her ass. "Spank it!" And Nick popped her on her ass. Katherine growled through her teeth. "Daddy knows what I like!" She fixed herself up and strutted to the front door turned blew a kiss to Nick, waved and left. Nick closed his door and said to himself; '*Damn it... this bitch gave me a hard-on again and then left me here all alone!*'

The Tortured Soul Trilogy
(A Tortured Soul)
Chapter 61
(You Still Know Nothing About Me)

Katherine picked me up at the bar across from the job about 8pm. "Is there a reason why we always have to meet here?"

"Yes there is…"

"And are you gonna tell me?"

"I could tell you… but then I would have to torture you…"

"Come on… seriously!"

Nick thought for a moment and called over to the bartender. "Hey Jimmy! Can I borrow your notepad?"

"Sure Nick!"

And Nick took out his pen and wrote on the paper, tore it off the pad, folded it and gave it to Katherine… "Meet me here tomorrow…"

Katherine opened the note and read it. "What is this place?"

"Somewhere… other than here… where I want you to meet me… Okay?"

"What time?"

"It's on the note…"

"Okay…! Any particular way you need me to dress?"

"Casual is fine by me…"

"Okay! Do you want to take me home?"

"Yes I do…" Nick kissed her on the forehead. "…But right now I have an errand I need to run…"

"But what about *tonight*… and you know… 'Our… plans'…?"

"Sorry kiddo… I'm gonna have to take a rain check."

Katherine poked out her lip. Nick kissed it.

"Do you need me to drive you somewhere…?" Katherine asked.

"No… I'm good… so I'll see you tomorrow?"

Katherine put the note in her purse. "I'll see you tomorrow at two…"

"See you." she said. Katherine kissed Nick and left…

"Stalk you!" Nick replied.

Katherine paused at the door, turned and blew Nick a kiss and waved goodbye. Nick turned to see Jimmy staring in the direction Katherine was standing.

"What Jimmy?"

Jimmy turned to Nick and smiled "…Nothing! Need a refill?"

Nick looked at his drink and shook his head no. "I'm good…"

Jimmy picked up his notepad from the bar and went to attend other customers.

- - -

The next day, Katherine pulled up to the block about 10 minutes early, but there was no parking anywhere. There were motorcycles parked in every available spot on the block. She drove up and down the side streets until she found a space about three blocks away. She got out and looked at her watch. "2:05! *Damn!* I'm already late!" Katherine briskly walked towards the address. She now had the opportunity to check out some of the bikes on the street. There were some beautiful bikes out there and some classic pieces, but she had no time sightsee right now. She was anxious to see Nick, especially since he had cancelled their last appointment on such short notice. She arrived at the address but she paused in front of the building. She knew it was some type of bar but the establishment had no sign out front, and the front door was very worn and beat up. Katherine took out the note and verified the address again. Yes… this was the right place; Katherine grabbed hold of the loose doorknob and entered. Katherine stood in the open doorway for what seemed like an eternity. The place was a hardcore biker bar. Marilyn Manson's '*If I Were Your Vampire.*' was playing on the sound system.

"Hey!" A voice yelled from the dimly lit bar out to her. "…In or out! But close the fucking door."

Katherine paused in the door for a brief moment, considering 'out' as her best option; when a biker and his girl bumped her from behind, pushing her into the club. The woman turned to her and checked her out up and down.

"You must be lost and looking for directions... cause you are in the *wrong* fucking place *honey!*" All the women in the bar laughed. Katherine looked around the room, clutching her purse in both hands in front of her. There was nobody in there except mean and ugly tattooed bikers and their bitches. She saw a biker sitting in a corner, getting an impromptu lap dance from a biker bitch wearing nothing but ass less chaps. The girl threw her hair around in a circle as she grinded her ass in his lap. The recipient looked at Katherine and motioned her to come over. That's when she heard a voice call her.

"Is there something I can help you with honey?" She turned to see the bartender. He was about 6'4", bald, about 350lbs in full biker regalia... his front teeth were missing and he slid his tongue in and out of the gap as he spoke... He was busy cleaning a beer mug with a dishtowel. "Can I help you? Cause we aint got no change for the bus..." The bar crowd laughed.

"I... I... um... I..." She couldn't speak she was so scared; she knew she didn't belong here.

He put the mug down on the bar and leaned towards her on the bar. "Honey! You keep stuttering like that around here... somebody's gonna stick a 'pacifier' in your mouth!" Two of the bikers drinking at the bar laughed, a third turned on his chair to face Katherine. He leaned back on the bar and took a long drink from his beer. He wiped his mouth with his sleeve and then he smiled at her.

She took a deep breath. "I'm... here to see Nick..." she said quickly.

The bartender froze. "*What* did you say?"

"I'm here... to see *Nick*? Nick Anderson...? He asked me to meet him here..." The patrons sitting at the bar cleared out. The bartender stared at Katherine.

"*You're* here... for *Nick*?"

"Yes..." Katherine looked around. Everyone that she felt was crowding her; had backed away.

The bartender took a step back away from the bar. "I'm... I'm sorry... I... I didn't know you were a friend of Nick's..." The bartended yelled into the club. "Hey Nick! There's a young lady

329

here to see you!" The bartender motioned her to sit at the bar. Katherine shook her head no. "I'm... I'm... really sorry...! I... didn't know... you were a friend of Nick's."

Katherine got bold and cut her eyes at the bartender. "You know if you stutter like that in here... someone might stick a 'pacifier' in your mouth..."

"Yes ma'am...!"

Nick came out of the back poolroom, wearing jeans, cowboy boots, and a leather jacket with a worn denim vest over it. He walked over to Katherine and kissed her gently on the lips. "Have any problems finding the place?"

"No..."

Nick turned to the bartender. "Have any problems... *while* you were waiting for me?"

The bartender looked intently at Katherine. "No..." Katherine replied. The bartender took a deep breath and walked away.

"Okay then... let's go..."

"We're not staying...?"

"You wanna hang out here for a while...?"

Katherine took a quick look around. "Not really...!" Nick escorted Katherine out. She looked around the room as he walked her to the door. The attitude of the patrons was quite different from when she first came in. She couldn't put her finger on it... but she felt... revered... As they stepped outside Katherine remarked. "I didn't know you were in a biker gang!"

"I'm not... I own the fucking place! So where's your car?"

"I parked it about three blocks away..."

"Sorry about that... I should have told them to leave you a spot out front..." Katherine had a newfound respect for Nick. About a block away, as they walked towards her car there was a man sweeping the street. He was tall, fat and wearing a torn 'wife beater' shirt. Nick allowed me to pass first. Just as Nick passed, the man spoke to him.

"How many times do I have to tell you biker bums to stay the hell off this street? And that goes for your filthy whores too!"

I didn't see what happened. All I heard was the crisp snap of denim. I turned to see Nick in a Tae Kwon Do stance. The heel of his right foot was in the air, one inch away from the man's face. The man was in total shock. He dropped his broom and ran back into his house. Nick held that position until the man closed his door behind him. Nick slowly lowered his foot and walked towards me and took my arm gently...

"So... where did you say you were parked?"

"...Over here..." I said nothing more about what just happened... but I was moist... I gave him my car keys and he opened my door for me, then got in the drivers side. Nick drove us to a place that looked like an abandoned warehouse. There were a few cars in the parking lot. "Is this another club?"

"Sort of..." He walked me inside and the place was just that... a warehouse with industrial shelves, wire racks and wide aisles. It looked like a Costco's, Big Lots or a Sam's Club. People were mulling around with carts... just shopping. There was one little difference though... the shelves were stocked with sex toys and gadgets, devices, oils and fragrances and costumes... lot's and lot's of costumes. A checker walked up to Nick and kissed him.

"Hey Nicky..." And she strutted back down the aisle.

"Don't tell me you own this place too!"

"No... I'm just a valued customer!"

"Uh huh! So why are we here?"

"My dear... for us, this is the world's largest candy store... and today is *your* birthday... let's go shopping!"

'It's *not* my birthday!'

"Work with me!" Nick grabbed a cart and we toured the store. I felt like Dorothy in the Land of Oz. this was a strange and amazing place. As we walked down the aisles, I saw something that looked like artwork from outer space.

"What the hell is that thing used for?"

Nick put it in the cart. "...Only one way to find out!" We shopped and browsed for about an hour and the cart was full of wonderful things, toys and costumes. I walked towards a leather display and checked out the different restraints, paddles and whips. I picked up a leather mask all covered with zippers and leather bindings. It matched my cat suit. I held it up to Nick...

"What do you think?"

"I don't like it...!"

"Why not...?"

Nick took the mask out of my hand and held it in front of my face. "A mask can be useful... it allows the wearer to feel 'safe'... it protects their anonymity... It's a '*What ever happens in Vegas*' kinda thing... It can allow the wearer to relax in its safety..."

"But that's a *good* thing... right?"

"If that's what you want... yes... But there is also a negative effect..."

"And that is?"

He held it in front of his face. "It also has the tendency to de-humanize the wearer to the beholder. Without a face to relate to, the beholder may lose their compassion... they become desensitized to the pain they inflict.... And that's how things get out of hand... and someone gets hurt... badly! But if you really want to get it..."

Katherine took the mask away from Nick's face and gently put it back where she found it. "I *never* want to hurt you like that...!"

Nick kissed Katherine on her forehead and hugged her... "So...? Got everything you wanted?"

"And more..."

"Okay... let's pay for all this stuff... unless..."

"Unless what?"

"Unless you want to steal it and find out what it's like to be 'incarcerated'!"

Katherine had a puzzled look on her face. Nick pointed to a sign on the wall.

Shoplifting will not be tolerated. Violators will be punished severely.
And NO!
That is not meant to encourage you!

"Oh!" And Katherine ran off down the aisle and turned the corner.

"What the HELL?" Nick exclaimed. She returned a few moments later holding two pairs of handcuffs and tossed them into the cart. Nicholas laughed.

"*What...?*" Katherine asked.

They rolled the cart to the check out. The young lady who greeted Nick was now working the register. "Oh my...! Is this a private party... or can anyone cum?"

"*Private party...!*" Katherine answered curtly.

"Hell-o... *jealousy issues...!*" I whispered.

Katherine cut her eyes. The checker smiled. "Lucky girl...! All this attention focused just on you!" And she winked at Katherine. As Nick put the items on the counter the girl rang them up and bagged them. Katherine looked up, and behind the girl, on the counter, Katherine saw *it*. It was about 13" tall, four to five inches in diameter... and made of stainless steel! Katherine's lips separated slightly and she sighed. Nick leaned over to her, Katherine stayed focused on the item, Nick whispered to her.

"Do you want one?"

"Yes...!" Katherine hissed. Nick whispered in her ear. Katherine licked her lips.

"You... *do*... know... That's... *her*... Thermos bottle!"

Katherine blinked, the girl laughed into her hand. "I knew that!" She said plainly.

"Uh huh!" Nick snickered.

The checker stifled a laugh. "...Cash or charge?"

"Charge please!" And the checker took Nick's card to process it. She let out a small chuckle. Katherine squinted her eyes at her.

"You do this to every new customer on purpose, don't you?"

The girl busted out laughing. "Yes! And it gets funnier each and every time!" she said.

Nick signed the receipt and he and the cashier looked at Katherine and laughed. Katherine hit Nick. "*Not* funny you guys!" As they walked towards the exit with their purchases, Katherine turned back to the checker to cut her eyes at her one more time. That's when she saw a young black woman on line sheepishly point to the Thermos. Katherine put her hand over her mouth and stifled a laugh. Nick turned to her.

"You okay?"

"Um Hmmm!" Katherine then covered her mouth and laughed.

Nick looked back at the checker. "Uh huh!" Nick looked at her knowingly.

"I'm sorry... but now that I think of it, that shit was fucking funny!" We went outside with our bags and we barely had room in the trunk of Katherine's car for everything. "Aren't you afraid of being seen coming out of this place?"

"Not really... there's no sign out front so nobody knows what this place is... unless they've been here before... and besides, then they would have to explain what *they* were doing here..."

"What happens in 'Vegas'...?"

"People in glass houses..." I put what I could in the trunk and tossed the rest in the back seat, and drove her home.

"Oh Ohh!" Katherine exclaimed.

"What? What's the matter? You wanna go back for the Thermos?"

Katherine hit Nick on the arm. "Noooo...! I just realized... where am I gonna put all this stuff?"

"Well... most of the costumes will stay at my place... I don't want you driving around dressed like that... people might talk!" Katherine giggled. "...As for the rest of it... I've got that covered..." Katherine raised her eyebrow but didn't question him about it.

"Now that I think of it Nick... Can I ask you a question...?"

"Sure... there are no secrets between us now!"

"You own 'The 'C' Cup' don't you...?"

"Nothing gets by you does it?"

"When did you buy it?"

"Well... right about a year after my 'unpaid vacation', I realized that I could be unemployed or worse at the whim of some faceless moron in marketing, and my pension from this company would keep me in dog food for the rest of my life when I did retire..."

"...But you don't have a... ewwww!" Katherine got the connotation.

"...*Exactly*! So I saved up my money, looking for an investment, that's when a friend of mine wanted to sell his biker bar. He was having problems with the I.R.S. so, I bought it cheap and with the profits I made, I bought the "C" cup and with the profits from both those places, I bought the building I live in now! So I'm pretty much set for life..."

"If you're rich..."

"I'm not *rich*... but I don't worry about bills..."

"Okay... so if you're 'well off'... Why do you still work at Data Corp.?"

"I've worked there for almost 30 years now. The people there are like family to me... besides if I had left... I would have never of met you...!"

Katherine leaned over and kissed Nick on the cheek. "...So you own the biker bar and the "C" cup, and you hired all the employees yourself?"

Nick rolled his shoulders. "I think I know where this is going..."

"Come on..."

"Yep... I hire everyone, *even* the strippers for the Biker Bar..."

"You *hire* strippers...?"

"Uh *Yeah*...! Bikers are not that into poetry readings like the patrons at the "C" cup... *go* figure!"

"We're gonna have to address your hiring process..."

"You know what...? On our next session... we *will* address your jealousy issues!"

When they arrived at her place Nick took all the bags inside. Katherine looked at all the bags and looked at Nick. "I meant to ask you...what did you mean before when I asked you what to do with this stuff and you said '*you had it covered*'...?"

"Go to your bedroom and you'll find out..."

Katherine had a puzzled look on her face but did as she was told. She took a bag into the bedroom and went to look. At the foot of her bed was a beautiful Victorian steamer trunk. It was made of mahogany and leather and had very ornate locks and hinges. "What is that?"

"It's a steamer trunk... I brought it for you and dropped it off while you were out... I hope you don't mind..."

"I love it… but how did you know I needed one so big?"

"Actually, I didn't think you would fill it in one shopping spree!"

Katherine's jaw dropped. "But you said…"

"Yes I did… yes I did… I know… now can you help me put the rest of this stuff away?"

Katherine reached into a bag and pulled out a device and purred. "…And where does *this* go?"

Nick reached into the bag a pulled out a bottle of lubricant. "Here… let me show you…!"

"*Okay*… but right now I don't *need* a lubricant…"

The Tortured Soul Trilogy
(A Tortured Soul)
Chapter 62
(Joe's Apartment)

Katherine enters Nick's apartment after work on Friday. She used her own key to get in. Nick is sitting at the dinner table with a strange looking box from a hardware store. "Hey Nicky... What's in the box?"

"Take off all your clothes..." he said plainly.

"...Just like that? No kiss, no 'Hi Katherine' first?"

Nick stood up and undid his belt... "Don't make me tell you again!"

Katherine knew that tone in his voice. "Yes Daddy..." Katherine slowly stripped down to her bra and panties.

"I said '*all your clothes*'... shoes too." Katherine did as she was told and stood there, naked, wondering what Nick had in store for her. Although she had been naked in front of Nick many times before, this felt strange to her, she felt more than just naked, she felt vulnerable. He opened the box and took out a pair of latex panties, a 'do rag', a spray can, a kerchief and goggles.

"What the hell?"

Nick quickly took his belt off. "Don't speak unless I tell you too..." Katherine was conflicted, she wanted to obey Nick but she also *wanted* to be punished... Katherine decided to keep quiet. Nick handed her a hair scrunchie. "Put your hair up please!"

"Yes daddy..." Nick stood close to her as she raised her arms to tie up her hair... he blew on her nipples... they responded, Katherine purred. He held out the panties.

"Put these on..." Nick held her hand to steady her as she raised her leg to put the panties on. Once she had put them on, Nick got the spray can and sprayed the inside edges on the panties around the legs and waist. Katherine bit her lip. She wanted to ask him what he was doing, but she bit her tongue. Nick sensed her inquisitiveness and held the can up to Katherine. "Spray glue... it's used by swimsuit models to keep their panties from riding up." (So that's how they did that! But why is Nick gluing my panties on for?) Nick then took the 'do rag' and tucked all her hair under it. "Follow me please…"

"Yes daddy." And Nick took the mask and goggles and led Katherine to the portal of pain… Nick strapped her wrists and ankles to it as he had done before but this time he strapped her waist in on the horizontal plain. "What's this for?" Nick's belt stung the round of her ass… Katherine moaned… and her jaw trembled. The pain is just what she wanted. She couldn't wait for what was to come next. Nick reached around her ankles and she heard a loud click. He then went to each of her wrists and she heard another click, then another. Nick stood behind Katherine.

"Trust me…?" Nick asked. Katherine nodded. Nick took his belt and put it around her neck from behind her. Katherine gasped. "Trust me…!" Katherine nodded but the belt cut into her throat a bit. Katherine was very scared, but she would not say anything. She had to trust Nick. "Lean back…" Katherine leaned back and Nick pulled on the belt ever so slightly and the ring tilted towards him into the horizontal position. She was suspended in mid air face up. Nick placed a pedestal with a pillow on it behind Katherine's head to support it. It was a very odd sensation. She felt like she was in the middle of a magic trick. Nick raised her head gently and tied the kerchief over her mouth and nose. "Can you breathe?" Katherine nodded. "Are you comfortable?" Katherine nodded. "That won't last long…" And he put the goggles on her. Katherine wondered '*is he gonna spin me around? What?*' It was then Nick turned on the music. It was Billy Idol's "*Flesh for Fantasy*". Just then she felt something strange on her body. "Don't move…"

"Yes daddy!" The she felt it again and again on different parts of her body. It kinda tickled. It was an odd sensation; she couldn't explain what it felt like.

"Try to relax…"

"Yes daddy…" Katherine closed her eyes and went with the strange feeling. It felt like thousand of little hands caressing her all over. She began to twitch and writhe with it. The music brought her into the proper mood. She bit her lip ever so slightly because now it tickled, but it was nice. She felt Nick bring her upright then face down. Now she began to feel the strange sensations on her back, ass and thighs. She still couldn't describe it but it was now all over her. She felt her back pop like it did when she was at the chiropractors. Nick then raised her upright, and turned the music up a bit. Now Katherine was dancing to the music and writhing to the sensations on her body. She shook and twitched and writhed with every moment. She felt it on her nipples her fingers and toes... everywhere. She moaned and cooed and purred. That's when she opened her eyes. There was something outside on the face protector of the goggles. She couldn't see what it was clearly because her hot steamy breath had fogged up the glass. She squinted to try to focus. That's when it moved. Then it crawled away. It was the biggest fucking water bug she had ever seen in her life.

Katherine didn't remember her screaming or fainting... she only remembered waking up in Nick's bed and almost jumping right out her skin brushing herself off. Her entire body had the heebie-jeebies and she couldn't sit still. Nick was sitting in a chair in the room, sipping tea.

I threw the pillow at Nick.... He blocked it with his hand. "What the fuck *was* that?"

"Those were Madagascar hissing cockroaches... They're quite harmless."

Katherine's body trembled. "You covered my body with cockroaches?"

"Uh huh... and some centipedes..." Katherine threw another pillow, barely missing Nick. "I guess we're not gonna add that to our repertoire!"

"Oh yeah... you aint never pulling *that shit* on me again!"

"Okay then...! I'll get you some chamomile tea!"

"Thank you!" she said as Nick left. "And I want the back rub that goes with it!" She shivered from the thought of what she just experienced. *"Bastard!"* She yelled. Katherine lay down but jumped up and began to rub her skin again. "Ewwww!"

The Tortured Soul Trilogy
(A Tortured Soul)
Chapter 63
(Shock the Monkey)

I answered the door and Katherine came in and kissed me. "So, am I allowed to ask what you have in store for me today?"

Nick thought for a moment. "Yeah sure... I think for this session I need you to understand what's going to happen..." Nick went to the couch and brought out a stainless steel case with leather straps around it.

"That's an interesting briefcase; I've never seen you with it before..."

I placed the case on the coffee table. "It's not a briefcase..."

"Then what is it?"

"In the 60's Russian athletes would use this to help stimulate their muscle growth without the use of drugs..."

"Does it work?"

"No... it was just a distraction so you wouldn't notice they were using drugs to make their muscles bigger!"

"So why do you have one?"

"Well the unit does have its uses..." I opened the case and pulled out the electrodes.

"It looks like an electro-cardiogram device... What are these?"

"They're electrodes..."

"You mean like in electricity...?"

"Don't worry... It's all powered by lithium batteries... it's the same voltage used in those ab-zappers they sell on TV."

"Do those things work?"

"Well... No not really, but when attached on the right spot it has an amazing effect..."

"And what *spot* are we talking about?"

"Do you trust me?"

"*Nooo*...! When can we begin?"

Anderson takes Katherine into the game room and helped her get dressed into a latex outfit with cutouts. Nick then took out a sponge and he began to wipe down Katherine's bare skin with it. "For better conductivity..." He then tied Katherine to the portal in an 'X' position and began to attach the electrodes to her exposed skin. One set went on her stomach, one above each nipple, a set on her buttocks and inner thighs and one on her clit. He handed her the control. "These buttons activate the different electrodes and this switch increases the intensity of the shocks. You don't have to worry about electrocution; the maximum level of shock is no more than a 9-volt battery. Okay?"

"Uh huh..."

He then brought out a red ball gag. "Because you have the briefcase control in your hand and there is real no danger... there is no need for a 'safety' word... Open..." And she opened her mouth and he tied the gag around her head. Nick then pulled up a chair and unzipped his pants and pulled out his cock and began to stroke himself. "Whenever you're ready...!" And Nick sat down to 'enjoy' the show. Katherine hit a button and a mild electric shock made her tits twitch.

"Ummmm!" Then she hit another and her ass twitched. "Um hmmm! Nice!" Then she found the prize button... the one that was connected to her clitoris... Katherine threw her head back and moaned. This went on and on for several minutes. Katherine would toggle the different switches as Nick masturbated. Katherine was now bathed in sweat and nearly exhausted. Nick walked over to the suitcase and showed Katherine a button on it.

"This one puts the machine on automatic..."

Katherine dropped the remote and nodded yes... Nick hit the switch. Katherine convulsed in the throngs of electric orgasm, until she heard Nick moan as he came and then she passed out. Nick carefully released her from her bonds, undressed her and took her to his bed. He was about to cover her with his blanket when he thought... *'Oh what the hell...!'* And he masturbated while watching her sleep naked on his bed. There still is nothing sexier than a woman at peace.

The Tortured Soul Trilogy
(A Tortured Soul)
Chapter 64
(Wax On... Wax Off!)

Katherine is naked and tied into the portal in an X. Nick takes out a bottle of baby oil that he has sitting in a bucket of ice. He moistens a rag and begins to rub her down with it all over her body. "That's cold!" and she began to shiver. Her nipples became hard immediately. Nick kissed them.

"I know baby... It'll only be cold for a few moments..." After a while the cool oil felt really good on her skin and it didn't hurt that Nick rubbed it in. Nick kneaded and rubbed her entire body deeply. He spent and extra long time on her nipples then he leaned into her and worked her ass. She liked that a lot. Katherine kissed Nick deeply as he squeezed her ass and grinded his hips into hers. She was shivering a bit from the chill.

"You keep that up... and I'm gonna cum...!" she purred.

"Oh really...?" And Nick reached down and concentrated rubbing on her clitoris and her labia. Katherine began to coo and purr and breathe heavy.

"I thought you said no sex before pain?" she gasped.

"I'm sorry...! Did I say *this* was going to be painful?" Nick stroked her faster and faster, Katherine gasped and smiled. She knew this was going to be a really good fuck. Katherine came and squealed. "Okay so much for the foreplay..."

"That was foreplay?" she sighed.

"Oh yeah...!" And Nick unhooked the portal and turned Katherine to the horizontal plane face up. Her head laid on the pillow on the stand under her. He then started to place lit candles all around the portal. When he was finished it looked as if she was in the middle of a medieval chandelier.

"Are you going to use hot wax on me...?" Katherine moaned in anticipation.

"Not exactly...."

"*Huh?*" And Nick got a pot of hot water with a smaller pot inside of it and a turkey injector and placed it on another stand off to the side. "What the hell is that?"

"The temperature of wax from a lit candle is unpredictable at best. So I cooled you down a bit and now I'm going to use warm oil to achieve the same effect in total safety... the candles around you are for ambiance only..." Nick filled the injector with the warm oil from the smaller pot and squirted a small amount on Katherine's body.

"Ohhh ho!" She moaned.

"You okay?"

"Oh hell yeah...! Let's do this!"

"Yes madam...!" Nick also had a bucket if ice nearby and he would take turns icing her down and dripping warm oil on her body. Sometimes he would pick a spot, sometimes Katherine would request specific placement. Katherine moaned and cooed with every drop. Katherine bit her lip.

"Nick?"

"Yes Katherine?"

"Can you just squirt that across my body?"

"Sure...!" And Nick emptied the syringe across her body. Katherine squealed. "Again!" Nick complied. Katherine squealed. "Again...! Again...!"

Nick continued as she requested. Katherine was totally aroused and writhed and gyrated in her restraints. "Katherine?"

"Yes Nicky?" she panted.

"I'm intrigued here... what are you sensing?"

"It feels like you're cumming all over me!" and she squealed again.

"Oh really...? Well then..." Nick filled the syringe with the last of the oil and positioned himself between her legs and rubbed her clit with a piece of ice. Katherine moaned and wailed. Then he took the syringe and slowly emptied it out full on her pussy and clit. Katherine went wild. Her pussy began to twitch.

"Ohhhhh mmm... mmm... myiii godd... dd... dd... dd...!" Katherine panted like an animal and began to breathe heavy. Her body shivered in the restraints and then she went limp.

"Well... *that* was fun... we're gonna have to do this again!" Nick said.

"Oh yeah!" Katherine barely whispered. Nick reached for the wheel to bring Katherine upright. "Wait a minute...!" Katherine said.

Nick paused. "Yes Katherine?"

"Once more…! Please!"

Nick looked into the pot. "There's no more hot oil and it would take too much time for me to make more…"

Katherine licked her lips and wiggled her tongue like a snake. "I believe… you have a special syringe set aside… filled with exactly what I want!"

"I hadn't thought of that…" Nick unzipped his pants. "Where would you like the money shot?"

"Right in my face please!" Nick got into position and began to masturbate over her. "If you don't mind…" Katherine cooed. "May I get my own?"

"I aim to please Madam…" Nick released her right hand from the restraint so that he could get into better position and he placed his throbbing cock into Katherine's waiting mouth. Nick reached over and fondled and stroked her nipples. Katherine stroked and sucked and licked him until… "I'm gonna *cum!*"

Katherine disengaged her mouth from his stiff cock. "*Me too…!*" She said. Nick took his left hand and stroked himself faster and faster while fingering Katherine's pussy with his right. Katherine continued to lick the head of his cock waiting for him to spurt. He then 'tea bagged' her and she licked and sucked his balls. "Give me! Give me baby! Cum for momma…!" Nick complied and threw his head back as he came. Katherine came hard once more and then she just started laughing.

"What's so funny?" Nick asked breathlessly. Katherine laughed.

"You missed… You *bitch!*" And Katherine laughed hysterically.

"Don't make me *laugh!*" Katherine and Nick both began to laugh uncontrollably. Katherine turned her head in the direction Nick shot his load.

"I think you shot out a candle!" she said. That did it… Nick was rolling on the floor laughing. "Do me a favor… before you pass out laughing… Get me down from here!" she said. Nick got up, blew out the candles, straightened out the wheel and untied her. They both laughed all the way back into the bedroom.

The Tortured Soul Trilogy
(A Tortured Soul)
Chapter 65
(She's Got Legs)

Katherine picked up the dirty dinner plates and put them in the sink. Nick returned from the liquor store with a nice dry white wine. "I have the wine... I'll get the glasses..."

"We won't be needing glasses..."

"Oh...? Why not?"

"Follow me... I wanna try something... Bring the wine..." Katherine tied her hair in a ponytail and Nick followed Katherine to the game room and to the portal of pain.

"What do have in mind, Katherine?"

"You sound nervous!"

"Should I be?"

"No daddy... you shouldn't." Nick took that to say he would be in control of whatever Katherine had planned. Katherine took off her skirt and panties and tied up her blouse in a knot above her stomach and stepped into the portal and grabbed the top of it. "Tie me off..." Nick reached for her ankles... "No... do my wrists first..."

"Yes Madam." Nick complied and he tied both of her hands to the top of the portal. Katherine took her right leg and raised it to 3 o'clock on the portal. She was wearing her leather shoes with the rings Nick liked.

"Tie that off for me please."

"Yes madam..." And Nick tied her right ankle to the portal using the ring on her shoe.

"Okay this is where is gets tricky... grab my left ankle and tie it at nine o'clock... Easy now!" Katherine held herself up with her arms as Nick carefully raised her ankle and tied off her left leg as she requested. She was now spread eagled in a Chinese split.

"Wow!"

"I told you... seven years of dance!"

"Now what...?"

"Flip me horizontal... face up please!"

"I'll have to tie you off at the waist first… for safety…"

"Do it then…"

"Yes madam!" And Nick cinched her by the waist and then unhinged the portal and slowly put Katherine into position.

"Now what…? I'm intrigued here."

"You have that bottle of wine?"

"Yes…"

"Open it and place it on my stomach with the neck facing six o'clock…"

"Yes madam…"

"Put the neck so the wine pours on my pussy." And he did as she requested; he had to place the winebottle under the knot Katherine tied in her blouse to keep it from falling. The wine slowly poured out as Katherine manipulated her stomach muscles.

"Damn… you're a nimble little minx aren't you…? Now what…?"

"You brought the wine… aren't you thirsty?"

"Why yes! Yes I am…" And Nick pulled up a chair, sat down and stuck his face between her legs and tongued and licked her wine soaked pussy. Katherine came in waves. Nick stood up and pulled the chair away.

"Will that be all?"

"No…" Katherine purred. "Pull your pants down please…"

"Yes madam…"

"Now flip me… face down towards you…" Nick moved the empty wine bottle and flipped her and now her face was in his crotch. "Come closer please…"

"Yes madam…" And Nick stepped closer and Katherine sucked and licked Nick's stiff cock. Some of the wine had soaked his crotch. Nick grabbed her ponytail with both hands and pumped her head on his cock.

"You've thought this out for a while haven't you?" Katherine moaned and sucked his cock with more intensity and vigor. "You don't have to answer… I'll take that as a yes…!"

Katherine disengaged herself. "Nick?" Katherine was breathing heavy.

"Yes Madam?"

"Does this count as a session?"

"Well… technically no… I haven't tortured you…"

"Well… if you don't get that cock in me right now… it *will* be torture!"

"Yes madam…" Nick quickly got a condom from his wallet and put it on… he grabbed the wheel. "Face up or face down?"

"Damn it Nick! Get in here NOW!" And she writhed in the straps. Nick quickly got into position and entered her from behind and started pumping her faster and harder… "Yes! Yes! Yes! Oh my…! Oh… you motherfucker! Oh you *mother… fucker!*" Katherine threw her head back. "You have no idea how much I want you to smack my ass right now…" Nick reached up and grabbed a paddle dangling from the ceiling above the portal and complied and smacked her on both cheeks of her ass. Katherine came like a banshee! Nick growled like a wolf. The both came like wild animals. Katherine huffed and puffed and moaned. She was totally exhausted and spent. Nick slowly flipped her upright and untied her in the opposite order that he tied her. When he untied her hands she laid them around his neck and she kissed him. "I *thought* you said… no pain after sex?"

"What I *said* was… 'You wouldn't have *the strength* for pain after sex' and I was right!"

Katherine shook her head… and licked her lips. "You *bitch!*"

"…Yeah… I love you too…" Nick replied. Nick kissed her and carried her semi-limp body to the bedroom so she could sleep it off.

The Tortured Soul Trilogy
(A Tortured Soul)
Chapter 66
(Tied To The Whipping Post)

Nick came over to the house at Katherine's request for a punishment session. When he arrived he took out several ropes and restraints laid them out on the floor. "What's all this?" Katherine asked.

"Today we're gonna try to get our merit badge in knot tying..."

"You're gonna tie me up?"

"At first yes... but then the method of tying you up is going to vary to make the restraints uncomfortable..."

"Nick... I don't know about this..." Katherine didn't mind being tied down but being tied up was something totally different. There was something surpressive about it she didn't like. It idea of it alone was somehow claustrophobic.

"I know you're not sure... but do you want to even try it?"

"I don't know... I don't think I'm gonna like this..."

"Do you *not* want to do it at all... or, do you want to see how it feels first?"

Katherine looked at all the ropes and paused. "I don't know... Nicky... I just don't know..."

"Okay then..." And Nick began to gather the ropes and restraints together to put them away. Katherine picked up one of the ropes off the floor and held it. Nick paused. "Katherine...?" Katherine held the rope in her hand. She felt its texture and wrapped it around her wrist. "Katherine...?"

Katherine held out the rope to Nick. "I wanna try this one..." Nick took the rope from her but he sensed her apprehension. "You *don't* have to..."

"I... I want to..." She wanted to be submissive to Nick.

"Okay... I want you to put on your leather cat suit so the rope doesn't burn your skin..." Katherine's leather cat suit was covered in rings that Nick would use to tie her onto the mahogany door to restrict her movements when he punished her. But

Katherine knew this was going to be very different. She came out wearing the cat suit, gloves, heels and all.

"What do you want me to do?" There was fear in her voice and Nick took note of it.

"Give me your hand…" Katherine complied and held out her hand. Nick methodically began to tie her wrist with the rope. It was a sensation she had experienced before, but still, this time, it felt very different. He wrapped her wrist with several turns. He then stood behind her. "Give me your other hand…" Katherine was hesitant, and slowly put her other hand behind her. As Nick began to tie her wrists together Katherine resisted. She never resisted before.   Now her wrists were tied together and Nick worked the ropes up the rings on forearms up to her elbows. Katherine sighed. "Are you okay Katherine?" Katherine nodded. "You know this stops when you say 'when'…" Katherine nodded. Nick took another rope and began to tie Katherine's ankles. Again she resisted having her ankles tied together. He then tied her legs together just below and just above the knees. She stood there, hogtied. Nick pulled out a large sharp pocketknife and showed it to her.

"What the hell is that for?"

"When… you say when… it will take too long to untie the ropes to free you… so I'm gonna have to cut your bonds off to get you out faster. I wanted you to see the knife so it wouldn't scare you…"

"Okay!" She took a deep breath and let it out slowly. Nick reached around her from the front and held her arms behind her.

"Kneel down please… I've got you… you're not gonna fall!" Katherine knelt down as Nick steadied her. She was now on her knees. The ropes cut into her shins. Nick removed the leather pieces covering her breasts. Katherine felt the cool air on her nipples. Nick stood before her and she leaned forward to reach Nick's crotch with her mouth. "*No!*" and Nick leaned back and away from her. Katherine shivered a bit. "Katherine? Are you sure you're okay?" Katherine nodded. "No… I want you to answer me… are you all right…?"

"Yes… Nick… I'm okay!"

Nick went into the kitchen and got a bowl of ice and began to ice Katherine's nipples from behind her. He was slow and methodical with that too. Katherine panted but not in a way she panted ever before. He leaned over her to see her face. "Katherine...? Talk to me..."

"I'm *alright* Nick... go ahead... let's do this!"

Nick went behind her again and grabbed her by her ankles and tied another rope around them and then hog-tied her to her wrists. Katherine was now leaned forwards and she kept her head down. Katherine began to pant again. He began to wrap the rope around her waist from behind and crossed the ropes bet around her breasts and shoulders like a medieval cross your heart bra. This placed more pressure on her arms and legs. From behind her, he iced her nipples again as he wrapped the rope around again and again. He put his knee between her shoulder blades and he pulled the ropes tighter to exert more pressure. As he iced her nipples again, that's when he noticed Katherine face as she was forced to lean back towards him. She was silently crying uncontrollably. The tears were streaming down her face. "*Katherine*!!!" Nick looked into her eyes. Her reaction wasn't from physical pain... she was scared to death. "Talk to me! Katherine... Say something!" Katherine couldn't speak. She just cried harder but silently. Her mouth was wide open but no sound came from her at all. Nick quickly got the knife and cut her loose with three quick slashes. He pulled the rest of ropes off and Katherine collapsed into Nick's arms and began to cry out loud now.

"I'm sorry! I'm so sorry Nicky... I'm sorry! I'm so sorry..."

"It's okay baby! Are you alright?" She said '*I'm sorry*' over and over again. Nick held her to comfort her. But she wouldn't stop crying and saying I'm sorry. Nick kissed her and held her but she still wouldn't stop crying. Katherine grabbed Nick crotch and began to stroke him. "*No... baby... no... stop...!*" And he tried to pull her hand away but she wouldn't let go.

"I'm sorry... I'm sorry!" she said as the tears streamed down her face. She just kept repeating '*I'm sorry*' as she tried to unzip his pants. Nick tried to stop her but she just wouldn't stop clawing at his crotch. Finally, Nick let her unzip him and she dropped to her kness and began to suck and lick his cock. It was the only thing that seemed to calm her down. She stroked and sucked him as she sobbed. She sucked him with determination at first, but then she calmed down and began to suck him with a fervent passion. Katherine moaned and sucked and bobbed her head up and down his shaft. Nick threw his head back. He wasn't expecting this to go this way and was caught way off guard. Nick put his hands on Katherine's shoulders and eased himself down into a full split. Katherine stayed on him and voraciously devoured and licked every inch of him. Katherine then reached for an ice cube and put it in her mouth and continued to suck Nicholas dry. Nicholas' body began to convulse as he came. Katherine grabbed her nipples and squeezed them hard and she screamed as he came in her face. She then rolled over on top of him, placed her head on his stomach and continued to kiss and stroke and lick his spent cock.

"I'm sorry... I'm sorry baby..." She said as she gently stroked his cock. "Please don't tie me up again" And she began to lick his cock like an ice cream cone. "Please... don't tie me up like that anymore. Please?" Nick looked at her and he realized, she wasn't talking to him... she was talking to his cock.

"I'll never do that to you again..." he answered.

"Thank you...!" She continued to stroke and lick and kiss his cock until he was fully erect again.

'*I can't believe I'm ready again!*' Nick said to himself. Katherine started sucking on his stiff member again. She deep throated him and Nick's body shivered. Nick fought the urge to say: '*You keep blowing me like this, and I will keep tying you up!*' He knew that he had touched something dark and evil within her soul and he had promised her, if she drew a line, he would *not* cross it, no matter how rewarding it was going to be for him. Katherine didn't stop until she made him cum two more times. Nick's cock was now numb and he was exhausted. She was adamant that she would not be tied up like that ever again. Nick got the message, when she finally allowed him to get up; he got rid of all the ropes he had purchased. When he got back to her, Katherine had slipped out of her leather panties and was spread eagled on the couch, masturbating and pinching her nipples.

"Thank you daddy...!"

"My pleasure Madam..." Katherine motioned for him to come closer. Nick shook his head. "I... *don't* have *anything*... left...!"

351

"I want you to... *eat me*! I want to feel your beard between my legs...!" And she spread her labia and stroked her clit.

"Yes madam..." And Nick knelt down and began to lick and tongue her wet pussy. Katherine held the back of his head and directed him as she saw fit. He would 'return' the favor and proceeded to give her multiple orgasms until *she* couldn't take it anymore. What's good for the goose...!

The Tortured Soul Trilogy
(A Tortured Soul)
Chapter 67
(The Reveal)

One Sunday afternoon, Nick and Katherine were just sitting around her house. Nick was reading the newspaper, Katherine was writing in her journal. Katherine got up and went into the kitchen. "I'm sorry Nick... I don't have any tea... would you care for a cup of coffee?"

"Sure... I'd love a cup... thank you..."

"Really...? All these years... I don't think I remember ever seeing you drink coffee..."

"I don't mind having a cup every once in a while..."

"So...? How do you take your coffee...?"

"Black and bitter... like my ex!"

"*What*?"

"I'm sorry... that was a private joke..."

Katherine filled the coffee maker and began the brewing. "You're ex-wife was black?"

"Still is the last time I checked!"

"No I mean... I..."

"You're surprised I was once married to a black woman...?"

"No... No... I..." Nick looked at Katherine. Katherine held up her hand to Nick. "Nick! I am not..."

"No one is sweetie... *until* they start stuttering..." And Nick went back to reading the paper. Katherine was hurt that she felt she had disrespected Nick and that he thought that of her. Nick looked up at Katherine and took out his wallet, opened it to a picture and handed it to Katherine.

"Is this her?" Nick nodded. "She is... gorgeous!"

"You think she's hot... you should see our daughter..."

Katherine looked at the next picture in his wallet. "Oh my... she looks like she could be a runway model!"

"She did a little runway and print work... but she gave it up..."

"Why?"

"Personal reasons..."

"I didn't mean to pry..."

"I told you before... there are no secrets between us..."

"So what does she do now?"

"She's taking courses in computer programming and computer language."

Katherine handed Nick back his wallet. "May I ask... what happened to your marriage?"

"Well, we had irreconcilable differences..."

"What could you two possibly have disagreed about that could have broken up your marriage?"

"She thought I was an asshole... and I disagreed!"

"...Seriously!"

"Seriously! Our marriage was doomed from the start... it was the late 70's. We dated while I was in college to prove a point, we got married to piss off our parents and we got divorced about fifteen years later because that wasn't a good enough reason to continue our relationship...."

"Was she into...?"

"No... but that's not to say it wasn't a *painful* relationship..." Nick smiled.

"You must have loved her... once!"

"I still do... we just couldn't get along in the same house..."

"You two fought all the time?"

"...When we weren't having sex... yes!"

"Surely you two agreed on some things?"

"We agreed that she should have full custody of Cynthia..."

"You miss your daughter don't you?"

"Lynn eventually took Cynthia to Europe to help her start her modeling career, when Cynthia quit... Lynn stayed in London. Cynthia came back to the states but we don't see each other as much as I'd like to..."

"Your ex-wife's name is Lynn?"

"It's short for Shao-Lynn..." Katherine raised her eyebrow. "Hey! She was born in the sixties..."

"So your ex is younger than you?"

"Only by six years or so..."

"I seem to notice a pattern here..."

"Oh yeah...?"

"You like your ladies younger than you..."

"Honey... at my age... they're *all* younger than me!"

Katherine laughed. "May I say something? And please don't take it the wrong way..."

"Sure!"

"My great grand-mother was..." Katherine hesitated.

"...Was black?" Nick added.

"Yes... how did you know?"

"Lucky guess... plus white girls don't *usually* sign up for African dance classes..."

"I didn't want to bring it up before because I..."

"Didn't want to sound like some phony liberal that goes around saying; '*I have 'black' in my family...*'"

"Yes!"

"Did you ever meet your grandma?"

"I spent all my summers with her in Georgia... she was the most wonderful, loving, compassionate woman I have ever known..."

"You knew you two were related?"

"Yes... she was family, first and foremost...! It was never hidden from me... I just never knew she was 'black', she was just grandma...!"

"You miss her?"

"...I think of her almost every day!" Katherine poured Nick a cup of coffee and handed it to him. "What about your second wife?"

"British... died of ovarian cancer... about two years after we were married..."

"Oh Nick!"

"It's okay... Amanda was a very nice lady... I *really* cared about her. I loved her so much that I married her even though we knew she was dying. She was cremated and sent back to England where she sits on her family mantel..."

"That's so sweet...! How did you two meet?"

"Visiting Cynthia for a runway show she was doing in London. Amanda was covering the show for a local paper and her daughter was in the show too. We hit if off… whirlwind romance, you know… the usual…"

Katherine thought a moment. "Wait… *Amanda…*? Nick is Mandy… Amanda's daughter…?"

"…Yeah from a previous marriage… Hey! You're good at this, quick… what number am I thinking of right now?"

"…Sixty-nine!"

(Damn! She *is* good!) "But she got me addicted to drinking tea…"   Nick sipped the coffee and spit it back. "…And I guess it's a habit *you're* not gonna get me to break! You do know when I said 'black and bitter', I was kidding?"

"…Too strong?"

"Ackk!"

"Okay! I'll stock up on tea…! Geez!" Katherine took Nick's cup and poured him a glass of wine instead.

"May I ask *you* a question Katherine?"

"Sure Nick? What?"

"I just put new batteries in my briefcase just a few weeks ago and they're already dead… any explanation?"

"Ooops!"

"*Ooops*?" Nick raised an eyebrow.

"I was gonna replace them before you noticed… I forgot, sorry!"

"And what do you think I would have done if I wanted to use that on you and the batteries were dead?"

"I would *hope*… you would beat my *ass*!"

Nick started to laugh. So did Katherine until Nick got up and took of his belt. "Come here…"

"Nicky no!"

"I *said* come here!"

Katherine began to laugh harder. "No!" She said.

Nick got serious; Katherine continued to laugh. "Are you defying me young lady?"

"*No!*" Then Katherine laughed nervously.

"Then come *here…*!"

"No!" The laughter became a bit more hysterical.

Nicky took a step towards Katherine, she ran behind the couch. "What do you *think* you're doing?"

"Uh uhh! You've gonna have to earn *this* ass whuppin'..." And Katherine made Nick chase her around the room until he finally cornered her and dragged her to the chair. They were both out of breath. She tried to fight him off before he was able to control her and get her over his knee. She covered her ass with her hands.

"Move your hands young lady!"

"*No!*"

"You're only making it worse for yourself!"

Then Katherine's voice became *very* serious. "Nick! Don't you *dare* hit me!" And Nick let her go... Once Katherine said 'when', Nick had to respect her boundaries and stop. Katherine was breathing heavy, but she did not get up from Nick's lap. She stayed there in that prone position.

"Are you getting up?" Nick asked. Katherine did not answer but she did not get up from his lap either. She continued to breathe heavy and then faster. She slowly reached for her elastic of her pajama bottoms and slowly shimmied out of them. She then slowly reached down in front of her and tightly grabbed the chair legs in front of her.

"Beat me... daddy!" Katherine realized that this had become a 'session' and that she was in full control of the pain she was about to receive.

"Yes madam!" I tore that ass up until Katherine passed out. I then lifted her limp body off me and gently took her to the bedroom and placed her on her bed. Katherine slept peacefully for the rest of the afternoon. She was completely worn out... I watched her sleep for a while; she looked like an angel floating away on a cloud. There is nothing sexier than a woman at peace. I went back into the kitchen, got myself the glass of wine Katherine had poured for me earlier. I then went to sit in the living room. Katherine kept the TV in her bedroom and I didn't want to wake her, but I didn't want to go home either. I decided to kill some time reading. I had already finished the newspaper so I reached over to the side table and opened it looking for some magazines or something. Inside there was a Victoria's Secret catalogue with several outfits circled. I guess I just found out what she was getting me for *my* birthday. The other book in the drawer was a Bible. I opened it and noticed that she had many 'post-it's inside in the

Book of Proverbs, Psalms and Lamentations. I wasn't interested in reading the Bible right now, so I put the Bible down and went back to refresh my drink. It was then I saw the journal Katherine was writing in. I looked at the open pages and it was hand written poetry and prose. I didn't think it would be problem to read some. I took it and sat back down on the couch. After reading a few pages, I realized that the poetry mirrored and were in harmony with the Bible passages she had highlighted. I cross-referenced the Bible passages with her poems. You could tell by the different inks used, that they were written in different times of her life. I sipped my drink as I continued to read.

The writings were a stark contrast to the sleeping angel I left in the other room. Katherine was a tortured soul and I had just discovered the window to her suffering. I read each and every word carefully and I felt all her pain and misery. How could someone so young and so beautiful have gone through so much heartache and pain? It wasn't until I closed the journal that I realized that I was crying... I wiped my eyes and sobbed. I put the books back in the drawer and that's when I looked up and saw that Katherine was standing in the bedroom doorway... watching me!

"I'm sorry... I didn't... mean to..." I whispered.

Katherine walked over to me and put her finger on my lips. "Shhhh!" She wiped a tear from my eye and she cradled into my lap, nestled her head into the crook of my neck and shoulder. She put her hand on my heart... and went back to sleep. I held her in my arms and gently rocked her... Katherine purred. I held her close to me and kissed her forehead. This was the very first time I truly realized how much I love her. The tears welled in my eyes. I never want this moment to end.

God... what has this woman done to me? And I thank you for her.

The Tortured Soul Trilogy
(A Tortured Soul)
Chapter 68
(The Masochist Yelled 'Beat Me! Beat Me!' And The Sadist Wouldn't Do It!)

Katherine is naked except for her shoes and gloves and is tied to the 'Portal of Pain' as usual. She has no idea what Nick had planned; he was being very secretive about it. It concerned her because after the last session, he would at least give her a heads up. "What are you going to do to me?"

"Do you trust me?'

"*No*… let's do this…" She had learned to tell him she didn't trust him, that way he knew that she would use the safety word if things got out of hand. Anderson tapes the remote to her right hand. "Why are you doing that?"

"For this… you're going to be gagged… you won't be able to say the safety word… I just wanna make sure you don't drop the remote… remember… the moment you press the button… it stops…"

"I'm scared!"

"You should be!" Anderson puts a blindfold on Katherine.

"I'm gonna be blindfolded?"

"Only for a few moments while I prepare you…" Anderson plays Pink Floyd's '*Comfortably Numb*', then returns and starts to rub her body down.

"Is that liquid latex again?'

"No… its olive oil mixed with just a little cinnamon to create a warm feeling… and protect your skin…"

"Oh… I like it… I really like that!" Anderson continues to rub her down. Katherine likes it. It was like a warm full body massage. "But when does the pain begin?"

"Just a moment… be patient…" Anderson takes the ball gag and tightly ties it in her mouth. She moans in anticipation. "Are you ready?" Muffled moans came from Katherine. "Okay then… here comes the pain…!" Nick grabs a 'cat-o-nine-tails' and begins to whip Katherine. He struck her all over her body, her back, her buttocks, her thighs, across her chest, her belly. With every sting if the whip; Katherine writhed and moaned. The pain was quite exquisite. The sharp sound and the sting of the whip on her body excited her more and more. Katherine didn't even consider hitting the remote to stop this. Nick even took the whip and struck her between her legs so that the middle of the whip would strike her clit. Katherine threw her head back and began to choke. Nick reached over and took the gag out of her mouth so she could breathe. But she still didn't hit the remote. Katherine began to moan and holler with every stroke of the whip. Nicky stopped whipping her and Katherine bathed in the sting of the whip. She let out a low moan and took a deep breath. A wave of adrenaline rush washed over her. She didn't care about the 'No sex after pain' rule.

She began to scream. "Fuck me! Fuck me…! Nicky please! I want your cock! Fuck me please… Please Daddy! Fuck meeeee!" Katherine began to cry and sob now. She desperately wanted Nick's cock… not a toy… his cock. "You bitch! You fucking faggot! You mother… fucker! FUCK ME!! Fuck me now!" Katherine was covered in sweat and bruises, her pussy was wet and hungry and her nipples were hard and tender. She writhed in her restraints. She couldn't even touch herself to get herself off. Katherine began to cry hysterically now… she pulled on the restraints like a captured animal… but she still wouldn't hit the remote. She then resorted to begging. "Please…! Please! May I have your cock? Please daddy… may I please have your cock? I'll treat it so nice… I'll do anything you want Daddy… Please! Please, daddy, please…! I just want to feel you deep inside me… I want to squeeze you and milk you… Ah ha! Yeah… give me! I want it… I want it now!" When he didn't respond she became furious… and she spat into the room. "You cock sucking son of a bitch! You're masturbating aren't you? You're jerking yourself off… aren't you? You fucking faggot! What about me? What about me! I wanna cum too! You selfish bastard! Do ME…! You fucking ass clown! You selfish son of a bitch!"

She pulled more and more on the restraints, they wouldn't give but she still wouldn't hit the remote. Then the pleading started… "Please daddy… don't waste it… let me have it… let me have it daddy… you *know* I'll do it right for you… I'll suck it for you… I'll swallow you whole… just please *give* me!" Then she

360

accepted. She began to pant heavily. "Okay...! Okay...! If this is what you want... go ahead... stroke your cock... stroke it for me daddy..." And she began to grind her body like a stripper. "Is that what you want...? Yes...? Does daddy like?" And she arched her back and wiggled her tongue like a snake. "Are you behind me? I know you are, cause I know you love looking at my ass.... Come get it daddy... I'll let you ass fuck me... You know you want to... Go ahead... lube me up and ass fuck me... I know you want to... I've seen you check out my ass when you think I'm not looking... go ahead... fuck me up the ass! Come on... bring it bitch!" And she rotated her hips slowly and then jiggled her ass like a stripper. "Ohhh! Does daddy like?" She then began to moan and move her body in waves. She had no idea where he was in the room, but she knew he was watching her. "Cum for me... cum for me please! Shoot your cum all over me... whatever you want... it's all for you... it's all yours... go ahead baby! Cum in my face... cum on my ass... whatever you want... Let me hear you cum... for me! Bite me... beat me... lick me... eat me... do whatever you want... it's all yours daddy! It's all yours!" Nick carefully removed her blindfold. Kitten looks at Nick's eyes intently. "Did that do it for you daddy?" Katherine panted and her body quivered just at the sight of Nick, but then she noticed a bright light behind him and a video camera on a tripod. She sees her image on a TV monitor off to the side. Katherine's eyes widen and she screams and fights to pull herself from the restraints.

"Use the remote!"

Katherine continued to struggle. Nick feels that she is about to hurt herself, and he steps in front of her blocking the camera.

"Use the remote Katherine... you're the only one in control here... hit the remote!" She finally hit the button and all the lights went off and the restraints loosened. Nick catches her as Katherine falls into the fetal position on the floor. Anderson holds her shivering body. "It's okay baby... its okay..." Katherine is now crying uncontrollably. Her whole body is shaking and shivering. She then starts hitting Anderson while she's crying. Anderson holds her hands and she continues to fight back. "It's alright Kitten, it's alright... there's no tape in the camera, there was never any tape in the camera!" Katherine cries hysterically,

Anderson goes over and opens the camera. "See...? There was never any tape in the camera!"

Katherine sits there wide-eyed and in total shock and dismay. "Why? *Why* did you do that?" She reverted to the fetal position shivering and crying. "I *trusted* you!"

"Sometimes the pain doesn't stop, just because we want it to... and sometimes the things that we do, doesn't stay a secret..." He calmly said. Anderson kneels down next to her and spoons her on the floor as she cries. "That's when you have to be strong for yourself... by yourself!" Nick rocked her in his arms and kissed her gently on her face.

"I... am... so *mad* at you right now!" she stammered.

"I know... I know..." And he rocked her in his arms and kissed her neck.

"I don't know *where*... I don't know *when*... but this *bitch* is gonna get *even* with you!" Katherine hit Nick again and again with the side of her closed fist.

"I know... there's gonna be hell to pay!"

"You're *damn* right there is!" And Katherine turned her head towards him and kissed Nick deeply. "I just wish I didn't fucking love you so much! *You bitch!*" She said. She hit him one more time and then she cuddled into Nick's arms shivering and shaking.

"I needed you to love yourself more..."

"That makes no fucking sense at all to me right now!"

"It will Katherine... it will..." Nick just held her in his arms until she fell asleep exhausted. Nick picked her up and put her in his bed, covered her up with his blanket and left her to get some sleep. Katherine turned into his pillow and caught a whiff of his scent. She nuzzled it, stuck her thumb in her mouth and began to masturbate... furiously.

"Oh yeah! *That's* what mama wanted!" She came hard and then she drifted off into a peaceful sleep. Fuck Nick and his 'No sex after pain' rule.

The Tortured Soul Trilogy
(A Tortured Soul)
Chapter 69
(Suspicious Minds)

One morning after spending the night, Katherine wakes up in Nick's bed all alone. "Nick? Nicky...? Are you there? I swear that man disappears every time I fall asleep!" Nick enters the room buttoning his jacket. "Where are you off to?"

"...To the store... I wanna pick up some breakfast... you want anything?"

"Whatever you bring me is fine... I trust your judgment..."

"You sure...?"

Katherine nodded... "Say Nick..."

"...Yeah sweetie?"

"I need to get on the Internet... May I use your computer?"

"As long as you don't download any viruses... sure!"

"What about downloading porno?"

"There's no more room in the hard drive for any more porn..."

"What's your pass code?"

"Don't have one... just click on the internet explorer..." Nick turns to leave and turns back. "You sure you don't want me to bring you anything special back?"

"...Just you daddy!" And Katherine blew Nick a kiss. Nick exited and she heard the front door close, and she got up from bed, closed her robe and sat down at Nick's computer. She was about to click on the Internet logo when she saw an icon on his desktop with a sub heading *'Filename; Svetlana'*. "...'Svetlana'...? Where have I seen that name before?" Katherine's jaw dropped when she remembered where she had heard the name before. "Isn't that *Lisa's* real name...? Oh I know he doesn't have a ..." Katherine hovered the cursor over the icon. She hesitated. Should she? Or shouldn't she? I should let him have his privacy, but the she remembered him telling her that they had no secrets between them. Besides, if he did get angry with her for prying, he could always punish her later. She bit her lip slightly, closed her eyes, considered the consequences and clicked on the icon.

The very first photo that came up was of Lisa with some strange woman on top of her naked oiled body. "Oh... you... *son of a bitch*! I knew it! I just *fucking* knew there was something going on between the two of you..." Katherine's finger hovered over the file delete button. "It would serve him right!" But then she paused, and clicked on the next picture... and the next... and the next... At first she was checking to see if Nick was in any of the photos, but then she became intrigued with the photos, and the things Lisa and her hot friend were doing. Katherine tilted her head. "So *that's* what that's used for!"

She continued to click from photo to photo. She leaned close to the screen to get a closer look at the action, and then she realized that she could enlarge the shots with the click of a mouse. She leaned back and crossed her legs and sat in the lotus position in Nick's chair. Before she realized it, her free hand was between her legs stroking her clit. Katherine cooed a bit as she stroked herself and fantasized over the photos. She let out a low moan and reached up and pinched her bright, hard nipples. Now she was moaning and purring with each new photo. She let out a huge sigh and threw her head back and came. It was different than any other experience she ever had. It was a mello orgasm. It felt like a sudden short drop instead of the rollercoaster rides she had become accustomed to. She actually felt... refreshed. She took a deep breath and that's when she realized, she wasn't alone. She placed her feet on the floor and slowly turned around in the chair. Nick was standing behind her.

"Don't stop on my account!" Nick said.

"How long have you been standing there?"

"I came in just as you crossed you legs..."

"And you came back without breakfast because?"

"I forgot my wallet... but I didn't want to interrupt you..."

"I see..." Nick got his wallet from the nightstand and began to leave. "Wait a moment..." Nick turned to her and Katherine got out of the chair and motioned for him to sit. He came over and sat down. Katherine spun him around slowly in the chair to face the computer. He reached for the delete button. Katherine stopped him and put his hand on the mouse. Nick didn't know what she wanted him to do. She clicked on the next picture of Lisa going down on Valerie for him. She then stood behind him and began to kiss his neck and ears. "You *like* that daddy?"

Nick answered cautiously, "*Yes...!*" She clicked on the next photo. Lisa was now on top and had Valerie's labia wide open with her fingers and was stroking Valerie's clit with her tongue. Katherine began to lick his ears and she clicked on the next picture. Lisa was on her back and Valerie's mouth was full on Lisa's pussy. Valerie had both of Lisa's nipples in between her thumbs and forefingers. Lisa was sucking on a glass dildo. Nick felt a little uneasy in this situation. Katherine then reached around Nick, unzipped his pants and reached in for his cock with her right hand and began to stroke him slowly. Katherine opened her robe with her left hand and her bare nipples were on either side of Nick's head. He turned his head to kiss her nipple, but she took his chin in her free hand and turned his head back to the computer screen. She continued to stoke him slowly. He now knew what she wanted him to do, and what she was going to do for him. With every click and every new photo Katherine stoked Nick's cock tighter and faster, tighter and faster. She took her left hand and retrieved her scent on her fingers and placed it under his nose. Nick inhaled deeply. Katherine rubbed her nipples on Nick's broad shoulders. And she continued to kiss his face and ears and to stroke him faster and faster and faster until... "AHHHHH! HA!" Nick was covered in sweat and was spent. Katherine kissed his lips tenderly, and whispered in his ear.

"So daddy... do you think I've resolved my jealousy issues?"

"I *do* believe you have..."

"I'm gonna get you a towel and then I'm gonna take a shower..." Katherine began to exit... "Oh and Nicky..."

"Yes Katherine?"

"Be a doll and E-mail that file to me!"

"Yes Madam..."

The Tortured Soul Trilogy
(A Tortured Soul)
Chapter 70
(Killing Me Softly)

Nick came over to Katherine's house to pick her up. She was dressed up a little too much for what Nick had planned that evening. She had on a nice blouse, slacks, pumps and a short jacket. Her hair was cascading around her face"Okay... we're not going to work today..."

Katherine did a turn and looked in the hall mirror. "What's wrong with what I wearing?" She thought she looked cute.

"It's a little over dressed for where we're going tonight..."

"I don't understand, you said; "dress casual"..."

"A little more casual..."

"What *do* you want me to wear?"

"Okay...! Put on those 'designer' ripped jeans of yours, your running shoes and a sweat shirt... and no bra... I want you to be loose and comfortable..."

Katherine didn't understand what this was all about but she learned to trust Nick so she went back into the bedroom and changed. "Is this what you wanted?"

"Yes... and tie your hair into a ponytail... "

She complied. "Okay?"

"Perfect... let's go..." They went outside and got into the car and drove off.

"So where are we going tonight?"

"Remember the night you danced for me?"

"*Hell yeah*! Every time I smell curry, my pussy twitches!" Nick smiled and thought of Pavlov's dog.

"And remember when I said to you that one of the rules was that we would never have an audience...?

Katherine became a little concerned. "*Yes...?*"

"And that I said that as time progressed we would decide when to change the rules?"

"*Uh huh...?*"

"Well... tonight is the night!"

"OH *HELL* NO! Stop the *fucking* car!"

"Katherine... *Listen* to me!"

"No! NO! NOO! I am *NOT* gonna strip for your biker buddies! No *fucking* way! Stop the car NOW!" Nick pulled the car over. Katherine was still heated and pissed. "*Okay...! Okay Nicky!* I have gone along with a lot of crazy shit since I've been with you... and I must admit I liked a lot of it... Hell! I LOVED a few of them and I want to do those again... one or two were a bit too much... but hey! I got into this so I can try out new things, get my freak on... but I am not... let me make this *real* clear... NOT...! Gonna strip naked for your *fucking* friends...!"

"I don't want you to strip... but you *are* gonna perform in front of an audience tonight...!"

"*What are you talking about*?" Now Katherine was totally confused. Nick got out and opened Katherine's door. When she got out they were in front of the "C" cup.

"What *the* hell? What are we doing here?" Nick didn't answer and led her inside. There was a moderate sized crowd listening to a spoken word poet just finishing to everyone snapping their fingers and lighting their cigarette lighters. Mandy walked over to them.

"You're just in time... you're on next!"

"... 'On next' for what?" Katherine asked. Nick reached into his jacket pocket and handed her a piece of paper. "What's this?" Katherine opened it. It was one of her poems from her journal; Nick had typed it out for her. She then realized what he wanted her to do. She looked at Nick and quite plainly said. "Okay...! I changed my mind... I'll *strip* for your biker friends!" Nick laughed and led her to the stage. Mandy introduced them to the audience and she handed Katherine the mike. Nick settled onto a bar stool, Mandy took out a guitar from behind the register and gave it to Nick. He began to play "*Stairway to Heaven*". Katherine closed her eyes and listened to Nick as he played. Then she heard him softly sing; "*and she's buy-i-ying a stairway to hea-e-van...* Katherine instinctively knew this was her cue and without even looking at the paper, she began to recite her poem. Katherine's voice was soft and soulful. She let herself go and she felt as if Nick held her in his arms with the music he played. She felt safe and

367

secure and had no problem at all bearing her soul. When they had both finished the room was silent... then the snapping began... and the lighters lit, a moment later they were getting a standing ovation. Mandy came over and threw her arms around Katherine.

"That was so beautiful..." And Mandy kissed Katherine on the lips, and hugged her. "That poem touched my very soul!" And Katherine hugged Mandy. "How did you know?" Mandy cried softly. "Exactly what I always wanted to say all of my life?" And they rocked each other in each other's arms.

"Hey...! Can I get in on some of this?" Nick interrupted. They both looked at Nick and waved him off. "Oh no... they *didn't*!" Katherine went over to Nick and hugged and kissed him.

Nick said to Mandy "...and you! Get back to work!" Mandy laughed and went to go serve customers. Katherine kissed Nick again.

"And what if we would have bombed?" Katherine wondered.

"Then... I would have made you strip! That's why I told you not to wear a bra!" Katherine laughed. "You wanna do another poem?" Nick asked.

Katherine took Nick's hand and put it under her sweat top onto her erect nipple. "What do you think?"

"I 'think' everybody can see us..."

"I don't care... the way I feel right now, I'd *fuck* you right now on this very stage!" She whispered.

"...So much for your fear of performing in public! But we shouldn't talk about this right now..."

"Why not...? What's the big deal?"

"The *big* deal is... you still have a *live* mike in your hand and everyone can hear us!"

"Ooops!" Katherine checked the mike and it was off all along, she hit Nick in the stomach with it. Nick laughed. Nick and Katherine actually stayed around long enough to have some tea and biscotti and mingle with the patrons awhile before going to her place and fucking like bunnies...

The Tortured Soul Trilogy
(A Tortured Soul)
Chapter 71
(A Quiet Storm)

Katherine stopped by Nick's house at about 2pm one weekend. Nick was watching TV at the time. "Hey Katherine...!" And Nick kissed her. "What a pleasant surprise..."

"I hope you don't mind... me just coming by like this?"

"Not at all... come on in..." Katherine stepped in and Nick took her jacket and hung it up for her. "I was just in the neighborhood and..."

"No explanation necessary..." Katherine smiled. "Sit... make yourself at home..." Katherine sat on the couch. "You're just in time..."

"How so...?"

"I just ordered pizza and I was just about to make some sangria..."

"You make your own sangria?"

"Its not so hard... just take a gallon of dry Spanish wine and add a can of fruit cocktail and top off with lemon, lime and orange slices... viola! Sangria...!"

"Can I help?"

Nick looked shocked. "You know *how* to use a *can opener*?"

"*Fuck you!*"

"I'll hold you to that later...!"Nick led her into the kitchen and gave the can of fruit cocktail and the can opener to her and he started to slice the fruit for the sangria. Katherine opened the can and was about to drain it. "No... save that... it helps sweeten the wine."

"Now what...?"

"There's a large glass pitcher in that cabinet..." Katherine got it and rinsed it in the sink. "Empty the can into the pitcher..."

Nick pulled out a gallon jug of red wine and handed it to her. "Fill the pitcher up to the curve..."

She did and Nick added the slices to the top and stirred the mixture with a wooden spoon and offered her a taste. "Ooh…! That's good…"

Nick took the pitcher into the living room and set it down on the coffee table and went back into the kitchen as Katherine came out with the wine glasses. Just as she put the glasses down the doorbell rang. "Oh Katherine… That's the pizza guy… The money is on the banister, could you get that for us?"

"Sure Nick…" Katherine paid the man and Nick came out with plates and put a trivet on the coffee table.

"Just put the pizza box on the trivet." Katherine put the pizza box down on the trivet and stared at Nick. "*What*…? What did I *do*…?" Nick asked.

"It's just…"

"It's just… 'what'…?"

"For a confirmed bachelor… you're broken in quite nicely!"

"Oh *stop*…! We're not all cavemen…!" Katherine laughed and began to grunt and pretended to pick fleas off Nick's body. Nick laughed. They sat down on the couch; Katherine kicked off her shoes and got comfortable while Nick channel surfed until he came to "*The Princess Bride*" without commercials. Nick stopped there.

"I *love* this movie!"

"Me too…!" Nick replied.

"Oh stop!"

"I'm serious… I've seen this movie over fifty times… I can recite every line by heart…"

"Me *too*…!"

"*Yeah* right…!" Nick said

"I'll tell you what…" Katherine said. "Either one of us starts a line and messes it up, has to take a sip of sangria…"

"Careful… sangria sneaks up on you…"

"…Shouldn't *you*… be more concerned about that than me?"

"Oh… that sounds like a challenge!" By the time the film ended both were quite mellowed out by *two* pitchers of sangria. Katherine had settled into Nick's chest. She kissed his neck and ears. Nick kissed her face and lips. Katherine took Nick's hand and placed it under her blouse. Nick gently stroked her nipples as they watched the next movie.

"This is nice... I like this..." She said.

Nick kissed her on her forehead. "Me too..."

"I meant... being here with you..."

"Me too... cause *this* movie *sucks!*"

Katherine laughed and they kissed each other deeply. Katherine settled back into his chest and squeezed him tightly. "Is there anything else on?"

"Do you really care?"

"Not really..."

Nick turned off the TV and they fell asleep in each other's arms. Katherine woke up about two hours later all alone on the couch. "Nicky?" she called out.

Nick answered from inside the kitchen. "In here baby...! I was just cleaning up the dishes..."

"*You're* doing dishes?"

"Yes... It's the maids' night off! But if you *wanna* throw on the uniform..."

Katherine laughed. "Let me help you..." She said. And she tried to stand up and fell back on the couch.

"Are you okay in there?"

"Yes... I'm okay... boy...that sangria sure does sneak up on you!"

Nick laughed. "Told you... I'll tell you what... give me a few more moments while I finish up in here and I'll take you home... you're in no shape to drive..."

"Okay..."

Nick finished cleaning the dishes and put everything away. "So... Katherine... you ready to go?" he said from the kitchen.

"Yes I am Nicky..."

"Okay... grab your jacket..." And Nick stepped into the doorway to the living room and stopped dead in his tracks. "Oh... *my*...!" Katherine was bent over his coffee table with her ass towards him. She was spread legged with her panties in her left hand on the table and her other hand was fondling her pussy in his full view. She was holding a condom package between her pinky and third finger of her right hand as she rubbed her clit and labia with the other two fingers. Nick watched her intently.

"Farm boy...?" She said. Nick smiled. "...Can you get this for me please...?"

Nick walked over and took the condom from her. "As you wish...!"

Chapter 72
(Welcome To My Nightmare)

A few weeks later Katherine went to Nick's house for another unannounced visit. This time Nick wasn't home. Because she had walked to his house this time, she waited for almost an hour for him to come home before she called his cell. Maybe he was at the 'C' cup or the biker bar.

"Hello?"

"Hey Nick... It's Katherine... where *are* you?"

"Hey Katherine... I'm in New Jersey, at Cynthia's graduation ceremony... why?"

"Oh damn...! Was that today?"

"Yeah... I asked you to come with me and you said you weren't ready to meet her yet..."

"I remember now... When will you be coming home?"

"Not until Sunday night... why...?"

"I really needed to see you..."

"Well tonight I'm taking my baby out to celebrate and tomorrow we're going to the Giant's game. I should be home about 10 tomorrow... I'm sorry baby."

"Me too...!"

"Rain check...?"

"I guess..." Katherine sighed.

"You okay Katherine?"

"I'm just a little disappointed... that's all..." Katherine got silent.

"Katherine...? Are you there...?"

"Yes... I just really wanted to be spanked tonight... that's all!"

"Phone sex later?"

"Not the same... but thanks..."

"You sure you're gonna be okay?"

"Enjoy your weekend baby... I guess I'll see you at work Monday..."

"I love you baby..."

"I love you too Nick..." Katherine started to walk back home from Nick's. It was getting late but now she had no place to go, and all night to get there. She toured the neighborhood until she walked by the club that Anderson told her not to go in. She hesitated near the door thinking if she should defy him and go in. Damn him, I need companionship this weekend. It's just not the same thing when you're all alone. She stood there for a moment as she watched some people enter and leave. *What harm could it do? I'll go inside, have a drink or two and then go home.* Curiosity burns in her mind, but then she heard Nick say to her *'Promise me you'll never go in there...'* Katherine is about to turn and walk away when 'Mistress Gothika' and her slave, 'Pet' came out of the club. Katherine stood there and just looked at them as Gothika lit a cigarette. She was wearing a black wife beater, elbow length black leather gloves. There was a studded wristband on one wrist, a gold shackle on the other. Her face was deathly white, her lips ruby red and her hair was blacker than black in a pageboy cut. Her long bang covered half her face in an odd angle. She had on biker jeans and work boots. She wore a gothic crucifix hanging from a choker on her neck. She also had on an ankle length black leather vest that looked more like a cape. Pet was dressed like a pink baby doll holding a pink teddy bear. Mistress Gothika had Pet on a dog leash. The black studded collar that Pet wore was a stark contrast to her pink attire.

"Hey honey...! You need a little help with something?" Gothika said to her.

Katherine was caught off guard staring at them. "Ah... No...! I was just waiting for a bus..."

"There's no bus stop anywhere around here chick... if you need a ride home... just say so!"

Katherine thought for a moment. "Okay!"

"Okay then..." Mistress Gothika tied Pet to a parking meter and put in two quarters.

"You're just gonna leave her there?"

"What business is that of yours? Get in the car!" Mistress Gothika opened the driver's door and got in. Katherine stood by the passenger's door. "I *know* you don't expect me to open the door for you do you?" Katherine stood there. "This aint a fucking date...! And I aint a fucking cab...you getting in or what?"

Katherine opened the car door and looked back at Pet. 'She'll be okay.' Katherine said to herself and got in, but she couldn't believe she was doing this.

"So... what's the address?"

They drove off. Katherine thinks to herself; 'Technically I never went inside..." That rationalization would be of little comfort to her later.

- - -

Monday morning Nick arrived at work, but Katherine was nowhere to be found. He thought that she may have had a meeting in the main office, but she would have told him or left a message if she did.

"Has anyone seen Katherine?" Nick asked.

"Why no... I haven't seen her all day... did she even come to work today?" Wilson answered.

"Sally... Call her at home..."

Sally dials the number over and over. "She doesn't answer; Mr. Wilson..."

"Try her cell..."

"Still no answer...! I hope she's okay!"

You know, sometimes she just doesn't come to work... after a rough weekend..."

"There was no reason to go there Anna..." Nick replied.

"Okay, but it's not like Katherine not to call... I hope everything is alright!" Anna replied.

"Me too..." Anderson picks up his cell and discretely dials Katherine's home phone, there's still no answer. "Wilson...?"

"Yes Anderson?"

"I have to leave the office for about two hours to check the proofs with the printer... The photos for the proposal they sent are cropped all wrong and wrong sized... I'm gonna have to correct the errors on their computers..."

"Two hours?" He looked at his watch. "By the time you get there and back... You might as well take the rest of the day then... I'll see you in the morning!"

"Yes sir..." exits. And if I get a chance, I'll stop by Katherine's place and see if she's okay...

"Do you have her address?" Wilson asked Nick.

"Ah... no but I'll get it from personnel on my way out..."

"I have her address Nick... I'll get it for you..."

"Thanks Lisa... you're the best..."

"Anything for you Nicky..."

Nick heads out of the office and heads straight for Katherine's house. "If that son-of-a-bitch Johnny came back and hurt Katherine again..." Nick tried hard not to think about it, but his blood was boiling. He never considered the possibility that someone else could be responsible if something ever happened to Katherine.

The Tortured Soul Trilogy
(A Tortured Soul)
Chapter 73
(Smooth Criminal)

Anderson opens Katherine's door with his key and enters. "Katherine? Kitten...? Are you here? *Katherine...?*" '*She has to be here.*' Nick thought to himself. '*Her car is still parked out front.*' That's when Nick hears a muffled whimper from her bedroom. He quietly goes into the kitchen, reaches into the drawer and gets a large butcher knife and holds it hidden to his side. He slowly enters the bedroom, to find Katherine naked, tied to the bedposts, badly beaten and gagged. He slowly and carefully removes the gag, Katherine sobs.

"She wouldn't stop! I used the safety word... and she wouldn't stop!"

Nick was more concerned about Katherine than upset with her. "I *warned* you... You still need to learn who you can trust..." Nick had to cut her ropes... Whoever *she* was, had taken great pains in restraining Katherine. Once she was cut loose, Katherine went into the fetal position.

"Owww!" And she cried.

"Its okay baby... its okay... let daddy see." Nick carefully checked her to see if any serious damage has been done. The restraints had left bruises on her wrists and ankles. The gag left red marks on her mouth and cheeks... Her neck had bite marks and she had bruises on her neck were she had been choked. Other than that, there were no bruises on her face. Her body was covered in black and blue marks. Katherine balled up into the fetal position again. "Let daddy see..." Katherine whimpered but opened up to him. "Okay... you have a lot of black and blues, a few bite marks, but no cuts, no open wounds... Nothing seems to be broken..." Nick noticed a spent cigarette that burned her end table. "...And no cigarette burns... thank goodness!" Katherine began to sob again. "Katherine ... Listen to me very carefully... did you eat or drink... anything?"

Katherine shook her head no. "She said... she wanted me... alert..."

"Do you know where your purse is?" Katherine pointed; Nick got the purse. "May I?" Katherine nodded. Nicholas opened her purse and checked her wallet. Her ID and charge cards were still all there. "Okay... she didn't rob you and your keys are still here... so I won't have to change the locks... but if you want me too I will... if it makes you feel any better..." Katherine nodded yes. Nick went to put her stuff back in her purse... he paused as he looked inside of it.

"That's mine..." Katherine whispered.

"Did she *use*... anything on you?"

"*No*... she never touched me there... she said I didn't *deserve* it..." Katherine began to shiver. "Daddy...?"

"Yes Katherine...?"

"Kiss it and make it better...!" Nick went over to her and Katherine raised her hands like a child who wanted to be picked up. She put her arms around him and he kissed her forehead gently. Katherine felt safe in her arms... she absolutely trusted him... Nick would have to do something very drastic to change that... But not right now... Nick took a blanket and wrapped her in it and got up and Katherine reached out to him. "Don't leave me..." And she whimpered. Nick sat back down.

"I'm not leaving you, I'm just going into the next room and I'll be right back." Nick gets up and Katherine returns to the fetal position and begins to suck her thumb. '*My Lord...*!' Nick said to himself. Nick winced a bit every time he saw her convulse a little as she lay there. Whoever did this to her fucked her up her head real bad. This was worse than any time Johnny ever beat her. He only beat her to get control of her or to get sex, once he got what he wanted, he would stop. Whoever did this; did it for the sole purpose of beating and humiliating her. She's worse off now, than when we first started... and he went to the bathroom to draw a bath for her. He added Epsom salts to the water. He then returned to the bedroom, picked her up in his arms and brought her into the bathroom. He took the blanket off her and slowly eased her into the warm water. She sighed as she entered the water.

"Uhhhhhh! Nick!"

"Easy now... *easy*!" He took a bag from his jacket pocket and took out a small plastic bottle and poured the contents into the water.

"What is that?"

"Lavender... it'll help you to relax... I had purchased it for another reason..."

"It hurts all over..." she sobbed.

"I know Kitten, I know!" He then moistened a washcloth and slowly bathed her, she winced every once in a while as he bathed her. "I know baby, I know... try to relax... I promise to be gentile..." Katherine would wince and then coo and purr as I bathed her, sometimes she would flinch if I touched an area were she really was in pain. But she allowed me to do anything to make it better. I had turned on the hot water and let it trickle into her bath water so it would slowly bring up the water temperature. It wasn't long before the bathroom was all steamy. Katherine in now totally relaxed and purred... Nick used a soft towel to pat dry her after her bath so as not to irritate her tender skin. He took her favorite terry cloth robe and covered her gently. Nick returned to the bedroom with her near unconscious body and gently put her in bed. He covered her and kissed her gently. He turned to leave.

"Please don't go..." Katherine whispered.

"I'll be in the next room... if you need me... I already called the job and left a message to let them know you won't be in for a couple of days... so you just relax... I'll have some dinner ready for you if you're hungry later..."

"Thank you Nicky..." As Katherine falls gently asleep, she mumbles. "I love you..."

"I love you too Kitten..." The lavender Nick had with him was purchased with the specific purpose of relaxing Katherine and soothing her nerves. Nick had hoped that today would have been the day he would make real passionate love to her. He had planned on it being a slow, comfortable fuck session, but plans often go awry... tonight Nick did make love to Katherine... he just didn't have sex with her... There wasn't any food to make in her cupboards so Nick made some coldcut sandwiches for her. She must have been tied up for at least two days without food or water, but right now she needed to rest. When she didn't come out of the bedroom after a few hours, he brought her the food and a glass of wine. Katherine ate it and drank the glass of wine, but in a guarded position. Kind of like a mouse trapped in a corner.

"Thank you Nicky..."

"Anytime Kitten..." Katherine smiled and Nick took her plate and covered her with the blanket. "Get some sleep..."

"Stay the night with me...?"

Nick wanted to, but he knew that she would bond to him in a way that was not going to be helpful. No, she needed to ride this out alone, for now. This is where she had to be strong for herself, by herself. "I'll be in the other room if you need me, but in the morning I'm going to go out to the hardware store so I can change your locks."

"Thank you!"

Nick kissed her gently and tucked her in. Katherine was fast asleep before he even left the room. Nick took the dishes and put them in her sink. He then settled down for the night to sleep on the couch, that's when he saw another cigarette was left on the coffee table and it left a burn mark there also. "Filthy fucking habit... and that bitch ruined two tables to boot!" Nick picked up the cigarette butt to throw it out and then he recognized the brand. Not too many people smoked that brand in the U.S. "No! It *couldn't be!* It's gotta be a fucking coincidence! That crazy bitch is supposed to be in Philly!"

* *Author's Note* *

Unbeknowst to Nick, Katherine had 'dated' Mistress Gothika for a while whenever Nick wasn't available. When Katherine tried to break off the relationship with her, Mistress Gothika decided to teach Katherine a harsh lesson. She beat and humiliated Katherine amd left her tied to the bed knowing that someone would find her. She knew Katherine was seeing a man, but had no idea it was her ex, Nicholas. Nick would have to do damage control, not only about Katherine's physical and mental injuries, but also at the office. Katherine had a well known reputation for getting herself 'hurt'.

- - -

The next morning when Anderson arrived at work, the office is all a buzz.

"Anybody know what happened to Katherine?"

"Oh please… you know what happened… her boyfriend beat her up again!" one of her co-workers from another floor said.

"I thought he was in California?"

"That's not what happened…" Nick interjected. "She was mugged by two thugs on her way home from the movies, they almost killed her!"

"Oh *my* God… What did the police say?"

"What do they *always* say? They're investigating it…"

"But how did it happen?"

"She was on her way home and as she got to her door they pushed her into her apartment and roughed her up…"

"Did *they*…?"

"No…! They didn't sexually assault her…"

The women in the office breathed a sigh of relief. No need to start a rumor that would frighten anyone or make any woman leary about traveling alone in the neighborhood.

"Did they take anything?"

"They must have thought someone called the cops so they hightailed it out of there. She'll be out for a long time…" Nick said.

"What did the doctors say?"

"She's gonna be okay… Her ego is bruised more than anything else. She just needs to rest…" Nick said.

"Did the police get a description…?"

"Not really… just two young punks… but the police think this was just a crime of opportunity… There've been no other reports…" (No lie there.)

"Do you think Johnny set it up so he could have an alibi?"

Nick shook his head. "You watch *way* too much TV…"

"Oh my… I hope she's going to be alright!"

"Yeah maybe we should stop by after work and cheer her up…" Wilson said.

"I don't think that's a good idea…" Nick said. "She doesn't want to be… *seen* right now… *you know…*" Nick couldn't take the chance of anybody seeing her rope burns and putting two and two together.

"Got you… But you think she'll be okay all by herself…?"

"Yeah, she'll be okay... she's got someone looking after her until she gets better..."

"Who...?"

"A close personal friend of hers..." (Still no lie...)

"Maybe we should chip in and get her a gift basket, maybe fruit or some flowers..."

"Maybe she would like a muffin basket..." Bob added.

"Great idea! We'll all chip in... Nick, would you mind dropping it off at her place after work?" Wilson said.

"No problem... it's on my way home, I'd love to!" Like I always said... *'Never let the truth get in the way of a good story...'* The office accepted that Katherine was the victim of a break-in and not a victim of bad judgement.

Nick went straight over to Katherine's house after work after picking up a basket of biscotti Mandy had made up and gift-wrapped for her. He arrived at her place at about 7. He knocked, she didn't answer. "Katherine...? It's me... Nick...!" Katherine opened the door.

"Why didn't you just use your key?"

"I didn't want to just walk in on you... I wanted *you* to open the door for me..." Katherine kissed Nick. Nick held her gently and gave her the gift basket.

"Oh! You shouldn't have..."

"I didn't... They're from the guys at the office..."

"But it *was* your idea?"

"Actually it was Bob's idea... which is probably why he felt he didn't have to chip in..."

"And how much did *you* chip in?"

"*Hey*! I brought it here what *more* do you want from me?" We laughed.

"Take off your coat... stay a bit..."

"No... I'm going on home..."

"You're leaving me again...?"

"You still need more time to recuperate..."

"But I feel fine..."

"Physically, maybe... but you need time to heal emotionally..."

"Come on... spend the night with me... I really don't want to be alone..." She licked her lips. "I'll make it worth your while..."

I kissed Katherine softly as not to hurt her bruised lips. I know it seems cruel but I didn't want to make love to her, not with her feeling like she just got out of a train wreck. "I don't want to take advantage of you..."

"But I want you... I need you to take advantage of me..." she cooed.

"You really need some 'alone' time..."

Katherine nodded. She knew not to push it with me. "When will I see you again?" She asked.

"I'll give you a call in a couple of days..."

"What will I do while you're gone?"

"Have some biscotti... watch some TV... I got you a couple of videos..."

"*Really*...?" Katherine said in anticipation. She hadn't seen any porn in a while.

"Calm down you... they're not *that* kind of videos... Gees, you're incorrigible!" Nick kissed her again. "Take care of you..."

"Nick?"

"Yes Katherine..." Katherine opened her robe and took both index fingers and pinched both nipples at once. The pain this time wasn't pleasurable.

"And that's another reason I'm gonna let you get some rest..."

"When you're right... you're right Nicky..."

"Katherine?"

"Yes Nick?"

"This won't happen again... will it?'

"No sir...!"

"As my grandfather once said to me; '*That'll learn you!*'..." Nick said. Katherine nodded. "I stocked your fridge and bought you groceries this morning, so that should hold you for a least a week. If you need me to bring you anything else... you call me..."

"What if I *need*...?"

"No… Not right now… Not when you're vulnerable like this…when you're fully recovered we'll go back to things as usual…" It was killing Nick that he shouldn't make love to her. But he wanted to wean her off pain first before taking the next step to pure passion. To make love to her now would undo everything that they had accomplished. Katherine kissed Nick again and he handed to her the keys to her new locks before he left. She closed and locked her door. She took a deep breath. No one had ever taken care of her like this before in her life. Sure she would get phone calls and visits from her co-workers on occasion while she was out, but Nick was special to her, so very special. It's a shame Nick didn't know that making passionate love to her tonight would have broken the cycle of abuse that Katherine was trapped in. Having him take her knowing that he wasn't responsible for her pain would have meant the world to her.

"Oh! I wanna *monkey fuck* that man so bad!" She looked at the videos Nick brought. "Oh…! *'My Fair Lady'*…! I *love* this movie…" And she went into the bedroom to put it in her video player while singing; *'Just you wait 'enry 'iggins, just you wait…!'*

* *Author's Note* *

The previous chapters involving Nick and Katherine's secret relationship, although in proper order, occurred during the time Jennifer was at Faber Co's main office and in training with marketing. In order to minimize any confusion over overlapping time lines, I separated the chapters in order to better focus on each storyline. We now have returned to the present; Jennifer has completed her training with marketing and has arrived to work in Katherine's dept. while Katherine is out on 'sick leave'.

The Tortured Soul Trilogy
(A Torured Soul)
Chapter 74
(The X Files)

Katherine and I had decided to 'give each other some space' until she was fully 'healed' from her misadventure. I would leave it to Katherine to contact me when she was ready; she continued to see Mercedes professionally during the time she was out. I knew she was in good hands until she came back to me. I can't begin to tell you how much I miss her. In the weeks to come, I went to work and took over the Monday and Friday progress reports.

"Hey Nick... what are you doing?"

"...Oh, Hi Lisa! Katherine is going to be out for a while longer so I figured I'd do these for her..."

"I heard... I feel so sorry for her... How's she doing...?"

"As well as can be expected..."

"If you see her or get in contact with her... let her know I was thinking of her..."

"I sure will Lisa..." And Lisa kissed me.

"What was that for?"

"I just wanted to... you're such a good man... I just wish my ex was half the man you are..."

"Oh stop!"

Lisa focused on Nick's crotch and put the tip of her index finger in her mouth. "No... I'm serious...!"

Nick put his hand on Lisa's chin and raised it till she was looking in his face, smiled and kissed Lisa on the cheek. "Behave...! I'm gonna start work on these reports..."

"Oh...! That won't be necessary..."

"What are you talking about? Of course it's necessary..."

"No... I meant let the new girl do it..."

"*What* new girl?"

"Jennifer Jones... the new girl they hired to replace Maggie... oh... you haven't met her yet?"

"No I haven't... I just got in..." (Damn! With what has been going on lately, I had totally forgotten about the newbie they hired! Besides, I thought it was supposed to be a guy! I wonder what took so long for her to start here, but no nevermind. I'll worry about that later.)

"Well... you'll like her..."

"Oh yeah?"

"Yeah... just don't 'like her' too much... Now that I've gotten rid of my stinking husband for good; you know I got 'dibs' on you..."

"O...*kay*...! By the way I meant to ask... who has the kids?"

"He does... for now until the holidays...!"

"Is that gonna work for you?"

"Yeah... He's a good father... just a lousy husband... we'll be fine... I'll... be... fine..."

I realized this was a touchy subject so I switched gears. "So where can I find... um..."

"...*Jennifer*..."

"Jennifer...?"

"She's at Maggie's desk... well I guess its Jennifer's desk now."

"Okay Lisa... I see you in a bit..."

"Nicky..."

"Yes Lisa?"

"You *can* call me 'Svetlana'..." She hissed. (Does she k*now*...?) And Lisa sauntered back to her desk. I turned around to leave only to be face to face with Bob.

"What do you want Bob?" (Not that I really wanted to know.)

"I know you don't like me Nick... but I don't care... You are a GOD...! And you're going after Jennifer next aren't you?"

"No Bob... I'm *not*..." And I walked past Bob towards Maggie's old desk.

"That's what you say *now*! You haven't seen Jennifer yet... Go get her... get her for those of us schlubs that will never have a shot like that in hell..." And Bob stuffed his Danish back in his mouth. I walked over to Maggie's old desk on the other end of the office. I wanted to find out what all the excitement was about and see who this new girl was and would she be a problem.

The Tortured Soul Trilogy
(The Confessions of Jennifer X)

Chapter 75
(The X Files)

I had made my way to the downtown offices of Faber Data. Again, my reception was lukewarm, but this time I think Hagen had warned them of my pending arrival. My cover was to replace Maggie, who was transferred to the main office. But Maggie was now being floated on occasion to help cover for Katherine, who was out on sick leave. Lisa, one of the girls that worked here, was very happy to show me around. I didn't know if she was a *hooker* or a *fluffer* yet, but I did know, she was checking out 'the new girl' to see if I'd be any 'competition'. I got right to work to see if I could handle the job. Piece of cake, I could do this on my lunch hour if I wanted to. I sat down at Maggie's old desk and contemplated my next move. The women here were the same as the main office, the men no different; I could handle this. But there was *something* different... in the air... I couldn't put my finger on it. I closed my eyes and I swear I could sense the presence of...

"Hi... Jennifer... I'm Nick... Nick Anderson... welcome to Faber Data Corp."

"*And... Here we go...!*" Jennifer thought to herself. I swiveled around in my chair to see my 'opponent' for the first time.

Nick held out his hand... her chair spun slowly around and there she was... the most beautiful woman I had ever seen in my life. Let me put it you this way... she made Svetlana look like a geeky nine-year-old boy. And when I say Svetlana, I mean the fantasy 'Svetlana'; I had *totally* forgotten what Lisa looked like.

"A pleasure to meet you Nick... I'm Jennifer X. Jones..."

She stood up, stepped from around the desk and she had legs for days and she took my hand. Jennifer was about 28 years old. She was a good two inches taller than me even without the heels. She wore a smart, light gray, ladies business suit with a mid thigh skirt. Her blouse was buttoned just low enough to get your attention but not enough for you to focus your attention. As phenomenal as this woman's body was, you *had* to focus on her face. Her make-up was flawless. When she spoke, she commanded attention without demanding it. Her silky dark black hair was pulled back, but not in a ponytail the way I like it. Oh well, nobody's perfect... I would have to work on that. Her hand was soft and supple but her grip was firm but not masculine. She was the world's most perfect dominatrix... and she knew it!

'*This old man is my worthy opponent...? Please!*' He shook my hand. Nice grip, but I could see he was taking me all in. The '*Jenny Mojo*' had trapped him, I own this guy!

"What does the 'X' stand for?"

(Not what *you* think! 'Chester'!) "Xiomara... It was my grandmother's name but you can call me Jennifer..." I pointed at the reports in his other hand. "What is that?"

"Oh... these are the Friday, Monday reports... I was told you would be handling these so I thought I'd bring them over..."

"...And give you a chance to check me out?" He bowed and nodded slightly to affirm my assumption. I smiled at him. "I like that..." And I bowed to him back. It felt as if two samurai had just met on a dirt road. Then I did a runway model turn for him to give him the full effect, just like I had done for Michael. "...So...? What do you think?"

"I like the package and the presentation... so far..."

I saw his eyes were now focused on my hair which I had in a French twist. He squinted, showing either slight disapproval or disappointment of the hairstyle. "But you don't like the way I wore my hair..."

"Amazing powers of perception... you have."

"Thank you..."

I handed her the files. She walked around her desk, sat down and threw them in the garbage. I raised my eyebrow.

"I picked those up about an hour ago... they've already been processed and filed."

I took my hands and crossed them in front of me at the wrists. She looked at the gesture and smiled. '*Damn! Did I just give the 'I'm protecting my crotch' signal?* I placed my hands behind me and leaned slightly back. "So... you're here to replace Maggie..."

"Let the game begin..." Jennifer thought to herself.

(**White Knight takes Bishop**.)

"No... I'm here to replace *you*... and *possibly* Katherine..."

(**Black queen takes Knight**.)

"I *beg* your pardon?" I leaned forwards.

(**White Rook protects King**.)

She leaned back in her chair and swung from left to right, right to left. "I'm not here to play games Mr. Anderson... I'm here to replace you and replace you, I will, and there's not a damn thing you can do about it!" She stood up and she displayed herself. "New hotness..." And she pointed at me. "...Old and busted..."

(**Black Queen takes Rook**.)

"Ms. Stark left specific instructions with Mr. Hagen... that I'm to be in charge of this floor in the event of her absence..." I said.

(**White Bishop to Black Queen's Rook 4,
Black Queen in Jeopardy**)

"*Really*...? Because Mr. Hagen and Mr. Theopolous hired and trained me... *personally*..." (No reason Nick should know the truth about my personal agenda.) "...And it's just a matter of time... before your wrinkled, old ass is gone!"

(**Black Queen protects King**)

"We will see Ms. Jones... we will see..." I leaned on her desk and whispered. "Old age and treachery *always* beats youth and skill..."

(*White Bishop to Queen's Rook 5,*
Black Queen in Danger.)

I straightened up and adjusted my tie. "…And just so you know… my ass is quite smooth and supple for a man my age!" and I winked at her.

He winked at me? This guy *really* thinks he's *my* match? Pfffttt! "Not as smooth and supple as mine is." Jennifer replied. He turned and began to walk away; I waited till he was 'just' far enough before I called him. "Oh Mr. Anderson…" He stopped and turned. "…*Love the suit!*" I said that just to get his goat. I wanted to throw him off his game and it worked. He left in a huff. This is going to be easier than I thought!

Oh *no*, she didn't! This *bitch* has absolutely no idea with whom she's fucking with! I have buried my enemies in unmarked graves. I was a corporate assassin when this little bitch was still sucking her mommy's tit! I walked back to my desk like a fighter returning to his corner after receiving his instructions. Wilson, who had been with the company as long as I have, was waiting for me at my desk.

"Nick…? Have you met Jennifer…?" Wilson asked; Nick nodded. "That woman is a pit bull in a push-up bra…" Wilson said. He had gotten the heads-up from a co-worker in the main office. He didn't know what was going on, but he knew it wasn't good. Nick sat at his desk and sipped his tea. "Nick… *Please* tell me you got this!" I looked Wilson square in the eye. Wilson relaxed and breathed a sigh of relief. "Whatever you need, I got your back… all my money is on you Nick…" And Wilson went back to his desk.

Ding! It was on… Now don't get it twisted… this is *not* going to be a physical battle… "*For we wrestle not against flesh and blood but against principalities… 'evil'… in high places…*" No… this was going to be a battle of wills and it's no holds barred! Nick knew exactly what to do… *absolutely nothing*!

When Napoleon tried to invade Russia, he failed miserably; because the Russians didn't fight back… they retreated! Allow me to explain… Every time Napoleon's army came, the Russians would burn down the village before they arrived and retreated farther and farther into the mountains, the cruel Russian

390

terrain and the Russian winter. As the French armies advanced, their supply lines became more and more strained. Something that the Russians had become accustomed to, the Russian winter, defeated Napoleon's army without a shot ever being fired! Nick Anderson would do the exact same thing... he would let the marketing protocols break Jennifer. Like quicksand, the more Jennifer would embrace the protocols... the more they would suffocate her! What Jennifer had was Mr. Hagen in her pocket... what she did not count on; is that she could not play that ace in the hole... not just yet! Jennifer had to resign herself to take over the office discretely. Although everyone 'knew' what she was doing, it wasn't 'official'. Officially, I was left in charge of the office as senior employee with Katherine's support. She had given me control and the office would follow my lead and my lead only!

The Tortured Soul Trilogy
(The Confessions of Jennifer X)
Chapter 76
(Beautiful Liar)

I knew that I was the alpha female, the HBIC here, but Hagen and Theo had placed me in a subservient position. That wasn't my plan, but the situation dictated it for now. I hated having to be perceived as being on the bottom, but I resigned myself to make the best of the situation. Because I was seen as being harmless, I was virtually invisible. This gave me almost unlimited access to juicy bits of information, and info was bandied about the office 'water cooler' in abundance. The women couldn't help but wag their tongues, the men... well, only needed a little 'encouragement' to spill their guts. This was a little too easy!

It didn't take me too long to get enough dirt on everyone in the office that I would be able use at any given time to leverage my goal to run this office. All I needed was dirt on Nicholas to get rid of him but I also wanted some dirt on Katherine. I don't want Nick's job, I wanted Katherine's but that would have to wait. The head office wanted Nick out first and foremost and that's why I was sent here, but I really didn't want a 'part time' job here. I had to make sure my position and finances were safe. I had come too far to go backwards into the abyss again.

Dig as she did, she found no dirt on Nick. The man had no skeletons in his closet. With Katherine on the other hand, she had hit the jackpot. Katherine was on medical leave due to being a crime victim where she was severely beaten, but Jennifer found out that prior to that, she was a constant victim of domestic violence. I can't believe Katherine actually allowed her boyfriend to beat her into submission... and the guy was at least ten years younger than her. How could this company put someone in charge that had no control in her own personal life?

"I don't know which is worse; a bitch-ass punk or a punk-ass bitch!" Jennifer sighed.

I could easily deal with Katherine when she got back. Right now, the only person standing in my way was Nicholas Anderson. I just couldn't understand why the company wanted him gone; he was very good at what he did. He was knowledgeable and friendly and a team player. None-the-less, this was no concern of mine, his head was on the chopping block and I was to be his executioner. It only bothered me that I couldn't find a kink in his armor. A man with no secrets is very formidable indeed. I had already made the mistake of being cocky by warning him of my intentions; Jennifer would not make the mistake of underestimating him again. Every Superman has his Kryptonite... Jennifer would have to find Nick's.

The Tortured Soul Trilogy
(A Tortured Soul)
Chapter 77
(It's Just A Little Crush)

Nick knew Jennifer could do Maggie's old job on her lunch hour if she wanted to. So she had all day to free try to get herself intertwined into the mix, try to make herself an indispensable part of the team she was determined to take over. Nick had to give Jennifer credit where credit is due. She did everything she could to take over the office. But without the perception of being in authority there was little she could do. She took on any extra work to try to make herself indispensable. It didn't work on me because as long as I had Lisa's help I didn't need to depend on Jennifer for anything. She even took over the marketing protocols... and the Lincoln-Hanna files... Well, she *thought* she took it over. Nobody wanted any part of that file, except for Katherine and she was still M.I.A., so it was given to her willingly.

The only thing Nick didn't know was Jennifer's real agenda.

(The Confessions of Jennifer X)

I didn't worry about Nick or any other of the '*Chester*' here. I focused on working on the company files. The more I knew about how the company ran, the easier it would be for me to take it over. Everything here was pretty much routine and ran the same way the main office ran. Except for one thing... a dinosaur, by the name of 'The Lincoln-Hanna' files. This thing was older than Lincoln and all you could say was holy Hannah when you saw it! It was the computer program that started this company and it was the lifeblood of the company, which explained *why* the company was on life support! This thing weighed about 50 pounds, printed in old computer language. It was even printed on that old style printer roll paper. I had to get down and dirty to try to make sense of this file. Weeks went by and I couldn't decipher it... I stayed up nights trying to figure how those codes worked... nothing! I couldn't make heads or tails of that program. I started to miss my hair and nail appointments, I was starting to look like these other busted ass bitches and that's just not me anymore! This system is not taking me down without a fight!

(A Tortured Soul)

After about a month and a half of banging her head against the wall and not getting anywhere, Jennifer went from a confident warrior to a babbling idiot! She ran around chasing her own tail for the most part... while Nick sat around doing nothing. Oh... he did his job... just nothing above and beyond like he did for Katherine.   Jennifer was harried and exasperated all the time. Her hair was out of place and she wasn't getting enough sleep at night... I think I actually saw bags under her eyes! She was becoming frustrated to the point of a nervous breakdown... She did anything she could to deploy the marketing protocols... without success. She begged, she borrowed... she even tried to seduce... nothing worked. Nick would just bide his time. As Nick expected, Jennifer was getting more and more frustrated with downloading the company codes.

"*Damn! This program is just... fucking quicksand! The more I learn about it, the less I know! I'm gonna have to grab one of the girls here to help me... I will not let this thing stand in my way!*" Jenny thought. She enlisted the help of Lisa, and they were at her desk trying to figure a way to download the new codes into the system. The old system crashed again and again. Finally Jennifer broke down and slammed the file on her desk and shouted. "*Damn it*! Isn't there anybody in this office or out in the field that knows how to program these codes into the system? Is there *anyone* familiar with the old company codes?"

I looked up from my desk. "*It's showtime!*" Nick thought. She looked around the room for an answer... and all at once, everybody on the floor stopped what they were doing, stood up... and pointed... Jennifer turned her head to the direction everyone was pointing to... She slowly turned to see... *me*!

"Oh *hell* no..." she mouthed.

I was sitting in my chair facing her with my legs crossed at the ankles, swaying left to right and right to left. I raised my hands and beckoned her while I mouthed; '*Come to daddy!*'

Lisa whispered in Jennifer's ear; "You better put on your knee pads and touch up your lipstick honey... cause in about five minutes you're either gonna be *kissing* his ass... or *sucking* his dick!" Lisa looked in Nick's direction and smiled; "*Personally*, I would do both!"

"Okay Lisa... you're a fluffer and a hooker!" Jenny said to herself. "...Son of a *bitch!*" Jennifer mouthed. I had sorely underestimated him. He was something that I had not come across at Faber before... He was a man who actually knew how to do his job! Jennifer picked up the files from her desk and took the long, slow walk to Nick's desk and placed the file on his desk. She opened her clutch purse, took out a compact mirror and her lipstick and applied it while Nick watched her approvingly. She put her lipstick and mirror away and pursed her lips.

"So...? What will it be?"

Nick stood up. "If you had only taken that attitude with me when you first got here... things would have been a lot different between us!" And Nick walked away.

Jennifer's jaw dropped "I can't believe that you're not gonna help me... are you?"

Nick turned to her and shook his head and mouthed; "Nope!" and he turned to leave.

"It's not over... I still have an 'Ace' up my sleeve..."

"I think...*now*... would be a good time to play it! If I haven't trumped it already...!"

Jennifer stood there and watched Nick walk away from her, out of the office and through the door into the hallway. She paused... and lost it! She was totally enraged now. Infuriated, she followed behind Nick into the hallway. (Damn it! I don't have time for this shit! I have got to get control of this office before Steven passes away! And now I need the help of the one man I was supposed to get rid of! SHIT!) "Nick...! Nick! I am *talking* to you!" Nick turned away from Jennifer and walked away. Jennifer was so frustrated at this point that she had had enough... She did not come this far to fail and not to some 'old man' who was on his way out. She stepped up behind Nick as he walked away. "Now *you wait* just one *damn* minute…" And she grabbed his arm at the bicep. Nick stopped and turned to her and stood there. Jennifer hesitated, not because Nick confronted her, but because she was suddenly amazed by the size and tone of his arm. Nick's arm was tensed up and felt like a steel cobra in her hand… She was taken aback by how pumped up he was… It reminded her of a boa constrictor she had once worked with on stage. She instantly flashbacked to the feeling of comfort it gave her to feel the power and strength in which it held her… She gently squeezed his bicep. "Oh… *my*…" She sighed.

Nick looked at her waiting for her to finish her response, that's when he realized that she was mesmerized. Nick pulled her hand off him. Jennifer blinked and sighed again. "What…? Jennifer?" Jennifer was at a loss for words. "*What*?" Nick repeated. Jennifer stumbled for her words.

"Can't we… I mean can't you and I…"

"What? Can't we what…? Can't we just get along…? I don't think so…"

Jennifer bit her lower lip. "No…! Can we… ummm!" And Jennifer… blushed! Nick looked at her and the realization of what was happening to her hit him like a bolt of lightning. Jennifer panted and quickly excused herself and walked away fiddling with her hair. This was not a trick… not a ploy… Nick stood there, closed his eyes, took a deep breath, opened his eyes and watched her walk away. He knew that scent she had left behind. She was in heat… Bob came from the hallway behind Nick and stood there as Nick walked back to his desk.

"*You… are… a…* GOD!!!" Bob muttered.

Jennifer walked past Maggie and headed back to her desk feeling flushed and exasperated. "What the hell is wrong with me?" She felt her forehead and she knew she was wasn't feeling well. She then checked her pulse… her heart was racing. Angie from the fifth floor was putting the days file reports on the desks and walked over to Jennifer.

"Oh oh… honey… You look like you caught a bad case of 'Anderson Fever'…"

Jennifer looked at Angie with a puzzled expression. "I have *what*…?"

"*Anderson Fever*...You got the *hots* for Nicholas Anderson... and from what I can see, you got it *bad* baby!"

"Huh...? What are you talking about?"

Angie sat and leaned over Jennifer's desk. "Have you ever seen the movie '*Michael*' with John Travolta...?"

"...The one where he's an angel?" Jenny asked; Angie leaned back. Jennifer had no idea where she was going with this.

"That's the one... Remember the scene where they're in the cowboy bar and all the women in the room just gravitate towards him?"

"Yes... I think I vaguely remember it..."

"Well in *this* performance, the part of Michael will be played by Nicholas Anderson... *and*... scene...!"

Jennifer suddenly was struck by an epiphany... '*Oh my god...! The part of 'Michael'... is being played by Nicholas!*' I continued my conversation with Angie. "Nick is in 'heat'...?"

"Uh huh!"

"You know this *because* you... were once 'affected' by him?"

Angie stood up, tossed a file on the next desk and winked at Jenny. "Yep... but I've had my 'inoculations' already... but damn if I couldn't use a 'booster shot' right about now honey...!"

"You've had sex...? With Nick...?"

"Don't act so surprised...."

"No... it's just... I mean... I..."

"You didn't think that sort of thing went on here...."

"Exactly... I would think the company would frown on that... especially after the company had paid for a sexual harassment seminar."

"What I do on my own time and with who aint nobody's business but mine..."

"So you two had an affair?"

"About a year after my divorce... yeah... for about two months..."

"So what... happened?"

Angie smiled a smile of knowledge. "You mean *during*...? Or *after*...?"

"After... I mean why didn't you two...?"

"Stay together...? I did something really stupid... I got back with my ex... Nick don't play that shit... He's an animal in bed, but he doesn't mess with people in a relationship..." Angie closed her eyes and took a deep breath. "I can still remember the first time he..." And Angie blushed and fanned herself with a file folder. She opened her eyes and looked at Jennifer. "...It's a crying shame you pissed him off honey... it's a damn crying shame... That man touched buttons I forgot I had!" And with that, Angie left. Jennifer turned on her desk fan and put it under her desk to blow up her skirt, unbuttoned her top button and fanned herself. Jennifer hadn't felt this way about any man in a very long time. Maggie, who happened to pass by, looked at her and shook her head and went about her business.

For the next few weeks, it was all about Jennifer. She went out, partied, networked and let her hair down. She didn't even care about the job anymore... she was focused on getting herself 'vaccinated'. She needed to get past this in order to focus on the job at hand. Nothing worked... It's not that she couldn't get laid... that was *never* going to be a problem for her... but her random encounters didn't scratch that itch, not at all, she couldn't even 'scratch' it herself. No... she could not substitute the cure for her problem with a generic, she would have to get it from the source. She would have to try to bed Nick, but not to get under *his* skin, but so she could get him out from under hers. She switched gears dramatically. If banging her head wasn't gonna work... then she would just bang the boss, and for all intent and purposes... Nick was the boss!

The Tortured Soul Trilogy
(The Confessions of Jennifer X)
Chapter 78
(Black Magic Woman)

Jennifer came to work one day and decided that she was determined to nail that man. She looked around the office to see if anyone was watching. There were too many people on the office floor so she went into the ladies room. Only Maggie was there, washing out her coffee cup. Jennifer opened her blouse, fluffed the 'girls' up, and sprayed her favorite perfume between her breasts and on her ankles. She did that so a man would focus his attention on her feet whenever she sat across from him. By getting a man to focus on her feet it would make him feel subservient to her. She left two buttons on her blouse undone and said: '*Ladies…the hunt is on!*' Jennifer was bringing her "A" game to bear. The 'Jenny Mojo' was set on a search and destroy mission. Maggie just stood there, shaking her head. I'm pretty sure it's been a long while since she's '*baited the hook*'. She walked back to her desk and opened the bottom drawer and took out her "Friday night 'do me' heels". They were 5" pumps that hurt her feet but made her calves look better, is as if that were at all possible… Plus the extra height worked to her advantage as well. Jennifer strutted her stuff down the hall straight to Nick's desk. Maggie was talking to him and Jenny gave her the 'get lost' look. Nick was sitting at his desk talking to Maggie when she just left abruptly. Jennifer walked up behind him. "Good morning Nick!"

I turned around to see Jennifer standing over me. "Good Morning Ms. Jones…'

"You can call me Jenny…Nick."

"Okay… 'Jenny'… how was your weekend?"

"Good… and yours?"

"Not bad… Stayed in… did a little reading…" Jennifer lingered around my desk. "So? What can I do for you? Jenny?"

"Oh… I ah… sent you the new codec's for the PMT-QMT you needed for the account you're working on…"

I opened the inter-office e-mail she had sent me.

"Thanks Jenny… this would have taken an extra two weeks to download without these corrections… Thank you!"

"Any time Nick… I umm… I'm going by the coffee room… would you like me to bring you some?"

I held up my cup of tea. "No… but thank you so much for offering… Jenny…"

"No problem…" She made a mental note that he was a tea drinker. Jennifer headed to the coffee room. She wanted to make sure Nick was watching her walk away. She turned her head slightly and noticed in her peripheral vision that he was. She stopped to bend down to pick '*something*' up off the floor. She noticed from the corner of her eye that Nick watched her 'drop it like it's hot' and she smiled. She returned with her coffee, black the way she liked it, and took a sip and sat down on the edge of his desk. All Nick had to do was look in front of him and he would get a peek at the *promised land*. His eyes remained focused on hers.

"Is there something else you need Jenny?"

(*Yeah there is…Nick!*) "No… I just wanted to make myself available you, in case you had a problem with the corrections I sent you…" With that Jennifer leaned back, put her hands behind her on his desk and crossed her legs. She swung her right foot to allow the perfume she sprayed on her feet to circulate… "I'm all yours today… use me anyway you like!"

"Actually… I'm good…"

"I can *make you* better…" Suddenly, Jennifer leaned forward towards Nick's computer screen and pointed to a line of code. "Are these the right codes for this account?" Her neck and breasts were inches from his face. Jennifer had less buttons fastened than usual and she was wearing a shear black lace bra. Her nipples were clearly hard and defined through the sheer fabric. Nicholas could see the bra unfastened from the front. She knew her nipples were exposed; she felt her blouse drift away from her. She turned into him so he could catch a glimpse. This fleeting glimpse was cut short by a whiff of Jennifer's perfume… it was a very popular brand with women on the prowl… Unfortunately, Nick doesn't like perfume; it only aggravated his sinuses. Suddenly, he quickly turned his head away from her. She leaned closer putting her hand on her exposed cleavage. "I'm sorry Nick… I hope I didn't embarrass you!"

"No… it's your perfume…"

Jennifer leaned back and away from Nick, slightly insulted… Nick looked at her holding his nose.

"Oh no…! It's not *your* perfume… it's any perfume… I suffer from allergies and most perfumes set it off…"

"I'm sorry… I assure you that not the way I intended to *set you off…*!"

Jennifer whispered to Nick. "I'll go wash it off… I'll be right back…" Mental note number two; cut back on the perfume. Jenny purposely left her coffee cup on Nick's desk to give her the excuse to return. Nick coughed and Jennifer walked right past Maggie who was going back towards Nick's desk.

"Maggie… you're back! So as we were saying… what have you been doing these days?"

"Oh I'm just gonna be back and forth from office to office for a few days… until Katherine comes back."

"Well you look fabulous… new dress?"

"…Just a little something I picked up with my pay raise!"

"Well *excuse me!* Miss 'Executive Secretary'! So you just came by to rub our noses in it?' Maggie laughed. "But you do look wonderful… your new position has done wonders for you! So are you going to be here all day?"

"No I'll be heading back to corporate this afternoon."

"You have time to have lunch with an old friend?"

"For you Nicky… I'll make the time…" And Maggie walked towards the hallway to the elevator banks. Nick called to her.

"Oh Maggie…!"

"Yes Nicky?"

"Lunch is on you!"

Maggie laughed and waved Nick off and got in an elevator.

Nick finished his reports and got them from the printer and took them to Katherine's office. He would only go into her office if he absolutely had to and he didn't stay in it very long. Although Nick was officially in charge, he preferred to work at his own desk… He respected Katherine's space… and did not allow anyone, especially Jenny in her office. Nick was a warrior from the old days, he knew that Jennifer's 'friendliness' was just a ruse and although he was going to play along, he wasn't going to fall for it. Jennifer would do anything and everything to get what she wanted. Nothing was beneath her; the problem was Nick realized, is that she now had another personal agenda. This was *not* about Data Corp. and furthering her own career.

Nick unlocked the door to Katherine's office and stepped inside. He placed the files of her desk, so that Katherine could properly file them when she came back. He turned to leave and then... for no apparent reason... he paused. Katherine jumped into his thoughts... it was as if she was in the office... waiting for him... he felt like, well... like the moment he opened the door and entered; he had released a genie in a bottle... He was instantly transported into her arms, memories of her and the times they had together flooded his thoughts... all at once and one by one. He stood there and reminisced. Nick took a long, deep breath and immediately vividly fantasized about her. His nipples got hard and his cock was awakened in anticipation of an encounter that wasn't occurring. He stood there and basked in the feeling. He had to catch himself... *'What the hell just happened?'* he said to himself. *'What power does this woman have over me that no other woman has?'* He stood there. *'Has this witch put a spell on me? Does she have some voodoo 'mojo' that she's using to captivate me...? Even in my very thoughts...?'*

Not even the two women Nick married had ever had such a profound effect on him... Nick felt a little dizzy. Nick sighed and then he was struck by an epiphany. He now realized why he never allowed anyone into Katherine's office, why he kept the door locked. He now knew why she was able to invade his thoughts like a succubus... He now knew what power she had over him. Nick took another long, deep breath... there she was... again. Katherine's 'scent' was in the room... There is nothing in heaven or earth more powerful than the scent of a woman in heat. Nick looked around the room and looked at her desk. That's when he fantasized of the things she did... alone... sitting at that desk. Nick closed the door as he left but not before his took one more deep breath.

He locked the door behind him. Nick headed to the men's room so he could splash some cold water on his face. As he headed to the men's room he saw Wilson step to the door, push it ever so slightly, mutter under his breath and head towards the stairs. Nick knew exactly what that meant... Bob was in the bathroom... No... don't misunderstand... it's not what you think... Bob was the kind of person who 'traps' you in the men's room. He waits until you're 'preoccupied' and then begins to have a conversation with you. More of a monologue really but I think you get the point. You are now his captive audience and it's very difficult to 'relax' when someone is speaking directly to you, especially while he's standing at your stall door. And he won't stop doing that, because it's the only time anyone will listen to anything he has to say that's not about company business... Although I feel sorry for Bob, I'm not in the mood for that bullshit right now... I followed Wilson's lead and headed towards the stairs to use the next floor's bathroom. Jennifer came out of the ladies room just as Nick passed by the bathroom door. Jennifer cut him off.

"Oh Nick...?"

I stopped. "Yes Jenny?"

I stepped up to him, leaned, turned my head away slightly away and pulled my hair back, exposing my neck to him. I knew if he leaned in, he would get an excellent view. "Is this better?'

As a courtesy, I leaned into her long neck and moved my face from her ear down to her shoulder. There was one less button done on her blouse from before. She was taller than me and in her heels I had a direct view of her ample cleavage and her hard nipples as they moved up and down as she breathed... it was a crying shame that I just didn't care... "Yes... Jenny... that's much better..."

He leaned close into my neck and inhaled. I felt his hot breath on my breasts. I liked it... a lot. Jenny leaned back and covered her neck with her hair again, and she whispered. "Are you alright Nick...?" she purred. "...You seem a little... *flustered...*!" And she smiled.

"Oh... yes... I was just on my way to put some cold water on my face... thank you..." (It's just too damn bad for her that she had no idea that she had absolutely nothing to do with the way I felt right now...)

"No... *Thank... You...*! If you need me for anything, you know where to find me..." She whispered, and Jennifer strutted away with a triumphant look on her face... "*Got you!*" Jennifer thought as she walked off but nothing could be farther from the truth.

As Nick stepped out of the fourth floor men's room, Maggie was coming out of the personnel office with a file in her hand.

"Hey, Maggie, perfect timing...! Where would you like to have lunch...?

"Actually... I'm in the mood for tea and biscotti!"

"I know *just* the place!"

"I know you do... just let me get my purse..." Maggie got her purse and folded the file she had in half and put it away.

"You're taking that file back to the main office?" I asked.

"Oh no..." She answered. "This is personal..."

"Shall we... madam?" And I offered my arm.

"...By all means sir!" Maggie took hold of my arm and we had a nice walk to the "C" cup arm in arm. We laughed and joked and talked. It was nice to spend some time with her again. I like Maggie.

The Tortured Soul Trilogy
(The Confessions of Jennifer X)
Chapter 79
(Beautiful Liar)

I had just gotten out of my shower and was drying my hair. Jennifer took her robe off and began to moisturize her skin. She stood in the mirror and checked out her body. "Now if I could only dance for Nick, I know I would have him in the palm of my hands... literally!" She danced in the mirror naked. She still had all the right stripper moves. The 'Jenny Mojo' was still in full force. She reached up and tweaked her nipples. It felt good. She hadn't been mounted right since Michael died... A wave of sadness suddenly struck her. She missed Michael... She went into her closet and took out one of Michael's shirts she had kept. She inhaled it deeply; it still had his scent on it. She then put it on and began to dance and gyrate until she was all hot and bothered. She reached over to her dresser and took a bottle of his favorite cologne and sprayed it into the air. She closed her eyes and let her sense of smell take it all in. She danced some more and then she took out her favorite dildo from her dresser. It was the one she took to college to *entertain* herself when she and Michael were apart. She took the dildo and rubbed her clit with it. She became moist and warm immediately. She bent over her bed's footrest with her ass in the sky she placed the dildo behind her in between the cheeks of her ass. Having Michael behind and on top of her was their favorite position. She squeezed her ass cheeks to hold the dildo as she repositioned her hand to grab it from between her legs. Jennifer worked it in and out, in and out, slowly at first until she was very moist and ready, then faster and faster. She pushed and pulled it. She pinched and worked her nipples and fondled her clit, harder and faster... faster... faster... and then... Nothing!

Jennifer lay down on the bed and began to cry. She couldn't cum, no matter how hard she tried. She was unable to re-create the feeling and the experience she had by having sex with Michael. This, at best, had become a very poor substitute. It only satisfied her, so many times before, because she knew it would hold her until she was with Michael again. This time the fantasy only served to remind her that she would never be fulfilled again. She needed to be held; to be desired... to be... made love to. She needed a man's touch. She needed to feel a man's strength and desire and passion for her. She *needed* an old-fashioned monkey fuck. That's when Jennifer knew... she would have to seduce Nick once and for all, if not to get control over him... to get her freak on. Nick was the first man since Michael to kindle raw passionate desire in her. She decided Nick would be the one to quench all her lustful desires.

The Tortured Soul Trilogy
(The X Files)
Chapter 80
(Devil in a Blue Dress)

The elevator door opened and Jennifer came to work wearing a blue suit with thin red pinstripes that looked as if it was spray painted on her. She wore no blouse or bra under the jacket. Only a silk scarf tied loosely around her neck covered her cleavage. Her lipstick was blood red and her shoes were... fierce! She had a pair of kid leather gloves on and her hair was layered in a feather cut. She even had the hair stylist add highlights to her hair. To say she looked fabulous would have been the understatement of the century. She purposely walked the long way around the office in order to strut her stuff. It was if she was doing a one woman fashion show for the office. Every man at Faber Data Co. stopped in his tracks as if time stood still as she walked by. Jennifer stopped in front of Bob's desk, who was looking as if he was about to have a heart attack. "Bob!" Bob stared at Jennifer. "Bob...!" He still didn't answer. "BOB!" Bob blinked. "If you pass out because you forgot to breathe... I am NOT giving you mouth to mouth... understand?" Bob nodded, Jennifer continued over to Nick's desk and walked pass Maggie.

"Don't you think that suit is a 'bit much' for the office?" Maggie said to her.

Jennifer totally ignored her and continued over to Nick's desk and sat in his chair to wait for him to arrive. She sat there for almost ten minutes and then looked at her watch. '*Where is he...?*' she thought to herself. Lisa came by wearing her 'skinny' jeans and an animal print blouse and dropped a file on Nick's desk.

"That is a beautiful outfit you have on Jennifer.... I love the hair..."

"Thank you... Lisa."

"Special occasion...?"

"I have a very important lunch date today..."

"Who's the lucky guy?" Jennifer didn't answer her. "Okay then..." and Lisa began to walk away... "It's such a shame Nick isn't here to see you in that suit... you look fabulous!"

"What did you just say?" Jenny asked.

Lisa stopped and turned. "I said; you look fab…"

"Before that…!"

"Before…? Oh… I said it's a shame Nick isn't here to see you in that outfit… he would have loved to have seen you in it!"

(I needed him to see me OUT of it! Damn!) "What do you mean? Nick isn't here?"

"He's in Boston… didn't you know…? Hagen sent him there to cover for Katherine in the presentation to the new client there… I thought you knew and was waiting here for Nick's files so you could cover for him while he's gone."

"When will Nick be back?"

"Not for two days… at least…"

"*Fuck!*" Jennifer said to herself.

"Anyway… have fun on your 'lunch date'… whoever he is… you should have him wrapped around your finger by dessert!" And Lisa left.

"*Fuck!*" and Jennifer picked the files on Nick's desk and walked to her desk. Wilson walked by her.

"Wow! Jennifer! You look…"

"Save it… Wilson!" Jennifer sat at her desk and started to work on the company files and reports for the day on her desktop. She had planned to wow Nick into taking her to a long lunch and then set the stage for them to have a 'fling' after work. Today being Thursday, he would have to leave her place early so that he could be to work on Friday. The plan was perfect… except for one small detail. Nick was in Boston. In frustration, Jennifer immersed herself in her work. She would have to rethink her strategy.

Lisa came around Jenny's desk later in the day and looked at her watch. "Jennifer?"

"What is it Lisa?"

"Didn't you have a lunch date? It's almost two o'clock!"

Jennifer looked at Lisa to see if she was being sarcastic, but she realized Lisa was truly concerned.

"Last minute cancellation…"

"What! I can't believe you called off your lunch date to work on these files…! Why didn't you tell me? I would have taken it over for you…"

Jenny again looked at Lisa. Again Jennifer sensed that Lisa's sentiment was honest. "Thanks... I appreciate your concern..."

"Honey... believe me, I appreciate the importance of a 'nooner'..." Jennifer tried hard not bust out laughing. "What really sucks is; knowing you; you won't wear that outfit again... I mean... It looks like you bought this outfit specifically for this date..."

"Oh... don't worry Lisa... I'll eventually find someplace else to show this outfit off...!"

And with that, Lisa left. Just as Lisa was out of sight, she began to giggle to herself. '*Stupid schiksa princess...*!'

- - -

Every attempt Jennifer tried thereafter to manipulate Nick into a sexual encounter failed for some inexplicable reason. It was if the universe had aligned itself against her. Either it backfired miserably or something came up to thwart her plans. The frustration of not getting what she wanted only served to intensify her desire to have it. At one point she thought Nick might be gay... Nah! No chance of that! Something is up... she just needed to find out what the hell it is. She was tired of trying to trick Nick into having sex with her, plotting and planning took way too much effort and subtleties were wasted on Nick. She was being distracted from the job she came to do at Faber. Jennifer tried to make the hard decision to let Nick go and focus on the job at hand, but there was something... holding her back. She couldn't figure out what it was. Why couldn't she let it go? Jennifer was walking to her desk with a file in her hands that she needed to upgrade in order to download it into the company protocols. "Damn it... this is going to take all day!"

Bob walked up to her. "Jennifer...?"

"What do you want Bob?"

"Nick asked me to give you these codes so you can upgrade the Lincoln-Hanna files for the new programs..."

Jennifer opened the folder and read the codes. She checked them against the file she had. "This would actually work... Thank you..."

"Don't thank me... Thank Nick!" And Bob walked back to his desk. Jenny looked around the office and saw Nick talking to some of the other employees. He was holding his tea mug and just... talking. She watched him. There was something about Nick. He wasn't all that good looking; he wasn't the smartest or even all that smooth... But there was... something *about* him. For the next few weeks, she studied Nick, what he did, who he spoke to and how he carried himself. She watched him laugh, she watched him work and she watched him do his job. There really wasn't anything all that special about Nick. Then one day, one of the workers from another floor came to Nick with an envelope for a co-worker whose wife had passed. She watched as Nick made a donation. '*Sucker!*' she said to herself and she watched Nick calmly walk away. She kept her eyes on him and for some reason, when he was out of her line of sight; she repositioned herself to watch him. It was then, she found out, why she couldn't let him go. Nick had gone into a quiet corner of the office and was standing there... crying! She watched him for a moment or two before deciding to let him have his privacy. As she stepped away, she felt something cold on her face. She reached up and it was her tears, Jennifer was crying too. Jennifer hadn't cried since... It was then she was struck by an epiphany of why she couldn't let Nick go. It *was* physical at first... nothing more than a bio-chemical reaction, but as time went on... something changed... Jennifer realized that Nick had touched her heart and soul. Nick had touched her in a place she thought was dead and buried a long time ago. Jenny wiped the tears from her face. She decided there would be no more trickery, no more schemes. She would find a way to just tell Nick how she felt about him. But, God help him if she gets hurt again! Every thing she tried in the past had failed... even her 'Jenny Mojo' failed her... This time I'm going for the direct approach... Tomorrow I will set the stage to nail that man... A simple note should do it. She sat down and wrote it out, but it needed a 'visual aide'.

The Tortured Soul Trilogy
(The Confessions of Jennifer X)
Chapter 81
(Changing Lanes)

At the end of a Friday of a three day weekend, Jennifer was heading out of the office. She was going to go out clubbing with her old friends when her cell phone rang. She looked at the caller ID... She froze in her steps. She answered it without speaking. The one-sided conversation lasted less than two minutes and ended with Jennifer saying '...*I'm on it!*' and then hanging up. She then dialed L.L's cell phone. "Tobey...? Its Jennifer... something came up... I won't be enjoying your... company... this evening... Rain check...? I love you babe!" And she hung up the phone. Jennifer's 'personal agenda' was going to have to wait. This was old business and all new business would have to take a back seat. "Damn it... I really wanted to see Tobey tonight...." It didn't matter, Jennifer was going to be up all night, and not the way she wanted to. She turned and went back to her desk and took out a blank data disc. She turned her computer on and accessed a file that she had encrypted with her security code. She unlocked the file and pressed 'copy'. It took over fifteen minutes for the files to download. "Damn this pre-historic computer program! I should have been out of here ten minutes ago!"

She looked at her watch. The CD drawer opened and Jennifer took the copy and placed it in a dummy music jewel case and put it in her purse. Hagen wasn't going to like this, he wasn't going to like this one bit, but she had a job to do. This was much more important to her than getting her freak on... But that didn't mean she couldn't use her 'influences' in the future to get what she wanted from Nick. She walked to the elevator just as the door opened and Jennifer entered. She paused the doors for a moment and looked around. She shook her head. '*I must be getting paranoid...*' She pressed lobby and the doors closed. The disc now contained everything Steven needed to hang Hagen out to dry. And Jenny could use the information she gathered to leverage Hagen and Theo to put the pressure on Katherine when she got back. It was just going to take a lot of time to decipher the information, and time was something Jenny and Steven had precious little of.

The Tortured Soul Trilogy
(The Confessions of Jennifer X)
Chapter 82
(I Feel Like Somebody's Watching Me)

Jennifer was not the last person on that floor as she had thought. As the elevator went down, the bathroom door of the men's room opened slowly. Bob peeked out. "She's gone!"

Wilson poked his head from the door as well. "Are you sure?"

"Yeah... she's gone..." They stepped out of the men's room and looked around.

"I'm glad you came and got me Bob..."

"No problem Wilson... what do you think she's gonna do with that disc?"

"I have no idea... but I think Jennifer is trying to pull off something big..."

"You really think it's something big?"

"You heard her... she broke a hot date to smuggle that disc out of here..."

"Who do you think she's working for...? A competitor...?"

Wilson looked at Bob with a look of bewilderment. "Bob! Do you really *think* she's a corporate raider sent to steal our programming codes for a... '*MySpace*' page?" Bob shrugged his shoulders. "It's obvious whatever she's doing... it's to screw over Nick... or maybe Katherine...!"

"What should we do?"

Wilson took out his cell phone and hit speed dial. "Hey Nick...? It's Wilson... I got some news for you about Jennifer..."

Bob gave Wilson a 'thumbs up'.

The Tortured Soul Trilogy
(Living La Vida Puta)
Chapter 83
(Take a Walk On The Wild Side)

Lady Latex hung up her phone. She wasn't happy that Jenny had broken their 'date' for the weekend. She didn't have anything special planned for the night; she just wanted to... girl talk. There was a lot on her mind and she needed to bond with her. Jenny was just so easy to talk to. They had been through so much together. She knew Jenny would understand how she felt. She tried to hide her disappointment and not let it affect her performance on stage. Her set was at best, lack luster. She just couldn't get into it no matter how hard she tried. No matter, the show must go on. Tobey walked into the strip club dressing room after her last set. She had the room all to herself. The other girls were either on stage, working the bar or lap dancing for the customers. Her feet hurt and she was tired. She wanted to get out of her costume; thigh high black latex stiletto boots, elbow length latex gloves and a matching latex thong. She wore seven delicate gold chains that connected her nipple rings to each other. Each chain was a little longer than the next and they cascaded down her chest when she danced. As she walked over to her dressing station she paused in front of the full-length mirror and posed in front of it. She took off her jet-black wig and ran her fingers through her own shoulder length light brown hair. She looked closely at her face in the mirror. Tobey was pretty close to being 40 years old and you could begin to see the small lines in her face. She turned around and checked out her ass in the mirror. She tightened her butt cheeks together and relaxed. She noticed her ass was beginning to sag. She turned to the front to check out her abs. She still had a six pack and her arms and legs were still firm and her tits were still perky... and yet...

"I know what you're thinking Mami..."

She turned to see Cisco standing in the open doorway. Cisco knew she was hurting and he knew this wasn't about Jennifer canceling their date. He was there to support and comfort his woman. "Do you?" She asked.

Cisco nodded. "You are *still* one hot looking woman…"

"Am I…?" she asked.

"You know you are…"

Tobey sat down in her chair and began to remove her gold chains one by one and place them carefully in her jewelry box. "The girls are getting younger and younger and I keep getting older…"

"So?"

"So… I think its time for me to step aside and let the kids get their shine on…"

Cisco sighed. "You're sure about this Mami?"

"I'm tired Cisco… I don't want to do this anymore…"

"Whatever you decide Mami… You know I got your back… I will support any decision you make."

Tobey closed her jewelry box and placed it in her gym bag and began slowly to get undressed, also placing her costume in the bag, piece by piece. She was now sitting in her chair, naked and began to lotion her skin. She also rubbed some Tiger Balm on her sore muscles. She stopped. "Please stop watching me…" She whispered not turning to look at Cisco. She didn't want to see him staring at her naked body, not right now.

Cisco averted his eyes and turned to leave. "So…? This is it?" he said over his shoulder.

"Yeah… tonight was my last night…"

Cisco nodded and reached for the doorknob. He was going to close the door behind him to give her some privacy.

"Baby…?" she said. Cisco turned to her. "Take my bag to the car and I'll meet you there after I settle up my tips."

She had begun to remove her make-up. Cisco walked back to her, took the bag and gently kissed Tobey on her forehead. He headed back to the door, stopped, turned and held the bag up to her. "But… you're still gonna wear this little outfit *for me…* right?" He whispered softly.

Tobey stopped in the middle of what she was doing. Her eyes began to well up with tears. She swiveled in her chair until she was facing Cisco. He said exactly what she needed to hear. She spread her legs, leaned the chair back and whispered. "Lock the door… and get your ass over here!"

Cisco licked his lips. "Yes ma'am!"

The Tortured Soul Trilogy
(Living La Vida Puta)
Chapter 84
(The Girl with Something Extra)

Tobey came out of the back door of the club and started walking towards the limo where Cisco was waiting for her. She smiled because she knew that they were going to continue what they had started in the dressing room. She was very up for that tonight. As she stepped towards the car, she thought she heard a sound. She paused. She heard it again. It was the faint sound of a moan. Sometimes stray hookers would work the back alleys near the club, but this was not the moan of a sexual encounter, it was the moan of pain. Tobey took out and opened her switchblade and slowly walked towards the car again. As she passed the alleyway, she heard the moan again. She continued to walk past it but then she stopped. "*A bitch has got a bitch's back...*" She thought to herself. She slowly walked backwards towards the alley entrance again. "Who's there?" No answer. Tobey squinted her eyes to try to see into the dark alley. She didn't see anything. "Anybody there?" Still no answer; She started to walk to the car again. That's when she heard a faint cry.

"Help me... please... help me!"

By now Cisco had stepped out of the car. "Baby...? What's going on?" He asked concerned that L.L. was alright.

Tobey placed two fingers under her eyes. It was the club signal to keep an eye on her. Cisco came a little closer towards the alleyway. Tobey tried to see where the voice came from but the alley was too dark. As her eyes became used to the darkness she saw a woman's body sprawled out near the back wall near a small pile of garbage. "Static!" she yelled. This was the club code that there was a major problem and the shit was going down. Cisco ran over to Tobey.

"What is it baby?" He asked.

"I got a chick down at the back of the alley..."

Cisco squinted. "I see her... you stay here and I'll check her out..."

"Be careful baby!"

417

"I will…" And Cisco headed slowly into the dark alley. He could tell that there was no one else there. He checked on her and she was nearly unconscious.

"Is she one of our girls?" Tobey called into the alley.

"No… but she's beat up pretty bad!"

"Is she a working girl?"

"I don't think so… she's a little too well dressed for that shit!" Cisco took off his jacket and covered her half naked body with it and carried her out into the light.

"What do you think? She checking on her boyfriend and he beat the shit out of her…?"

"I don't think so…" Cisco said. Cisco turned around and Tobey saw the cum on her face.

"Oh my god… do you think she was raped?"

"Her dress was up around her thighs… I'm sure *HE* wasn't raped…"

Tobey raised her eyebrow. "You mean…?"

"Yeah… she's a chica sin crica…"

"I can *hear* you…" the girl moaned.

"Get her in the car… we'll get her fixed up…" Cisco carried her to the car.

"My shoes…" she moaned.

"I'll get them…" Tobey said. And she went down the alley and got them. "Damn girl! These shoes are fierce! Where did you get them?"

"Tobey! Focus! You two can girl talk later…" And Cisco put her in the back of the limo. Tobey climbed into the back with her and tended to her wounds and cleaned her up. Cisco drove off. He was a very petite man and if it wasn't for the peek Cisco got, nobody would have believed she was a man. He wasn't wearing a wig; that long luxurious hair was all his. His face and body would make any woman jealous. Tobey took a bottle of water from the limo fridge and began to clean her up and check her wounds.

"You wanna tell me what happened back there?" Tobey asked her as she wiped her face.

"I was walking home from work when I was mugged…"

"Cisco… Pull over and let this bitch out here!"

"No don't!" she said.

"Lie again to me bitch!"

"Okay... okay! I was 'working' the corner when this guy picked me up... after I... finished... he wanted more..."

"And he got pissed that you wasn't selling what he was buying..." Cisco added.

She nodded. "He beat me... took my purse and left me in that alley..."

"He could have killed you! Where was your backup?" L.L. asked.

"I think the other girls must have found out what I really was... and they set me up... they let me take this guy even though it wasn't my turn..."

"You need to get a better class of friends..." Cisco said.

"Or... you need to stop lying to your friends... maybe if they knew the truth... they would have had your back!" She closed her eyes and nodded in agreement.

"So where do you live?" Cisco asked.

"I'm... in between places right now...!" she said.

LL looked at Cisco. Cisco nodded. "You're gonna stay with us until you can get back on your knees again..." Tobey said.

"No...! No more... I can't keep this shit up anymore... This isn't the first time this has happened to me. I may not survive the next one. I have to get a real job... I have almost enough for my last operation... I'm not in a rush..."

"So... What can you do... besides... you know... to earn some money?" She didn't answer.

"Okay..." Cisco said. "You'll stay with us until you're feeling better... I happen to know of a club that needs to hire a new dancer...!"

"You think she can?" LL asked.

"I don't see why not... she's got nicer tits than you do...!"

"The fuck he does!"

"*Hello...?* I *can* still hear you!" she said. Cisco and Tobey laughed.

"Okay... Three questions..." Tobey said.

"You just saved my life... why not?"

"What's your name?"

"My real name is Juan... but I go by the name of *Iris..."
(Pronounced E-reese.)

"Who's your plastic surgeon...? Cause I'm really thinking of getting some work done eventually..."

"These are real... they're from the hormone injections..."

"Damn!" Tobey said.

"You said you had three questions..." Iris said.

"Yeah... where the fuck did you get these shoes? They *are* fierce!"

Iris laughed. "Don't make me laugh! I think I have a cracked rib!"

The Tortured Soul Trilogy
(Living La Vida Puta)
Chapter 85
(Three's Company)

They took her to the emergency room to get her X-rayed and make sure she'd be okay. The doctor came out and didn't know how to let them know... She kept stuttering and hesitating. "Spit it out... how is she?" L.L. demanded.

"Well... um... your friend... is..."

"What? What? She's what?" L.L. asked getting a little annoyed.

The doctor took a deep breath. "Well... she's... a... man...!"

L.L. took a deep breath. "Okay, *Queen* of the land of the painfully obvious... can we talk to your sister, the *Princess* of the merely obvious...?"

Cisco turned to the doctor. "Is '*she*' going to be alright?"

"She'll... be just fine... he... *she* just needs to rest until her bruises heal... I'll give you a prescription for a mild pain reliever..." The doctor had a quizzical look on her face.

"What?"

"How do you know *her*?"

"She's a friend..." They both answered simultaneously.

"Anything else you need to know doc?" L.L. said crossing her arms.

"No..."

They took Iris to their place. Fortunately there was no permanent damage. Iris only had black and blues, a busted lip, a black eye and a bruised rib. She was better in just a few weeks and eventually worked at the club for Tobey and Cisco. They told all the girls the deal. Iris wasn't the first pre-op tranny that had worked there. She just wasn't allowed to give any lap dances to the clients. She would only dance on stage. When she wasn't dancing she would help Jackie bartend for some extra cash.

"How's Iris doing?" Tobey asked Cisco.

"She's good... She logs in top three in tips almost every other night... soon she'll have enough money to get her last operation..."

"Soon she'll be moving out and getting her own place..."

"Good...!" Cisco said.

"Was it a problem her living with us until she got herself together...?"

"No... it's just..."

"Baby... if you had a problem with her living with us... why didn't you say something...?"

"It's just... nothing..."

"Come on baby... tell me!"

"It's just..."

"Just what?"

"Well... you being a lesbian for all those years and Iris does have 'the best of both worlds'... I was getting a little worried that... you know!"

"Yeah... he does have a bigger dick than you do bitch!"

"Pussy!"

"You should be glad I have one!"

"I am... but every once in a while I gotta check!"

"Later when we get home... I'll make sure you do a thorough inspection..." L.L. said

"Oh yeah!" Cisco licked his lips and kissed Tobey. "I got to cover Jackie at the bar... I'll talk to you later!"

"I'll be in the office if you need me..." Tobey replied.

Cisco walked to the bar, Tobey headed towards the office.

"Damn! Cisco can't fuck worth a shit but that man eats me out like it's nobody's business... but I must admit... If Iris *was* into women... Cisco's fucking bags would've been packed months ago!"

Cisco was behind the bar helping Jackie when Iris came over after her set to help bartend. Jackie excused himself so he could restock the bar from the back room.

"So Cisco... how's it going?"

"Good... how about you Iris...?"

"I'm sure L.L. told you I'll be moving out to get my own place soon..."

"You know you can stay as long as you like..."

422

"And you know that's not true…"

"What are you talking about?" Cisco asked.

"You know I love you guys and I really appreciate what you've done for me… but you two have enough drama in your lives… The last thing you need is a third wheel in the mix. Especially *this* third wheel! Cisco… I'm not attracted to Tobey… and no… I'm not attracted to you… but I know that idea has been festering in the house. I don't want to be the one to break you two up, because I have never seen two people so much in love with each other like you two…" Cisco nodded in agreement. "I have a close friend I met in therapy… We're going to be moving to another state where we can start fresh…"

"When will you be leaving?"

"In a few weeks…"

"You know Tobey and I are going to miss you!"

"I know… I'm gonna miss the both of you too. You two are the parents I never had… you accepted me without judgment; you supported me when no one else would. You saved my life by giving me a reason to live. I don't know how to repay you…"

"You wanna repay us…? Be happy!" And Cisco kissed Iris on the cheek. "Now get back to work! I don't pay you to stand around and bullshit!"

Iris laughed. "Yes sir!" she said. Iris went behind the bar to serve customers. "Cisco?"

"Yeah Iris?"

"I hope I find someone who will love me the way you two love each other!"

"You will… just don't settle… you deserve better!" Jackie returned with the stock. Cisco headed over to the office. He entered and Tobey was going over the books. Cisco locked the office door.

"What are you doing?" Cisco cleared the edge of the desk with a sweep of his hand. "What the fuck are you doing? I was working on those books!" Cisco loosened his tie and pulled up a chair to the opposite side of the desk and sat down. "What the fuck…?" L.L. exclaimed.

"Shut up woman… and get your ass on this desk… now! I'm not waiting for tonight… for your pussy 'inspection'…"

Tobey's nipples got hard and she was wet. Normally she didn't like aggressive partners, but Cisco was different than any sex partner she ever had. She came around the desk to where Cisco was, she kissed him and he lifted her up onto the desk. He reached under her skirt and tore her panties off. He leaned her back on her desk. Tobey unbuttoned her blouse and she began to squeeze her nipples. Cisco couldn't fuck worth a damn, but that man made damn sure she got off at least two times before he got his off. Tobey's jaw shook as he licked and sucked her clit. "Oh god I love this man!" she muttered as her eyes went to the back of her head.

Nick was busy helping Lisa and John clean up the account codes they were working on. He went back to his desk and was in constant instant messaging with Lisa at hers to help her finish correcting the account. He then rewrote the corrections so he could send it in a company e-mail to her. Jennifer was on another floor in a conference call with Hagen. Probably snitching her little ass off... Nick hurried to see if he could finish before she came back. He didn't want to take the chance that she would see what he was doing and be able to duplicate the process on her own. Knowing that Jennifer was back on track with her agenda to take over Katherine's job, made him want to make sure that she wouldn't succeed.

"I'm glad to see you haven't been slacking off while I was gone!"

Nick stopped and spun around in his chair. "*Katherine*!!!"

"You miss me...?" Nick jumped out of his chair. Katherine held out her hand. "Easy *tiger*...! Easy!" Nick stood there excited like a puppy whose master had just come home. Katherine glanced at Nick's crotch. "Is that a..."

"Hell *yeah* it is...!" He didn't even give her a chance to finish the Mae West line.

"Watch it...! Office gossip and all..." Katherine remarked.

"*Fuck' em!*" and Nick hugged Katherine tightly.

"I missed you too...!" Katherine whispered in his ear.

"So? You're 'okay'...?"

"I'm getting there..."

"Let me look at you! You look great!"

Katherine glanced at Nick's crotch again. "Yeah... I'm... getting that impression!"

"Uh uhh! Look at you...! You dropped some weight..."

"Yes!"

"I'm *so proud* of you!"

"Thanks!"

"Good... now stop it before your tits fall off!"

Katherine's jaw dropped and she hit Nick on the arm. "*What...*? I think I look good!" And she did a models turn for him.

"Well thank goodness you didn't lose any of your ass..." Katherine hit him again. "But seriously... *stop it* before your tits fall off!"

"Speaking of 'tits'... since the subject came up... among other 'things'... did you nail the new girl yet?"

"...Define 'nail'...?"

"Did you introduce her to 'Little Nicky' yet?"

"No... but I have 'nailed' her..."

"Dish... she gonna be a problem?"

"Big time... but I have her all tied up right now..."

"Lucky girl..." Katherine smiled. "Step into my office and bring me up to speed on her... and Nick..."

"Yes Katherine?"

"Leave the door open..."

"Yes Madam..."

Nick and Katherine sat in her office for about an hour catching her up on Jennifer and Katherine caught Nick up on Johnny. Johnny was going to go 'away' for a while to consider his actions. Can you say 'aggravated assault'? Funny thing is; time in the joint would actually help his career. "I can't believe you finally filed assault charges against him...!"

"Not me... his 'Baby Mama'..."

Nick stopped and turned his head in an odd angle like a dog. "Ex... *squeeze* me? I *beg* your hardon...? His *Baby... Mama...*?"

"You heard me right...!"

"Peter Pan gots kids?"

Katherine cut her eyes at Nick. "You wanna hear this... or not?"

Nick settled back into his chair and threw up his hands. "Dish sister..."

"She's some rap groupie from California, he knocked her up and then he tried to knock her out... She didn't play that shit and threw his ass in jail..."

"You know anything about her?"

"His girlfriend's name is Marie-Claire... She's 22, his daughter's name is Jordan, and she's five..."

Nick did the math. Johnny had been cheating the entire time he knew Katherine. "Oh shit...! I'm so sorry Katherine...!"

"It's okay... I'm okay... But I gotta give the chick credit... he tried to pull the shit on her that he pulled on me... and she had his ass taken out in handcuffs."

"Really...?"

"Yep... and it seems that Johnny didn't like being handcuffed as much as I do... so he took a swing at the cops..."

"Oh boy!"

"Yeah... so they added assaulting a police office to the charges... Even if she drops the charges, he's gonna do at least 3 months..."

"So... all the times he was in California... 'On tour'..."
Katherine lowered her eyes. I knew that this was still an open sore. There was nothing to gain by talking about it. "So does this mean it's officially finally over between you and Johnny?" I said.

"Oh *hell* yeah...!"

"So what did you do with your engagement ring?"

"She has it... As for my 'replacement' ring, I hocked that piece of shit and bought myself a new Ipod..."

"You're gonna let her keep your ring?"

"Why not? It's a small compensation for her having to keep Johnny too...!"

"How do you know all this?"

"While Johnny is in jail... she checked his cell phone... my number came up... She called me... we had a nice *long* talk."
Katherine leaned back in her chair. "So... back to the business at hand, where are we in performance levels...?"

"32%... I made sure you a little wiggle room..."

"...And exactly what do you expect me to *wiggle* in return?"

"Okay... if we keep this conversation going... I *will* lock that door and have my way with you on your desk."

"The blinds are still open you know!"

"Whatever!"

"We'll talk more about that later..."

"Yeah, let me get back to the corrections before 'you know who' gets back..." Nick stood up and had to 'adjust' himself before her walked out of her office.

"Oh I forgot to say; It's good to see '*you*' too!"

"Stop it!" And Nick went back to his desk. Katherine made a quick phone call and just as she walked out of the office, Jennifer had just come down from the ninth floor trying to get priority codes from Hernandez to decipher the disc when she noticed a woman she had never seen before come out of Katherine's office. Jenny had never been in there herself so she decided to find out who this woman was.

"Excuse me...? But what were you doing in that office?"

"You mean; 'What was I doing in *my* office?' Don't you?"

Jennifer stepped back. "*You're* Katherine...?"

Katherine eyed her. "And *you* must be Jennifer..." Katherine was quite surprised that Nick didn't try to bed her in spite of what was going on.

"It seems that our reputations have preceded us!" Jennifer said. Neither one held out their hands to shake the others'. "May I have a moment of your time?" Jennifer said. And Jenny reached for the doorknob to Katherine's office.

"Certainly... *your* desk...!" Katherine closed her door and led Jenny back to her desk.

"*Oh! This chick is good! But I still have her number*! Jenny thought."

Katherine and Jenny jockeyed for the lead position as they went back to Jennifer's desk. Jenny snickered to herself. It was like a slow motion version of roller derby. Each needed to be perceived as the lead dog. Nick watched them as they subtly jockeyed for position as they walked and thought to himself; '*If those two ever get along... I will be the luckiest man on the planet!*' Luck was something Nick was not gonna have...

428

For the next week or so, Nick and Katherine worked together and apart to make sure whatever Jennifer had planned would fail. It wasn't easy. Jennifer was very good at what she did and the company protocols didn't want to play favorites. They were literally fighting a battle on two fronts. By the end of the week everybody needed some down time.

"Katherine... I'm on my way out to hang with the guys... you sure you don't wanna come with...?" Katherine shook her head no. Nick whispered to her. "It's just a group of us from the job... You would be with all of us..."

Katherine kissed Nick. "You go ahead... have fun... I have things to take care of..."

"Call me tonight for some phone sex?"

"Absolutely...!"

"Walk you to your car?"

"I'm good... now get out of here! You're friends are waiting..." Nick blew a kiss to Katherine and left. Katherine got all her things together that she needed for the weekend. She really did want to hang out with the boys and she didn't mind that Nick would be there, but she really needed to catch up on these files and she didn't want to stay in the office tonight all alone. As she stepped into the parking lot she felt... anxious. She started to get goose bumps all over her body. Something wasn't right. She looked around but didn't see anything. She shook her head. '*It's nothing.*' She said to herself. She got to the car she opened the trunk and put her briefcase in. She then walked over to the driver's side and just as she was about to put the key in the lock, she heard a familiar voice.

"Hey! Lookie here... I think I see somebody I know!"

The sound of the voice almost made Katherine pee on herself... She took a deep breath. She turned on her heels and saw her. The Mistress Gothika was in the parking lot with her 'Pet'. "*Oh shit...! What the hell was she doing here?*" Katherine thought.

Mistress Gothika walked over to her. "Hey? It's… 'Kitty'… isn't it…? What…? No hug and a kiss for an old friend?" Katherine puffed up and held her car keys tightly in her hand. Mistress Gothika walked over with her Pet in tow and paused. Mistress Gothika looked at Katherine and tilted her head from side to side. Katherine had a cold and dead look in her eyes now. Ice water was in her veins. "What? Kitty cat gonna… scratch me? Huh? Is that what you're gonna do… Huh?"

"No…! Maybe I'm just gonna kick the living shit out of you and take your little Pet to be my very own!" Mistress Gothika's 'Pet' had a hopeful look on her face as if to say '*Please!*'

"Oh *yeah*?" Mistress Gothika puffed up.

"Fucking 'A'… *bitch!* You want some? Come get some! I still owe your ass for burning my coffee table." Katherine motioned for her to come closer. Mistress Gothika held her ground and looked into Katherine's eyes and stared. Katherine didn't blink. She didn't flinch. Katherine was in a very dark place now. Mistress Gothika broke eye contact first.

"I'm so sorry… I thought I knew you… but I must be mistaken… you're *not* the girl I once knew… not any more…" Gothika said. Mistress Gothika turned away and then turned back and winked at Katherine. "Good for you!" And she smiled. Mistress Gothika lit a cigarette and began to leave. 'Pet' hesitated and looked at Katherine with a desperate look in her face. Katherine shook her head and mouthed '*I'm sorry!*' Mistress Gothika pulled Pet's leash and they walked off together. 'Pet' was gonna have to free herself; otherwise she would only go from one bad situation to another if she couldn't stand up for herself. That's when she realized that's what Nick and Mercedes had told her about herself. Katherine took a deep breath and was… renewed… She felt… vindicated, but she was clearly shaken by the confrontation. She looked around to make sure nothing else was going on in the parking lot before she got in and drove off.

Nick stepped out of the shadows where he was hiding and watched as Katherine drove off. He combed his fingers through his hair and took a deep breath. He was the one who had left an anonymous note at the club for Mistress Gothika to meet at the parking lot. He hated to have to do that to Katherine… but he knew he had to... besides he was right there, if she needed him. Katherine had to take a stand on her own to get over the pain she put her through; just like Nick had to get over the pain that Mistress Gothika had caused him several years ago. Nick felt his side where she had broken his rib during rough sex. Nick took another deep breath. Strangely, the pain he felt for so long... was suddenly gone. Mistress Gothika and her kind would never fuck with either one of us ever again. '*I need a drink*'... he said to himself and walked over to the corner bar where everybody was waiting for him. Nick would have to wait for Katherine to call him later tonight.

The Tortured Soul Trilogy
(A Tortured Soul)
Chapter 88
(On A Clear Day)

Nick walked into the office about mid-afternoon after had worked most of the day on the ninth floor. Bob quietly called him over to his desk.

"*Nick... Nick*! Come here!" He whispered.

"What is it Bob? What's going on?"

"Where... have you been all morning...?"

"I've been on nine in a meeting with Hernandez... why?"

"Katherine has been looking for you all morning!"

"So... why didn't somebody just call me?"

Bob had no answer. "I... I... I just thought..."

"Bob! Whenever you think, you hurt yourself... Where is Katherine now?"

"Standing *right... behind...* you..." he whispered.

"Bob... why didn't you tell Nick I was looking for him?" She said as she walked up to them.

"I... I just did!"

"Nick?"

"Yes Katherine?"

"May I see you in my office... please?"

"Do you need me to bring anything?"

Katherine paused a moment. "Yes...! Bring the Lincoln-Hanna file with you..." Katherine went back in her office and closed the blinds.

"Oh Shit!" Bob whispered. "That *file* is all screwed up... you're gonna be stuck in her office for the rest of the day!"

Katherine spoke from inside her office. "Nick...! *Now...*!" she said sternly. Bob winced and Nick went to get the file. The Lincoln-Hanna files were over 1200 pages of outdated codes. The book looked as if it was run over by a tractor-trailer. Half the pages were old and torn. It was mostly used as a buffer. If you didn't want anyone to bother you, all you had to do was open that file and leave it on your desk. You were treated like a leper. Nobody actually *worked* on that file... Nobody... but Katherine...

and sometimes Jennifer. Nick lugged the file into her office. "Close the door and make yourself comfortable. *This* is going to take a while..." She said to him. Nick heard the door lock as he closed it. He then placed the heavy file on the side table and opened it and sat down in the chair opposite her.

"Where do you want to begin?"

"Let's start with; where the hell were you all morning?"

"I was with Hernandez on nine going over..."

Katherine cut him off. "I needed you *here* Nick!"

"Everybody knew how to reach me..."

Katherine slipped her feet out of her shoes and placed her left foot on top of her desk." "Yes...! But do *I* know how to reach you?" And she placed her right foot on the opposite end of the top of her desk. Nick stood up and walked closer to her and focused his eyes between her legs. She wasn't wearing panties. Katherine was clean-shaven.

"Yes... you obviously do...!" Nick loosened his tie. There was already a towel under her. She had been planning this all morning.

"Put both of your hands on my desk and don't you dare move unless I tell you!"

Nick complied. "...Yes Madam!"

Katherine took her right hand and began to stroke her clit and coo and purr. "Do you have *any* idea how important it was for me to see you?"

"I believe I'm starting to realize the severity of the situation..."

"Really...? Cause I don't think that you do..." Katherine licked her finger while she rubbed her pussy. She then spread her labia apart exposing her swollen clit. She took her finger out of her mouth and began to flick her clit, slowly at first, then faster. Katherine began to masturbate harder and faster. Katherine was very wet and horny. She moaned as her eyes went to the back of her head. Nick began to sweat. He was about to take out his hanky to wipe his face when Katherine spoke. "I told you *not* to move unless I said so..."

"I just...!"

Katherine cut her eyes at him. "Do you *want me* to stop?"

"No...! Madam..."

"Then do as you're told..." she snapped. He placed his hands back on the desk. She unbuttoned her blouse, unhooked her bra and revealed her rock hard nipples. She blew on them and purred. Nick licked his lips. "Hand me my purse please..." Nick slowly reached for her purse on her desk never taking his eyes off her. Katherine began to pinch her nipples. Nick held her purse out for her. "My hands are a little busy right now... do you mind...? I believe you *know* what I want from my purse." Nick nodded and opened her purse and took out her 'Travel Buddy" and put it on the desk in front of her. "Be a doll and turn that on for me!" Nick picked it up and turned it on. Katherine reached out and took it from him. Nick was totally amazed by how limber she was. She had actually reached forward while remaining in a spread eagle position. Katherine winked at Nick. "Merci..." Nick stood there and reached into her purse again and removed a small bottle of personal lubricant. "That *won't* be necessary... but thank you!" Katherine stroked her nipples with her 'friend' and cooed. "Both hands back on the desk... please." Nick leaned closer forward this time before putting his hands on the desk. "Oh! Daddy wants a *closer* look, *does* he?" Nick nodded. Katherine took the device and stroked the inside of her thighs and purred. She teased Nick for over five minutes with its placement. He really wished that she would just.... And then she did! Katherine pumped her special friend in and out, twisting and turning it back and forth and in and out. This went on for another five minutes and Nick watched every move... until.... Katherine's eyes went to the back of her head again. "Ohhhhhhhhhhh! My...!" she moaned. Katherine's entire body quivered and shook, her hands, her thighs and her head shook and then she threw her head back. "Ohhhhhh! Yeah! Oh yeah!" Katherine sat there and panted like a small animal. Nick was exhausted, even *his* arms were shaking. "That's what mama *wanted*!" she whispered. Nick closed his eyes; he was a little dizzy. Katherine took the towel and wiped herself and her 'friend' off. "You okay Nicky...?"

"Yes... I'll be okay..."

"Need to borrow my towel?"

"Yes please..." Katherine handed Nick the towel and he took a full whiff of Katherine's scent. She then placed the towel in a plastic baggie Katherine had prepared and then she put the bag in a gym bag by her desk.

"Take a moment or two to get yourself together before you go back out there..."

"Thank you..."

"No... thank *you*.... and Nick...?"

"Yes ma'am?"

"Make sure I know where you are in case I *ever* need you... so that next time, you can be a little bit more *involved* in my personal projects! Okay...?"

"I'll put my number on speed dial on your phone for you...!"

"I would appreciate that..." And Katherine came from around her desk and kissed Nick. "And so would you...." And she allowed Nick compose himself and to catch his breath, while she put her panties back on. To tease him more she bent over, ass towards him and so very slowly pulled them up. Nick reached his hand out to touch. She slapped his hand away. "No...! You get to *look*... only!" and she smiled a evil grin.

About two minutes later Nick came out with the Lincoln-Hanna files. Bob was just coming back from the copy room. Bob looked at his watch. "Boy! You were only in there for half an hour... you sure got off easy!"

"That's what *you* think, Bob!"

The Tortured Soul Trilogy
(The Confessions of Jennifer X)
Chapter 89
(I Need a Hero)

It was a Saturday afternoon and Jennifer was bored out of her mind. She was starting to get cabin fever. She hadn't gone out clubbing in weeks. The office politics was getting on her nerves. Katherine was getting on her nerves and Nick wasn't being... co-operative on any level. "I got to get some fresh air before I lose it!" Jennifer got her car keys and decided to do some window-shopping at the mall. Maybe get a facial or something. She needed pampering and she needed it bad. It had been a while since she had done that with Ramona. She called Bonnie to see if she wanted to hang out with her, but she had to go to some school recital her niece was in. Jenny parked her car in the lot and strutted her way to the lobby doors. She was wearing her skinny jeans, black pumps and a light sweater top. As she stepped towards the doors a young man stepped up and held the door for her.

"Good morning sweetheart!" he said enthusiastically.

"Thank you... you're so sweet!" She knew perfectly well that he was making his move because at least three other women entered that door and he basically ignored them. This was a concerted effort on his part. A few years ago she would have not spoken to him at all but she realized that nobody likes a stuck up bitch. He followed her in, a little to close for her comfort. She stopped short and he tried to start a conversation with her. "I'm sorry..." Jennifer interrupted. "I just came here to do some shopping..."

"Maybe you would like some company? Let me walk with you..." He interrupted.

"No... no thank you... I'd rather just do my shopping alone..."

"Okay... so how about giving me your number and I'll call you later...?"

Jennifer smiled. "I don't think so... I'm not in the habit of just giving men I don't know my contact information..."

"Oh but I know you..."

"I'm sorry but I'm quite sure we've never met before... but that was a nice try!"

"Oh I'm sure you don't remember me... but I sure do remember you..."

"Tell me... does *anyone* you try that line that on fall for it, Chester?" Jennifer shook her head and turned away from him. She was sure this was just a ploy to get her to talk to him. She took exactly two steps away from him until he spoke.

"The Kitty Bar in Philly..." he said.

Jennifer stopped dead in her tracks. (Damn it! It never dawned on me that someone might recognize me in this city!) Jennifer played it cool, turned on her heel and looked at him. "I beg your pardon...? The what...?"

"The Kitty Bar... You *know*... it's a strip club in Philly."

Jennifer laughed and she shook her head trying to bluff him. He wasn't going for it.

"I spent every other weekend at that club just to see you... you were the hottest dancer I've ever seen... then one day... poof... you where gone. Imagine my surprise when I saw you just walk up towards me..."

"I appreciate that you think that I'm this girl you fantasized about... but you've mistaken me for someone else... Sorry!"

"Look... I *know* it's you... Why don't you just cut me a break and give me your number...?"

"Even if I *were* her... I told you... I don't give my contact information to people I don't know... go chase another dream..." Jennifer wasn't getting anywhere with this, she just wanted to make space between them and disappear into the mall crowd. She got about ten steps away.

"Stuck up bitch!" he yelled across the floor. A few shoppers stopped in their tracks. Now this asshole was drawing attention to her. This was the last thing she needed. She took two more steps. "Fucking whore!" he yelled at her and he threw a couple of dollar bills into the air.

(Okay... now this motherfucker went too far.) Incognito or not, she was going to have to deal with him. She was about to turn around when she heard another man's voice. A voice she vaguely recognized. She turned to see Nicholas all in the guys face. Jennifer didn't know what to think. '*How much did Nick hear?*' was her only concern.

"What did you just call me?" Nick said angrily.

"What...?" The guy was confused as to why Nick was in his face.

"You just called me a bitch and a fucking whore..."

"No I... didn't..." The guy stuttered.

Nick's tone became more was more intense. "What? So *now* I'm a liar...?"

"No! No... I didn't call you a liar...!" The guy was totally caught off guard by Nick's verbal attack.

"Oh so... now I'm just fucking stupid... Is that it?"

"No...! Look man I don't have a problem with you..."

"Is that right...? You call me a bitch... you call me stupid... and a liar... and now you *don't* have a problem with me?"

The guy tried to puff himself up to Nicholas. He didn't know who this guy was but he was in no mood for any shit. "Look man I don't know what your problem is but I'm not afraid of you!"

Nicholas spoke through his clenched jaw. "Good! I just love kicking the living shit out of someone who's not afraid to die!" and Nick's nostrils flared.

The guy had about enough and put his hand on Nick's chest to push him away. That's when he felt what kind of physical shape Nick was in. The bravado drained from his face.

"I'll give you two choices... you can either leave through the front door or the front window... tick tock!" Nick said.

The guy slowly backed away from Nick. The crowd was now focused on them. The guy eased his way out the door not looking back. After he left and the small crowd dispersed, Nick walked over to a totaly surprised Jennifer.

"What the hell was that all about?" she asked.

"Ah that? I was over there and I saw him giving you a hard time so I figured I'd fuck with his head..."

"And what if he took a swing at you?"

"Then... I would have kicked the living shit out of him!"

"You would have done that... for me?"

"I don't go for men going around disrespecting women... I have a real problem with that... a real big problem with that..."

"Women...? Including me?"

"Hey... we're 'family' and we've had our personal problems. If I don't have the right to call you a bitch... who does that guy think he is?"

Jennifer grinned. "So... you're just upset that he cut in front of you in line?"

Nick grinned. "Something like that..."

Jennifer just looked at Nick. She felt her heart skip a beat. She wanted to fuck him so bad, she could taste it. She stared at him and pictured herself bent over with him on top of her.

"What?" he asked.

"Huh? Oh nothing... so, other than being my knight in shining armor... what are you doing here?"

"It's like... a mall...! I'm here to shop. Duh!"

Jenny laughed. "So... would you like some company?"

Nick shook his head no. "I'll see you at work... are you gonna be alright?"

"I'll be fine... thanks Nick..."

"No problem Jennifer..." And Nick walked away. Nick was acting aloof to her, but still, she felt a connection was there. If he didn't care anything about her, he wouldn't have stuck his neck out for her honor. Jennifer saw this as an opening. She was going to bide her time and make a bold move for him before this week was over.

The Tortured Soul Trilogy
(A Tortured Soul)
Chapter 90
(Wicked Games)

Friday afternoon Nick started to get his things together to leave for the day. Katherine wasn't in her office; she was in a meeting on nine with Hernandez to go over the office performance levels. She probably wouldn't finish before the end of the day so Nick resigned himself to call her later that evening. He was getting ready to go to lunch and as he was about to turn off his computer he found an invitation by the power button. He opened it. The note had an address he didn't recognize and contained a flavored condom. There was a note:

Dear Nick;

My place, nine o'clock Saturday. Bring this with you and we'll find out if it fits! And if it does...there's more where that came from. Call me!

No signature... just a lip print on the card... This isn't Katherine's address or phone number and she knows quite well that this condom is too small for me... Who the hell left this? Oh! Maybe it was Lisa...? I did tell her to put her 'meat' order in early next time... Nick turned the card over to see if there was a signature on the back and that's when he got a whiff of Jennifer's perfume... Oh ohh! This aint good! Nick put everything back in the envelope and was about to throw it in the trash but decided that this was something he could *not* allow to fall into the wrong hands. He would get rid of it in a safer environment. He put the invitation in his jacket pocket and left. Jennifer sat at her desk and watched him leave. Jennifer turned to see if anyone was watching her and she put her hand in her blouse and fluffed herself.

"Got you!" she purred and she got her purse and left to go home for the day. Jenny had scheduled a half-day so she could prepare for her date with Nick. She had considered the possibility she would only get one shot at him so she was going to make sure she took full advantage of their time together. At the end of the day, Nick dropped of his Friday reports in Katherine's office. She was there waiting for him.

"I thought you already went home Katherine..."

"I was going to meet you at your place but I decided to wait for you..."

Katherine kissed Nick. "So what do you have planned for me tonight? Are we eating in, or out?" and she smiled wickedly.

"Actually, I can't see you this weekend..."

"*What*? Why not?"

"I have other plans..."

"What other plans could you possibly have? The weekends are our special time together ... and I haven't been 'mounted' in a long time... You know I can't wait to see you..."

"I'm sorry Katherine...!"

"*Sorry*? Sorry my ass! What is going on? You have another 'acquaintance' you need to see?" Nick looked around the office to see if anyone was still there. He and Katherine were the only ones left on that floor. Everyone else had either gone home or they were at the bar down the street. She took a little umbrage to him scoping the floor before talking to her. "What? Are you ashamed of me now?"

"Katherine, don't be ridiculous..."

"Oh... now I'm ridiculous? I'm *ridiculous*? Was I ridiculous when I was all tied down in that latex French maid uniform...?" Nick tried to calm me down. I pushed him away. Nick crossed his arms.

"No one on this job or this building knows anything about our 'special' relationship, not because I want it that way, because YOU want it that way... all you have to do is tell me different, and I'll yell it from the rooftop."

"You would do that...?"

"Actually No... I have a fear of heights... but I would send it out in a company e-mail..."

"Don't try to make me laugh... I'm so pissed at you right now..."

"As you should be..."

"Tell me what's going on Nicky..." Katherine was getting mildly upset. "I'm trying not to be jealous...who are you going to see...?" She asked. "I don't mind if you're going to see Lisa or Valerie... or even Mandy, just tell me what's going on..."

I could tell she really didn't want to hear the answer. "What if it's Jennifer...?" I asked her. Katherine dropped her eyes. She didn't want to hear that. She tried very hard to cover it up, but the mere mention of her name and the possibility of me having sex with Jennifer hurt her.

"No problem...!" She didn't lift her eyes to me. I knew she was lying, but I also knew this was a huge step for her. I wasn't gonna let her twist in the wind.

"Cynthia is in town for the weekend, I rarely get to spend time with her. So, I'm gonna hang out with her. I'm taking her out to dinner tonight and tomorrow we're gonna do a tour of the city."

"And she just *happened* to pop in for the weekend?" Nick held out his cellular phone and handed it to her. "What's this for?"

"She's speed dial 10... call her..."

"You think I won't?" Katherine fingered the phone buttons.

"You want me to dial it *for* you?"

"You would let your daughter know about me?"

"She already knows about you..."

"*What*? She... *knows*...!" Katherine's face blushed. She placed her hand on her bosom.

"No... not *that*... jeez! That you and I are *you know...* 'dating'..."

Katherine let out a sigh of relief. "So she's okay with it?"

"Yes... actually..."

"And she's not into... you know...?"

"Not that I know of..."

"You don't know?"

"Hey... not an ordinary topic of conversation between father and daughter... '*So Dad... spank anyone new lately?*'... '*No honey, say that reminds me, I fixed the crack in your studded paddle, let me know if it pinches your ass anymore*'... '*Gee, you're the best dad a girl could have!*'"

Katherine stifled her laughter. "You are crazy... but I'm not... Give me your daughters number... if I have to, I will check up on you this weekend..."

"I thought we resolved your jealousy issues...?"

"This is not a 'jealousy issue'… It's a 'you're standing me up again' issue…" Nick gives Katherine the phone number and kisses her and turns to leave. "Oh Nick…"

"Yes Katherine?"

"Just so you know…"

"Yes Katherine?"

"…I'm gonna put on the leather cat suit you love so much and spend the night paddling my own ass until it's pink and tender… just so you think *only* of me when you jack off tonight…"

"Isn't *that* a jealousy issue?"

"Okay… maybe a little…"

Nick looked around again to make sure the floor was clear. Nick turned back to Katherine and slowly unbuttoned her jacket and then her blouse. Katherine did not resist. He roughly pulled her bra down under her breasts and took his index fingers and flicked both her nipples hard at once. Katherine's eyes widened, her shoulders pushed forward as her back hunched over. She gasped and let out a high moan.

"What was *that* for?" she sighed.

"Just a little something to get your weekend started…" Nick kissed her and turned to leave then turned back. "And just so *you* know…"

"Yes Nick?" Katherine sighed deeply.

"You *did* look a little ridiculous in the maids' uniform…" Katherine giggled and Nick left. Katherine pinched her nipples and let out a sigh before fixing her clothes. She went back into her office, locked the door behind her, turned off the lights and grabbed her purse. She placed her legs on the desk, leaned back and took out her 'favorite travel toy'.

"Damn that man… there's no way I was gonna go straight home feeling like this…" The low hum of the device was quickly replaced by Katherine's low moans. "Ohhhh yeah…!"

Chapter 91
(Torn Between Two Lovers)

Nick came to work Monday morning and Jennifer was sitting on his desk... in full 'hunting gear' and she was not pulling any punches. "No more games Nick!" Nick put his cup on his desk and took off his jacket and put it on the back of his chair.

"What's... going on...? Jenny?"

"Who is she?"

"... 'Who is she'... who?"

"The woman that has you... all locked down that you're willing to pass up all of 'this'..." And she stood up.

"What... *the hell...* are you talking about?"

"Don't play with me... You know damn well what I'm talking about... you stood me up on Saturday night..."

"We *didn't* have a date on Saturday...!"

"You knew full well what Saturday was all about... I think I made it *perfectly* clear for you... and you didn't show! You didn't call!"

"Something came up... dang!"

"*Something came up...*? Don't toy with me... I saw you *with* her..."

"*Her...*?" Nick knew she couldn't possibly be talking about Katherine. Nobody knew about their relationship but did Jennifer catch them together somehow? No, because then she would have said 'Katherine' and not 'her'. Who the hell is she talking about?

"The hot little mulatto chick I saw you coming out of that restaurant with on Friday night..."

"You mean... *Cynthia*... my daughter...?"

Jennifer paused. "Your *daughter...*?"

Nick nodded and pulled out his wallet and showed Jennifer a picture with him when she was younger. "What...? Are you following me now?"

"*No...*! I was in the neighborhood... doing some shopping... And I happen to see you two coming from the restaurant... "

Nick put his wallet away; he knew there was only one store in that neighborhood that was open at that time of night on a Friday. "*The Warehouse...*?"

Jennifer eyes widened. "How do you know about 'The Warehouse'...?"

Nick smiled and winked. "How do *you* know about it?"

Jennifer looked into Nick's eyes and realized that he was at *least* at her level of sexual prowess and awareness. She was now more than ever determined to get Nick in bed. Jennifer leaned in and whispered. "Let me tell you something right now Nick... I *will* have your naked, sweating body on top of me... or I will know the reason why..."

"Hey... *how about...* I don't *sleep* with the enemy...?"

"*Please...*! Even with considering the situation at hand here... that excuse is mighty thin..."

"You're pretty full of yourself aren't you?"

"I am *very* full of myself... I just need you to 'top' me off!" And Jennifer stepped up to Nick and fondled his crotch. "It seems to me that I have an ally...!" And she stepped away.

"Its not gonna happen... Jenny."

"You sure...? Cause I don't seem to remember you stepping back just now!" Jenny took a step and paused. "I'm sorry Nick..."

"You should be..."

"I mean; I'm sorry that the condom I bought for you was too *damn* small... but I think I know your size now...!" She held up three fingers and stroked her tongue across the top of them. "I should have purchased magnums... I won't make that mistake again..." Jenny walked away knowing that she had him where she wanted him, so to speak, but she was all hot and bothered now; knowing the kind of damage '*Little Nicky*' could do. Tonight, her 'warm-up exercises' would produce the desired results.

Nick sat down and put his head in his hands. Before he met Katherine, he would have been all over Jenny like cold on a glacier. Jenny finally got to him. *Damn it! Why didn't I back up just then?*

"Nicky...? Are you okay?"

Nick lifted his head to see Maggie standing there. "Oh Maggie...! Yeah I'm okay..." Maggie handed Nick his tea mug. "Thank you... you're a sweetheart Maggie..."

"Anything for you Nicky..." And Maggie dropped a file on his desk.

"Don't you worry Nicky... everything is gonna be alright..." Nick blew a kiss to Maggie as she left and he picked up the file.

"Gee... I wonder where Maggie got this file..." Nick suddenly realized where Maggie had just come from. He turned in his chair slowly to see Katherine sitting in her office, at her desk, working diligently. *"Okay Jenny... you wanted to fuck me so bad...! I think you just did!"* He thought.

Katherine looked up from her desk. "Nick... may I see you for a moment?" Nick mouthed; *'Dead man walking'* and went into her office. "Close the door please..."

"Yes ma'am..."

"It seems to me that Jennifer has been acting a little... 'distracted'... lately...!"

"Yes she has..."

"It's affecting her work..."

"Really...? That's a good thing isn't it?"

"Yes it is..." Katherine put on her glasses. "Nick?"

"Yes Katherine...?"

"Please make sure that whatever is 'distracting' her... doesn't 'resolve' itself any time soon...!"

And *'The Mean Green Mother from Outer Space'* rears its ugly head again! Damn! "Yes ma'am... I'm on it... I mean... I won't...I mean..."

"Just say; 'Yes Katherine'..."

"Yes Katherine!" and I turned to leave. Katherine called to me.

"Nick!"

"Yes?"

"But when I give you the word..." Nick listened intently. "I want you to flip that bitch inside out! Understand...?"

Nick had a confused look on his face. "...No! I... *don't...*"

446

"When the time comes... you will..."

Nick left Katherine office a little dazed and confused. Did Katherine just tell me that she was gonna let me... Nah! I must have misunderstood her! Nick went back to work. '*I don't remember my life being this difficult...*' Nick said to himself.

- - -

The next few months at Faber Data Corp. were a living hell for Nick. The job sucked to begin with, but now he had to contend with office politics, and the strangest relationship that he has ever had in his life. He had to find a way to juggle his love life and do his job at the same time. It was all so simpler when he was just getting by at work and got laid with anyone he wanted to, whenever he wanted to. He began to hate to come to work in the morning. He didn't get up early anymore to have tea and watch the news. He went to bed earlier and got up later and later. He needed to get control back of his life. Katherine was exhausting him on and off the job. Jenny's newfound knowledge of the damage that 'Little Nicky' could do only served to make her advances more and more aggressive. Even flirting with Lisa gave him no pleasure anymore... He couldn't even think of revisiting or starting a sexual relationship with anybody else right now. He was off his game and it showed. He became introverted and paranoid. He felt like every thing was either his fault or his responsibility. Fortunately, Mandy was able to run the "C" cup on her own and the biker bar needed no managing so that was one less thing on his mind. Nick was slowly, but surely going crazy. He had no idea what to do. He noticed that he was losing weight and his appetite for everything had become stale. He found himself drinking more and more. After finishing off another bottle of wine all by himself, he took stock of his situation. "*Fuck ME! The bastards are winning!*" Nick said to himself. "*How did I get myself into this mess and how the fuck do I get out?*"

The voice of reason came from a most unexpected place... He came to work one day and sat at his desk. He actually just sat there with his head in his hands and just when he thought he was about to break down and cry... he felt a comforting hand on his back. He sat up to find Maggie standing there with a folder in her hand.

"Maggie...! How are you doing today sweetie?"

"I'm good Nicky... here... this is for you..." She handed me the folder.

"What is this Maggie?"

"It's your vacation request..."

"I didn't put in for a vacation...!"

"I know... I put it in for you..."

"You did...? Why...?"

"Cause you need a vacation... duh!"

"Maggie... this is not a good time..."

"This is the best time..."

"I really appreciate this but..."

"But nothing..." Maggie said.

I stood up and hugged Maggie. "Thank you!"

Maggie kissed me on the cheek. "Now I'm gonna say something to you... that I said to my first husband..." Nick had a puzzled look on his face. "...Get the *fuck* out of here!" she said to me. A shocked look came over Nick. "You heard me! *Out*...!"

"My vacation starts now?" I opened the folder and there was a two-week cruise ticket inside for a ship that departed the next morning. "You didn't?"

"I did... now... git!"

"You didn't have to do this, you know!"

"What else was I gonna do with by bonus check?"

"I love you Maggie!" And I hugged her again. She kissed my cheek and wiped off her lipstick of my face.

"If I was thirty years younger, I'd of made you *prove* that to me... now get to going before an old lady shows you how it's really done!" Maggie smiled and slowly licked her lips. "Oh yeah... That's right...!" she said and she winked at me. "Grandma still got skills..."

I stifled a laugh; Maggie smiled knowingly. As I left the office and blew a kiss to Maggie, I turned to go back to Katherine's office to tell Katherine, but Maggie blocked the way. She then bum rushed me to the exit. I passed Bob's desk on the way out. He just sat there with an amazed look on his face. "Don't even say it Bob!"

Bob mouthed: "How *does* he do *that*?"

I was conflicted, I want to get out of here, but my sense of duty.... you know what... fuck this place... *I'm on vacation*...! I left the building and I wasn't gonna get in contact with anybody from the job! Who am I kidding here? I called Katherine from the parking lot the moment I got outside.

"Hey baby?" she answered.

"Katherine... I just wanted to let you know..."

"...Enjoy your vacation baby!"

"You *knew* about it?'

"Who do you think signed off on it?"

"I love you!"

"I love you more... and I'll prove it to you when you get back..."

"You gonna be okay while I'm gone?"

"Don't worry about this place... Momma's got this!"

"Thanks!"

"Nick?"

"Yeah baby?"

"I know you won't have any problems finding 'company' on the cruise but if you do happen to get lonely..."

"Phone sex?"

"Oh yeah!"

"I'll call you tonight!"

"Make sure you have a towel handy..."

"You too...!"

The next two weeks was absolute bliss for Nick. It wasn't the best cruise ever, but just the fact that Nick got away from everything and was being treated like a king took all the weight of the world off his shoulders. He gained his weight back, he relaxed, he got laid whenever he wanted to and he called Katherine every night. When Nick got back he was totally refreshed... The same was not true for Katherine; with Nick away she had to deal with the office and Jennifer on her own. The office employees were not the problem; it was the performance levels. Although the levels were above 30% when Nick left; they crashed in his absence. Katherine didn't have the computer savvy to maintain the levels even with the office on her side. Jennifer wasn't any help and frankly; no one expected her to be. After all, Katherine's failures were Jennifer's stepping-stones to her management position. Katherine was being chewed out constantly by the head office, much to Jennifer's delight. Nick came back to an office that was worse than when he left. Nick went straight to his desk to see if he could get the numbers back up to get Katherine out of the dog house.

(The Confessions of Jennifer X)

For the next few weeks Katherine and Nick were in constant private meetings, working closely together, trying to keep the productivity levels up. I had to work even harder to decode those files on the disc. It was now two on one and the odds were not in my favor. Bedding Nick would have to take a back seat again, but I had caught a break... Nick had gone on vacation for two weeks leaving Katherine and I on an even playing field. She was quickly falling apart without his help on the floor. Katherine even had the nerve to confront me once! I put that silly bitch right back in her place! Right quick and in a hurry.

- - -

Katherine found out that Jennifer was taking credit for her hard work and 'snitching' to the head office when things went wrong. Katherine decided to finally confront Jennifer.

"Ms. Jones... A moment of your time... please?"

"Sure Kitty... anytime!"

Katherine cut her eyes. "You *will* address me as Katherine or Ms. Stark... Do I make myself clear?"

"Yes... *Katherine*... I didn't mean to be... *disrespectful.*"

"It has come to my attention that you haven't been pulling your weight around here lately..."

"What *ever* do you mean? I believe I'm doing Maggie's job better than she *ever* did... and let's face it... that's *all* I'm responsible for around here... *now*, if there's a problem in this office... that would fall under... let me think... oh yeah... *your* jurisdiction...! Katherine!"

"I know what you're doing... Jenny."

"Knowing... *what* I'm doing and being able to *do* something about it... are two *very* different things..." And Jennifer walked back to her desk, stopped and turned. "This is all about power and who has it... You're gonna have to learn that... the hard way... Oh and Katherine... just so *you* know... you may call me... *Ms. Jones*, don't you *ever* call me 'Jenny'...!" Then Jennifer mouthed; "*Bitch*!" Jennifer walked away from Katherine, feeling a little triumphant that she had won a minor victory. "*Now I knew for sure I needed Nick on my team to fulfill my goals. I'm gonna stay on him like white on rice!*"

Jennifer thought she had Katherine's number. But Katherine still had a trick or two up her sleeve. Katherine looked in my direction; I was already looking in hers. She raised her hand to eye level, palm up and quickly turned it palm down. I immediately knew what she meant. I looked in the direction that Jenny was walking away in. She wanted me to 'drop the hammer' on Jennifer. I turned back to Katherine... Katherine nodded. I shook my head and I mouthed to her... "No, I *won't* do it!"

Katherine smiled and mouthed; '*Good answer!*' and went back into her office.

"Damn it! This bitch was testing me...! Good thing I passed!" But I still needed to get something straight between Katherine and me. I stepped into her office. Katherine had her head focused on a file on her desk. "Katherine...?"

"Is there something on your mind Nick?" She said without raising her head.

"I need to get some clarification here...!" And Katherine continued to work on her files without looking up.

"What's on your mind?"

"I want your undivided attention..."

Katherine still didn't look up. "You have my attention... Just ask your questions... Nick!"

"I don't believe I *have* your attention..." Nick closed the door to her office and closed the blinds. He then unbuckled his belt. Katherine immediately stopped what she was doing and had a look of amazement on her face.

"You *wouldn't... dare*!"

"Would you like to *test* me young lady?"

"No...!"

"No… *what*…?"

Katherine shivered. "No daddy!" Katherine's lip quivered. Nick slowly removed his belt and folded it in half.

"I'm going to ask you some questions… and you *will* give me straight answers…"

"Yes daddy!" Katherine kept her focus on the belt in Nick's hand.

"What was on your mind when you said you wanted me to 'flip' Jennifer?"

"I thought that by having sex with you it would throw her off her game…"

"And you would be right… Now…! What made you *think* that I would have done that… just because *you* said so?"

"I… I… I…"

Nick leaned into Katherine's desk; she trembled. "I… am… *not*… your… personal… *Hit man!*"

"Yes daddy!"

"My dick is not a weapon that you can aim and fire at your discretion…"

"Yes daddy…"

"If *I* choose to have sex with Jennifer, I *will* do so… at *my* discretion… to please her… to please *me*… not to *fuck* with her head… Understood?"

Katherine nodded. "Yes daddy!" Nick pointed to Katherine with the belt in his hand. Katherine shuddered and winced.

"I *warned* you… there is a line I do *not* cross… and I draw that line… *right here!*" Katherine shivered again. She didn't know what to think. This wasn't like any session they ever had. Nick was truly angry with her.

"Are you going to punish me?"

"No… but just so you know… the punishment would have been… I sever our relationship… got it?"

Katherine had a tear in her eye. She realized that she had overstepped her bounds. "Yes daddy… I'm sorry!"

Nick took a step back from the desk and unzipped his fly and pointed to the floor in front of him. "Come here…"

"Yes Daddy!" Katherine stepped around from her desk and kneeled before him. She reached into his pants, slowly took out his cock and began to perform fellatio on him. She was crying. Nick did not enjoy any of this, but he felt it had to be done... When she finished she stood up. She couldn't look at Nick.

"Make sure you *never* try to pull this shit ever again!"

"Yes sir!" Katherine sobbed. Nick fixed his pants and Katherine went to sit back at her desk. She was crying and sobbing. "Why did you do that to me?" She sobbed, wiping the tears from her eyes.

Nick sobbed. "I needed you... to experience... for yourself... what you wanted me to do to Jennifer...!"

Katherine began to cry. So did Nick... "I'm sorry daddy...!"

"...Me too baby!" Nick motioned for her to come to him.

"I don't want to..." and she cried and sobbed. Nick opened his arms. Katherine slowly got back up and came into his arms. Nick hugged her and they both cried in each other arms.

"Tough love stinks..." and he kissed her on her forehead.

Wilson walked towards Katherine's door to knock when Bob stops him. "Don't go in there...!"

"Why not...?"

"Nick is in there with Katherine... and she's not happy...!"

"Really...?"

"Nick had to close the blinds..."

"That's *not* good... Jennifer again...?" Bob nodded. "Damn...! I bet you she's chewing Nick out right now!"

"I wouldn't doubt it...!" (*Bob, if you only knew*!)

"Do me a favor...!"

"Sure Wilson..."

"Let Katherine know I want to see her when she done..."

"Are you sure you *want* to be next in line?"

"You're right... I'll catch her up with later... Thanks for the heads up!"

"No problem!"

The Tortured Soul Trilogy
(A Tortured Soul)
Chapter 92
(Under My Thumb)

One of the vice-presidents, Mr. Theopolous decided to be the keynote speaker at the end of the fiscal year at our offices... Uncle Theo, as he liked to be called, was not a compassionate man... his management technique was at best, heavy handed to the point of being cruel. He would put you in the mind of Alec Baldwin in *"Glengarry, Glen Ross"* or Kevin Spacey in '*Swimming with Sharks*". He was a vicious pit bull of a man and was known to take no prisoners. Personally, I didn't give a shit; he wasn't my direct boss, so his threats were nothing more than a bunch of hot air from a blowhard to me. It was only middle management that had to put up with his crap... There were only six floor managers in this office and that wasn't enough of an audience for him to perform in front of, so everyone in the office was called into the meeting in the third floor conference room. I sat near Katherine to make sure she had my moral support.

(The Confessons of Jennifer X)

I requested that Hagen hold the company meeting at the downtown office. I wanted to beat Katherine in her home court. I wasn't happy when Theo showed up, but he was in charge of this office and Hagen didn't want to look too involved. The meeting was just a ruse to rip Katherine a new one, to bring her down in front of everybody. Once she was eviscerated, I was there... to finish her off. After the bloodbath, I would be seen as the changing of the guard. I'm going to bypass Nick and go straight after Katherine. Hagen and Theo didn't like it, but I'm not here to make them happy.

(A Tortured Soul)

One by one Theo took apart the floor managers, pointing out all their faults and failures over the past year. Jennifer strategically placed herself to the right and just behind Theo... She was clearly visible to every employee but safely out of the line of fire. This was an excellent move on her part... It gave you the impression that she was Theo's right hand and immune to his scrutiny. When he focused his attention on Katherine, 'the golden child'... Jennifer stood 'at ease' behind him, at this point her face was emotionless, but she had an icy stare focused right at Katherine. Theo 'fired' at will and Jennifer was now perceived to be Theo's 'enforcer'. Jennifer was playing her 'ace'. She was bypassing me and going straight after Katherine.

Theo attacked Katherine's business sense; he attacked her management skills and he came a little too damn close to attacking her character. I saw tears well up in her eyes... Theopolous smelled blood in the water and went in for the kill... He wouldn't fire her, but he wouldn't turn down her resignation either. That would give Jennifer a pass straight to Katherine's position. Katherine tried hard not to break down, Theo saw that she was on the verge and became more determined to push her over the edge... Jennifer glanced in my direction for split second, I bowed slightly; the gesture was not returned. Jennifer refocused her gaze on Katherine. I no longer had a trump card... The increase to 30% in performance levels meant nothing to Theopolous, It wasn't gonna protect Katherine. It was too little... too late...

(*Black knight protects Black Queen,*
White Queen in jeopardy)

Katherine was a trooper... as much as she looked like she was about to break down, she had a look of determination that she would not let him have the satisfaction... silently we all rooted for Katherine to stand up to this Greek bastard... No way did anyone want Jennifer in charge. Not even the bitches in the office that despised Katherine. They would rather go with the devil they know. Theo continued his attack on Katherine and Jennifer looked as if she was waiting to pounce. I waited silently for Katherine to say 'when' and end all this. She was stronger than I thought. I taught her well. It felt like it took forever but the meeting ended without incident, we all went back to our desks.

455

Theo spoke with me afterwards in private. He wasn't happy with me changing his plans about getting rid of Nick. My only concern was taking over the company, and to do that I had to take Katherine down. And once I did that, I needed Nick... in more ways than one. I wasn't concerned with Theo's plans, which probably included getting rid of me. Without revealing myself, I reminded Theo of who was running the show here. He left in a huff, but not before he agreed I would have Katherine's position. He fell right into my trap! Afterwards I walked past Nick in the hallway.

"Nick?"

"Yes Jennifer..."

"I just wanted you to know... Once Katherine is out of here... There is always going to be a place for you under me... Even here at Faber..."

"*Cute...!*"

He began to walk away; I stopped him. I was being a little too cynical then, so I corrected myself. I was still on an adrenaline rush from besting Theo. I need Nick on my side in more ways than one. "Nick... I'm serious... no games... all you have to do, is ask... I will drop *whatever* I'm doing for you... And I do *that* for *no* man..."

Nick looked into Jennifer's eyes looking for a tell. There was none. "You're *serious!*"

"I need you... in more ways than you or I can ever imagine..."

Jennifer slowly approached me and she hesitantly kissed me. She was waiting for me to push her away. I wasn't going to... I was going to find out... right now... the truth. Jennifer leaned in and kissed me deeply. She was *not* playing games. This wasn't a kiss of seduction; she let herself go and gave herself freely to me. She did the one thing she had *never* done in her life before. She gave control to someone else, and that someone was me. Her kiss lingered after she pulled away.

Although Nick was an amazing kisser, the spark wasn't there at all. I imagined what his face would feel like between my legs, or his hips thrusting into my loins. I was all hot and bothered but I knew that he wasn't interested in me. I sighed and there was a tear in my eye. I gently wiped my lipstick off his face. He would give me his body; someone else owned his heart.

"You okay?" he asked.

Jennifer sobbed a bit. "I'm *never* gonna have you... am I?"

"It doesn't look like it... I'm sorry...Jenny..."

"Then why... did you...?"

"I had to know... *You*...?"

Jennifer chuckled under her tears. "I *had* to try..." Jennifer walked away and stopped and turned. "I know she wouldn't want to share you... *but I would*... if I had to...!" I walked away feeling empty inside, but at least with that finally out of the way... I could now concentrate on eliminating Katherine.

(A Tortured Soul)

And she left. I stood there... I felt... as if... *my* heart was breaking...! I turned around to go back to my desk and there was Bob, just standing there. Before I could say '*Bob you son of a bitch! Will you please just get the fuck out of my face?*' I saw a tear in his eye.

"That was heartbreaking... and so beautiful... I used to envy you... but now... I *see* the pain you must always be in... where do you find the strength...?" I lowered my eyes and put my hand on Bob's shoulder then walked past Bob back to my desk. "That was absolutely fucking beautiful... How does he do that?" and Bob wiped the tear from his eye.

Katherine had gone back into her office and closed the door slightly behind her... I gave her a few moments before I walked over. Just as I was about to knock on her door, that's when I heard her... at her desk... sobbing... I closed her door all the way. The office was starting to empty and everyone was going home. I was gonna wait for Katherine so I could take her home. I would just give her some privacy for now. I walked out of the main office into the hall, mad as hell and I waited there to catch my breath. I rang for the elevator so I could go outside and get some fresh air. As I stood there waiting... Theo came out of the men's room... he stepped right past me onto the elevator as if I wasn't even standing there... I followed him in and he said to me: "Lobby!"

I pressed the button and the moment the door shut I grabbed that little sanctimonious bastard by his lapels and lifted him three inches off the floor and pinned him to the back wall of the elevator. Theopolous was in near shock; he was totally caught off guard by my actions.

"What *the fuck* are you doing? Do you *know* who I am?" He said. He tried to struggle out of his predicament and I stuck my thumb right under his chin, hitting his pressure point. He gasped and stopped struggling. I put my face right next to his as if I was about to kiss his cheek and I whispered in his ear.

"Listen to me, you *miserable* little piece of shit... If you *ever* speak to Katherine the way you spoke to her today again, I will take *great* personal pleasure in breaking every fucking bone in your body...!"

"After I fire you... I'm gonna throw your ass in jail!" He stammered.

I pulled my face away until I was nose to nose with him. "Do I... *look...* like I give a flying fuck?" Theopolous gulped. "I *will* grind your body into hamburger, feed it to my dogs and then... make them take a shit off of a cliff... Have I made myself... perfectly clear?" The elevator doors opened in the lobby and I put Theo down and adjusted his jacket. "You have a nice day!" Theopolous stepped out of the elevator and huffed at Nick. Nick focused his stare at Theo. *"Don't... you... test... me... Theo...!"*

The Tortured Soul Trilogy
(A Tortured Soul)

Chapter 93
(Jungle Love)

And the doors closed and I rode it back upstairs to get Katherine so I could take her home. Nick came out of the elevator, thinking to himself; *'That's gonna come back to bite me on my ass...'* Just as he stepped into the hallway Katherine was standing there waiting for him. "I was just looking for you Nick..." Nick nodded. "May I see you in my office for a moment?"

"Of course Katherine..." Nick walked two steps behind her to respect her authority on the floor. She opened the door and let him in the office and closed the door behind her. He felt that he shouldn't sit down for this.

"Nick... I need to ask you something..."

"Katherine... you don't need my permission to ask me something, just ask... I told you there are no secrets between us..."

"How do you define our relationship?"

"How do *I* define our relationship?"

"Yes..."

"And you want an honest answer?"

"Please..."

"Right now... at this very moment... we are 'friends with benefits'... you only come see me when you wanna borrow a 'cup of fuck'... I'm just your booty call...!"

Katherine dropped her eyes... "I can't believe you think that of me!"

Nick took her chin in his hands. "Look at me..." Katherine averted her eyes... "Look at me Katherine..." She looked up at him and she had a tear in her eye. Nick wiped it with his hankie. "You don't 'love' me... not right this moment... you're in love with the thrill... and I have to tell you... because I know for a fact... eventually, the thrill fades... the grass is always greener on the other side and you will eventually find someone else to mow your lawn."

"So...? You don't love me...? Or am I just your punching bag...? *Your* booty call...?"

"First of all… I have never punched you nor have I ever touched you in any way that you didn't like or caused you permanent physical harm… Second, I am *absolutely* in love with you… which is why I do these things for you, your pain is my pleasure, your pleasure is my ecstasy… and third of all and most important…" Nick looked deep into her eyes.

"Yes Nick?" she sighed.

"Hell *yeah* you're my booty call!"

Katherine's jaw dropped and she hit Nick on the arm. "I can't believe you said that! You *faggot!*"

"Honey… If I *were* a faggot… I would *not* be tapping that ass like I do!" Katherine hit him again and laughed. Katherine hugged Nick tightly. Nick rocked her. Katherine got very serious.

"What gonna happen to 'us' Nick?"

"Right now… what happens to 'us' is entirely up to you…" Nick took a deep breath and leaned his chin on the top of her head. "…It always has been…"

Katherine kissed Nick under his neck and looked at him and licked her lips. "You in the mood for a booty call right now?"

Nick nodded. "You…?"

Katherine nodded and kissed him again. They left the office together and he walked to her car. He opened her car's passenger door for her.

"Nick?"

"Yes Katherine…"

"No kinky stuff tonight… I just want an 'old fashioned' monkey fuck…"

"Would you like me to stop and pick up a bottle of wine on the way home?"

"Yes please… that would be nice… and maybe a little something to nosh on for later…"

"Yes madam…" Katherine kissed him again. She got in and he closed the door for her and Nick got into the drivers side and closed his door.

"Are you packing…?"

"Of course I am…"

It was late and dark and theirs was the only car in the company parking lot… This was a business district and the police never made rounds there after 7pm… Their car never left the

parking lot. An old fashioned monkey fuck is just what it is...
wherever it is... and that's all there is to it...

The Tortured Soul Trilogy
(A Tortured Soul)
Chapter 94
(Hit The Road Jack!)

The next morning Jennifer received a phone call at her desk from Theo. He sounded a little upset but he sounded very pleased with himself as well. Jennifer wondered what this was all about. "Yes Theo?"

"Good news Ms. Jones…!"

"Good news for who…?"

"For you Ms. Jones!"

"Oh…? Well, don't keep me in suspense… what is it?"

"Congratulations… As of today… you have Nicholas Anderson's position in the company!"

"What are you talking about…?"

"I fired the son of a bitch this morning!"

"*You what*…? How? Why?"

"After the meeting yesterday he put his hands on me and threatened me!"

"*What*…? Why would he do that?"

"He realized you were gonna take Katherine down and he couldn't take having you in charge of the office… so he attacked me!"

"I find it hard to believe he would do that to just keep me from taking over the office! That makes no sense at all…"

(Theo did not catch Jennifer's slip of the tongue.)

"Believe it! Now I want you to tell him to call Hagen right away, so he can tell him the good news!"

"Why don't I just have him speak with you…?"

"NO…! I mean… I… promised Charles he could do it…"

Theo was in charge of this building; there was no reason why Nick had to speak to Hagen… except…

"Coward!"

"What did you say?"

"I'm sorry… we must have a bad connection… I said *COWARD*…!" And Jennifer hung up the phone. "Damn it! Why did Nick do that for…? Without him I can't run this office… even if I *did* take Katherine's spot! He's the only one that knows how to break those codes on that disc! Damn... I'm gonna be struck in Nick's job for thirty years like he was... This sucks!" Then another realization hit her. "He's gonna hate me! He'll think I set this all up! SHIT! There's no way in hell we'll ever get hooked up together now! Damn, damn, *damn*...! I need time to think, I gotta somehow spin this in my favor! *Right*! How the hell do you spin doctor getting them fired? Damn it!" Jennifer wrote the note to call Hagen and left it on Nick's desk for when he got in. "I need time to think... Think Jenny, *think*!" Jenny went back to her desk compose herself.

Nick arrived back at his desk and there was a 'post-it' on his computer terminal in Jennifer's handwriting. It said he should call Mr. Hagen... immediately. Nick knew something was very wrong. He knew it was all over. He could feel it in his bones... Nick sat down, opened his cup of tea and took two sips. "Damn! Earl Grey... I really need chamomile right now!" Nick picked up his headset and dialed the number to Hagen's office. Hagen's secretary put Nick right through. Nick knew this was bad... Hagen usually left people on hold a moment or two whether he needed to or not... He felt that it was important to let people wait on him. It gave him a feeling of power. "Yes Mr. Hagen...? Yes Mr. Hagen... Yes, Mr. Hagen... I understand.... Yes sir...!" Nick hung up the phone, and dropped his headset on the desk. Jennifer came up behind him and put her hand on his shoulder. Nick thought it was Katherine and he put his hand on top of hers without looking. He smelled the perfume, that's when he realized it was Jennifer. Nick let go and turned his chair around to look at her... "Came to gloat?"

Jennifer paused. "*No*... I didn't..." Nick looked at her and there was a tear in Jennifer's eye. "I didn't want *this*... I mean... I *did* when I first came here, I wanted it more than anything, but that was before... I... I..." Nick stood up and held Jenny's face with both hands and gently kissed her on her lips. Jenny held his hands to her face. "Nick, believe me... if there were something, *anything* I could do... to stop this... I would!"

"I believe you..."

"I know... this is gonna sound selfish... but... my 'offer'... still stands... Not for me... I want to do 'it' for you... I really do... If you'll have me..."

"Thank you... Jenny...!" I paused. "You're still gonna go after Katherine... aren't you...?"

(Damn... He still thinks this is about Katherine... He'll never agree to help me break those codes now!) "No matter how I feel about you Nick... I gotta look out for me...! I just wish you had my back instead of Katherine's... we could have done amazing things together... I just wish I could start all over, knowing what I know now, so that things between us would have been different." Jennifer kissed Nick again and walked back to her desk wiping her tears with her kerchief. She was *not* happy with the way this turned out. It was like that old Chinese curse; '*May you get what you wish for!*' Jennifer sat at her desk and began to rethink her strategy.

Nick got a storage box and began to pack his things... This was a day he never considered would happen. I mean... he knew it *would* happen, someday... Just not today, not like this... Katherine came out of her office and sat down on the edge of Nick's desk.

"Hey Katherine...!" Katherine didn't answer him. Nick looked at her and then continued to pack his things. "I guess you heard..."

"I just got off the phone with Hagen... so? This is it?" She asked.

"I guess so..." And Nick continued to pack.

"Do you want to stay?"

Nick thought for a moment and looked around the office. "This office has been my home away from home for over twenty years now... I have a lot of good memories of this place. I'm gonna miss it and the people I worked with..."

Katherine whispered; "Even Bob?"

Nick laughed. "Yes... *even* Bob!" Nick paused. "But I guess with all the free time I'll have... I can always stop by and visit anytime I want to... and I can focus my efforts on the 'C' Cup and the bar now... I guess it was a good idea to go into business for myself... I knew this day would come someday..."

"Do you wanna stay?"

Nick sighed. "Katherine, I've been let go... The company finally got what they wanted... Jennifer has my job now!"

"Do... you... *want*... to...stay...?" Katherine said deliberately.

Nick looked deep into Katherine's eyes. A tear formed in his eye. "Yes...! I want to stay..."

"You should have *never* put your hands on Theopolous..."

"I know..."

"I could have handled him myself..."

"I know... I just..."

Katherine stood up and kissed Nick so very gently. "Thank you for defending my honor... Now...! *Unpack* your things..."

"*What*?" Nick raised an eyebrow.

"You heard me... unpack your things..." Katherine left Nick standing there wondering what she had cooked up in her mind. She headed towards Jennifer's desk.

"What are you going to do?" he asked.

Katherine stopped and turned on her heel. "Relax... Momma's got this!" and Katherine continued to head towards Jennifer's desk. "Ms. Jones?"

"Yes Katherine?"

"My office please..." (Okay Katherine... This *is* it...! Without Nick you're in the same boat I'm in... let's see which one of us makes it to shore.) I followed Katherine to her office. Only one of us was getting out alive. I took a deep breath as I walked past Nick who had been packing his stuff. I wanted so bad just to hold him, but right now I have things to do. Katherine led Jennifer into her office and closed the door behind them. "I believe this is the first time I've ever been in your office..."

"Well drink it all in sister... cause you're never gonna see it again!"

"...I *beg* your pardon?"

Katherine walked over to her chair and sat down. "I want you to pack your things and get out!"

Jennifer looked at Katherine as if she had just lost her mind. "You can't *fire* me...! You don't have the stroke!"

"Maybe I *can't* fire you from the company... but I, sure as hell, *can* have you removed from *this* building!"

"And how do you expect to get away with that?" Katherine reached for a file on her desk and tossed it on Jenny's side of the desk. "What is this?"

"Open it..."

Jennifer defiantly picked up the file and began to read it, unemotionally at first, then puzzled; then her face turned pale. "You *must* be joking...!"

Katherine sat in her chair, crossed her legs and began to swivel, right to left... left to right... "*Believe it!*"

"There's no way you can make these charges stick!" Katherine smiled, reached into her desk drawer, took out another file and tossed it on her desk just in front of herself, farthest from Jennifer's reach. "And what is *that*?"

"...Only *one* way to find out!"

Jennifer held out her hand... Katherine smiled and sat back and swiveled back and forth in her chair... Jennifer wasn't so confident now. Jenny had to bend way over across Katherine's desk to reach for the file. This was the ultimate act of submission. She was forced to bow to Katherine. She picked up the file, straightened up, opened it and read the papers inside. "I don't get this... what does Tim Connelly's retirement have to do with me? I don't get this at all!"

"Tim was charged with sexual misconduct and was forced into early retirement... to protect the company..."

Jennifer shrugged her shoulders. "...And?"

"...And they had less evidence on him than I have on you!"

"*You* filed these sexual harassment charges against me?" Katherine shook her head and glanced at the open blinds on her inner office windows. Jenny turned to see Maggie standing there, waving to her. Jennifer was aghast. She put her hand on her bosom. "I... *never*...!" That's when the realization came to me; Maggie was the one that filed the charges, because I was pursuing Nick. I never once thought that old biddy would turn me in... for sexually harassing Nick! Threw my head back and closed my eyes. (*I can't believe I fucked myself!*)

466

Katherine stood up and put her hands on her desk and leaned forward. "I don't care that you tried to take my job, I don't mind that you did all my work for me... *Hell*... I don't even mind that you took credit for my all my hard work and ideas... Oh yeah... I know it was you that gave Theo a disc with all the computer data that I had to rewrite and circumvent against marketing protocols; I didn't even have a problem with that... business is business...! But when you *fuck* with my *man*... that's when I stop the show!"

Jennifer mouthed '*fucked with your man?*' (*What is she talking about?*) Then Jenny looked around to see Nick at his desk unpacking his stuff. She turned back to Katherine, who nodded. That's when Jennifer came to the sudden realization that it was Katherine that Nick was in love with all along... "But Nick has been fired by Hagen and Theopolous! Getting rid of me *won't* get him his job back!"

"That's what *you* think sister... I just got off the phone with both of them and I traded *your ass* for Nick! It seems that they need to keep this all hushed up more than they want Nick out of here!"

Jenny chuckled. "I know you won't believe me when I say this Katherine..." And I got very serious. "But... I'm actually *okay* with that!"

"*Uh huh*... pack your things... and get to stepping... *bitch!*"

Jennifer placed the files on Katherine's desk. Katherine dismissed her with a sweeping motion of her left hand. Jennifer exited Katherine's office and closed the door behind her, smoothed her skirt, fixed her jacket and walked back to her desk not looking up from the floor. She didn't want to see the expression on the other employee's faces. Half way there, Bob yelled out '*Dead man walking!*' Jennifer stopped in her tracks and closed her eyes waiting for the laughter that didn't come. She took a deep breath, opened her eyes and walked a little faster to her desk. There was already a storage box on her desk waiting for her. She quickly packed her things and just as she was about to pick it up she heard a voice behind her.

"Need some help with that?" She turned to see Nick standing there.

"No... I've got it..." I whispered.

Nick ignored her and took the box. "I'll walk you to you car..."

Jennifer bowed slightly; Nick returned the gesture. Jennifer mouthed 'Check and mate!' They walked out together and Nick put the box in Jennifer's trunk. Jennifer held out her hand.

"No hard feelings... Nick?" Nick pushed my hand away and hugged me; I hugged him back. Nick rocked me from side to side. It felt real good to be in his arms. I really needed to be hugged right now. I miss my Michael so much. "I'm so sorry Nick..."

Nick leaned back at looked at her. "Why...? You got thrown out of this office to go to work in corporate headquarters... knowing you... you'll *own* this company before you're 35!" Jenny smiled. (*If you only knew!*) Nick stepped back and held out his hand. "Good luck Jenny!" Jenny pushed Nick's hand away and gently kissed him on the lips.

"Katherine is so lucky to have you..." Jennifer got in her car. "I guess I'm never gonna see you again..."

"I'm just a phone call away... besides... I believe... I still have a 'rain check'...?" Nick said.

Jenny looked at him and her heart quickly skipped a beat, but then she looked into Nick's eyes and realized what he really meant. She was okay with that, Jennifer nodded and smiled. "Yes you do... and it doesn't have an expiration date on it... You can use it *whenever* you like!" Jenny was so envious of Katherine right then, but then again why shouldn't she be happy? After all, I had Michael... one time, and I didn't like it when I lost him. I drove off without looking back.

Jennifer had failed at her goal spectacularly, Theo and Hagen were going to have a field day with her now, and there's not a damn thing she could do about it. That's when her cell phone rang. She looked at the caller ID... It was Ramona. The game was all over! Jenny drove straight to the airport to go back to the Callahan Estate; she didn't even bother to go home to pack first.

Nick turned back to the building to see Katherine standing in the building doorway, watching him. He walked over to her.

"...You checking up on me?"

468

"Don't flatter yourself!" Nick and Katherine watched Jenny's car hit the highway.

"Who taught you how to do that?" Nick asked her.

"*You* did!" Katherine answered.

"You're *damn right* I did!"

And Katherine kissed Nick long and hard. Katherine then gently wiped off her lipstick from Nick's face. "Now get your ass back to work! That pole isn't gonna dance around itself!"

"Yes Ma'am!" Nick stepped into the building.

"Oh Nick…?"

He paused. "Yes Katherine…?"

"Come to my house tonight… be there about 8…"

Nick smiled. "Why can't I just take you straight home from here?"

Katherine voice became authoritative. "Because I *said* so…!" Katherine smiled a wicked little smile.

"…Eight huh? Two quick questions…"

"Yes?"

"Shall I bring a bottle of wine?"

"Yes… and…?"

"What do you want for breakfast…?"

Katherine thought for a moment. "…Homemade French toast with fresh strawberries…"

"You want honey or syrup on that?"

Katherine turned to Nick. "…Are we still talking about breakfast?"

"I don't think so…"

"…Make it honey then!"

The Tortured Soul Trilogy
(A Tortured Soul)
Chapter 95
(Wrapped Around Your Finger)

Katherine is sitting at the breakfast table finishing up the last of the French toast just as Nick comes downstairs with his overnight bag in his hand. He put it down and opens the front closet and began to take his stuff out and put it in the bag. "What are you doing?'

"Packing up my stuff…"

"Why? Where are you going?'

"Remember when I promised you that I would make love to you until *you* were finished?'

"…Yeah?"

"Well… *you're* finished!"

Katherine stands up and holds her robe around the neck. She was caught surprised by his comment. "But… what am I going to do now?'

"Anything you want to do…!"

"But… what if I want to do… *you*?"

Nick smiles and walks up to her. "Who said you can't?" Nick kisses her on the cheek. "Take care of you…" He says. Nick goes towards the front door and reaches for the doorknob, Katherine calls to him.

"Come back here and sit down…" Nick paused and turned to Katherine. She put the last strawberry in her mouth and chewed it up and swallowed it.

"Huh…?"

"I said… *Sit…! Down…*!" Nick's eyebrow raised, among other things. He turned to Katherine, bowed slightly and said. "Yes… madam…" Nick put down his bag and as he walked back towards the dinning room, Katherine pulled out her kitchen table armchair and slid it to the center of the living room. Nick watched as she slid it on its back legs and then he followed her eyes. Katherine sat the chair down in the middle of the room and that's when Nick noticed the leather restraints in her left hand. Nick paused and shuddered, ever so slightly. He looked back into

Katherine's eyes and realized that she saw him shudder; that's when there was a change in her face. Instantly her eyes changed from the look of a frightened deer, to the look of a confident predator. She slapped the restraints on her thigh. "I said... *SIT*!" Nick walked over and sat down. Katherine tied his wrists to the armrests. Nick watched her very intently as she tied him down. Katherine then walked away.

"Where are you going...?"

Katherine turned on her heel. "Do NOT speak... unless I tell you to..."

"Yes... madam!"

Katherine took a scrunchie off her wrist and tied her hair up into a ponytail. She then reached over on the table and put her glasses on. She turned back to Nick. "You like?"

(*How the hell did she know?*) Nick shivered in his chair and stammered. "Ye...ss...s madam..."

Katherine slowly began to remove her terry cloth robe, very... very slowly. As she dropped the robe to the floor, Katherine's naked body shivered a bit in the cool room. A bead of sweat formed on Nick's brow and worked his way down his nose. Nick tried to reach up and wipe it. He had forgotten his hands were tightly bound. "Let me get that for you..." Katherine strutted slowly over to Nick, slowly she straddled him, her warm breasts so close to his face. She sat on his lap, legs spread and she was face to face with him. Nick's breathing was hard. Katherine breathed on his face. Her warm breath on his skin was like a soft caress. Katherine deftly switched her position to where she was now facing away from him; her soft ass was now in his lap. Her alabaster shoulders were on his chest. He could see her bright erect nipples from just over her shoulders. He wanted to touch them, pinch them so bad, but he was still bound to the chair. Katherine leaned forward and grabbed her ankles giving Nick an excellent view of the shape of her full round ass still in his lap. She gyrated her hips just a little and then... she slowly sat back up and snapped her head left to right, right to left; her ponytail whipping Nick's face. Nick gasped a bit as her hair slapped his face. She then slowly rotated her neck, stroking his face with her ponytail. Nick could smell the herbal shampoo she had used. *'Damn,"* he said to himself, *'she learned way too much about me...'*

Katherine then stood up, rubbing her ass up his chest, stopping just short of his face. As he leaned his head down to place his lips on her, she walked away. Nick stayed focused on her ass and suddenly felt as if she had just left him naked, tied to the chair. He had it, and just like that, she took it away. Nick had never felt so vulnerable in all his life. He felt like a trapped animal, his breathing became heavy and quick. Katherine slowly strutted away from him, paused, quickly kicked her feet shoulder width apart and slapped herself on her ass. It left a small pink mark. "Did I get it for you?"

Nick gasped and stuttered. "Ye..yes... Madam!"

Katherine turned on the ball of her foot and faced Nick. "Really...? Cause I don't believe I did...!" Katherine reached up and took the index finger of each hand and flicked both her nipples one time in unison. Katherine cooed. Nick whimpered. Katherine walked back to him; bent over him, her nipples in his face. She reached around his neck and loosened his tie and pulled it off him. "Open..." Nick opened his mouth and Katherine gagged him with his silk tie. That's when Nick realized... there wasn't gonna be a safety word... Katherine was in full control of this session. Katherine ran her fingers through Nick's hair and pushed her erect nipples gently into his face. Katherine moaned deeply. She suddenly pulled his head back with a fistful of hair. "Do you trust me?" Nick could only mumble and nod yes. "Well... you *shouldn't*..." Katherine let go and walked back to her robe on the floor and picked it up and folded it neatly and held it in her hands. (*What the fuck is she doing?*) Nick thought to himself. He pulled on the restraints, but they wouldn't give. Then he saw the knife in Katherine's hand. Nick began to struggle to get out of his bonds. Katherine was on top of him in an instant, the knife was under his chin. "Shhh! Easy now... I really don't *want* to cut you..." Nick tried to focus on the knife on his neck. "Remember the time I told you this bitch was gonna even with you...?" Nick eyes widened. "Don't look so surprised... you *knew* payback was coming... Didn't you?" Katherine whispered in his ear. "Its payback time... *baby*!" Beads of sweat formed on Nick's brows. Nick was hyperventilating. Poor baby...! You need some air..." With that Katherine slowly and methodically cut the buttons of his shirt off, one by one... from the top to the bottom. A muffled scream came out of his mouth. Katherine pulled Nick's shirt open and fondled his chest and abdomen, knife still in hand. "You have an amazing body... Better than most men half your age... I can't wait to see the rest." Katherine placed her head on Nick's chest. The knife in her hand was very close to his crotch. She could hear his heart beat a mile a minute. Katherine looked Nick dead in his eyes. "You said you trusted me... *trust* me..." Nick began to cry softly... "Do I have your undivided attention?" Nick moaned and nodded yes. "I don't *believe* that I do...'

Katherine threw the knife across the room and it stuck in the far wall. Katherine undid Nick's belt and pulled it off him. She folded the belt and snapped it; it made a very loud pop. Nick flinched. She turned her back to him and snapped the belt on her ass; it left a bright pink line on her ass. Katherine cooed and dropped the belt on the floor and walked back to where she left her folded robe. She placed the robe between Nick's feet and kneeled before him. Although Nick's feet weren't tied, he couldn't fathom kicking her. She undid his pants and gently reached in and took out his cock. Nick took a deep breath and shivered in the chair. "Don't be afraid... trust me!" Katherine began to stroke Nick gently, taking great care to stroke the head of his cock with her thumb. Katherine kept full eye contact with Nick. Normally this would be an incredible turn on, but Nick could only think of the knife impaled in the far wall. When would it come into play again, and how? He almost didn't realize that Katherine was now kissing and licking the head of his cock. She paid special attention to the little fold of skin between the head and the shaft by sucking and licking it gently. Nick became erect quickly and Katherine cooed and moaned. She held his balls in one hand and stroked him slowly with the other. She breathed on it so softly... "It's so beautiful... I just love your cock!" She exclaimed. And just like that, Nick's throbbing cock disappeared into Katherine's voracious mouth. Nick's head fell back into the chair and he leaned his hips into it. Nick could see the tight ponytail on back of Katherine head as it bobbed up and down on his shaft only stopping to lick him like an ice cream cone before resuming sucking and licking him whole. Katherine reached over with her left hand and untied Nick's right hand, without ever breaking her rhythm. Nick again leaned into it. Katherine stopped and stroked his cock slowly with her right hand.

She looked up at Nick. Nick looked into her eyes. (Why did she stop?) "Does mommy *have* to do everything?" She took his right hand in her left and slowly placed it on her ponytail behind her head. Nick took hold of it tightly and guided her head back onto his cock. Katherine had given control back to Nick. Nick pushed and pulled Katherine's head any way he wanted and Katherine was fine with that. Then, suddenly, he pulled her off him. She tried to re-engage but he held her ponytail tight and away from him. Nick was breathing rapidly. She looked into his eyes. "What's wrong Nicky?" She looked deep into his eyes and smiled. Nick let go of her ponytail. She smiled knowingly. "I *know* what *you* want..."

She took off his gag and then reached down into the pocket of the robe on the floor under her knees and took out a condom and opened it with her teeth. She positioned the condom over the head of his cock and with one swift deep throat; the condom was on. No muss, no fuss! She got up from her kneeling position, turned around and pushed her ass up in the air. She smacked her ass and pulled her checks apart at sat while Nick held his cock and guided it in. Once inside, Katherine crossed her wrists behind her. Nick held her wrists with his free hand. Katherine pumped her ass on Nick's cock to the rhythm Nick held her wrists with. In and out, up and down. Every once in a while she would twirl her head like the chick at the biker bar; her hair would slap Nick's face. Suddenly Nick let her go and she put her hands on her knees and she began to pump her ass faster and faster up and down on his cock. Then she hesitated at the top of the stroke, fingered her clit, waited a moment and dropped it like it was hot in one bold stoke. They both came at once. Katherine leaned back and slumped forwards, she had actually passed out. Nick was covered in sweat. He held her around waist so she wouldn't fall off his lap. He pulled her back so that she lay fully on him. He repositioned his free hand around her waist and held her close to him. He watched as her naked, spent body, breathe, in, out, in, out. Nick gently kissed her neck and shoulders. Nick was still inside her and he felt as her vaginal muscles contracted in waves. Katherine let out a low and deep moan.

"I can't believe you're cumming in your sleep..." He whispered. Nick let out a low moan as her vaginal muscles caressed and squeezed his cock and milked him dry. He continued to kiss Katherine's neck and ears. I've said it a thousand times before and I'll say it again; 'There is *nothing* sexier than a woman at peace!' Katherine came to about ten minutes later.

"That... was... fucking amazing!" She moaned. Katherine stood up and put her robe back on. *"Now...!* I'm finished...!" And she went back up the stairs. "I take it you can find you way out on your own?"

"Yes madam..." And I began to untie myself, as I got myself together and headed to the door I yelled upstairs. "I'm gonna have to go home and put on a new shirt... I'm gonna be a little late for work..."

"It's okay..." Katherine said back as she turned on the shower. "The boss doesn't mind..."

Nick smiled and headed out the door. As I walked down the street the cool morning breeze touched my moist skin and it felt like a quick dip in a pool. I closed my eyes, took a deep breath and paused to take in all in. I felt as if I had just run a marathon. I just wish she had done all this to me last night... I could sure use eight hours of sleep right now...

The Tortured Soul Trilogy
(A Tortured Soul)
Chapter 96
(You Oughta Know)

Katherine is walking down the street, bold and confident; everyone stops and turns to watch her pass. Katherine was wearing a short dark gray skirt with a waist high slit, open toed black stiletto heels and a low cut, white, see through blouse with ruffles that covered her nipples. Every once in a while if a breeze hit the ruffles in just the right way, you could catch a glimpse, not a good look, but a glimpse… she had on a smart pair of soft black kid leather gloves with a zipper on the back of the hands. On the end of the zipper, was a pull ring about an inch and a half in diameter. The gloves were part of her cat suit and matched her shoes; that Nick would use to tie her to the Portal of Pain. Her hair was in that fabulous ponytail and it bounced up and down as she walked. And …yes… she was wearing her eyeglasses. Two cars actually almost got into an accident by watching her as she walked by. She arrived at the office building when suddenly Johnny pops up from behind her, seemingly from nowhere and grabs her left arm.

"So Kitty Kat, you miss me…?" Katherine turned to Johnny who had a grip on her wrist. "I just got out a few days ago and I decided to give you another chance… *Damn* bitch…! You're looking mighty fine these days… you been working out or what…?" Johnny talks tough to Katherine trying to use his new 'prison cred' trying to get a rise out of her, Katherine is totally emotionless. Johnny raises his voice and pulls on her arm. She twirls her hand quickly in a counter clockwise motion and Johnny can't keep his hold onto her. His face shows discomfort from his thumb being twisted in a direction it's not meant to bend in.

"My name is… Katherine… only my friends and lovers get to call me Kitty… and *you* do *not* qualify…!"

"What *the* fuck? Who you think *you* *are* bitch? I'll knock your skinny ass into tomorrow!"

"You *used* to knock my ass into tomorrow… but that shit don't wash with me no more…" Just as Johnny tries to step up to

Katherine, she raises her hand in his face. Johnny pauses in mid step. "When!"

"What?"

"Not 'what'... when!"

"*When...*? What the *hell* does that supposed to mean?"

"It means; I decide how much pain I allow you to give me... it means; *I decide* where I draw the line... and I draw it... right *here...*!" Katherine motions a line between them; Johnny's eyes follow her finger. Johnny balled up his fist and raised it menacingly; Katherine doesn't flinch. He swings at Katherine and stops inches from her face. Katherine doesn't even blink. The bravado drains from Johnny's face. Katherine motions a back slap with the flick of her wrist to Johnny. "Get to stepping... *bitch!*" Johnny just stood there, emasculated by that one simple gesture. Katherine now had full control, and Johnny knew deep in his heart that even if he did beat her. Even if he did make her cry, her spirit could not be broken. She was now totally in charge, and nothing that he could do, could take that away from her. She was now, and would be from now on; be in charge of 'when'. From this day forward that decision was hers and hers alone. Johnny stepped back away from her. He didn't want to turn his back on her. He wasn't afraid of her... but he knew... that she was no longer afraid of him and even in his immature mind, he knew, that she was dangerous... very, very dangerous... and he wanted no part of that.

Katherine turned on her heel and walked boldly to the front door of the F.D.C. building just as Nick stepped up to get the door for her. As she entered the door, Nick gave her a 'high five'. As she enters the building, Nick turns a does a 'Yes!' Nick stayed just inside the door to keep an eye on Johnny and to watch what would happen next. The first person to see Katherine enter the lobby was Bob, who was waiting for the elevator. He was mesmerized as she approached him and almost dropped the Danish he was stuffing into his face. Katherine ignored his presence and rang for the elevator.

"Why Katherine! Good morning...! You look very..."

"Don't even think about it Bob!"

Bob paused, and stammered. "...But... I..." Katherine threw him a look. Bob hesitated. "...Yes ma'am..." He turned around and took the stairs up to the third floor. As Bob disappeared around the first turn of the stairs, Lisa walked up to Katherine and she stopped dead in her tracks.

"Good morning Lisa…"

"Good Morning Katherine…"

"Where did you just come from?"

"Oh…! I was waiting over by the vending machines until Bob got on the elevator… so I could take the next one…"

"…Understood!" Lisa continued to stare at Katherine. Katherine seemingly paid no mind. "Is there something wrong Lisa?" She asked without turning to her.

"Katherine…? Is that really you…? Girl! You look… great! Where did you get that fabulous outfit?"

Katherine turned to Lisa. "You like?"

"Girl… you are so hot in that outfit… I… would fuck you!"

The elevator door opened and Katherine stepped in and turned to Lisa. *"Really…?* So… What are you doing for lunch Lisa? Cause I understand you like to eat…*raw fish*…!" Lisa blushed… and followed Katherine into the elevator. "Oh by the way Lisa…"

"Yes Katherine?"

Katherine pulled her glasses down and gave Lisa the once over. "…*Love the suit!*" And the elevator doors closed. I waited for the next one.

"That's my girl!"

Chapter 97
(The Bitch Is Back)

About two weeks later, Hagen and Theo entered Hagen's office laughing and joking only to find Jennifer sitting at Hagen's desk with her feet up, smoking one of Hagen's cigars.

"Well Jennifer... I see you finally found the nerve to come back here! How was your two weeks 'vacation'...?" Jennifer just puffed on Hagen's cigar and blewn out a smoke ring. "Do make yourself at home... why don't you?" Hagen said.

"Don't mind if I did... Thank you... You know... smoking cigars is such a filthy habit... How can you stand to have this thing in your mouth?"

"Oh... I'm quite sure you've had very similar experiences with something just as filthy in your mouth Miss Jones..." Theo smirked and laughed.

"Good one Theo... good one!" Hagen said.

"I have good news and great news Ms. Jones..." Theo said.

"Please... Don't keep me in suspense... do tell..." Jennifer put the cigar out on Hagen's floor. Hagen became angry but smiled.

"First... the good news, you're fired! As I believe Katherine once said to you... *'Pack your shit and get out!'*..." Hagen said.

"And don't let the doorknob hit you on the ass... although I'd really like to see that..." Theo added.

"And why am I being fired?"

"Failure to complete the duties for which you were employed... not that you ever really worked here... you were just a nuisance that we had to put up with that's all...'

"And the great news...?"

"Steven Callahan is *dead*!" Hagen announced.

Jennifer cut her eyes at Hagen. How dare he revel in that news? Hagen wasn't fit to polish Steven's shoes. "I know... I just attended his funeral on Sunday... it was lovely... you *should* have sent flowers..." Jenny said calmly.

"And with him dead, the leverage over me goes over to someone else, and I don't have to put up with any more of your shit anymore... now... get your feet off my desk and get to stepping, bee atch!"

Jennifer laughed. "I really hope you got *all* of that out of your system Hagen...." Jenny said. And as Theo opened the office door to throw me out, there were two men standing there.

"Who the hell are you?" Theo said.

"I'm sorry gentlemen... where are my manners? Allow me to introduce you to my 'associates'..." Jenny said. The two men entered the room and closed the door behind them.

"What the hell is going on here?" Hagen said.

"This is Mr. Cisco Torres... and this is Mr. Jinx Alexander... These gentlemen have 'inherited' Steven Callahan's 'stock' portfolio after his untimely death..." Hagen looked at them in shock and dismay. "And just before that... they were my 'personal' bodyguards..."

Jinx reached into his pocket and took out the data disc and showed it to Hagen. Hagen's jaw dropped.

"That's right... bitch! You're *my* little puppy now!" Cisco said to Hagen and he scratched his face with his right hand sporting his favorite 'jewelry' (you know what I'm talking about!)

"What are you two going to do?" Hagen asked.

"The question is... What are *you*... going to do...?" Jinx said as he put the disc away. Hagen stood there, speechless. Jenny liked watching him sweat and twist in the wind.

"Would you like a suggestion here Hagen?" Jenny said. Hagen nodded. "Mr. Theopolous is going to take a much needed early retirement and I'm going to take over *his* position in the company..."

"Why in the hell would I do that for...?" Theo said.

Cisco punched Jinx as hard as he could in the stomach with the brass knuckles; Jinx barely flinched. Theo couldn't believe what he just saw.

"Care to pick *your* dance partner Mr. Theo?" Cisco said.

Theo gulped and turned to Jennifer. "But why *me*...? Why don't you make Hagen quit?" Hagen cut his eyes at Theo.

"We own Hagen..." Jinx said. "You're the problem here... do you... *want* to be a problem?" Theo shook his head no. Jenny picked up a folder and Cisco took it and handed it to Theo.

"Sign these..." Cisco said. Theo opened the folder, signed the papers inside without even reading them.

"Don't worry about packing your things... I'll have the janitor box your things... and throw them out! Get to stepping bitch!" Jenny said. Theo left hurriedly. He didn't even speak to or acknowledge Hagen.

"What's gonna happen to me?" Hagen asked.

"You mind your P's and Q's and *nothing* is gonna happen to you. You and I will run this company; Theo was just dead weight... Oh by the way... I'm going to try to find a competent computer programmer to update the company's systems... it should have been done years ago..."

"Where are you getting the money to budget that?"

"Let's just say... Christmas is postponed at the Hagen household... indefinitely...!"

Hagen was about to protest when Jinx leaned on his shoulder. "You okay with that Hagen?" Jenny asked.

"Yes..."

"Yes 'what'...?" I asked.

"Yes... *Ms. Jones*..."

"You're damn right, '*Yes, Ms. Jones*'..."

"Will there be anything else...? Ms. Jones...?" Hagen said.

"No... you may leave now..." Hagen looked around. "Oh... you can have Theo's old office... I *like* this one... and your personal secretary too..." Hagen left sheepishly and Bonnie entered bringing coffee.

"I brought you some coffee Ms. Jones... black... just the way you like it!"

"Why thank you Bonnie!"

"My pleasure Ms. Jones..." Bonnie handed her the coffee. Jenny took a sip and nodded in approval. Bonnie smiled and turned to leave.

"Have lunch with me this afternoon Bonnie?"

"I would love to... *Jenny*..." And Bonnie walked to the door.

"Love you!" Jenny said.

"Love you back!" Bonnie replied and closed the office door behind her but not before she glanced at Jinx.

"Say... Ms. Jones...?"

"Yes Jinx?"

"Is *she*... you know... seeing anybody?"

"What am I...? Her pimp?"

"No...! I'm just saying..." And Jenny and Cisco laughed. "Ah come on...!" Jinx said.

"Jinx... would *you* care to join us for lunch?"

"I would love to...Ms. Jones."

"Jinx?"

"Yes Ms. Jones...?"

"...You take it easy with her...! I like her a lot! And I can replace you faster than I can replace her..."

Jinx threw his hands up. "Kid gloves Ms. Jones... kid gloves! I kinda like her too. She's friendly..."

"Yeah, Jinx was having a very nice conversation with her while we waited outside." Cisco said.

Jenny nodded approvingly. "Speaking of 'nice conversation' how are you and L.L. coming along?"

Cisco smiled and fixed his tie. "You know how I do...!"

"Do I have to keep my eye on you too...?"

"Excuse me Jenny? Have you *met* L.L.?"

"Pfffttt... I forgot!"

"I didn't!" Cisco joked.

Jenny sipped her coffee. "Jinx... I have got to ask you something..."

"Yes Ms. Jones?"

"How in the *hell* did you take that *punch* from Cisco?" Jinx opened his shirt a bit. He was wearing a thin bulletproof vest. Jennifer laughed and shook her head. "I should have known!"

- - -

So that's how Jennifer X. Jones, former stripper, survivor of child abuse and all around tough ass bitch... with a heart of gold, became the vice-president of Faber Data Co. Like she said, *'You can take the girl out of the hood...'* You know it would have been so much easier if she had just brought Jinx and Cisco with her the first day she arrived… But then her story wouldn't have been as good or the payoff so rewarding. A year later she still hadn't found a computer programmer who could properly update the companies systems, but she worked closely with Nick to patch whatever programs they could to get company's overall levels to at least 25% above standards. Marketing didn't like it, so she fired their company. She didn't need them either; *they* were the albatross around the company's neck and the biggest waste of money. That meant even more money for a new computer program and peripherals that would work. The additional profits were pooled to be able to pay the programmer once he was hired. System updates were slow but steady.

Jennifer still continued to work closely with Nick until a competent programmer could be hired. Breaking the codes on the disc was no longer a priority. Who needed the codes when she had Nick? Eventually, she went back to working *on* Nick. He was still a tough nut to crack… even with a standing rain check. There was no rush right now… Jennifer would just bide her time. Eventually she *would* seduce him. There were many opportunities. Nick and Jenny even spent a week together at a business seminar once, and although the timing was right, the 'time' was wrong! (Please don't ask me to explain! You know damn well what I meant about the 'time' being wrong!) It would take a while before the two of them would finally have their 'magic' moment… and Jennifer didn't plan it. I guess sometimes you just have to let things… happen naturally.

The Tortured Soul Trilogy
(The Confessions of Jennifer X)
Chapter 98
(Jenny - 867 -5309)

Jennifer rolled over in bed and snuggled into her pillow. She was just waking up from a long night of drinking and dancing. The last thing she remembered was passing out but she couldn't remember if was from the drinking or a night of wanton sex. She looked around her room. *'What time is it... what day is it... for that matter?'* Her head felt like someone used it as a soccer ball. *'I need an aspirin...'* She got out of the bed and she was naked. *'Shit!'* she said to herself. *'What... or, who... did I do last night?'* This wasn't like her. It wasn't that she cared whom she had sex with, but at least she had an idea when she woke up what she did the night before. She heard a sound from the bathroom. Someone had just gone into the shower. She knocked on the door.

"How long you gonna be...?"

"I'll be out in just a few moments..."

"Damn it... I don't recognize that voice. Who the hell is that?" I thought. "Don't use up all the hot water..." I went to the kitchen to get some aspirins. *'Who the hell did I sleep with last night?'* then I heard the man's voice behind me.

"Um... *I* usually *dress* for breakfast!" I turned around to see Nicholas Anderson standing behind me. "Nick? What are *you* doing here?"

"Um... I brought you home last night from the club..."

"You stayed here... last night?"

"Yes... Um... I know this is your place and you can walk around any way you like... but aren't you cold...?"

I looked at myself and I was standing there naked... so what? I used to make my living walking around like this! "That was *you* in the shower?" He nodded and went into the other room and came out with a bathrobe and put it on me. "What is your problem? We had sex last night... now you have a problem seeing me naked? What? You can fuck me but now you can't look at me...?" I said to him.

"Jennifer... I don't know where you got the idea that we had sex last night..."

"You mean...?" "Nick shook his head no. "We *didn't* have sex last night?"

"No...! Trust me... you would have remembered *that!*"

I cut my eyes at him. "Then what are you doing here?"

"I told you... I was at the club where you were partying last night and you got so drunk that I had to bring you here... It was late, so you asked me to spend the night..."

"So you just brought me home...?"

"It wasn't *that* easy..."

"What do you mean...? It wasn't that easy?"

"Well... you had a few too many last night and you jumped up on the bar and started dancing... quite well I must say... Then the crowd started yelling 'Show your tits'..." Then you started to unbutton your blouse..."

"I didn't!" Jenny said in horror.

"No... that's when I snatched you off the bar and took you home... I was almost lynched by a drunken mob!"

"So, where did you sleep last night?"

"On the couch..."

"How did I get undressed?"

"I would have to assume you undressed yourself, took a shower and then got into your bed naked..."

(Oh... That's why my bed felt wet... and I probably played with myself as I often do before I go to sleep. That would explain why I thought I had sex...) "And you just stood there watching me while I stood here naked!"

"You didn't seem to mind a moment ago... and I still don't mind!"

"And you *didn't* take advantage of me last night...?"

Nick put his hands in his pockets. "I don't take advantage of unconscious women..."

"I'm not unconscious now..." Jenny said seductively.

Nick smiled. Jennifer realized this was her golden opportunity to have him. "No you're *not...!*" He said. "And I *believe...* I have a rain check with no expiration date on it..." Nick pulled out the invitation Jenny once gave him and he fanned himself with it.

(That's how he had my address!) "Would you like to use it now?"

Nick nodded. Jennifer slowly took her robe off and let it drop to the floor. She reached up and pinched her nipples and began to gyrate for Nick. She danced like she did when she worked the pole in Philly. Like the time she first worked as a fluffer on that porn shoot. She turned away and did the 'body wave' towards him. She then leaned into him and he reached around and felt her breasts. She felt his stiff cock through his pants on her naked ass. She bent over and grinded her ass into his crotch. The 'Jenny Mojo' was working... finally! She stepped away from him and turned and danced for his some more. Nick began to remove his shirt. Nick had an amazing chest and upper body for a man his age. Jennifer knew from her last attempt to bed Nick that Nick was packing heat. Nick unzipped his pants and took out his thick, long cock. Jennifer paused. She knew Nicky was packing heat... but this man was a fucking mutant! Normally Jennifer didn't like to give head, but she was so focused on his cock that she didn't realize that she had dropped to her knees and was devouring him like a bomb pop. She just could just barely get the head of his dick into her mouth. She held him with both hands and still didn't have all of him. This only served to excite her even more. Nick placed his hands on the back of her head and guided her head on and off him. There was no way she was gonna be able to deep throat him. She kneeled up and placed his cock between her tits and stroked his shaft with her breasts while she licked and sucked the head of his cock. Nick began to moan. After a while her jaw and knees started to hurt.

Nick sensed this and helped her up to her feet and bent her over the sink. She gyrated her ass in anticipation of his cock deep inside her. He took a little longer than she expected and she looked back to see what he was doing. He was putting a condom on. She kicked her legs open and he mounted her. She hadn't felt such exquisite pressure since the time she first fucked Michael Callahan. It had been more than six years since then and right now she felt exactly the way she did the day she lost her virginity.

Nick hit a spot no man had hit since Michael. The flashback damn near sent her into a fuck frenzy. She kept regressing into the past and coming back to the present. She was in the exact same position. Her ass was in the sky, her nipples were rock hard and she fainted in just the same way, but with one major difference. This time when she woke up, Nick was not asleep from exhaustion. He was still pumping her ass as if this was the last piece of pussy he was *ever* gonna get. Not only was he a mutant... he was a fucking *machine*! Jenny's tits were in the sink and Nick had filled it with warm water and it kept her hot and moist. Nick had held on to her hair so her face wouldn't go in the water. Jennifer eyes rolled to the back of her head. He was in total control of her. Jennifer lifted her knee onto the counter and began to scream. "Fuck me daddy! Fuck me hard! Come get this pussy... daddy... *FUCK ME*!" What Jenny didn't realize is that by calling Nick '*Daddy*', he regressed to the last time he had sex with Katherine. If it were at all possible, Nick pumped her juicy pussy with even more wild abandon. Jenny felt as if she was about to swoon and faint again. "Don't you have a heart attack on me, *old man*...!" Jennifer moaned.

"I got your 'old man'... right *here*!" And Nick pulled back and rammed his cock into her, deep and swift. Jennifer reared back, her jaw trembled and she slammed her hands on the counter on either side of the sink.

"Oh you... mother... fff... fff...fff...! Keep doing that! Don't... Stop...!"

Little did either one know, but they were both in a sexual time warp. A vortex of passions for another partner, in another place, another time, in an instant they were mentally switching partners back and forth; Jennifer and Michael, Nicholas and Katherine, Nicholas and Jennifer.

"Oh! Ohh! Ohhhh! Don't stop! Keep it up... right there...! Oh... oh... you... I love your cock! I *LOVE* your *COCK*! It's all yours daddy... its all yours! Ahhhhh! Ahhhh! Ahhhhh! Right therrrrrrre!" Jennifer pinched her nipples roughly. She couldn't breathe. She was actually sucking in short breaths of air violently. "Ah... Ah... ahh!"

"Come on! Come on! Give up that pussy you *BITCH*!" Nick demanded. And Nick slapped her on the ass hard. Jenny began to beat her hands on the countertop again.

"Come get it daddy! Fuck my ppp... pppus... seeeeeeeeee! Yeah! Oh... right there you... fff... fff..." Jenny's eyes went to the back of her head again. "Ohhhh!"

"Give... *me*...!" Nick demanded.

"You want it...? Spank that ass daddy! Spank it!" Nick complied and spanked her ass hard as he pumped her. "Gggg... ggg... ggg!" Jenny choked out. Jenny and Nick were now in perfect harmony; they were like a well-oiled machine, a very 'well-oiled' machine. The sound of Jennifer's ass smacking Nick's hips became louder and louder. Jennifer screamed loud and her pussy gushed. Then her vaginal muscles contracted violently. "Why didn't you ever fuck me like this before?" she screamed. She took a handful of water from the sink and splashed it on her face and neck. She wasn't gonna let him knock her ass out again... not now! He pumped her harder and harder, faster and faster. '*When is he gonna finish*?' She couldn't believe the stamina Nick had. Nick suddenly pulled out of Jenny. Jenny slowly turned to him. Her thighs were quivering and she could barely remain standing up.

"I can't cum...!" he panted. He was still fully erect and ready to go.

"The *hell* you can't...!" she panted and moaned. She wasn't about to keep this shit up until *he* was finished... She slowly lowered herself onto her knees onto her robe on the floor. She used her hands to slide herself across the floor towards him. Nick stood there shivering. Jenny peeled the condom off Nick and the moment she touched his cock with her bare hand, Nick moaned. That when she realized, the condom was blocking the biological reaction one has skin on skin. She began to stroke him gently and Nick howled gently. She took her tongue and licked around the head. Nick began to pant and moan. With every lick, Nick shuddered. That's when she realized, down on her knees, that she wasn't subservient to him. She was... in charge! This was the ultimate act of trust a man could bestow a woman. He had placed his most prize possession in her absolute control. Every time she sucked and licked him, she watched his face. His gratification was her gratification. Nick leaned his head back and simply whispered '*Please...?*' That did it. She looked at his throbbing cock. '*This... belongs to me!*" She whispered. Jennifer relaxed her jaw and began to devour him voraciously. She worked his cock in her mouth as if she was working her dildo in her pussy. After sucking him hot and heavy for ten more minutes...

"I'm gonna cum!" He yelled.

"Cum in my face bitch!" And she stroked and licked Nick's cock with wild abandon. Again, Jenny inadvertently had said the 'magic' word to Nick and he came like a fountain. When Jenny felt his spurt on her face and tits, she came like a banshee. This was *her* moment of triumph. When they had cum together it felt as if the room was spinning. Nick then took a towel and lovingly wiped her face and body. They both slowly collapsed into a heap on the kitchen floor. Just before she lost consciousness again, Jennifer whispered. "I thought you said... you don't take advantage of unconscious women?"

To which Nick replied. "I thought *you* said... you didn't *like* giving head..."

"I guess we both learned something new about ourselves today!" and she nestled into Nick's arms.

She got up a few moments later and went into her bathroom to wash up. Nick brought her robe and covered her and carried her back to her bedroom. Later that day, in Jennifer's bed, Nick was still lieing down next to her, spooning her. She rose up and felt her head. "Oh...! I could really use some of 'the hair of the dog that bit me'..."

Nick pulled back the covers. "Your wish is my command!" he said.

Jenny looked down at 'him' and was awestruck. "You can't be serious!" she said. Nick was very serious; Jennifer was very pleased.... Twice!

The Tortured Soul Trilogy
(The Confessions of Jennifer X)
Chapter 99
(Woman to Woman)

A few weeks after, I received a call from Katherine Stark. I hadn't seen or spoken to her since the day she had me 'removed' from her office almost a year ago... She asked to see me privately at her home... not her office... *her home*... I think I know *why* she wants to see me... I should have never had sex with Nick... I should have respected her space... I should have respected her feelings... I should have... Oh FUCK her! I'm not responsible for her man cheating on her with me! She's just gonna have to get over it! I don't owe that bitch a damn thing! But I'm still gonna go see her... I don't back down from anybody... We are gonna get this resolved... one way or another... And if I work it right... I'll have Nick all to myself... I *like* that! I got to Katherine's house a little before 3pm. She wanted me there about 2:30, but I decided to make her wait on me... put her at a disadvantage... make her play my game... my way. I called first to make sure she was home waiting for me. I waited outside her house to make sure she wouldn't make believe she wasn't home if I knocked on her door. I looked at my watch, stepped out of my car and went to her door and rang the doorbell. Katherine opened the door wearing a casual but smart outfit. Her hair was in a ponytail and she was wearing plain eyeglasses. She had been writing in a journal while waiting for me.

"Come on in Jennifer... Make yourself comfortable..."

"Thank you Katherine..." I entered her simple but stylish apartment. My place was much bigger than hers, but I like the way she set her place up. I looked at Katherine; she was somehow different from when I last saw her. If possible she was more confidant... more secure. This was *not* the same Katherine I once knew.

"So... did you have any problems finding my address?"

"No..." I said nonchalantly.

"Oh...? Cause... I was wondering why you sat in your car for over 20 minutes after you called me to tell me '*you were on your way*'..."

'*Shit!*' I thought to myself, '*I should have parked where she couldn't see my car... That was an amateur mistake!*' No... this isn't the same Katherine... not by a long shot...

"Sit down... make yourself comfortable..." I sat on her couch and crossed my legs. "Would you care for a glass of wine?"

"Is it safe to drink?" I joked.

Katherine laughed. "Yes, it's safe... I'll even have a glass with you..."

"Yes please... thank you..."

"Red or white...?"

"Whatever you have is fine..." Katherine went over to a wine rack and pulled out two bottles, put one back and opened the other and poured us each a glass. I swirled the wine glass and inhaled the bouquet. "Very nice nose..."

"I like it..." Katherine said.

She took a sip and so did I. "It's very nice... I'm quite impressed..."

"Thank you..."

"Okay... now that we've exchanged our pleasantries... Why did you want to see me?"

Katherine looked at her watch. "That didn't take long did it?"

I took a deep breath. "Look... we both know that you and I didn't meet under the best circumstances and we got off on the wrong foot..." I said.

"You *think*?" I laughed and so did Katherine. This was the first time we ever dropped the act and just be ourselves...

"I just want to say... I'm sorry..." I didn't expect to hear myself say that.

"You're *not* sorry... But looking back on the situation... you do wish you hadn't been placed in that position..." Katherine took off her glasses and picked up her wine glass and took a sip.

I tipped my glass to her; she returned the gesture. No, this isn't the same Katherine I knew. "Well having said that... there may be something else... that is going to put a damper on our newfound 'understanding'..." I said.

"You mean... you having sex with Nick?"

I was taken aback. "You *know* about me and Nick...? And don't insult my intelligence by using that old line; *'No... but you just told me'*..."

Katherine sipped her wine. "Of course I knew... Nick and I don't have *any* secrets between us...!"

"And you're *okay* with that...?"

"Obviously...!"

"You're *really* okay with that?"

"Uh huh..."

I was almost at a loss for words. After what happened between us before because of Nick, I knew there would be more drama than this!

"I'm so sorry Jennifer... did I take the wind out of your sails?"

"I did have this long, drawn out scenario played out in my head..."

"...Was there a cat fight involved...?"

I smiled at Katherine. "Maybe...!" I took another sip of wine, she offered to refresh my drink, I accepted. "What did he tell you about us?"

"Everything..." she said.

"I'm just so... amazed that you don't have a problem with this... after all, it was my going after your man that made you retaliate against me in the first place..."

"Well... *that*... among other things..." I nodded in agreement. "Nick... helped me get over my *jealousy issues*..."

"So... dish... what *did* Nick tell you exactly..."

"Well... he told me that the first time you two tried to get together didn't go well at all..."

I nodded. "True... I expected so much that weekend... then my 'family friend' showed up unexpectedly... How was your first time with Nick?"

"Actually our first attempt was a comedy of errors... I'm getting the impression Nick isn't very good on 'first dates'..." Katherine confided, Jenny laughed. "How was your second 'date'...?" Katherine asked.

"Well... I had gone out to dinner... business related... and then I went out for a few drinks and dancing and Nick was at the club... I had a 'few too many' and..."

"He had to drive you home...?"

"I... made him *think* he had to drive me home..." Katherine laughed. "What's so funny?"

"He made *you* think that he *thought* he had to drive you home...!"

My jaw dropped. "He said that?"

"Nick... is not stupid by any definition of the word."

"Why that little..."

"Uh uh uhh... remember... *you* tried to trick *him* first..."

"Accepted..." and I tipped my glass.

"So what happened next?"

"He didn't tell you...?"

"I want to hear it from you..."

"Okay..." I took another sip of wine. "He dropped me off at my place, it was getting very late, so I asked him to spend the night... and he did. The next morning... I seduced him..."

"And of course... again *he* was okay with that!" I cut my eyes at Katherine. She laughed. "Again... it was *your plan* to begin with... not his fault he went with it!"

"He was all over me in a few minutes..."

"If you're saying that to get a rise out of me... don't bother... remember... I already know what happened..."

"Okay... we spent a lot of time on foreplay and by the time we..." I took a deep breath.

"And...?" Katherine prompted.

"It was fucking amazing...!" Katherine sipped her wine. I took a sip of mine. I paused a moment and asked. "Katherine... may I ask you something?"

"Go ahead..."

"As far as you know... is he... taking... *anything*?"

"Anything for what?"

I held my elbow to my side and raised my fist towards me. "To keep him... 'armed and dangerous'?"

Katherine shook her head no. "No he's not... that is all Nick honey...!"

"*Really*...?"

"Oh *yeah*!"

"How can you be so sure?"

"We've had too many impromptu encounters and you have to take a pill at least and hour before... and unless he takes a pill... *everyday*...!" Jennifer nodded in agreement. "We had a marathon once... it lasted over 27 hours..." Katherine added.

(Damn! Michael and I did almost 18 hours once and we were both sore as all hell afterwards! We couldn't fuck for two weeks afterwards.) "*27 hours*...! Straight...?"

"Oh no...! On and off... but after a quick nap or two, he was back on the saddle and good to go... and there aint no pills for frequency..."

"How many times did you two...?"

"Girl...! I lost count..."

"How many times did you...?"

"Seven...!"

"Damn!"

"Oh yeah!"

"Was it *that* good for you?"

"It was great!!! But I got to tell you... my pussy was sore as hell for two days...! But the pain was well worth it... A word of advice; make sure you have plenty of lubricant handy... just in case *you* ever catch him when he's in the zone..."

"I'll stock up... thanks!" Katherine offered to refresh my drink. "So... it's all over between you two...?" I asked as I held out my glass.

Katherine pulled the bottle back. "Oh honey! You've had too much to drink! You got a better chance of getting a crack head to give up the pipe than for me to give up that man!" I smiled and Katherine refilled my glass.

"Then why did you ask to see me?"

"Nick and I discussed it and we felt that it wasn't fair to you to make you think that you two were 'sneaking around'... so we felt it would be better if you heard it from me... and here you are..."

I still couldn't believe my ears. "And you're *really* okay with all this?"

"I believe we covered that already honey! The question is; 'Are *you* okay with this?'..."

"I guess I was always okay with it... it's just out in the open now!"

"Then we're okay... By the way, Nick mentioned that he was very impressed with your 'skills'..." Katherine refreshed her own drink.

I took another sip. "I still have a few tricks I haven't shown him yet..."

"Really...?"

"Oh yeah...!"

"Maybe you'd like to show them to me?" Katherine put her eyeglasses back on and stood up and walked over to her bedroom door and pushed it open and leaned in the doorway. I watched her. There was something about seeing her standing there in the doorway. She was now enveloped in the orange afternoon sunlight coming from her bedroom window. There was a raw sexual energy that exuded from her. It was if she had her own 'Kat Mojo' working for her. She was beautiful and desirable. I have never been attracted to a woman before. Okay, maybe Tobey once, but we were more friends than 'girlfriends'. Oh... women have tried, I just was never interested... until now. "So...? Care to dance...?" Katherine whispered. I focused in on her eyes. The eyeglasses she was wearing had a profound, almost hypnotic effect on me. She had an authoritative look about her. She was the alpha bitch and I succumbed to her will. There was a scent, in the air, but was that her? Or was that me?

I don't know if it was the wine, or if talking about the 'affair' made me horny. I paused for a moment emptied my glass and then stood up, slowly unbuttoned my blouse and took off my bra and dropped in on the floor. Katherine smiled and had a look of approval on her face. "Don't mind if I do..." I walked over to Katherine and kissed her deeply while I unbuttoned her blouse. She wasn't wearing a bra. She very was firm and perky for a woman her age. If I didn't know any better, I would have sworn we were the same age. I fondled her nipples and she cooed and purred. She reached under my skirt and fingered my clit. I was already wet. "Katherine..." I whispered.

"Call me Kitty..."

"Kitty... I've... *never...*"

"It's okay… I understand… it's your first time… I *promise* to be gentile…!"

I couldn't believe I was saying this to her. I took a long deep breath. "It *is* my first time… with a woman but… I… *don't…* want you… to be gentle…!"

"*That*… actually works for me…!" And Katherine took off her belt and I panted in anticipation… It had been so very long since I felt the sting of leather on my skin… a very long time. "Before we do this… there are rules we must follow and they are NOT negotiable…" She said as she led me in and closed the door behind us. She explained that a safety word would be used to stop the discipline if I couldn't handle the pain. This chick had no freaking idea the amount of pain I could handle. I just nodded in agreement.

Katherine's bedroom was very feminine but not frilly. Not the bedroom of a 'princess' but that of a queen. She walked over to a steamer trunk at the foot of her bed and opened it. It was a treasure chest of pain and torture. My nipples were hard again and I had goose pimples. I was amazed at the 'toys' she had. I mean, I'd seen them at the warehouse but I never would have conceived this about Katherine. I knew her 'ex' used to physically abuse her, but abuse is forced… these are the tools and trappings of consenting adults. I panted heavily with anticipation of what was about to happen.

"Take off your clothes but leave your shoes and panties on…" Jennifer hesitated and Katherine slapped her thigh with her belt. "Now!" Jennifer complied and removed her clothes. Katherine watched her intently; she was very impressed with Jenny's hot young body. Katherine began to pant ever so slightly. "Face down on my bed please…" Jennifer kneeled up on the bed and as her ass was up in the air, Katherine smacked her on the ass with the folded belt.

"Ohhhh! My…!" Jenny moaned. Jennifer shivered a bit and had a flashback to when her mother beat her while her father watched. Jennifer instantly became hot and moist from the sting of the leather belt on her ass. As Jennifer lay down she could see that the bedposts were worn where she could tell Katherine had been tied to… on several occasions. Katherine took out two leather restraints and tied her wrists to the bedposts. Jenny held onto the leather and twirled it around her wrists to make it tighter.

"Are you *sure*... this is your first time?" Katherine said as she placed her eyeglasses on the end table.

Jennifer didn't answer, she only whispered. "Beat me... mommy!" Katherine became excited at being called mommy and reached into the trunk and pulled out her favorite cat o'nine tails and tore Jennifer's ass up. On occasion Jennifer would rear up on her knees to give Katherine a better angle to strike her buttocks. This also gave her the opportunity to rub her nipples on Katherine's silk sheets. The sensations were strangely comforting. Jennifer screamed and cried out with every lick, but never said the safety word. Time passed and Katherine slowly untied her. Jenny purred and cooed at the pain she had received. "Are we done...?" Jenny asked. Katherine shook her head no. Jennifer eased herself off the bed and Katherine pinched her nipples.

Katherine held the whip out to her. "I have only one question for you... can you dish it out as well as you can take it?"

Jennifer's hand trembled as she reached for the whip. The thought of wielding a whip was a totally foreign concept to her. "I don't know if I can do this..."

"You mean to tell me... you've *never* thought of beating my ass?" Katherine whispered humbly.

Katherine yielding to her is just what she needed. Jennifer slapped the whip into her open palm. "Yes I have!" And the alpha bitch was back. Katherine slowly removed her blouse and skirt and laid herself over the trunk in a prone position. Her ass was the most beautiful thing I had ever seen, and I've worked with strippers. She took hold of the bed's footrest and squeezed it tightly.

"Then beat my ass... *bitch*!" Katherine said softly as she turned her head away from me giving me control.

"Oh! I'm gonna show *you* who the *bitch* is...!" There was a lot of anger in Jennifer. Anger at her father, anger at her mother, anger at Katherine, anger at the world and her lot in life in general. Jennifer took all that anger out on Katherine's ass... and Katherine didn't mind it one single bit. Every stroke evoked an emotional release from both of them. By the time Jennifer was finished Katherine's ass was beet red. Jennifer's naked body was glistening with perspiration. Between the beating she had just taken and the

497

physical and emotional demands of disciplining Katherine, Jennifer was high on an adrenaline rush. She basked in its glow as Katherine lay there in her prone position. She dropped the whip on the floor; she didn't have the strength to hold it anymore. Her hands and fingers trembled uncontrollably. She was exhausted. Jenny stood there shivering and shaking until she heard Katherine moan and sob.

"Uhhhhh... ohhhh!" Katherine moaned softly as her jaw trembled.

(*Oh my God! I forgot all about Katherine!*) "Katherine! Are you okay?"

Katherine moaned again. "Ohhhh... The pain...! That... was... fucking... delicious...!" And Katherine tried to get up but her arms were weak and her legs were shaking. She could hardly move as she crawled over the trunk into her bed. Jennifer tried to help her up but she too, was as weak as a newborn kitten. Katherine got into bed finally and turned to Jennifer and motioned her get in the bed. "Come to mommy!" Jennifer smiled and got into bed with Katherine and nuzzled into her breasts. Katherine held her close as she took the blankets and tucked the both of them in. Jennifer began to suck Katherine's nipple. Katherine began to suck her thumb and they both fell fast asleep.

The Tortured Soul Trilogy
(The Confessions of Jennifer X)
Chapter 100
(Me and Mrs. Jones)

Jennifer woke up the next morning to the smell of pancakes and sausages and eggs. She was still in Katherine's arms and she turned to see Nicholas standing there holding a TV tray with breakfast and set it on the end table on Katherine's side of the bed.

"Good morning ladies…"

Jennifer grabbed the covers and covered herself up. "What are you doing here?"

"Good morning Nicky." Katherine said. And Nick kissed Katherine, pulled down her covers and kissed her nipples. Katherine cooed.

"What are you doing here?" Jenny repeated.

"And good morning to you too…!" And Nick came around and kissed Jenny on the forehead. "It's obvious you're *not* a morning person…!" Jenny pulled the covers tighter over her. "Relax… I just came over to take Katherine to breakfast, but you two were sleeping so peacefully, I decided not to wake you and serve you breakfast in bed instead… French toast?"

Jenny nodded and ran her fingers through her tussled hair. Nick fixed a plate of French toast and sausages and put two strawberries on top.

"Eggs?"

"No thank you…" And he handed the plate to her. Jennifer sat up and held the blanket close and took the plate from Nick. "Thank you…" He then fixed a plate for Katherine they way he knew she liked it and handed it to her.

"You want butter or syrup on that…?"

"Are we still talking about breakfast?" Katherine asked.

"Behave yourself… from the look of you two, you had enough fun for one day. By the way, how was she…?"

Katherine kissed Jennifer on the corner of her lips. "She was fucking fantastic!"

"Told you...!" Nick said. And Katherine bit into a strawberry and began to eat her breakfast. Jenny looked around the room. She couldn't believe how nonchalant they both were about all this. She was very concerned about Nick seeing her this way. She was so embarrassed to be caught in bed with Katherine. Especially after the night she just had.

"I have... to go..." Jenny said. But Jennifer didn't get up; she hoped that Nick would leave to give her some privacy so she could get dressed. Nick sat down on the edge of the bed.

"Don't go on my account... stay... I was going to take Katherine to the movies this afternoon... you're welcome to come along if you like..."

"Yes Jennifer... come with us... to the movie... and then cum with us tonight..."

"I'm up for it if you are..." Nick said.

"Okay!" Jennifer blurted out. She couldn't believe she just accepted an invitation to a ménage a trios. Even *she* wasn't that sexually liberated. "But... I don't have a change of clothes..."

Katherine looked at her. "I have a skirt you can borrow I think will fit you..." She pulled the covers down off Jenny so Nick could see her breasts. Jenny didn't struggle. Then she squeezed Jennifer's breasts and pinched her nipples so very tenderly. "But I don't have anything to cover these up with... is that a problem?" Jennifer cooed and moaned. It excited her to be fondled in front of Nick. She wasn't as embarrassed any more.

"I can wear the blouse I wore yesterday..." Jenny said, trying to make it seem every thing was normal and she was okay with what was happening, but she was very confused.

"So... it's a date... I'll leave you ladies... to finish your 'breakfast'..." And he turned to leave.

"Nicky...?"

"Yes Katherine?"

"Could you bring us the syrup you promised...?"

"As you wish..." Nick left and returned with the syrup bottle and left again. Jennifer took her plate and reached for the bottle in Katherine's hand.

"Silly girl... did you really think I was going to waste this on French toast...?"

Jennifer's eyes widened. She couldn't think of how to reply to that. "Won't that ruin the sheets...?"

Katherine smiled. "You let *me* worry about that...!" Katherine pulled the sheets off Jennifer and poured dollup of syrup on her nipples and licked it off. Then she poured a line of syrup in between her breasts to her navel. Jennifer shivered at the feeling of the cold syrup until Katherine began to lick her way down her body. And then Katherine took the squeeze bottle and disappeared under the blanket. Jennifer threw her head back and grabbed the headboard behind her. No one had gone down on her like that since Michael...

"Ohhh mmm mmm mmm my G... g... g... g... gaahhh!" Jennifer moaned.

Nick went back into the bedroom about an hour later, looking at his watch. The two of them were in the sixty-nine position perpendicular to the bed going at it like there was no tomorrow. "Are you two *still* at it?" Neither one stopped to answer him. "Sorry... you shouldn't talk with your mouth full... I get it..."

And he turned to leave. Katherine spoke while breathing heavy. "Wait... I have an idea..." Nick smiled. He really liked it when Katherine had an idea. "Come here please Nick..." Nick complied and came over to where Katherine's face was. "Are you packing?" Nicky looked at her.

"Have we *just* met?" He answered sarcastically.

"Then get 'dressed' you have work to do..." Nick took out his wallet and took out his condom and unzipped his pants and he was about to open the package to put it on. "Wait a minute...!" Katherine panted. Nick paused. He wondered what as on Katherine's mind. "Jenny?" Katherine said while finger flicking Jenny.

"Uh huh?" Jennifer didn't stop licking and sucking Katherine's pussy; she was too into it right now.

"Do you have a problem with Nick riding bareback?"

"Uhh uhh!" Jenny moaned. Nick raised his eyebrow. Katherine already knew Nick had checked out that Jenny was in perfect health and fully 'protected'.

"Come here daddy..." And Nick came closer and Katherine held him by the base of his shaft and began to suck him.

After a moment or two, she guided him to enter Jennifer's hungry wet pussy. Jennifer moaned and licked Katherine's pussy with a new abandon. Katherine took turns licking and sucking Nick and guiding him into Jennifer. After ten minutes of the sex roulette Nick cried out.

"I'm gonna cum!" Katherine eased him out of Jennifer and sucked him dry. "Ahhhh haaaa!" Nick moaned. And Nick came all over Katherine's face. Katherine's vaginal muscles contracted in waves. Jenny didn't stop licking and sucking on Katherine's clit. Katherine screamed and moaned. After a moment or two Jennifer pouted.

"What's wrong Jenny?" Katherine asked.

"I wanted to play too!"

"You sound like that's a problem..." Nick said. And he positioned himself to where Jennifer's face was. And they began all over again. Because Jenny was on the bottom, Jenny 'tea bagged' Nick whenever he was in Katherine. This time Jennifer came and squealed like a banshee, Katherine made damn sure of that. They played the game for the rest of the day. They never made it to the movies. They tried different variations on a theme, using a toy in place of Nick when he needed to rest and 'reload' with the same results time and time again. They even took turns alternating straddling Nick's cock and face as he lay in the bed. They ended the game with Katherine sucking on Nick, Nick sucking on Jennifer's clit and Jennifer sucking on Katherine's. By the end of the day the three of them were knocked out on Katherine's bed. Nick in the middle, Jennifer and Katherine nuzzled into him on either side, sleeping peacefully. Nick opened his eyes and looked at each one of them and thought to himself. (Today ...ay ...ay I consider myself ...elf ...elf to be the luckiest man in the world ...orld ...orld!) And then he whispered. "You two are the horniest bitches I've ever seen..." And they both, at the same time, punched Nick in the stomach. "Oooop!" Nick groaned. And they all giggled and went back to sleep, Katherine sucking her thumb and Jennifer holding Nick's cock.

Hours later Jennifer was leaving the apartment to go home. They all had to be at work first thing in the morning. She had borrowed one of Katherine's skirts and one of Nick's shirts. At the door she kissed Nicky deeply and then kissed Katherine deeply and then whispered in her ear. "And don't think I don't know what you did, bitch!"

"What are you talking about?" Katherine asked.

"You know perfectly well what I'm talking about... You made Nick come for you *first*!"

"You noticed that did you?" And Katherine giggled; Jennifer nodded.

"Ladies... this is not a competition!"

"That's what you think!" They said in unison.

"Don't make me have to paddle both your asses!" he said. Jenny looked at Katherine and they both smiled. Jenny walked to her car and drove off.

"Nicky?"

"Yes Katherine...?"

"I don't care what you do with... or to Jenny... when I'm not around... Just please don't..."

"...Jenny or no other woman will *ever* go into the game room... That room is for you, and you only Katherine... I promise!"

Katherine kissed Nick deeply. Nick had *never* broken a promise to her. "I can't believe how much I fucking love you!" She said.

"You know... I *still* have that condom we never used!"

Katherine sighed and pinched her nipples. "And you called *me and Jenny* the horniest bitches you know..."

"Excluding me... of course!"

And Nick carried Katherine back to the bedroom. Katherine smiled and thought to herself. And I'm gonna make him cum for me last! Yay! I win!

(The Confessions of Jennifer X)

After we had established our newfound 'understanding', Nicholas and Katherine confided in me, the truth about their relationship. Oh... they were very much in love with each other, but they had an open relationship and could see anyone they wanted to, whenever they wanted. What I'm talking about is how they came *to be* lovers. Katherine was a domestic abuse victim and Nicholas came to her aide. He taught her how to take control of her life by her taking full responsibility for the amount and the quality of pain she will accept. He introduced her into the world of bondage and discipline, and Katherine took to it like fish takes to water. Having had a session with her, I allowed Nick and Katherine to involve me as well. I became their #1 pupil. I learned to like our discipline sessions at Katherine's place as much as I liked sex. We alternated sessions with one-on-one sex and threesomes at will... I'm beginning to enjoy this new level of sexual awareness. A girl can really get used to this!

The Tortured Soul Trilogy
(The Confessions of Jennifer X)
Chapter 101
(Suspicious Minds)

Jennifer received a call from Nick asking her to meet them at Katherine's house at 8pm. "Should I bring anything... *special*...?"

"No... Oh...! By the way... Are you wearing your calf high boots and a skirt today...?"

"Yes I am...!"

"Then come as you are..."

"I'll be there at 8..."

"Jennifer...?"

"Yes Nick?"

"If you're late... we're going to start without you...!"

"I *won't* be late...!" Jennifer did not want to get sloppy seconds of Nick this time if she could help it. She arrived at Katherine's at a quarter to; she knocked on the door. She heard Nick's voice call out.

"It's open!" Jennifer entered but didn't see them anywhere in the house. "We're in here!" She heard Nick call from Katherine's bedroom. She walked towards the open bedroom door.

"I'm early! I know you two didn't start..." Jennifer stopped in the bedroom doorway. "With... *out...me*...!" Katherine was naked except for some leather gloves and high heels. She was kneeled over the treasure chest, wrists tied to the bedposts and she was wearing something that looked like a latex cocoon tied around her legs but her ass was bare. She had a red ball gag in her mouth. Nick was seated facing her in one of Katherine's dining room armchairs. Katherine was crying but she had not been punished as far as I could tell. "What is this...? What's going on...?" I asked. Nick stood up and turned to Jenny. He was wearing a gray Armani suit, silk shirt and tie. He was barefoot. He was holding his folded leather belt in his right hand. He looked at Jennifer.

"Take off your skirt..."

"Why should I...?"

Nick slapped the belt on his thigh. "NOW!" Jennifer took a half step back and balled up her fist. She didn't know what to expect. "I said... NOW!" he said with authority. And he slapped his thigh with belt again. Nick had used his belt on her in the past, but this time was somehow going to be very different. Jennifer hesitated but complied and stepped out of her skirt. She would submit herself to Nick's authority. Nick took her skirt and took off his jacket and tossed them on the bed and rolled up his cuffs. His forearms were strong and thick. The veins in his arms were pronounced. The mere thought of those powerful arms taking a belt to her naked ass made her wet in anticipation. "Have a seat please..." He said calmly. Jennifer cautiously sat down. "I'm sorry if I scared you, but I don't have time to explain right now, everything will all be quite clear to you in just a few moments."

Jenny nodded. "Okay!" she said nervously and she sat down and crossed her legs.

"Please place your knees over the armrests..." Jennifer spread her legs slowly and placed the armrests under her knees. Nicholas took two leather restraints out of his pockets and secured her ankles to the chair legs. Jennifer began to pant.

"Nick...? What are you doing?" Jenny asked.

Nick then tied her wrists together behind the chair. "I need you to witness this..." He gauged the distance between Katherine's naked ass and me. "...But you're just a little *too close* right now..." Nick grabbed the back of the chair and leaned it backwards suddenly. Jenny screamed as she went back. Jenny didn't like the sense of helplessness it caused. Nick dragged the chair back on its back legs about two feet and leaned it back a little farther. Jenny was totally fearful in this position. She wanted to yell out, but Nick leaned into her and kissed her. "Trust me... nothing is going to happen to *you!*" And he sat her back up.

"What are you going to do...?" Jenny asked.

"It has been brought to my attention that Katherine is still harboring some jealousy... and she asked me to *help* her deal with it..."

"And why am I here...?"

"Visual aide..." Jenny didn't know what the hell Nick was talking about. Then Nick went over to Katherine and whipped her one time with the belt. Katherine let out a muffled yelp.

506

Jennifer's ass twitched and she got very wet. "Can you see clearly from there...?" He asked Jenny.

"Yes!" Jenny moaned.

"Good!" And Nick began to tear Katherine a new one. Jennifer immediately had a flashback to the porn shoot and the dominance scene. With every sting of the belt she became conflicted, she was getting wet and moist and horny, but she didn't want to *stop* it this time. What she really *wanted* was to take Katherine's place. She wanted Nick to beat *her* ass instead. She could tell Katherine was in complete and utter ecstasy. But she couldn't understand... how was *this* teaching Katherine a lesson about jealousy? After many, many strokes of the belt, Katherine's ass was beet red and the strap made stripes all over her buttocks. She was cooing and moaning uncontrollably. Jennifer's nipples were hard and sensitive now, just from watching and from the fabric of her bra rubbing them. Jennifer wanted so badly to masturbate right now, but her hands were still tied behind her. Nick slowly untied Katherine and placed a pillow on the trunk and sat her down on her tender ass. Katherine let out a stifled moan. He removed her gag but left her legs tied together.

"Thank you baby!" Katherine cooed.

"Don't thank me just yet..." And he pinched her nipples. Katherine moaned again, but I somehow knew... that wasn't for her benefit... it was for mine! Nick walked over to me. (Good! Now it's my turn!) "So... did you enjoy the show?" He asked me.

"I'm all wet and horny... is it my turn?"

"Yes it is...."

"Katherine?" Nick said.

"Yes... Daddy?"

"Pinch your nipples for Jennifer please...."

"Yes... daddy!" And Katherine began to stroke and rub her breasts and nipples, cooing and purring the whole time. Katherine was really getting into it now but she couldn't reach her clit because the cocoon that kept her legs tied together came up to her waist. She kinda looked like a latex mermaid. "Untie me...please..." She begged.

"No... continue to fondle your breasts please..." Katherine pouted but obeyed. Nick then stood behind me and began to fondle me over my blouse... My eyes went to the back of

507

my head. I really needed to be touched right then. My hands, although tied, could feel his erection, I worked my hands up and down on his shaft; he leaned into it. "Katherine?"

"Yes Nick?"

"Does it *bother* you that I'm touching Jennifer like this?"

"*No…!*"

"*No…?* Then I guess you won't mind *this…*" And Nick reached into my blouse with both hands and began to rub and stroke my breasts and nipples.

"Damn it Nick… I'm *already* all hot and bothered…!" I hissed.

"I'm so sorry Jennifer… allow me…" And Nick unbuttoned my blouse and unhooked my bra from the front clasp and exposed me to Katherine. Katherine sobbed but continued to fondle her nipples. She was clearly lying about this bothering her. "Please be a bit more patient with me…" He said to me. And he went back to squeezing and fondling my breasts.

"Okay…!" I moaned. "Whatever you want Nicky…" Nick then reached between my legs and down into my panties and began to finger flick my clit. He then reached deep inside me, wet his finger and stuck it inside my mouth. I licked and sucked his finger and he squeezed and pinched my nipples with his other hand. He then went back to rubbing and stroking my clit and labia. I closed my eyes as Nick stroked me almost to the point of orgasm. I opened my eyes and I peeked in Katherine's direction. She was very distraught and upset. (Oh…! This bitch is *jealous*… of… *ME…!*) *That's* when I put on a show for *her*. This bitch was gonna get her full money's worth! I began to moan and coo with every stroke of Nick's strong hands. He continued to knead and massage my breasts and nipples. It felt soooo good! I only wish he could get his hands on my ass. I leaned my head back and Nick kissed me. I leaned forwards to watch him fondle my nipples. "Pinch them… pinch them hard…!" He reached into his pocket and pulled out a pair of alligator clips that were attached by a chain. He clipped one on each of my nipples and then he gently pulled on the chain. It felt like electricity went through my body straight to my clit and I screamed. "Oh Nick eeee!" I thought of L.L. and her seven gold chains she wore on stage. I imagined how they came into play in her bedroom.

I couldn't see what Nick was doing but seemed like he had pulled a step stool behind my chair. (What is he doing now?) He placed his left hand on my chin and stuck his thumb in my mouth. I began to suck his thumb and every once in a while he would tug the chain. The shock went through my body. I closed my eyes and then I felt something heavy on my shoulder and Nick pulled his thumb out of my mouth. When I turned my head to the right, Nick had stepped onto the stool and his hard and throbbing cock was now on my right shoulder. I looked dead into Katherine's eyes and kept my eyes focused on her as I stuck my tongue out and tickled the tip of his dick with the tip of my tongue. Katherine began to rock back and forth... I realized she would give anything to be where I was right now... I had something she wanted... very badly! And that got me horny as all hell! I began to lick the head of his cock, kiss the rim around it and nibble and lick the shaft. Never once did I take my eyes of Katherine. Katherine was so very frustrated at this point.

"You *bitch*!" She screamed at me.

(Oh *yeah*...? Really now? Oh... *I'm just getting started*!) I opened my mouth wide and began to suck Nick's cock with a new purpose in life. I wanted this bitch to have a front row seat of him cumming all over me! Damn that Nick and his stamina! I was blowing him like there was no tomorrow and after a while I didn't want to waste it. I wanted him in me... now! All of a sudden, Katherine, who was so upset moments ago about what was happening; became my personal cheering section. She started to moan and pant and egg me on! Well all right then! I *guess* she got over whatever jealousy issues she had! After ten minutes or more of sucking Nick's cock, I disengaged myself. "Nicky...?" I panted.

"Yes Jennifer?"

"I want to cum... *please*?"

"Your wish is my command..." He turned to Katherine. "Katherine?" He said.

"Yes daddy?"

"Crawl your ass over here and eat Jennifer out until she cums..."

"Yes daddy...!" And Katherine got down on all fours and shimmied like an inchworm towards me. She raised herself up by putting her hands on my knees. "May I untie myself now?"

Nick knew she desperately wanted to finger her clit while she went down on me. "No... this is all about *Jennifer* and *her* needs!" Katherine nodded and was about to bury her head between my spread legs when Nick stopped her.

"Oh... I almost forgot... let's get these out of the way!" And he reached between my legs and tore off my panties. I sighed and moaned at the wedgie it gave me.

"Now... you can begin...!" And Katherine buried her face between my legs. I rotated my hips forward so she could have better access. She licked my clit with wild abandon. Every once in a while she would finger fuck me with her glove on. It was a little rough but I liked it; and then went back to sucking and licking my swollen clit. She reached up and began to tug on the chains still attached to my nipples. At one point a clip popped off. The sudden shock made me cry out and my jaw trembled, it felt so good! Nick placed the clip back on my nipple and put his cock back in my mouth. I had the best of both worlds and I came like I had never cum before; and not once during all that time, did I feel like I was being used. I felt as if all this was to focus attention on me. I like that!

Afterwards, we all took a shower together. Even in the shower they both focused on washing and bathing me. I got so horny that Nick entered me from behind while Katherine washed and fondled me. I never felt so... special, so... adored. When we got out of the shower, Katherine did my hair while Nick gave me a manicure and pedicure! I have never felt the way I felt then, and I've had top-of-the-line spa treatments! After they were finished pampering me, I got dressed. On my way out, I stopped and asked Katherine. "So...? Are we 'cool' now...?" Katherine kissed me deeply and acted as if she wanted to go down on me again... Yeah...! We were cool. I turned to Nick. "And you...!"

"Yes Jennifer...?" Nick asked.

"You owe me $35 for the panties you ripped!"

"Can we take it out in trade?"

I looked at Katherine and she nodded approval. "We'll talk..." and I kissed Nicky and I left.

After Jennifer drove off, Nick turned to Katherine. "I hope we never have to do that ever again, young lady!"

"Oh... *let's*...! Do... *that*... again...!"

Nick shook his head. "Okay... but if it's okay with Jennifer... we'll tie you to the chair... next time...!"

"Or... maybe you...!" Katherine replied

Nick smiled. "We'll see...!"

The Tortured Soul Trilogy
(The Confessions of Jennifer X)
Chapter 102
(Tonight, Tonight, Tonight)

Katherine took Nick out to dinner for his birthday and they had a great time... except for the part when all the waiters came out and sang '*For He's a Jolly Good Fellow*!' while bringing out a custom birthday cake that was shaped like a mountain with a sign that read '*Over the Hill*'.

"Happy birthday baby!" Katherine cooed.

"Thank you Katherine..."

"I love you Nick!"

"I love you too Katherine..." And they kissed passionately.

"Damn!" A waiter whispered to the waitress. "I thought she was his daughter...!"

"I know I don't kiss *my* daddy like that!" she whispered.

"I don't think you kiss *anybody* like that!" He replied.

"We can *hear* you!" The wait staff cleared out quickly and left them kissing each other softly. "What do you say we... take this cake home... and 'eat it'...?" Nick said seductively.

"Hmmmmmm! I like to sound of that... but I have a surprise gift for you at home I *think* you're gonna like better..."

"Better than cake...?"

"Much... better... than cake!"

"So... why are we... still here?" They had the staff wrap the cake up and left to go to Nick's place. When they arrived there was nothing special there. "So... where's my 'surprise'...?"

Suddenly Katherine's voice became very serious. "Go into your bedroom and take off all your clothes..."

Nick turned to her and looked into her eyes. He knew that look and the tone of her voice. She was going to be 'in charge' of *this* session. "Yes madam!" Nick walked towards his bedroom while loosening his tie and removing his jacket. He entered the bedroom and saw that there were leather restraints already on each post of his bed. He hesitated. Katherine reached up between his legs from behind him and fondled his balls.

"I said... take your clothes off!"

Nick moaned from the pressure she exurted. "Yes Madam..." Nick got undressed and stood there.

"Lie down on the bed face up please..." Nick got on the bed and Katherine began to tie him to the four posts. She then propped a pillow under his head. She went over and stood at the doorway. "Can you see me clearly?"

"Yes Madam...."

"Are you comfortable?"

"Yes... madam..."

"Well... you won't be... for long..." And then Katherine... left! Nick lay there, helpless and without a clue what Katherine had planned for him. Katherine was the only woman Nick could trust enough to put him in this 'predicament' but he was still... concerned. Beads of sweat started to form on his brow as he waited. After what seemed like forever, the bedroom door opened and Katherine stood in the doorway. She was wearing a fedora and a trench coat. She was wearing her plain dark rimmed glasses. Nick smiled. He knew this was going to be good. She slowly stepped into the room and paused. He heard footsteps behind her and in walked... Jennifer! She too was wearing a trench coat and a fedora, but she had a pair of huge D&G sunglasses on. Nick laughed.

"You two look like spies..." That's when Nick noticed a stainless steel briefcase in Jennifer's hand. He immediately recognized it. It was his 'muscle zapper', a device that stimulated muscle growth with electronic pulses. He had used the device on Katherine before. Now... it looked as if it was *his* turn...!

"You have been keeping... something we want from us... Nicholas!" Katherine growled.

Nick looked at them and immediately got into character. He did his best Sean Connery impersonation. "You won't get any information out of me... ladies!"

"Porque usted crees, que nosotros quieremos... informacion?" Jenny said as she put the briefcase down.

Nick never heard Jenny speak Spanish before. "Si no quieren informacion, que ustedes buscan de mi?" Nick replied still using Connery's accent. Jennifer immediately became all hot and

513

bothered and panted heavily. She didn't know Nick spoke Spanish. It was just another turn on for her.

"You know what we want..." Katherine cooed.

Nick smiled and stayed in character. "Even tied up as I am... I can still take the two of you on..."

"Yes... we know..." Katherine said. "Which is *why*... we brought some help..." Nick looked at the briefcase; Katherine and Jennifer shook their heads no. Nick was confused, what had they planned for him? "Svetlana!" Katherine called out.

Nick's eyes opened wide. "What?" he said out of character, and in walked... Lisa!

Lisa was their co-worker, a hot Russian 'Amazon' minx. Lisa had pursued Nick in the past, but Nick would only fantasize about her as a Russian Bond girl named 'Svetlana'... He wouldn't go after her because she was married... *until* recently. Lisa had E-mailed Nick X-rated pictures of her but Nick never followed up on it... he was kinda 'tied-up'... Only Katherine knew about his fantasy and she already had developed a 'special relationship' with Lisa, so it wasn't difficult at all for her to set this all up for him. 'Svetlana' sauntered in wearing a leather cat suit that looked as if it was spray painted on. As she walked past Jenny and Katherine, they dropped their coats. They too, were wearing tight leather cat suits. The three of them walked over to the bed. Katherine was on his left, Jenny on his right and 'Svetlana' at the foot of the bed. As they climbed up on the bed, the last thing Nick remembers is hearing them say. "Happy Birthday Nicky!"

Nick woke up the next morning. There were parts of leather cat suits strewn all over the room. Katherine was asleep to his right, sucking her thumb. Jenny to his left snuggled on his chest, and 'Svetlana'...? Well, she was kneeled up on the bed sucking and licking Nick' cock like there was no tomorrow.

"Well good morning to you too... Lisa!"

Jenny woke up next. "Girl! Are you at it *again*? Damn!"

Katherine woke up and looked at Jenny and then at Lisa. "Uh uhh! This bitch has *got* to go!"

"Yeah...!" Jennifer chimed in. Lisa reached up and started to fondle Jenny and Katherine's clits with her thumbs while still sucking on Nick. They both eased their legs open and she finger fucked their pussies as she continued to go down on Nick. Jenny's jaw trembled and Katherine moaned.

"Ohhh! But let her... finish... first!" Katherine moaned. Jenny agreed. Nick closed his eyes and took a deep breath. "I don't have a problem with that..." he said.

It took a while but they all eventually had some of Nick's birthday cake. Nick was making coffee while the girls had cake in the living room.

"How the hell does he do it?" Jenny asked.

"He must be taking something..." Lisa exclaimed.

"Nope!" Katherine interrupted "... He doesn't do drugs..."

Lisa shook her head but Jenny nodded in agreement. "But... *how*...does he...?" Lisa asked.

Katherine motioned them to come closer. They all leaned in. "I'm gonna let you in on a secret... don't you dare tell him I told you...!" Jenny and Lisa nodded. "I'm *serious*! Not a fucking word out of either of you!"

"Tell us..."

"Yeah bitch... dish! How does he do it?" Jenny said.

Katherine looked to see if Nick was in earshot. They leaned in closer in to her. "Nick... *lasts* longer... if he's... fully 'dressed'...!"

"Really...?" Lisa said.

"Of course!" Jenny said. "That's why the first we had sex he couldn't cum..."

"Until you gave him head... you had to take the condom off him first..." Katherine said. They all leaned back and smiled at each other. "Remember... not a word..."

"Trust me..." Lisa said. "That is something I will definitely keep... 'under wraps'..."

They all laughed until Katherine interrupted them. "Ah...! You two bitches do *know*... that's *my* man... *right*...? You two are only 'visiting'..." Jenny and Lisa both turned away from Katherine and each other and continued to eat their cake. "Oh *hell* no!" Katherine said. Jenny and Lisa laughed. Nick entered with the coffee.

"You ladies behaving yourselves?"

"Yes Nicky..." They harmonized.

Author's Note

I was extremely conflicted about including the following chapter: 'Queen of Hearts'. It shows a side of Nicholas Anderson that most people will not find 'appealing'. I struggled and pondered for many weeks over it while I was editing this book before I made my decision.

Some will condone what Nick felt he 'had' to do. Some will condemn him. Many will feel that the situation could have been handed differently. Although I could 'sugarcoat' it... it's not my place to make any of this easier for anyone to deal with.

Nick is only a human being... not a superhero, he is subject to the same trappings as the rest of us. He laughs, he cries, he makes mistakes...

I finally decided that I was not writing a tribute to Nick. This is what happened, when it happened, how it happened and whether you or I like it or not... It is what it is...Jennifer and Katherine dealt with it, got over it.

I suggest... you do the same.

The Tortured Soul Trilogy
(The Confessions of Jennifer X)
Chapter 103
(Queen of Hearts)

Nick came home from shopping one Saturday afternoon to find Katherine sitting his living room, drinking a glass of wine. She had a strange look on her face. "Hey Katherine...! To what do I owe the pleasure...?

Katherine sat there; she was shivering. "Hi baby..." she said.

Nick immediately knew that something wasn't right. He put his bags down. "Katherine...? What's wrong...? I don't like the way you look... are you okay...?"

"I'm okay Nicky..." She reached for the bottle of wine on the coffee table but her hands were shaking so badly, she could barely refresh her drink. Nick took the bottle out of her hand and poured her a glass. She could barely raise it to her lips.

"Baby, something *is* wrong... Talk to me..." Nick asked with a concerned look on his face. Katherine tried to take a sip but she hit her teeth with the glass. Now Nick was really worried. He took the glass from her hand, went into the kitchen and got a drinking straw and put it in the glass. Katherine smiled. Nick handed her back the glass.

"Thank you baby!" She stammered.

Katherine was able to sip the wine without hurting herself. "Kitten... talk to me... what's going on...? You know I'll do anything for you... just talk to me..." Katherine began to shiver. Tears started to well in Nick's eyes. "Baby... please... talk to me... please...!"

"It's okay Nicky... it's nothing bad... I just can't believe I'm going to say this..." Nick was now very scared. He had no idea what Katherine was about to say. Katherine had totally freaked out during a rough session once, but this was different, very different. "Nick... I feel so silly... I... I..."

"Baby... *What*...?

Katherine paused and laughed nervously. "Nicky..." She paused. She couldn't look Nick in the eyes.

"Damn it Katherine...! WHAT?" Nick couldn't take it anymore.

Katherine cowered and started to cry. "I'm sorry... Nicky..."

"*What* did you *do* Katherine...?"

"Re... remember... when I made you promise never to let Jenny into the 'game room'...?" she sobbed.

"Yes..." Katherine started crying again. Nick turned to the door of the game room... it was ajar.

"*Katherine*! What did you *do*...?" He slowly walked towards the door and pushed it all the way open. He looked in. Jennifer was naked, tied to the portal of pain. Katherine walked up behind him and desperately hugged Nick from behind.

"I'm sorry... I know I made you promise never to bring anyone into the game room... but I just had to... Nicky... I'm sorry... please forgive me...!" She sobbed.

"No forgiveness is necessary..."

"*What*...?" Katherine looked at him with caution.

"You made *me* promise *never* to bring anyone into this room... I never made *you* make that promise..." Nick said quietly.

"You're okay... with this...?"

Nick grabbed Katherine's wrist roughly. "I'm okay with this... but that doesn't *mean* you're not going to be... punished!" Nick said sternly.

"Why? You *said* you never made me promise...!"

"I shouldn't have had to..." Nick said quietly. Katherine's eyes got wide as Nick dragged her to the portal. Nick dragged Katherine over the portal and released her.

"Nicky... what are you going to do?" Katherine was very afraid now. She had previously overstepped her bounds with Nick in regards to Jennifer and he almost left her. He had warned her that there was a line that he would not cross. He warned her that if she crossed that line, he would sever their relationship... forever! "Nicky... Please!" Katherine sobbed.

"Take off all your clothes..." He said plainly.

"Yes... daddy!" Katherine began to cry as she got undressed. She knew that this punishment was going to be severe. It was *not* going to be pleasurable at all. Nick went over to Jennifer on the wheel.

"Jennifer...? Are you okay...? Did she 'hurt' you...?" Jennifer slowly opened her eyes and licked her lips.

"Not in any way... I didn't like..." Nick kissed her and reached up to untie Jennifer's hands. "No... don't..." She whispered. Nick stopped. "This is as much my fault as it is Katherine's... We were waiting for you to come home... for a booty call... we started... talking... about this room... The things you two did in here... I became... intrigued... The next thing we knew..."

"I understand... but that doesn't excuse your behavior...!"

Jennifer cried. "I'm sorry... *daddy*!" Being called daddy by Jennifer almost softened his heart... but... lines had been crossed. Something had to done about it. Nick reached down by Jennifer's ankles and she heard a loud click. He then reached above her wrists and heard another loud click. Nick had released the wheel and it was able to spin freely. Nick spun Jenny slowly until she was upside-down. Nick fingered Jenny's clit and labia and finger fucked her. He then licked his finger and looked at Katherine.

"Come here please..."

"Yes daddy..." She sobbed and she walked over to Nick.

"Face Jennifer and place your hands at the top please..." Katherine complied and Nick tied her wrists to the portal and then her ankles. The two of them were now in a 69 position but the two parallel wheels kept them at least 12" apart from each other. They each had a perfect view... but no access. Nick then flipped the wheel horizontally with Jenny on the bottom, facing up. "Jennifer...?"

"Yes daddy...?"

"I'll be with you... in just a few moments... can you be patient?"

Jenny sobbed. "Yes daddy..." Nick took a red ball gag and gagged Katherine and got out a cat-o-nine tails and began to beat Katherine. Jennifer cried and screamed for him to stop it. This was not something that either one wanted...

"I thought I told you... to be... patient..." Nick then flipped the wheel to place Jenny on top, gagged Jenny with another gag, and started in on her. After he was finished, all three of them were exhausted and covered with perspiration. Nick then got a condom and got 'dressed'. Nick took turns fucking Jennifer and then Katherine. Just when one of them was about to cum, he would pull out, flip the wheel and start on the other. Each had to watch the other get all of Nick without any of the rewards. Nick was not, I repeat, *not*, enjoying any of this... Eventually, Nick could not maintain his erection. Tough love sucks! Nick flipped the wheel vertically and released Jennifer first and flipped Katherine upright and then released her. Both were crying and sobbing but not in the 'good' way. "The two of you... get dressed... and get out!" They both nodded. Jennifer was more angry than upset than Katherine was. Nick sensed it. "Do you... have a... *problem*...? Jennifer...?" Jennifer stared at Nick. Nick stared back. "Well...? *Do you*...?" he demanded.

Jennifer averted her eyes. "No..."

"No... *what*...?"

"No... daddy..."

"Then get dressed... and get the *fuck out*!" He whispered. They both got dressed but they waited at the front door for Nick to come out. Katherine had put Nick's groceries away. Nick came out of the bathroom after he finished masturbating. "You two still here...? *What*?"

There was a pause... Jenny spoke. "When can we come see you again... daddy...?"

Katherine nodded. "Yes... daddy... when...?"

Nick shook his head no. "Get out..." He whispered and went back to his bedroom.

Katherine leaned into Jennifer and cried. Jenny hugged her and tears welled into her eyes as well. The tears were not from the pain they just received, but from the pain they had given... to Nick. "Let's go... give him time... He'll call us... when he's ready..." Jenny said. Jenny closed the door behind them as they left. Nick started to cry. He really hated himself right then. It was at least a month before he was able to call Jennifer. Katherine was more difficult for him, they worked in the same office and she was his boss. Katherine gave Nick his space. She waited patiently for him to forgive her. Nick called them to take them out to dinner and dancing about two weeks later. They never left his house. They all spent the night crying and apologizing to each other. They all slept in Nick's bed. They just held each other and cuddled; there was no sex or any 'sessions' that night. They all promised this would *never* happen again. They all continued their relationship from where it had left off. No one ever talked about that day and Katherine never allowed anyone else in that room ever again. Jennifer would from now on, respect Nick's space and so would Katherine.

The Tortured Soul Trilogy
(Living La Vida Puta)
Chapter 104
(Testing, Testing, 1, 2, 3)

Three months later, L.L. was pacing up and down in her bedroom. She kept looking at her watch. "Damn it! How long does this shit take?" Five minutes later, she checked again. It was the third time she took the test... there was no doubt in her mind now. She held up her hand and looked at the one and a half carat engagement ring Cisco gave her and she picked up the phone and called him. "Baby...? I think we're going to have to move our wedding date up...!"

"I don't mind... but why?"

"You're going to be a father..." Cisco shouted for joy. "You son of a bitch!" L.L. whispered.

"I love you baby!"

"I love you too..." and she paused. "I better get my tight body back after this or you are in a world of trouble!" Cisco laughed. There was no way L.L. was going to get married without having Jennifer being her maid of honor. They got the car packed and drove out to see her.

"Does she know we're coming?" Cisco asked.

"I tried to call her on her cell but I got her voice mail... I'm pretty sure she'll be home, if not we'll do a little shopping or some sightseeing until she gets home..."

Cisco called Jinx, and he said he had the day off so there was a good chance she was home. L.L. and Cisco arrived at Jenny's house about two hours later and her car was still in the driveway. Cisco and Jinx used to work together but when Jinx started to date Jenny's personal secretary, she took him on as a driver and bodyguard so those two could be close to each other. Jenny was cool like that. She would make an excellent maid of honor.

Nick was at Jennifer's house in the middle of a session. Nick was kneeled over Jennifer's naked body and they were experimenting with asphyxiation. Jenny had developed a yearning for dangerous sex. They had purchased a pressure mask from the Warehouse and Nick was pumping it up and checking her vitals very carefully. Nick didn't like doing this and he knew that one wrong move could cause brain damage or death from a lack of oxygen. Nick held Jennifer's pocketknife open in his hand just in case he had to cut the bag open in a hurry. The session wasn't having the desired effect. Jenny wasn't experiencing the feeling of 'dread' she wanted, maybe she trusted Nicky too much. It was only making her dizzy and *not* in a good way. Nonetheless, Jennifer was very disappointed and wanted to stop; Nick was very relieved, besides he didn't like to use masks or anything that dehumanized his companions. They would not be adding this to their repertoire. He took the bag off her head and tossed it away. "Any other ideas Jenny...?"

Jenny pouted and thought for a moment. "Okay... How about you just tie me face down and you just monkey fuck me?"

"That's doable!" Nicholas went into her dresser and got her leather restraints out and Jenny rolled over and got into position. Nick then tied her wrists and then her ankles to the bedposts.

"Before you we start... how about one of your famous massages I heard so much about?"

"You got it!" Nick couldn't believe that he and Jenny had sex but he never gave her a massage before. "Where do you keep your moisturizer?"

"Top drawer..."

Nick opened the drawer and found six new bottles of KY personal lubricant. "What's with all this?" Jenny turned to look and began to laugh. "Oh... you've been talking with Katherine I see...!" Nick said.

"She said I should 'stock up' just in case..." She laughed.

Nick placed a bottle on the nightstand beside her. Jennifer's eyes widened. He also put her knife down next to it. He then took out the bottle of moisturizer. "Well it's always good to be 'prepared'..." He took a squirt of moisturizer rubbed it into the palms of his hands and began a deep tissue massage. Jennifer moaned and cooed with every rub.

"Damn! That's good... real *nice*... you ever think of charging for your massages?"

"There's a name for men who charge to give women pleasure..."

Jennifer laughed and moaned again. "Do my lower back." Nick worked down and kneaded and rubbed her lower back. Jennifer moaned again. "Lower!" she giggled. Nick started to knead and mold Jennifer's ass. "Ohhhhh! My! Ahhhhh! Yeah baby! That's the spot!" Nick then worked his way down her long lean legs and thighs paying special attention to her muscular calves. Jenny moaned and purred and cooed. "Damn that's *good*! So *good*!"

Then Nick took hold of one foot. "Did I ever tell you, you have the body of a stripper?"

Jennifer jumped, surely Nick didn't know! "Don't do that! My feet are ticklish!" She said to cover. Nick rubbed her arches and worked her toes. "Never mind!" She said. And Jennifer settled back into the massage. "You keep that up and I'm gonna fall asleep...!"

"Oh... I have better way to put you to sleep..."

"Oh yeah?"

"Definitely!" And Nick worked his way back up to her buttocks and rubbed them again. Jennifer had a marvelous ass and if you didn't know it yet, Nick was an ass man. The massage started Jennifer up all over again.

"You missed a spot!" she cooed.

"Where?"

Jennifer wiggled her ass. "Under!"

"Yes ma'am!" And Nick got some more oil and began to rub the inside of the thighs nearest her pussy. Jennifer was already very moist and wet and ready.

"Ohhhh! Ho! That's nice... real nice... I *like* that!"

"If you like *that*... you're gonna *love* this!" And Nick spread her labia with his thumbs and rubbed them. Jenny threw her head back and moaned. Nick took two fingers, spread her labia again and stroked her clit with his finger. Jennifer began screaming

524

into her pillow. He stuck his face in her ass and started to lick her pussy. Nick's rough beard felt good on her thighs. He kneeled up and lay on her, he was about to enter her.

"Wait!" Jenny said. Nick hesitated. "Suit up first...!" Nick didn't understand why he needed to. He had ridden her bareback before, but if she requested it, he would honor her. Jenny wanted this one to last a long, long time. Nick got up and got 'dressed' and then eased up on top of her again. "Nick...?"

"Yes Jenny?"

"Could you..." She paused.

"What...?"

"Could you... hold the knife to my throat... please...?"

"You *want* me to...?"

Jennifer began to pant heavy. "Yes!!!" If Jennifer wanted a rape/abduction fantasy Nick would deliver. Nick reached over and picked up the knife. He got back on top of her and held the knife, blunt edge, to her throat and entered her slowly and began to pump her pussy to his hearts content. He pulled her head back by her hair so he could keep his eye on the knife. Even the blunt edge could do damage if you don't pay attention. She felt the cold steel on her throat and gasped in excitement. She could now experience the dread and fear of death... safely. She reared up and he began to bang away. Nick had learned how to change the rhythm of his stroke to Jennifer's delight. He would switch from fast and hard, to slow and deep. This went on for about fifteen minutes. Jennifer's vagina began to involuntarily contract in waves. Nick pumped her ass harder and faster. Nick reared up and placed his hands on either side of the bed near Jenny's waist. He used his forearms to control her hips and lock her down. He may have to use the lubricant today after all! Jenny screamed. "Aye Papi...! Da me...! Dame duro!" Nick pumped her pussy in ernest; Jennifer let out a primal scream.

As Cisco opened the car door for L.L. he heard a scream come from the house. It was Jenny. He handed L.L. his gun. "Baby... there's static... take my gun and watch my back. I'm gonna check it out!"

L.L. cocked the gun. "I got you baby... please be careful!"

Nick placed the knife under Jenny's throat and pulled her head back by her hair again. "Venga puta cabrona! Give up that pussy! Damelo! Dame la crika tuya" Nick knew that's what Jenny wanted to hear. Jennifer's body quivered and she screamed out loud. That's when Nick caught a glimpse of a Peeping Tom just outside Jenny's window. Cisco had quietly made his way to the back of the house and didn't like what he saw in her bedroom window. A moment later he ran towards the front door. He motioned to L.L. to keep her eyes on him. L.L. ran up behind him, gun at the ready.

"Baby? What?"

"Static! Some guy has Jenny naked on her bed and he has a knife to her throat!" Cisco whispered.

"Oh my god! *Jenny*!" L.L. exclaimed.

"Shhhh! I'm going to pop open the front door... just stay behind me in case I get into any trouble..."

"Shouldn't we call the cops?"

"No time... Jenny is in trouble now!"

L.L. nodded and Cisco broke the side window panel to open the front door. That didn't work because Jenny had a lock that needed a key from the inside. Cisco rammed the door with his shoulder and it popped open. He carefully entered the house. He did not want to startle the intruder and have him hurt Jennifer. Cisco didn't know the layout of Jenny's house but he knew her bedroom was in the back to the right. He worked his way back and L.L. followed slightly behind him. Nick heard her front door get kicked in. He jumped up off Jenny and stood by the bedroom door. "Not a fucking sound out of you!" He whispered. Jenny didn't know what was going on, she hadn't heard a thing between her screams and burying her face in the pillow. Nick stood near her bedroom door and listened. Someone was in the house. Jenny now heard it too.

"*Untie me!*" She screamed.

"I told you to keep quiet!" Nick barked.

As Cisco made his way back, he heard the intruder bark at Jenny to keep quiet. He knew he had to get to her quickly. He got to the bedroom door that was slightly ajar. He peeked through the door crack and could barely see that Jenny was still face down on the bed. She was moving so she was okay, but the guy wasn't on top of her anymore. Cisco was going to burst in and see if he could take this guy by surprise. He pushed the door open but the guy was

526

behind the door, he twirled his arm under Cisco's, grabbed him by the back of his head and had the knife to his throat in an instant. He leaned Cisco back to stop him from squirming. This guy definitely had military or martial arts training.

"And who the fuck are you?" Nick asked him.

Before he could answer, Nick felt cold steel on the back of his head and heard a gun hammer click. He then heard a woman's voice. "The question is... '*Who the fuck are you*'...?"

Nick tightened his grip and held the knife tighter against the man's throat. It was a *Mexican standoff*. He had this guy and this woman had Nick. But Nick was at a huge disadvantage; Jennifer was still tied to the bed. L.L. felt the same way. She had this guy but he had Cisco and there was still Jennifer to think of. L.L. didn't know what to do and the longer she waited, the more intense the situation became. L.L. could not live with herself if anything happened to Cisco. She thought of her unborn baby.

After what felt like an eternity, Jennifer spoke. "What *the fuck* is going on?"

"A bitch has got a bitch's back... Jennifer! Are you alright?" The woman said.

"L.L....? Is that you?"

"Yeah bitch! I'm about to blow this rapist away... cover up your ears girl!"

"NO! No! noooo! Don't shoot Nick! L.L. he's a friend! Don't you dare shoot him...!"

"A *friend*...? The way you were screaming...? Oh! *Ohh*...? My bad! I had no idea!"

"Hey pal... you wanna ease off with the knife now?"

"Cisco...? Is that you?"

"Yeah Mami! It's me... Can you get your *friend* to back the fuck off?"

"Nick! Stop! Let Cisco go!"

"Just as soon as your girlfriend pulls back the hammer on the gun!"

"Sorry!" L.L. pulled the gun away from Nick's head.

"It's cool... the safety was still on..."

Nick looked at her gun. "No... it's not!"

"You sure?"

"Yes!"

L.L. looked at it. "No... this is on; and this is... oh! Oh well... no harm done..."

"*Hello...?* Still have a knife to my throat here!" Nick eased off on Cisco. Cisco looked over at Jenny. "You okay?"

"Turn around... don't look at her!" Nick said to him.

"It's okay Nick... Cisco's seen me naked before." Jenny said.

"That's right!" and Cisco adjusted his jacket.

"Cisco?"

"Yeah Jenny...?"

"Get out!" Cisco exited the room.

L.L. turned her attention to Jenny. "So? What? Are you so frozen in fear you can't get up and say hi to an old... *Oh!* I didn't... see the... *leather*... restraints..." L.L. said.

"Do you *mind*? Can we have some privacy here?" Nick demanded.

"Look... I don't care if you are a friend of Jenny's..." And L.L. looked down. "Daaammmmn! No wonder the bitch was screaming...! And *why* you had to tie her ass down...!"

"L.L. *out!*" Jenny said. And L.L. left; but not before singing; "*My bologna has a first name...*"

"Out!" Jennifer said.

"What did you say L.L.?" Cisco asked as L.L. entered the room.

"Nothing Cisco... Let's let them get dressed..." L.L. took one last look. "Damn! Just... *damn!*" and she closed the door behind her.

The Tortured Soul Trilogy
(The Confessions of Jennifer X)
Chapter 105
(I Aint No Holla Back Girl)

Nick and Jenny came out fully dressed about ten minutes later.

"What are you two doing here?" Jenny asked them.

"What? Bitch! We can't stop by and make a surprise visit to an old friend?"

Jenny tilted her head in Nick's direction. "*Duh*...! NO!"

"*Excuse Me*! How was I *supposed* to know you were getting your freak on?"

"It's called a... *telephone*...!"

"So, how do you know Jenny...? I mean besides..." Cisco asked Nick while pumping his fist.

"We're business associates..." Nick curtly replied. He didn't like Cisco and the way he referred to their relationship. "And how do *you* know her...? That you've seen her *naked* before?" Nick asked.

"We're... *business associates* too..."

Jenny interrupted them. "Actually... I'm Nick's *boss*... And I *believe* Nick was just *leaving*...?" She needed to cut this conversation quickly. She did not want Nick to know too much about her past or present dealings. Nick bowed; he knew he was intruding on the intrusion. He reached for the busted front door knob.

"You sure you don't want me to come back and fix your door for you?"

"No... Cisco broke it; he'll fix it. Thanks!"

Nick was about to leave when he turned back, and kissed Jennifer very passionately. "Call me..." and he left.

Jennifer moaned as he left and turned to her friends. She knew Nick was now on his way to Katherine's to finish what he started. Jennifer was not a happy camper about this. L.L. and Cisco ruined what could have been a fantastic afternoon. "*What the fuck are you two doing here*?" she exclaimed.

"Damn... girl, with that attitude, maybe we shouldn't ask you to be my maid of honor... Let's go Cisco..."

"Yeah go... but not before Cisco fixes my..." Jenny did a double take. "What the fuck did you just *say...*?" Jenny asked surprised.

"You heard me right!"

Jennifer screamed and hugged L.L. then pulled back. "You better *not* be pregnant!"

"Get the fuck out of here!" L.L. said. Jenny laughed. "Of course *I'm* pregnant!" L.L. said.

"*What!*" Jenny screamed again.

"Yeah... but she didn't get pregnant until *after* I proposed!" Cisco said.

"Yeah... Damn 'celebration' lasted all night!"

"I'm so happy for you two!" Jenny beamed. And   they spent the rest of the day going over their wedding plans and all the arrangements. Cisco fixed Jenny's door and window while she and L.L. talked about their future together. After they left, Jenny was very sad. She almost had it all too and now she was reminded that it was all gone. That night Jenny cried herself to sleep.

- - -

Nick wanted to ask Jenny about Cisco and L.L. but he repected her space. After all, they all had an open relationship and Nick couldn't be hypocritical about private 'boundaries'. Jennifer continued to have sex and 'sessions' with Nick and Katherine, one-on-one and in threesomes on several occasions. She even went out with them to the movies or for dinner and dancing. (Katherine was a much better dancer than Nick.) But in her heart she knew she was just the third wheel, and she was just a little too self-centered to be anybody's fall back girl or booty call.

After L.L. and Cisco's wedding she knew it was time for Jennifer to find her own man and get on with her life. Nick and Katherine realized it was for the best, and they were okay with it. Slowly but surely, she eased herself out of the relationship. Jennifer would never forget the times they had together. Katherine gave Jenny her favorite cat o'nine tails as a 'memento'.

The Tortured Soul Trilogy
(The Confessions of Jennifer X)
Chapter 106
(I Can't Find My Baby)

This is it. Jennifer was going out on the hunt, only this time; she wasn't looking for Mr. Right Now. She didn't need to find *a* man; she needed to find *her* man. She wore the blue pinstripe suit that Nick never got to see. She had told Lisa she would find a place to show it off. Tonight, was as good time as any. She didn't wear the silk scarf around her neck this time. She took out a list of all the clubs she was going to hit. These clubs were known to be the hangout spots of all the eligible bachelors in town. She stepped into her limo and gave the driver the list.

"Start at the top… and I'll work my way down…"

Her driver nodded. "Yes Ms. Jones…" And she was off. The first club was a big disappointment. It was jam packed with women with the exact same game plan. The men there were just a bunch of losers trying to take full advantage of it. The next club wasn't any better. It was filled with semi-celebrities, posers and paparazzi. The third club was the charm. It was a target rich environment. The man to woman ratio was about 3:1 and the men were good looking, upper income, and semi-professionals. They were the crème de la crème but they weren't full of themselves.

"This is the place…" She sighed. As she entered the room, she tossed her hair back. One third of the room turned their eyes to her, men and women alike. "Yeah… I own this place…" She walked over to an empty table towards the back and sat down. Needless to say, all eyes were on her. The waiter immediately brought her a drink. "Excuse me… I didn't order this…!"

"Its compliments of the gentl…" and before he could finish, Jenny cut him off.

"I don't care… I'm quite capable of purchasing my own beverages… now take that away and bring me a 'Cream Soda'… thank you…" The waiter complied and as he walked away, he shrugged his shoulders at the unknown benefactor. Jennifer wasn't here looking for a man that would pursue her; she was looking for the man *she* wanted to pursue. She was giving the 'Jenny Mojo' the night off. Jenny danced and worked the crowd. She met a lot of nice men and got a lot of phone numbers, but that's not why she was here. She wasn't here to network; she was looking for the spark of romance. Jenny was about to call it a night so she stepped over to the bar to call her driver. This was the right spot, tonight just wasn't the right night. As she finished her call a man slid up next to her.

"A 'Cream Soda' please…" he requested.

Jenny turned to see a very handsome, distinguished young man standing there. The bartender placed the drink in front of him.

"Oh no… it's for the young lady…"

Jenny closed her phone and looked at him. "I can buy my own drinks… thank you!"

"Oh… *you're* paying for it…! I'm just paying you back for turning down the drink I sent to your table earlier…"

Jenny's jaw dropped. "Well… aren't *you* just bold?" He shrugged his shoulders and smiled. "Well… you're going to have to pay for this one *too*… I was just leaving…" she said.

He paused a moment. "You wouldn't happen to have any crazy glue in your purse, would you?"

"Yes… why?"

"I just want to borrow it… so I can glue my face back on…" Jenny smiled, opened her purse and gave it to him.

"Thanks!" he said.

Jenny took two steps away and turned back to him. "I *said*… I was just leaving…"

"I heard you…"

"Well…? How do expect to return my property to me?"

"Oh…? Ohhhh…!" The young man paid the bar tab and then he escorted Jennifer to her limo. He opened her door for her.

"So… what's your name?" She asked as she got into the limo.

"Armand…"

"Jennifer…"

"A pleasure to meet you Jennifer…"

"Armand?"

"Yes Jennifer?"

"Get in the car…" Jennifer figured that the night shouldn't have to be a total loss. She had her driver take the long way home to give them a chance to get acquainted first. "So Armand...? Why did you wait so long before approaching me?"

"I figured I'd give you a chance to check the room out, eliminate my competition and well... here we are..."

Jenny smiled. *'He'll do nicely for this evening.'* They continued their conversation and even stopped to get something to eat. They went to her house and Jenny tossed her purse on the couch. Her house phone rang. She answered it. It was her driver, Jinx. He had used the information gathered from their conversation to check out Armand. He even got Armand's credit history from the info he got from Armand's credit card he used to pay for drinks at the club. He checked out okay. Jennifer had learned a lot from Steven. Jennifer hung up the phone and turned to Armand. "I'll have my driver take you home..." she said as she took off her earrings.

"Oh... of course!" Armand sounded a little disappointed. He turned to leave.

"Not *now*... I meant... in the morning...!"

Armand tried hard not to smile and ruin his chances. "Okay...!"

"So Armand... are you 'packing'...?"

"Huh? What...?"

"Do you have a condom?"

"Actually... I have three..."

"Were you expecting to use all three tonight?"

"I hadn't planned on it... but I wouldn't mind!" Jennifer took off her jacket. She was now naked from the waist up. Armand was focused on her body. "My lord! You are a goddess!"

"So...? What do you have on your mind Armand?"

"The same thing I was thinking all night long... I just want to bury my face between your legs...!"

"I think that can be arranged..." She led Armand into the bedroom. As she entered her room Armand pulled her chair from her dresser to the middle of the bedroom. She looked at him.

"With your permission... I know this is your home and this is a mutual encounter... But if you don't mind following my lead... I promise you won't be disappointed!" Jenny was quite impressed with his chivalry. She allowed him to direct her, besides, after Nick and Katherine, what could this guy possibly do to shock her? "Please take off your pants and panties." He sat in the chair, and of course you know... Jennifer knows how to take her clothes off to inspire a man. Armand was very *inspired* to perform... "Now please come towards me." She stood in front of him and began to do a little dance for him. It reminded her of when she used to do lap dances for clients. "Please turn around." She did. "Come closer..." She did and he grabbed her hips and gently pulled her closer. That forced her to spread her feet around the legs of the chair. "If you can... grab your ankles for me..." (No problem!) The moment she grabbed her ankles he placed both his arms between her legs and worked her nipples. He then stuck his long tongue deep inside her pussy. He had complete and amazing muscle control of his tongue. He was able to roll and twist and curl his tongue at will. In between he would pull his tongue out and take long, slow flicking licks of her clit and labia. Jenny had hit the cunt licker jackpot! She cooed and moaned with every stroke of his tongue. Jenny reached up between her legs and unzipped his fly and pulled his cock out. Now she knew *why* he was so good at oral foreplay. All she could think was '*I wonder if he has a sister?*' Once Jenny was properly warmed up, Armand would put a condom on and drop Jenny's ass on his lap. When he was done; he would lift her up and continue to eat her out to her hearts content. Armand finished Jenny off on her bed with an oral examination the lasted the rest of the night. Only Katherine had ever come close to going down on her like that before. Armand was a very accomplished cunnilinguist. He more than made up for the fact that he only used two condoms that night. Well, she didn't expect him to have Nick's stamina. She didn't expect to find any man with Nick's stamina. Jenny's driver took Armand home in the morning.

Author's Note

Okay... I had to condense the last chapter a bit to make a long story short. I don't want you to think that Jennifer would just sleep with anybody at whim and she never rode a first date bareback. Jennifer and Armand actually dated for over a month before they had sex. It actually took Jinx about two weeks to have Armand checked out and Armand took another two weeks to check out Jennifer. No he wasn't checking her background or credit references...

Jennifer isn't going to be too happy I wrote this. But hey! She gave me the info and creative control... so here goes...

Armand had become gun shy. He had, on two other occasions, been burned by dates that he had picked up. He wanted to be very sure that Jennifer was...

You see, as you know, Jennifer is a very sexually aggressive person, and Armand wanted to make sure that she was...

This wasn't easy for him, he had to make sure and he didn't want ruin a good thing or to insult Jennifer by just asking her outright...

Well... what he did was, make an appointment with his doctor for both of them to take blood tests together so he could be absolutely sure that Jennifer was...

Born a woman! There...! I said it!

*Armand had learned the hard way, that if she's too good to be true... she's probably a he! The last two 'women' Armand had picked up at a bar were later discovered to be post-op trannies... fortunately **before** he had sex with them, but still, it was quite humiliating for him. Armand was not gonna take any more chances. Jennifer was a little put off that Armand had his doubts but she understood, besides, it gave her the opportunity to make sure Armand was in perfect health.*

And YES! Jennifer X. Jones is in fact a genetically born female with all the original factory-installed accessories. But times are crazy and hey... you gotta check'em... if not for gender, for diseases!

How can I be so sure that Jennifer is a woman? First, she was admitted to a mental hospital as a child and they did blood work up on her. Second, she was arrested for murder, they too did

blood work to check her DNA in that CODIS thing and three...
Some men can tell if something aint right. And I'm one of them.
But I gotta tell you... I am SO glad I'm married now and don't
have to test my abilities any more! Whew!

Okay... let's get back to the story...

Jenny knew Armand wasn't the one, but he sure as hell made the top ten. Armand knew the deal and he was quite okay with it. Jenny would continue hitting that club until she hit the jackpot. She went every other weekend and visited their restaurant as often as she pleased. She and Armand hooked up every once and again, but he knew nothing would come of it... I mean there was no future in the long term... I mean... oh to hell with it. He had a little dick... *okay*?

Almost 18 months later, still no Mr. Right. She would continue searching until she would find him.

Chapter 107
(UnBreak My Heart)

Jenny's cell phone rang; she checked the caller ID... It was Katherine's home number. She hadn't spoken or seen Katherine or Nick in almost two years, unless it was related to business, and that was very rare. She was too busy trying to develop her own to revisit that relationship. Also, she was still trying to find someone with the right computer skills to upgrade the systems. It was a 24-7 job and Hagen wasn't much help, but she had to admit, he was taking his job more seriously than he ever did before. Getting rid of Theo really straightened his ass up.

'*This is a booty call... I know it...*' she said to herself. She contemplated just letting it go to voice mail when she said to herself. '*What the hell... why not? I could use a little three way diversion right about now.*' She hadn't gotten a major freak on in a long while. She answered it. "Katherine! It's been a while... what's going on?" Silence. "Katherine?" Still silence. Jenny held her phone away from her to check the signal strength... that's when she barely heard Katherine's voice.

"Jenny...?"

"Katherine? What's going on girl? How you doing?"

"I need you to come by the house as soon as you can..."

"I can't come by right now... how about tonight? Is that good for you...? What should I bring...?"

"Jenny... Nick is dead..." Then silence.

Jennifer froze; she couldn't believe what she just heard. "Wh... wh... *what*!!!" Her voice trembled.

"Nicky is dead Jennifer...!" And Katherine started to cry hysterically.

"Katherine! Calm down...! What happened to Nick?" Katherine couldn't speak, she was crying so hard. "Katherine...? *Katherine*...? What happened to *Nick*? *Damn it...! Answer me!*" Silence... Suddenly there was another woman's voice on the phone.

"Jennifer...?"

"Who *is* this?"

"Mandy…"

"And *who* the hell are you…?" My mind was so screwed up; I thought she might have been someone I was 'replaced' by.

"I'm Nick's step-daughter… there's been a terrible accident…!" she sobbed. Even though Mandy was crying and had a thick British accent she was still a lot more coherent then Katherine.

"What… the… fuck… *happened*… to Nick?" Jenny tried to be calm but her voice was clearly shaking.

"Nick was killed last night by a drunk driver! How soon can you get here?" Mandy sobbed.

"I'm on my way right now!"

"Please drive carefully…" Mandy sobbed. When Jenny arrived, Katherine looked like hell. She was heaving and sobbing uncontrollably. Katherine did not cry 'pretty'. Jenny held her and kissed her. Katherine was inconsolable. Jenny held her close and rocked her; Mandy came out of the kitchen with tea and biscotti. She put them on the coffee table. "You must be Jennifer…"

Jennifer acknowledged her without letting go of Katherine. "You must be Mandy…"

"Yes… I'm sorry we finally meet under these 'circumstances'…" She sobbed.

"What the hell happened…?"

"Nick was walking home from the 'C' cup…"

"The *what*…?"

"The 'C' cup… it's a coffee shop Nick owns… I work there…"

"Okay… *and*…?"

"And… as he was walking home… some kid was coming home from a party…" And Mandy started crying.

"Come on… butch up! What happened…?"

"He was… drunk… and speeding… he hit a parked car… he flipped over and went up on the sidewalk and crushed Nick…! It was awful!" Mandy sobbed. "It happened so fast… he never saw it coming…" Mandy blew her nose in her hankie. "It… was… so sudden…" Hearing those exact words immediately sent Jenny into a flashback to when she learned Michael had died.

"Noooooooo! No! No! Nooooooo!" And she screamed and began to cry uncontrollably. "Maa-mmmmmmmmieeeeee!" And Jennifer lost it. Mandy and Katherine grabbed her before she fell to the floor. Katherine was shocked right out of her grief. Jennifer was a rock; no one had ever considered the possibility that she would break down like this. Jennifer was shaking and trembling and crying uncontrollably. Katherine and Mandy took her over to the couch. Katherine had hoped that Jenny would be able to be strong for her, but now the roles were reversed. Finally, after all these years, Jennifer grieved every tragic event that happened in her young life. Nick's sudden horrendous death; was the last straw.

Mandy and Jennifer hugged and cried together. Katherine got up, composed herself and had to step-up and take over alpha female spot. Katherine served them the tea and sat with them on the couch, Mandy cuddled to her side, Jenny laid down with her head in Katherine's lap. She rocked Mandy as she stroked Jenny's hair. Katherine hummed a spiritual song her grandmother used to sing to her. Her singing calmed them all down until they all fell asleep in each other's arms. Strangely enough, having to take care of Jennifer and Mandy in their grief helped her cope with her own. It 'changed' Katherine in a way she had not expected. It had awakened her maternal instincts. Katherine tapped into a source of strength and power that every woman was born with. Katherine chuckled to herself under her tears. Nick promised her that he would help her any way he could; to help her get over her self-esteem issues. (Nick has *never* broken a promise to me...) Katherine shook her head; her transformation into a self-assured woman was now completed.

The Tortured Soul Trilogy
(The Confessions of Jennifer X)
Chapter 108
(I Wanna Know What Love Is)

Nick's funeral would be in a few days. Jennifer was doing some spring cleaning... you know... getting rid of things that she didn't need to hold on to. Old clothes, old papers, and... stuff, you know... old memories... There are some memories that you can put aside... but you can never get rid of. Jennifer was going through some old letters and getting rid of junk mail that had accumulated over the years. That's when she came across a phone number, a number she hadn't called in over five years. "I wonder if... nah!" She was about to toss it out in the trash, but she hesitated... She called the number. A woman answered whose voice she did not recognize. "Hello?"

"Hello?" Jenny replied, "May I speak to Ms. Crystal please...?"

"Who is this?"

"My name is... Jennifer... Ms. Crystal used to take care of me... back in the day..." There was silence for a moment.

"I'm sorry... but my mother doesn't stay in touch with former patients..."

"You must be Emily... I understand..."

"How did you know my name?"

"Your mother and I spoke of you... we used to have long conversations... just the two of us..."

"Wait... You're *that*... Jennifer...?"

"I... *guess*... I am..."

"Hold on..." Jennifer held on until another woman's voice answered.

"Hello?"

"Hello Ms. Crystal...?"

"Who is this?"

"Jennifer... Jennifer Jones..."

"Jennifer...?" Then there was short pause then Ms. Crystal squealed. "*Jenny*! I remember you!" And Ms. Crystal laughed, but it was a little huskier than Jenny remembered. "How you doing baby?"

"I'm good..."

"No you're not! I can tell it in your voice... don't tell me you're having problems with your husband Michael...?"

That's when Jenny realized that she never told Ms. Crystal what had happened. "I... I... never married...Michael."

"*What*...? You didn't marry that boy? The way you talked about him? What did he do... girl?"

"He... he *died...* Ms. Crystal... I'm sorry I never called you to tell you it's just that I..." And Jennifer began to cry.

"Jennifer... where are you now?"

"I'm home..."

"All alone?"

"Yes..."

"We can't do this over the phone... Give me your address... I'll be right over..."

Jennifer knew that wouldn't be possible, they were in different states, but it was only a four-hour drive so Jenny asked permission to come visit her instead. Ms. Crystal agreed. Jenny packed an overnight bag and made the long trip over the next morning. Jennifer was very excited that she was going to see her again. Ms. Crystal was the only person in her life that was like family to her, other than Steven and Ramona. Jenny pulled her car up to the driveway. She was very nervous and excited. She got out of the car and stepped up the door of a very modest semi-attached house. The front lawn needed some attention, but the flowers in the garden were very well kept. Before she could even knock, the door swung wide open.

"Who the hell are you?" Ms. Crystal demanded.

Jenny was taken aback by the confrontation. "Ms. Crystal...! I'm *Jennifer*... Jennifer Jones!"

"No you are *not*! There is no way in the world you are the snot nosed little girl that was so full of piss and vinegar that walked out of the clinic ten years ago...!"

Jennifer smiled. "Yes I am!"

Ms. Crystal hugged her tightly and Jenny reciprocated. "Get in here girl... you're just in time... I'm making some jerk chicken... You look like you haven't been eating proper..." Jenny stepped inside and Ms. Crystal noticed her ass. "But I can see the red beans and rice have been good to you!"

Jenny put her hands to cover her behind. *"Ms. Crystal!"* Jenny laughed.

"Don't mind her..." Emily said as she entered the room. "I *know... you* know how she gets..."

"I sure do... how do you put up with it?"

"Practice... lots and lots of practice..." They laughed.

"You know... you two little bitches know where the door is... must I show you how to use it?"

Emily ignored her and escorted Jenny into the dinning room. The three of them sat and talked for hours, catching up on lost valuable time. Ms. Crystal had gained about thirty pounds since retiring from the clinic. Emily didn't live with her but she came over on weekends to spend time with her mother. Dr. Imani quit a year or two after Jenny left, the patients kept attacking him and the staff wouldn't lift a finger to help him. Emily was divorced and her son was in college doing very well. All the while that they talked and laughed and cried together, Jenny felt as if she were floating above the room, watching the three of them. It felt... so right. Jenny was in a good place. There was an over abundance of love in this house. *"Why didn't you let me move in with you?"* she thought to herself. *"My life would have been so different..."*

"Different isn't always better..." Ms. Crystal said.

"What...! Did I...?" Jenny put her hand over her mouth.

"No... you didn't say it out loud." Emily said. "My mother has always had a discerning mind..."

"Which is why you never got away with any shit when you were younger!"

Emily nodded.

"Wait! Can she really...?"

Emily nodded again and Ms. Crystal held out her left hand vertically and smacked it hard with her right. Jenny leaned back and blushed. "Mama knows things you don't think she knows..." Ms. Crystal said. Emily left the room quietly. *Now...* the conversation began. She and Ms. Crystal spoke until well past midnight. Jenny bared her soul knowing she could not lie to someone who already knew everything. When they were finished,

Jenny felt as if a huge weight was taken off her. She was refreshed and exhausted at the same time.

"Can you help me, Ms. Crystal?"

"No daughter... I can't... but I can put you on the right path..."

"What does that mean...?"

"It means... go to bed... We have church in the morning..."

"I've never been to church!"

"Do you think I don't know that? And don't you think it's about time you started?" Jenny nodded. Emily came in and took Jennifer to her room.

"How does she...?" Jenny asked.

"She's not psychic... if that's what you're thinking..."

"Okay... so... how does she do it...?"

"After so many years of working at that clinic she became extremely observant. She can tell things about you by the way you walk, how you reach for something or how you... just stand there. It's a learned trait and she extremely good at it. It's a good thing she never chose to take advantage of people with her ability."

"Are you coming to church with us too?"

"I'm sorry... have you *met* my mother...?" Jenny laughed and went into her room.

"Goodnight Emily..."

"Goodnight Jenny..."

"Good night... And I better not hear any buzzing sounds coming from your bedroom..." Ms. Crystal added.

"*Ms. Crystal*!!!" Jenny said.

"I was talking to my daughter... But I'm keeping my eye on you too..." Ms. Crystal went into her bedroom.

Emily whispered. "If momma don't get none... nobody get none..." and they giggled.

"I hear *that*!" Ms. Crystal said. They ran into their rooms.

The next day they all headed to church. It wasn't a very big church; there were more people in the choir than in the pews. The pastor was an excellent speaker but the message just wasn't for Jennifer. She just didn't 'get it'. What was supposed to happen? What was she supposed to do? Jennifer sat there and just enjoyed the sermon... it wasn't all that bad. The choir began to sing '*I Need*

You to Survive'. In the middle of the song the choir sang chorus softly.

> *'I pray for you, you pray for me,*
> *I love you; I need you to survive...*
> *I won't harm you, with words from my mouth,*
> *I love you; I need you to survive...'*

Over and over again, then the pastor made an altar call. Anyone who wanted to give his life to Jesus just had to step up and receive. No one stepped up. The choir continued to sing, the pastor continued to ask for anyone to come forward. The choir sang louder and louder.

> *'I pray for you, you pray for me,*
> *I love you; I need you to survive...*
> *I won't harm you, with words from my mouth,*
> *I love you; I need you to survive...'*

I closed my eyes and swayed with the music. Back and forth, back and forth, the singing got louder and louder. I opened my eyes when I heard applause. I didn't realize it. I was standing at the altar with my arms raised up like a child waiting to be picked up. How did I get up here? No one was near me. I wasn't escorted up here. Ms. Crystal and Emily were still where they were but they were dancing and stomping their feet.

> *'I pray for you, you pray for me,*
> *I love you; I need you to survive...*
> *I won't harm you, with words from my mouth,*
> *I love you; I need you to survive...'*

I looked up and the pastor was praying over me. He took a vial of oil and broke it open and poured it in his hand. He reached up and touched my forehead with it and prayed some more. I started to stomp my feet. Tears came to my eyes and then... I passed out quietly. When I woke up I was in Ms. Crystal's arms on the bench. Emily was sitting next to us praying silently. "What happened...?"

"You fell out..." Emily replied.

"I *what*...?"

"You 'fell out' baby..." Ms. Crystal said. "It happens when you're filled with the Holy Ghost and have a revelation..."

"*What*? What revelation did I have...?"

"I don't know, baby... only you know, and if you don't know... it's for you to figure out...!"

After services we went back to Ms. Crystal's house; I had to pack to go home. Emily was going back to her place. I don't get what happened to me. I think the pastor slipped me a 'Mickey' in that oil he anointed my head with. Yeah... that's what happened... it was all for show. I'm a little too smart to fall for it. I went to my car and I hugged Emily and turned and hugged Ms. Crystal. "So...? Am I 'saved' now?"

"Not yet... you don't believe what happened to you today and you're going to try to rationalize it away... if you haven't already have." Ms. Crystal held out a book to me.

"What's this...?"

"You know darn well what it is... take it!" I took the Bible from her and put it in my car.

"I'm not going to change my ways... you know!"

"You're not supposed to change your ways... trust in the Lord... and change will come..."

Emily nodded. I hugged Ms. Crystal again. "I love you..."

"I know baby... I love you too!"

I hugged Emily and said my goodbyes. I felt a little better having visited them. I was getting in my car when Emily handed her mother a bag. Ms. Crystal handed it to me.

"What's this?"

"Just something else I wanted you to have... don't open it until you get home..." I put the package on the passenger's seat. I put the car in gear and waved and as I drove off. When I got home I put my bags down, I'll unpack later. I tossed the package on my bed and I put the Bible on my nightstand. It was the Bible that she read to me every night at the clinic whenever I couldn't sleep. I laid down on my bed. I was exhausted from the drive home. That's when I rolled over on the package. '*What is this*?' I opened it. It was the rag doll I wouldn't let go of as a child when I was in the clinic. '*I can't believe she kept it after all these years*!' I held the doll in my arms and fell asleep. I had a funeral to go to tomorrow afternoon. As I closed my eyes I thought to myself. '*Ms. Crystal does love me…*'

The Tortured Soul Trilogy
(The Confessions of Jennifer X)
Chapter 109
(I Don't Wanna Close My Eyes)

Nick's funeral was beautiful. Everyone came from Faber and some hardcore bikers too. '*What was that all about?*' and lots and lots of distraught women. '*Who are all these women? When did Nick ever find the time?*' Nick was to be cremated and Katherine was going to keep his ashes. Katherine was a rock. She took care of everything. A grief counselor from Faber named Mercedes escorted her around, just in case. As I walked around commiserating with everyone, I saw his daughter Cynthia sitting by herself, crying. I sat next to her.

"Hi... My name is Jennifer, you must be Cynthia, Nick's daughter...?"

She looked up. "I'm so sorry... have we met before?"

"No... I once saw the two of you together having dinner... he told me about you... How are *you* holding up?"

"I'm so confused...!" Cynthia sobbed.

"I don't understand..."

"I don't know if I should be sad because of what happened to daddy or upset... about... what he did... with all these... *women*..." And then she whispered. "They keep telling me... *stories*...!"

Jennifer smiled. "Your father was a very giving and loving man and although I don't know what he did with most of these women... I do know I loved him very much! And he loved you very much..."

"What about Katherine?"

"Other than your mother and Mandy's mother... Katherine was his favorite... He loved her more than anyone in this world!"

Cynthia cried some more. "I really like Katherine... She's the only 'one' daddy spoke of to me..."

"Same here...!"

Cynthia dried her tears. "But *all* these women…!" She paused and looked at me. "I'm sorry! Are *you*… one of them…?" I nodded. "Oh…! I didn't mean to…"

"No offense taken… we are what we are…!" I smiled and hugged her.

"But *what* are you…?" Cynthia asked.

"*We*… are women who have had some serious problems in our lives… Some *more* serious than others… your father… *consoled* us… counseled us…he helped me and others like me to… handle and deal with our problems…" Jennifer sighed. "And to some of us… he was an *amazing* diversion…!"

Cynthia giggled. "Is that how you met my father?" she asked.

"No… We worked together for a while and I was his boss at Faber…"

"Oh yes… I know who you are now… You're Jennifer Jones…"

Jenny nodded. "So… what do you do?" Jenny asked.

"I'm a computer programmer and systems analyst…"

"*Really*…? You wouldn't happen to know anything about the Lincoln-Hanna files would you?"

"*That* dinosaur…?" Cynthia scoffed.

Jennifer looked away disappointed.

"I remember daddy bringing that file home on weekends and we would work on it together when I was a teenager… That's the file that made me want to get into computer programming in the first place. I always wanted to rewrite those codes for him… they suck!" Cynthia dabbed her tears.

Jenny looked back at her. "*You*… can *rewrite* those codes…?"

"Pffftt! Sure… it would take some time… but yeah! I can update them so they are compatable with current computer programs and won't crash …"

Jennifer's jaw dropped. (It couldn't be *this* easy? Could it?) That's when Mandy walked over to us. "Come on sis… I'll take you home now!"

"Mandy… do you mind if I take Cynthia home… I believe we have business we need to discuss…!" Mandy raised an eyebrow. "No seriously, *business*!" I said. Cynthia nodded approvingly; Mandy let me drive her sister home. Mandy left the viewing with C.J. Cassidy, a spoken word poet who recited a poem at the funeral. They had met at the coffee shop where she worked.

"So how long have Mandy and C.J. been together?" I asked Cynthia on the drive home.

"About three years now, she really likes him…"

"Is it serious?"

"They really love each other. If he asks her to marry him she'll say yes…"

"Really…? And how does he intend to keep her? I mean… how much does a spoken word poet make these days?"

"*Well*… he is *thinking* of writing a book…"

"Pffftt! A book? What kind of book…?"

"I don't know… but he did mention to me he wanted to speak to you about it…"

"Me…? Why would he want to talk to *me* about writing a book?"

Cynthia shrugged her shoulders.

The Tortured Soul Trilogy
(The Confessions of Jennifer X)
Chapter 110
(A New Beginning)

Jennifer got into her limo at about 2 o'clock. She had an important meeting to go to and she had to pick up the guest of honor. Afterwards she had to go back to the main office and take care of a few things. She reached over to the bar and was about to fix herself a 'Cream soda', her favorite beverage made with vanilla vodka and ginger ale. She paused. She didn't want the drink, not now. She poured herself a straight ginger ale.

"Jinx...?" she said to her driver. "How much time do we have before we have to be there?"

"About two hours, Ms. Jones... plenty of time to pick up..."

She interrupted Jinx. "Have you had lunch yet?"

"No ma'am, but I'm okay..."

"Tell you what... if you see a place on the way where you want to eat... go ahead and take an hour for lunch... I'll wait in the car..."

"Are you sure Ms. Jones?"

"I'm sure... I just need a little quiet time..."

"Anything you say Ms. Jones..."

(Damn right, *'Anything I say Ms. Jones...'*) Jinx pulled over to a fast food restaurant and parked the car in the lot. He got out and went to the rear door, Jennifer rolled down the widow. Jinx leaned into it.

"Is there anything you want me to bring back for you Ms. Jones?"

Jennifer placed her hand tenderly on Jinx's face. "No thank you Jinx... I'm good... I just need a little... space..."

"Do you want me to turn on the tinted windows so that you can have some... privacy?"

Jennifer giggled. "No... thank you Jinx... I don't need 'that kind' of privacy right now..." Jinx smiled and walked towards the fast food place. Jennifer rolled up the window. "Now... I'll have that drink..." She added a shot of vanilla vodka to her drink; took a sip and settled into her seat. "That's nice... real nice..."

Jennifer turned on the car CD player to her favorite soft jazz music mix. She sipped her drink again. "That's *real* nice..." She nodded to the music and sipped her drink. Jennifer was beginning to relax. She really needed to relax... She put the drink down and closed her eyes... sleep came to her slowly... but it was a troubled sleep. Jennifer had gone through so much in her young life, so much... pain, so much... heartache. "*Good Morning Heartache*" sung by Billie Holiday began to play on the stereo. Jennifer drifted off to an uneasy sleep. Hers was a hard life for such a young woman. She had gone from victim to villain to...

Jinx woke Jennifer from her sound but restless sleep in the back of the limo. She felt almost unburdened. "Where am I?" she asked.

"At the downtown offices of Faber Data Co." Jinx answered

"How long was I out?"

"About two hours..."

"Oh my god... the meeting!" Jennifer jumped up.

"Not to worry Ms. Jennifer... I picked up Ms. Anderson in another car. You where sleeping so hard I didn't have the heart to wake you..."

"Where is she now?"

"Waiting for you in the lobby... she's a little nervous but okay."

Jennifer quickly got herself together and entered the office building and met up with her.

"How was your nap?" Cynthia asked.

"Not as refreshing as I had hoped." Jennifer answered. "How are you holding up?"

"I'm good..." They both entered the elevator and went up to the third floor where everyone was waiting for their arrival. They headed for the renovated conference room and everyone followed them in and settled into their seats. "May I have everyone's attention please...?" Everyone paused and paid careful attention to what Jennifer had to say. "I want you to meet the young lady who was finally able to upgrade all our computer systems so that the download times have been cut in half and

551

raised performance levels back to a respectable level and increased productivity and... oh yeah... your salaries!" The office gave Cynthia a standing ovation. She bowed slightly and waved to everyone. "...And as a reward for all her hard work, she has been promoted to building manager, a position that I had slated to go to Katherine, before she left to pursue other interests... but I have no doubts in my mind that my protégé will excel in her new position..." Jennifer paused. "And if anyone gives her any shit... They *will* answer directly to me! Do I make myself perfectly clear?" Everyone nodded and agreed. "Bob?"

"Yes Ma'am! No shit!" Bob put down his bran muffin. Bob had a stroke a while back and was now watching what he ate.

"Very well then... I will leave you all in the very capable hands of Ms. Cynthia Anderson... Please treat her like she's family!" Jennifer leaned over to Cynthia and whispered. "I wish your father could have been here to see this... he would have been so very proud!"

"Thanks... he would have been so proud of you too Jenny!"

Jennifer left Nick's daughter, to handle the offices and get settled in. Everything was right with the world. Jenny was now the CEO of Faber Data after Hagen retired. Cynthia had finally corrected all of their computer problems. Now the company was being hired to handle computer animation programs for major film companies. Profits were up and Jenny and the company's future were pretty much secure. *"Thank you Steven, I love you Michael..."* She whispered to herself.

Jennifer did a last check of the floor to see if anyone needed anything to help with his or her job performance quotas or if Cynthia had any questions. Cynthia had a handle on things so Jennifer said her goodbyes and headed towards the elevator. Yep... everything was right with the world... her personal life, on the other hand, still needed a serious overhaul. Jennifer was still very distraught over Nick's sudden death. "Damn it! Does every man I love or ever loved have to die? What the fuck? Am I some kind of jinx? Did someone put a hex on me when I was born? Did I do something in a previous life that I deserve this shit?" Jennifer knew she wasn't jinxed, but she did know that her life was nothing more than a series of tragic events. She was just feeling sorry for herself.

She suddenly felt that she had to 'do' something to redeem herself. She had a strange feeling that something was left 'undone', some unfinished business, but she couldn't figure out what. She looked up to heaven and channeled what Ms. Crystal instilled in her when she read the Bible to her for so many years at the clinic. "Lord...! I know you haven't forsaken me... show me a sign! Tell me what I have to do, to get back in your good graces? I know you love me and I have a purpose here... use me as you wish... I know I wouldn't be the first harlot you've used to further the glory of heaven. All I ask for is a chance. Lord, into thy hands I commend my spirit!"

The elevator door opened, she entered and she pressed the lobby button, but the elevator went up instead. 'Darn!" she looked at her watch. She still had to get back to the main office before quitting time. 'Oh well... I can always just go back tomorrow. After all, I am the boss around here.' She said to herself. The elevator doors opened on the fifteenth floor and she looked to see if anyone was getting on. There was no one there. *'I guess they took another one.'* She pressed the button for lobby again, and just as the doors were about to close, she put her hand to block it. She looked at the sign of the company that was headquartered there. *'La Sociedad De La Mujer Muda'.* She stared at it for a moment. She didn't know that their corporate offices were in this building. Suddenly an office door opened and she saw a familiar face. The woman stood there and acknowledged her presence but did not 'confront' her. After a brief moment she spoke to Jennifer.

"May I help you with something?" She asked Jennifer softly. It was Marisa... the woman who had given her the brochure in the mall that day. Marisa did not recognize her. Jennifer took a deep breath and exhaled. Marisa saw that as an opening. "Please...!" Marisa said. Marisa sensed her apprehension and motioned for her to step off the elevator. "We're all friends here..." Jennifer stepped off the elevator and walked up to Marisa. Marisa had a look of empathy on her face. "Did Mercedes recommend you to us?"

"Who?"

"Mercedes Ramirez, she's a counselor... did she recommend you to us?"

"No... I... You gave me a brochure in a mall... once..."

"Oh yes... I remember you now... it's Jennifer... right?"

"Yes! It is..." Jennifer was quite surprised that she remembered her name after all these years.

"What can we do for you Jennifer?"

Jennifer took another deep breath, and steadied herself. Her path was now clear as a bell. She knew what she had to do. "I understand you help abused women find their voice and you need volunteers for the cause..." Marisa nodded. "Sign me up...!"

Marisa smiled, and then hesitated, and then she gently hugged Jennifer. Jennifer hugged her back. "I'm so surprised you found us here..."

"Why would you say that?" Jenny asked.

"We only just moved our headquarters into this building a few weeks ago... it wasn't even listed in the brochure I gave you." Jennifer's jaw dropped. Then she smiled. "Come on in... I just made a fresh pot of coffee... would you care for some biscotti? There's a little bistro in the neighborhood we get them from..."

"I know the place... Thank you, I'd love some!" Jennifer followed Marisa until she saw the photograph of Maria Suarez on the wall. It was in the same frame. The duct tape still covered her mouth. Jennifer stepped up to it and reached for the tape. She paused... Marisa didn't stop her this time. She gently tugged at the tape and pulled it free. Jenny rolled it into a ball and threw it in the waste can. "No more silent woman, no more mujer muda... from now on, this bitch is gonna make some noise!" Marisa smiled. Jennifer called Jinx on her cell to let him know she would call him later in the evening to pick her up. Marisa led her back into her office. Jennifer smiled, threw her head back and exhaled. She pointed her finger to heaven. Now... Nick could truly be proud of her...

Nick had left his brownstone to his long time lover and companion, Katherine, where she still resides to this day.

He left The 'C' Cup to his stepdaughter, Mandy Smyth.

Cynthia eventually closed down the biker bar and it was replaced by a donut shop, much to the delight of the surrounding neighborhood. She used the profits of the sale to continue her education. She is presently engaged to a nice young man she met while working at Faber.

Lisa and Valerie moved in together after her divorce was finalized and Lisa now runs Valerie's web based business of photo-erotica and on-line fetish community

Nicholas was given a simple closed casket funeral that was attended by family, bikers, co-workers and a dozen or so of Nick's 'acquaintances'. Katherine brought Nick's guitar along and sang Seals' 'Kiss from a Rose' at the funeral. The guitar was cremated with Nick and the ashes are kept with love and care in an urn on the living room mantle next to the video of 'My Fair Lady'.

Katherine eventually left Faber Data Corp. in order to help Mandy manage the 'C' cup. There, they carry on Nick's legacy of helping women with their problems and issues, not with whips and chains but with tea and biscotti. Their first and most challenging 'client' was 'Pet'. She was also their very first success story.

Although Katherine still 'reminisces' about the 'adventures' she had in the game room with Nick, she has never allowed anyone else inside that room... After all, Nick once confided in her that the reason no one had ever been in the room before her is because he had designed the room... especially for her...

Jennifer has been working very closely with Marisa and Mercedes and they have been helping to spread the message of hope to many abused and battered women.

Jennifer offered to pay Ashley's college tuition just as Michael had done for her. It wasn't necessary. Ashley had received a full scholarship to the school of her choice. With her family's permission, she got Ashley a new car.

After a while Jennifer and Katherine resumed their relationship... It was something they both needed and besides, they were closer to each other than anyone else on the planet.

Strangely enough, one of the characters in this biography I have been asked the most about is Johnny 'Precious'. There is no 'Johnny'. He is one of the merged characters that actually represent several men (and women) in Katherine's life, who either abused her mentally, physically or financially (or in any combination thereof) during the course of her life. Yes, she was engaged (to two different men) and broke it off, and as a result of that, Katherine turned away from men and sought solace in a woman's arms only to find that the negative characteristics exists in both sexes. It wasn't until she had totally exhausted all her options that she finally turned to Nick for help. I hope that clears a few things up for you!

Cisco and Tobey had a little girl and named her Jenny. They still run what's left of Callahan's businesses, but L.L. is a stay at home mom. Oh... she still collects the 'rent' from the cathouse... Come on... a bitch's gotta get paid! What

The Tortured Soul Trilogy
(Living La Vida Puta)
Chapter 111
(Of Vice & Men)

With Michael and Steven dead, and having a daughter to take care of, running the strip club and a brothel was too much to handle. The strip club only made money because it was used to funnel and launder money from the Callahans' other 'businesses', but those had been taken over by his other partners. There was also a 'controlling interest' in Faber Data, the company Jenny took over at Steven's request. Jenny was now the CEO but she was the one who actually 'inherited' the stock in the company, but she opted to be a silent partner and have it look like Cisco owned the stock.

That left only the brothels, and although they brought in good money, the expenses were a little out of control. Cisco had to make a very hard decision to get them back in the black. He went to several financial advisors who made a plan to refinance his debts and get them out from under. It was a bold plan and the bank was on board... there was just one person standing in his way... L.L.!

Cisco came home straight from the bank. His nerves were a little shot. Money was tight and with a four-year old daughter it was time for him to buckle down and stop acting like a 'playa' and start acting like a father with responsibilities. He had to find a way to refinance four mortgages (Three brothels... excuse me... *'rooming houses'* and his home.) So he could have a strong future for his daughter that would have nothing to do with strippers and pimps and whores. *Oh my!* It was a great plan, but the best laid plans of mice and men... His wife was a co-signer of all the mortgages and true to L.L.'s spirit, she had a wait and see attitude. He knew that time was not of the essence, but the prime rate was at a new low and what they would save in mortgage payments could put little Jenny through college! There was even enough of a savings to get Jenny into special schools and get tutors to help get her into an Ivy League school. Hell, there would be enough left to clear off all the credit cards!

"Why does she do that?" Cisco wondered. "This is our child for crying out loud! She has to care what happens to her!" Cisco thought about L.L.'s past and the fact that her parents abandoned her at such a young age should not have to be a factor in her blatant procrastination issues. He knew his wife, she wasn't being evil... she was being hardheaded, and he knew a hard head made for a soft behind! Cisco became a little distracted thinking of L.L.'s 'soft behind'. He shook the thought of her bent over the couch while he... That was the 'playa' talking; Cisco the father had to take control here. "I got to talk to her about this... even if this wasn't about little Jenny... it's still good business! L.L. has good business sense... I don't know why she just doesn't get with the program!"

Cisco got home and sat his wife down and pleaded his case. He showed her all the figures and projections that he made and the bank manager made for him and the prospectus two financial advisors made for him. They all agreed that this was a sound plan and the soonest they could put it into motion the better...Everybody except L.L. of course!

"Let's just see what happens and I'll think about it..." She said very plainly.

It was as if she wasn't listening or just didn't want to listen. Cisco was livid with his wife. They had discussed her selfishness before and they thought they had gotten past it. And here it was, rearing its ugly head all over again. Cisco looked at his wife with a bit of disdain. How could she be so cruel? So insensitive...? After all they had been through in their lives together? He should have earned her respect a long time ago. She should have learned her lesson about opportunities lost by now. He tried again to convince her that it was a good move and she went ballistic on him.

"What is so fucking important that this has to be done right now? Why can't it wait? Why can't you for once... do things my way? Don't you think I know what I'm doing? Huh? You're my husband... why don't you act like one and support my decisions for once? I can't believe you you're bringing this shit to me now, knowing what I'm going through with the girls and with the strip club...!" She shook her head. "I swear you treat me like shit sometimes! I'm so mad at you right now I could spit!" She turned her back on him. "You son of a bitch!"

Cisco just stared at her. "*Is she serious? No really? Is she fucking serious*?" "I'm the 'son of a bitch'? *I'm* the 'son of a bitch'...?" He replied. He was mad as hell right then, but he counted to ten before he spoke again. He looked at his wife and said calmly: "So... let me get this straight... I *don't* drink, I *don't* smoke and I *don't* use any drugs... I *don't* gamble, abuse you *or* my child. I've *never* cheated on you although I have had motive *and* opportunity... and the only thing you have to *complain* about... is that I don't agree with you, when you're *wrong*??? Well *somebody* dial *9-1-1*! Cause I must be the biggest *fucking son of a bitch* on the planet!

L.L. cut her eyes at Cisco. "Why don't you come down off that cross, take the wood and nails, build yourself a bridge and get over it?" L.L. said. Cisco then turned his back on her. She was really pushing her luck with him. "You know what your problem is?" She paused. "You fucking take it for granted that that I'll be here when you come home..."

Cisco turned back to L.L. and said quietly and calmly. "You... take it for granted... that I'm coming home!"

L.L. was taken aback by that. She hadn't expected to hear that remark from him. She thought she had his number. "You wouldn't *dare*..." and she cut her eyes at him. Cisco shook his head at her. Did she have *any* idea of what he was capable of? L.L. grabbed her purse and car keys and headed to the door.

"You're just gonna walk out of here? We haven't finished discussing this yet."

"You can 'discuss it' by your goddamn self... I have things to do..." She headed to the front door.

"Aren't you even gonna kiss me goodbye?"

L.L. kissed two fingers of her right hand and smacked her ass with it and left. Cisco just shook his head and ran his fingers through his hair. He loved L.L. but this bitch went too far... She really needed a wake up call. Cisco went into the bedroom and got out his Bible. He opened it, began to read it and began to pray. "Lord... Give the wisdom and strength to deal with this woman you gave me!" Even with the shit L.L. just pulled there was still a way to save his plans for his family's future. But it was a little drastic. L.L. just had to be left out in the cold on this one. A man has to do what a man has to do... Cisco began to seriously consider an offer he got a while ago to go back to Miami and run with his old crew. At least there, they respected him as a man...The money wasn't bad either! That's when the phone rang. "Yes...?" Cisco nodded his head. "Sure! I understand... You know what? I'm coming right now... Thanks!" Cisco took a deep breath and grabbed his coat and went out the door. Just as he closed the door, he looked back into the house, shook his head... and exhaled!

L.L. was half way through her list of things to do and placed the last of her purchases in the trunk of the car. Just as she was about to open the car door, her cell phone rang. She looked at the caller ID. It was Cisco. She was too angry at him right now and didn't want to hear him piss and moan anymore about her attitude. Let him leave it on voice mail. She would erase it later. She almost finished up her daily errands and looked at her watch. "Damn... I still have things to do but I have to pick up Jenny at daycare." She pulled out of the mall and headed out to pick up her daughter. She would get there in plenty of time. She pulled into the parking lot of the Tiny Tots Day Care and went inside. She went to her classroom and Jenny wasn't there. She looked around the room to see a few stragglers, but there was no sign of Jenny. She went to the attendant who was putting a jacket on one of the kids whose parents had arrived to pick him up. "Sylvia? Where's Jenny?"

Sylvia answered without looking up at her. She remained focused on the rambunctious child she was dealing with. "Oh! Her father picked her up about an hour or two ago..." Sylvia did not see the look of shock and dismay that flashed across L.L.'s face. Before Sylvia could say another word, she quickly ran outside, got in her car and peeled out of the parking lot like a maniac and headed straight home. She called the house several times but the machine picked up.

(Cisco's Voice) "Hi... this is Cisco..."

(L.L.'s Voice) and L.L...."

(Jenny's Voice) "Ad Jenny... (Jenny giggles)

(Together) "We're not home right now, but you know the drill..." Beeeeep!

"No one is home! Damn it!" L.L. exclaimed and she hit the gas. She didn't know why. They weren't there, what's the rush? She pulled up to the house and barely parked in the driveway before she jumped out of the car. That's when she saw them, six or seven garbage bags and some of Jenny's toys on the curb. She slowly walked over and carefully opened up a bag. Inside were some of Cisco's clothes, shoes and suit jackets. She took out a shirt of his and held it in her hands. *"Fuck Me!"* She thought. *"He left me and took the baby! My baby!!!"* She dropped to her knees on the hard sidewalk and began to cry, softly at first, then harder and harder. It was at that very moment her very own words came back to taunt and humiliate her. *"That... is your punishment... you treacherous bitch!"* She threw her head back and screamed at the top of her lungs. It was a scream that would make strong men weak in the knees.

"You hear that Fezik? That is the sound of ultimate suffering. My heart made that sound the day my father was slaughtered..." Inigo Montoya in 'The Princess Bride'

The tears flowed down her face as she screamed again. That's when the front door flew open and Cisco came running out to his woman who was in agony, a butcher knife was in his hand at his side.

"Baby! What's wrong? What happened? What is it?" He asked her as his eyes darted up and down the street desperate to find whatever it was that caused his woman this much pain that it made her cry out so.

"Cisco???" She sobbed. "What are you doing here?"

"Where else would I be baby? Are you alright?" he replied and his eyes still darted back and forth and then he finally focused on her still kneeling on the street.

"Where's Jenny, Cisco? Where's Jenny?" She sobbed.

"She's inside watching 'Dora the Explorer and Diego'...! Baby? Tell me what's wrong? What happened?" And he helped her up off the ground and hugged her while still keeping an eye on the street like a meerkat.

"Why did you pick her up from daycare?"

561

"They called and said she wasn't feeling well so I picked her up and brought her home and made her some chicken soup... didn't you get my message?" (*That's why he called me!*) L.L. grabbed her husband and never wanted to let him go. God, she loves this man, this sweet, wonderful man. She had been so stupid and so selfish! "Honey...? What...?" He started to ask her what happened.

She interrupted him. "Why are these bags on the street?"

"They're my old clothes and some toys that Jenny doesn't play with anymore. I left them here for Good Will to pick them up... I told you yesterday...! Why?"

(And the phone probably rang inside the house while he was taking the bags outside!)

He held his wife close and she walked with him back inside. The moment she saw Jenny sitting calmly in front of the TV she ran to her and hugged her like she hadn't seen her in years.

"Mama loves you baby!" and she kissed her.

"I love you too mommy!" and she hugged her mother back.

"Are you ever going to tell me what just happened?" Cisco asked.

"No..." she laughed. "It's over... it's all okay now baby!" She said as she wiped her tears. Cisco shrugged his shoulders and put the knife back in the kitchen drawer where he got it from. When he came back into the room, she sat her husband down at the dining room table; the folder with Cisco's plans for the family's finances and Jenny's future was still on top of the table. L.L. fingered the folder nervously.

"Cisco...?"

"Yeah baby?"

"Don't be mad with me..." she whispered.

"Talk to me..." he said plainly.

"If it's okay with you..." Cisco leaned a little forward to hear what his wife had to say. "Can I have Jennifer look this over for me...? And if she signs off on it... we'll go ahead and do it!"

Cisco had a broad smile on his face, He took a deep breath and exhaled, this was a huge leap for his wife and he was okay with the progress she was making. "Sure baby... I trust Jennifer's judgment..."

They stood up and held each other in their arms. L.L. kissed her husband passionately. "Isn't it time for Jenny's nap?" L.L. smiled and winked at him.

"No... it's still early..." Cisco answered looking over L.L.'s shoulders at the hall clock.

L.L. turned to look at Jenny to make sure she was focused on the TV and pulled down her tank top exposing her breasts. She then coyly played with her nipple rings... "Are you *sure*... It isn't time for Jenny's nap... *baby*...?" She cooed.

L.L. pulled her top back up. Cisco walked over to Jenny and picked her up in his arms. "We're going to go sleepies mami... *you* wanna go sleepies?" Little Jenny rubbed her eyes and nodded. She still didn't feel well and really could use some bed time right now. So could mommy and daddy! Jenny cradled into daddy's neck and when he turned around she waved bye-bye to mommy. L.L. blew her a kiss. Jenny reached out and 'grabbed' it and touched her mouth. L.L. smiled. A wave of calm enveloped L.L. She was at peace for the first time in her life.

"Don't it always seem to go, that you don't know what you've got 'til it's gone?"

Cisco took Jenny to her room and tucked her in bed with her favorite rag doll she got from her Aunt Jennifer. He kissed her forehead and she didn't have any fever. She was fast asleep in a matter of moments. Cisco went back into the living room but L.L. wasn't there. "Honey? Where are you?"

"In here baby..." L.L. answered from the bedroom. Cisco entered the bedroom to find his wife sitting on the edge of the bed wearing leather chaps, black stiletto heels and seven gold chains which connected her nipple rings and cascaded down her abs, and nothing else but a big smile. L.L. seductively spread her legs, fingered her clit and whispered to her husband. "Lock the door... and get your ass in here!"

Cisco licked his lips. "Yes... Ma'am!"

The next morning they called Jennifer who looked at the proposals, conferred with the company's accountants and she signed off of their plans. It was a good investment. It would help secure the future for L.L., Cisco and her god-daughter Little Jenny.

The Tortured Soul Trilogy
(The Seduction of CJ Cassidy)
Chapter 112
(99 Luftballons)

Katherine had spent the night at Jennifer's house and got up in the morning to make breakfast. Katherine turned on the internet radio to an 80's station and sang to the songs she liked as she got the pans out. Jennifer came into the kitchen all disheveled and kissed Katherine good morning. "Morning baby!"

"Good morning Jenny… what would you like for breakfast?"

"Hmmmm!" Jenny moaned seductively. "You know what I want…!" and she kissed Katherine again.

"What do you want to eat…?" Katherine caught herself when Jenny put a smirk on her face. "I mean… what do you want me to cook?"

"May I have pancakes?" Jenny chuckled.

"Coming right up…" And Katherine began to fix breakfast. Just about then, as Jenny was reading the morning paper, the song '*99 Red Balloons*' came on. Katherine turned it up and began to sing with it. Jennifer picked her head up from the paper.

"Why do like that song? It's so fucking stupid!"

"It's a great song!" Katherine remarked. "It's very deep and has a very positive message…"

"Please!" Jenny answered. "I don't even know what the song is about… and neither do you…"

"I *do* know what the song is about…"

"And is there any way on earth to stop you from telling me what that is…?"

Katherine ignored Jenny and answered her anyway. "The song… is about a child who gets a bag of balloons, 99 red balloons in fact, and one day, decides to fill them up and release them as a message of hope to the world…"

Jenny dropped her head on the table. "Please make her stop!"

"And…" Katherine continued, ignoring Jenny's remark. "…The neighboring country saw the balloons on their radar screens and thought it was an air attack and sent out their jet fighters to counter-attack..."

Jenny lifted her head. "Okay...?" Now she was interested.

"The two countries each thought that the other started a war and they eventually destroyed each other..."

Jenny shook her head. "How the fuck does this song, have a 'positive message'...? The kid started a war that destroyed both countries!"

"...After the war was over, and everyone was dead, the child found a red balloon in the rubble and filled it and released it..."

"And started another war...? What the fuck?" Jenny was now really confused.

"No... It showed that even after all the death and destruction... after all the pain and heartache, the child still had hope for the world... She still had faith in the power of love..." Katherine served Jenny her pancakes.

"I still don't get it..." Jenny said and she poured the syrup and cut into her pancakes.

Katherine kissed her forehead gently as she poured her a cup of coffee. "...Then why are you crying...?" She whispered into Jenny's ear.

"Cause your coffee tastes like shit?" Jenny replied. Katherine put her hand on her hip and laughed. Jenny sobbed a bit and Katherine held and rocked her while she cried softly. Jenny knew full well the meaning of the song. The next song on the radio was *"Safety Dance"*. "Now *this* song... is fucking stupid!" Katherine said and she went over and changed the station. Jennifer laughed uncontrollably. Jenny ate her pancakes as Katherine turned the radio until she got to a Latin station; Hector LaVoz's *"El Dia De Mi Suerte"* began playing. Jennifer began to sing along as she ate.

> *Pronto llegara... el dia de mi suerte,*
> *Se que antes de mi muerte,*
> *Seguro que mi suerte cambriara.*

Katherine joined in.

Pronto llegara… el dia de mi suerte,
Se que antes de mi muerte,
Seguro que mi suerte cambriara.

Jennifer stood up and began to salsa with Katherine. They danced all over the kitchen as if they didn't have a care in the world. When the song ended, they held each other tightly. Today they made up their minds that their luck would change… for the better.

The Tortured Soul Trilogy
(The Seduction of CJ Cassidy)

Chapter 113
(What I Did On My Summer Vacation)

Katherine had gotten a hold of a religious novel by a little known author. She liked the novel and the novelists' style of writing. He was able to write a compelling story with the ability to allow the reader to be personally involved. His way of telling a story enabled the reader to envision the characters through their own personal perceptions. He also was not afraid to touch upon subjects that most would shy away from. She felt that he could, in his own way, write a story based on the events of her life. She contacted him via 'snail mail' and asked if he would write her biography. As an 'honorary' deacon of his church and involved in women's issues, he jumped at the chance to write her story.

He continued to communicate with Katherine through regular mail channels because it was the only safe way to make sure her identity would remain a secret. The return address was always a P.O. Box. With no electronic trail to follow, her identity would remain safe from prying eyes. He began to write "*A Tortured Soul*" under the pen name C.J. Cassidy based on her letters. The book was beginning to come together, but once the storyline drifted into the world of BDSM, he was morally unable to continue. He stopped mid-way through the chapter "*Hanky-Panky*" and informed Katherine of his decision. Katherine was upset that her story would not be told. She didn't want to start over with a new author. He consoled her by telling her that he could turn the project over to a friend of his. Katherine was a bit put-off but soon agreed. He put me in contact with Katherine, and I continued the novel where my friend had left off. That is how *I* became C.J. Cassidy.

Halfway through the novel, I felt that I needed more personal contact with Katherine. There were some details that required face time in order to expidite the novel. To ask her a question by mail, only to have to wait a few days for the answer and to find that the answer only brought up more questions; slowed the writing process down to a crawl. When we needed to have two-way conversations, she mailed me a pre-paid 'burn phone' to communicate with her directly. Still, I wanted to interview her person to person. It took a while, but she agreed.

I had signed up for an acting class in the town where Katherine lived. I knew about The 'C' Cup and I stopped by after an audition. I figured that this would be a nice common neutral ground to meet Katherine in person to interview her. While I was there I was smitten by an olive skinned waitress named Mandy. She asked me to read some of my poetry on open mike night. That night as I finished my set, Nicholas got on stage with a beautiful young woman. It could have been his daughter, but I felt there was something more between these two, so I thought better of it. My suspicions were confirmed when after they finished performing their set, they almost had sex right there on stage. Mandy introduced us later and much to my surprise, the young lady with him was his lover and co-worker, Katherine Stark. The woman whose biography I was in the process of writing. There was something about these two, something I just couldn't put my finger on. Then it dawned on me as we sat and talked over tea and biscotti. They were absolutely in love with each other. I became fascinated with them.

I had begun dating Mandy and that brought me in contact with Nicholas and Katherine more often. (Mandy happened to be his step-daughter.) I got to know them better and we talked openly about life in general. One day Nick invited me to come to his home to go over my notes and to help me edit some pages I was stuck on. I came over to his house and Katherine was there. She was not the most beautiful woman I had ever seen, but there was something about her. I realized that when the two of them were together, she lit up the room. It was like he completed her. Don't get me wrong, he wasn't Svengali. They deeply loved each other and of that there was no doubt. As Nick and I spoke, Katherine made some suggestions on the storyline. They were damn good ideas. Slowly but surely the conversation shifted from their sex life to their relationship. I was blown away as to how they met and why they became lovers. Nick became a little hesitant about the project and wanted to back out. I tried to convince them that their story needed to be told. They agreed, but only if I would promise that I would never reveal their true identities. I told them that I would protect

Katherine like a lioness protects her cubs. My assurances calmed their fears. I began to write their story with a whole new passion.

Before I was able to finish and publish the novel Nick died in a tragic accident. Katherine was absolutely devastated. Mandy and I tried to console her as much as humanly possible but she was inconsolable. Nick never got a chance to read the final draft. Katherine helped me tweak it and finally gave me permission to publish it. It was titled *"A Tortured Soul – The Unauthorized Biography of Nicholas Anderson"* It was published by BookSurge on Valentine's Day, Feb 14th 2008 with Katherine's blessings.

After the book was published to rave reviews, I began to get very bad feedback about Jennifer X. Jones, who was an antagonist in the novel. The more I heard on how much everyone hated her, the more intrigued I became with her story; especially when Katherine began to defend her. That was strange. Why would she defend this cold conniving bitch? I felt the same way about her as my readers did. I had met Jennifer briefly at Nick's funeral and to say that my description of how beautiful this woman is an understatement; is an understatement in of itself.

Katherine put me in contact with Jennifer and I interviewed her to get her side of the story. Again, I was flabbergasted by the ordeals Jennifer went through. I discovered that she was more victim than villain. It took me almost five years to write *"A Tortured Soul..."* I wrote Jennifer's bio *"The Confessions of Jennifer X"* in only three months! After all, the story was written already, I just had to re-tell it from her vantage point. Again my new novel garnered critical acclaim. (Not huge book sales, but hey, I'll take critical acclaim over 'the book stinks' any day!) Jennifer was now being seen in a whole new light. She was no longer reviled for her actions and she even has developed a large following in the Hispanic community. She is now seen as a tough as nails survivor and nobody argues with that.

I stayed in contact with the both of them as I promoted the two novels. I needed their feedback and began a MySpace page to write blogs and bulletins on these two amazing women. I was touched to the very core of my heart when I began to receive E-mail from abused women who said that the stories of Katherine's & Jennifer's heartache and triumph moved them and gave them hope. I tried to be supportive of them as much as humanly

569

possible. I like to think that my life was meant to be focused for that very purpose. The message had been passed on; learn to say 'when!' and that my friends, is priceless!

Now, not everyone took to the biographies, the girls, or to me with open arms... C'est la vie! I didn't expect the whole world to accept my novels. They are brutal and stark. The abuse is real. The sex is raw and passionate. I took a position of; this is what it is, deal with it, or don't. But still, I believe that the subject matter isn't for everyone. There are things that I believe that even adults should not be subjected to!

In the course of my dealings with Katherine and Jennifer, something happened, my respect and admiration of these two amazing women, changed. We had become best friends but I no longer loved them; I fell *in* love *with* them.

> *I shall be telling this with a sigh.*
> *Somewhere ages and ages hence:*
> *Two roads diverged in a woods and I,*
> *Took the one less traveled by,*
> *And that has made all the difference.*

Robert Frost

The Tortured Soul Trilogy

(The Seduction of CJ Cassidy)

Chapter 114
(The Seduction)

After we published '*A Tortured Soul…*' and '*The Confessions of Jennifer X*' and I became very good friends with Katherine and Jennifer. It was no big deal for us to visit each other and stay overnight at each other's homes. Being in Nevada, their house was close to wherever I had an audition. I focused on my friendship with the girls as we stayed in contact while I was pushing their biographies. As you may or may not know by following my MySpace blogs, I spent a week with Katherine and Jennifer at Jennifer's house. Jenny's place is like a palace. We had a wonderful weekend together bar-b-cueing by the pool and we went to a local amusement park and acted like kids again, and then they asked me to stay to help Jenny paint and redecorate her house. We spent another week together shopping and hanging out. It was like a weeklong slumber party. Don't get me wrong, they worked me like a government mule, but, oh the benefits! Katherine is an excellent cook and Jenny… can't cook worth a hill of beans but she likes to prance around her house naked. So does Katherine! Who's got it better than you CJ? Nobody!

One night they took me to a strip club L.L. and Cisco owned. We got comp'd at the door; given V.I.P. seating and we were given a free bottle of Moet. I'm not partial to champagne myself, so I ordered a 7&7. We watched a couple of the girls do their thing on stage.

"So? Jenny… you miss working the pole?" I remarked.

"Hell no…! But I know I could get on that pole right now and out earn all these bitches!"

"I'd give you a hundred right now if you jump up on that stage!" Katherine said laughing.

Jennifer smiled and then looked at me.

"Don't look at me… I'm not going to pay to have other men stare at your tits! Besides I get that floorshow for free. Forget I brought it up!" I laughed.

Jenny smiled at me and grinned, she knew I liked looking at her naked body. Hell, who wouldn't? I had gotten my first peek when they house-sat for me when I was on vacation a while back. I came home in the morning and Katherine was making breakfast, Jennifer was knocked out on my bed buck-naked. Have I told you Jennifer has an amazing body?

We sat and drank and watched the show. A couple of the girls offered to give us lap dances. Katherine had one after Jennifer had one. I didn't want a lap dance, especially after I was able to see the girls up close. When I was in my twenties I would have loved to have a hot young woman grind her naked ass into my lap. Now that I'm in my fifties I didn't enjoy myself. I developed a problem seeing girls younger than my daughters taking their clothes off and gyrating for money. The mere thought of it skeeved me out. I know these girls are of 'age' but I just felt like an old pervert. Seeing grown men 'making it rain' and then seeing the girls on their knees scooping up the money, kinda made me sick to my stomach. I had the same reaction when I went to a strip club for my brothers' bachelor party. I never realized before how degrading all this really was.

"CJ...? What's the matter? You're not enjoying yourself?" Katherine asked me.

"I'm good..." and I sipped my drink.

"Bullshit!" Jenny cut in. "What's wrong? These girls aren't hot and sexci enough for you?"

"I've seen better..." and I winked at Jennifer. Jenny smiled and I stirred my drink and took another sip. "They're cute and all... I just have other things on my mind..."

I had married Nick's step-daughter, Mandy, but because of a lot of baggage that both of us carried, we separated and got an annulment after only two years. That was my third failed marriage. I'm 50 years old, single and my carreer still hasn't taken off. I was having the worse mid-life crisis ever!

Jenny offered to spend $50 on a lap dance for me; I declined. They finished off the bottle and we went home early. They asked me why I really didn't enjoy the club and I told them. They tried to make up for it later by ordering porn on PPV. As much as I like porn, I was a little put off watching porn at their house. I mean; you know men don't watch porn for the plot! I didn't want to get caught doing anything stupid that would get me banned from visiting them ever again. I resigned myself to just spend the rest of the time with them finishing painting and decorating the house.

That Friday, the girls were out shopping all day and I was left in the house alone to finish painting the last room to be decorated. I spent the morning clearing out the room and moved all the furniture into the spare bedroom I was staying in. I would just have to sleep on Jennifer's sofa bed tonight. The girls came home just as I had finished painting the trim and the molding. Katherine put the groceries down on the counter for tonight's dinner. Jinx, Jenny's chauffer and personal bodyguard, put Jennifer's purchases in the guest room where all the furniture was being stored. Tomorrow we would put the rooms back together.

Katherine kissed me and pulled back. "Ewwww! You stink! Go take a shower!"

"What? I've been working hard all day."

Jennifer walked past me and scrunched up her face. "We know... forget taking a shower... go soak in the tub and don't come out until you're clean and fresh!" Jenny said.

"And do not put your stinky clothes in the hamper... put them right in the wash! Ewww!" Katherine added.

I left the room, but not before fanning my armpits at them first!

"Ewww!" They chimed together.

I got in the shower and rinsed off first before I filled the Jacuzzi tub to soak. Jennifer's tub could comfortably fit three people; mine could only hold one. As I lay there I imagined what it would be like, the three of us in the tub, naked and all... soapy. I added some lavender bath salts to the water and hit the jets. I hadn't realized how sore and tired I was from working at Jenny's house all week. It felt good just to lie there and soak. Jenny's favorite soft jazz station always played in her bathroom. I reached over for the bottle of lavender and added a little more to the water. What? Men can't be pampered a little? "Calgon... take me away!" I must have fallen asleep in the tub because the next thing I remember is Jennifer knocking on the bathroom door.

"Did you drown in there?"

"No... I'll be out in a few... I'll be all 'pruney'... but I'll be out!" Jennifer laughed and went downstairs. I went downstairs wearing only my jeans. I was only supposed to stay for one weekend and I had only packed an overnight bag. The girls wanted to buy me clothes, but I didn't want to impose. They said it was only fair, seeing that I helped so much the last two weeks. I declined. I've been married and women like to dress me like I'm their personal Ken doll. I didn't want to hurt their feelings if I didn't like the clothes they bought. I'm very casual in my style and I like it that way. (Katherine says homeless men dress better than I do!) I went into the kitchen where Katherine was cooking dinner. I came behind her and put my arms around her and kissed her neck. "Better?"

Katherine turned into me and sniffed me. "Much...!" She was only wearing her terrycloth bathrobe. (Cooking with hot oil, naked... not a good idea! Pffftt!) I tried to sneak a peek at Katherine's nipples as she cooked but she held her robe tight over her. I could swear I saw her wink at me. "Now git while I finish making dinner." She said.

"Yes ma'am." And I kissed her. I made my way into the living room and Jennifer had already pulled out the sofa bed and was watching TV while eating a fresh fruit salad. Jennifer was propped up there naked, which did not surprise me; the girls always walked around the house naked any chance they had; although Katherine was the modest one and usually wore only panties and her robe. Jennifer scooted over and patted the bed to get me to lie down next to her. I got in bed with her and she began to feed me fruit from her bowl as we watched TV.

"Dinner should be ready in an hour." Katherine called out.

"Good... cause I'm starved... what are we having?"

"She's making salmon cakes and Spanish rice..." Jenny answered.

"I love Katherine's salmon cakes!"

"I know... she's making them especially for you!" Jenny said. And Jennifer snuggled into me and fed me a piece of cantaloupe. I put my arm around her and continued to watch TV until she put her hand on my chest and began to stroke my nipple. She then took a strawberry, bit into it and rubbed my nipple with it and began to lick and suck it off. I was very excited but I was also very uncomfortable. I didn't know what was going on. Katherine was in the next room. What if she walked in on us? What if this upset her? What the fuck is wrong with me? This sensuous, beautiful, naked young woman is licking my nipples and I'm scared as shit! She then moved her way up and began kissing my neck and ears. I began to pant and she pulled back to look into my eyes. "Relax… I promise I'm not going to hurt you!" She cooed.

"My getting hurt is not what I'm concerned with right now…" I whispered as I glanced towards the kitchen opening.

"Don't you want to have sex with me?" She asked seductively.

I looked at her; she was hot, horny, naked and sexy as all hell, this *had* to be a trick question. "Of course I do… I've wanted to make love to you since I first met you…" I paused. "But…? What about Katherine?" I couldn't believe the situation I was in. I have an unbelievable shot at paradise, and I'm turning it down because our best friend and her lover was in the very next room. Jenny looked into my eyes and smiled again; she then leaned in and started to kiss me just under my jaw, worked her way back to my ear, blew on it and softly said:

"Okay, if that's how you feel about it…! Do Katherine first…!"

My heart almost jumped out of my chest! Did she just say what I thought she did? *"What?"* I whispered incredulously. Jennifer kissed me deeply and got up and headed towards the kitchen. My gawd! Her ass is magnificent! She stopped and turned to me. "If you think you might need… a little something… to help you to keep up with us tonight… there's a bottle of Viagra in the medicine cabinet in the downstairs bathroom." She met up with Katherine just as she was entering with our dinner tray. Jennifer whispered something to her, kissed her, took the tray from her and headed back into the kitchen. Katherine stepped up to the edge of the sofa bed.

"Hi…" she said sweetly.

"Hi Katherine..." I whispered nervously.

"Are you okay with this?" She asked

In my mind, I was shouting *"HELL YEAH I'm okay with this...! Now drop the robe and get your hot little ass in this BED!"* It came out... "Are you sure *you're* okay with this?" I stammered.

Katherine smiled and dropped her robe slowly on the floor. She climbed up and nestled into me and began to kiss me passionately. I was so turned on and so scared that I hadn't even realized she had unzipped my pants and was stroking me. As much as I fantasized about this, I was not prepared for it. I was sweating bullets. What if I didn't... *'measure up'?* She began to work her kisses down my body until she got to my belly button and the tip of my hard cock was inches from her mouth. Then she looked at me and said: "May I?"

Did she *really* have to ask permission? "Please do..." I whispered. And she slowly kissed her way down my throbbing member and began to lick and suck me. My eyes went to the back of my head and we were only getting started. Katherine held my cock in her left hand and got up on her knees to straddle me. "Katherine! Stop!" I moaned.

"What's wrong CJ?" Katherine said softly.

(*I can't fucking believe I'm doing this! What the fuck is wrong with me?*) "I know the rules... and I'm not... 'prepared' for this. I didn't think this would happen... I mean... I hoped it would... but..."

"Oh...!" She smiled. "I almost forgot..." She rolled off of me and reached into the end table and took out several different condoms. I wondered how long they had been planning this. "We didn't know what size you were or what you would like to use..." She eliminated the ones she knew wouldn't fit and held up the three that were left. I had no idea which one to pick. I haven't needed a condom in years. Hey, why buy an umbrella when you don't expect any rain?

"The silver one!" I said. She began to open the package for me and I still can't believe I said this... "Is it true that you can put that on a man without using your hands?" (*DUDE! What the fuck is wrong with you? I can't believe you just said that to Katherine! You just blew getting laid!*)

She just smiled and put the condom in her mouth and HOLY COW!!!! She *can* do that! Just when we were about to 'engage', we both said to each other. "Please be gentile with me!"

And we both laughed nervously. I'm not going to go into details on what happened next, but it was the most romantic, passionate love making experience I have had in a very, very, very long time. I really like Katherine, she is so warm and gentile and the sweetest woman I have ever known. I could not imagine or conceive of why anybody would ever want to hurt her! I made sweet love to her for almost twenty minutes. I wanted to experience her, all of her. I had no idea if I would ever have another chance like this ever again.

After the foreplay, I was going at her like it would be the last time I would ever get any pussy. After we were finished, we cuddled and lay there and basked in the moment.

"That... was beautiful CJ... thank you..." And she kissed me and she snuggled into my chest. "I really needed that!"

I kissed her on her forehead. "You're welcome Katherine...!"

We were about to fall sleep, when we heard Jennifer clear her throat. "Ah hem! I know you two did not forget all about me!" I laughed, Katherine giggled and got up out of the bed and went back into the kitchen. "So CJ...? You think you're ready for round two?" Jenny said.

"Bring it BITCH!" I ordered and I made the '*come here*' motion with my hands.

(Okay, I know what you're thinking right now. No... I did NOT lose my last mind. I know Jennifer very well and that was exactly what she wanted to hear!)

Her eyes widened, her lips parted and she let out a slow sigh as her heaving bosom rose and fell. Her nipples were rock hard and she smiled at me and she smacked her ass... hard.

"If I bring it... you *better* fucking deliver!" I got up, went to the bathroom and washed up. When I got back to the living room, Jenny was bent over the back of the couch, masturbating nice and slow. I got my hard-on back immediately. I watched her perform as I put a new condom on. "You took so damn long... I had to start without you..." she moaned. "You know how hard it was... being in the very next room... hearing the two of you going at it... and I wasn't getting any?"

"Was it this hard...?" And I came up behind her and eased my cock into her.

"Damn!" She exclaimed. "That's what mama wanted!" Again, I'm not going into any details, but we did break a lamp. Having already had an orgasm with Katherine made my 'curtain call' with Jennifer last that much longer. And that was a good thing because Jennifer is a world-class sexual athlete in bed. That night she won two gold medals and a bronze! (I won Miss Congeniality, Pffftt!) Katherine, soft and gentile; Jennifer, rough and nasty, together they were the most fantastic sexual experience I've ever had! They are the best of both worlds. And if I ever couldn't carry the burden, they would do each other! We had dinner together and we all finished off the evening in Jennifer's bedroom. Although she had many trappings of bondage and discipline in her room, they knew I wasn't into that. We just monkey fucked each other all night long. Now I'm not vain and I'm not embarrassed to say that I did have to use one of *daddy's little helpers* to get me through the night. I had NO intentions of disappointing either one of them! It was an amazing and magical night!

The next morning I had a reaction I did not expect, I woke up sullen and moody. I don't know what we did last night. Oh, I know *what* we did... I just didn't know what the ramifications of our actions would be. I've had friendships ruined by entering into a sexual relationship and I did not want to have jeopardized our friendship for sex... amazing sex! But was it really worth it? I didn't want to live the old Chinese curse; *May you get what you wished for!* Katherine entered the kitchen where I was having a cup of coffee and kissed me.

"Good morning CJ... you're up early..."

"I couldn't sleep..."

"Are you okay?" She asked with concern in her voice.

"I'm okay..." then I hesitated.

Katherine sensed my anxiety and got herself a cup of coffee. "Hold that thought... I'll get Jennifer..." She returned moments later with a groggy Jennifer in tow.

"This better be important...! I like to sleep in when I get a good fucking!" And Jennifer rubbed her eyes and kissed me. "And you were great last night!"

"Jenny... this is serious..." Katherine said.

Jennifer looked at Katherine then at me. I had a tear in my eye. "What's wrong? What's going on...?"

"We all need to talk…" Katherine said.

"Yeah… we need to talk…" I said. We sat in the kitchen and talked about everything… anything… you know… things. We discussed things we should have talked about last night, before we… got intimately involved.

"Is this going to be a problem for you CJ?" Katherine asked.

"What…? Having sex with the both of you? Please! I've been married twice and I've been around the block more than a few times… I can certainly handle whatever you two can dish out!"

"CJ…" Jennifer said softly. "Just because you spent four years in high school, doesn't mean you have a college education…"

I looked at Jennifer and then Katherine. Katherine nodded her head. "She's right CJ; you have no idea what we are capable of dishing out…" Katherine sighed.

"We're *not* talking *about*…?"

Jennifer kissed me softly. "No baby… we're not talking about B&D…"

"We have needs that most men can't fulfill…" Katherine whispered. "We don't want you to feel… *obligated*…"

I looked at them with a look of disappointment on my face. I thought I got the job done. "Wow…! So… last night…?" I began to ask. I really didn't want to hear the answer.

"Oh No! You were great last night… you far exceeded my expectations!" Jennifer cut in.

"Ummm? Thank you?" I didn't know if that was a compliment or not.

"That's not what she meant… We knew we were going to enjoy your 'company', we just didn't expect that your… skills… and your willingness to satisfy our needs would go so far above and beyond the call of duty."

"You sure that wasn't just the Viagra talking?" I said.

"Honey! If there is a pill out there that can make a man eat me out like you did last night, I wanna invest in the company!" Jenny giggled and stroked her pussy fur gently.

"Yeah CJ… that's a skill you brought to the table on your own!"

"Well!" I laughed. "You don't care how your man is hung, once you get Puerto Rican tongue!"

Jennifer snickered. "Honey! Don't kid yourself!" My jaw dropped. "Oh baby…!" Jenny quickly said apologetically. "You're more than adequate in your package…" She turned her head away. "I'm just saying…!" and Jenny ran her hand through her tussled hair.

"Ignore her! I like the size of your cock!" Katherine cut in. "And… your skills with your tongue!" and she kissed me.

"Deep throating you isn't ever going to be a problem!" Jenny said aside.

"*JENNIFER*!" Katherine exclaimed.

"I'm kidding!" Jenny smirked.

"No you're not… but I don't have an ego problem… its okay! I'm used to working with what little I have!" I said. Jennifer smiled and kissed me.

"Size doesn't matter… you know that!" Katherine said to Jennifer.

"Ri-ight…! Which is why breast reduction and cock shortening are the two biggest plastic surgeries performed today!" Jenny said sarcastically.

"JENNIFER!!!"

"*What…?*"

"Don't worry about it Katherine! We all know Jennifer gets '*ugly*' when she doesn't get her beauty sleep!" I said. Jennifer dropped her head and started to snore. We all laughed it off. "Okay… so… where do we go from here?" We drank coffee and ate Danish and talked, and cried, and hugged each other. We came to the understanding that whenever they needed to borrow a cup of 'sex', they could call me. If I needed to borrow a fuck, all I need do is call, anytime. I was officially inducted as a friend with benefits, not a booty call… a friend, with benefits. Nothing of our previous relationship would ever change. We were BFF and they were my BBE (Best Bitches Ever) I found out that the girls had planned this all along, They wanted to spend some personal time with me and taking me to the strip club was supposed to get me in the mood, (That back fired). Watching porn with them only made me feel self-conscious… Sometimes you just have to let the love-making process progress naturally. Let passion and desire take control and the results are amazing if you truly care about each other. We spoke for about an hour or so. Jennifer really wanted to go back to bed.

Katherine took my hand. "Come on… let's get you back into bed…"

"I'm not sleepy…" I said to her.

Katherine kissed me deeply. "Neither am I…!"

"Well I'm going back to sleep…" Jennifer chimed in. "Wake me when you two are finished and I'll put your ass to sleep CJ!"

"And just how are you gonna do that?" I asked seductively.

"I'm gonna put your ass to work motherfucker…! You still have to move all the furniture out of the spare room and get my house back in order…!" Then Jennifer kissed me. "After you do that… then and only then…will I fuck your brains out again!" She turned to go back to bed. "And you owe me for the lamp you broke!"

"Technically… *you* broke the lamp while I had you bent over the couch!"

Jenny stopped and thought a moment. She remembered that she kicked the lamp over when she threw her leg up to give me deeper access. "Okay… culpa mea!"

"If you two don't mind, is it okay if I cook tonight?" I said.

Katherine laughed; "You can cook?"

"When I wasn't trying to make it as an actor or a poet, I tried to get my degree in culinary college…"

"You have a 'degree'…?" Katherine asked.

I shook my head. "Not really! But I did pretty well in my classes, before I ran out of tuition money…"

"Hell yeah you can cook tonight!" Katherine said.

"You didn't graduate…? You better taste it before I eat it!" Jennifer grumbled towards Katherine.

"Don't I always?" Katherine laughed.

"Oh… no… this bitch didn't!"

Katherine rolled her head. "Oh yes this bitch did!" Katherine led me to the spare bedroom. Jenny went into her bedroom.

"I don't want to disturb Jenny's sleep. I hope you don't mind?" Katherine said.

"If you don't mind it being full of two rooms of furniture!"

"I forgot...!" Katherine thought for a moment. "Sofa bed?" I nodded.

"When you two finish... somebody get up and make breakfast... Maria has the weekend off..." And Jenny went back to bed.

"You want to watch that porn film we rented yesterday?"

"I don't think we'll be watching TV..." I was already making a pup tent in my pajamas. Katherine smiled and took me to the living room.

The following chapters describe and chronicle our developing sexual and personal relationship that spans the next three years. Because I live in New York and the girls live in Nevada, each encounter may have been separated by weeks or even months. For most part we had a long distance love affair. We saw each other whenever we could. I could only go see them when I had time off from work. If we all had that week free or a three-day weekend, we would all stay at Jennifer's. Katherine or Jennifer could come over and visit me anytime they wanted, but Jennifer was very busy running her company most of the year. Katherine's schedule was much more open and would visit me at her whim. I only saw them both if I stayed at Jenny's place. Our sexual relationship was simple at first and didn't become more provocative until we got 'familiar' and more 'comfortable' with our situation. At first, it was just about the sex but then things got more and more complicated.

The next chapter occurred after I had not seen the girls for almost six months. My daughters were now back living with me and all our schedules were crazy. Sometimes Jennifer had business conferences in different cities back to back. Katherine was busy with her 'volunteer' work with abuse victims and I was trying to help out my MySpace friends with their personal problems. The three of us would talk on the phone or e-mail each other almost every day. They say that absence makes the heart grow fonder. Well, being physically away from each other only showed us that our relationship was not just sexual. We had developed a bond, a bond that would be tested in the times to come.

I'm not into the rough stuff the girls are into, but they later cultivated a desire in me to enjoy kinky sex and get into role-playing. (Yeah, like they twisted my arm!) I draw the line to anything that I think is too rough or physically abusive, but as long as I think it's fun and playful, I'm very willing to play along. They know not to take it too far as far as I'm concerned. They respect my wishes. I enjoy 'learning' new things. Boy! Do I enjoy 'learning' new things! I just have to keep an eye on my limitations. It's up to me to make sure we don't cross that line.

The Tortured Soul Trilogy
(The Seduction of CJ Cassidy)
Chapter 115
(A New Morning)

Monday morning about 11am, I got up out of bed and Katherine was in the kitchen making me breakfast. To my surprise, Jenny was up and already out of the house. "Where'd Jenny head out to so early in the morning?"

"She had an appointment with her doctor..."

"She okay...?"

"Just her routine check-up... you know she doesn't play when it comes to her health. She should be back soon." I nodded. "Hungry?"

"I could eat a little something..."

"Greedy!" I laughed as she put a plate of home baked muffins in front of me. "Have one of my blueberry surprise muffins..."

I took a fresh warm muffin and bit into it, it was good. I took another bite. "Honey...? They're no blueberries in this...!"

"SURPRISE!!!" I shook my head. Katherine laughed. Just about then Jenny walked in the door.

"Hello?" Jenny called out as she put her jacket away.

"We're in the kitchen baby!" Katherine answered. Jenny came in and kissed me and then kissed Katherine. "How was your check-up...?" she asked Jenny.

"I swear, if I ever get my hands on the motherfucker who invented the mammogram... I'm gonna put his dick in it!"

Katherine laughed; I grabbed my crotch. "Owwwww!"

"My tits still hurt..." and she opened her blouse and unhooked her bra from the front. "Free!" she exclaimed and she kneaded her breasts so very gently. "...Don't get any ideas CJ... and you neither, Katherine!" I stood up behind her and began to rub and massage her shoulders. Jennifer cooed. "Oh what the hell... go for it C.J.!" Jenny leaned back into me and arched her back. I reached around her and gently massaged her breasts being very careful not to touch her tender nipples. "Oh that's feels so fucking good! Now if only this is what a mammogram felt like, more women would get checked more often." Jenny raised her arms and put her hands behind my neck. I kissed Jenny and she reciprocated. I knew it felt good to her because her nipples perked right up.

"Other than that, how was the rest of your check up?" Katherine asked.

"Huh?" Jenny cooed.

"Your check up…? How did it go?"

"Oh! My blood pressure, blood sugar, and cholesterol are all good. I'm a little anemic so my doctor is giving me some vitamin and mineral supplements."

Katherine passed her the plate of muffins. "Have one of Katherine's blueberry surprise muffins…" I said. Jenny picked one up and bit into it.

"Oh Katherine this is delicious!" I looked over Jenny's shoulders, and there were blueberries in the muffin. I looked puzzled.

"Your muffin has blueberries?"

Jenny looked at me as if I were an idiot. "Of course… They're Blueberry Surprise Muffins!" And she shook her head and looked at me funny. "What the fuck is wrong with you?" Katherine busted out laughing. Jenny looked at her.

"Am I missing something?" Jenny asked. Katherine got me again.

"You gonna take the rest of the day off?" Katherine asked.

"No… I just came home to shower and change… I have a new client I have to schmooze this afternoon. But I'm coming straight home to you two as soon as it's over… CJ?"

"Yeah Jenny?"

"You think you can keep your dick out of Katherine until I get home?"

"I can guarantee it… at least until 3 o'clock this afternoon…"

"Why 3?" Jenny asked.

"That's when I should be back from an audition I booked last Friday…"

"What are you going for?" Katherine asked.

"What else? They need a thug for a scene where the lead gets beat up…"

"When are they going to realize that you can actually act?" I shrugged my shoulders. "Well, I hope you get it baby!" Jenny said as she went to go upstairs to shower.

"Whether you get it or not… you will get 'it' when you get home…" Katherine whispered.

"CJ!" Jenny yelled out from the stairs.

"Yeah Jenny?"

"What time is your audition?"

"I have to leave out of here in about an hour… why?"

"Get your ass in this shower with me… I'll have Jinx drop you off! But right now… I need you to get me off! That bitch can wait!" Katherine and I laughed as I headed upstairs.

The Tortured Soul Trilogy
(The Seduction of CJ Cassidy)
Chapter 116
(If You Can't Stand The Heat!)

I was visiting the girls while I was suspended with out pay for two weeks from my regular job. I got to Jenny's from working out at the local gym after an audition I had for a local Indy film. I hit the shower when I got home. Jenny has a gym on her property but I need something just a little more 'hardcore'. Their gym has ballet bars, Yoga mats and Pilates machines. I need a gym that smells of sweat and testosterone, not perfume and potpourri, especially when I had a bad day of auditions. When I came downstairs, Katherine was just getting in from doing food shopping. I grabbed the bags she had.

"Hey sweetie…" and I kissed her.

"You just got in?"

I nodded. "A while ago."

"Did you get the part?" I shook my head no. Katherine knew not to question me any further about the audition. If I had gotten the part, it would have given me the excuse to stay a few more days. I would have used my vacation time. "Your time will come." And she kissed me gently.

"Are there any more bags?" I asked, changing the subject.

"Jinx got them…" And Jinx entered with the rest of the shopping bags.

"I'll take those off your hands Jinx…"

"Thank you Mr. Cassidy…" and he handed me the bags. "Will that be all Ms. Stark?"

"Yes Jinx thank you so much… you're a doll…" and Katherine kissed him on the cheek. I puffed up as Jinx got in the car and drove off. "What are you *doing*?" Katherine asked in bewilderment.

"Brother moving in on *my* territory!" Katherine laughed hard. "What???" I said.

"Jinx would *breathe* on you and you'd go down like a drunken prom date!"

"What...? Have you seen these guns?" And I flexed for Katherine. She smiled.

"Actually those are quite impressive... You just got back from the gym?"

"Yep!" and I flexed again. "I'm just six sit-ups away from being a Greek god!"

Katherine busted out laughing again. "Bacchus...?" She remarked.

"What...? I know you didn't!"

Katherine did the 'head move' "Oh yeah I did!" and she laughed again.

"You... have been hanging around Jenny way too much!" Katherine laughed again. "Speaking of which... where is she...? I thought she'd be home by now."

"She sent Jinx to pick me up and drop me off so I could start dinner... she'll be here..."

"Just in time to sit down to eat..." I said to complete Katherine's thought.

Katherine cut her eyes. "I believe we discussed Jenny's cooking shortcomings..."

"One of these days I'm going to get her alone in this kitchen..."

"You've done that already..." Katherine snickered.

"...To teach her how to cook..."

Katherine kissed me. "Like I said; 'you've done that already...!' Now Mr. Greek god, you wanna put those muscles to work putting away the groceries while I start dinner?"

"I thought you were going to let me cook tonight?"

"You don't mind a little help do you?"

I grabbed the grocery bags and flexed one more time. Katherine shook her head. "What are we making?" I asked as I put the canned food away in the pantry.

"I picked up some free range chicken..."

I kissed Katherine. "I'll put these away and I'll help you with the biscuits..."

"Great... but help me cut up the chicken too!"

"No problem, your wish is my command!" And I kissed her again. The kiss lingered.

"Dinner first!" Katherine whispered and she kissed me again. I put the rest of groceries away and as Katherine made the seasoned flour for the chicken, I began to quarter the chicken. "You're pretty good at that..." she said to me.

"I was a butcher for about a year..."

"Is there anything you haven't done?'

I snapped my fingers in the air twice. "There is one thing!" I lisped. Katherine laughed and got the peanut oil ready and started pre-heating the oven for the biscuits. I handed her the cut chicken and she shook a drop of water into the oil to check if it was hot enough. She dipped the chicken in an egg and buttermilk coating, floured the chicken and slid them into the hot oil. I got the biscuits out of the fridge and tapped it open and buttered the pan. I handed Katherine the pan of biscuits and she slid it into the oven and started the timer. I continued to coat and flour the chicken as she put a pot on the stove to start the vegetables. We moved through that kitchen like a well-oiled machine. Not once did we bump into each other and we anticipated what the other had planned to do next. I reached into the freezer and took out two bags of frozen vegetables. "Broccoli or mixed veggies...?"

"Mixed veggies... Jennifer won't eat broccoli..."

"Sure she will..." I had a look of surprise on my face.

"Okay... I don't want her eating broccoli!"

I laughed my ass off! "Mixed veggies it is..." Suddenly I heard Katherine scream and grab her hand. "Baby what happened?"

"The oil popped and I burned myself!" She put her hands under the sink and ran cold water on them.

"Let daddy see..." She held out her hand and I could see it was starting to blister. I put the frozen broccoli bag on her hand. She held the bag on it as I took the last of the chicken out of the oil. I checked the biscuits and they were ready so I took them out and basketed them. I went back to check on Katherine. "Let me see..." She showed me her hand. "That's not too bad... just keep the frozen bag on it." Katherine pouted and sighed. "You want me to kiss it and make it better?"

"Ah huh!" and she pouted again. And she held her hand out and I kissed the boo-boo.

"Better?"

589

"Uh-uh…" and she smiled. I kissed her hand again, and again.

"What are you doing?" she said and she began to breathe heavy. I didn't answer her and I began to kiss the tips of her fingers. Katherine exhaled deeply. "What are… you… doing?" I kissed the palm of her hand and placed my other hand on the back of her neck and drew her head gently towards me. "What… are…?" And I kissed her passionately. I then began to kiss her neck and ears. "You… doing?" she moaned. I continued to kiss and nuzzle her neck. She threw her head back and took a deep breath as I nuzzled her breasts. "Oh… my…!" she moaned. I just love the look in a woman's eyes when she wants me to make love to her. I held her face in both my hands and caressed her face as I kissed her and she kissed me back. Our tongues probed each other's lips and tongues. Katherine blushed as our lips touched and we French kissed passionately. I again nuzzled her neck while I held her waist and worked my hands under her blouse up under her breasts. She breathed hot and heavy. I blew in her ear as I gently stroked her nipples with my thumbs. She gasped as I pinched her nipples. "Stop!" She whispered breathing heavily.

"Do you really want me to stop?" I whispered in her ear making sure my hot breath touched her ear.

"No…!" She whispered. She unbuttoned my shirt and began to lick and suck my nipples. She pinched my nipples as I unbuttoned her blouse. I returned the favor and she gasped for air. I held her and I began to lick and suck on her nipples. Her legs were getting weak. I licked around and around her areola and nibbled her nipple so very gently and she moaned. "Ohhhhhhhh! Myyyyyy!" I kissed her between her breasts and she kissed the top of my bald head. She grabbed my head, leaned me back and kissed me again. She then reached down and fondled my stiff throbbing cock over my pants. 'Ohhhhh ummmmm! That feels… so… nice… and hard!" And she continued to stroke me over my pants. I lifted her into my arms and carried her into the living room. We were still kissing as I gently lay her down on the couch. She unzipped me and began to stroke my cock in her hands. I was working her nipples gently and pinched them and she cooed. I reached under her short skirt and pulled off her panties while placing both her ankles on my right shoulder. I gently kissed her calves as I took her panties off. Katherine started to coo and purr. She giggled as my kisses tickled her. I then placed her right foot on my left shoulder and again kissed her calves as I slowly worked my way down kissing the inside her legs. She grinded her ass as I got closer and closer to her pussy; I paused and just looked at her stroke her labia gently. She closed her eyes and moaned. She opened her eyes to see me staring right into hers. She blinked and then she reached up to pinch her nipples. I knew what she was doing. She was trying to make me break eye contact with her. She closed her eyes and turned away. I put my hand on her chin.

"Don't..." I whispered. "I think you're beautiful...!" I tried gently to get her to turn her head back to me, she resisted. A tear came to her eye.

"Eat me!" she whispered. And she did not mean that in the good way.

"As you wish..." I whispered.

She turned back to me and sighed. "Oh CJ!" and her countenance softened. I then buried my face into her hot, moist pussy. I licked and nibbled her clit and she swooned with every lick. She took my head and directed me wherever she wanted me to be and I had no problem with that. She threw her hands above her head and I reached up and pinched her nipples again. She trashed her head back and forth and moaned deeply. "Mmmmmmmmmmmm ahhhhh!" I had taken the opportunity of while I was tonguing and licked her pussy and labia to get out a condom from my wallet and put it on. She held my arms and pulled me up to lie on top of her. She placed her left leg on the back of the couch and her right foot on the floor. Katherine was so wet and juicy that my cock eased into her pussy like a heat-seeking missile. Her eyes and mouth opened wide as I entered her so very slowly. "Right there... Ohhhh, you feel so good!" And she thrashed her head again and tears welled in her eyes.

"Am I hurting you baby?"

"No... give me...!" And she put her hands on my ass and pulled me inward. Again her mouth opened wide and I put my finger in her mouth and she began to suck my finger and gasp for air, and I haven't even started pumping her yet! I slowly pulled out and entered her again. "Muuuuuuuuu maaaaaaa ahhhhhh haaaaa! I love your kkk... kkk... cock!" And she pulled my ass towards her again and I pumped her as fast as she pushed and pulled my hips. "ggg… ggg… ggg…. Ahhhh haaaa! Nice! That feels so good… so ggg… ggg…" Tears welled in her eyes as did mine. I buried my face into her neck and began to bite and suck her neck just behind her ear. "Mmmmmmmmmmmmmmmmm ha haa haaa!" And then… I lost my mind. I began to pump her like a jackhammer. "Yeah… yeah oh yeah right there… right there… don't stop don't… mm mm mm myyyyyyy ggg… ggg… gggg" And she made a strange gurgling sound and her eyes went to the back of her head. I then began to ram my cock hard and deep into her. "Mmm… mmm… yeah! Yeah! Ohh yessssss!" And her voice got deep and rough. She put her hands behind her and sat up from her position. "Oh you motherfucker… you mother… fucker! You! Mmma mma muuuuuu! Ayiiiiiiiiiiiiiii!

I threw my head back. "Ahhhhhhhhhh!"

"Yeah right there… cum for me… cum for me baby… it's all yours… cum for meeeeeee!" I put my full body weight on Katherine and changed my stroke to where my hips were slamming into hers. The sounds of our loins smacking together were emphasized by the sound that a wet pussy makes when you're ramming your cock into it hard! "Oh yeah! Oh yeah! Give meeeeeee!" and she let out a high-pitched squeal. I came hard and the sweat poured off me onto Katherine. She rubbed my sweat off my face with her hands. "Yeah baby! Yeah… cum for me…." I only wished that I could feel her pussy on my cock and not through a condom. I threw my head back and spurted hard again! She rotated her hips for me.

"Stop! Stop… stop!" I moaned. It felt too damn good. And I eased my cock out of her. Her jaw dropped.

"Ohhhh hohhhhh!" and her eyes went back in her head again. "Mmmmmmmm" she cooed and I laid down on her and she held me and put her thumb in her mouth and we both fell asleep.

I just don't get it, and I will NEVER understand why anybody would want to tame or hurt this beautiful and vivacious woman! When her sensual spirit lets go… it is an amazing experience! I am thankful for the honor and privilege to be able to share in it! I don't know how much time had passed but I was shocked awake by something extremely cold on the small of my back. I jumped up and screamed! It was Jennifer; she had placed the bag of frozen mixed vegetables on my back. Katherine jumped too when I screamed.

"You made biscuits and fried chicken but you couldn't wait five minutes to heat up the vegetables before you two started to fuck on my couch?" Katherine laughed as Jenny went back to the kitchen to fix herself a plate. "And you better had left me some dick for dessert! That's all I have to say!" We both laughed at her. "Ha-Ha shit! One of... or both of you is fucking me tonight...! Just like the two of you... I need some loving too... one of ya'll better give me some or I'm gonna know the reason why..." She came back in with her plate, eating but still fussing. She sat down on love seat opposite the couch. "I'm out busting my ass making this paper and you two are in *my* house... getting *your* swerve on... Mama needs some loving too... shit!" We just laughed at her watching her eat and fuss. She pointed at us with a piece of chicken. "I aint laughing... This aint funny... as a matter of fact... one of you should be licking my pussy right now! I'm serious...!" She bit into a chicken thigh. "Damn... this chicken is so good!"

Katherine got up and kneeled in front of her and started to unbutton Jenny's blouse and I undid her bra from behind. As Katherine went down on her I began to suck and lick her nipples. Jennifer moaned. "Yeahhhh! That's what I'mmmmmm talking about... show a bitch some... l... l... love... mmmmmmmmm!" And she calmed the fuck down as I reached under her skirt and fondled her wet pussy. Katherine kissed my hand. "Ya'll have no idea how horny I got watching just you two... laying... there... knowing that you just... mmmmmm! Yeah... right there..." And she threw her head back while we all enjoyed dessert. We got chicken fat all over... well... everything! LOL!

Author's Note

I did try to get Jennifer one-on-one in the kitchen to have a cooking lesson. It did NOT turn out anywhere near like this chapter... the chicken she made was under-cooked and made me sick! From now on Jenny is banned from cooking! She's allowed to make coffee and reservations and that's it!

BTW I won't eat her cooking but I WILL eat her out! I aint stupid! Pffft!

The Tortured Soul Trilogy
(The Seduction of CJ Cassidy)
Chapter 117
(Bridge Over Troubled Water)

Joanna was a friend of ours who, with Katherine's and Jennifer's help, got the courage to finally leave her abusive husband. They had been together for almost ten years and he beat and abused her for eight of those years. He broke her jaw on two separate occasions. She had two daughters, seven and five and one day when he beat the oldest, it was the last straw and their last day. She waited and when he went to work the next morning, she packed her shit and got out. She took what little she owned and her two girls and started her life anew. It wasn't that easy... Jimmy did not just go away. He did not just let it go... She had an order of protection... for her, and one for each of her two daughters. It meant nothing after he beat her again. It was too little, too late. Sure he was arrested; sure he was brought up on charges. Sure he was released, to do it all over again. This had gone on for another two years. Joanna came by to visit Jennifer one day when I was spending the week with her; her hair was swept over the right side of her face. "I love the new hairstyle!" I said as I went to kiss her but she pulled away. That's when I saw the black and blue bruise on her jaw. She was using her hair to hide it. "He hit you didn't he?" She cried and held me but not to hug me but to hold me back.

"Please don't CJ... he's not worth it!" I kissed Joanna and held her close to me.

"But *you* ARE worth it...!" Don't get me wrong, Joanna aint no day at the beach. She is a handful at times, but she's never done anything to deserve to be hit by any man. I have a real problem with men who hit women just because they think they can. If you feel you have to hit someone, you can just walk away. Leave the bitch! I've done it. I grabbed my pool cue case and headed to the bar he usually hung out at. Halfway there, Jenny buzzed me on my cell. Joanna must have called her from the house. I told Jenny what I was about to do.

"Stay right there..." Jenny said. "Cisco and Jinx are on their way..." I waited at a coffee shop on the corner for them. I wasn't concerned with what they thought about it, but I did not want to disrespect Cisco and Jinx by not waiting for them. The limo pulled up about ten minutes later. Cisco and Jinx came out and walked up to the coffee shop just as I came outside to met them. I was still a little pissed.

"You are not going to talk me out of this... you know that, right...?"

"We're not here to stop you bro... we're here to make sure nothing happens to you... In case you get in over your head. Jenny knows a man's gotta do what a man's gotta do..." Cisco answered.

"Get in the car Mr. Cassidy..." Jinx said. I was hesitant but Cisco gave me an approving nod so I got in the car. They pulled up to the bar about fifteen minutes later.

"Nobody touches the asshole but me..." I said as we exited the car.

"It's all you bro!" Cisco said. "We got your back... that's all..." I took my pool cue case, walked into the bar and walked over to the pool table. There was no one playing. I racked up and played solo while Cisco and Jinx sat at the bar and ordered some beers. Jimmy, not knowing who I was or why I was there, walked up to me.

"Would you like a game?" and he turned to the wall to grab a cue. I slowly unscrewed my cue...

"Sure... but the game I wanna play... you're not gonna like..."

"What's that supposed to mean...?" He chuckled until I cracked him over the head with the thick end of my pool cue. Two of his buds jumped up to get involved until Cisco and Jinx drew their guns on them. His buddies froze right where they stood. No one else moved or said a word; they just watched me as I beat Jimmy down. Having back-up with me, they must have thought that I was a 'bill collector'. Jimmy had a problem betting on the ponies. He kept betting on the wrong ones. His luck wasn't getting any better. He got a few good shots in before I clubbed him hard and he went down like a ton of bricks. He looked at me in shock as I played a drum solo on his body. When I had enough, I motioned Jinx to come over and Jinx laid the guy face down on the pool table. By this time Joanna got worried and impatient and had taken a cab there and entered the bar at that very moment. I guess she was there to stop me. Pffftt! Too late! I lifted his head off the pool table towards Joanna.

"You see that little filly right there?" He moaned. Jinx held his head up as I walked over to her, pulled her hair back and gently kissed the bruise on her face. "She's a friend of mine... She's like family to me. If you ever touch her again... I will come back here, and *not* in the forgiving mood I'm in now... and kick the living shit out of you! Comprende amigo?"

Joanna was about to walk me out when Jimmy spoke. "I never touched that bitch..." He moaned. Not a good idea seeing that Jinx still had a hold of him. I walked over to the bar took Jinx's beer bottle and broke it on the bar. Joanna flinched.

"Jinx...? Did this dumb son of bitch just call me a liar?"

"I believe he did Mr. Cassidy..." And Jinx held him tighter as I approached.

"No! No...! I didn't... I'll never touch her again! I promise!" He stammered. I nodded to Jinx who let him go. He got up, limped into a chair and tended to his wounds. Cisco put his gun away. Asshole's friends had gone to sit down in the corner with their heads turned away. Amazing how you find out who your real friends are. As Cisco escorted Joanna out, I walked over to the bartender and tossed about $200 on the bar.

"That should cover the beer my friends had and any damage that I might have caused..."

Jinx and I turned to walk out. The bartender spoke to me. "Mister...?" I turned back. The bartender pushed the money on the bar back towards me. "The beers are on the house... and as for any damage... the son of a bitch got what he deserved... it couldn't have happened to a nicer guy!"

I bowed slightly to the bartender as I placed my hand on my heart. "In that case... I'd like to buy a round for the house..." The bartender nodded and the waitresses served everyone except Jimmy and his friends. I got my cue and case and put my cue away. Jinx and Cisco escorted Joanna back to the limo.

As I walked outside, the sheriff's car was already outside and was cutting off Jenny's limo. I walked over to the sheriff still sitting in his patrol car. Cisco, Jinx and Joanna were already in the limo. I guess I'm gonna do a little cell time, but it was worth it. "Is there a problem officer?" I asked.

He motioned for me to come closer to the squad car. I came to the door. "What are we doing tonight son?" he asked.

I held up my cue case. "Playing a little pool..."

"Is Jimmy in there?" Obviously the sheriff knew what was going on. My concern was, is he a friend of Jimmy's?

"Yes sir..."

"He still breathing...?"

"When I left out of the bar... yes sir!"

"I take it you won't be coming back here... to play any more '*pool*'...?"

"I'm hoping it won't be necessary officer... I beat who I came here to beat..."

The sheriff smiled. "Then good night to you sir..."

"Good night officer." And he pulled out of the parking lot. I got in the limo and we pulled out.

"I appreciate what you did for me, but you do realize that what you did was no better than what Jimmy did..." Joanna said to me.

I kissed Joanna on the forehead. "I know baby... but it felt good as all out!"

"Thank you, but please don't do that ever again... After all, he's still the father of my kids... I loved him once..."

I nodded. "I love you Joanna..." I said.

"I love you too..." And Joanna hugged and kissed me. We dropped off Joanna and then Cisco and Jinx took me back to Jenny's. Jenny had taken a cab home and was waiting at the front door. She was very anxious to see me.

"You okay CJ?" and she kissed me. "You look like you got as good as you gave."

"Trust me... he looks and feels much worse than I do!" I rubbed my jaw where Jimmy caught me with a left hook.

"You sure you're okay?"

"I'm good... I'm just hoping Joanna is gonna be okay..."

"She'll be just fine... But you look like you need a good fucking..."

I was confused. "Why would I need...?" And I looked into Jenny's eyes. I shut up cause that's when I realized that Jenny was really turned on by what I did and wanted desperately to show her 'appreciation' to me. She led me inside the house and we barely made it upstairs... We did it on the stairs actually. I just love a passionate monkey fuck! Jimmy never fucked with Joanna again, not because of what I did, but because Jinx and Cisco visited him one more time about two weeks later when they found out that Joanna called the cops on him again. They were not as gentile as I was; they too, it seems, have a big problem with men hitting women. Joanna is not only getting on with her life and met a nice young man who loves her and the kids, and she now gets her child support checks on time.

The Tortured Soul Trilogy
(The Seduction of CJ Cassidy)
Chapter 118
(The Narrator)

It was a warm Saturday afternoon, and Jennifer who was sunning herself while naked in the back yard hammock, had just fallen asleep. Katherine was reading a book and I had just finished bar-b-queuing and was just listening to the ball game on the radio. Katherine took off her glasses, put her book down and got up to make herself a drink. "Would you like a glass of wine?" She asked me.

"No thank you Katherine..."

"How about a pina collada?"

"No... I'm good..."

Katherine smirked. "Oh...*val*...tine?" She said with a pseudo-German accent. I busted out laughing. I recognized the line from 'Young Frankenstein'.

"Nothing!" I said abruptly and Katherine laughed.

"How about a '*Sloppy blow job*'?" she said abruptly.

"Is that a drink?" I asked.

"Depends on what side of the blow job you happen to be at!" she said seductively.

I turned around and looked back and forth. "Out here?" We knew no one could see us in Jennifer's back yard. And if Jennifer woke up she surely would not mind.

"No... come upstairs..." And she walked towards the house while dropping her robe. I turned to the sleeping Jennifer and then looked back at Katherine's amazing naked ass as she walked away. Katherine was a classically trained dancer and had a set of stems to match. Her back and shoulders were muscular but feminine. She had the body of a woman who played beach volleyball. Katherine stopped at the patio doors. She then removed her bikini top and dropped it. I turned to Jennifer again. "Let her sleep..." Katherine said. "She can always join us later..." And she stuck the tip of her finger gently in her mouth and sucked it a little. Jenny is not the sort of person you want to wake up once she gets into a good sleep mode so I turned off the barbeque and walked towards Katherine and kissed her in the doorway and she led me upstairs to the bedroom. "Go wash up…"

"Join me?" I said.

"Don't mind if I do…" And we both took a shower together. The water was hot and steamy and so was the foreplay. We took turns washing and soaping each other up. I was very horny and erect from her using her hands and a washcloth to wash me. I paid particular attention to soaping her ass and nipples, and we held each other close and kissed each other as we scrubbed each other's backs. I tried to enter right there in the shower, but she held me off. "No! Not yet, don't be so impatient… you're gonna get all the pussy you can handle soon enough!"

I smiled. "Sorry… I'll behave…" And I continued to wash her down.

"You missed a spot…!" she said.

"Where?" And she lifted her leg, grabbed her foot and placed it on the built-in towel bar of the shower. I used my foot to steady the one she was standing on.

"Right here…" she said and she stroked her pussy.

"I thought you said…"

"Wash it… Don't stick your dick in it…" she whispered. "At least… not yet!" And she bit her lips gently.

"Okay…" And I took my hand and placed it on the leg she was standing on and bent down until I was holding her ankle and I began to lick her clit.

"What are you doing?" She moaned.

"You said '*wash it*' you didn't say what I could use!" And I dove my tongue in and out of her pussy and nibbled on her swollen clit.

"Ommmmmmmm muuuuuuuu!" she moaned. I continued to eat her to my (and her) hearts content. She couldn't hold her foot on the towel bar and keep her balance in that soapy water while I was eating her out. "Stop… Stop!" she said as she lowered her leg.

"You want me to stop?" I said as I fingered her pussy and labia.

"Hell no, I don't want you to stop, but unless you want to explain why I fell in the shower to the paramedics…" She moaned. "We better take this to a more secure location. Besides… we used up all the hot water…"

"You shouldn't worry about me having to call the paramedics..." I said.

Katherine started to stroke my cock again. "Why? Would you give me cock to mouth resuscitation?" She moaned.

"Of course!" and I smiled broadly. Katherine has an oral fixation and amazing skills.

"Do you have your certificate of proficiency?"

"Uhhhmmmm!" I couldn't think of a snappy reply while she was jerking me off so softly.

"Well... we're just going to have to... cram until you can take your exam..."

"Okay... can we cut this witty banter out... and go in the bedroom so I can monkey fuck you now?" Katherine laughed out loud, quickly rinsed off and got out of the shower. I turned off the water and we dried each other off and headed to the bedroom. Katherine led me there holding my erect cock. We got to the bedroom door and Jennifer was sitting at her dressing chair, her feet up on the edge of the bed, sipping on a glass of red wine, waiting for us.

"And what... were you two planning to do... without me?" she asked.

"What would you want us to do?" Katherine asked while she stroked my cock in Jennifer's direction.

"Well... if had to direct you..." Jennifer said.

"Please do..." Katherine cooed. Jennifer put her finger into her glass of wine, stirred it a bit and then put her finger in her mouth and sucked and licked it seductively.

"And you two would do... whatever... I tell you to do?"

"I'm an actor and take direction quite well, thank you..." I said. Katherine stroked my cock and sighed; Jennifer crossed her legs, took a sip of wine and started to narrate our 'sex scene'. (As an actor, I don't normally like 'improvisational theatre', but I got the impression this would be just fine with me!)

Jennifer began to narrate: "And she brought her clandestine lover to the bed and sat him down on the edge and she slowly got on her knees before him and began to kiss his throbbing cock." I sat down and Katherine pursed her lips and only kissed my cock, the head, the shaft, my balls and did nothing more. She continued to so this until Jennifer spoke again. "She licked the head of his dick, paying close attention to the rim and to the little fold of skin at the base, flicking her tongue, wildly..." She flicked her tongue on me and gave me long wet laps on my shaft. It was amazing to be the recipient of a tongue-lashing. "She then held his balls with loving care and began to devour him, all the while stroking his shaft."

And Katherine followed direction to the tee. Jennifer just watched intently while Katherine bobbed her head up and down the head of my dick sucking harder whenever she pulled back on it. Jennifer continued to give directions to Katherine and all I had to do was sit there and enjoy. I enjoyed what was happening and I enjoyed the look on Jennifer's face as she watched. Jennifer's voice became sultrier and more soulful as she got hornier from just watching. And every once and again Jennifer would wet her finger in her wine and suck it dry or use it to pinch her nipples while she spoke. "And then CJ stood up and switched places with Katherine, who lay back, held her ankles apart, and CJ began to repay her in kind by licking and sucking her clit." Katherine began to writhe and rotate her hips to intensify my eating her out.

"Mmmmmmmmmmmm!" She purred. "Kitty like!"

"She than grabbed the back of his head and maneuvered his tongue wherever she wanted. CJ would then take his tongue and slip in and out of her pussy, licking her clit whenever he came out and licking it again before he went in." I was starting to get the impression that the girls had set all this up previously, because I could have sworn Katherine would on occasion give Jennifer hand signals to direct me as she wanted. OH... I didn't MIND... it's just an observation.

"Ohhhhhh! Yeah! That's nice.... That's nice... I like that!" Katherine moaned.

"Finally CJ reached on the end table and put on a condom while Katherine took the palm of her hand and rubbed her pussy faster and faster, making sure she stayed good and wet until he was ready..." It took a moment to put the condom on. Then the damn thing broke. Jennifer didn't miss a beat. "And Katherine became impatient and licked her finger and thrust it deep within her..."

Katherine complied. "Ohhhh! Ohhhh! Muuuuuuuuuu! Ahhhh!"

"She fingered herself faster and harder, faster and harder!" Jenny said as I got another condom.

"Oh ah! Oh ahhhh I want your cock, give me, baby please... hurrrrrrrrrieeeeee!"

I got the condom on as soon as I could and I was about to enter her when... "Wait for it!" Jenny said. I looked at Jennifer like she was fucking kidding me! She raised her eyebrow and said: "Trust me... I know what I'm doing!" I stood there for a moment and I focused my eyes on Katherine who was wailing and hollering for my cock while finger flicking herself wildly. "Wait...! Just a little longer..." Jenny said. Then Katherine started to smack her pussy with the palm of her hand, and rubbing her clit faster and faster, she then began to pant like an animal and began to claw at me to get me on top of her.

"Give meeeee! I want your cock! Give meeeeee! NOWWWWWW!"

"Not... yet..." and Jennifer started in on herself, rubbing and fingering her own swollen clit.

"YOU BITCH! FUCK MEEEEEEE!!!!! NOW!" Katherine screamed and she arched her back, threw her leg on my shoulder and smacked herself on her ass hard. She then stuck her thumb in her mouth and began to suck it.

"Now!" Jenny said, "Flip that bitch on her knees and fuck her!" I reached over with my opposite hand and grabbed Katherine's leg off my shoulder and swing her around to her stomach and she reared up on her knees and took both her hands and spread her cheeks exposing her reddened pussy to me. Katherine's ass was absolutely magnificent! The red welt of her smacking herself was starting to appear. I stood there... mesmerized... "What are you waiting for damn it? I said fuck her now!" Jennifer had straddled the armrests or the chair with her legs and was masturbating hot and heavy now. I grabbed Katherine by the waist and she grabbed my cock and I slid right into her pussy with no effort! "Pump that bitch! Pump her hard!" Jennifer moaned.

Every once in a while Katherine would 'prompt' Jennifer to say 'faster, faster!' and I would follow direction. My body was glistening with a light layer of sweat and so was Katherine. I was in the perfect position, behind Katherine staring into Jennifer's eyes. If I leaned back at just right angle it looked as if Katherine was going down on Jennifer as I pumped her pussy. Jennifer looked at me as if she knew what I was thinking. I had my knees propped on the side of the bed frame using it for leverage while I held onto Katherine's waist while I pumped her like mad. I refocused my gaze on Katherine's ass. Katherine was now teasing her anus with her finger. I knew she liked to experiment with a butt plug and wanted to try the real thing, but like Jenny, I'm not into anal sex. Katherine got the hint that I wasn't going to 'double dip' and stopped. I pumped her pussy harder and harder. Katherine was moaning and cooing and kept sucking in short bursts of air while she slammed her hands on the bed. I looked up and Jennifer, who had stopped narrating and was now licking and sucking her nipples as she worked her clit with her right hand. I looked at her and said: "And the narrator finally couldn't take it any more..."

Jennifer took her eyes off Katherine and looked up at me and panted heavily.

"She got up and reached into her dresser drawer and took out her favorite play toy..." Jennifer nodded and did as I said as I was banging away at Katherine's ass. "She sat back down, turned on her special friend and began to tease her clit with it..." Jennifer followed my directions and cooed. "She slowly eased it into her sweet, wet and hungry pussy... in and out... in and out... every once in a while she would pull it out, lick it and work it back inside her... After a while she used the same rhythm that CJ used to fuck Katherine so she could fantasize that it was her getting the full benefits of CJ's thick, hard cock instead of Katherine..." I now began to play follow the leader with Jennifer. What I did to Katherine she did to herself with the vibrator. If I went hard and fast so did Jennifer. If I took long deep strokes, so did Jennifer. Katherine squealed and I began to pump her with wild abandon. Faster and harder, my thighs were slamming into her ass harder and harder and the bed shook and Jennifer kept right up with us. They were both moaning and panting with wild abandon. Jennifer then broke script, closed her eyes and went for hers; I then concentrated all my efforts on Katherine. All of a sudden Jennifer started to cum, and Jenny does not cum quietly! And so did Katherine at the same time. Katherine's pussy started to contract hard and she almost squeezed me out of her pussy involuntarily. I grabbed her hips and thrust myself in and held on tight. This bronco bitch was not gonna throw *this* cowboy... I held on for dear life. Katherine threw her head back and screamed:

"Fuck meeee... I'm cumming... I'm cumming! OH! OH Ohhhhhhh! NICK EEEE!" And Katherine gushed a bit just as I let go of her. She collapsed in a heap face down on the bed. Jennifer sat there. Her mouth was wide open and she was in shock. Jennifer put her hand over her mouth. Her eyes were focused on my face and my reaction.

"CJ!!!! I'm so sorry!" Jennifer said, and she began to cry. Katherine looked up at Jennifer crying and that's when she realized that she had blurted out Nick's name. Katherine put her hand on her mouth and turned to me, tears welled in her eyes.

"My god... CJ...! I didn't mean to..." And Katherine began to cry. Jennifer got up and hugged Katherine.

'CJ... she didn't mean it...! CJ...?" And Jennifer couldn't stop crying and neither could Katherine. She pulled Katherine off the bed and they dropped to their knees on the floor and Jennifer kissed Katherine lovingly and held her. "CJ!" Jennifer cried. "She didn't mean it! Please...!" I started to get dressed. Jennifer continued to implore me to forgive Katherine.

"It's okay..." I said quietly... "I'm going to take it as a compliment..." Katherine turned to me but she couldn't look me in the eye. "Obviously, I brought Katherine to a place that only Nick had ever taken her before... I'm not insulted... I'm honored..." I walked over to where the girls were. They didn't know what to think. They had no idea what I was about to do. "Can I have a hug?" And I held out my arms. They both got up and hugged me tightly.

"CJ... I'm sorry... I'm so sorry baby! I didn't mean to..." Katherine said through her tears.

"Forgiven." I said. It was something the girls said to each other when one of them fucked up accidentally.

"Love you!" Was the response I got from both of them.

"Love you more!" I answered which meant it was over and forgotten.

"It won't ever happen again... I promise...!" Katherine sobbed.

I kissed Katherine on her lips and her forehead. "Oh... It will happen again... and I'm going make damn sure it does! Don't you ever feel ashamed that you miss Nick...!" and I looked at Jennifer. "That goes for you too Missy Foo!"

They both hugged me tighter. I just raised my head to heaven and took a deep breath and for some strange reason the line from "Spiderman" came to my thoughts. *"With great power lies great responsibility..."*

I prayed that I could satisfy these two wonderful women, not only in the bedroom, but also in life in general. We all lay down on the bed and I gently kissed them both and that's when it happened. Jenny's brand new bed... BROKE! It crashed to the floor with a loud thud. The girls began to laugh hysterically! I just looked around amazed. Katherine laughed, looked at me and said. "There's something Nick never did!" I busted out laughing. It was the ultimate tension breaker. You have no idea how much I love these two bitches!

"You owe me a new bed... bitch!" Jenny said to Katherine while laughing.

"It's all CJ's fault!"

"Fuck you, it's my fault! The bed is under warrantee, get it replaced!"

"The *mattress* is under warrantee... not the bed frame!" Jenny said.

"So...? Go buy a new one then... I'll help you break that one in too!"

Jenny busted out laughing. "If you can break the bed with me under you like you just did with Katherine, I won't mind replacing it!" Jenny ordered a new bed frame on-line. She was able to get it delivered in about three hours. We spent the rest of the evening trying to recreate the events leading to the bed being broken with Jennifer playing the part of Katherine. Did I tell you I love these two crazy bitches?

The Tortured Soul Trilogy
(The Seduction of CJ Cassidy)
Chapter 119
(Mystery Shopper)

Katherine was getting cabin fever from staying in the house for ten days straight. She had been sick from the flu and stayed in bed most of the time. She felt much better today and it was a nice day so she decided to do a little window shopping at the mall. She decided to leave her car home and walk. She could use the fresh air and exercise. She went bright and early so she could avoid the crowds. The mall was near empty when she got there. She liked that. She could shop comfortably without attracting any attention. She window shopped at first, her main concern was just to get out of the house. Nothing caught her eye, so she stepped into a shoe store when she saw a cute pair of stilettos in the window.

She just asked the clerk to get her a black pair in a size 7. (Hey you never have enough pairs of black shoes!) Just as the clerk went into the back, she felt like someone was watching her. She was just about to turn around when someone's face came close and kissed her neck behind her ear. She spun around to see who it was.

"Jennifer!" Katherine beamed. "What are you doing here? I thought you where at work?"

Jennifer looked around to see if anyone was watching and kissed Katherine on the lips. Katherine fought the urge to pursue the kiss further. "I don't have to be at work until 2 today, so I thought I'd go shoe shopping. I see you're feeling better."

"Much better... now that I've seen you!" Katherine's nipples became hard almost immediately after kissing Jenny. "So? Did you see anything you like?" Jenny gave that wry little smile she always gives when she get a dirty thought in her mind. She leaned into Katherine's ear and whispered.

"No I didn't... Unfortunately you're wearing a bra today!"

Katherine blushed. "JENNIFER!" Katherine whispered in shock. She then looked around to see if anyone heard that. "You are so bad!" She whispered.

"Really? Maybe I need a spanking?" Jennifer whispered back. If Katherine wasn't already hot and bothered, she sure was now. That's when the clerk came back with Katherine's shoes.

"Here are your shoes..." And he opened the box, sat before Katherine and helped her slip on her shoes. Katherine stood up and strutted up to the mirror in them. Jenny turned to the clerk.

"Do you have those in a nine?" Jenny asked.

"A what?" Katherine teased.

"You didn't let me finish!" She turned to the clerk. "Do you have those in a nine... and a half?" And Jenny cut her eyes at Katherine, who shrugged her shoulders and giggled. Jenny wears a ten... and a half!

The clerk smiled. "I'll check for you Miss..." and he went back into the storeroom. Jenny walked up behind Katherine.

"So? What do you think?" Katherine quickly rephrased the question. "About the shoes...?"

"I think..." Jenny hissed. "That the clerk looked up your skirt when he put those shoes on you!"

Katherine let out a small breath of air. Jenny knew she was getting to her. The clerk came out with two boxes. "I don't have them in black in your size but I have these other colors you might like..." Jennifer sat down and the clerk helped her put the shoes on, the sandy brown shoe on one foot, the leopard print on the other. "Thank you..." And Jennifer strutted around to the mirror to check them out.

Katherine thought that turnabout was fair play. "So? Did the clerk catch a glimpse of your panties?" She whispered to Jenny.

"I'm quite sure he didn't..." Jenny replied while switching sides in the mirror.

"How can you be so sure?" Katherine smirked.

"I'm not *wearing* panties!" Jenny hissed. Katherine was really hot and bothered now. She could feel her nipples get hard and tight. "I'm also sure... he's not gay..."

"And how do you know that?"

"Because he caught wood and had to go behind the counter to hide it!" Now Katherine couldn't take anymore. Jenny's 'Mojo' was on full blast.

Katherine walked over to the clerk with the shoes. "I'll take these…" He boxed up my purchase and turned to Jenny.

"And how about you Miss?" Jenny shook her head no. Jenny had a hard time buying shoes. She was a shoe fanatic but shoes that look cute in small sizes looked like hell in bigger sizes. Jenny was resigned to buying shoes on-line or in stores that catered to transvestites. The clerk rang up the purchase and turned to Jennifer. "If you give the store your number, we can call you if the shoes become available in black…"

"Nice try…" Jenny was talking about him getting her number, but she decided to be nice. "I wouldn't buy the same pair she has… that's a little tacky!" They left the store together.

"So… what do you want to do know?" Katherine asked.

"I have an idea…" And Jenny led her to a store that had bathing suits on sale. The two of them picked out a few outfits, but the sign said that only two suits would be allowed in the dressing room at one time. Jennifer went in first and came out with the first suit then the second. Katherine liked what she saw. She liked the suits as well. Jenny called the clerk over.

"I'll take these but give us a moment while she tries hers on…" The clerk took the suits to the cashier and then tended to another customer in the store. Jenny turned to Katherine. "Go ahead… try them on…!"

"I didn't come out to buy a bathing suit…"

"Neither did I… try on the suit…" Katherine acquiesced and went into the dressing room and tried the suit on. When she came out, Jennifer inspected the suit very closely while touching the ruffles around the breast seductively. Jenny copped a quick feel of Katherine's nipple under the ruffle. Katherine took a deep breath. "I don't like it… let's try the other one on…" Jenny said. Katherine nodded and went back into the dressing room and Jennifer followed her in. Katherine got undressed and asked Jennifer for the other suit. Jenny just sat on the bench and spread her legs. She really wasn't wearing panties. She began to stroke her labia.

"Jenny!" Katherine whispered. "What are you doing?"

Jenny licked the tip of her finger and reached into her blouse and fluffed herself. "You know damn well what I'm doing... do you really think I brought you here to try on bathing suits? It was the perfect excuse... to get you naked... and alone..."

"We are NOT alone you crazy bitch!" Katherine whispered. "We could get caught!"

"So?" Jenny said as her finger disappeared into her hot, wet pussy. "If you're scared... put you're clothes back on... and leave..." Jenny then pulled her blouse open and pinched her nipples hard. "Or... you can get your hot, naked ass over here... and eat me..." Jenny moaned oh so quietly. Katherine looked up and around the dressing room. "They don't have cameras in this store... lawsuits and all... That's why I brought you in here!" Jenny licked the tip of her fingers, hiked up her skirt, spread her legs and held her labia wide open. "Well? Are you in? Or out?" Katherine watched nervously as Jennifer fingered herself slowly then faster. Jennifer's nipples were hard and tight, so was Katherine's. "Are you going to let me have all this fun alone?" Jenny hissed. Katherine didn't answer; she just slowly got down on her knees and placed her head between Jenny's thighs.

"You have no idea how much I missed you!" Katherine whispered as she placed her hands on Jenny's thighs and rubbed them and then kissed her moist pussy.

"I missed you too... real bad!" Jenny moaned and Katherine licked and tongued Jennifer's clit.

Katherine had to take it easy and slow. Jennifer is a screamer and the last thing she wanted was to draw attention to what they were doing. Katherine wasn't into dangerous sex... but Jennifer was starting to develop that fetish in her. Jenny reached down and worked Katherine's nipples roughly as Katherine licked and nibbled her clit. Now Katherine was afraid that she might make a sound that would draw attention. It was hot and scary at the same time. It was sensual rush on so many levels. Jenny threw her head back. "No! No! Don't you dare!" Katherine whispered.

"I... I... C... ccc... can't help it! Ohhh!" And Jennifer's voice was about to hit high 'C' as she was prone to do when she came. Katherine quickly grabbed the swimsuit and jammed them into Jenny's mouth. Even with the gag, Jenny made too much noise for comfort. The clerk began to make her way back to the dressing room. Katherine had to think fast. She took the first swimsuit and stuck it out from the cracked door. "Could you do me a favor? This is too tight... can you get me the next size up?"

The clerk took the suit. "I'll see if I can find the next size... do you want the same pattern?"

"Yes please!" And the clerk walked off. Katherine was shaken. She looked at Jennifer who still had the suit in her mouth and had a look of complete look of bliss on her face.

"Okay? Can we leave now?" Katherine asked.

Jenny took the suit out of her mouth and sighed. "Not yet...!" And Jenny reached in between Katherine's legs and began to stroke her clit. Katherine tried to step back but there was no room in there.

"STOP!" Katherine said sternly but quietly.

"Shhhh! They'll hear you!" and Jenny began to work Katherine with her fingers. Katherine's eyes rolled to the back of her head.

"The clerk will be back in a minute..." Katherine moaned.

"Then we shouldn't waste any time..." Jenny stroked Katherine slowly and then faster and faster. Now it was Katherine's turn to lose control. Katherine placed her hand over her mouth as she felt the adrenaline rush hit her. Jenny played her like a fiddle and the piece was "The Flight of the Bumblebee". Katherine knees got weak, her face was flushed... orgasm hit her in waves and then...

The clerk knocked on the door and opened it to see Katherine wearing the first bathing suit and Jennifer sitting on the bench, talking on the phone. "We don't have that print in a larger size... I'm sorry!"

"You know what? Never mind the other suit..." Jennifer said placing her hand over the mouthpiece of her phone. "She'll take this one..." And Jennifer returned to her phone call. "Oh... do you mind?" The clerk nodded and left them alone for a moment. The girls left the store with the three bathing suits. Katherine was nervous as a cat. Even the security guard outside the store looked at her a little funny.

"I'm... I'm going to go home..." Katherine said breathing softly.

"I'll take you home..."

"I thought you had to work?"

Jennifer had called her office and cancelled her appointments. "Did you forget? I'm the boss... besides... I have a sick friend who needs some TLC!" Katherine smiled broadly as they got into Jenny's limo.

"So Katherine... I want to see what those shoes look like..."

Katherine pulled out the shoe box. "I thought you saw what these shoes looked like in the store?"

Jenny took them out of the box. "Put them on!" Jenny asked.

Katherine slipped them on and turned her leg to the side. Jennifer nodded approvingly.

"Jinx?"

"Yes Ms. Jones?"

"Take the long way home... Please... and be a doll and put up the security partition in the limo."

"Whatever you say Ms. Jones..." As the partition went up, Jenny lifted Katherine's skirt above her waist and pulled her panties to the side. "I wanted to see what they would look like... on my shoulders... This is going to tickle a bit..." Jenny moaned as she spread Katherine's legs open placed her head between her thighs. Katherine threw her head back and enjoyed the ride home.

The Tortured Soul Trilogy
(The Seduction of CJ Cassidy)
Chapter 120
(Ladies Night)

I called Katherine Friday afternoon on my way to Jenny's and asked if she would be coming over to Jennifer's tonight, and I would meet them there later in the evening. I could bring over a bottle of wine and make dinner for us. "Sorry baby!" she said. "Tonight it's just going to be the two of us... We're going to spend the night at my place, I hope you don't mind?"

"I don't mind..." I was a little disappointed. I didn't like traveling all that way and not see them. Anytime they spend the night at Katherine's meant that they were going to have a bondage and discipline session. And although I was welcome to come and enjoy the festivities, it just wasn't my thing, and as far as I was concerned, watching was just one step away from getting involved. And I don't go for that shit, but I would never deny the girls their fun and games. Now that Katherine learned not to equate pain with sex, those two had carte blanche to do any thing and everything, without fear. I guess I would just spend tonight at Jennifer's alone until they called me. "You two have a good time... I'll call you in the morning..."

"How about you come over in the morning and serve us breakfast in bed?"

"What would you like?"

"You...!" After one of their sessions and after a good nights sleep, the girls were always horny as all hell afterwards; I knew that if I came over, I had better come prepared.

"I'll take two pills and call you in the morning..."

Katherine cooed. "I can't wait until tomorrow; I'll let Jenny know so she can send Jinx to pick you up..."

"Katherine...?"

"Yeah baby?"

"Please... try to keep the bruises down to a minimum? You know how delicate your skin is..." I didn't mind their sessions but the bruises and black and blues did bother me. The three of us would get kinky and wild sometimes, but I had my limits. Jenny would joke that I liked my meat rare.

"Hmmmmmm!" Katherine pouted. "I'll try..." she purred. "But I can't make any promises..."

"Katherine?"

"Yeah baby?"

"You're masturbating right now aren't you?"

"Uh huh! I'm so wet...! Talk dirty to me... Help me get off Papi..."

"Ummm I'm on a public bus and it's packed... and unless I want to be arrested for public indecency... no!"

"But baby! But I'm so wet and horny... I just want you tell me what to do...!"

"Improvise...! Then show me later what you come up with!"

Katherine giggled. "Ummmmmmm! I like that idea! See you tomorrow baby!"

"Bye Katherine..."

"Whisper it..."

"Good bye Katherine..." I whispered.

"Uhhhhh.... Bye baby!" And she hung up.

- - -

Jennifer came over to Katherine's house and used her key to get in. "Katherine...? Kitty? Are you home baby? Where are you?"

A low moan came from the bedroom. "I'm in here Jenny..." Jennifer walked over to the bedroom and the door is wide open and so is Katherine. Katherine is working her vibrator in and out of herself with wild abandon. "Bitch! I know you did NOT start without me!!!"

"I'm so horny! I'm so wet... I couldn't wait! I needed to get off!" She moaned. And she continued to work the vibrator in and out, in and out. Jennifer just went to Katherine's steamer trunk and opened it and took out her restraints. Katherine did not stop what she was doing.

"Bitch... roll over..." Jennifer demanded. Katherine complied, and laid face down keeping her legs spread and working the vibrator and fondling her clit. Jennifer tied her ankles to the bedposts. Katherine then grabbed the other bedposts in anticipation of being tied. "Uh uhh... I'm not tying your hands... keep on working that rubber dick..." Katherine reached for the vibrator still deep within her and began to work it in and out faster and faster. Jennifer took off her top and bra got a bottle of baby oil and began to rub it all over her own breasts and nipples. She then oiled Katherine's ass. "Does that feel good to you... you bitch?"

"Yes... it feels so good... Kitty like..." Jennifer took a riding crop out of the trunk and smacked Katherine on the ass as hard as she could. "Owwwwwwwww! Ohhhhhhhhhh! Nice! Mama likes that!" Jennifer struck her again. Katherine reared her ass up to let Jenny get a good swing. "May I have another...? Bitch!"

"Oh...! I know you didn't just call me a BITCH!" And Jenny began wailing on Katherine's ass. Katherine howled with every stroke but she wouldn't stop working the vibrator in and out of her hot, wet pussy.

"Oh Ohhh Ohhhhh Muuuuuuuuuuuu! Ahhhhhhhh Haaaaaaaa! Spank me, spank me you fucking bitch! Beat my ass! You bbb... bbb... bbbitch!" Jennifer accommodated her every whim, they both knew, Katherine, being the recipient was in charge of the session and it would stop only if Katherine said so. Katherine's nipples were rock hard and sensitive to touching her silk sheets. Katherine's ass was now beet red and tender and she came so hard that she actually squeezed the vibrator out of her gushing pussy. Katherine let out a high-pitched squeal and dropped face forward into the pillows. She tried to reach for the vibrator, she wanted to 'top off' but it was now out of her reach. Jenny was covered in perspiration from giving her a whipping. Jenny got the vibrator and showed it to Katherine.

"You want this?"

Katherine reached for it. "Gimme..." she moaned. Jenny pulled it away and opened the end table and took out a condom. Katherine was perplexed. "What do you need with that?"

"You'll find out..." and Jennifer put the condom on the vibrator. Katherine had a confused look on her face. The Jenny took the bottle of baby oil and stood behind Katherine. "On your knees bitch!" Even tied to the bedposts she was able to rear up on her knees and put her ass in the sky and began to rotate her hips.

The sting of the whip was burning her flesh and Katherine loved it when Jenny turned on the ceiling fan and the cool air caressed her ass.

"Oh yeah... that feels so good..."

"I have a present for you..." "What is it?" Katherine cooed. Jenny shoved the bottle of baby oil tight against Katherine's anus and squirted some of it into her ass. Katherine's eye widened and a look of shock came across her face. "What the fuck are you doing?" She moaned.

"I'm going to give you what no man has ever given you!" And Jennifer oiled the condom-covered vibrator and eased it deep into Katherine's ass. Katherine's jaw opened and her lip quivered. Katherine let out a gasp and moaned.

"Ohhhhhh that's fucking amazing..."

"Oh yeah...? Wait till I turn it on...!" and Jenny did. Katherine howled at the sensation. Katherine had used a vibrating butt plug before, but it was only 3", the vibrator was a full 10" long and deep in her colon. Jenny then put her head down on the bed under Katherine's hips and began to lick and suck her clit while working the vibrator in her ass; in and out, in and out. Katherine slammed her hands on the bed in wild abandon. Jennifer began to fondle and caress her own pussy. It looked like the most erotic game of limbo ever!

"Oh! Oh! Ahhhhhh! Ohhhhhh! Fuck ME! Fuck me in the ass! That's so gggg... ggg... ggggaaaaa!" Katherine was looking around the room in desperation; she didn't know what she was looking for. She couldn't move from her position because her ankles were still tied to the bedposts. Tears came to her eyes and she when came, she came hard. "I can't hold it any more...!" Katherine screamed.

"Don't you spray that ass funky oil on me bitch!" Jenny yelled. Jenny jumped out from under her. "Hold it!"

"I... kkk... kkk.... Can't!" Katherine's pussy contracted and her clit twitched.

"Hold it!" Jenny barked. Jennifer grabbed a towel that Katherine kept near the bed, because both of them were gushers, and held it to Katherine's ass.

"I can't... I can't... untie me! Untie ME!" Jennifer held the towel on Katherine's ass and released the quick clips on the restraints.

"Go!" Katherine grabbed the towel and ran to the bathroom and closed the door behind her.

"Owwww!"

"Katherine, are you okay in there?" Jenny asked.

"I fucking forgot you just beat my ass!"

Jennifer almost passed out from laughing so hard. Katherine's sore ass had touched the cold toilet seat and it stung like hell!

"It's not fucking funny bitch!" Katherine laughed.

"Then why are *you* laughing? And you better spray in there... or light a match or something!"

"Fuck you bitch!"

"Whatever!"

Katherine came out looking like something the cat dragged in. She was covered in sweat and her hair was all sweated out.

"Holy cow... I feel like I lost ten pounds...!" And Katherine breathed heavy.

"Next time warn me when you're gonna pull that shit on me... and I'll take an enema beforehand!"

"What was it like?" Jenny asked.

"You wanna try it?" Katherine asked seductively.

"Fuck NO! Only Captain Kirk will go where no man has gone before! I am not gonna stick anything up my ass, and I'm not gonna let someone else do it either."

"Oh...? But you had no problem whatsoever ramming my vibrator up *my* ass!"

"Hey... That was your fantasy! Not mine...!"

"By the way... thank you for putting a condom on my vibrator first!"

"No problem..." Jennifer looked at it. "But I'm not going to unwrap it... I'll leave that up to you!"

(*You may think that considering their festishes and sexual adventures that anything goes, but there is a line the girls don't cross. Katherine hates needles and Jennifer is totally against anal sex.*)

Katherine had a feeling of euphoria sweep over her. "You okay Katherine?" She had a stupid grin on her face.

"I feel fucking amazing! I feel like I came like I've never cum before!"

Jennifer peeled her panties off and got spread eagle at the foot of the bed and fingered her clit and wet labia. "I'm glad you do... cause I didn't get mine off yet..."

Katherine sucked her finger. "Don't mind if I do...!" And she went into the end table and took out Jenny's favorite dildo, got a chair and a pillow for her tender ass, and pulled up to Jenny so she could sit and bury her head in Jenny's moist loins. But then she pulled back.

"What's wrong? You better not be changing your mind..."

"How about... I shave your pussy for you?" Katherine asked.

Jenny's eyes widened. "You wanna shave my pussy?"

"Uh Huh!" Katherine grinned. Jenny stroked her thick, nappy pussy fur, spread her moist labia and fingered her clit.

"How close do you want to trim me...?"

"Bald!" She whispered.

Jenny spread her labia and moaned. "That's gonna itch like a motherfucker when it grows back!" She moaned

Katherine smiled. "I know..." She whispered.

Jenny's was now wet and anxious, and she fingered herself deep. "Go get the razor!" Jenny began to breathe deep and hard as she fingered herself. No one else had ever shaved her pussy before... not even at the spa, for some strange reason; just the thought of it turned her on. The strip clubs she had worked in didn't allow full nudity, so Jenny never showed her pussy on stage. She always wore panties or a thong. Her pussy fur was always neatly trimmed but never shaved. Katherine returned with a safety razor and took the baby oil and squirted a little into her hands. She sat down and began to stroke Jennifer's pubic hairs with her wet, oily hands. Jennifer purred and cooed with every stroke. "Rub my clit..." Jenny moaned. Katherine complied and stroked her clit with her thumb while running her hands through Jenny's thick fur. "Oh that feels so good..." Jennifer began to stroke and pinch her nipples. Katherine reached for the bottle of oil and squirted a bit on

Jenny's breasts. Jennifer rubbed it all over herself and purred. "Oh that feels so... slippery!" and Jenny rubbed and stroked her breasts tightly.

"Ready?" Katherine asked.

"Uh huh!' Jenny purred. Katherine took the razor and gently began to shave Jennifer all the while working her oiled fingers in and out of her swollen pussy. Every once and a while Katherine would gently blow the cut hairs away. Jennifer would moan seductively. "I want your mouth on my pussy..." Jennifer moaned as she massaged her nipples covered in slippery oil.

"I'm going to have to use your 'pacifier' until I'm finished shaving you..." Katherine reached for Jenny's toy and buried it deep inside her.

Jenny moaned and cooed. "Hurry! Please hurry!" Jennifer writhed and rotated her hips.

"Stay still..." Katherine said. "I don't want to cut you..." Jennifer moaned and her eyes went to the back of her head. Katherine continued to slowly and carefully shave Jenny and work her dildo in and out of her. Jenny arched her back and moaned and panted like an animal.

"Aren't you done yet?" Jennifer was in total agony.

"Just a little bit more baby! I'm almost there..."

"Me too...!" Jenny moaned. And Katherine blew on her exposed and swollen clit. Jenny's clit twitched, Katherine knew she had her right where she wanted her.

"Hurry baby... I want you to eat me... Ohh eat me... Lick my pussy!!!" Katherine finished shaving Jennifer and blew off the last of the loose hairs. Jennifer jumped at the cool breath on her freshly shaved snatch. Jennifer threw her head back and reached for her pussy, she could not wait any longer. She wanted to get off, and she wanted to get off now! Katherine held Jenny's hands away. Jenny was now thrashing in the bed. "I wanna cum! I wanna cum... oh my ggg... ggg...! I wanna cum!" And Jennifer screamed in frustration. That's when Katherine pulled the dildo out and dove into her pussy and clit with her tongue and sucked and nibbled on it. Jennifer threw her head forward and gasped. She grabbed Katherine by her ears and positioned her tongue deeper and deeper into her swollen pussy. Katherine hummed and licked and sucked on her clit and labia, and stuck her tongue deep inside her and flicked her tongue inside her while spreading her labia with her thumbs. Katherine squeezed and manipulated Jenny's clit in between her thumbs and Jennifer squealed in delight as she licked and nibbled her. "Oh yeah! Oh yeah! Ohhhhh yeeaaaaaah right therrrrrrrrrrrreeeee you cunt licking bitch! That's so good, so ohhhhhhh!" Jennifer squeezed her nipples hard and came the same way. Jennifer fell back on the bed exhausted and spent. She licked her lips and moaned. "Ohhh that was so good…" That's when Jenny heard the crack of a whip in the room. Katherine had gotten her cat o'nine tails, and stood on the bed over her.

"Now you roll over you BITCH!" And she cracked the whip again. Jennifer could barely roll over on her stomach with her knees on the floor, before Katherine started to tear into her ass. Each stroke of the whip sent chills up and down Jenny's spine. She writhed in pain and pleasure all at the same time as Katherine beat her until Jenny passed out. When they woke up the next morning, Jenny was nuzzled into Katherine's breasts and Katherine was sucking her thumb.

When I arrived the next morning about 10am, I walked in on them because they didn't answer the doorbell. I knew they had a good session cause they didn't wake up when I called out their names. I looked at the two of them, sleeping like angels in each other's arms. Both of their asses were an amazing shade of pink. Katherine having a lighter complexion showed hers more than Jenny, but you could see hers was pink too.

As I've said before, I'm not into the whole take a beating, give a beating shit these two are in to, but seeing their pink little asses got me horny as hell! I just stood and stared at them for a while, contemplating getting on top of each of them and humping the shit out of them, but I decided to let them sleep a little longer. They were going to wake up hungry before they would want to fuck so I went into the kitchen and began to make banana pancakes with whipped cream and some bacon. Just as I plated the food, they came out of the bedroom arm in arm, more holding each other up than walking together. The smell of fresh homemade pancakes had woken them up. They each took a plate just as I added a dollop of whipped cream on top. "Bacon?" I asked. Each shook their heads no and began to eat breakfast, they both stayed standing up to eat. I muffled a laugh as I chewed on the bacon they turned down. "Soooooo...? How was your night?" I smirked.

"Fuck you!" Jenny answered. (You *do* know she is NOT a morning person!)

"We had a great time last night thank you for asking..." Katherine replied.

"Ah... you two bitches did brush your teeth before you came down to breakfast?"

They both busted out laughing. "Yes! We did!"

I laughed and Jenny cut her eyes at me. "By the way Jenny... I love the new hairstyle..."

Jenny placed her hand on her head and then turned to the hallway mirror and looked at herself. She turned back to me confused. "What new hairstyle?" Katherine laughed and pointed at Jennifer's crotch. Jenny looked down and busted out laughing. "You like?" and Jenny did a models pose for me.

"Oh yeah!" And I bit into another strip of bacon. "So how's your breakfast?"

Jenny took her finger and dipped it into the whipped cream on her plate and placed the whipped cream on Katherine's nipple. "It sucks!" and she licked the cream off Katherine's nipple, Katherine threw her head back and cooed and moaned. Katherine then returned the favor.

"Personally... I love your banana pancakes..." Katherine cooed. And she stuck two fingers into the tub of whipped cream. "But it's not the banana I want right now..." And she stuck her fingers into her mouth and sucked the cream off. "Jennifer?"

"Yeah Katherine?"

"Are you thinking what I'm thinking?"

Jennifer stuck two fingers into the tub of cream, spread her fingers apart and licked the cream off while flicking her tongue and winked at me. "Maybe...!" Katherine dipped again and Jenny eased towards me and undid my zipper and took my hard cock out. Katherine stroked my cock with the whipped cream and Jennifer gently licked it off my stiff dick. (Don't worry... I knew something like this would happen so I showered before I came over!) Jenny deep throated me and I almost choked on the bacon I had in my mouth. Jennifer then dipped her fingers into the whipped cream, covered my cock with it and grabbed Katherine by the back her

621

hair and made her kneel before me. Jenny stroked me with one hand and forced Katherine to suck me with the other. Jenny took turns stroking me and pushing Katherine's head on my cock. Jenny turned to rub her ass on me so I reached up and kneaded her breasts and pinched her nipples. Jennifer cooed, leaned back and I kissed her passionately as Katherine sucked harder and harder on my cock. I then grabbed both girls by the back of the head twirling their long hair in my hands. I made Jenny kneel down and pulled Katherine up to her feet. I worked Jenny's head all over my cock and pulled Katherine's head back so I could suck her cream covered nipples. I then made Katherine kneel again. And then I made them both get down and take turns sucking and licking me. And when they got to the tip of my dick, they tongued the head, and then kissed each other. They also lip locked onto either side of my cock and sucked as if they were fighting for control of the head. It was fucking amazing! (Where do they learn this shit?) I threw my head back while working them by the hair. I was so into it I actually head butted them once! "Oh shit! I'm sorry!" I said as I pulled them back away. "How's your head?"

"I haven't heard you complain yet!" Katherine said.

"Pfffft!" Jennifer scoffed and she went back to sucking me whole.

"You think you got enough strength for both of us?" Katherine said.

"I took a pill before I got here and I jerked off while you two were sleeping, so honey... I... am an all day sucker!" Katherine cooed and they both took turns playing Russian roulette, each taking a hard suck before letting the other suck on me. My eyes were gone to the back of my head and I was panting in deep short breaths. Jenny then started to jerk me off quickly, harder and tighter, harder and tighter. Katherine locked her lips on the tip of my dick and puffed on it like a cigar. I was totally out of breath but I was not going to cum.

"Oh fuck this!" Jennifer said. If you can't cum then I'm gonna make the best of it!" She spun me around and leaned over the countertop and arched her back. "Fuck me Papi! I want to feel your cock deep inside me...!" And she hiked her right leg on the counter and stoked her tender ass. I got a condom and put it on. "Come get this!" Jenny cooed. "Come fuck my pussy!"

I was about to enter her when Katherine also bent herself over the counter and threw her left leg on the counter. They began to kiss each other and I started in on Jennifer while she fingered Katherine's pussy and smacked her ass, gently, but enough to invoke a response from Katherine. Whenever Jenny pulled her fingers out of Katherine I would switch and enter her. Katherine would reciprocate by fingering Jenny and smacking her ass. After about five or six turns Katherine screamed out: "I'm gonna cum!"

"Me too!" cried Jennifer. I looked at them both and then I realized, there was only one way I was gonna pull this off. I pulled out of Katherine and stuck my finger in each of them and worked both their pussies as fast as I could. They both threw their heads back and Katherine came first and Jennifer was a close second! The both gushed and their pussies twitched. I immediately entered Katherine first to feel her pussy suck me and then when she slowed down I entered Jennifer and she worked her snatch like a vacuum! My balls felt like they were going to explode. I pulled out of Jenny and moaned.

"I'm gonna cum!" Katherine gently peeled the condom off me. They both dropped to their knees and began to kiss and stroke me until I came on both their faces! My dick actually made a sound like a spray bottle; I shot my load so hard! "Ohhh Ohhhh! Ahhhhhhhh! Haaaaaaaaa!" I moaned. And I almost fell back but the girls grabbed my legs and held me steady. I took the roll of paper towels and I gently wiped my cum off their faces and hair. I was still erect so Katherine sucked on me one more time. Jenny stroked me so very softly. I was still erect and ready.

"You look like you still have something to give…"

"I'm gonna need a moment…or two!" They walked me into the bedroom leading by my stiff cock. Jenny said to Katherine:

"Grab what's left of the whipped cream!"

Katherine grabbed the tub and the maple syrup. "Just in case!" she replied.

To paraphrase Rick James: "Viagra is one hell of a drug!"

The Tortured Soul Trilogy
(The Seduction of CJ Cassidy)
Chapter 121
(Three Can Play That Game)

The next day, Katherine and I were cooking dinner and Jennifer had excused herself and went upstairs to get ready for dinner. She decided to take a hot bath instead. We were half way through making dinner and Jennifer still hadn't come down. "Amazing how Jennifer disappears or goes to sleep whenever it's time to cook…"

"Jennifer doesn't cook… you know that, but she has never failed to pick up a check when we go out to dinner…!"

I threw up my hands. "Oh! We're going to go there are we?"

Katherine kissed me. "You'll never have to pay for dinner the way you cook… And I mean in the kitchen too!"

"Oh so…? I'm just your 'man whore'…?"

"When you're not cooking… Duh… yeah!" And I smacked Katherine on the ass. Katherine moaned.

"Don't start something you don't want to finish!" She cooed.

"Okay… I'm going to wash up for dinner and check to see what's taking Jennifer so long…"

"Okay, tell her dinner will be ready in about half an hour…"

"Righty'o…" And I kissed Katherine and went upstairs. I got upstairs and Jenny wasn't in the bathroom. Her wet towels were on the floor. That's when I heard a moan come out of her bedroom. *"I guess she's having at it…"* I thought to myself. *"I'll just let her have her alone time…"* I started to head back downstairs when I heard Jenny's trembling voice through the door.

"CJ? Is that you?"

"Yeah baby, it's me…"

"You're just in time… Get your ass in here…" she moaned.

"Let me wash up and I'll be right there…"

"Hurry... Please!" she begged. I washed up and went into her bedroom. Jenny was bent over her dresser, wearing nothing but her black pumps and a look of happy diversion. She was watching her face in the mirror as she was stroking her clit and manhandling her pussy. She was humping the air with her ass and fingering herself furiously. "Suit up and get your cock in here now!" She panted in a commanding tone. I sat down on the bed behind her and just watched her. She turned to me while still fingering herself. "What the fuck are you waiting for? I said get suited up!"

I leaned over to see her face in the mirror and smiled. "Trust me... I know what I'm doing!"

"You BITCH!" and Jenny turned back to the mirror and continued to finger herself deeper and harder. Jenny moaned. "Damn it! You *do* know what you're doing...!" and she laughed passionately.

"Dance for me bitch!" I said. Jenny began to gyrate and grind her ass and did not stop fondling her hot, juicy pussy.

"You like that papi?" She moaned.

"You know I do..."

She finger flicked her clit with one hand as she rubbed her ass with the other. "Ohhhh! Ohhhh...! I like it too..." and she smacked herself on the ass and used her whole hand to manipulate her wet labia.

"If you like that... you're gonna fucking love this...!" I said. And I smacked her gently on the ass. (Hey! I was not going to take the chance that she didn't want to go there!) "Harder!" she moaned. (Okay! I guess she does want to go there!) I slapped her ass harder. "Damn it CJ...! Slap my ass harder!" I slapped her ass harder, her head went back and she moaned. "...Call me a dirty girl!"

"You dirty little girl! You nasty dirty little girl!" And I smacked her ass hard again and her thighs hit the dresser.

"Again, Papi... Do it again...!" I smacked her ass hard again but I was a little concerned that she might get hurt hitting the edge of the dresser, so I came over to her left side facing away from her and hooked my arm under her waist with my left arm. I began to spank her with my right. She turned to me with her mouth wide open and panted like a caged animal. Her eyes widened and she cut her eyes at me and purred. "Where did you learn to do that?" She cooed.

"Did I give you permission to speak puta??" and I smacked her ass again.

"Ohhhh!!! My!" she cooed. I could tell she really liked that. I continued to spank her and she continued to masturbate with her left hand, using her right to steady herself by holding the dresser or putting her hand on the mirror.

"What are you doing? I asked her.

"What...?" She moaned.

"I asked you what are you doing with your other hand? You dirty little whore!" And I slapped her ass.

"I'm playing with my pussy!" She moaned seductively.

"You're WHAT...?" I said angrily and I slapped her ass again.

"I'm playing with my pussy daddy... I'm playing with my... wet... juicy... pussy. I'm taking my fingers and rubbing my swollen clit. It feels so good daddy... it feels so good...!"

With every word I said next I smacked her ass. "You... Nasty... Dirty... Little... Puta... You... Nasty... Slutty... Bitch...!"

Jenny's ass was now a bright red, which is not an easy task on her olive skin. My hand was beginning to sting. She masturbated faster and deeper and she started to moan and wail. "I can reach it! I can't... reach...!" and she took her right hand, pulled the drawer open and pulled out her vibrator. I grabbed her right hand and stopped her.

"Oh no you don't!"

Jenny's face was in agony. "What are you doing? Give me!" She said.

"Oh...? Now... you want it, do you?"

"Let go...! I can't reach...

"I *can*...!" Jenny was so aroused right then she didn't know if she wanted to fuck or fight. I took the vibrator from her and tossed it on the bed behind me. I unzipped my pants. "Do you want that...? Or do you want this...?" She stared at my erection and swooned. She reached behind her and stroked me gently.

"I want your cock!" She moaned.

"Beg for it!" She was breathing through her mouth and she looked like she was about to pass out. She couldn't believe I was gonna make her beg for it... she couldn't believe what she did next.

"Please...? May I please have your cock...?" And she cooed and moaned and humped the air again.

"I'm not convinced... Beg harder...!"

"Ohhhh... harder... I want your hard... cock... I want your stiff, hard, throbbing cock deep inside me daddy... Give me please...! Please...?" She didn't even realize that I had released her and was putting on a condom while she begged for it. She continued to dance and gyrate with her hands on the dresser. "Give me... give it to me... ram your thick, long, cock deep in my pussy... push it in and pull it out and out and in... smack my ass with your thighs and call me your dirty whore!" She licked her finger seductively. "Give me your..." And I slipped my swollen member deep inside her! Her head swung back. And her hair slapped my face. I thought she was going to break her neck! No need to prime her pump any more... She wanted to come and come right now! I banged away at her ass like a jackhammer. She began to choke and slam her hands on the counter. "Gggg... ggg... ggg... Fuck my ppp... ppp.... Oh haaaaaa! Haaaaa..... ah haaaa! Ffff... fff... ffff... Fuck that pussy CJ...! I love your cock!!! FUCK Meeeeeeeee!!!"

Now, I don't have an ego problem... my cock isn't all that big and from this angle, her perfect ass gets in the way! I'm okay with it and she knows just what to do about it! She took her right hand and cleared the dresser and put her leg up to give me deeper access. That's all I needed. My back arched. I rammed my cock to the hilt and I came so hard that I swore I shot the condom off! Jennifer's pussy contracted in waves, milking me dry. My eyes went to the back of my head and I howled! A feeling of euphoria swept my body... I felt like I had just run a marathon. My legs were weak and I could barely stand up... And then... Jennifer... fainted. I almost fucking dropped her! I held onto her waist and swung her limp body around onto the bed behind us. She purred and cooed and balled up into the fetal position. I could see her shiver ever so slightly. Then I saw a stupid smile come across her face and she nestled into the bed, pulling the pillow closer to her. I leaned my head back and took a deep cleansing breath. I lowered my head and opened my eyes; that's when I heard a moan that was not coming from Jennifer. I turned towards the bedroom door. It was wide open and Katherine had pulled up a chair outside and had propped her feet on the doorway and her body was shaking and quivering as she too was having an orgasm from masturbating while watching us. Jennifer's vibrator was still in her trembling hand. She had actually entered the room, picked it up and used it on herself and we were so caught up in what we were doing, we didn't even realize she was there the whole time.

She licked her lips and fondled her twitching pussy and cooed. "I came up to tell you... dinner's ready...!"

"Does Jenny know you play with her toys?"

Katherine laughed. "I eat her pussy... I didn't think she'd mind...!" she panted. "Besides... aren't you... one of her toys? And we share that!" Katherine stroked her nipples with Jennifer's vibrator and cooed.

"You said dinner is ready?" I asked.

"Yeah... it's downstairs if you wanna eat..."

I walked over to Katherine and grabbed her ankles and held it to the doorframe. "What are you doing?" She asked me.

"You said; "Dinner was downstairs and I haven't eaten yet!" And I kneeled down and began to lick her swollen clit.

"Oh my god! You're gonna make me cum again!"

- - -

Katherine and Jennifer are in the bed fast asleep. Katherine is sucking her thumb and Jennifer is nuzzling Katherine's breasts. My cock is totally numb and feels like I left it in Katherine's mouth. I'm at the dinner table having seconds. Those two are the best aerobic workout that a man (Or woman) can possibly have. I better leave them something to eat in case they wake up hungry later.

The Tortured Soul Trilogy
(The Seduction of CJ Cassidy)
Chapter 122
(Criminal Acts)

The doorbell rang at Jenny's house between 7 and 7:30PM. She had just gotten home from work. She didn't get a chance to get comfortable. "Who could that be at this hour?" She checked the security camera at the door and saw a police officer standing there. "Is there a problem officer?" She said over the intercom.

"Could you open the door ma'am?"

"CJ...? Is that you?" She replied.

"Ma'am... could you open the door... please...?"

"Okay...?" She came down and opened the door. "What's this all about CJ...? Did you just come from an audition?"

"Ma'am? Are you Jennifer Jones?"

Jenny looked at me strangely. "CJ...? What the hell are you talking about...?"

I took out my handcuffs. "Ma'am... I have an arrest warrant for Jennifer Jones... are you her?" I said sternly.

Jennifer looked at the cuffs and sighed and her eyes widened. See looked at herself in the reflection of my mirrored sunglasses. I had planned on that. I knew she had narcissistic tendencies. I knew it would be a turn on for her. "I'm Jennifer Jones...!" she moaned softly.

"Ma'am, turn around and place your hands behind your back please..."

Jennifer complied and I handcuffed her. "What is this all about officer...?" She cooed. "I'm sure I'm innocent..."

"A likely story..." I then took out a ball gag from my pocket, reached around her and placed it in her mouth and tied it under her hair. "You have the right to remain silent..." And I pushed her into the house and closed the door behind me. "Are you carrying any concealed weapons?"

She shook her head no. "Uh uhh!" she mumbled.

"I don't believe you... I'm gonna have to strip search you..." And I pushed her face up against the wall and patted her down. I took my time grabbing and fondling her ass. She leaned into it and moaned. I unzipped her skirt and pulled it down around her ankles. She stepped out of it and she was wearing white silk panties. I fondled her ass some more. She grinded her hips into it. "Spread'em..." I barked. And she kicked her legs open and I held her face against the wall with one hand while I pulled her panties over and fingered her wet pussy. Dipping my finger in slowly as she moaned and cooed. I roughly turned her around until her back was against the wall. I then fondled her breasts over her blouse. Jenny didn't wear a bra today and her hard nipples looked like they wanted to poke right through her blouse. I pinched her nipples hard. She moaned. "No concealed weapons... huh? And what are these?" And I ripped her blouse open and the buttons hit the floor. I roughly pinched her nipples and massaged her breasts. I saw her legs were getting weak and she was so very turned on right now.

"Okay... lady... you and I are going downtown..." She sighed and moaned at the thought of '*going downtown*'. And I roughly pushed her to the bedroom by holding on to her arms. I pushed her face down on her bed over the footrest. I smacked her ass and she cooed again. I held her facedown on the bed. "Don't you move...!" I barked at her. Jenny laid there and waited. I went to her dresser and got her leather restrains and tied her ankles to the legs of the footrest. She was now cuffed, bent over, spread-eagled and grinding her nipples on her silk bed sheets. She stroked her ass and patted it for me. I went back to her dresser and looked until I found her dildo. I took it over to her, pulled her head back by her hair and showed it to her. "Is this yours?" She nodded. "Really? This belongs to you...?"

"Mmmm hmmmm!" She mumbled.

She nodded again and I walked behind her. "If this is yours... Then it should fit... right here!" And I slowly eased her dildo into her hot, wet, hungry pussy. Jenny threw her head back and let out a muffled scream. I worked the dildo in and out and twisted and turned it. Jenny began to tremble and shake and let out moan after moan. I worked it faster and faster until she was in a full frenzy. She was wet and horny and screaming at the top of her lungs. I worked it deeper and faster until she almost couldn't breathe. I untied the gag because I was afraid she might choke. She inhaled roughly and panted like an animal. The she hollered:

630

"Right there... ohhh... ohhh right there! You mmm... mmm... mother... fff... fff... fff... Oh! Oh! Ohhh! Ahhhhhhhh! Aiiiiiiiii!" And she started to gush and her pussy started to twitch. I knew that she could go on like that for at least five more minutes. I let go of the dildo still inside her and put on a condom. I was not gonna let her have all the fun alone. I pulled out her dildo and eased my cock inside her. "Ggg... ggg... ggg oddd... that's soo... mmmm.... Oh!" And her pussy's contractions pulled me deeper inside her. I swear this chick is half vacuum cleaner! I let her pussy dictate the speed and duration of my stroke. Every time she contracted, I pushed in deeper. If she relaxed, I pulled out to just the tip. "Whh... wha... the fff fuck are you doiiiiiinnnnngggg?" I pushed in as deep as I could while holding her hips and her pussy clamped down on me hard! I couldn't move, but I really didn't have to. Her pussy did all the work and then... she let out a high pitched squeal... and then... and then... Lights out! Her head hit the bed and her ass dropped and my dick fell out of her.

"Damn! I knocked her ass out... again!" I couldn't believe it; I have only knocked out two other women out with sex once before and here it is number three or four with Jenny! I didn't know if I should be proud... or scared! I checked her breathing and she was fine. She was panting in small breaths. I started to untie her legs so I can put her in bed until from my vantage point I saw that her pussy was still puckering and twitching! *"Well... I didn't get off yet..."* I said to myself. So I pulled up a chair behind her and started to masturbate as I enjoyed the show. I can't begin to describe how amazing it is to see a woman just have an orgasm and then another and then another. I was totally focused on her throbbing pussy and her sweet ass, so focused that I didn't realize that she had come to. It's funny how a man becomes embarrassed when he's caught masturbating, even by the woman he has sex with.

"Mmmmmmm... ohhhhh!" she moaned. "That was soooo good!" She turned her head as much as she could to see me behind her. She reared up and gyrated her ass round and round and jiggled it for me. "You like that baby?" She moaned.

"You know I do..." I whispered. She looked at me as I masturbated faster. I felt it was okay as long as she was turned on by it.

"Oh baby… you didn't cum yet?"

"Not yet…"

"Come here…" I came up behind her. "No… lay down on the bed, across from me…" I lay down on my back, perpendicular on the bed; my stiff cock was inches from her mouth. "Closer…" I shimmied over. "Closer…" I shimmied a little closer. "Okay… now you're fucking with me… do you want me to suck your cock or not?" I slid right under her and she giggled and she deep throated me. My eyes went to the back of my head. She used her tongue to guide my cock in and out of her mouth. She sucked me until I felt like I was about to swoon. She then started to lick and nibble the head. "Do you have the keys?" and she shook her handcuffs.

"Yeah…"

"Then you better un-cuff me… before *you* pass out and I'm stuck here like this…" I reached into my pocket and unlocked the cuffs. She rubbed her wrists. "Now… where was I?" she said. I grabbed the back of her head and gave her a gentile reminder. Now with her hands free, she went at me like nobody's business. She finished me off by jerking me off as she sucked the little fold of skin at the base of my head. I shot my spurt high into the air and then… I passed out. When I woke up, she was lying next to me gently stroking my cock and looking at me deeply and lovingly. She kissed me. "So… how did the audition go?"

"What audition?"

"The one where you needed to wear this uniform."

"Oh this…? I rented it just for this occasion…"

"Really…? So… what other costumes do they have?"

"For me… or for you…?"

"Do they have a website?" I nodded. She went on line and ordered a women's police uniform, a nurse outfit and a cheerleader outfit for herself. "Aren't you going to order anything for Katherine?"

"The nurse's uniform is *for* Katherine…"

"Oh? My bad!"

"CJ…?"

"Yeah Jenny?"

"They have a 'Wonder Woman' costume…"

I smiled and kissed her gently. Just her mentioning it to me gave me wood. "Okay... but you don't need it...!"

I think I created a monster with Jennifer. It seems that she really likes role-playing... a lot! She has ordered for me a deliveryman's uniform, a pizza guy outfit, a construction worker, a Marine captain's uniform, (I guess she has a thing for 'An Officer and A Gentleman!) I'm starting to feel like a one man "Village People"! Her favorite 'costume' she likes me to dress up in; is a gray Armani suit she bought for me in a men's store. I don't wear it outside her house, I wear it only for her when she's 'frisky'. I know it reminds her of Michael or maybe even Nick. I don't mind... I do it to make her happy... and she gets very... 'appreciative'!

The Tortured Soul Trilogy

(The Seduction of CJ Cassidy)

Chapter 123

(Jealousy)

Weeks later, I was back home in New York. I had just come home from work. It was a Friday and Jennifer had to work this weekend, she's in Boston doing a client seminar, so I didn't expect to speak to her at all, and I couldn't get in touch with Katherine. She's probably hanging out with a friend. I came home from work, took a shower and was about to settle into working on my new novel. That's when I was hit by writers block. I tried to E-mail Bella to get some more background on her, but she must have been hanging out with her friends. I left her an E-mail and I would check for a reply later. Friday night and I'm home... all alone. I didn't expect any of my daughters back until Monday night. It was too early to go to bed, nothing was on TV and I didn't have any movies except porno. I tried to write something down, anything. Nothing, I just wasn't inspired. "Fuck this... I'm going out and have a few drinks and try again later tonight... or tomorrow..." I threw on a shirt and sneakers and was about to walk out the door. I opened the door and... There was Katherine standing there with an overnight bag! "Katherine!!! Baby!"

"Surprise baby! You happy to see me?"

"Hell Yeah!" And I hugged her and lifted her off her feet.

"What are you doing here?"

"I came to spend the weekend with you, I hope you don't mind?"

"I don't mind!" and I hugged her then I looked around. "Does Jennifer know you're here?"

"She had Jinx drop me off at the airport..."

"Is she coming too...?"

"Can we NOT talk about Jenny this weekend?"

"Jenny who?"

Katherine laughed. "See... this is why I love you so much..."

"I love you more!" And I kissed her.

"Aren't you gonna invite me in?"

"Get your ass in here girl..." And I took her bag inside.

"Your timing is perfect. I was just about to head to the bar, would you like to join me?"

"Do I have time to take a shower?"

"Absolutely!"

"Wanna join me?"

"I just got out the shower, but maybe I missed a spot!"

Katherine laughed and kissed me. "Wait for me here... I'll be down in a minute..." And she went upstairs.

"I'm so glad you came...!"

Katherine peeked from around the corner of the stairs. "I haven't cum yet!" and she giggled.

"I know how this weekend is gonna turn out!"

Katherine laughed. "Did you say you want me to turn you out?"

"Let's keep it simple okay?" I said. Katherine slipped out of her thong and spun them on her fingertips. "Or not...!" I finished saying. I took her bag upstairs and put it in my bedroom. She turned on the shower. I started to put her stuff away and make room in my closet. Katherine got in the shower. "You have no idea how happy I am to see you!" I said.

"Would you have been happier if it was both of us?" she said from the shower.

"Both of 'who'...?" Katherine giggled. "That's right!" I said." I aint falling for that shit tonight... It's just me and you Katherine, we're gonna have some quesadillas, get our drink on..." Katherine came out drying herself off with a towel. I hugged her. "And come back here and fuck like bunnies...!" I continued.

"And what makes you think you're gonna get some pussy tonight?" She said seriously. "Did you make plans for tonight with another woman?"

"You know damn well you did not come all this way... just to use my shower...!" I pinched her nipples. She pulled back, covered up and laughed.

"Stop it!" She giggled. "Now get out so I can get dressed!"

"Why do I have to get out so you can get dressed?"

Katherine kissed me. "Because if you stay here... you won't let me get dressed... now git!" And she smacked my on my ass. Damn, she knows me so well. She got dressed and we went out to the local bar, had a few drinks. I had the quesadillas and she had the buffalo hot wings. We got back home about 2:30 in the morning and the bar is only down the block. We were both drunk and laughing when we got home. Katherine kissed me at my doorway.

"This isn't a date... I'm not dropping you off... I live here too!"

Katherine's lips parted slightly and she looked at me. "You think I live here?" She whispered.

"Don't you have a key?" She shook her head no. I gave her my keys and she opened the door. She turned back to me, pushed her breasts forward and she kissed me passionately. I lifted her up and carried her inside. We... never made it to the bedroom. I wrote it in 'A Tortured Soul...' and I meant it... A monkey fuck is what it is... where it is... and that's all there it is to it! When I woke up the next morning we were both naked on my living room floor. I had a couch pillow under my head and Katherine was still asleep, ass up, on my sofa cushions stacked on the floor. I took one look at her magnificent ass in the air and said to myself: "Don't mind if I do!" I reached into the end table and got another condom and got dressed for battle. I licked my finger and rubbed her pussy until she was wet. She cooed in her sleep and she woke up just as I entered her.

"Ohhhhhh! Myyyyyy! Good morning to you too CJ!" I banged away at her ass like jackhammer. Katherine was very wet, very horny and very appreciative. "Yeah... yeah... right there... you got it... right therrrrrrrrrree! Ohhhhh!" I tried something with Jennifer a few weeks ago and got away with it so I decided to press my luck. I slapped Katherine on the ass. She threw her head back "Oh baby!!! Smack me... smack my ass baby!" I slapped her on the ass again as I pumped her harder. "Oh! You know what I like... spank my ass baby! Spank me!" I took turns slipping my cock into her and slapping her ass hard.

"Whose pussy is this?" I asked.

"It's your pussy baby! It's all yours! Fuck me Papi! Fuck that pussy... Give me!" I locked onto her hips with my forearms and began to very slowly pump her. In and out, in and out. I did not want to cum before she did. She threw her head back again.

636

"Aye Papi! Fuuuuuuu ckkkkkkk meeeee! I'm so juicy! Am I wet enough for you Papi? Is it wet? Do you like my pussy Papi?"

I leaned into her ear and kissed her back and shoulders and whispered. "Yes *Katherine*... I love your pussy! Now give it to me... you conniving bitch!" She turned to me with her mouth wide open. I knew what she was doing... she was speaking Spanish trying to get me to fuck up and call her Jennifer! Only Jennifer called me Papi and she knew that. I pounded her pussy like a jackhammer again. My thighs slammed into her ass harder and faster. Katherine's head thrashed up and down and looked like it was going to pop off.

"Oh yeah!!! Oh yeahhhh! Fff... fff... fff... ohhh! M... mm... mmm... my.... I'm gonna cum.... I'm gonna... ggg... ggg... ggg!" She began to suck in air, she could barely breathe. She bit the edge of the sofa cushion. "Oh you mother fff...fff...ff... fucker! I'm gonna... ayiiiiiiiiiiiiiii!" And Katherine... passed out! Damn! I've knocked out Jenny before but never Katherine! Then it happened, her pussy swelled up and began to contract and suck on my cock. Holy cow! I thought only Jennifer's pussy did that! I couldn't pull myself out. (Not that I really wanted to!) Every time I tried to pull out, her pussy sucked me back in! It actually felt like I was getting head! Then I felt a feeling of euphoria, I threw my head back and I came... hard!

"Oh... Ohhhh Uhhhhhhh! Shiiiiiiitttttttt!!! Ah HAH!!!!!" And then Katherine gushed and involuntarily pushed my cock out of her pussy. I fell back and lay down on my cold wood floor, but I didn't care. I felt the room spin and I started to laugh... I couldn't stop laughing! I put my hand over my mouth. And I began to hyperventilate, I couldn't breathe, the sense of euphoria gave me the giggles and I could not stop! I felt myself get dizzy, my body trembled and then I passed out! The phone ringing at about 10am awakened me. I answered it and it was Jennifer. I turned at looked at Katherine. She was still ass in the air but she was sound asleep with her thumb in her mouth. That's how I knew I gave her a good fucking.

"Hello...! CJ...! Are you there?" Jennifer called out.

"Yeah I'm here Jennifer... I just woke up, what's up baby?"

"Let me talk to Katherine..."

"Pfffft... sorry baby... I *just* knocked off a piece of pussy and her ass is out cold! She aint waking up until the crack of noon!"

"Well damn! Go ahead then! She came hard huh?"

"She came like you cum... I don't know what you taught her... but thank you!"

"I see she's been using my Ben Wah balls..."

"Your what...?"

"Ben Wah balls, they're like those kung-fu balls that you use to work your hands. They help develop your vaginal muscles..."

"Like Kegel exercises?"

"Yeah... only with weights..."

"That reminds me... where *are* my kung-fu balls?"

"You really *wanna* know?" Jennifer laughed. "I'll be here until my meeting at two today... Have the bitch call me when she can unless you have her mouth otherwise pre-occupied!" And Jennifer laughed again.

"I'm so surprised you're not jealous..." I said.

"Oh... I'm gonna get mine when I see you... don't you worry!"

"You got it!"

"Love you!"

"Love you more!"

"You better start making breakfast for her; you know she eats like a horse after a good fucking...!"

"Who you telling? She eats, you sleep! I got this covered!"

"Call me later okay!"

"Okay! By the way Jennifer..."

"Yeah baby?"

"You're masturbating right now aren't you?"

"Damn it...! How did you know?"

"As different as you two are, you're still pretty much the same... and I can hear it in your voice... Tell me what you're doing..."

"You want me to tell you what I'm doing...?" She hissed.

"Yeah! You dirty, slutty little whore... this aint no fucking webcam bitch! Tell Papi what you're doing..." I said putting a little baritone in my voice. Jennifer began to describe what she was doing to herself in vivid detail. She panted and cooed and moaned. The more she spoke, the more her voice became hot and seductive. I just kept calling her a dirty whore and a slutty bitch. It only turned her on more. I had my hard-on back. After about ten minutes she cried out. "I'm gonna cum...!"

"Cum for me... cum for Papi!" And she wailed and moaned and let out a high-pitched scream. After a moment I spoke. "Jennifer? Are you still there?"

"Yeah baby!"

"You're welcome..."

Jenny giggled. "I love you... you bitch!" she said.

"I still love you more!"

"Call me later!"

"You got it! Now go take a shower... you still have a meeting this afternoon!"

"I just want to suck your cock right now!"

"Good BYE Jenny! I'll talk to you later!"

"Bye!" and I could hear the pout in her voice, she knew I had a hard-on and who would reap the benefits.

"Bye!" and I hung up. I turned around to see Katherine had put the cushions back and was sitting on the couch. She was all pouty and had her bottom lip poked out. She stared at my hard-on.

"I... see... you've been talking with Jennifer..."

"Hey... you said not to talk 'about' her, not 'to' her, besides she called to talk to you..." Katherine pouted again. "Okay... what's going on? You two have a fight...?" I asked.

"No..." and she crossed her legs and held on to the pillow. That's how I knew something was very wrong. I sat down next to her and put my arm around her and kissed her forehead.

"Tell me... what's wrong baby?"

She nuzzled up to me and cuddled. "Would you have rather have me here, or her?"

"Truth be told...? I would rather have both of you here, but you know I'm glad you're here."

She stroked my erect cock gently and then paused as if she needed to think of the next question, although I knew this was already on her mind. "Do you love me? I mean do you really love me?"

I kissed her on her pouting lips. "You know I do... Now tell me what's going on between you and 'what's her name'...?"

Katherine laughed. "It's nothing..."

After two marriages and two daughters, I speak fluent 'Womanese'. "Oh hell no... I know that when a woman says 'it's nothing'... it's 'something'... what's going on?"

Katherine snuggled into me tighter and kissed my neck. "That bitch is getting on my fucking nerves...!" She continued to stroke my cock.

"She gets on my nerves too sometimes... so why do you stay with her?"

"I think I love her..."

"You do love her... and so do I... And she loves both of us..."

"Then why does she piss me off sometimes...?"

"Welcome to the real world baby... it's not supposed to be easy... it's not supposed to be *kittens and giggles*' all the time... You're supposed to have good times and bad times... after you add up all the numbers, it only matters if you still love each other!"

Katherine hugged me. "Thank you CJ!" And she kissed me.

"Come on... I know you're starved, let me fix you something to eat..."

Katherine went back to stroking my cock. "I am a little hungry..." And she started to lick and suck my cock. I threw my head back and breathed little puffs of air. (Damn... I just love this horny bitch!!!!)

After we had breakfast... I mean pancakes... we called Jennifer. Katherine stayed on the phone with her so long that Jenny was late for her meeting. But this was much more important than a business meeting on a Saturday... things got put out there... things got resolved. Afterwards Katherine handed me the phone. "Yeah Jenny?"

"Thank you CJ... I knew you were just what she needed... thank you for being a good friend! I love you!"

"Prove it!"

"I will when I see you... now go take her to bed and fuck her brains out! I want her nice and 'happy' when she gets back to me..."

"You got it... Bye baby!" and I hung up.

"What did she say to you?"

"She said I should take you upstairs and fuck your brains out!"

Katherine kissed me passionately. "Well... no sense pissing her off now!" And Katherine led me upstairs to the bedroom. I don't know if I have the strength.

"Did you notice that I packed the nurse's uniform Jenny got for me?"

Problem solved!

- - -

Two weeks later when Katherine and Jenny were back in Nevada and I was still in New York; the girls were hanging out at Jennifer's house after work watching TV and spending some quality time with each other. Katherine was about to start dinner, when the oven wouldn't light properly and wouldn't stay on.

"Oh... I need to tell CJ to look at oven when he gets home, it's not working properly... maybe he can fix it... It probably needs a new heater thingy..."

"Katherine?"

"Yeah Jenny?"

"CJ is in New York... he's not coming here tonight! We don't expect him back for another month."

"Damn it!"

"What's wrong?"

"I got used to having a man around the house..."

Jenny sighed. "Yeah me too!" and she hugged Katherine. "You wanna give him a call?"

"No... I wanna give him some pussy!"

Jenny laughed hard then pouted. "Damn... now that I think of it, so do I!" and she pinched her nipple. "I'll call a handyman..."

"JENNY!"

Jenny shook her head. "For the *stove* you sick bitch!"

Katherine laughed. "Well it's not getting fixed tonight, so you better order delivery."

"What are you in the mood for?" Jenny asked.

"I told you what I was in the mood for... CJ is in New York! Order anything you want... I'm not very choosy tonight."

"Okay... I'll have Jinx pick up some pasta with lemon sauce from Vito's."

"Sounds good... oh! And order some seafood to go with it!"

"Absofuckinglutely!" Jenny went to the phone and began to dial Jinx to pick up dinner. He said he'd be there in about twenty minutes with their dinner. Jenny hung up and was about to go back into the living room with Katherine; she hesitated, pinched her nipple again, sighed and dialed another number, a number she hadn't called in a long while. "Hi... this is Jenny... How you been?"

The Tortured Soul Trilogy
(The Seduction of CJ Cassidy)
Chapter 124
(Reality Bites... My Ass!)

Two months had passed and I went to Nevada to visit Katherine at her place. We were going to see Jennifer the next day. I was coming out of the airport and was going to catch a cab to Katherine's house, when I saw Jinx standing next to the limo parked right out front of the gate. He waved me over. I came over, shook his hand and gave him the bodyguard hug. "Hey man! Long time, no see, how are you doing?"

"I'm good... but Ms. Jones needs to speak to you before I take you to Ms. Stark's place..." He said.

"Is Jenny okay?" I asked.

"I'll let her tell you..."

"Okay... take me to her...!" The back door of the limo opened and Jennifer came out. "Jenny!" and I hugged her but she was a little 'off' with me. "Baby, are you okay?"

"I need to talk to you... get in the car..." Her attitude concerned me. No return hug, no kiss... she was all business. The '*I need to talk with you*' has always been me. This was not like Jenny at all. If I didn't know any better, I thought I was about to get whacked! I got in the car and she sat across from me. She was already drinking scotch... straight.

"It's a little... early to be hitting the sauce... isn't it?" I asked cautiously.

"Do you mind if we stop off at my place first...?" she replied dryly.

"No problem..." Jenny cut her eyes at me and sipped her drink and poured herself another. She didn't even offer me a drink. I couldn't wait to find out what the hell was going on, even though I wasn't sure if I was the problem or not. Neither of us spoke to each other the entire drive. I tried to start a conversation, but Jenny turned on the CD to drown me out. I understood she did not want to talk about anything until we got to her house. I stayed silent; Jenny kept drinking. We got to her house and Jinx opened her car door and she handed him her empty glass and walked straight to the front door without even waiting for me. I knew she was a little drunk because she wasn't very steady on her feet. It took a minute before she could open her door. She cussed twice. I turned to Jinx.

"I'm worried about her..." Jinx said.

"Me too..."

"Please take care of her... You have no idea how much I love her..." Jinx said. I knew what he meant by that. He and Jennifer go back a long way.

"I meant to ask you Jinx... how are things between you and Ms. Delafield?"

"I think Bonnie is the one..." And Jinx smiled a broad smile. Bonnie Delafield was Jenny's personal secretary at work. I smiled at Jinx; they were the strangest couple I had ever seen. Jinx was 6'4" and built like a line backer; his girlfriend Bonnie was a petite woman who barely came up to his waist. Okay... I can see how that can work but I digress. Jinx loved her and treated her like a queen. She adored Jinx. "Go handle your business Mr. Cassidy...! Ms. Jones needs you..."

I tapped Jinx on his broad shoulder and shook his hand. "Thank you Jinx..." and he got in the car and drove off. Jinx would take care of my bags for me. I knew that Jinx trusted me to take good care of Jenny, and that I would do anything in my power to try to fix whatever was wrong. I barely stepped into the house when Jenny threw her arms around me and began to cry hysterically. I held her close as she cried on my shoulder. I didn't say anything to her at that moment. I instinctively knew she needed to let it out before she could talk about it. I walked her over to the living room, helped her off with her jacket and sat her down on the couch. She kicked off her shoes. I then went to the bar and fixed us both a mixed drink. I gave her one and I sat down next to her and she cried again.

"Thank you..."

"Baby... Tell Papi what's wrong." She sobbed and took a sip of her drink and she sobbed and cried again. I took the drink from her, put it on the coffee table and held her close to me. She just wouldn't stop crying. I took a napkin and gently dabbed her tears. I was scared now; I still had no idea what was going on. "Baby... if you don't tell me what's wrong... I won't be able to help you..."

She nodded and wiped her eyes. "I did a bad thing...baby!"

I looked at her as if to say; "*And...? How is this something new?*" She saw my expression and hit my chest quickly with the palm of her hand and sobbed. Now I knew this was serious. She turned her head away. "What did you do? You know you can tell me anything!" I said empathetically.

She cried and nodded her head and leaned into me hugging me tightly. She curled her legs under her on the couch. "You won't be upset with me?"

I kissed her forehead and leaned her head back and kissed her lips so very gently. She reeked a little of liquor. She must have been drinking long before she picked me up at the airport. "I promise I won't be upset... tell me... what happened?" She nodded and nuzzled into my arms again. She took a deep breath and exhaled.

"I slept with another man..."

I know she couldn't see my expression right then, but it was '*Yeah...? So what?*' She knew I had sex with Bella during one of our 'hiatus' when we hadn't seen each other for months. We didn't have an exclusive relationship at the time and we don't keep secrets from each other but then I realized this really was bothering her. "You slept with another man?" I asked. She leaned back looking with tears in her eyes and her lip quivered. I knew that Jenny wasn't anybody's 'one night stand' so this was with someone she knew. She must have sensed what I was thinking.

"I knew you would be upset..." And she buried her head into me again and sobbed and cried some more. It was at that moment I realized, she was upset, that she cheated! I had no idea how much it hurt her to think that she had been unfaithful!

(Now here is where it gets dangerous. If I don't get upset, she'll think that I don't care. If I get upset too much, it will only hurt her more. I had to have just the right amount of indignation to satisfy her need to be chastised, but not seem overbearing and possessive.)

Because I didn't respond, she pulled back to see my reaction. "You must think I'm a whore!" she sniffed.

I gently guided her head back on my chest and hugged her. "I have NEVER thought that you were a whore..." She sobbed then smiled ever so slightly. "You're a slut!" I said nonchalantly. She coughed. "Unless you charged him... then you're a whore!" She pulled away, laughed and then a moment later began to cry again. I almost had it! I was this close but I missed it by a hair! I tried to pull her back to me but she resisted.

"Get away from me... You think this is all a joke." She sobbed.

"I do *not* think this is a joke... I am *very* upset with you right now young lady." I said sternly. "But I love you too damn much to make you feel worse about something that you are obviously already beating yourself up about!"

She looked up at me; her mouth wide open and her lower lip trembled. "You *love* me?" she stuttered and she dried her tears with her hanky.

"You know I do..." And she hugged me tightly. I got it right this time. "Tell me what happened..." and I rocked her in my arms.

"I had sex with Armand... I went over to his place. We had a few drinks, I kissed him and before I knew it I had unzipped his pants and he put his hand..."

"NOT the details... you silly rabbit!" Jenny laughed and wiped her tears. I was a little relieved it was Armand. He and Jenny had a special relationship once before but it didn't work out. I oddly felt safe. I knew I wouldn't lose her to Armand but I also knew she was searching for something. Jenny smiled at me and then she got serious again.

"I don't know what happened... It happened so... quickly..."

"But you didn't really regret it until you realized that you couldn't cum..."

Jenny nodded her head. She couldn't believe that I understood what she was going through. "I didn't enjoy it at all... In fact I hated it. I hated myself for doing it... I felt so... dirty!" She sobbed. "I haven't felt that dirty since..." And I kissed her to stop her from speaking, I knew where she was going with this and I did not want her bringing up her past working as a fluffer. There was no reason to open any old wounds. She cried and said softly. "What the fuck is wrong with me?"

I held her and rocked her in my arms. "There's nothing wrong with you... sweetheart. You're just not the same person you were a few years ago... My little girl has finally grown up!"

"I don't know what you mean..."

I kissed her again. "It's so very simple... you can't just 'fuck' anymore... you have to care about the person you have sex with... you have to love them... they have to love you. It's no longer about the physicality; you have to be emotionally involved too!"

"I don't feel wrong when I fuck you... or Katherine..."

"That's because Katherine and I love you... and as much as you don't want to admit it... you love us too!"

"You mean that? You really do love me?"

"Is that such a surprise to you...?" I said; Jenny paused, licked her lips and suddenly attacked me so very passionately. She kissed me hard and began to peel her clothes off and tore at mine. She began to kiss me and grab for my crotch. As much as I really wanted to monkey fuck her right there and then, I remembered that Katherine and I had a date for tonight and to occupy myself with Jenny now, would upset and disappoint her. "Jenny stop! Please... I know you don't want to hear this... But we're forgetting all about Katherine!"

"No you're not..." I heard from the top of the stairs. Jenny continued to kiss my neck and open my shirt and lick my nipples. It was Katherine wearing just a bathrobe. I was a little surprised to see her here. She slowly came halfway downstairs. She already had spoken with Jenny about this and sent her to get me at the airport. She had been patiently waiting upstairs until Jenny had a chance to talk with me privately. "You two go ahead... fuck each other silly..." She said approvingly. "I'll be upstairs... waiting... for the both of you!"

I began to pinch Jenny's nipples and she cooed and kissed my neck. "We'll meet you upstairs..." and I kissed Jenny. "In about twenty..." I kissed Jenny again. "No... say 30 minutes?" Katherine nodded at took a step back upstairs. "Katherine?" I called to her as Jenny unzipped my pants and began to stroke my cock and leaned in to lick and suck me.

Katherine paused. "Yeah baby?"

"Hot tub and lavender?" I knew Jenny needed to relax and calm her nerves.

Katherine opened her robe, tweaked her nipples hard and sighed. "Oh yeah! You read my fucking mind!" Katherine started up the stairs.

"Don't forget the 'tub toys'…!" Jenny added as she stroked me.

Katherine didn't pause this time. "Please! Have I EVER forgotten the tub toys?" Jenny laughed and then deep throated me. My eyes shot to the back of my head.

- - -

Viagra & a Red Bull: $20.

Cab to the airport: $60 plus tip.

Round trip airline tickets: $250.

Corporate limo that picked you up at the airport: $135,000.

Saying just the right thing to get a young, sexy, Latina horny enough to suck you dry while you finger and lick her wet pussy and knowing that there's a young, hot, horny, blonde haired, brown-eyed beauty waiting to finish you both off in a hot tub scented with lavender… and your weekend is just STARTING!!!

Fucking Priceless!

Imagine if I HAD a MasterCard!!!

The Tortured Soul Trilogy
(The Seduction of CJ Cassidy)
Chapter 125
(Afternoon Delights)

I was staying over at Katherine's (Nick's place) for a few days over another three-day weekend. Jennifer was away on business and we were having a really nice time just being together. I'm beginning to learn that I have a tendency to fuck up a good thing. I stir things up to see what would happen or because I'm nervous that something can't be right; or just because... My friend Bella, who happens to be a 'sanguine vampire', explained that it's not a feminine side but my emotional or sensitive side of me that gets in the way. Damn she's smart for a 19 year old.

We were sitting in the eat-in kitchen, Katherine was reading the morning paper; I was on the computer working on a script. Katherine will let me use my laptop. Jennifer takes it away from me when I visit her house. Last night we had a great sex. It wasn't a romp. It was nice and sensual. It was a slow, passionate evening of touching and groping and experiencing each other and being in the moment. We kissed each other's bodies. We caressed each other. We spent the night being aroused by arousing each other. We made love to each other, slow and deliberate. No monkey fucking, no sports fucking, just a slow comfortable screw. We had to turn the ceiling fan on because the room got hot and stifling. The cool air on our naked, glistening bodies only revived our desire to continue our lovemaking. We changed positions several times during the night. She positioned me; I positioned her. We both gave of our hearts and bodies freely last night. When I woke up in the morning, I was spooning her. I was still inside her, slowly pumping her in and out. Even in our sleep, we were still at it! Katherine moaned. "Baby? Aren't you finished yet?"

"You want me to stop?"

Katherine pushed her ass deeper into me. "No..." I lifted her leg into the air and began to pump her pussy in earnest. This was not going to be smooth sex... this was going to be a monkey fuck. I began to pump her harder and faster. Katherine's eyes opened wide and she let out a sigh. "Yeah... yeah... give me! You like that? You like that baby? Cum inside me baby... give me!" That's when I realized that I wasn't wearing a condom. Katherine must have sensed my concern. "Ride me baby... go ahead daddy... cum inside me... give me... I want to feel your hot spurt deep in my pussy... Cum for me... take it! It's all yours baby!" She started fondling her clit. No way I was going to stop now. I pumped her harder and faster. "Give me... give me! Cum for me... cum for me baby!" I threw my head back; my body was racing with endorphins. "Yeah baby! Yeah cum on! Cum on! Give me!" She took my finger and began to suck on it and I came hard! She felt my juices fill her void and she lost it! "Yessssss! Give meeeeeeeee!" And Katherine let out a high-pitched squeal. I love when she does that! She grabbed both my hands and wrapped them around her. I squeezed her nipples. She did not want me to pull out. I rammed my cock as far as it would go and held it there. "Mother fuuuuuuuuuccccccckkkerrrrr! Ahh ahhh! Ahhhhhhhhhhh! Haaaaaaa!" And she came hard. Her pussy twitched and she grinded her ass into me. "Mmmmmmmmmm haaaa!" I kissed her neck and she purred and cooed as her pussy massaged and milked my cock dry. I slowly pulled out and Katherine groaned and moaned softly. "Mmmmm... nice!" I got up and got a towel, wiped myself off and then wiped Katherine off. I spent special attention to wiping her pussy and clit. Katherine grinded into it. "Thank you CJ..."

"No... Thank yooo Mr. Acabano!"

She smiled and giggled. "Breakfast?" I asked.

"Please?" She smiled; Katherine loves good food after sex.

"In bed...?"

"Uh uhh... I think we've had enough 'breakfast' in bed time... I wanna get vertical otherwise I'm never getting out of his bed..."

"You say that like it's a problem..." I said.

Katherine laughed. "You know, you can't keep taking those little blue pills... you need to let your body rest!"

"Katherine..."

"Yeah baby?"

"I didn't take a pill last night... or this morning..."

Katherine's eyes opened wide and she put her hand on her chest and sighed. "You didn't...?"

I slowly shook my head no. "That... was all you baby!" I turned to leave. "I'll have breakfast ready in twenty minutes... don't use up all the hot water when you shower..."

"CJ...?"

I turned back and smiled at her. "It was all *you* baby... *all* you...!" She smiled. I paused. "Pancakes?" I asked

"Yes please..."

"Thank you Mr. Acabano..."

Katherine replied: "No... thank yooo Mr. Acabano!" I laughed, went to the bathroom to wash up and Katherine got in the shower behind me. I fought the urge get in with her and headed to the kitchen.

As I was saying, after breakfast, we were sitting in the kitchen, going about the morning as usual. I looked up at Katherine, just sitting there; she was content. I stared at her as her head nodded to some song playing in her head as she read the paper. She was at peace. Katherine is the most beautiful woman, I have ever seen in my life. I am totally taken by her. She's so beautiful. Not drop dead gorgeous, Jennifer is, but there is an aura that is around her when she's happy. It draws you to her. It's like an irresistible force. She looked up at me and smiled. My blood pressure dropped slightly and my cock got hard. I swear Katherine and Jennifer can put Viagra out of business!

"Katherine?"

"Yeah baby?"

I took a deep breath. "Can we talk?"

"Sure... would you like some coffee?"

I winced. "Your coffee...?"

"Fuck you! What's wrong with my coffee?" I grabbed my throat and made a gagging noise. "I promise not to make it too strong okay?"

I laughed and she slammed the paper on the kitchen table. She made me a cup and served it to me. She stood over me as I creamed and sugared it. I lifted the cup slowly to my lips. I stopped the cup just short of my mouth and turned to her, hovering over me. "What???"

"Drink it!"

"I am…"

"I'm waiting…"

I smiled. "You wanna back up a little?"

"No…! Drink it!" I slowly raised the cup to my mouth. "Drink it!"

"Okay! Give me a moment…" I took a sip. It was good, surprisingly good. I took a bigger sip. Katherine shook her head and sat back down in her chair. "When do you learn to make coffee?"

"Fuck you…"

I took another sip. "May I have some more?"

Katherine smiled wryly. "I'll think about giving you some more…"

"Okay then while you think about '*giving me some more*'… how about I have another cup of coffee?"

Katherine smiled. "You bitch!" She got up and freshened up my cup. Her breast slipped out of her robe as she stood near me to pour. I leaned in and kissed her nipple. She jumped a bit and covered up. "Stop that you nasty buzzard!" She giggled. I smacked her on the ass. She growled and then pinched her nipple, shook her head and she went back to sit down.

"Are you *always* this horny?" I asked.

"You know I am… and you know you like it!" I nodded and took another sip of coffee. "I suppose you want to talk about what happened in bed this morning?" I looked up at her from my cup. "I know you too well CJ… you just can't leave well enough alone… She put the coffee pot down and sat next to me. "Did it bother you that I wanted you to cum in me? You know I'm on birth control and I can't get pregnant… We were in the moment; I didn't want to break our rhythm…"

"No form of birth control is perfect… My youngest was born holding the I.U.D. in her hand… but that's not it…"

"I don't believe you…"

"If you want… I'll bend you over this table and monkey fuck you bareback right now!"

Katherine sighed, took a deep breath and shook her head as if she was shaking off the thought of being bent over the table right now. "Hold that thought! Okay… then what *is* bothering…?"

Katherine paused, cut her eyes, got up and poured herself a cup of coffee and sipped it. "This is about Jennifer... isn't it?"

"Yes... and no..."

"The fuck is that supposed to mean?"

"It's about me and you... and Jennifer..."

Katherine took another sip of her coffee. "Okay... let's have it..."

"I know you don't like it when I bring up Jennifer when it's just the two of us..."

"Get *on* with it... please...?"

"Look...! You love her... I love her; we both... love her..."

"And she loves us both... we've been through all this..."

"Are you gonna let me finish?"

Katherine dropped her eyes. "I'm sorry... Go ahead..."

"A while ago Jennifer was beside herself because she slept with another man..."

"I know... she felt like she cheated on you..."

I shook my head no. Katherine had a puzzled look on her face. "She felt... she cheated on *us*!"

Katherine's eyes widened. "I never thought of it that way...!" Katherine put her cup down. "But what does that have to do with what happened with us this morning?"

"When I'm with you, I'm with you, when I'm with Jennifer, I'm with Jennifer... when I'm with the both you... it's like the fucking Fourth of July... But I need you to understand. This is not a competition; I love you both, in different ways, for different reasons, but equally. There is no reason to try to one-up each other... As beautiful and marvelous as this morning was... It felt like you were trying to... I don't know... *win*?" I wasn't sure if I expressed myself correctly. Katherine sat quietly and after a few moments she began to cry softly. "Katherine...? What's wrong? Why are you crying?"

Katherine sobbed. "I did a bad thing CJ..."

I was concerned. "Katherine? What did you do...?"

Katherine began to hit her thigh with the heel of her hand and cry. "I... I... lied to you..."

My eyes opened wide. "*Katherine*! Don't tell me... You're *not* on birth control?"

"No! Not *that*! And besides... why would that be such a bad thing?" She snapped back.

"*Don't*... change the subject bitch! What did you do? How did you lie to me? I want to know right now!" Katherine sobbed into her hand. I dropped my eyes not to look at her. "I'm not falling for the tears... what did you do?"

"Jenny isn't away on business... she's in town. I just told you that so I could have you all to myself this weekend..."

I stood up and pointed at her. "See? This is what I'm talking about..." Katherine started to shake and shiver. "Why didn't you just tell me you wanted to spend the weekend alone with me? Why did you find it necessary to lie to me... you *know* I *hate* being manipulated like this..."

Katherine was crying hard now. "Please don't be mad at me... I'm sorry!"

"Jennifer would *never* do something like that to you..."

Katherine shook her hands. "I know... I know...! I'm sorry..."

"And what if she found out? Did you think of that?"

"No..."

"Pick up the phone and call her..."

"What?"

"You heard me... pick up the phone and call Jennifer, right now!"

Katherine shivered.

"Why?"

"Because I fucking told you to!"

Katherine picked up the phone and speed dialed Jenny. "What do you want me to tell her?" She stammered.

"Tell her the truth... that I came over last night to spend the weekend with you and is it okay with her that it be just the two of us..."

"Jenny? Hi baby... I'm good... I just called to tell you... CJ came over last night to spend the weekend ... is it okay with you if it's just him and me alone this weekend...?" Katherine listened quietly. "Thank you baby! I love you!" Katherine cried.

"What did she say?"

"She said it's alright with her if we spend some quality time alone together and she wants to talk with you..."

"I told you..." I mouthed. Katherine handed me the phone and left crying into the living room. "Jenny? Hey baby? How are you?"

"I'm good baby... what's with Katherine? She sounded a little upset..."

"You know how she gets sometimes... I just came over to help her get through some things..."

"You mean like inviting you over to spend the weekend with her... without telling me anything about it first?" I looked at the phone. "Come on... you would have not come all this way without telling me, unless you thought I was out of town!" Jenny said.

"You know you're too smart for your own fucking good, don't you?"

"I didn't get where I am by letting people bullshit me... and I know Katherine too well and besides, I'm going to have you all to *myself* next week..."

"I won't be in town next week... I'll be back in New York... "

"I'm going to have a sleep over at your place... just like Katherine does... do you have a problem with that?"

"HELL no, I don't have a problem with that... a whole week? You can manage that?"

"I'm the fucking boss here... I do whatever I want, and fuck whoever I want, whenever I want for as long as I want..."

"I can't wait..."

Jennifer was silent and then her voice got very serious. "CJ?"

"Yes Jennifer... what's up?"

"Katherine... is probably going to ask you to do something... that you're not going to want to do, but I really need a huge favor here..."

"What? What do you want me to do?" I was worried about Jennifer's tone in her voice. I didn't like it, not at all. Jennifer was silent for a moment. "Jenny? What is it that Katherine is going to ask me to do?" I asked.

"I know that bitch like the back of my hand..." she whispered. Jennifer paused again.

"Jenny... What do you think Katherine is going to ask me to do?"

"CJ... Katherine is probably going to ask you... to punish her... I want you to go ahead and do it!"

"Why can't you just come over later and do it yourself...?"

"It's not me that she needs to punish her right now; she needs you to discipline her... I'll tear her ass up good about this later, but right now, we both need you to do it... please?"

"Jenny, you know I don't like getting into that shit... I leave that up to you two. I don't want to get involved in any part of it..."

"I know baby, I know..."

"Jenny... I want the truth here... did you two bitches set all this up?"

Jenny was horrified. "No CJ! I swear! I would *never* do this to you on purpose! The very thought of you getting uncomfortable with our relationship and leaving us... scares me! Papi, I swear to you, we did *not* set this up... please believe me..."

I waited and listened patiently as Jenny pleaded her innocence. Jenny was sobbing. "What do you want me to do...?" I said softly.

Jenny sobbed. "Tie her down... and beat her...! You... you don't have to be too rough with her... you don't have to use anything on her... just spank her ass with your hands... just make her sorry she betrayed your trust..."

"Okay! I'll take care of it..."

"CJ... I promise... I will fuck you silly all next week if you do this..." she pleaded.

"No thanks..." I said dryly.

"What!!!?"

"Oh... you're *gonna* fuck me silly all next week... I just don't want you to do it because I did this... I don't want to be 'rewarded' for what I'm about to do to Katherine."

"Baby...?"

"Yes Jennifer?"

"I know you don't want to hear this right now... but you *will* be rewarded for doing this... It's going to make Katherine respect you... and if you think she has fucked your brains out before… is nothing compared to the way she is going to fuck you once she has learned to respect you… Just like I fucked you that time after you spanked me…"

"I *knew* that was going to bite me on the ass the moment I did it…"

"Baby… I will bite you *anywhere* you want me to… if you do this…!"

"Okay… I'm going to hold you to that…"

"CJ?"

"Yeah Jenny?"

"I am soooo wet right now!"

"Jenny?" I whispered.

"Yeah baby…? Talk to me…" she whispered.

I put some baritone in my voice. "Would *you* like to be punished right now?"

Jennifer let out a long soulful moan. "Yes I do…" she hissed.

"Would you like me to tie your ankles together and make you bend over…?"

"Yeah baby! I do…" she cooed.

"Would you like me to pull your panties down and slap your ass and call you a dirty little whore?" I whispered.

"Spank me Papi… call me una puta desgraciada…" She moaned.

I knew she was masturbating right then, I could hear that sound a wet pussy makes when you stroke it hard. "Goodbye Jennifer…" I said abruptly.

"Damn you CJ…! You're better at this than you know!" She moaned woefully.

"Whatever…" I hung up the phone and went into the other room. Katherine was leaning on the closed game room door, shivering, holding a thin leather belt in her hand. She turned and she leaned her head on her forearm on the door.

"CJ… I need to ask you for a favor…" she slowly held the belt out to me. I walked over to her shivering body and took the belt from her hand. She bent over and slowly hiked her robe to reveal her sweet naked ass. She then placed both hands on the door and braced herself. "Beat me… please…?" she sighed. "Beat me Daddy!" I stood behind her and pushed up on her and I now had her pinned between the door and my body. Katherine opened her mouth wide and let out a deep moan. "Ohhhhhhhh ahhhhhhh!" I took both ends of the belt and put it over her head and held it gently to her throat. "Ohhhh my!" she sighed. Katherine began to grind her ass on me. I gently pulled back on the belt like a rider pulling the reins on a wayward horse.

"Jennifer seems to think that I need to '*teach*' you to respect me..." I whispered in her ear. Katherine began to pant like a small animal that was trapped. I used the belt around her neck to gently straighten her up. She continued to grind her ass into my crotch and moan. "Stop that!" I barked at her. Katherine jumped a bit, stopped and lowered her head. I then quickly pushed up against her pinning her to the door with my body again. "Look at me!" I barked. She turned her head towards me and focused in on my eyes slowly. I still had her pinned face first to the door.

(Damn I wish she didn't look so sexy right now as the ingénue, but I was pissed at her.)

"Personally..." I whispered "I don't feel that I should have to teach you respect me, seeing that I should have already earned that from you... but it seems that I am going to have to get actively involved in earning it..." I leaned in closer, still holding the belt across her throat. Katherine shivered as my hot breath caressed her neck and shoulders. "First and foremost, learn this... I will *never* enter *that room*... you two bitches are not going to trick me, maneuver or anger me into entering that room... *ever*...! Do I make myself perfectly clear?"

"Yes sir!" Katherine whispered.

I put both my hands on the door on either side of Katherine's head and twirled the outstretched ends of the belt in both my hands tightly. It came off her throat and was now stretched across the door in front of her. "Second..." I snapped the belt hard and it snapped in half. Katherine yelped. "I am *never* going to beat you... or Jennifer... no matter how poorly you two behave. There is a line I do *not* cross..." I clenched my teeth. "And I draw that line right here and right now..."

Katherine nodded. "I'm sorry!" she sobbed. I turned her around to face me.

"I have left women *better* than you because of this bullshit... and I can walk away right now... no skin off my ass!"

Katherine's jaw dropped and she began to cry and she grabbed me by my waist. "No! Please! Don't leave me! Please don't leave! I don't want you to go... I'm sorry... just don't leave me...!"

I lifted Katherine's chin and kissed her deeply, she kissed me with a desperation as if she thought this was to be our last kiss. I backed away from her slowly she tried to make the kiss linger. "Now..." I said quietly. Katherine wiped her eyes. "I want you to go into the bathroom and put some cold water on your face, have a glass of wine, do whatever it takes for you to calm your nerves... Use one of your toys... whatever. Get in the bed and you and I are going to have a repeat performance of last night... all of it... even the bareback part..."

Katherine nodded and smiled. "Okay..." And she slowly approached my lips and kissed me deeply. "I love you!" she panted.

"I love you too... but just so you know... don't you ever try to pull this bullshit on me again... or on Jennifer... got it?"

"Yes sir!" She stepped away from me towards the bathroom.

"Katherine?"

"Yes CJ?"

"You have no idea how much I love you? Do you?"

"I think I'm starting to get an idea..." She took one step away.

"Katherine?"

"Yeah baby?"

"Jennifer is going to come over to stay at my place all next week and we're going to fuck like rabbits... do you have a problem with that?"

Katherine slowly shook her head no and cupped her breasts and squeezed her nipples. "If you have anything left for Jenny after this weekend is over... go for it!"

"It's not over you know..."

"What do you mean?"

"Jennifer is going to come over here after we're finished... and tear you a new one for lying to her..."

Katherine sighed. If she wasn't already aroused, the thought of Jennifer whipping her later; brought her there. I don't have a problem with what those two do in private. I just don't want to be involved in it, any of it.

"That's later... right now... you and I have a prior commitment..." Katherine said seductively. Katherine paused for second. I knew there was something she had to ask but she felt out of place asking me.

"What is it Katherine?"

She took a deep breath. "So... no more kinky sex for you and me...?"

"Huh!" I huffed. "Baby... I will handcuff you... spank you... *playfully*... use your toys on you. Tie you up, tie you down, whatever it takes to get you off *at least* three times before I do... but... I *will not* beat you! You okay with that?"

Katherine moaned. "I am *very* okay with that..."

"Good! Cause that's all I have to give you... or Jennifer...!" I waited until she went into the bedroom before going to my carry bag and taking a Viagra. I didn't take one last night, and although I'm very horny right now, I'm too old for this shit... daddy needs a little help sometimes!

The Tortured Soul Trilogy
(The Seduction of CJ Cassidy)
Chapter 126
(It Sucks To Be Me Sometimes!)

Okay, so, you just read the last chapter and you know how my weekend with Katherine went. I got back home to New York and started to clean my place up. Jennifer does not like a messy house and I have no intentions of giving her any reason not to have sex with me, although, nothing so far has ever stopped her before. Jennifer had a short business meeting in New York and she decided to stay with me the rest of the week. I was running the vacuum, when I heard the doorbell. I looked up at the clock. "What the fuck? Her plane shouldn't have even landed yet!" I grabbed two bottles of this new KY his and hers lubricant just in case she would monkey fuck me at the door. (She's done it before!) I opened the door. "You're here early..." And standing at the doorway with her suitcase was...

Not who you think...

Guess!

Nope! Not her either...!

I just want you to get the same feeling of eternity I felt standing in my open door...

Just a little longer...

Wait for it!

Okay...! Now!

"Mandy! What are you doing here? With a... suitcase?"

Yep! It was my ex-wife Mandy. You know, Mandy? Nick's stepdaughter? You know Nick, Katherine and Jennifer's former lover? Mandy? The one who works with Katherine at the C Cup??? Yeah... I know... I know! Be glad you don't have to deal with crazy shit like this!

Mandy looked at the bottles of lubricant in my hands. "Please tell me... you were expecting someone else?"

I held up the bottles. "Well... if she doesn't show... would you mind?" And I shook the bottles.

"Bullocks! I've been right put off screwing your sorry arse a long time ago...!"

"A simple no would have been just fine thanks!"

"Come kiss me you ole bugger!" And she threw her arms around me and kissed me.

"I'm so glad to see you honey! But what are you doing here? With a suitcase...?"

"I was passing by and decided to drop in..."

"You were passing by? The shortest plane ride here is three and a half hours!"

Mandy walked into my house and sat down. I haven't seen Mandy since she got engaged to Thomas. I mean; I've stopped by the C Cup to see her if I was in town visiting Katherine. She knew we were 'dating'. "Am I interrupting something?" she asked

I brought her bag inside. "What if I told you that you being here is gonna screw up my getting laid?"

"Would make my bloody day it would!" And she crossed her legs. I had almost forgotten how great her legs were. She caught me staring. "Take a good gander Luv! That's as close as you're gonna get!" Then she squeezed her ample bosom. "To these too!"

"Damn! And here I was so hoping you would fancy a fuck!"

"Pffftt! Aren't you banging Katherine like the rusty barn door you are?"

I looked at the watch I wasn't wearing. "That didn't take long! I believe it's a world record! And it's a 'rusty *screen* door'..."

"Oh, don't get your knickers all in a twist... I told you I don't mind that you and Katherine are together... and humping each other like stray dogs!"

662

"Are you *sure* you don't fancy a fuck?" I asked sarcastically.

"I'm sure... but I do fancy some tea..." She got up and went into the kitchen. "And don't be staring at my arse as I walk away..."

Damn, you know if you say don't, you have to do it! Mandy didn't have a great ass, but I have seen it up close and personal. I caught wood almost instantly.

"You know where everything is... Make me a cup too, if you don't mind!" At that moment, the doorbell rang. I smiled as my asshole puckered. "Mandy?" I said towards the kitchen.

"Yeah Luv... I know... no cream in your tea..."

"No! Uh... yeah but, remember when you said you were okay with me and Katherine being together?"

"Uh yeah! I just said it a moment ago! Why?"

"I need you to hold that thought!" And I opened the front door, and before I could say a word, Jenny's blouse and bra was on the floor and she was unzipping me. Jenny froze when she heard the two teacups shatter on the floor behind us.

"What the fuck is Jennifer doing here?"

"Exactly what I was going to ask CJ... about you!" Jenny said.

"Don't ask me... I just got here myself..." I said.

"You wanna cover up your tits Luv?" Mandy said nonchalantly.

"Not really!" Jenny said defiantly.

"I can't believe you're cheating on Katherine!" Mandy exclaimed.

"I'm not!" both Jenny and I said simultaneously.

"Buggers?" She pointed at me. "You're fucking Katherine...!" I nodded, she pointed at Jennifer. "And *you're* fucking Katherine?" Jenny nodded. "And you two..."

"Are fucking each other... Or at least we were just about to..." Jenny said, nodded and looked at me. "Yep, that just about covers it, unless you have something to add to that CJ...?"

"Nope... I was about to get into Mandy's knickers for the old 'in and out', but then you stormed in..."

"Fucking bullocks, so you three are...?"

Jenny nodded. "All making love to each other... yep!" I sat on the couch and motioned committing Hari-Kari with an imaginary sword.

Mandy looked at Jennifer. "I always meant to ask you Jennifer... are those real?" Jenny nodded yes. "They're quite nice!" Mandy commented.

"Thank you! Would you like to cop a feel?"

Mandy grabbed hers and jiggled them. "No, I have my own to play with, but thank you so much for offering!"

"Jenny, could you please put your blouse back on?" I said.

"Why?"

"Cause you're half naked, Mandy's nipples are hard and I can't concentrate!" I adjusted my cock.

Jenny picked up her blouse and began to put it back on. I zipped up my pants. "You sure you don't want to cop a feel?" She said to Mandy leaving her blouse open.

"Maybe later Luv..."

Jenny looked at me and flashed them. "CJ... I know you want to touch them..."

"CUT THE SHIT OUT!" I barked. They both jumped. "Okay... Katherine and Jennifer and I are all lovers... she's here to monkey fuck me this week, because I was with Katherine all last weekend. I hope to go and monkey-fuck the both of them at Jenny's house later this month..."

"I'm going to be in San Francisco the week of the 21st... so you better make it the week after..."

"Stop fucking around Jennifer!" I said. She had a smug look on her face. She liked that I was twisting in the wind here. I slowly looked at Mandy. "Now that we all know why Jennifer is here... Why are *you* here Mandy?"

Mandy dropped her eyes and paused. "Thomas threw me out!" She whispered.

"*What*?" Jenny exclaimed. "That son of a bitch...! Sit down, tell me what happened!" and Jenny brought Mandy to the couch and they sat next to me.

"And it gets better!" I said as I motioned tying a rope around my neck and hanging myself.

"*CJ*! Mandy is in pain and you're making jokes..."

"You're right! I should be making tea." I got up and cleaned up the mess Mandy left and went into the kitchen to make everybody tea. When I came back Jenny was rocking Mandy who was crying into her shoulder. Jenny's blouse was still open and Mandy had her arms around her waist. Mandy's lips were just *that* close to Jennifer's nipples. Damn my eyes... it was hot as hell to watch and here I was being so insensitive. I served them the tea.

"Thank you baby!" Jenny said.

I motioned for Jenny to close her blouse and she did as I served Mandy her tea. "Thanks Luv..." They both sipped their tea.

"But that doesn't explain why you're *here* Mandy..." I said.

Mandy looked at me and averted her eyes. "I thought that maybe I could crash here for a bit and..." And Mandy cried on Jenny's shoulder again. Jenny pointed at me and then at Mandy discretely. That's when I was hit by an epiphany. Mandy *did* fancy a fuck! *"Oh hell no!"* I mouthed.

Jenny cut her eyes at me. *"If she wants to... do it..."* She mouthed back.

Don't get me wrong; I would love a little slap and tickle with the ex. We were 'friends with benefits' after we split up and before she met Thomas, but I'm with Jennifer and Katherine now, and I don't have the emotional or physical strength for this. What? I'm a porn star all of a sudden? And since when is Jennifer okay with me fucking the ex? She's here because she has a problem with me fucking Katherine! Besides, I don't want to give Jennifer a 'free cock' card to sleep with another man... again!

"Mandy, you can stay here as long as you like... I'll sleep on the couch... it'll be just like old times..." I finished off sarcastically. "...And as for Jennifer...?"

"I'll stay at a hotel..."

"Hey! I can stay with Jennifer at the hotel..." I chimed in. Jenny cut her eyes at me. I finished with: "But I don't think you should be alone right now!" Damn! Damn! Damn! It sucks to be me. I'm not gonna get any pussy from Jenny. I shouldn't even try to get pussy from my ex. And I sure can't leave Jenny and Mandy alone together! When Mandy and I were going through our problems with our marriage, it was Mandy who suggested that we try adding a third person to our lovemaking and she, of course,

665

suggested Jennifer! Why do I feel like my world is imploding in on me?

Did I happen to mention; it sucks to be me?

"So Jennifer... how long have you and Katherine been having at it?" Mandy asked Jenny.

"We've been together for almost eight years now..."

"And you're okay with CJ having sex with Katherine?"

"I'm okay with the arrangement..."

I looked at Jennifer. I knew she was being facetious.

"And... exactly how long have *you* been fucking my husband?" Mandy asked her.

I cut my eyes. This situation is sinking fast. Mandy looked at me. I always knew she suspected that when I was interviewing Jennifer for her bio, we were having an affair. It's really not that big of a stretch of the imagination. After all, we are together now.

"I've never fucked your *husband*..."

Mandy raised her eyebrow. "Oh really? I thought that's why you're here..."

"Katherine and I didn't get involved with CJ until about six month's after you got engaged to Thomas... CJ wasn't your husband then, timing is everything sweetheart...!"

"Katherine told me about her relationship with CJ... she just never told me that she had a relationship with you or that you were involved with CJ..."

"Yes... Well... Katherine does seem to like to keep me her 'little secret'..." Jennifer cut her eyes at me. She was not happy with Katherine right now.

"Jennifer...! We're working on it... give her time..." I said.

"I would think eight years would be more than enough time..." Jenny got up. "I'm going to call a few hotels that my company has standing reservations in and I'll call a cab."

"Jenny may I see you for a moment... privately?"

"Sure CJ!" and she stepped towards the kitchen.

"No... I'd like to see you in private... upstairs..."

"What can you say to me upstairs you can't say to me in the kitchen?"

"Jennifer! Get your ass upstairs... right now!" Jenny sighed and went upstairs. I turned to Mandy. "I'm going to talk to Jenny for a moment and let her call the hotel from the upstairs phone. I'll be back down in fifteen minutes... twenty tops." I went upstairs where Jenny was already on the phone with the hotel. "Jennifer... you know Katherine has a secretive nature..." Jennifer held her index finger up to me. She wanted me to be quiet while she was on the phone. "You know that she's a very private person, especially when it comes to us..."

Jenny held her hand up. "Whatever... She had no problem telling Mandy about you..."

"First of all, I'm Mandy's ex-husband and they work together, of course she would have to confide in her that we're sexually involved, she didn't mention you because she doesn't want anybody to know she's bisexual...!"

"So am I! What? Is she ashamed of who and what she is? Cause I'm not!" Then Jenny mumbled under her breath. "She's the bitch that turned me out in the first place '*for fucks sake*' as Mandy would say!"

"Actually Mandy is British, that's an Irish saying..."

She cut her eyes, turned her back to me and turned back. "And I have a problem with you as well..."

"*Me*...? What did *I* do?"

"You obviously didn't tell Mandy about me... are you ashamed of me too?"

"I am *not* ashamed of you. I write about you and me and Katherine on the Internet everyday! I'm writing a new novel about us for crying out loud. I just didn't think it proper to rub my ex-wife's nose in it!"

"And when were you going to tell her about us...? When the next book came out?"

"Honestly, I thought she knew or just didn't care, she's with Thomas, or she *was* with Thomas, besides, she doesn't read any of my stuff..." Jennifer must have sensed I was lying to her. I knew Mandy didn't know about our three-way love affair. Oh sure, she knew about Katherine and she suspected Jennifer, but she didn't know Jenny and Katherine were having at it. She didn't want Mandy to know about it so I wasn't going to tell her about it either.

She pursed her lips. "Phhhsss... *what ever*! Hello? Yes I need a room tonight... My company has a standing reservation... Faber Data...! Yes I'll hold, thank you!" She turned to me. "I am *not* your secret whore!" She spoke into the receiver. "Yes... that will be fine...the name is Jennifer Jones... I should be arriving in an hour or two... yes... thank you!" And Jenny put the phone down. She leaned back on my dresser, crossed her arms and just looked at me. I knew that look, Jenny was horny as all hell, she gets that way when she's agitated. I could see her hard nipples right through her blouse. I unzipped my pants and began to stroke my cock.

"What are you doing?" she whispered. I continued to stroke my cock until I was hard and I walked towards her. "Oh? You think I'm just gonna *give you* some pussy now...?"

"You're not my '*secret whore*', but you are... *my* whore... and I believe you came all the way here so we can fuck... and fuck you I will..." I opened my dresser drawer and took out a condom and put it on.

"You... just put on a condom so you can jerk yourself off... cause I'm *not* gonna fuck you!" I reached over and pulled open her unbuttoned blouse. She didn't try to stop me. I looked at her and her nipples were rock hard and very sensitive. She let out a low moan as I pinched and worked her nipples. "Damn it! That feels so... good!" She growled. I slowly reached under her skirt and fondled her pussy; she still didn't try to stop me. She was very wet. Jenny let out a low moan.

"You're ready to fuck somebody... and I'm the only man here..." I leaned into Jenny's ear and whispered. "And Mandy is off-limits... for both of us!" I roughly turned Jennifer around, lifted her skirt, ripped off her panties and bent her over the dresser. I grabbed her arms and held them tightly behind her and I monkey fucked her. It turned her on that Mandy was just downstairs, plus Jenny gets hot and juicy when she's agitated a bit.

"Call me your whore baby...!" Jenny moaned.

"You filthy fucking whore... give me that pussy Puta! Cabrona!" And I rammed my stiff cock in her hard and deep. I put my hand tightly over her mouth, cause Jenny is very loud and my ex was just at the bottom of the stairs. She took her free hand and she pinched her nipples hard. Jennifer came hard and you could barely hear her muffled screams. She then finished me off with amazing oral. Like I said, nothing has ever stopped Jenny from having sex with me. I went back downstairs while Jenny got herself together. Mandy cut her eyes at me. Jennifer came down behind me two minutes later after having called a cab.

"Your lipstick is smeared dear!" Mandy said nonchalantly.

Jenny took out a tissue and wiped it all off. "I'll fix it when I get to the hotel..."

Mandy held out Jenny's bra to her. The cab bonked his horn as he arrived.

"I'll come back to get that some other time..." She looked at Mandy. Mandy knew that Jenny was marking her territory. Mandy tossed the bra on the couch. I took Jenny's bag to the cab. When I came back inside the house, Mandy looked at her watch.

"Congratulations!"

"For what?"

"You made her orgasm in under fifteen minutes and it still took her ten more minutes for her to get your rocks off... I'm impressed..."

I put my hands in my pockets. "You know me... if I don't deliver under 30 minutes... it's free!"

"You just *had* to fuck her... right *now*?" Mandy said as she threw Jenny's bra at me.

"It was her now... or you later... and up until right now, I couldn't trust myself with you..."

"And now you can?"

"The animal desire is gone... but no... I still can't trust myself with you... Katherine and Jennifer have taught me... how to... regenerate desire at a moments notice. I'll masturbate before I go to bed... you'll be pretty safe then."

"Bastard! What about my needs?"

"Mandy... that's not fucking fair! You wanted a man that was faithful and not a mangy dog... and when I decide that I don't want to be a dog... you deride me for not breaking a trust with someone else so you can satisfy your needs... what about me? What about my needs? What about my feelings?" Mandy cut her eyes at me. "Don't look at me like that... you didn't know about Jennifer, but you damn sure knew about Katherine... you should have called me. Maybe I could have spoken to them about this... see how they would have felt about it first..."

"Did you ever love me?"

"Bitch! I *still* love you... That's why I'm having such a fucking problem here!"

Mandy sobbed. "May I have a hug?" She sobbed.

"I thought you would never ask!"

We came together slowly and hugged. "I guess it too late to ask you if you fancy a fuck..." She asked.

"I love you way too much to fuck you..." I kissed her forehead and then her lips. "But had you called first, it would have been my pleasure to make love to you tonight!" I held my ex-wife and rocked her and kissed her forehead. We danced to no music for over fifteen minutes. Later, I ordered a pizza, sausage and peppers, the way she liked it and we sat down and talked all night. We fell asleep on the couch, fully dressed, Mandy nuzzled into my arms. I kissed her forehead and she kissed me, I kissed her deeply. We both knew. It wasn't going to happen. But we were closer now than we ever were before. I really do love Mandy, but I love Katherine & Jennifer in the now. I leaned over, kissed Mandy again and whispered. "You want me to kill Thomas?" Mandy busted out laughing. "No I'm serious... something slow and painful... and you know Jennifer has friends who can make the body disappear!"

Mandy giggled. "So tell me, what would you do to him?"

"Oh did I tell you? I'm working on this script... "*Psychosis Y Dementia – A Love Story*", It's about a demon of retribution who avenges a maiden beset by evil forces... There are some great kill gags in it..."

"Who's writing the script?"

"Hector and I..."

"How's he doing?"

"He's good... He's at the Comics Convention at The Javitz Center, playing 'Psychosis' to see if we can get funding for the film or the graphic novel..."

"Tell me more about this script you two are working on..."

I made breakfast and we talked. Mandy listened to my screenplay. She even had some good suggestions. Funny, she never really cared about my 'career' when we were married. She didn't even bother to read *"The Confessions of Jennifer X"* after she read *"A Tortured Soul..."* she lost interest. Maybe if she had read my second book, some of this wouldn't be such a shock to her. I liked being able to sit and talk with her again; I really missed doing that with her. I guess when you're too close to the trees; you can't enjoy the forest. Jennifer called me from the hotel after her meeting and we made the arrangements for Mandy to go back home that afternoon. Mandy was ready to go back home but she didn't go back to Thomas. Katherine was going to let her stay in an empty apartment in Nick's brownstone as long as she wanted. I'm glad, that poor kid has gone through too much shit in her life. She shouldn't have to take any from anybody anymore. It's funny, Mandy and Katherine help abused women find strength and courage. And here Mandy was, looking for a chance to exhale. I guess we all still need a little help every now and then. Jenny arrived in a cab later that afternoon; she was going back with Mandy. Mandy hugged and kissed me and got in the cab. I took her bag outside and put it in the trunk. I then took Jenny's bags out. Jenny rolled down her window.

"What the hell are you doing? I'm going back to Nevada with Mandy!"

I came over to her open window. "Young lady... Get... *your* ass... out of *this* cab... into *that* house... out of *those* clothes... and into *my* bed... now!" The amazed look on the cab drivers face was priceless! "You came all the way to New York to monkey fuck me all this week and you've wasted two whole days... get your hot little ass in my house now! Move it!" The cab driver shook his head and laughed to himself, that is, until Jenny got out of the cab and went into my house while taking off her jacket. "Cabbie!" He turned his attention to me.

"Yes sir!"

I walked over and handed him a twenty. "You make sure my wife doesn't miss her flight..." He looked towards the house. "Not her..." I pointed at Mandy. "Her!" Mandy rolled down her window. I kissed her.

"Take care and have fun!" Mandy said.

"You know I will."

"What the???" The cabbie was totally puzzled.

"Hey! Plane to catch…! Cab… drive!"

"Yes sir!" And the cabbie drove off shaking his head. Jenny stuck her head out of my bedroom window. She was already naked.

"Hey you! Are you coming up here? Or do I have to start without you?"

"Go ahead and get started without me… I'll be right there!" I heard the buzz of Jenny's vibrator as I slowly made my way back to the house. Hey! The more warming up she does, the easier it is for me! I am 53 years old for crying out loud… and speaking of crying out loud. You know Jenny is a screamer? Woo hoo!

The Tortured Soul Trilogy
(The Seduction of CJ Cassidy)
Chapter 127
(Pushing the Envelope)

I was in my eat-in kitchen, at the breakfast table, working on a new novel for my friend, Bella, who is a self-proclaimed modern day vampire. The working title is '*Blood Moon Rising*'. Jennifer calls her "Little Sis" because other than the blood lust; she's just like Jennifer was at her age and there is a striking resemblance. Nonetheless, Jennifer doesn't like it when I spend my time with her on my computer. She demands my undivided attention, but I can go on-line if she's asleep or otherwise occupied. I'm in the zone right now and I won't stop writing when I'm on a roll. Jennifer came down from the bedroom dressed and ready to go out. She was wearing a light pullover sweater top, her short black skirt with the slit on the side, and her 5" 'do me' heels. Her hair was cascading around her face. She looked hot, and she knew it. She came up behind me and kissed my neck and fondled my nipples. "What are you working on?"

"Doing some research for the novel I'm doing with Bella. You look nice... you going out?"

"I wanted to take you to out dinner and maybe we could go clubbing..."

I don't dance very well and I can only salsa with Jennifer cause she has to do all the work. Most of the time she dances with other men, and I sometimes get the feeling that I'm her 'safety' date. If a guy gets too pushy, she can tell him she's with me. I don't mind, cause when Jenny has a night out, she's very horny afterwards and making her cum doesn't require too much effort on my part. (No, it's not that I'm lazy... but sometimes you have to put in a little overtime to satisfy Jenny, and let's face it... I'm not a spring chicken anymore.) "Okay... let me just finish this last paragraph, I'll hit the shower and get dressed..." I only had to rinse off and getting into a pair of nice slacks and a shirt would take no time at all, I could be ready in 15 minutes, 20 minutes tops. I continued to work. Jennifer went to the coffee pot, poured herself a cup, black the way she always liked it and took a sip.

"Mmmmm that's good…" She turned to me. She had that 'look' like she was upset that she was being ignored. She wanted to be the focus of my attention. I could tell that she was somewhere between horny and angry. "I didn't come over to watch you work on that computer, you know I want your undivided attention… turn that shit off and at least talk to me…"

"I have to get this done… I'm working on a new novel and I'm on a roll…" I continued to type.

"Can't it wait?"

"No…! Can't YOU wait?"

Jenny's jaw dropped. She couldn't believe what I just said to her.

"Oh no you fucking didn't!"

"Oh yes I just fucking did!"

Jenny looked around the room as if I didn't know to whom I was talking to. She had a look on her face as if to say; '*I know you did not just tell me to go fuck myself!*' "Turn that computer off right now!" she barked.

"Blow me…!" I barked back.

"What did you just say to me…?"

"You heard me bitch! I said get under this table and blow me!" (I know, I know, but trust me… I know what I'm doing… I… think!)

Jenny poured the rest of her coffee into the sink. "I know you don't think I'm gonna blow you just because you asked me too!"

"I didn't ask you to blow me… I 'told' you to blow me… now are you getting under this table or not?" I continued to type out the next chapter, ignoring her.

"NO! I'm not getting under that table!" she said not believing my sudden boldness.

"Okay then…!" I paused. "Katherine blows me better than you ever could anyway…"

Jenny looked at me as if I had lost my fucking mind, and to be honest with you. I wasn't too sure of my sanity at this point either! That was way out of line with her considering what's been going on with the three of us lately. "I know what you're doing CJ!" She said angrily.

"I know what you're 'not' doing... now be a good little whore and get under this table and get to sucking my cock... I'm getting a little impatient with you right now."

Jenny cut her eyes at me. She couldn't believe what she was hearing. "How about I just bite your cock off... bitch?"

"Either way it *will* be in your mouth..." I said nonchalantly. I pulled the chair that was next to me out to give her access under the table. I continued to type. "You want my undivided attention? Wrap your luscious lips around my dick..." I could see Jenny clearly in my peripheral vision. I had to keep her in sight, just in case I pushed too hard, but she wasn't moving so I kinda knew I was still safe. After what happened at Katherine's, I knew I had a 'get out of jail free card'. Even though I was trying to cash it in now, I had to decide how far I could push her buttons before endangering my life. I stopped typing and looked at her. I could tell she was becoming aroused. Her eyes were wide and her nose was open. Her breasts heaved as she took slow deep breaths.

This was the first time I ever stood up to her and she liked it! She liked it a lot! "Don't make me angry... you won't like me when I get angry!" (I don't think she got the "Incredible Hulk" reference.) Jenny's lips parted, she let out a deep breath and she blushed. Now she was really horny. She took a step towards me. "No!" I said and she stopped. "Now you pissed me off! Take your blouse off..." She slowly reached around her waist, pulled her blouse out of her skirt and pulled it over her head. Now I knew I was in full control of her and she wanted me to be. "Now the bra..." She reached behind her and undid her bra and shimmied out of it. Her nipples were already hard and firm. "Pinch them for me..." She complied and pinched her nipples hard and cooed. "Now get your hot little mocha ass under this table..." And I pointed under the table. She took a step towards me. "No!" I said, she stopped; now she was confused. "Grab those two pot holders on the fridge and kneel on them..." She turned and did as she was told. "Now... slide your ass over here... like you did for Nick!" Her jaw dropped and she panted. She had forgotten that I knew everything about her and Nick, after all, it was me who wrote her biography. It turned her on that I knew her most intimate secrets. She realized that she had trusted me with things only a very select few knew about her. She put her hands on the floor and slid

675

towards me. I spread my feet and she slid under table and positioned her head between my knees. She unzipped me and began to stroke my cock with her hands. I continued to type.

"What do you want me to do Papi?"

"I told you what I want you to do... now you're just stalling... get to sucking my cock, you dirty little slut! You fucking whore!"

She reached for my belt buckle and began to try to pull it off me. "Are you going to punish me?" She said seductively.

I grabbed her hand to stop her. "No..." I said plainly. She blinked and acknowledged that I would never beat her. She began to kiss and lick the head of my dick. I had forgotten that she had worked as a fluffer for a porn film. She knew how to give just enough head to keep me erect but not make me cum. She got off her knees and was now sitting side saddle on the floor with her head on my thigh. She flicked her tongue up and down my shaft and she paid close attention to the little fold of skin near the rim. Then she sucked on it until I thought I would faint.

"You like that Papi?" She said as she stroked me softly and gently.

"I think you have my undivided attention now!" I said with a low moan. I reached down and fondled her breasts and squeezed her nipples. She kissed my hand and forearm. I stopped just as she deep throated me. I grabbed the armrests of my chair. Jennifer looked up at me from under the table.

"Please keep your hands inside until the ride stops..." and she took my hands and put them back on her nipples and smiled. And she began sucking my cock, sucking harder as she pulled back off it. She then began to suck on the tip as if she was puffing on a cigar! Where the fuck did she learn to do that? I put my hands on the table and pushed the table away. That gave her room to bob her head up and down on my shaft. She reached up and took my hands and put them on her ears. He wanted me to direct what she was doing. She began to flick her tongue in and out of her mouth while she had my cock in her mouth. I pulled her off me and leaned back on the chair. She stroked the head my cock with her thumb. I swung my head right and left violently. "What's the matter Papi? You told me to do for you what I did for Nick!" And she deep throated me again. "You *still* think Katherine can blow you better than I can?" She went down on me again and I violently swung my head from side to side again.

"I think you're about to take first place!" I moaned.

She took a deep breath and buried my cock deep in her mouth. She began to hum and my eyes went to the back of my head. I have no idea what she did next. All I remember is my balls tightened and I felt my hot spurt shoot hard into Jennifer hungry mouth and she sucked me dry while she moaned. I peeked under the table and Jenny's panties were around her ankles and she had been masturbating the whole time. She pulled her fingers out of her wet pussy and held it to my mouth. I licked her fingers. I leaned back on the chair and Jenny came out from under the table. She rubbed her breasts and nipples in my face. She took her fingers and put them under my nose and I breathed her scent in deeply. She leaned into me and whispered. "I'm going upstairs and freshen up... get your ass upstairs and I want you to do for me what I just did for you!"

I saved my pages and turned off my computer just as she stepped towards the stairs. "Yes ma'am!" I got up went to the fridge and got an energy drink. "I'm gonna need two..." I took two out, opened one and guzzled it and opened the second one just as I got to the stairs. Papi is going to have to put in some serious overtime! By the way...? Have I told you how much I love this crazy bitch?

Not including Katherine, Sex with Jennifer is absolutely the most amazing experience I have ever had in my life. She's raw, passionate and when she gets 'romantic' and playful... Sorry, I have to stop. I'm getting a hard-on just thinking about it. Sometimes I get scared. I don't understand why Jennifer and Katherine chose me to unleash their animal passions on. They have each other. Why do they need me? I mean besides the equipment? It's funny, I don't think of them as lesbians or bi-sexual. They use each other as if it's to occupy their time until I get there. They need a release? They get it on with each other. If I'm there, they involve me in their lovemaking. Each of them would like my undivided attention when we make love. When we are all together, they rarely make love to each other. They concentrate on me. I don't know what I'm saying here, but it's as if Katherine and Jennifer treat each other as a 'safety fuck'. They have become comfortable with each other. They get it on with each other; so they don't have to go 'outside' for sexual release.

Whatever you may think of Katherine and Jennifer, they are not whores or sluts. They are beautiful, dynamic, powerful, sexual beings, who have found a unique way of expressing their passions for life and for each other... and for me. And whatever you may think of me for taking advantage of the situation... you're probably right! I'm enjoying the hell out of this! Shit! I'm a 53 year-old man and I'm having amazing sex with two young, hot, sexy women and *they're* okay with it? What? Who's got it better than you CJ? Nobody! I don't know how I got so lucky and I sometimes wonder if a time will come that I won't be the focus of their passions. I'm not the kind of guy who lives in the now... I need a sense of security. I need to know that they will always be there for me, and I can always be there for them. Not just sexually but emotionally as well. But that story is best saved for later. Right now I want to tell you what happened the day before Jenny was going to go back home.

Let me recap here. I spent the weekend with Katherine at her place and now Jennifer is spending the week with me at mine. The week was postponed a day by a surprise visit from my ex-wife. Mandy has gone home; Jennifer is here with me aaannddd scene...!

The Tortured Soul Trilogy
(The Seduction of CJ Cassidy)
Chapter 128
(It Sucks to be me... Part two!)

I came home from work on Thursday and Jennifer was sitting in the living room having a glass of wine. I immediately knew something was up because she was fully dressed. Jennifer avoided wearing clothes and would prance around the house naked all the time. In fact I got used to coming home to a naked woman. She jumped up and hugged and kissed me. "Hey baby! I'm so glad you're home."

"I'm glad to see you too baby!" I put my briefcase down.

"Are we going out somewhere tonight?"

"No? Why do you ask?"

"Because you're dressed..."

She looked at what she was wearing. "I just have jeans and sneakers on..."

"I mean... you're wearing clothes..." I paused a moment. "Oh! Is it...?"

Jenny looked at me then shook her head. "No! It's not that time of the month... You're still gonna get some pussy tonight!" And she giggled and hugged and kissed me again.

"So what's going on?" Jenny's face got serious. I didn't like it. "What's going on Jennifer?" I asked. She looked down at the ground. She knew that I was serious because I called her Jennifer.

"Baby..." she said quietly.

"What?"

"Please bear with me... I'm so scared right now..."

"What did you do? What's going on?" I didn't like where this was going.

"Come with me..." she said softly. And she took my hand and led me into the kitchen. I looked around and the kitchen was spotless.

"You cleaned the kitchen?" I was amazed. Jenny has a maid to do all her housework.

"Yes... but that's not it!" She sat me down at the table and went over to the oven and opened the door. I looked at her. *"What the hell is she up to?"* I said to myself. She took out a plate wrapped in aluminum foil, unwrapped it and carefully brought it to me and placed it in front of me. She was shaking and wringing her hands. She bit her lip and fidgeted with her hair. I smiled at her. "I hope you like it baby!" she said. I looked down at the plate. It had two fried pork chops, red potatoes and asparagus with pearl onions. Jenny went to the cabinet and brought me a knife and fork and a napkin. She then went to the fridge and poured me a drink and placed it on the table in front of me.

"You... cooked... this...?" I smiled at her.

Jenny nodded nervously and fiddled with her hair. "Uh huh..."

I looked at her and I squinted my eyes at her. "*You*...? Cooked *this*...?" She nodded again and bit her lip. "Where did you get the recipe?" I asked cautiously.

"I called Katherine... and she walked me through it..." I nodded. I took my knife and wiped it with the napkin and looked at it. Jenny just stood there rocking back and forth. I felt bad making her twist in the wind but you have to understand, Jenny fucks like a porn star but she cooks like shit! But at least Katherine walked her through it. I tried to teach Jenny how to cook once. I promised myself I would never let her back in a kitchen again. I only drink her coffee, which she taught Katherine how to make. I took the knife and fork and cut into the pork chop. I knew I was taking my life in my own hands here. She tried to fry chicken for me once. The outside was well done but it was raw at the bone. The chicken only made me sick, raw pork could kill me! Jenny watched my face intently. I held up the piece of pork chop on my fork and she watched me as I slowly placed it into my mouth and chewed. She rocked back and forth as I swallowed. I cut into the potato and she watched me intently as I ate that. The pork chop was dry and tough, overcooked and under seasoned and the potato was undercooked. "How is it...?" she asked nervously.

I looked Jennifer square in the eye and said: "It's delicious! It's really good baby!" I was not about to break her heart when I know she tried so hard to cook this just for me.

"You're a lying bastard!" she whispered. I looked into her eyes, cut into the pork chop again and took another bite. "But I love you, you lying bastard!" She said. And she ran over to me threw her arms around me and began to kiss my neck and face.

"Do you mind? I'm trying to eat here...!" I said plainly.

She threw right her leg over me to face me and sat down on my plate. She peeled off her top, unhooked her bra and put her tits in my face. "You wanna eat that shit or do you wanna fuck?" she moaned.

"I don't wanna eat it now that you stuck your ass in it... so I guess... we're just gonna have to fuck!" Jenny giggled and I began to suck and bite her nipples. Jenny moaned and cooed. I really think she came the moment when I ate the meal she prepared for me.

"Was it really that bad?" she asked me.

I kissed and licked each of her nipples very deliberately. Jenny took a deep breath and sighed. I kissed her neck and whispered. "I noticed you didn't fix yourself a plate!" A tear came to her eye and she threw her arms around me. I grabbed her thighs and stood up. She wrapped her legs around my waist and I carried her upstairs. "So... just a question... what did you have in mind for dessert?"

"You're carrying it up the stairs..." She cooed.

"You have no idea how much I love you!"

"I love you too you lying bitch!" Jenny cooed.

"So... pizza?"

"Half cheese, half pepperoni?"

"You got it baby!"

"It's already in the oven..." I stopped and looked at Jennifer. "What...? It's always good to be prepared!" She said.

We didn't make it all the way up the stairs. We had dessert on the top steps.

The next morning the doorbell rang. I got out of bed. Jenny was still knocked out from last nights fuck fest. She was snoring like a busted chain saw. Jenny always sleeps in after a good fuck. If she jumps out of bed in the morning, well... your days are numbered pal.

"Who can that be? I'm not expecting anybody..." I put my pants on and went to the front door. They kept ringing the doorbell. "Keep your pants on! I'm coming!" I opened the door and Katherine was standing there with her suitcase.

"You sure you want me to keep my pants on?" She said seductively.

I crossed my arms. "What in the hell are you doing here Katherine? You just couldn't let it be? This is Jenny's week, you just had to ruin it didn't you...?" There was a look of shock on her face.

"Is that Katherine?" Jenny yelled out from the bedroom.

I looked at Katherine when I realized what was going on. "Jenny invited me..." she had a sad look on her face. "I thought you knew... I thought... she told you..."

"Jennifer!" I shouted upstairs. "Get your ass out here!"

Jenny came to the top of the stairs. "Baby? What's wrong?" She saw that Katherine was at the door and very upset. I looked up at Jenny; she realized I was upset too. "I invited Katherine to come spend the rest of the weekend with us... It was a surprise... for you!"

Katherine had tears in her eyes. She had no idea this would backfire on her.

"Damn it!" I pulled Katherine into the house and closed the door. "You two bitches always do this to me... you do things without telling me and I look like the bad guy!"

"I thought you wouldn't mind..." Jenny said surprised.

"I wouldn't have minded... but I just fussed out Katherine because I thought she was being selfish by being here and interrupting our time together... We just discussed this... You can't do just things without telling me..." Katherine was sobbing now. Jenny felt really bad that her surprise had backfired. "I'm sorry Katherine... I'm sorry I fussed at you." I began to kiss Katherine passionately and kissed her neck and face. "This is all Jenny's fault... you okay?" Katherine nodded. I hugged her tightly. "Daddy's sorry he fussed at you... you didn't deserve that! Go on upstairs and wash your face." Katherine slowly went upstairs and I went back outside for Katherine's bag. Katherine just got to the top of the stairs and was hugging Jennifer. "I need a huge favor from you two..." They turned to me. "From now on... if you two make any plans... that involve my dick... please let me in on it in advance...!" They nodded. "Now you two kiss and make up…" They kissed each other gently and then again and then more and more passionately. I stood there at the bottom of the stairs and watched them as they kissed each other deeper and harder. Jenny opened Katherine's blouse and began to stroke her nipples. Katherine sighed and began to suck on Jenny's tit. They began to kiss and fondle each other at the top of the stairs. They seem to have forgiven each other and I sure as hell wasn't all that mad at them right now either!

"CJ?" Jenny moaned as Katherine sucked her nipple.

"Yes?" I whispered.

"Katherine and I have just made plans that involve your dick… Would you like to come upstairs?"

"I'll be right up… you two go in the bedroom… and continue making up…"

Jenny turned Katherine to face me and she kneaded and stroked Katherine's breasts for me, she then reached down and fondled her crotch. Katherine almost swooned. "We both owe Katherine an 'apology'…" Jenny cooed as she grabbed Katherine's crotch and squeezed and rubbed it.

"Okay… I want Katherine eating your pussy with her ass in the air and when I come upstairs I'm going to fuck her from behind… Is that okay with with the two of you?"

Katherine's legs got weak and Jenny held her up. "I think that's a yes…" Jenny said.

I shooed them off and they went towards the bedroom. I went and took a Viagra. I swear those two bitches are going to drive me crazy, but I'm loving every minute of it!

Have I told you how much I love these two horny bitches?

The Tortured Soul Trilogy
(The Seduction of CJ Cassidy)

Chapter 129
(Yeah, I Fuck Up Too!)

I was spending a week at Jennifer's house. Katherine would come and spend the night with us whenever she wanted to or she would come spend a week at my house without Jennifer. I hadn't seen Katherine all this week. I figured she was just giving Jennifer and me some alone time. I got to Jennifer's about 5pm from working out at the gym and Katherine was in the living room watching TV. Jennifer hadn't gotten home yet. "Hey baby?" and I kissed her. She seemed a little moody.

"Something wrong...?" I asked.

"No... Nothing's wrong..." (First clue) I went upstairs to shower and when I came back down she was still watching TV. As I passed by the kitchen, I noticed that there was no dinner ready. I get it... She does not have to cook for me... I am not the 'master' of this house, besides I guess Jennifer was bringing dinner home or we would order delivery when she got home. I went back into the living room and sat next to Katherine. "What are you watching?" No answer. (Second clue) I didn't care for the show she was watching, but I wasn't about to change the station, so I went over to my briefcase and took out my laptop. I began to check and answer my e-mails. "What are you doing?" she asked.

"Just checking my E-mails..."

"Do you have to do that now...?"

(Major fucking clue... and I'm oblivious!)

"I'll be off in a moment... You know Jenny hates it when I get on line, so I figured I'd get this done before she came home..."

"She's not coming home tonight... She called me and said she has an emergency meeting in Boston, she won't be back until tomorrow morning or afternoon..."

"Oh! I didn't know... should I whip something up for dinner?"

She didn't answer and raised the volume on the TV. Okay...! I guess she's not hungry. With Jenny out of the house tonight I went back to checking my messages. After a while, Katherine spoke. "How much longer are you going to be? I want you to sit with me..." She said.

(BIG FUCKING CLUE... but did I get it? Noooooooooooo!)

"I'll be right there... I just have two more messages to answer and I'm all yours..." By the time I finished, Katherine was gone. The TV was still on, but she wasn't in the room. I thought she went to make a sandwich or use the bathroom. I sat on the couch to wait for her to return. After about ten or fifteen minutes I called out to her. "Katherine? Your show is almost over... do you want me to save the ending for you?" No answer. "Katherine...?" I hit the record button and TiVO'd the show for her. "Katherine...? Where are you baby?" Did she leave the house without telling me? I went upstairs to the bedroom; all my stuff was thrown out in the hallway. "Oh fuck me! What did I do?" I said to myself. I tried the bedroom door. It was locked. "Shit!" I knocked on the door gently. "Katherine...? Are you alright...?"

"Go away!" and I heard her sob.

"Oh FUCK me!!!! What did I do now?" I thought to myself. (No... she was not on the 'rag' and NO... I did not ask her that! I've been married three times. I know that trap, thank you very much!

"Honey? Are you okay? Is it that time of the month...?"

"You son of a BITCH! You think that every time I'm mad at you is because it's that 'TIME OF THE MONTH'!!!!"

Uh uhh! I've been to that dance before and I don't like the DJ! I need help here. I'm lost with no map and no clue. That's when I thought of calling Jennifer. Yeah, Jennifer can help me out, but where is she in Boston? Oh I know, call her cell. I only called Jenny on her cell if it was an absolute emergency. This most certainly was an emergency. I picked up the house phone to call her.

"Do you fucking mind? I'm on the phone with Jennifer!" Katherine yelled through the phone.

685

"Sorry!" and I hung up. "*FUCK ME!*" Katherine is throwing me under the bus with Jennifer driving right now! I went into the living room and sat down in the dark. I felt like a condemned prisoner waiting for the footsteps of the guards to take me to the guillotine. About twenty minutes passed. The phone rang once. Katherine picked it up.

"CJ! Pick up phone... I'm not your goddamn secretary!"

I heard the bedroom door slam. I picked up the phone; it was Jenny. "CJ...?"

"Jenny? I..."

"Be quiet and do what I tell you..."

"But..."

"What part of '*shut the fuck up and do what I tell you*' didn't you understand?" Jenny said sternly over the phone.

"Sorry!"

"Go to the store and pick up some Double Deep Chocolate ice cream and bananas and whipped cream and chocolate syrup and make Katherine a sundae the way she likes it and tell that bitch you're sorry..."

"But... I don't know what I did wrong!"

"DO... IT...!"

"Okay... when will you be coming home...?" Jenny hung up without even saying goodbye to me. Great! Now I'm in the doghouse with both these bitches! I went straight to the store and came back to make the sundae like Katherine likes it, heavy on the chocolate and whipped cream. I even spiked the chocolate with some Kaluha. I took it upstairs and gingerly knocked on the door. "Katherine...?"

"What the fuck do you want? Go away!"

"I... I made you a sundae and I... I just wanted to say I'm sorry... I was insensitive and... I should been more... empathetic to your needs... I'm just a big dumb animal... and I'm sorry!" At that moment the door swung open and I jumped a little. I held out the sundae and Katherine took it and took one spoonful into her mouth. She left the spoon in her mouth and looked at me and cut her eyes at me. I just knew I was going to be wearing the fucking sundae! She paused... she smiled and she grabbed me and she pulled me into the bedroom.

When Jennifer came home from Boston about 5am, we were still in bed. There was ice cream and whipped cream and chocolate... everywhere! I guess I did wind up wearing the sundae after all!

"What the fuck!!! What the hell have you two been doing while I was away?" Jenny was royally pissed. Not only did 'we' interrupt her meeting with our bullshit, her bed looked like a chocolate hurricane hit it! Katherine quietly left the room. "Answer ME! What the fuck is all this?" Jenny yelled at me. I just sat on the edge of the bed. The sheets were sticking to me. Jenny looked like she was about to explode. I didn't know what to say and Katherine had left me to fend for myself. It seemed like an eternity until Katherine returned with a tray of ice cream, chocolate, whipped cream and a peeled banana. Jenny looked at her like she was crazy. "And what the fuck to you think you're going to do with all that?"

Katherine dipped the tip of the banana into the bowl of whipped cream and licked it clean. "You said you wanted to know what we did all night..." and she sucked the banana clean. Jenny looked at her again like she was crazy. Katherine winked at me... I knew what she was thinking. "Take your clothes off and get in the bed..." she said to Jenny.

"What??? I am *not* getting in that nasty ass bed..."

Jenny turned to me. I was standing there holding Jenny's leather restraints. "What part of '*shut the fuck up and do as you're told*' didn't you understand?" I said. She turned back to Katherine.

"You heard him. Shut the fuck up... and do as you're told... bitch!"

"Fuck you! I... am... not..." And I came up and from behind Jennifer I reached around her and took the banana from Katherine and dipped it in the chocolate and held it to Jenny's mouth. She pushed it away. "Get that shit away from me... If you get chocolate on me I swear I'll..."

"There's Kaluha in the chocolate..." Katherine said. Jenny looked at Katherine and sighed. Jenny is the kind of woman that when she gets angry, she also gets sexually aroused. She looked at Katherine licking whipped cream off her spread fingers and Jenny parted her lips and let out a deep breath. I saw this as my opportunity to gently stick the banana in her mouth. I held it out for her and she leaned forward and took it in. Jenny moaned and sucked on it seductively. I gently pushed the banana in and out of her mouth and she moaned again. As I pumped the chocolate covered treat in and out of her mouth, I reached around with my free hand and began to unbutton her blouse. Katherine undid her bra and began to paint her body with the whipped cream and lick it off. We both took her clothes off as we massaged the chocolate and whipped cream all over her while she sucked on the banana. Jenny was about to swoon as I lifted her onto her bed I tied her wrists and ankles to the bedposts and Katherine got the ice cream and fed me a spoonful. Just before she put a spoon of ice cream in her own mouth she said; "This... is going to feel... a little cold..."

We both took turns putting ice cream in our mouths and licking and sucking Jennifer wherever we pleased and wherever it pleased her. We kept 'reloading' the banana with chocolate for her. She sucked on the banana as we pleasured her body. After a while, I replaced the banana, with my stiff cock. I straddled Jennifer as she sucked my head and shaft and Katherine focused her attention on licking her pussy and using Jenny's vibrator on her.

"Papi... give me! I want your cock!" Jenny moaned. I put my hands on either side of her and positioned myself on top of her. I was about to enter her.

"CJ! No!" Katherine moaned. I turned to look at Katherine who was now holding a condom in her hand. I nodded in agreement. I wasn't packing. Although Katherine and I were now riding bareback, I did not have Jenny's permission. I rolled off Jenny and Katherine opened the wrapper and placed the condom in her mouth. She deep throated me in order to put the condom on me. I love it when she does that! "Now..." Katherine moaned. "Go ahead and fuck her!"

I rolled back on top of Jennifer and began to pump her pussy nice and slow. She was so wet and juicy. Jenny moaned and cooed. "Yeah Papi... that so good... that's so fucking good... I love feeling you on top of me...! Give meeeee!" Katherine watched us fuck until she couldn't take it any more. She tapped me on my shoulder so I could ease my face away from Jenny's. Katherine straddled Jennifer's face, to face me, while holding on to the headboard behind her. I sucked Katherine's nipples as she grinded her pussy on Jenny's sweet lips. Jenny tongued Katherine's moist pussy with smooth long stokes. All the while I pumped Jenny's juicy pussy. Katherine then grabbed and stroked Jenny's nipples. Jenny howled softly as she came. I then grabbed Katherine by her hair and led her to the end of the bed. I bent Katherine over the footrest and told her to eat Jennifer out as I doggy styled Katherine. We kept Jennifer tied up the entire time as we took turns fucking her and fucking each other. This wasn't a sports fuck... it was nice. We enjoyed each other's sensuality in a passionate and loving way. We finally untied Jenny and they both lay on the bed as I stood next to it and they took turns sucking and licking my cock. It took a long time for me to cum. I liked doing what we were doing and I didn't want it to end. Neither did they.

When we finished I took all the bed sheets and pillowcases and I put them in the washer. We all got into the shower and... Oh what the hell! I don't feel like being 'romantic' here... We got in the shower and monkey fucked the day away. Jenny has a six-foot by eight-foot open shower. It has six of those rain head sprinklers and it is in a rain forest motif. You can set the shower to light drizzle all the way to thunderstorm! And there is an Aztec pyramid waterfall on the back wall and the tiles are different shades of green with exotic animals painted on them. She has a live plant in one corner and a birdcage with parakeets in the room. I kid you not; when the shower is set to thunderstorm there is even a random flashing light to simulate lightning! Her bathroom is off the fucking hook! I fucking love it and I love fucking in it! Oh by the way... I still don't know why Katherine was pissed at me in the first place, but it did have to do with her wanting and needing my undivided attention and I didn't realize it until it was too late. I'm so glad Jenny helped me fix it... and we did show her our appreciation!

The Tortured Soul Trilogy
(The Seduction of CJ Cassidy)
Chapter 130
(You Can Fool Some of The People...)

I was on my way home to Jenny's and I stopped dead in my tracks. "Damn! Katherine isn't coming over until late tonight, which means there'll be no dinner... unless I cook..." I did a quick mental inventory of Jenny had at home and there wasn't enough of anything, except rice, to make a full meal for everybody. I certainly didn't want delivery tonight and I didn't want to eat out, so I stopped off at the grocery store and picked up some fresh shrimps. *"I'll make shrimp scampi and some Spanish rice... the girls will like that..."* I thought to myself. I arrived at Jenny's about four o'clock, I knew she was still at work, and besides, she wouldn't help me cook if her life depended on it. I put the groceries away and began to get ready to cook when I noticed through the kitchen window, a woman wearing only a bikini bottom, tanning herself by the pool. It certainly wasn't Maria, the housekeeper, and Jennifer didn't say anything to me about having guests tonight. I watched her as she just lay there and then she began to rub suntan oil on her body. I shouldn't be watching, but this bitch was hot! She was about 5'6', 29 years old, long legs, auburn hair past her shoulders and she was built like a brick sh... and that's when I noticed that she saw me in the window staring at her.

"Take a picture... it'll last longer...!" she said nonchalantly.

I doubted that. I didn't want to yell through the window so I went out to the pool to talk to her, yeah, yeah and to get a closer look... what? *What?* "Hi..." I said. "Are you a friend of Maria's?"

"Nice try..." She said. "But you and I both know this is Jennifer's house..." She got me. I knew the maid wasn't stupid enough to allow a friend or relative sunbathe nude at her employers, and if she said yes; she was lying. She just lay there and didn't even bother to cover herself up. Yeah, this was one of Jennifer's 'friends'.

"I just thought..." I didn't get a chance to finish my sentence.

"Did you really think I broke in... so I could sunbathe nude by the pool?"

"Well... there have been reports in the neighborhood of a beautiful woman breaking into homes in the area and sunbathing nude by the pool..."

"There've been complaints...?" she asked quizzically.

"Oh... I didn't say anybody '*complained*'...!" She laughed heartily and her breasts jiggled. Yeah, they were real! I couldn't help but stare at her. I was used to having Jenny and Katherine naked by the pool, but she had a great body that I've never seen before. Funny thing though, as beautiful and sexy as she was, I wasn't sexually aroused by her. Something just wasn't... right.

"Do you mind?" she asked.

"Not at all... thank you for asking..."

She took her finger and twirled it in the air signifying for me to turn around.

"Oh...? Sure..." and I turned my back.

"And don't be checking my ass out in the reflection in the patio door..."

I pulled my baseball cap over my eyes. "Better?"

She walked up behind me and rubbed her bare nipples on my back. "Yes Papi... that's much better..." And she went inside as she put on her bikini top back on. I followed her inside to the kitchen. Yeah, I stared at her ass... what?

"So...? How do you know Jennifer?" I asked her.

"I don't, we have a mutual friend..." She smiled. "I just flew in to visit her and I stopped by here and she's picking me up in the morning... I hope you don't mind having an extra overnight guest?" And she took a banana out of the fruit bowl, peeled it back and began to seductively suck and lick it.

"I don't mind... but Jennifer might have a problem with you trying to seduce her man..."

She deep throated the banana and then flicked the end of it with her tongue and smiled. "What makes you think that I'm trying to seduce you...? Papi?" I gave her a look of disappointment and disdain. She threw the banana out and she had an embarrassed look on her face. "Sorry... I didn't mean to..." She said as she dropped her eyes.

I quickly changed the subject. I didn't really mean to embarrass her. I just wanted her to know my situation. I should have handled it better. I knew she was just flirting and playing around. "I'm making Shrimp Scampi and Spanish rice for dinner, if you're allergic to seafood, I have a steak or some chicken I can prepare for you..."

"I'm okay with shrimps... thank you for asking." I turned and started the water for the rice. "Can I help?" she said meekly.

"Sure... By the way, I'm CJ..." I held out my hand, she shook it gently.

"I'm Iris... pleased to meet you." And I smiled. Now I knew why I didn't find her sexually attractive. This was Juan, Lady Latex and Cisco's pre-op transsexual friend. I guess she didn't know I wrote Jenny's bio and I knew all about her. Well... as much as I needed to know about her! Juan wasn't a really a transsexual, he was transgender. A transgender is a rarity; he is a man who has the body of a woman, naturally. Literally, Juan was a man trapped in a woman's' body. His breasts were real, (Except for some hormone shots), that luxurious hair was his, his feminine voice, his thin waist, his 'breeder' hips; all of it was natural. As a boy he dressed as a boy but only looked like a girl, dressed as a boy. As a child he was a target of bullies and endured many taunts from small-minded people, as a young man he was sought after by bulldyke lesbians. As an adult, he struggled everyday with his sexuality and finally opted to be the beautiful woman he had grown up to be. Once he moved away, where nobody knew him, no one questioned his gender. He lived his life as a woman, but not without certain... complications. He finally saved up enough money to have the one operation he needed to fully transition into womanhood, but he couldn't do it. He was still emotionally 'attached' to his penis. It was the only part of him that reminded him of who he really was. To this day he is in therapy trying to decide if he should have the operation and fully embrace his womanhood. She helped me cook and we had a very pleasant conversation once she learned to behaved herself.

"Boy, you sure know your way around a kitchen, Jennifer must let you help her cook pretty often..." she said to me. I busted out laughing, yeah, she only knew Jenny through L.L. and Cisco. She looked at me. "I take it, Jennifer doesn't cook…" she said.

"Not in the kitchen she doesn't!"

Iris laughed and hit me on the shoulder gently. "Desgraciado!"

"I am what I am baby!" Iris laughed again. Iris was pretty good in the kitchen herself. We continued to prepare the meal and the girls arrived in the limo just as we finished. Iris had gone upstairs to freshen up for dinner. I greeted them at the door and kissed Jenny and then Katherine. "Where's Jinx?" I asked as I looked out the door.

"I gave him the night off… he has a date tonight so I said he could use the limo… you didn't need him for anything did you?" Jenny asked.

"Nah… I just wanted to say hi…"

Katherine took a deep breath. "Oh, what smells so good?" Katherine asked.

"I made Shrimp Scampi and Spanish rice for dinner."

"How sweet of you… Do you need any help?" Jenny asked. I made a face.

"You know darn well dinner is ready…"

Jenny looked around the room. "Oh… I meant… like open a bottle of wine or something…"

"How do you manage that?" I asked her.

"Manage what?" Jenny asked.

"To show up when dinner is ready and not a moment sooner?"

"Practice!" Katherine answered dryly.

"Bitch!" Jenny said. Katherine shook her head and went to her room to freshen up for dinner. Jenny looked around the house and then looked out the patio window. "So… CJ… have you met our overnight guest yet?" And she smirked.

"She's upstairs taking a shower…"

"Really…? Is she… all wet and soapy?" And Jennifer smiled wryly. That's when I knew she planned this.

"I want to talk to you about her…"

And an impish grin came across her face. "Really? What about her?"

"May I speak with you in the library, Jennifer?" I didn't want anyone walking in on us while I spoke to her. Her smile dropped. She could tell by the sound of my voice I was not happy with her. She followed me into the library and I closed the doors behind us.

"It was just a joke CJ..." She said quickly as if trying to diffuse my anger.

"And was 'Iris' in on... the 'joke'...?"

"Yes..." She whispered guardedly.

"Good! Because if I thought for one minute that you just used her like that to play a joke on me..."

Jennifer's countenance changed and she put her hand on her hip in defiance. "Excuse me? You are not the boss of me! I don't answer to *you*!"

"No..." I whispered. "I'm not the boss of you... but I am your lover... and right now..." I circled my finger in her direction. "...with this 'attitude' you're giving me... I'm not liking you very much right now!"

She hesitated a moment and looked at me. "Oh FUCK you!" She barked at me. "It was just a joke! Get over it!" And she turned her back to me and crossed her arms.

"I know it was just a joke... I didn't have a problem with that... I get it... what you're not getting right now is that Juan is not a joke! He's a human being with feelings... and so am I..." And I opened the door and as I shut it behind me, I could hear Jennifer begin to cry softly. She realized her little joke had backfired. I turned to see Iris standing off to the side.

"Don't you think you were a little hard on her...? It *was* just a joke Papi!"

"I don't like it when someone uses someone else's 'situation' to play a joke on anyone. Even though you knew about it ... and you were okay with it... I didn't know that... and then when I called her out about it, she acted like my feelings about disrespecting someone like that, didn't matter... I don't play that shit... and she's a grown ass woman... and she should have known better!"

Iris' jaw dropped and she just looked at me.

"What?" I asked her trying to figure out what she was thinking right then.

"You have no idea how much I wish you were into trannies right now!"

I smiled and hugged Iris and kissed her on the cheek. "Tell you what... If I ever do decide to take a walk on the wild side... you'd be the first person I'd call!" I let her go but she held onto my hand and led me back to the library and opened the door.

"Oye chica! You betta get your ass out here and apologize to your man!" Jenny came out slowly wiping the tears from her eyes; hugged me and kissed my neck so very gently. Then she held me tight and I rocked her in my arms. "I don't hear an apology!" Iris said cupping her hand to her ear.

Jenny turned to Iris. "CJ... is fully aware of how I 'apologize' when I've been a bad girl! Thank you!"

Iris put the tip of her finger on her lower lip and kissed it. "You know CJ... I've been a bad girl and I'm sorry too!"

Jenny laughed. "Bitch! You better back the fuck up!"

"Well damn! Go ahead then! I'll give you two some privacy!" And Iris headed to the kitchen to fix herself a plate.

"Bitch better recognize... I don't share my man with nobody!"

I looked at Jennifer askew. "*Nobody...?*"

Jenny sucked her teeth. "Okay! Katherine... but that's where I draw the line!"

I kissed Jenny and her lips were still salty from her tears. "Me too... I hope you don't ever pull any shit like this again!"

"Were you really that mad at me for what I did?"

"You pissed me off! You know I don't like it when you're being bad."

Jenny's lips parted slightly and let out a soulful sigh. "You know damn well you like it when I'm being bad!" she said and then I kissed her again deeply.

"There's bad and there's 'bad'... Now... let's get something to eat before those two finish off what we made for dinner."

"I might not be in the mood to 'apologize' later..."

"When...? Have you ever not been in the mood...?"

Jennifer sucked her teeth. "You know... one of these days... I'm going to surprise you!"

I held her face and kissed her deeply again and her bosom rose and fell and she breathed soft breaths of air. "You... never fail to surprise me!" I said to her softly.

"But you won't be as angry with me later..." She pulled her lips into her mouth and licked the salty tears off with her tongue. "And I kinda like it when we have sex... when you're a little agitated with me... you get a little... nasty... and I like that!" Jenny grabbed my shirt collar and tried to pull me into the library.

"Uh uhh!" Katherine said from the hallway. "Dinner first... pussy later!"

Jenny stomped her foot. "Damn!"

"Besides... in case you forgot... we have a house guest..." and Katherine whispered. "And I'm not doing her!"

"Well... You know how I feel about it..." I turned to Jenny. "Jenny...?"

"I'd try almost anything one time..." and she shook her head no. "...but not tonight!" We all walked towards the dining room. Iris was sitting at the table with her plate in front of her and was waiting patiently.

"What are you waiting for Iris?" I said to her. "Dig in... you know it's good, you helped to prepare it!"

Iris just looked at us. "Aren't we gonna sit and say grace together before we eat?" she said.

"I know you weren't going to sit there and wait for an hour until CJ and I was finished before you were going to eat... were you?" Jenny asked Iris.

Iris smiled and laughed, but then she noticed that no one else was laughing. "...An hour...? Really...?" She asked incredulously.

Katherine raised her eyebrows and nodded.

"...A whole hour...?" Iris started to say.

"Drop it sister!" Jenny said. Iris fidgeted with her hair and took a sip of water. We all fixed our plates, sat down and Katherine said the blessing for the meal. We ate and spent the rest of the evening talking, laughing and playing cards.

Cisco came over the next morning to pick Iris up. It was good to see him again. I asked about the family. They had invited Iris to spend a few days with them and to baby sit for a few more days while he and L.L. went on vacation.

"Why didn't you just have Jenny baby sit...?" and I stopped asking in mid question. "Cause then the poor child would starve!" And I scratched my neck. Cisco and Iris laughed; Jenny hit me in the stomach hard!

"I'll be out of town on business all next week! Besides, I'm babysitting *you* this weekend!" Jenny smiled and bit her fingertip. "And besides you have never complained about anything I've given you to... eat!"

Iris looked at Jenny. "Oye! Mire esta puta!"

"You betta recognize... bitch!" We laughed and we walked Cisco and Iris to the car. Cisco and Iris drove off. I like Iris. She's good people.

"So Jennifer? If you had the chance... you would really do a trannie?" I asked her. I really wanted to how freaky this chick really is.

She kissed me softly on the lips. "You're the only chick with a dick I would fuck!"

Katherine laughed. "Well... with a 'real' dick anyway!" We all went back inside.

"So... ah? How does that... 'work' anyway?"

"Would you like to see a 'demonstration'?" Jenny asked.

Hell yeah I would!

The Tortured Soul Trilogy
(The Seduction of CJ Cassidy)
Chapter 131
(The Naughty Librarian)

I was staying over at Jennifer's house for about a week. I was watching a little TV in the spare bedroom... Okay, I was working on this novel. I have to take whatever opportunity available to get some work done when Jenny isn't around. I was in the middle of a chapter and decided to check my E-mails and that's when I heard noises from inside the house. I figured it must have been Maria, the maid. She came two or three times a week to clean and on occasion she would cook for Jennifer. She wasn't officially the cook, but sometimes she would spoil Jenny with a down home cooked Spanish meal. Jenny liked that. I didn't mind either, I wouldn't have to cook. The noises intrigued me, it didn't sound like someone was cleaning, or cooking. It didn't sound like someone was breaking in either. I stepped out of the room. "Maria? Is that you?" I said out loud. No answer. But I still heard the noises. I put on some pants and went downstairs to where the sounds were coming from. "Maria?" Still no answer. I heard the sounds and they were coming from Jennifer's private office and library. I knew Jenny was still at work. As I slowly opened the door, I saw Katherine sitting behind the desk working in a ledger. She was wearing a white, button down blouse with ruffles, a black wrap skirt, black pumps, she had her hair in a ponytail and she was wearing her dark rimmed glasses. She looked hot. There was a sensual, sexual aura around her that could draw any man or woman to her like a moth to a flame. She was like a black hole... you could not resist it if you came too close. "Katherine!" I exclaimed. "I didn't know you were here baby... when did you come in?"

Katherine looked up at me and placed her finger on her lips. "Shhh! Please!"

I looked at her strangely. I thought that maybe she was on the phone but I didn't see a receiver in her hand and she didn't have an earpiece on and she wasn't talking to anyone. She then continued doing whatever she was doing. "Katherine?" I whispered, "What's going on?" She shushed me again. I looked at her as she worked on something on Jennifer's desk. I came closer to see what she was doing and then she leaned back in the chair and put her right foot on top of the end on the desk. I watched her eyes and then she put her left foot on the other end of the desk. She was now spread-eagled in her chair. My jaw dropped. I had written her biography and I knew what this meant... or at least I hoped I knew what this meant. She took her finger and silently called me over. As I approached the desk I could begin to see over the desktop that she was sitting on a towel in the chair and she wasn't wearing any panties. She had played this game with Nick in the past, now it was my turn. I stood there as I watched her as she stroked her pussy. I leaned forward for a better look. She stroked her pussy fur so very gently. I was so very turned on right now. It's show time!

"I understand you like to role play with Jennifer?" She whispered.

"She told you about that, did she?" I whispered and smiled.

Katherine smiled and nodded. "I got wet and horny just hearing her talk about it."

"Jenny has that effect on people... And where the hell was I?"

Katherine stroked her clit. "Don't cry over a missed opportunity... You're here now... seize the moment!" And she dipped her finger in and took it out and licked it seductively; like she really had to do that to get my undivided attention.

"I don't have a costume..." I said.

"You don't need one... today we're playing 'The Naughty Librarian'..."

"And how do we play that?"

"First... you have to be very quiet..." I chuckled to myself. She picked the one game Jennifer can't play! I leaned on the desk as Nick did when they played this game in Katherine's office at Faber. She shook her head no and waved me back. As I took a step away Katherine leaned forward and pushed the ledger off the desk onto the floor. She did that without ever taking her feet off the desk. (Did I mention that Katherine is a flexible little minx?) "Could you get that for me?" and she leaned back. I bent down to get the book and as I looked under the desk, I had a direct view of Katherine's moist pussy as she stroked and caressed it. I paused to watch her. She put on a show for me for almost five minutes. "Crawl under the desk and eat me." Katherine moaned. I lifted my head to look Katherine in the eye. She already had her blouse open and her nipples were bright and hard.

"What?" I said.

"Shhhh! I *said*, get under this desk and lick my pussy... eat me!" She whispered.

I smiled. "I see Jennifer told you about that too!"

"You did it to her... she did it to me... now it's your turn to do it for me!" And she pointed under the desk again. "Get on your hands and knees, crawl under this desk and eat my pussy." And she squeezed her nipples and moaned. "Hurry... please?" I wasn't about to disappoint her. I bent down slowly and began to crawl under the desk. Closer and closer I came towards Katherine's pussy while she held her labia open and was stoking her clit. As I came closer and closer to her hot, wet, moist, juicy pussy, it dawned on me how demeaning this all was. I'm a big man and I barely fit under that desk. It was a bit claustrophobic. I tried to focus my mind on the prize. But I couldn't, you would think that after all these years, I would have learned to see a situation from the other's person's viewpoint. Now I was learning that lesson again, the hard way. I got close to Katherine's moist pussy and when I looked up she was pinching and twisting her nipples hard. I stuck my tongue in her pussy and began to suck and lick her labia and nibbled her clit with wild abandon. I wanted so badly to immerse myself in the moment and forget how I felt right then. Katherine moaned and cooed. She was most certainly lost in the moment. She held my head and directed my face wherever she wanted it. I desperately wanted to keep my mind on what I was doing and not on the position I was in while I was doing it. It didn't work. Katherine sensed that something wasn't quite right. She took her hands and gently pulled me away from her. "Baby? What's wrong?" And she stroked my face.

"It's... my knees... this is a little painful for me..."

Katherine knew I had bad knees but she could tell that the angst on my face was from something else all together. She rolled back on her chair and helped me out from under the desk. I scraped my back standing up. "Jennifer loved doing it for you... I loved doing it for her... I'm sorry that I forgot that you're not into the slave/master lifestyle." And she kissed me.

"I feel like such a hypocrite... I place you and Jennifer in all these subservient sexual positions all the time... and then I fall apart when I'm in one..."

Katherine kissed me again gently. "Don't beat yourself up about this." she said. I looked at her askew. Katherine laughed. "No pun intended... Nick didn't like it either... we all have our roles to play. As an actor you should have known that you were just 'miscast'... and I'm sorry to have put you in that position... literally!" She gently kissed me again. "Jennifer doesn't have a problem with you taking charge..." She kissed me again. "And neither do I..." We kissed passionately. Our tongues probed each other in wild abandon. Katherine stepped back, sighed, got back into character and said. "Do you know what the penalty is for having an overdue book?"

"I suppose you're going to tell me!"

"You get a tongue lashing!" and she reached for my zipper. I pulled her hand away.

"You first!" And I lifted her up with one arm and cleared Jenny's desk with the other. I carefully lay Katherine down on the desk and held her ankles apart. Katherine only weighs about a buck twenty and she likes it when I 'manhandle' her. "Now... where was I?" I asked. Katherine motioned me to come closer, placed her hands on my ears and pulled me towards her. She guided me right onto her swollen clit.

"Right... Here...! I book marked it for you!" Katherine and I had sex all over Jenny's office and while I was lying down on the desk with Katherine sitting on top of me, dropping it like it was hot on my cock, we were interrupted by Maria entering the room suddenly.

"I sorry Missy Katereene!" She said in her Spanish accent. I was surprised that we had never been busted long before this. Katherine hopped off me and I put myself away while she covered up.

"No te apures Maria... creemos que usted tenia el dia libre..." I said while zipping up.

"Si Senior Cassidy... I clean de other rooms and I com back later... Si?' She knew the deal and she wasn't shocked or surprised by anything that went on at Jenny's house. She's had to clean up behind us after our romps. And she's cleaned Jenny's bedroom before and it's full of all kinds of 'devices'. Maria got and kept her job because she was discreet. Maria turned to leave us to our own devices and finish what we started.

"Maria?" Katherine called out.

"Si Missy Katereene?"

"Quedate seguro que tu sabes que yo no quiero que tu tocas a CJ! Entiendes?"

"Ai no! Missy Kathreene! Missy Jennifer me mata si yo toca a ese hombre!"

"Pues... estamos de aqcuerdo..."

Maria nodded and left abruptly.

"And when did *you* learn to speak Spanish?"

"Oh please... you always knew I was... bi-lingual!" and she unzipped me and started in on me again.

"I can't believe you threatened Maria... she's a 62 year old woman!"

"Please! She wouldn't be the first grandmother who tried to take a shot at my man..." She began to suck and lick my cock and then she stroked me gently. "CJ...?"

I looked into her sad eyes as she kissed the tip of my cock. "I get plenty of offers and opportunities..." I said softly. "Only to you and Jennifer do I give access to... I like to keep it that way!" I said. Katherine deep throated me. My eyes went to the back of my head. Gentlemen please take note here... when you're faithful; you don't have to be afraid to answer any questions when your woman has your cock in her mouth. Trust and honesty has its own rewards. "So... tell me about the pool boy..." I said. I had never seen him, but I knew Jenny has to have one cause I've never cleaned the pool.

Katherine choked and laughed out loud. "He's older than Maria!"

I nodded and smiled and put my cock back in Katherine's mouth. "Okay then..." I said and Katherine finished me off.

The Tortured Soul Trilogy
(The Seduction of CJ Cassidy)

Chapter 132
(Wednesday's Child)

I was sitting out by the pool waiting for the girls to come home. I was having a glass of white wine. I had just finished cleaning Jenny's house, threw out the trash and finished doing my laundry. Anything else, Maria the maid, would take care of when she came to work tomorrow. Maria usually came two days a week, three days if Jenny had company over. I poured myself another glass just as the girls came home. Jenny had picked up Katherine from her house, on her way home from work. Katherine had gone grocery shopping and Jinx was putting the bags in the kitchen. Katherine kissed me and then Jenny kissed me. Katherine looked at the bottle of wine, got a glass and poured herself a drink. Jennifer began to unbutton her blouse so she could get comfortable. "Could you do me a favor Jenny... can you keep your clothes on?" I said. She looked at me strangely. She always went topless and especially by the pool when she came home and it was a nice day. She knew I liked to see her naked but she stopped unbuttoning her blouse at my request.

"Okay...?" Jenny said and she buttoned her blouse leaving only the top three buttons unfastened.

"Are you alright CJ?" Katherine asked.

"Yeah I'm good..." and I sipped on my glass of wine.

Katherine knew something was wrong. I'm not really a wine drinker and she's never known me to ask Jennifer to keep her clothes on. "Have you eaten?"

"I'm not hungry..."

"You sure...? I was going to make a pot roast..." I lifted my eyes to her.

"Hmmm... I haven't had a pot roast in a long time..."

"I'll get it started... you want red potatoes with that?"

"Yeah... that would be nice... Thank you..." And Katherine went inside to the kitchen: I didn't expect Jennifer to follow her.

"May I join you in a glass of wine?" Jenny asked. I nodded and she held out her glass and I poured for her. I refreshed my glass and she took a sip of hers and settled into the chair across from me. "Did I do something wrong?" She quietly asked. I shook my head no. "I know Katherine didn't do anything wrong... she's 'Little Miss Perfect'..."

"I thought she was 'Princess Littlefoots'?" Jenny called her that because she hated that Katherine wore a size seven shoe and Jenny wore a ten... okay... an eleven!

"That too...!" and she took a sip of her wine. "Is it something I said?"

"It's not you... or Katherine..."

"I know you're not gonna give me the '*It's not you, it's me*' bullshit!"

"No..." I smiled awkwardly.

Jenny took a sip of wine and picked up a strawberry from the fruit basket on the table and bit it. "I know it's not the sex..." I turned my eyes away slowly. Jenny caught on immediately. "Are you shitting me...? You have a problem with our sex life? How could it possibly be any better?"

"It's not the quality..."

She paused. "You want more? Cause... we can give you all you can handle..." I looked away and sipped my wine. "You want... *less*...?" Jenny was almost speechless. "Are you... breaking up with us...?" and Jenny almost dropped her glass.

"Hell no... you have a better chance of taking downtown Tokyo away from Godzilla than to take me away from you two..."

"Then what the fuck is it...?"

I freshened up my drink just as Katherine came back outside. She put her arm around my shoulder and I hugged her.

"What's going on?" Katherine asked.

"I don't know... he's...I don't know... freaking out about something and he won't tell me what the fuck it is..."

"CJ...? What's wrong baby...?" Katherine asked as she rubbed my shoulder.

Tears started to well in my eyes, Jennifer looked at me and the sudden realization hit her. "Oh my god...!" and Jenny put her hand on her chest.

"Jenny? What...? What do you think it is...?" Katherine asked.

"I'm so sorry baby...! I am so sorry!" and Jenny hugged me and I sobbed in her arms.

"What...? What is going on...? Tell me...!" Jenny kissed my neck and consoled me. "I didn't realize baby..."

"What???" Now Katherine felt totally out of the loop.

"CJ thinks that I... we... are using him only for sex..."

"What...?" Katherine said unbelievingly. "CJ... you know we love you dearly..."

I nodded. "I know... it's just..." I couldn't speak.

"You thought you were just a plaything?" Jenny said. I nodded. "Oh baby... You *are* our plaything but you mean much so more than that to us... we love you and we would do anything for you..." Jenny said

"Just tell us what you want..." Katherine added.

"I know... that there must be thousands of men... who wish... hell, they would kill... just so they could take my place with my situation just as it is... but... could we..."

"Could we 'what' baby?" Jenny asked.

"I feel so stupid... saying this..."

"What CJ...? What do you want us to do...?" Katherine asked.

"Can we just have dinner... like a family... no sex... and maybe... just play Scrabble tonight...?"

"Sure baby!" Katherine said.

"You know that bitch cheats...?" Jenny said.

"Fuck you! I don't cheat... you're the one who can't play..."

"Fuck me...? Fuck you! I know you hide tiles until you need them..." They argued for about two minutes until I stopped them and kissed them both on the lips. "What?" Jenny said.

"Now...! I feel like we're family!" and I smiled.

"Oh Fuck you too CJ...! Living with you is like having a third bitch in this house..." Jenny said. And she sipped her wine, put her glass down and walked towards the house, stopped halfway and took off her blouse and bra. "...And If I want to walk around with my tits out... I'll walk around with my tits out... This is my fucking house... and I'll do whatever the fuck I please!"

Katherine shook her head, smiled and followed Jenny inside. "Dinner will be ready in about two hours... I'll get the scrabble board." Katherine said as she got to the door.

"You need help with dinner?" I asked.

"I'm good... and I'll see if I can get Jenny to throw on a robe..."

"Don't try *too* hard..." I smirked.

Katherine smiled and shook her head. "You bitch! You just wanted to start shit, didn't you?" Katherine said to me.

I smiled. "I just don't want to take anything for granted... or be taken for granted..." And I tipped my glass to her.

Katherine shook her head and smiled. "All right then..." She stood by the patio doors. "What vegetable would you like with dinner?" I raised my eyebrow. "Right... string beans...! God forbid I don't serve string beans!" Katherine got the recipe for string beans from her grandmother. I loved Katherine's cooking as much as my own. Katherine paused at the patio doors again. "You... *sure*... you don't want any pussy tonight?"

"Let's see how dinner and the game goes first..."

Katherine went inside just as Jenny came out topless and had a bottle of suntan oil and began to oil herself down. "Do you have any idea how much I love you right now?" I said to her.

"I love you too... you fucking prima Donna... now do my back..." She handed me the bottle and I began to lotion her back so very gently. "You sure you don't want *any* pussy tonight...?" She moaned. I handed her, her glass of wine.

"Let's see how the night goes..." and I kissed her back and shoulders.

"You missed a spot...!" She leaned back on me and I rubbed the lotion on her shoulders, chest and belly. "Don't forget my nipples..." I smiled and kissed her. She placed her arm around the back of my neck, leaned back and sipped her wine as I lotioned and massaged her tits. She smiled broadly. This bitch knew I treated her like a queen. She liked that... so did I.

We had dinner by the pool, we had more wine, we played scrabble and yeah... we caught Katherine cheating... and... No, we didn't have sex that night. We went inside into the living room, enjoyed each other's company watching TV, eating peaches and ice cream until the wee hours of the morning and we all fell asleep naked, and cuddled in each other's arms.

I end each chapter almost the same way.

I love these two bitches!

The Tortured Soul Trilogy
(The Seduction of CJ Cassidy)
Chapter 133
(No Sex in the Champaign Room!)

So, you have read the previous chapters about the lives and loves and sexual experiences of Katherine and Jennifer, and you may get the impression that it's all about the sex. Don't get me wrong! The sex is fucking amazing, but that's not all there is to it. When I say I love these two bitches, I mean I love them... all the time. I came from New York to Jenny's place on a Friday morning to spend the three-day weekend with the girls. Katherine greeted me at the door.

"Hi baby!" and she kissed me. I entered the house and Jennifer was wearing sweatpants, flip-flops and a t-shirt, no bra. She came over and kissed me as well.

"Hey Papi... come on in."

"So? How are we doing?" I knew something wasn't right, Jennifer always walked around the house naked. It just wasn't like her, she liked it and she looked forward to it... So did I...

"I'm sorry CJ..." Katherine sighed.

"Sorry... for what?" I asked cautiously.

"It's her time of the month..."

"Oh... that's okay..."

"Me too!" Katherine said cautiously.

I looked at my hands. "Good thing I brought these along with me..." Jennifer busted out laughing.

"We're not 'totally' out of commission you know..." and Katherine stuck her thumb in her mouth.

"That's great for Katherine... and as much as I love sucking your cock, if mama don't get none... aint nobody getting none!" And Jenny yanked Katherine's thumb out of her mouth.

"Sorry CJ... rain check?" Katherine whispered seductively.

"Aint gonna be no 'rain checks', I'm not letting you two bitches out of my sight this weekend!" Jenny said.

"Being *in* your sight never stopped us before..." Katherine giggled.

Jennifer pulled Katherine away from me. "It will this time, bitch!"

"Come on... I'm sure there's a lot of things we can do this weekend... that doesn't involve sex..." I said.

"And NO gambling!" Jenny added.

"And no gambling..." I repeated. "I told you, no more casinos for me..."

"Good!"

"But I still buy lottery tickets..." I replied; Jennifer huffed. "Oh please! You buy them too... and you're rich!" I said

"I'm not rich, but I do like to buy tickets..." Jenny admitted.

Katherine shook her head. "You guys know those games are rigged, why do you play?"

"It's the thrill of maybe you might win with the deck stacked against you..." Jenny replied.

"Fuck that! I wanna be rich like you two bitches... I don't mind that you two make more money than me... but I would love to pick up a check once in a while..."

Katherine was raised in 'The Dirty South' and came from 'old money'. Her father didn't want her to become one of the idle rich. He hated to see young wealthy heiresses on TV or in the papers acting stupid, so he set Katherine up with a special trust fund. She could take out as much money as she pleased providing that she was working and had her paycheck directly deposited to the account. As long as money went in, she could take money out. The amount didn't matter; he just wanted to make sure she was busy. If she ever tried to cheat the system, like, by taking a fake 'job' with a friend, Big Daddy would just close the account once and for all. Katherine actually liked the idea and besides, she wouldn't do anything to make 'Big Daddy Stark' upset. She loved her father dearly and wouldn't do anything to disappoint him. Once she turned 40 and 'Daddy' knew she was past the 'sowing wild oats' stage, he dropped the work requirement and Katherine has had full access to her inheritance since.

Now, Katherine had and still has some emotional problems, but she is not stupid by any definition of the word. She kept her lovers close but she didn't tell them everything about her. She likes to keep her private life very private. There are very few friends or even close family that know everything about her. Even with her past lovers and the way they treated her and took her money at times; not one of them knew how much Katherine was really worth financially. Not even Nick... The only reason I know is because we were friends before we became lovers and even with that, I have never asked her for money, for any reason. Not even to invest in any of my projects; She even offered me the money to publish my books, I declined. I don't even allow her to 'pay my way' when we go out. If it's out of my league, we don't go or I let Jenny pay for me. What? I'm no gigolo, but that bitch has got bank too!

Jenny came to her money the old fashioned way, she worked the grind. (No! I'm not talking about her stripping!) She worked hard, went to school and with her 'connections' she took over and successfully runs a major corporation. This chick pulls down six figures a year!

As for me, I'm the broke-ass friend. Oh, I have a good job and make almost 60G's a year, own my own house, but I am *not* anywhere near these two bitches league when it comes to money. But God love them, they never make me feel like I'm inferior to them in any way. Don't ask me why I feel I need to say this, but hey, it's my bio and if I feel I need to discuss it. I will. I have never met Katherine's parents and no, she's not ashamed of me, but she does realize that 'Big Daddy' would never approve of me. (Her parents don't know about Jennifer either! There are just some things 'Big Daddy' can't handle and Jenny and I are on a 'need to know' basis and 'Big Daddy' doesn't need to know!) You may think that I'm bitter about that, but I'm not. I'm a big boy and I can certainly understand and respect Katherine's feelings on the matter. I don't have to be everything and everywhere in Katherine's life. I respect her, and I respect her space.

Yes, 'Big Daddy' knew about 'Johnny Precious'. After all, they were engaged to be married. And HELL NO, he didn't approve! He was so mad; he could spit nails! He even cut Katherine off until they 'broke up'. This is why I respect Katherine's wishes to keep our special relationship secret from him. Although I truly believe that Katherine would tell her father about me before she would ever mention her relationship with Jennifer. Jenny knows that, and she's not happy about it, but she too loves Katherine more than enough to respect her wishes as well.

"So... have you two eaten?"

"You know we haven't..." Jennifer said sarcastically. Katherine laughed.

"I meant... lunch!"

Jenny smiled with that mischievous grin she gets. "No, we haven't, what do you have in mind?" Jenny said.

"Well seeing that I'm officially off the menu and you two are 'out of season'... They cut their eyes at me. "How about I cook us something?"

"Let's go out... We've been struck in the house all day and we're beginning to get cabin fever, besides I'm in the mood for burgers and some wine..." Jenny said. Rare burgers and red wine was Jenny's favorite comfort meal when it was... you know... that time. Katherine's was Buffalo wings. I knew just the place they wanted to go.

"Well I'm buying..." I said.

Katherine looked at me and then at Jennifer. "You're buying...?"

"With what?" Jennifer asked.

"With... this!" And I held up a check.

"What the hell is that?" Jenny took it out of my hands.

"That... is my paycheck from working three whole days on an independent film!"

"What film?" Jenny asked excitedly.

"It's called 'Caged Rage'; it's about a street fighter in a prison fight tournament. I spent three days body slamming the stunt double for the lead actor."

"CJ! Are you serious?" Katherine beamed. "You're finally gonna be seen on the big screen?"

"Uh... no... the scene was cut out of the final edit... but I still get paid!"

Jenny shook her head, but she was supportive of me and my career. "Okay then..." And she handed me back the check.

"Ladies?" I asked as I put my arms out so they could latch on to them.

"Let me put on a bra and some walking shoes..." Jenny said as she exited the room. She returned with her jacket and had put on a skirt. "We ready?"

Katherine nodded and we all went out to the local pub for lunch. We had a great time together just eating and talking, playing beer pong, laughing and joking. We also talked about work, our relationship, you know, serious stuff. Afterwards we walked through the neighborhood to walk it off and do some window-shopping. After a few hours of just walking around, Jenny called Jinx to pick us up and take us home.

"You want to see a show later tonight?" Jenny asked.

"Sure!" Katherine said approvingly.

"I'm game if you two are... but ah... no drag shows okay?"

Jenny tilted her head at me. "Whatsamatter tough guy? Afraid of getting too close to your... *feminine* side?" and she pinched my nipple and laughed.

"You wanna take that chance?" I said dryly.

"Hell no! You act too much like a bitch as it is... we need to go somewhere and man you up!" Jenny shot back with.

"And no..."

"I got it! No strip clubs... Katherine and I will take care of that for you when we get you home tonight...!" I looked at Jennifer and shook my head no. "What? Why not...? Oh! I forgot! Damn!"

"Yep! *No sex in the Champaign room, No sex in the Champaign room...*" I sang.

Jinx picked us up about ten minutes later in the limo and we went home. There wasn't anything we all wanted to see that night, but Jenny scored three tickets to a college football game for Saturday evening. They weren't great seats but hey, it was last minute and it was something to do tomorrow. That night we ordered pizza and zeppolis and watched videos. I slept on the couch; the girls had the bedroom to themselves. The next afternoon we made a picnic basket for the tailgate party and headed to the arena. I like hanging out with these two. The game began about 6pm and we headed to our seats. "This is perfect... you get to see blood and violence and we get to see big, sweaty men with big..."

"Jenny!" Katherine exclaimed. "Behave yourself!"

"Bitch please…! I know you're checking out the ass on that defensive tackle over there!"

"I am… and you're cock blocking, bitch!" We all laughed and I shook my head. We watched a great game, had some bad hot dogs, warm beer and again enjoyed being in each other's company. During half-time Katherine reached under our blanket and started to stroke my cock over my pants. Jenny reached over and tried the same thing. She pulled Katherine's hand off me.

"Bitch! What are you doing?"

"What are *you* doing?" Katherine replied dryly.

"I… was making sure you weren't doing… what I just caught *you* doing!"

"Yeah right Jenny!" I said.

"Fuck you! I see you didn't say shit about either one of us touching your dick…!"

"What am I? Stupid?"

Katherine looked at Jenny. "You sure you don't want to bend this weekend's rules… just a little?"

I looked at Jennifer's eyes and she was horny as hell right then. I began to say; "NO! As much as the idea of you two going down on me under this blanket excites me right now…" But then I stopped when I noticed that a woman sitting in front of me turned, looked at me and smiled.

"Excuse me…" Katherine whispered to her. "You are not invited to this party… turn back around and watch the game!" At that moment a man on the other side turned to Jennifer and smiled at her.

"Oh HELL no!" She then pointed to the woman from before. "Maybe you should hook-up with this chick here…" The woman turned around and looked at the man, who looked at her and smiled. She got up to sit with him. Katherine put her hand over her mouth and tried to stifle a laugh. They cuddled under his blanket for a moment, kissed and then her head disappeared under the blanket. "Do you see this SHIT?" Jenny exclaimed unbelievingly. "What is this? The fucking hook up section?" The guy gave us a thumbs-up. We looked around and noticed that more than a few couples were 'engaged' in some type of sexual activity. We all raised our right hand, snapped our fingers and said: "Check please!" simultaneously, got up and left the arena laughing our asses off! When Jinx dropped us off at the house, Katherine was still laughing.

"Do you believe that?" Jenny said. "I mean did you fucking see that?"

I closed the door as the girls took off their jackets. "Why are you so surprised?" I said. "If I hadn't stopped you, you two were about to do the same thing to me…!"

"Yeah!" Jennifer said. "But we know you… at least I know where your dick has been…"

Katherine then snuggled up to me. She was still a little aroused by the idea of dangerous sex. "Yeah… we both know where your cock has been…" Katherine said and she sighed deeply. "Over and over again…"

"Back it up bitch! Don't make me hurt you!" Jenny barked. I knew she was talking to Katherine, but she didn't move away from me so I took a step away from her. Katherine bit her lip and fondled her breasts and nipples over her blouse.

"Jenny…? Why do you think that telling Katherine that you're going to hurt her… turns her off?"

Katherine slowly walked over to Jennifer and kissed her lips and took her by the hand and led her towards me and put Jenny's hand on my bulge. "Jenny? Can't we please bend the rules?" She whispered. "Just this once?" Jenny began to stroke me and then grabbed my throbbing cock over my pants. She bent slightly at the knees as if she wanted to get down on them and blow me right there. But then she straightened right up, but she didn't let go of me. Katherine began to kiss my neck and reached into Jenny's blouse and stroked her nipple.

"CJ?"

"Yes Jenny…?"

"I… we… have a confession to make…" She panted and she grabbed my cock harder.

"What? That it's not your 'time of the month'? Or Katherine's…"

Katherine looked at me surprised. "How? How did you know?" Katherine asked.

"I fell for it at first. Jenny dressed… her wanting burgers and wine. You, wearing your 'loose' pants…" I gently took

Jenny's hand off my cock. "But then... there was no... 'evidence' in the bathrooms of anyone having their period..."

"*What*?" Jenny said.

"I've been married two or three times and I have two daughters... I know the signs..."

"And what gave us away, Sherlock?" Jenny said.

"One or both of you always leaves a box on the side of the bathroom sinks, just in case... and Katherine didn't bring her 'big purse' she carries when she goes out that 'time of the month'. And Jenny's big feet aren't swollen and nobody asked me for a foot rub since I've been here..."

Jenny paused. "Fuck you! How about I kick your ass with my big feet?"

"You knew? And you didn't say anything? You kept up the charade? Why?" Katherine asked.

"I figured you two had a good reason to not have sex this weekend with me... it was to test me, or to test each other... and by the way... you two bitches failed!"

"You know what? You know way too fucking much about us!" Jenny said.

I kissed Jennifer deeply and then Katherine. "That's because I love you two bitches! It's my responsibility to know everything about you, to anticipate what you want and make sure you get it..."

"So... about what we want... and making sure we get it..." Katherine cooed. "Take us upstairs!" Katherine gently bit my nipple through my shirt. Jenny kissed me and tried to lead me upstairs but I resisted.

"Please?" Jenny begged. "Take us? Take us now? We're sorry and we want to make it up to you... real bad..."

"As much as I want to take you two upstairs and fuck you both silly... I kinda liked the idea of having a no sex weekend..."

"Really?" Katherine said.

"Yeah... I had a really great time the last two days... I *like* being with you two..." I kissed them each on the forehead. "You two are fun to be with... didn't you have fun?"

"I sure did..." Katherine said.

"Me too... I like being with you too CJ..." Jenny added.

"So… let's continue… what will it be then… a movie? Or going out dancing?" I asked.

"You wanna go out dancing?" Jenny said.

"I thought you hate to go dancing?" Katherine said.

"I do… but there's a lot of 'energy' here that needs to get burned up, and right now… dancing is safe…"

"Okay… we'll go upstairs and get dressed and we'll be down in about… an hour?" And Katherine looked at Jenny. "Maybe… a little longer…?"

I looked at them, shook my head and laughed. "Go ahead upstairs and fuck each other silly! I don't mind!" And they ran upstairs. Katherine stopped and turned back to me.

"You know… you *do* know way too fucking much about us!"

Jenny stopped at the top of the stairs. "You really think you can last the whole weekend with us… without any sex?"

"As much as I love you two… I'll try the best that I can…" I paused. "But… after we get back from dancing tonight… if you two have *any* 'energy' left… all bets are off!" They closed the door to the bedroom and I went into the living room to watch some TV. I noticed that Jenny picked up some new D.V.D.'s I haven't seen. I put one in and settled down to watch it. After the girls, finished… they never got dressed to go out. They came downstairs and snuggled on the couch with me and we watched TV all night long. We ordered in Chinese and spent the night laughing and talking and watching TV.

And no, we didn't have sex, or more correctly, I didn't have sex with them that weekend. But I would rather be with them and decide to have sex or not, than to be away from and have no shot at all! I was a little concerned that our relationship was just about sex; this weekend proved that there was more to it than that!

I really do love these two bitches. I love them more every day.

Okay, the story doesn't exactly end right there. Monday afternoon, Jinx took us all back to Katherine's house before they were going to drop me off at the airport. As we all headed towards Katherine's door it suddenly opened and there was a woman standing there. "Where have you been all weekend Katherine? I was worried sick!" She said sternly

Katherine just stood there in shock; she didn't know what to say. "Aunt P... P... Pamela?" she stuttered.

"Who the hell is this...?" Jennifer began to whisper in my ear.

"Jennifer!" I interrupted. "This must be Pamela Stark... you know... Katherine's aunt! From back home...? Big Daddy's sister...?" I turned to her. "I'm sorry, where are my manners...? I'm CJ Cassidy and this is..."

"Jennifer..." Jenny said and stopped.

"Jennifer Jones, she used to work with Katherine at Faber Data, Katherine spent the long weekend with us and we were just dropping her off... You must be Aunt Pamela...?" I said as I held my hand out.

"Oh yes, Jennifer... Katherine spoke of you... I'm sorry, but who are you again?" Pamela said to me as she shook my hand.

"CJ, CJ Cassidy..."

"He's..." Katherine began.

"I'm Jennifer's... fiancée..." Years of improvisation made me quick on my feet. Jennifer grabbed my arm tight, this is the first time Jenny was ever speechless. Katherine just stood there frozen. We were all busted. I had to think fast. There is no better cover than the truth. Jenny grabbed my arm even tighter.

"She's a skittish little thing isn't she?" Pamela asked about Jennifer who was shaking like a Chihuahua. I've never seen Jennifer react like that before, for any reason, for anybody.

"She's not a morning person and she gets a little shy when she meets new people..." I whispered to Pamela.

"Katherine? Aren't you going to invite them in dear?"

"Yes Aunt Pamela..."

Aunt Pamela led the way and Katherine looked like she was about to faint. Jenny just motioned for Jinx to wait for us.

"Just tell the truth... and everything will be fine." I whispered. "We'll just leave as planned and then you and Aunt

Pamela can catch up…" I said aside to Katherine. We all went in, sat down and had a lovely afternoon tea. Pamela is very nice; I really like her.

"Aunt Pamela?" Katherine asked. "I didn't know you were coming to visit…"

"Well actually I was in town to hit a few casinos while I was here… There was a big Texas Hold'em tournament in town over the weekend…" Aunt Pamela sometimes came to visit with Katherine when she was in town. It's one of the reasons I stay most of the time at Jenny's when I visit, or at Nick's place when I come to visit Katherine.

"You like to watch Texas Hold'em?" I asked.

"Aunt Pamela 'plays' Texas Hold'em…" Katherine replied. "She's actually nationally ranked…"

"*Oh ohh!*" I said to myself. "*This is someone who knows how to call a bluff!*" I would have to play my cards close to my vest to pull this off.

When she was in town for a tournament, she was usually comp'ed a hotel room by the casino, but this time she decided to stay at Katherine's. Jennifer was as nervous as long tail cat in a room full of rocking chairs. Not my analogy, Aunt Pamela's. After a while everyone got more comfortable but Jennifer would not let go of my hand. I looked at my watch.

"Oh dear… I'm so sorry, but I have a plane to catch… and Jenny's driver has been waiting. Aunt Pamela it has been such a pleasure to meet you!" I got up and I gently kissed her on the cheek. "Jenny? Say goodbye to Katherine's aunt…"

Jennifer kissed Pamela ever so lightly on the cheek. "Goodbye Aunt Pamela… it was pleasure… we have to do this again sometime…"

"Yes of course dear…"

And Katherine walked us to the door. I kissed and hugged her and she kissed and hugged Jennifer. "See! That wasn't so bad now… was it?" I said.

"No…" Katherine replied.

"Just don't let her into your bedroom…" I said.

Katherine's face turned pale. "Oh my god! She's been here all weekend!"

"Relax!" Jennifer said. "Your 'toy' chest is locked…"

"But my closet... my *costumes*..."

"Are just 'costumes'... If she asks, they're Halloween costumes!" I said. Katherine took a deep breath and relaxed, she could find a way to make that work. Jenny and I walked over to the limo and as we got in Pamela came out and waved to us and we drove off. Jennifer hit the limo bar almost immediately.

"Jennifer seems very nice, not at all the bitch you made her out to be..." Aunt Pamela said.

"Oh yeah... she's mellowed out a lot since she's been dating CJ..."

"Katherine...?"

"Yes Aunt Pamela?" Katherine said as she closed the front door.

"We need to go out and buy you a new bed frame..."

"Why?" Katherine was confused by her concern.

"The bedposts are all worn... they just don't make furniture very well here, it's all shoddy material. We'll have to get you a sturdier bed..."

"Yes Aunt Pamela..."

"How did that happen to your bed anyway?"

Katherine shuddered; she had to think quickly. She couldn't tell her aunt that the posts were worn from her and Jennifer taking turns being tied to them with leather restraints. "I don't really know. I bought it like that at a flea market. It was damaged so I got the set at a good price; I just never got around to getting it refinished..."

Aunt Pamela nodded. "Nothing wrong with second hand, but we should get a handyman to touch it up... No reason it shouldn't look nice..."

"Yes Aunt Pamela..."

"And then we'll go pick up your dog at the kennel..."

"I... don't have a dog..." She answered, confused by the statement.

"Really? I found a dog collar and leash under the couch when I was vacuuming... isn't it for *your* dog?"

"Oh...! I was dog sitting for a friend... We wondered where that was... I'll make sure he gets it back..." Katherine was getting a little better with covering her tracks.

"Oh…! Okay Katherine…" and Aunt Pamela took the teacups into the kitchen. Katherine breathed a sigh of relief; she was going to get through this visit just fine. All she had to do was remain calm and… "I just can't wait to hear how you're going to explain away the 13" dildo you left in the bathroom tub…!" Pamela said.

Katherine felt the blood drain from her face. She paused, took a deep breath and steadied herself. "Aunt Pamela…?" Aunt Pamela stuck her head out and stood in the kitchen doorway with her hand on her hip.

"Yes…? Katherine…? I'm listening…"

Katherine steadied herself. She could not believe what she was about to say to her aunt. "I'm 42… I'm not married… I don't sleep around… and a girl has needs…!"

Aunt Pamela paused, nodded her head in agreement. "Okay then…!"

Katherine went into the kitchen and they did the dishes and had a lovely visit. Aunt Pamela didn't interrogate Katherine anymore about her private life. Katherine knew Aunt Pamela understood more than she let on. You can't bluff a card shark but there is no better bluff… than the truth!

"When we were growing up… we had to use cucumbers…" Aunt Pamela remarked.

Katherine placed her hand over her mouth and blushed. "AUNT PAMELA!!!"

"Now you know why we never ate any of Grandma Mildred's cucumber sandwiches!"

"AUNT PAMELA!!!" Katherine exclaimed again. Aunt Pamela laughed her ass off! Katherine wanted to be shocked and appalled but Pamela was a young woman once too. As the week went on, they developed a brand new relationship. Katherine still hasn't told her the truth yet, although she suspects that Aunt Pamela already knows.

The Tortured Soul Trilogy
(The Seduction of CJ Cassidy)
Chapter 134
(Just Another Tuesday...)

Jennifer went over to Katherine's house after work one day. Katherine was just hanging out watching TV and crocheting a scarf or something. "Hey baby!" Katherine said as she kissed her cheek. "What are you doing here?"

"I didn't feel like going home tonight so I figured I would come over... and maybe spend the night... I hope you don't mind? Should I have called first?"

"Bitch please! You know you're welcome in my house anytime..." and Katherine kissed Jennifer passionately. "... and anywhere else... you want to be!"

Jennifer started to nuzzle Katherine's neck. Just as Katherine was getting into it, Jenny saw the knitting bag on the couch.

"What the hell is that?"

Katherine turned quickly. "What? Where? What is it?"

"That knitting... shit, you're doing...?"

Katherine sighed. "Bitch! You scared me! I thought you saw a water bug or something! It's just my crocheting..."

"When did *you* start crocheting?"

"One of the girls at the coffee shop does it to help calm her nerves, so I thought I would try it..."

Jenny walked over to the couch and picked it up. "What is it supposed to be?"

"I don't know yet... maybe a scarf, or a sweater or a shawl..."

"A... shawl...?" and Jenny started to look around the house as if she were looking for something.

Katherine turned her head left and right to where Jenny was looking. "What are you looking for...?"

"Your cat... here puss-puss... here puss-puss... here kitty, kitty...!"

"I don't have a cat...!"

"Are you sure? Cause I thought all old biddies that knit shawls have a cat... or two or three..."

"Bitch, fuck you!" And Katherine sat down and picked up her knitting. Jenny laughed her ass off. When she saw Katherine wasn't laughing she stopped.

"I'm sorry baby! I didn't mean to hurt your feelings. I didn't mean to call you an old biddy..."

"If I'm an old biddy... so are you!"

"Oh hell no, I'm not!"

"Really? Then where's your man...? Oh that's right... you don't *have* a man...!"

"Bitch! I have the same man you do!"

"Then you better call him... cause you aint getting any pussy here tonight!"

Jenny's mouth dropped wide open. "Ahhh come on! Katherine, don't be that way...!" Katherine continued to work on her project not saying a word. "All right then... be like that! I can wait... you can't stay mad at me forever!" And Jenny sat down next to Katherine leaving a space between them. "Besides... sooner or later... *you're* gonna want some pussy..." Jenny said. Katherine put her knitting bag on the couch between them and continued crocheting. Jenny looked at her. "You're really pissed at me? Really?" Katherine nodded slowly. "Then tie me down with that knitting... and spank me!"

Katherine shook her head slowly no. "I am not spanking you tonight... that... is your punishment!"

"Did you learn that shit from CJ?" Katherine was not amused. She continued to crochet her... whatever it was. "Damn... I guess we'll just watch TV... What are you watching?"

"I'm watching a tape of 'The Judge'..." Katherine stopped what she was doing and looked at Jenny, who was staring at her intently and Katherine busted out laughing. "Bitch, I am *not* turning into an old biddy...!"

"What... ever!" Jenny got up to get herself a glass of wine. "Would you care for a glass...?"

"No... pour me a scotch... wine is for 'old biddies'..."

Jenny laughed and poured them both a shot of scotch. She handed her the glass and toasted: "From one old biddy to another!"

"Score!"

"Salude!" And they sipped their drinks. Jennifer moved Katherine's bag over and lay down with her head in Katherine's lap. "I love you…"

"I love you too…" and Katherine leaned down and kissed Jenny deeply. "But you're *still* not getting any pussy tonight!"

"I'm okay with that!" and Jenny kissed Katherine again. "But we are not watching 'The Judge' together either!" Katherine handed her the remote and Jenny changed the channels. Nothing was on. "Damn!" Jenny sat up. "No pussy, nothing on TV… CJ is in New York…"

"You wanna cook dinner?"

Jenny cut her eyes at Katherine. "Have we *met*? Hello, my name is Jennifer… I burn *water…*!" Katherine and Jennifer laughed. Jenny took another sip of her scotch and looked at what Katherine was making. "That's pretty… I like the pattern…" Jenny paused at looked at Katherine.

"What?" Katherine asked.

"Is that hard to do?"

"Not at all… you wanna try it?"

Jenny paused. "Yeah… let me try it… but don't laugh!"

Katherine shook her head no. "I won't laugh." Katherine picked out a yarn and handed Jenny the needles and showed her how to get started. After a while Jenny got the hang of it. Every once in a while Jenny would show Katherine what she did and Katherine would undo it if she made a mistake and helped her correct it. They both sat there crocheting and talking and drinking. Katherine turned the TV back on and found an old movie and watched it as they crocheted throughout the evening. "Jenny?"

"Yeah Katherine?"

"Are we turning into two old biddies?"

"No… we're not…" and Jennifer kissed Katherine oh so softly. "But you might want to update the fames on your glasses…"

"I'm thinking about getting contacts… or Lasik." Katherine said as she took her glasses off.

"That would be nice…"

They continued to work on their projects until the movie was over.

"Jenny?"

"Yes Katherine…?"

"You wanna go upstairs so we can just fuck…?"

Jenny put down her crocheting. "Bitch, I thought you'd never ask!"

The Tortured Soul Trilogy
(The Seduction of CJ Cassidy)
Chapter 135
(Two Weeks in Paradise)

I couldn't wait for my vacation. Not only was it an all expense paid trip to Jamaica, it was two weeks alone with Katherine and Jennifer and I haven't been with them in almost two months! We had a lot of catching up to do! I needed to get laid and I needed to get laid bad! I knew the girls would most certainly make up for lost time. I packed my bag two days early. I was very anxious to see the girls again.

I started out for JFK airport at 7am for an 11am non-stop flight to Montego Bay. I arrived in Jamaica about 3pm. I spent an hour on line in customs. They made the guy in front of me unpack all his bags and because I look like "the usual suspect" I got pulled off the line and searched too! Then… I had to go through immigration! I got the hotel limo at around 4:30 and I got to the hotel around 8pm where Katherine booked a private villa. What? What? 11 hours traveling air, sea and land to get to the hotel in Ocho Rios? I was too tired to get laid now. I just wanted to get something to eat (I hadn't eaten since the night before!) and get some sleep! They checked me in and offered me a glass of champagne and fresh fruit. There was a huge welcome party for the new arrivals but I wasn't interested, I just wanted to go to the villa and see the girls. They got me a jitney to take me there. If you've never ridden a jitney, it's a glorified golf cart! I arrived at the villa in the dead of night. I opened the door and… nothing! The girls weren't there. I checked the bedroom and their stuff was there but no sign of them. I guess they went to the welcome dinner that was being held for the guests. I started to put my stuff away from my carry-on when I heard the door.

"Hello?" I called out. It was the valet with my other bag. Damn! By the time I unpacked my things I was way too tired to eat or to go to the party and look for the girls. I settled onto the huge four-poster bed. But not before checking the height of the mattress. *"Hey just right! I won't have to strain my knees!"* I turned on the TV and checked out what kind of channel line-up they had there. I was watching a Jamaican music channel when I heard keys in the door.

"CJ? Baby? Are you here?" Katherine said

"I'm in the bedroom sweetie... where else?"

She ran in, jumped on the bed and kissed me. "Welcome to Jamaica mon!" She said with the worse Jamaican accent ever.

"Tank yah dah ter!" I replied. "Where's Jennifer?"

"Ummm... we have to talk..."

I looked at her, Katherine has dumped Jenny in the past to spend alone time with me but we had discussed this and I told her I wasn't having it!

"Katherine...? Where is Jennifer?" I said with a stern voice. Just then I heard a hacking wheezing cough come from the other room. "What the hell was that?" I asked.

"*That*... is Jennifer... she's sick as a dog!" And Jennifer entered the room and looked like death warmed over.

"I'b thick!" she said.

"Your big ass sure is thick, but I heard you weren't feeling well!"

"Fuck you CJ!" she honked.

"Obviously not on this trip..." I retorted. Jenny looked as if she was about to cry. "Baby, I'm sorry... I was just kidding..." and I got up to hug her she backed off.

"Ged away from me!" And she turned her back.

"Ah come on! I was just playing..."

"No sday away... I dun wand you gedding thick too!" And she sat down in the far chair and blew her nose.

"What the hell happened? How did she get so sick?"

"Knucklehead here went swimming and then stayed outside in the sun to let her hair air dry. She fell asleep, naked of course, and got sick when the temperature dropped suddenly..."

"It got cold in Jamaica?"

"No... this happened back home... before we left."

"Have you taken anything for it?"

"She's tried everything short of voodoo..." Katherine said.

"I'b tried ebrethin...!" and she coughed. "Why dun you two go out... hab sum fun... I'b be otay..."

"You sure you'll be 'otay' Buckwheat?"

Jenny gave me the finger. "Fuck you CJ! dats not fuddy!"

I went over to her and although she tried to push me away I gently kissed her forehead. "I'm too tired to go out tonight... I'm just going to bed... Hey how come you're so well rested Katherine?"

"Oh, we got here on Friday... we've been here three days already!"

"You've been with her for three days? Okay then, I'll sleep on the couch and seeing that you developed immunity, you can sleep with 'Typhoid Mary' here!"

"I thwear CJ, Ib gunna beat yur ass when I get bedder!"

"Yeah... after you monkey fuck me...!" And I started to leave the room.

"I'b gunna take a shower before I oh to bed..."

"Hey that's an idea..." I said, "Take a steamy hot shower... it might help you clear your sinuses!"

"I'll try anytin..." Jenny got a bathrobe and started to disrobe.

"Wait... let me turn off the air-conditioning first... I don't want you catch pneumonia..." Katherine said and left the room. Jenny went into the bathroom and started the shower running. Suddenly she screamed and came running out dripping wet, wrapping a towel around her waist. Katherine ran into the room.

"What happened? CJ what did you do to her?"

"It wasn't me! I didn't do anything!"

"Dere's a wader bug in da badroom!"

I went to go check; Katherine looked at Jenny. "A water bug? Jenny? Seriously, you screamed for a water bug?"

"Fuck you bidch! Id wad a big ass waderbug!"

I came out of the bathroom. "I got it... you can go take your shower now!"

"Ib not going in dere alone!"

"It was just a water bug Jenny... Grow up!" Katherine said.

I held my hand up behind Jenny and held my fingers apart to show Katherine how big that sucker was. Katherine shivered. She's had a bad 'experience' with water bugs before. I was a little put off too, that sucker had wings!

"Well CJ killed it, go ahead and take your shower."

"Well Ib not going in dere alone! Dere could be more of dem!"

"Well I'm not going in there!" Katherine said.

"I'll stay with her..." I said.

"Otay... bud dun try anytin fuddy!"

"You... naked... in a shower... getting wet and all... soapy? And you think I'm gonna try something funny?" I took her hand and led her back into the bathroom. I led her into the shower but she wouldn't get in before she made me check for more bugs. I made her put on a shower cap so her hair wouldn't get wet and I sat on the toilet seat while she showered. After a while she began to feel better and she started to dance in the shower. "Remembering your old stripper days when you showered on stage?" She pulled back the curtain and danced for me in the steamy shower. She was definitely feeling much better. She gyrated and began to soap herself seductively. She then started to 'wash' her pussy.

"You gunna just sit dere... or are you gedding in dis shower wid me?"

I started taking my clothes off. "What took you so long to ask? Move over!" Sick or not, I needed to touch her, feel her body on me. I knew we weren't going to fuck. I didn't have a condom with me, but hot steamy foreplay never hurt nobody! I took a washcloth and soap and began to wash her down. She turned around so I could wash her back. She pushed her ass up against my hard cock. I reached around and soaped and washed her breasts and nipples.

"Ib you drop dat...I'b not bening ober to pick it up!"

I held the soap in front of her and turned my hand over and dropped it. "Ooops! Can you... get that for me?"

"Bidch!" And she bent over grinding her ass into me. I almost slipped and fell in the hot soapy shower. That's when Katherine came in, naked.

"What?" I said.

"I knew I could not trust you two alone! You're the only people I know that need a chaperone and a lifeguard in the shower!"

"Shut up and get your ass in here already, we're almost out of hot water." I said to her.

728

"This villa has instant hot water... it won't run out!" And Katherine got in the shower with us. We took turns washing each other in the hot shower. They took turns washing my cock slowly. I was really turned on. After a while the girls couldn't take it anymore. They knew I wouldn't get involved without a condom but that didn't stop them from getting it on with each other. They stood at the opposite side of the shower under the water and began to kiss and lick and then stroke each other. I stepped out of the shower and sat back on the toilet seat to give them more room to work their magic. I did not mind the show they put on for me. They both came hard. I was sitting there stroking myself. Katherine looked at me.

"Oh my... what ever are you doing CJ?"

I kept jerking off. "Hey... it's my cock and I'll wash it as fast as I want to!"

"You know..." Jennifer added. "For sum one who just took a shower... yur a dirty liddle fucker aren't you!"

"I can think of only one way for you to get me to stop what I'm doing..."

Jennifer pouted. She still didn't feel well enough to give me head. Katherine stepped out of the shower and kneeled in front of me and began to devour me voraciously. Jenny stayed in the shower and fondled herself for me. I leaned forward, reached over and grabbed Katherine's ass cheeks and spread them. Jenny looked at Katherine's sweet pussy. "Dun mind if I do..." Jennifer stepped out of the shower and went into her travel kit and took out her 'travel buddy', turned it on and worked Katherine's pussy from behind. Jenny masturbated as she worked the vibrating dildo in and out of Katherine as she gave me head. It got dangerous at one point when Katherine bore down on my cock when Jenny hit her spot!

We got out of the shower and decided to go ahead and sleep in the same bed. Jenny put on some pajamas she brought with her because she was sick and the resort we were staying in wasn't clothing optional. Jennifer slept in between us, I spooned her and she spooned Katherine. It was the first good night sleep Jenny had since she got there. Jenny always sleeps well after a good fucking but this time, the poor kid was just exhausted. Katherine was the first one up and dressed and she tapped me on the shoulder to wake me up.

"Do you think you can get up without waking her?" she whispered. "I want her to get as much rest as possible..."

I pulled back the covers slowly. Jenny's PJ bottoms were around her ankles, so were mine. "I doubt it... I'm still in her..."

Katherine was shocked. "How the hell did you get out of bed, get a condom and fuck her... without waking me?" She whispered.

"It wasn't easy... I had to gag her twice, but you *were* sleeping pretty hard."

"Well if you had to gag her two times... she's not getting up anytime soon, pull out and let's go get some breakfast."

I eased my cock out of Jennifer and she cooed and moaned and rolled over to sleep on her stomach. I got out of bed and Katherine pulled her pajama pants back up and tucked her in. I went into the bathroom to clean up.

"I can't believe you took advantage of her, knowing how sick she is!"

"I did not 'take advantage' of a sick woman! We were spooning and then she pushed and grinded her ass into me..."

"And what is that? The universal signal for 'stick your dick in me'...?"

I put my hands on my hips and looked at Katherine. "Bitch please...! Like *you* never used that signal to get me to kick it between the uprights when we're in bed...?"

She shook her head; she knew I was right. "You owe me one CJ!"

I peeked out of the bathroom door. "Technically... I owe you two!" I got dressed and we went to get breakfast and brought back tea and toast for Jennifer. When we got back she was still in bed knocked out.

"Damn! Is this bitch still alive?" Katherine said.

At that moment Jennifer rolled over and she was, in fact, still alive. "Where did you two disappear to?" She moaned.

"We went to get breakfast and we brought you some toast..."

Jenny smacked her lips. "I'm not hungry... I just want some hot tea..."

I held up the tea bags. "Hot tea... coming right up!" and I headed to the kitchen.

"You sure you don't want some toast?" Jenny shook her head no. "You sound better than yesterday; I guess the hot steam helped."

"Yeah and my fever broke last night…"

"That must have been from CJ taking your 'temperature' last night while I was sleeping!" Katherine added.

"Oooops!" Jenny said.

"Yeah… Oooops!" Katherine replied

That's when I came in to give Jenny her tea. "What?"

- - -

Jenny did not get better. Her fever was gone but she was still sick and the congestion came back by the end of the day. It didn't help that it rained every other day and every night we were there. Katherine and I spent the first week just caring for our sick lover.

"I'b so sorry I fucked up yur vacation!"

"You're not ruining anything baby! I love you and I love being with you, in sickness and in health…"

"What did you say CJ?" Katherine asked.

"I said I don't mind being with you if you're sick or not… why?"

"No reason!" And Katherine shook her head.

Jenny hugged me, "I lub you so much, you're too gud to me!" she said in her congested voice. "Now ged out! I want to ged some sleep and I'm tired ob seeing you two!"

I kissed Jenny on her forehead. "You sure?"

"Ged the fuck out!" Jenny rolled over and was fast asleep before we even got out of the bedroom.

"Poor kid… she exhausted!" I said as I closed the bedroom door behind me. I turned around and Katherine was at the open balcony doors. It was raining, a little more than a drizzle but much less than a downpour. "I guess we're not going out in that…" I said. "And the only TV is in the bedroom… you want to order room service?"

Katherine turned to me and smiled. "Yes… I think it's about time I got some room service…" And she walked out onto the balcony in the rain.

"Katherine! What the hell are you doing? Its bad enough Jenny's sick, you wanna get sick too? Does it always have to be a contest between you two? Katherine? Do you hear me? Get your ass back in here!" Katherine ignored me and leaned over the wet balcony rail which was about five or six inches wide. (That fact will become very significant in a moment. Trust me!) She looked across the field. There was no one out in this rain, except her. "Katherine! I said get your ass in here!" Katherine bent over the railing and slowly lifted her skirt over her waist; she wasn't wearing panties. She gyrated her sweet naked ass in the rain and cooed. The sight of the rain hitting her on the ass was a great turn on. She spread her legs open, reached under herself and began to fondle her pussy.

"I have a better idea... Instead of me, getting my ass in there... maybe you should come out here... and get in this ass!" The rain gently showering her ass was an amazing effect to the show Katherine was putting on for me. She gyrated her ass as she fingered herself. She dipped into her sweet pussy again and again. Then she licked her fingers and dove in again deeper and deeper. She was wet in more ways than one. "You gonna let me do this all by myself?" She cooed and she turned to look at me and I was gone. "What the...?" she said confused.

I appeared in the doorway wearing a condom. "You didn't think I was going out there... without a rain coat?" Katherine laughed and bent over the rail again. I stepped out onto the balcony, the rain was warm and my cock slipped into her hot pussy like a guided missile. I entered her slowly from behind and she cooed and moaned. This was going to be a slow comfortable fuck in the rain. I eased in and out of her and she pushed her hips up against the railing as I pushed in deeper and deeper. I forgot that Katherine liked dangerous kinky sex. I thought having sex leaning on the railing of a three-story building where anybody could see us was dangerous enough. Not Katherine!

"Hold me by my waist tight!' she said. I did. She grabbed my wrists and put her left leg on the railing. She then swung her right leg onto the other side of the railing. She was in a full split like she was working an x-rated routine for the balance beam. She took my hands and put them on the railing in front of her hips. "Don't worry... trust me, I won't fall!"

The hell she won't! What if she faints? What if I slip in the rain? What if I break the railing like I broke Jenny's bed? How in the hell do you explain this to the hotel staff? Or the local authorities...? "See officer what happened was... I swear you're going to laugh...!"

I was worried but I wasn't about to stop. I entered her again and fucked her so slow and easy that it took her to the most mellow place she had ever been. Well, as mellow as you can be on the edge of death! She rocked her hips up and down on my shaft. She cooed and purred the entire time. Her body gave off an amazing heat and passion. The rain on her body became like steam coming off a hot plate. This was too much for me. I really wanted to bang that ass, but not here. I hooked my arms around Katherine's waist and eased her off her precarious perch and backed us into a wicker chair behind us and sat her down on me. I pulled her top open and began to work her nipples as she booty shook her ass down on me faster and faster. She let out a high-pitched squeal that dropped down to a low soulful moan. Her pussy contracted and she cinched into me. "I'm gonna cum!" I panted. She got up and pulled the condom off me and began to suck me dry. I really wanted to cum between her legs but I wasn't going to stop her from doing what she liked to do.

Three way sex in the shower... Amazing.

Sex in the rain in paradise... Priceless!

We went inside and dried off with beach towels the hotel provided. We sat on the balcony watching the rain while cuddled in each other's arms. Some people are so busy with their lives they forget to enjoy their lives. They forget to just sit, and watch the rainfall... they wait and pray for sunny days. They forget that in every life, some rain must fall.

"You know you still owe me one!" She purred.

"You want it now?"

"No... let's just watch the rain come down." And she nuzzled into me. I kissed her forehead gently. It rained for the rest of the day. We sat there cuddled up and the sound of the rain lulled us both gently to sleep. It was Jennifer screaming in the bedroom woke us up suddenly a few hours later. At first we thought she had seen another water bug. But this was different. We ran into the bedroom and Jennifer was jumping up and down the bed screaming.

"Jennifer! What? What the fuck is wrong? What happened?" Katherine said pleading with her. Jennifer began to cry. But she wasn't upset. These were tears of joy. I grabbed Jennifer by the waist to get her to stop jumping on the bed. She threw her arms around me and laughed. That's when we heard the sounds of people rejoicing from the other villas.

"Jenny? What is going on? What is it?" I asked.

She looked at us as if *we* were crazy. Like we should know why she was screaming and crying.

"What? Bitch! What?" Katherine demanded.

Jenny just pointed to the TV. We looked at the news broadcast. "Barach Obama is the President!" Jenny screamed.

We had totally forgotten today was Nov 3rd!

The Tortured Soul Trilogy
(The Seduction of CJ Cassidy)
Chapter 136
(Vacation: Day 2)

I was in the living room finishing off a drink from the nights' celebration while I let the girls sleep it off. Jenny was still sick and Katherine was exhausted from partying and taking care of her. I fell asleep on the couch. In the morning Katherine came out of the bedroom first. "How is Jenny doing?" I asked as I kissed Katherine good morning.

"She's still pretty sick but she's horny as hell too!"

I shrugged my shoulders. "Nothing I can do about that right now."

And that's when I felt Jenny come up from behind me and began to kiss my neck and shoulders and reached over and pinched my nipples. She was naked from the waist up.

"I thought you were sick?"

"And horny... real horny!" and she continued to kiss my neck.

"Well at least you don't have a fever..." I whispered.

"The hell I don't!" and she reached from behind me and began to stroke my cock over my pants.

"Behave yourself! You're gonna start something you can't finish..."

"Who said I'm the one that has to finish?" I looked in front of me and Katherine was already taking her top off and stroking her hard nipples and licking her lips. Jennifer unzipped my pants and reached in and took my cock out and stroked it in Katherine's direction. Jenny continued to kiss and lick my neck. "Come here Katherine..." Jenny said and Katherine eased her way towards me. Jenny continued to stroke me in long deliberate strokes with her right hand. As Katherine came closer, Jennifer reached around the other side of me with her left and grabbed the back of Katherine's head and pulled her closer and kissed her deeply. She then took her by the hair and pushed her gently down to her knees in front of me, keeping control of her head with her hair. As Jenny held the shaft of my stiff cock she guided

Katherine's mouth on the head on my cock and pumped her head on me. Katherine licked and sucked; Jenny guided me and kissed my back and neck. I had two free hands so I stroked and pinched Katherine's nipples. That drove her wild. I then reached behind me and began to stroke Jenny's pussy under her pajama bottoms.

I turned to Jenny who kissed my lips. "You wish you had one... don't you?" I whispered. I knew this wasn't the first time they played this game.

"Bitch... I have three... four if I count yours!" She then began to gyrate her upper body so she could rub her nipples on my back. "Take off your shirt... I want to feel your skin on my nipples!" I unbuttoned my shirt and she pulled it off behind me. Now I could feel Jennifer's soft natural breasts on my bare back and her nipples as she rubbed them on me, Katherine's lips and mouth on my cock as she sucked me gently, all the while Jennifer stroked me with her right hand, guiding Katherine with her left. Jennifer stroked me gently at first but then she heard Katherine moan. I guess that was the signal to go faster. Jenny began to jerk me off in earnest now, faster and tighter, faster and tighter. Jenny's right hand touched Katherine's lips as she stroked me faster and faster.

"Where do these two get these ideas from?" I thought to myself. But I wasn't about to ask any questions right now! "I'm... I'm gonna cum!" I moaned. Jenny pulled Katherine off me and held her in position as she stroked me faster while kissing my neck. Katherine tongue lashed the tip of my throbbing cock quickly in anticipation of my spurting right in her mouth. "Ahhhhhhhhhh shhhhhhhhhiitttttttt! Haaaaaaaa!" I screamed.

Jennifer took her left hand off Katherine and hugged me and pinched my nipples. That's when I heard Jennifer coo and moan. She actually got her cookies off on that! Katherine got up and kissed Jennifer so very softly.

"I feel dizzy..." Jennifer said and Katherine took her back to bed.

"Jenny?" I said.
"Yeah baby?"
"You said you had three, four counting me?"
"Yeah baby..."

"Count me in again... but next time... I want *you* on your knees!"

"Oh yeah... I got you Papi! Just as soon as I feel better!" And Katherine smiled and put Jenny back in bed.

The Tortured Soul Trilogy
(The Seduction of CJ Cassidy)
Chapter 137
(Rainy Days)

The sun did come out during our vacation, but it was rare and short lived. We tried to take advantage of the sunshine whenever we could. One day it looked like it was going to be nice all day so all three of us went out to sit by the main pool. We thought the fresh air would do Jennifer good. Katherine sat by the pool, sunning herself and reading a novel she brought with her. Jennifer was also reading by the pool but she had shorts and a t-shirt on. She was still sick and didn't want to take any chances. I looked at them and thought to myself: "*I wish they were both naked...*" Katherine continued to read and Jennifer was fidgeting. She couldn't get comfortable. She couldn't relax. Something was bothering her and it wasn't about being sick. I could tell she was starting to get on Katherine's nerves. "Jenny?" I said.

"What?"

"Come take a walk with me... show me around the resort... you two have been here a few days and I never got the nickel tour... Maybe we'll take some pictures!" Jenny loves to get her picture taken.

"No thanks..." she said curtly.

My head turned to the side and I looked at her. "Okay... who are you and what did you do with my Jennifer?"

Jenny scrunched her face up. "I don't want my picture taken looking like this..."

"Okay then... we'll just walk around just the two of us... show me the sights!"

"What about Katherine? We can't just leave her here alone..."

I turned to Katherine. "Katherine?"

She looked up from her novel. "Yeah CJ?"

"Mommy and Daddy are going to go walkies... do you need a babysitter?"

Katherine went back to reading her novel. "The two of you take a hike and leave me the fuck alone!"

"Ewwwww! I see somebody's not getting any frozen yogurt for dessert!" I said. Katherine stood up suddenly and began to walk away. I thought I had pissed her off. "Where are you going?" I asked her.

She turned and smiled at me. "Fuck you two... I'm getting some frozen yogurt!"

I looked at Jenny and held my arm out. "Shall we?"

"Fine!" and she reluctantly took my arm and we took a walk around the resort. The entire time she kept fiddling with her top.

"You wanna get naked, don't you?"

"Fucking 'A' I wanna get naked!" and she tugged at her top again. "This t-shirt is rubbing my nipples raw!"

"Come with me..."

"Where are we going?"

"There's a drug store near the concierge..." Normally my saying something like 'cum with me' would have illicited a nasty response from her or at least a wry grin from her. That's how I knew she was uncomfortable and still not feeling well. I took her to the store and picked up a box of sheer strip bandages. "Here..."

"What's this for?"

"Put one on each of your nipples. It'll stop your top from irritating you..."

She grinned at me. "You do it for me!"

I smiled at her. "If I reach under your top... it won't just be your nipples that will get some first aide!" She took the box from me and went into the dressing room and came out five minutes later a bit more relaxed. "That work?"

"Yeah, but not until I licked my nipples first!"

"Do you have any bandages left?"

"Sure! Why?"

"Cause right now my shorts are irritating my cock!"

"I don't think I have a bandage small enough...!" I dropped my jaw. (Oh NO she didn't!) Jennifer laughed hard. I knew she felt a little better. We walked around the resort and I took pictures of everything I could. I tried to take Jenny's picture... Big mistake!

"Stop that please!"

"Okay!" and I stopped; I didn't want to piss her off... too late!

"Are you sure Katherine is okay?" She asked me.

"She's fine... she's a big girl and can take care of herself!" Jenny kept looking back towards the pool area.

"You know I don't have any pictures of me..." I said. Jenny ignored me. "Jenny?"

"What?"

"Take my picture..." I said.

"You hate getting your picture taken!"

"Come on... We're on vacation!"

She quickly took the camera from my hands and snapped a picture of me. "There! Happy now?"

"Oh come on! Let me at least pose first!" I looked for something to stand in front of. The moment I found a spot and stood there she took the picture. She came towards me and pushed the camera at me.

"Can we go now?" and she turned and walked away. I didn't have a good grip of the camera and it fell from my hands and hit the floor. I picked it up and the lens was cracked.

"JENNY!" I exclaimed. I looked up towards Jenny but she was still heading back to the pool area. She was determined to check on Katherine.

"Sorry!" she said half-heartedly and continued to head back to the pool.

I opened the back of the camera and took out the photo chip and put it in my pocket. I then took the camera and smashed it to the ground and threw it in the nearest trashcan. It was then I heard the voice of a southern gentleman standing behind me.

"That was a waste son! You could have just replaced the lens!"

I turned to him. "I'm sorry?"

"The camera... you didn't have to break it... it could have been fixed!"

"I'm sorry..." I said to him politely. "You were focused on the camera... you're *still* focused on the camera... It's just an object; it *can* be replaced. That isn't the problem right now. The problem is that my girlfriend is upset and preoccupied with something. I purposely broke the camera so I could focus on my

740

girlfriend!" His wife who was standing with her husband stepped up to me and touched my shoulder. She understood; her husband didn't get it."

"If you hurry… you can still catch up to her!" She said.

"Thank you… I always give her a four minute head start…"

His wife smiled at me. "You are wiser beyond your years, young man!"

"Actually I'm 53!"

Her husband smiled at me. He saw what Jennifer looked like and he was impressed. I headed back to the pool but it began to rain. I knew the girls would head back to the villa. They couldn't risk Jenny relapsing. I took the next jitney back. I arrived just as Katherine came out of the bedroom.

"Is everything okay? When Jenny came back without you and I thought something happened between you two." She asked concerned. I knew Jenny didn't say anything to her.

"Nothing happened… she just didn't feel well and wanted to go back to the pool and sit with you… I didn't start back until it started to rain."

Katherine knew I was lying, but she wasn't going to pull me out on the carpet about it. We both knew about Jenny's mood swings. Besides, she wasn't feeling well so she let it slide. "Where's your camera… did you forget it by the pool?"

"No… It fell and I broke it!" (No lie there!)

"Oh no! All our vacation pictures are gone?"

I took the chip out of my pocket. "No… I got'em right here baby!"

Katherine had a sigh of relief. At that moment Jenny came out of the bedroom topless… well… almost topless!

"JENNIFER!" Katherine exclaimed. "You didn't!!!"

Jennifer looked around the room.

"Didn't do what?"

"Don't tell me you went and got your nipples pierced!" Jenny looked down and that's when she noticed she still had the sheer strips covering her nipples. Jenny and I laughed our asses off! "What's so fucking funny?" Katherine demanded.

We ordered room service and spent another night in our room. It wasn't the best vacation in paradise, but I wouldn't want to have spent it with anyone else.

The Tortured Soul Trilogy
(The Seduction of CJ Cassidy)
Chapter 138
(Cutting the Vacation Short)

Between Jenny being sick and there being a hurricane warning and it raining almost every other day, we opted to cut our vacation a week short. Katherine made the arrangements to cancel our stay and change our flights. Instead of my going back to New York, she fixed it so I would fly back home with them and stay there for the second week. We would leave to go home in two days. Jenny was not too happy about it, but she certainly didn't want to be stuck in paradise, sick, during a hurricane. Katherine booked a spa session and an all day shopping spree for herself at my request. I wanted her to have some alone time, without worrying about Jennifer. I stayed behind and took care of her instead. Jenny was up and out of bed about 11am, which is pretty good for Jenny even when she isn't sick.

"Where's Katherine?" Jenny said, her voice cracking from her cold.

"She's having a spa session and then she's going into town to do some shopping."

"She's in town... shopping... alone?" Jenny was amazed.

"Yeah..."

"And you fucking let her go by herself? What is wrong with you?"

"I suggested it but it wasn't my decision, it was hers. She wanted to do this... I think it's a big step for her... and if she doesn't deal with it eventually, she'll be a recluse all her life..."

Jenny just nodded. "Okay... maybe you're right... Maybe I have been coddling her too much. She's a big girl and she has to learn to deal with it..." I nodded. "But if this blows up in her..." Jenny paused. "YOU are going to deal with putting Ms. Humpty Dumpty back together again...!"

"You know I'll be there for her... even if it means with dealing with her pain."

Jenny hugged and kissed me. "You're such a good friend CJ... I love you so much right now!"

"I love you too baby!"

Jenny went to the window and noticed that it looked like rain. "At least if it rains, she'll wear her scarf..."

"Don't worry about her... she'll be just fine."

It started to drizzle and then rain but not very hard. "She'll be fine... but I can't go out in this... I can't take the chance of getting sicker." I walked up behind her and put my arms around her and held her. She snuggled into it. "Damn... It is going to rain all week?"

"Does it matter... as long as we're together?" I said.

Jenny became visibly upset. She began to pout. Normally I hated pouty women, but Jennifer actually looked cute pouting. "I've been sick all week, it's rained every other day... our vacation is almost over and I didn't even get a chance to wear any of my new bikinis..."

"Is that's what bothering you honey?" And I kissed her lower lip. "Go put them on now!"

"Now?"

"Yeah... do a little fashion show for me... I want to see you in your outfits."

"Really?" Jenny's face lit up. "You want me to put on a show for you?"

"Yeah... but let's see your bathing suits first!" Jenny frowned up her face and punched me on the arm. "Go ahead... I'll even put some music on so you can walk the runway." Jenny squealed, kissed me and ran into the bedroom to get ready for the show. I knew Jenny always dreamed of being a high fashion runway model. She had the looks and build to be a Victoria secret model. I think she even auditioned once but it didn't work out. She was in the bedroom for a while. "What's taking so long to put on a bra and thong?" I called out. She came out in her first bikini. She did her hair, make-up the works. "Wow! You look fantastic!"

"Thank you..." and she did a models turn for me.

"Damn... just... damn!"

"A little runway music please?" I went to the CD player and threw on one of Jenny's jazz CD's. "Give me something a little more upbeat." I put on a reggae CD we picked up at the gift shop and Jenny pumped her hot ass across the floor like a veteran model. She loved every minute of it. I could see it in her eyes she was having a ball performing for me. It felt good to see her enjoy herself finally. It was a shame the camera was broken; I could have taken some amazing shots of her! I even began to do commentary for her as she walked. She would walk up to me, tell me the facts of the outfit she wore and I would repeat it using my 'stage voice' and she would take it from there. Every outfit she came out in she became more confident and she became radiant. I'm telling you, Jennifer is one hot smoking b... uh, young lady! We all knew she had an amazing body but in her young life she used it in ways she really wasn't very proud of. She was good at it, just not proud of it. She got so into the fashion show that she came out in mixed and matched suits with props. The show went on for about and hour. "Well... this was my last outfit... how did you like the fashion show?"

"Baby... you were amazing! I loved it!" And I clapped my hands and gave her a standing ovation. Jenny bowed and curtsied for me. And she laughed. Then she just stood there watching me look at her. Her breasts began to heave gently as she took long, slow breaths. She began to fiddle and fidget with the straps from her top. "You want me... to take this off?" She hissed seductively. Well as seductive as one can be with a frog in her throat. She panted with anticipation as she awaited my answer. "CJ...? Do you want me to take this off... for you?" She whispered.

Hell yeah I wanted her to take that off! It came out as: "No... keep it on... It looks so beautiful on you... you look so beautiful... wearing it...!"

Jennifer eyes softened and her lip quivered. She took her hand and put it on her perfect cleavage. "You... think I'm beautiful...?" She whispered.

"I'm sorry...? Do you even *own*... a mirror?" Jenny slowly approached me and pushed me back down on the couch and straddled me by placing her knees on either side of me on the couch and kissed me like she had never kissed me before. This is the first time ever that we kissed like this... and still had our clothes on!

When Katherine came back from shopping, Jenny and I were still laying down on the couch fully dressed and making out. Well I was fully dressed. Jenny still had her bikini on. "I'm sorry... did I come back too soon...? I see you two are just getting started!" I looked at Jenny and we quietly knew not to tell Katherine what we actually did all afternoon. Jenny got up off me and kissed Katherine.

"Well you look fabulous! You look like you're feeling better!" And Katherine touched Jenny's forehead. "No fever..." And she smiled at me. "But I did come home too early!"

"Never mind me... How was shopping?" Jenny said.

"It was okay..." And Katherine put her bags down.

"You sure?" Jenny asked unsurely.

"Yeah... I had fun... After a while I didn't think of it... so it didn't matter... it felt good to get out on my own."

"I'm happy for you baby! I'm glad you had a good time." I said.

"There was one woman... in town, who asked me what had happened..., to me..."

A tear formed in Jenny's eye. "Oh baby!" and Jenny stroked Katherine's face.

"I'm okay... its okay... I told her... what happened... She hugged me."

And Jenny hugged Katherine and kissed her so very gently on her lips.

"I'm so very proud of you baby!" I said as I hugged and kissed her.

"Okay, fuck all that shit... Did you bring me any presents?" Jenny interjected. And Jenny started going through Katherine's bags. I laughed my ass off!

"Yeah she's feeling better..." I said.

"Simmer down dah ter!" Katherine said. Her accent was getting better. "I bring some ting for everybodee!" Katherine went into the bags and pulled out jewelry for Jenny and clothes for me. We thanked her for all the beautiful things she got us.

"What's in that bag?" I asked.

"It's personal... for me... and Jenny..." Jenny peeked in the bag and squealed.

"I don't want to know what it is..." I said.

"Lying bitch! You *do* want to know but I'll never tell..." And she waved her finger like Brittany Murphy in '*Don't Say A Word*'." Jenny giggled. Jenny looked into the bag and began to squeeze her breasts and nipples and she kissed Katherine again. This time it lingered. I really wanted to watch them make out.

"CJ?" Katherine moaned.

"Yes Katherine?"

"Aren't you late? To be somewhere... else?"

"Nope..." (And miss this show? Hell no!)

"CJ?" Jenny hissed.

"Yes Jenny?"

"Get the fuck out... or get involved!"

I knew what 'get involved' meant. I looked at the imaginary watch I wasn't wearing. "Oh! Look at the time... I'm late... to be somewhere, anywhere else!" I grabbed a light jacket and walked out. "Be back in an hour..."

"Better make it two!" Jenny moaned.

I closed the door and headed for the jitney station to take me to the main hotel. Surely something was going on there, or I could just sit at the bar and drink. When I got back to the room I was a little schnockered on Appleton's rum. I knocked before I opened the door. "Housey keeping! You wanna me makie bed?" They laughed.

"Give us a minute!" I sat in the living room for a moment. "You can come in now." Katherine said. I went into the bedroom and Jennifer was face down laid at the foot of the bed. Her ankles were tied to the bedposts and she was in a full split. Katherine was sitting in a chair eating her pussy out. "Suit up... I warmed your dinner for you!" Katherine said. I got a condom and put it on. I stood at the foot of the bed where Katherine had pulled the chair away. I entered Jenny's wet, swollen, juicy pussy. I began to slowly pump her. Katherine moaned and climbed into the bed, got on top of Jenny and did a full split too. "Let's get this fucking vacation started already!" Katherine said as she kissed Jennifer neck and ears. I took turns easing my hard cock into Jennifer and then Katherine. Katherine would have to slide down a bit for me to reach her but her sliding on Jenny's ass only excited Katherine more. Katherine stroked Jenny's nipples whenever I fucked Katherine. I tried not to focus on the welts and bruises forming on their bodies from their private session. I tried to focus on their pink freshly spanked asses. I'm really not into the shit they're into, but I must admit a freshly spanked ass and a hot pussy is a big turn on for me, and these two bitches knew it. Katherine rolled off Jenny and kissed her passionately.

"Jenny?" I said.

"Yeah baby?"

"Grab your ass for me..." Jenny looked at me and cut her eyes at me. She wasn't into anal but that's not what I wanted. Katherine's eyes widened and she let out a sigh. I knew she wanted anal but she hadn't gotten the courage to ask me yet. She was excited and little upset that I might do Jenny instead. "I said grab your ass!" Jenny cautiously grabbed her ass and I grabbed her by the wrists and rode her pussy like a pony!

"I'm gonna cum!" she yelped. I began to pound her pussy in earnest and she squealed and came hard.

"Come here Katherine..." She looked at me and didn't understand what I wanted. I told her to get her face on Jenny's ass and hold her ass open for me. I pumped Jenny's pussy as Katherine playfully spanked her ass for me. I pulled out of Jenny and peeled off my condom. I stroked my cock as I looked into Katherine' hungry eyes. "Wanna finish me off?" She nodded, licked her lips and slid forward and began to give me head. I was about to cum so I pulled away, held her by the back of her head and she jerked me off until I shot my load on her tits and Jenny's ass.

"Damn!" Jenny said. "I should have been tied face up... so I could eat out Katherine!"

I loosened her restraints. "So...? What's stopping you?" And I sat down in the chair and watched while Jennifer topped Katherine off. Being with them is like being in a porn film and watching it at the same time. Jenny wanted so bad to stay in Jamaica another week, even if it was to stay indoors, but she still really didn't feel well and she was homesick. She wanted to sleep in her own bed. We wanted to sleep in her bed too. The next day we sat by the pool and drank like fish, the day after that we packed to go home to the states. Jenny settled into her sickness once she got home and was able to relax. She got worse than when she was in Jamaica. We spent the next week every day catering to Jennifer's needs and Katherine spent every night, catering to mine.

Jenny was feeling much better by the end of the week and Katherine let us have a day alone. Katherine went home first and I spent my last vacation day tending to Jennifer's needs. That night

Jinx took me to the airport so I could catch my flight home. Jennifer and Katherine also came to see me off. It was going to be another two months before I could see them both again. I didn't want to go back home. I wanted to stay but our situation doesn't allow that just yet. Katherine could fly down to visit me anytime she wanted but Jenny's schedule was as tight as mine. I did not want to leave them... I went back to visit Katherine just as soon as I could. Jenny met me there the moment when I arrived.

The Tortured Soul Trilogy
(The Seduction of CJ Cassidy)
Chapter 139
(Sometimes A Little Rain Must Fall)

I was spending a week at Katherine's house. Katherine had things to do for the whole weekend and she said it was okay with her if I spent the weekend with Jennifer rather than be here in the house all alone by myself. Bedsides, she knew Jenny would just come get me anyway. Katherine called Jenny to make the arrangements. I kissed Katherine goodbye and waited for Jinx to pick me up and he dropped me off at Jenny's about an hour later. I entered the house with my keys. "Jenny? Are you home baby...? Papi came to spend some time with you..." No answer. "Jenny?"

"I'm in the living room CJ... watching TV..." I walked in. Jenny was dressed. Okay, I was hoping she was naked but I was just as glad to see her anyway. I went to kiss her but she turned her cheek to me. "Hi baby... sit down..." and she patted the couch next to me.

"What are we watching?" No answer. She just stared watching the movie. I settled in and watched it too. It wasn't too bad. Some time travel movie with Nicholas Cage. During a lull I got up to make popcorn for us. I offered Jenny some but she waved it away.

"So, what did I miss?" Jenny didn't answer me. We sat there watching the movie, eating popcorn and suddenly Jenny sounded like she was laughing to herself. It wasn't a funny part. "What's so funny...?" I asked. She just shook her head. That's when I realized, that she wasn't laughing, she was upset, not angry upset, but sad upset. Concerned, I asked her. "Baby? What's the matter?" No answer. "Jenny...? Are you okay?" She nodded her head yes but then she sobbed. I paused for a moment.

"You want to talk about it?" She shook her head no, coughed and left the room quickly, crying as she left. I watched her as she left the room. "*Damn it!*" I said to myself "*Now what...?*" I had a feeling of déjà vu. I went through this shit with Katherine before; I guess it was Jenny's turn. I put the popcorn down. She's crying, she needs a friend, but she left the room, so she needed her privacy, but still she wants me to check on her. I wish I had that power Nicholas Cage had in that movie, to see two minutes into the future... I could really use a heads up here. But I'm just a mere mortal and I'm subject to following the rules.

(Gentlemen, take note here; learn the proper procedure; timing is everything!)

I gave her exactly four minutes before following her into her bedroom. The door was wide open. (That's the signal that it's okay to go in!) She was on her stomach on the bed, hugging her pillow and sobbing uncontrollably. She was holding the rag doll Ms. Crystal gave her when she was a child. I knew this was bad. Damn I'm such a man... I just kept staring at her ass. "I don't want you to see me like this!" and she turned over to her side, buried her face in her pillows and cried harder.

(Gentlemen, this does *not* mean 'go away', it means 'stay with me, but turn around!')

I sat on the edge of the bed with my back towards her. I gently put my hand on her outstretched leg and rubbed her calf.

(Outstretched means I'm reaching out to you. Touch me. If she doesn't quickly pull away it's okay. If she then slowly draws her legs towards her, it means come closer to me.)

I came up behind her and put my hands on her hip and gently rubbed her back and shoulders. She continued to cry into her pillow.
"CJ...?"
"Yeah Jenny... I'm here..."

(Gentlemen, if she calls you by your name, answer using hers. She wants to hear you say her name, not 'baby' or 'honey' or some other generic form of affection, her name! And she knows you're there physically; tell her you're there for her, emotionally!)

"I love you Papi..." she said softly.

751

(Now, is the time to express a generic form of affection.)

"I love you too Puddin!" (Okay, I wasn't supposed to mention her pet name to you here... oh well!) I continued to rub and stroke her back and neck gently. "You sure you don't want to talk about it?" I asked again.

"Uh uhh!" and she cried some more into her pillow and sobbed and her body shook.

(Wait for it!)

And then she began to cry hysterically.

(Now!)

I reached over and turned her around and held her in my arms as she cried on my shoulder and began sucking breaths of air as she sobbed. I just wanted to hold her and take all her pain away. "Tell Papi what's wrong baby!" She looked at me with red and swollen eyes. I kissed her pouting lip and then she hugged me. I held her close as she began to calm down and then... round two! She began to cry all over again. "It's okay Mami...! It's okay. Let it all out baby... It's okay... Papi's here... let it all out!" She cried in my arms for about ten minutes until it all began to subside. I lifted her head up and I kissed her ever so gently. "You okay now?"

She nodded "Yeah baby... I feel better..."

"You sure you're okay?"

She placed her hand gently on my face and kissed me again and then threw her arms around me. I felt the heat coming off her body. I could smell the faint scent of her salty tears. "Yeah baby... I'm okay! Thank you." She slowly let go of me and I kissed her again. She began to wipe her tears.

(Gentlemen, now her saying '*Thank you*' is where you leave her alone. She's letting you know you can go now. She needs time to recuperate and she can't do that with you there, she needs her privacy now. Hey, three wives, two lovers, two daughters and countless nieces, I know what I'm doing!)

"Okay... I'll give you some time to get yourself together and I'll see you downstairs in a few, okay...?"

"I love you CJ!"

I gently touched her face with the back of my hand. "I love you too Jenny!"

(Remember! Your name spoken must be followed by her name in the response!)

I got up to leave and she got a tissue to blow her nose. I stopped at the doorway and turned to her. "Eventually... I'm going to want to know what this was all about... but take your time... I'm here for you whenever you need me!" I turned to leave and that's when I saw it. It was a pale blue, man's silk shirt, crumpled up in her bedroom trashcan. I knew exactly whose it was. It was the shirt that Jennifer kept as a memento and would wear whenever she missed Michael terribly. She would dance in it to whisk her away to a better place. Sometimes she would spray her pillow with his cologne if she couldn't sleep. Now the shirt was in the trash. Without getting closer I also saw the empty cologne bottle. I must have paused a little too long because Jenny came up behind me and hugged me tightly and sobbed.

"I'm scared!"

"I know baby... I understand..." I placed my hand behind her and gently guided her to my side. I now knew what happened. Why she was in such a sad mood. She was feeling nostalgic and put on Micheal's shirt and realized that she was out of his cologne, a brand that was no longer available. The sudden realization that 'it', her connection to Micheal, was gone and that she could never get it back tore into her emotions.

"No... you don't understand..." She said with a sad look on her face. "I don't want to lose you CJ..."

I held her hands to my waist. "I'm not going anywhere baby... You know I'll never leave you...!"

"That's what they all said!" and she hugged me tighter. I'm about 20 years older than Jennifer and I know why she's scared. She lost Michael, her first true love. She lost Steven, a man who was like a father to her. She lost Nick... I turned into her and held her close to me.

"I can't guarantee what the future will hold, no one can... I can only promise you that I will never leave you of my own volition...!" I kissed her again on her trembling lips.

"CJ...?"

"Yes?"

"I... I don't miss Michael anymore... Am I a bad person?"

"No baby... you're not a bad person. You've just gotten over your grief and you wanted to make sure it was okay to move on with your life..." Jenny held on to me as if she never wanted to let me go, I held her tightly and a tear came to my eye. I love this woman as much as I love Katherine and Katherine loves us both just as much! That's when I realized; Katherine set this all up so I could be alone with Jennifer. As much as Katherine acts like she has problems with Jenny, she absolutely loves her. So do I!

"CJ... there's one more thing..." I nodded my head. "The plot next to Michael..." she began.

"If you still wish to be buried next to Michael when the time comes... I don't have a problem with that..."

"You don't?"

I shook my head. "It doesn't matter where our bodies are... our souls will always be together..."

Jenny kissed me passionately and I reciprocated. "CJ?" she hissed.

"Yes Jenny?"

"Make love to me... I don't want a monkey fuck... I want you to make raw passionate love... to me..." Her eyes dropped and then she focused into mine. She bit her lower lip. "Please?"

"Silly rabbit!" And I kissed her gently. "I'm making love to you right now!"

"Ohhhhhhhh!" She moaned and she held me close and we slow danced in her bedroom to our own music. Sex is the greatest thing on earth, but love is the most powerful force in the universe!

The Tortured Soul Trilogy
(The Seduction of CJ Cassidy)
Chapter 140
(Crossing The Line)

Making love and having sex with Katherine or Jennifer is the most amazing experience any man could ever want. To have both of them is anybody's ideal fantasy. Not even porn stars have got it like I got it right now! Porn stars only perform the act; I have the unique situation of being truly in love with these two women. But still, like in any relationship, there are problems, differences of opinions, and personal conflicts that have to be dealt with. Sometimes you have to make sacrifices and compromises to make things work. But there are some things that can't be negotiated. There are lines that you just can't cross. With Jenny its lying and anal sex, with Katherine it's being restrained in a 'closed' position and disrespecting her privacy. With me, it's the giving and receiving of pain. I cannot for the life of me, hit a woman in any way that causes her pain, even if she enjoys it. I don't see that as a bad thing, but remember; I'm in love with two women who are into bondage and discipline. I like to role-play. I've tied the girls down. I've spanked them (playfully) until they got a rise out of it. I've taken the dominant position in our lovemaking. I've allowed the girls to take charge of our sexual encounters. I don't have a problem with that. It's always new and exciting, but there was an occasion when I felt it went too far. The girls crossed the line with me once, and it almost cost us our relationship. We don't talk about it anymore, but I wanted to mention it here. I feel that it's important.

Katherine has a 'game room' in the house Nick left her, used for the specific purpose of bondage and discipline. Jenny has all her 'toys' in her bedroom for when Katherine stays over. I mostly stay over at Jennifer's when I'm in Nevada when I visit. On one occasion, Katherine asked me to beat her with a belt; I refused. I wish it had ended there. The three of us were in bed cuddling, things got heated, (Well duh!) and we started rough foreplay and we were about to get into a little kinky sex. It was fun and playful... at first. Jennifer was maneuvering Katherine all over my body as she had done in the past. I closed my eyes as I enjoyed being the recipient of Katherine's tongue lashing when I heard a smack. Now, the girls will smack each other on the ass at times but this was a little louder than usual. When I opened my eyes I saw that Jenny had Katherine's arm in a 'chicken wing' hold and had used a leather paddle she pulled from under the mattress to hit her!

"Jennifer! Please let go of Katherine and put that away..." I said quietly.

"It's okay CJ... I don't mind..." Katherine moaned.

My face became very serious. "But I do mind!" I said sternly. "I told you two I'm not into that shit!"

"Oh CJ... bitch please!" Jenny said with a scoff in her voice. "You've been with us when we've been frisky before... besides, technically, you're *not* involved... Let us have our fun!"

I didn't say another word. I just got out of bed and started to get dressed. "CJ? Where are you going?" Katherine said.

"Oh let him go sleep on the couch!" Jenny cut in. You could tell she felt I was being high and mighty. I put on my socks and sneakers.

"CJ...?" Katherine asked with a very concerned tone in her voice. "Where *are* you going at this hour?"

"I'm leaving... I'm going back to New York..."

"*What*...?" Jenny said totally surprised as I left the room while putting on my shirt. Katherine ran up behind me with Jennifer a close second.

"Come back to bed!" Katherine pleaded. "I'm sorry! We're sorry!"

"Oh come on CJ! We just got a little carried away..." Jennifer said apologetically. "I didn't think you would mind! I... I wasn't thinking... CJ! Please!"

I grabbed my bag and picked up the phone and called Jinx. Jinx was on 24-hour call from Jenny's phone, but it bothered me that I may be disturbing him. "Sorry to wake you Jinx... could you stop by and take me to the airport?"

Jenny grabbed the phone out of my hand. "Jinx... never mind... CJ is staying..."

I grabbed the phone from Jenny. "Jinx? I know Jenny is your boss and it's her limo... but I would really appreciate a ride to the airport... If it's a problem for you, I'll just call a cab..."

"I'll be right over Mr. Cassidy…"

"Thanks Jinx… I owe you one…" I hung up the phone.

"I can't believe you're leaving over this!" Jenny said.

"When." I said quietly.

Katherine's eyes got wide. "CJ! NO!" and she put her hand over her mouth. "When" was the safety word they used when someone has had enough pain or the other was about to go too far. Katherine hugged Jenny and they started crying. They spent the next fifteen to twenty minutes trying to get me to stay. I didn't say a word to either of them. I quietly waited for Jinx to come get me. When Jinx arrived he looked at me and then looked at Jennifer.

"Take CJ to the airport Jinx…" Jenny sobbed.

"Yes Ms. Jones." And Jinx took my bag to the car. I kissed Katherine and Jenny goodbye and followed Jinx to the car. Jinx didn't say a word to me the entire ride. When he dropped me off he took out my bag and gave me the bodyguard hug.

"Mr. Cassidy…?"

"Yes Jinx?"

"It's none of my business, and I don't know what happened… but please find it in your heart to forgive them."

"Tell them, I forgive them… I just need a little time away… to teach them a lesson…"

"I understand Mr. Cassidy…"

"I just hope they understand Jinx… I hope they understand…" I traded in my return trip ticket for the next flight to Newark airport. Just when I was about to board is when I realized that I didn't have cab fare to get me back to New York. I took out my cell to call my house to see if my youngest was home and if she could pick me up. That's when I saw a text on my phone. It was from the girls. It simply said; *We're sorry! It will never happen again. We love you!* When I got home there were six voice mails from the girls on my machine. I called them without listening to any of the messages. Jenny answered the phone.

"CJ? When are you coming back?" Jenny said.

"Yeah baby… when we see you again?" Katherine said on the extension.

"I don't know yet… I'll have to think about it…'

"CJ? Come on… it was just…" Jenny said sobbing apologetically.

I breathed heavy into the receiver. "I thought Nick already taught you two bitches to respect a person's boundaries... now I guess I have to do it!" and I hung up. I just gave those two bitches a wake up call. I grew up being beaten by my mother almost every day straight for five years. It got to the point that I couldn't sleep unless I had a beating. As a child, acceptance was my survival mechanism. As an adult I put away childish things. I understand that the girls have pseudo-masochistic tendencies that they developed from years of abuse and I respect that they have learned to deal with it in their own unique way. I grew up in a house where my sisters were constantly beaten and abused. My sisters never found an easy way out. I don't ever want to remember what it's like to get used to the idea of being beaten. The girls brought me to a place that I thought I had left behind forever. I questioned our relationship, where was the line being crossed? Where does harmless fun become harmful? Most people will think that I over-reacted. That I should have just gone with the flow. But I cannot give any quarter; I cannot go back. I do not want to be ever brought back to that point in my life. I went to bed without even getting undressed and cried like a baby. I didn't want to lose these two, but a man has to do what a man has to do! They both called me everyday for the next three days. I took their call on the fourth day. We talked on the phone everyday for two months until I was able to see them again. We never spoke about that day again and they never pushed the issue ever again. I'm not into that scene and as amazing sex is with them; I have no problem cutting all sexual ties with them if they can't or won't respect me, or my wishes. I truly do love them, but I will not compromise who I am for them, not for anybody! I have no desire of being caught up in a situation where I may be involved in intentionally causing pain to any woman... It's just how I am, and I like me this way! I know I'm not the pick of the litter, but I'm quite sure I wouldn't have problems finding a woman who is okay with who I am. And if I don't, I have absolutely no problems with living the rest of my life all alone.

When we finally did get back together, we had to redefine our parameters. We renegotiated our limitations. Every relationship is based to some degree on a slave/master relationship. There is always a give and take that is necessary in order for there to be a balance. There has to be a mutual respect of each other's space and for the person that they are. Boundaries must be set and you have to develop a level of trust that allows each partner to say 'when'. It doesn't require pain and punishment.

We talked over dinner; we talked over the phone. We talked over a few bottles of wine. We even talked while having intense sexual relations. Communication is the key to any successful relationship. We arrived at an agreement we could all live with. It's hard to believe, but sex with them... got better! They became more willing to satisfy my needs once they learned to respect me. It was my simple act of passive dominance that took them to a higher level of sexual performance. They discovered that I didn't have to hit them for them to acquiesce to my authority.

Jenny was right, sex is better once you learn to respect your partner.

The Tortured Soul Trilogy
(The Seduction of CJ Cassidy)
Chapter 141
(Thanksgiving Is For Family)

The following chapter is about what happened over the Thanksgiving weekend. My daughters had made Thanksgiving dinner and we were about to sit to eat when the doorbell rang. To my surprise, my daughters had arranged to have Katherine and Jennifer spend the weekend with me. We had a very special Thanksgiving, my four girls and I. After dinner, my daughters drove to PA to stay with family so that we could have our privacy. My daughters knew that our vacation in Jamaica didn't work out the way we planned so this was their gift to us. I love my daughters. I love Katherine and Jennifer. I could not have had a better holiday. The next day, Katherine, Jennifer and I spent the day taking full advantage of the Black Friday sales. Katherine and Jennifer made the centurion on their Amex cards cry!

The next day the girls woke up late, I was downstairs, checking my website, sending out holiday cheer to friends and family. Once Jennifer got up I had to get off the net. Jenny still doesn't like it when I'm on my computer if we're together. It cuts into our quality time. We had the last of the leftovers and then settled down to watch TV. We were catching up on all my favorite cop shows, the CSI's, Criminal Minds, House, The Closer and Boston Legal and we just enjoyed our time together. Finally we watched a 'chick flick'.

There we sat cuddled into each other, one on either side of me. It felt good to be close to them. It gave me warm feeling to have them near me. I was in the most peaceful state of mind I have ever been in my life. It was at this point that Jennifer unzipped my pants and pulled out my cock. I kissed her forehead as she gently stroked me. She continued to watch TV and stroke me until I was hard. Katherine then leaned into me and began to kiss and suck my cock. I don't know how to say this. It wasn't at all sexual. I know, I know, how could one beautiful woman stroking my cock while another was giving me soft, sensual fellatio not be sexual, is hard to fathom. I placed my left hand on Katherine's head and stroked her hair and my right around Jennifer's shoulder and gently stroked her nipple while I kissed her. We sat there and comforted each other. That's what it was, comfort. We each knew what the other wanted right then, and we allowed each other to give each of us what we needed. It was the ultimate showing of trust between three people. We allowed each to have what we needed without having it have to go any further than the gift of trust.

Now I truly know in my very soul that I love these two amazing women.

The Tortured Soul Trilogy
(The Seduction of CJ Cassidy)
Chapter 142
(What's Love Got To Do With It?)

A few months later we were staying at Jenny's. We had gone to bed early. We had a quick romp and fell asleep in each other's arms. I got up because I couldn't sleep. I had something on my mind. I guess Katherine woke up first and realized that I wasn't in bed and came looking for me.

"CJ...? CJ are you here? Where are you?" Katherine called.

"Marco!" I said.

"Polo!" She answered. She found me sitting in the living room with the lights off. "What are you doing sitting in the dark all alone?" And she turned on the lamp. "What's wrong baby? Is something bothering you?"

"Yeah... we need to talk..." Katherine just nodded her head. It was at this point that Jennifer wandered into the room rubbing the sleep out of her eyes.

"Why is everyone up? What's going on?" She closed her silk robe because the house was a little chilly.

"CJ needs to talk with us..."

"Again??? I thought we settled all our shit already!"

Katherine held Jenny's hand. "Come on... you know we'll always be there for each other, no matter how many times it takes to get things right...'

Jennifer sat next to her on the couch "You're right Katherine... I'm sorry CJ... you know how I get when I don't get my beauty sleep..."

"Yeah... you get 'ugly'..."

"Bitch!" and she gave me the finger.

"I love you too!" I answered.

"I need a drink, you want anything?" Katherine asked.

"Get me a glass of wine please..." Jenny mumbled.

"CJ?"

"No... I'm good..."

"You sure?"

"Yeah baby... I'm sure..." Katherine went to the wine rack and pulled out two bottles.

"You want red or a white Jenny?"

"Pour me a white..." Katherine poured the wine and brought Jenny her glass. Katherine sat down and they both sipped their wine.

"So? What do you want to talk about CJ?" Jenny asked.

"I've never broken the law before and I don't intend to start now... I'm too cute to do hard time..."

"What the fuck are you talking about?" Jenny said concerned. I now had her undivided attention. Katherine just put her hand on Jenny's knee to calm her.

"What's going on CJ... why would you say something like that...?" Katherine asked me.

"You know I love the both of you..."

"We love you too..." Jenny said. I held up my finger to stop her. "I'm sorry... go ahead speak your piece..." Jenny sat back and sipped her drink.

"I love the two of you more than I've ever loved any one person in my life and finding love with one person is rare enough, but to find two..."

Katherine looked at me concerned. "CJ... what are you getting at?"

I stood up, reached into both my pockets, pulled out two ring boxes and kneeled down. I opened the two boxes with my thumbs and held them out to each of them. "It's time I made honest women out of the two of you... Would you both do me the honor of being my wives?" Jennifer put her hand on her bosom and was rendered speechless; Katherine's mouth was wide open.

"W...W... what?" Katherine stuttered.

"Are you fucking kidding me...?" Jenny exclaimed. They each put their wine glasses down, reached for the ring boxes and stood up and stared at each other.

"I know the three of us can't have a legal ceremony..." I said. They exchanged the boxes with each other and looked at them. They seemingly had forgotten I was there. "Hello? Bad knees here... anyone listening to me?" They took the rings out of the boxes and placed them on each other's fingers and said to each other. "Will you marry me?" Both nodded to each other and kissed passionately. I raised my arms to them. "Hello...? I'm still in the room... and technically... I asked first!" They slowly turned to me, screamed and tackled me.

"Of course we'll marry you... you bitch!" Katherine gushed.

"Yeah bitch! What the fuck took you so long to ask us?" Jenny added.

"Hey... I knew I would want to marry either one of you but I couldn't figure out who I should ask. Then it dawned on me... '*Why break up a set*?' and I only got the nerve to ask the both of you about an hour ago!"

"If you were thinking about asking only one of us...why did you buy two rings?"

"I thought it would be tacky to propose to the other with the same ring if one of you turned me down." They showered me with kisses. Jennifer started to give me a hickey. "Hey!" I said. "No need to mark your territory now!"

Katherine laughed but Jenny didn't stop. "How did you pay for the rings...? Are the books doing that well?" Katherine asked.

I had a hard time answering Katherine with Jennifer making me a little woozy. "Not really... I worked some overtime... I had to sell some blood... work the pole... you know, the usual...!"

"So that's why you've been broke the past few months?" Jenny said as she stroked my fresh hickey.

"Pretty much!" I said. "Did she leave a mark?" I asked Katherine.

Katherine checked it. "Oh yeah!" She then turned my head around and gave me one to match on the other side.

"Anything else you two wanna suck on?" I said sarcastically. They both looked at me and smiled. "No! That's not what I meant... right... this... minute!"

They laughed. And we all went back to bed. None of us could sleep. Oh don't get it twisted, we weren't having sex, they were up all night planning the wedding! I had to go on-line to check sites for whatever they needed for the event. Oh sure! NOW Jenny has NO problem with me being on-line!

About six weeks later, we had a mock four-ring wedding ceremony. One I bought for each of the girls and they had the jeweler meld the two weddings rings they each bought me into one ring bridged with three diamonds signifying the three of us being together forever. They looked absolutely stunning as they came down the aisle in their coordinated wedding gowns. Cisco and Jinx brought each of them down the aisle and L.L. was the matron of honor for Jenny, my ex-wife Mandy was Katherine's. My daughters made the most beautiful bridesmaids. Katherine and Jennifer stood on either side of me as we recited our vows witnessed by close friends and family members (Those who actually showed up, there are a few people who still have issues with our relationship! Fuck'em!) As we finished our vows I whispered to them. "I can't believe you two wore white!" They both punched me in the stomach... Hard!

We now have taken permanent residence in Jenny's house and Katherine kept the brownstone that Nick left her. The girls use it so they can have their B&D sessions. I still don't get involved in that and I don't interfere with their right to privacy or to enjoy their fetishes. Oh, we do a little spanky-spanky every once and again, but I still leave the really rough stuff between the two them.

Have I ever told you how much I love these two crazy bitches?

The Tortured Soul Trilogy
(The Seduction of CJ Cassidy)
Chapter 143
(It's Not All Kittens & Giggles!)

We're on our way to church... (Yeah church! What?) Jenny just ran up the stairs for the third time because she doesn't like what she's wearing. We call that *"The Jenny Twist"* She walks towards you and then her hips kind of rotate quickly around and she's going back the way she came while saying *'Give me a minute, I'll be right back!'* now, for those of you who are *'hating on me'* as Jenny would say, life is not easy. I'm not going to give you a fairy tale ending here. It's not all 'kittens and giggles'. We still have our drama. We still have our ups and downs like any other... illegal... extended family. Yeah, we know we're not technically married. (Not even in Utah!) There was no marriage license and no one presided over the ceremony, but we did commit our lives to each other. There are too many legal marriages preformed where there is no commitment at all! Times are good; times are bad... Sex is great; sex is so-so! Sometimes these two bitches get on my last nerve and sometimes I have to seriously reconsider falling asleep in their presence! But... we're generally a very happy... *triple*? And I wouldn't trade my life with these two for anything in the world... And after all is said and done... isn't that the true nature of a happy marriage?

Sure the sex is amazing and exciting, but I am also spending time with them, laughing, crying and sometimes just 'being'... with them. It's nice... I not only love these two, I 'like' them. I don't mind having a heated conversation with them; I don't mind that Katherine cheats at cards. I don't mind that Jennifer snores like a busted chain saw sometimes. They don't mind that I'm perfect in every way... Pffftt! (Even I couldn't keep a straight face on that one!)

I'm not caught up in just the fantasy; I'm caught up with the reality. And that's nice... real nice!

I was on my way home to our main place at Jennifer's when Jinx detoured the car and went towards Katherine's brownstone that Nick left her instead. "Jinx? What's up? Is there a problem?"

"No sir... Ms. Jones... I'm sorry... Mrs. Jennifer Cassidy asked me to take you there instead..." and Jinx smiled.

"Okay then..." And I leaned back on the seat and fixed myself a drink. I knew there wasn't any problem... the girl's said they were going to redecorate the brownstone and probably needed my help painting or moving furniture. We arrived about twenty minutes later and Jinx let me out and shook my hand.

"Good luck Mr. Cassidy..."

I looked at Jinx. "You know you make me nervous when you call me 'Mr. Cassidy... Call me CJ..."

"Good luck CJ...!" and he patted me on the back just as the front door opened and Jenny and Katherine waved to me. Jinx got in the car and drove off. I headed towards the house.

"Hey baby!" Katherine said; she kissed me and so did Jenny.

"How are my girls?"

"We're good!" Jenny said and she handed me a drink. I love coming home to these two wonderful women.

"What's going on?"

"Nothing... we're just happy you're here..."

"Ah huh!" I was a little nervous. I still didn't know what these two were up to. I looked around the apartment and nothing was any different. "I thought you two redecorated in here?"

"We only redecorated... one... room..." Jenny said guardedly.

I looked at them. "Which room?" Katherine took my hand and led me to the game room. I resisted a bit. "You've shown me that room before... I'm not really interested in any changes you made in there..."

Jenny got behind me and nudged me a bit. "Please... just take a look at what we did..." Jenny asked. Her voice was soft and reassuring, I looked at Jenny funny. It was almost like she was begging for approval. I took a sip of my drink, nodded and allowed the girls to lead me to the closed door, but we all knew I would never go in there.

"Close your eyes..." Katherine said; I complied. I heard the door open.

"Open your eyes..." The girls said with excitement but concern in their voice.

I opened my eyes and... "HOLY SHIT!" I exclaimed. Jenny took the drink out of my hand and I slowly entered the room and slowly took in everything I saw in wonder and amazement. They had taken a room that was full of toys and trappings of pain and torture and turned it into...

A baby nursery!!!

Tears welled into my eyes as I looked at the crib, the changing station and all the kids' toys all around me. I turned to the girls, who were now standing in the doorway waiting for my reaction. They both had tears in their eyes. I pointed to them each very excited but confused. "Which one of you is...?" They both shook their heads no. Now I was even more confused. "We're... gonna... *adopt*...?" I asked. Katherine cried tears of joy, Jenny smiled and both girls ran in the room and hugged me.

"If you want to..." Jenny said. "But we're hoping to have our own..."

"We just wanted you to know that we want to have your children and..." Katherine hesitated.

"And... we're giving up the pain...! No more B&D! We're gonna give it up for you Papi!" Jennifer finished.

"You're joking? You two are gonna give up kinky sex? For me?"

"Aint nobody said that shit!" Jenny laughed. "We're still gonna get our freak on... all three of us..."

"We're just giving up the whips, chains and handcuffs... no more chastising, no more beatings... no more pain... I hope you don't mind?"

I looked around the room and shook my head no. "I don't mind ladies *but...* can we... *keep* the handcuffs...?" The girls hugged and kissed me. "You're giving up 'the pain'...? For real...? For good...?" I said. Jenny nodded.

"Besides... we're getting a little old for that..." Katherine said.

"Speak for yourself bitch... I'm still young and hot and I'm making a huge sacrifice here...!" Katherine shook her head and laughed. "I'm serious!" Jenny said. "But seriously... I'm over it... it's time to let that shit go... once and for all..." Katherine nodded and hugged Jennifer. "So? You never said if you liked the room?" Jenny said.

"I love it... but..." The girls looked at me.

"But what?" Katherine said.

"I think there's another room in this house that needs some serious work done in..."

"What room...?" Jenny asked.

"The bedroom... you two get your hot little asses in there... right now!" The girls sighed and ran into the bedroom. Jenny came back and held up her handcuffs...

"Katherine wants to know if you... wanna put on your policeman's uniform?" I nodded. Jenny ran back to the bedroom. I opened my wallet, took out my condoms and threw them in the garbage. I went to the bathroom and took a Viagra. Papi is gonna put in some overtime this weekend!

I know I've told you, I know I've said it before, but I really do mean it... I just love these two bitches! And they love me!

I was sitting at Jenny's desk editing my last novel in preparation to send it to my publisher, when Katherine came out of the kitchen ad kissed my on top of my head. "I love you!" She said.

"I love you too baby!" and I kissed her hand.

And she kissed my lips and put her arms around my neck and hugged me.

"CJ...?"

"Yeah baby, what?" I said as I typed.

"I want you to tell them..."

I stopped typing and looked at her.

"You want me to 'tell them'...?" I repeated quizzically.

"Jenny and I had a long talk about it... I think it's time I finally came out..." I could not believe what I was hearing. I have been keeping her identity secret for almost ten years now!

"You sure you want me to tell everybody who you really are? Are you sure you want to do that?"

"No... I'm not ready to tell the world who I am..." she paused and took a deep breath. "I want you to tell everybody what happened to me..."

I shrugged my shoulders and shook my head. What did I miss? I thought to myself.

"All of it..." she sighed.

My eyes opened wide. "What brought this on?"

"Your friend Carrie posted pictures of her surgery... If she can be that brave..."

"Baby? Are you sure about this? You really want to do that?"

She nodded. "I deal with it, Jenny deals with it and God bless you, you deal with it. I don't care what anybody else thinks, they're just going to have to deal with it too!"

"If I tell... eventually everyone will figure out who you are...! Are you really sure you want to go there?" She kissed me and nodded yes, a tear came to my eye.

"Yeah... I want to go there." She whispered. And she kissed me again and went back into the kitchen where Jenny was helping to cook dinner. (Yeah Jenny helps out in the kitchen now... she's getting better but we still won't let her fly solo yet... but I digress...)

Now that you have read this biography, you'll understand why what Katherine has asked me to do is so hard for me to do. I don't agree that I should reveal this, but it is Katherine's wish and I have done and will do anything for her to make her happy. This is a very big step for her and I am so very proud of her right now.

Here goes...

Just after *"A Tortured Soul – The Unauthorized Biography of Nicholas Anderson"* was published. Katherine was stalked and ambushed by one of her previous abusive partners. Sometimes you can't just walk away; sometimes they come back, when you least expect it. Katherine held fast to her strength and she was not going to go back to the abuse that she had endured for so very long. "Johnny" wasn't going to have any of it.

One day while Katherine was doing some shopping and returning to her car 'Johnny' came up behind her and threw a chemical in her face, disfiguring her for life. She turned her head in time to save her beautiful eyes, but she was badly burned on the left side of her face, ear and neck. She has had several surgeries to correct her features. Only if you look very closely, can you tell that something 'isn't quite right'. For all intent and purposes she looks normal and the scars have healed, but the emotional scar of the attack... still lingers. It is the reason I will NEVER reveal her true identity. I will not allow anyone to hurt my Katherine, under any circumstances. You may find this strange, but she has been attacked in the 'media' and our networking sites for being a coward and a hypocrite; a coward for not revealing her identity and a hypocrite for claiming that she hates abuse and yet still lives the life of a B&D fetisher.

I say here to all the women who have thanked Katherine for standing up to her abusers and for allowing her story to be told, that she does NOT regret her decision. She does not regret the 'insult' she endured by making that decision. Instead of regret, she only feels convinced and convicted that she doesn't have to put with abuse from any man or any woman. Her resolve to say 'when' has not been shaken by the repercussions of her taking control of her life. Yes, the result was severe, but Katherine has told me that she would not go back and change her mind to free herself from the abuse... for any reason! That might not make sense to some, but what she endured in the past made her the woman she is today. She became the woman that Jennifer and I love very dearly. It tempered her spirit. It strengthened her will. It taught her how to truly love herself and to know who truly loves her. She is a better person because of it. Jenny and I are better persons, for knowing and loving her. I cry each and every time I receive an email from someone who tells me "Thank You!" for telling a story that they themselves could not tell; thank you for alleviating my pain, by sharing yours. I cry when I hear that someone freed themselves from their own personal hell, because of Katherine's story and sacrifice!

(You ladies know who you are because even to this day I still tell each and every one of you how much I love you!)

The plaque in the game room says: "That which does not kill us, only serves to make us stronger" It's still in the nursery to remind us.

I was once asked a hypothetical question; "If the person you loved was suddenly disfigured... would you stay with them?"

I could not answer the question. Sure, the 'proper' answer is yes, but saying the right answer and doing the right thing, don't always go hand in hand. Until you experience it, you never truly know what you would do. Now I know what I would do, I will stay with Katherine for as long as she will have me.

Oh yeah... Jennifer too!

Love You! Cherish You! Adore You!
The Cassidy Family

"Over Time"
By Katherine Inez Stark

Over Time - You notice that he's always been your best friend.

Over Time - You notice that no one else has ever made you laugh as hard, or held your hand so tightly.

Over Time - You notice that you've always had a shoulder to cry on with the strongest arms to hold you up and to lean on.

Over Time - Flaws become endearing. Quirks bring a smile to your face. Every complaint was nothing more than a mere cry for his attention.

Over Time - Every conversation was a learning experience.
Every disagreement drew you closer to each other. Every second apart felt like an eternity.

Over Time - Comfort lived in his eyes. Strength lied in his voice. And together you moved mountains of pain and hurt.

Over Time - The hard days seemed small. The biggest problems seemed menial. And you've never gone a day without hearing 'I love you!'

Over Time - There was no more 'I' but 'we'. There was no more 'me' but 'us'. And you never questioned the unity of your heart.

Over Time - No one deserved more of your respect. No one deserved more of your understanding. No one deserved more or your love.

A love that started when God brought us together and blessed our union and created a standard of trust, loyalty and admiration that was strengthened... *Over Time*.

One of the greatest lines in a film was the final line in the classic movie; "The Maltese Falcon" starring Humphrey Bogart and Sydney Greenstreet. In the last scene a detective holds the black bird and asks Sam Spade.

"What is this?"

To which Sam Spade ponders and responds: *"The stuff that dreams are made of!"*

The End.

Great film, great cast, great line; there is mystery, intrigue, murder, mayhem, lovers betrayed, sacred bonds broken, a treasure hunt for a statue of a black bird worth millions... everything that makes a movie great. And that wonderful closing line: *"The stuff that dreams are made of!"*

Poignant, stirring, deep... until I realized something, something I never had realized before. I was struck by an epiphany that changed the entire meaning of the film. It changed how I felt about too many things in my life...

"The stuff that dreams are made of!"

A poignant line, but even more poignant when I realized... The Maltese Falcon... was revealed at the end of the movie... to be a fake! Not worth millions but made of lead painted over with black lacquer...

There was no shorter route to India; Columbus discovered America...

There was no fountain of youth; Vasco DeGama explored Florida...

The moon isn't made of green cheese... man headed to the stars!

What's more important? The goal? Or the journey? Or does the mirage only lead us down a path to own destruction? Why do I say this here? What am I trying to express? It's quite simple. The novel I have written here is based on the actual events of our lives and those of very close friends of mine, but the stories have been altered and romanticized to the point that the fine line between reality and fiction has been blurred. Did The Maltese Falcon really exist? Or was it a just a figment of someone's imagination with the sole purpose to inspire to achieve more?

You decide.

"It becomes easier when you realize the truth…"
"And what is the truth?"
"There is no spoon!"
'The Matrix'

- - -

"Life isn't about waiting for the storm to pass; it's about learning to dance in the rain!"

Anonymous.

"Pain and fear is the final hurdle that we must overcome, in order to survive."

C.J. Cassidy.

"Our pain may define who we are, but it does not have to control how we live."

Katherine Inez Stark.

"Sometimes… we just put our big girl panties on, and deal with it!"

Jennifer X. Jones.

If you or anyone you know is the victim of:
Domestic Violence, Spousal Abuse
Or Sexual Harassment

- - -

Seek Professional Help - Get Professional Help
Talk to Somebody!

- - -

You Are *NOT* Alone!

- - -

Get help to learn how to say: *WHEN*! You do NOT have to put up with it! I know you can do this! Nick did, Katherine did, Maggie and Mandy did, even I did... So can YOU!

Look Under State Resources in the Government Section of the Yellow Pages or Under the Crime Victims Board.

Or Call The National Abuse Hotline
1-800-799-SAFE

There IS help out there for you!

Love You! Cherish You! Thinking of You!

"May you have all the love and passion, and none of the heartache and pain!"

Katherine, Jennifer and C.J.Cassidy

This novel is the edited works of these novels
Written by Erotic Author C.J. Cassidy
All are available from Amazon.com

Living La Vida Puta - CJ Cassidy w/T. Oceanside
ISBN-10: *1-4392-6445-7*

The Confessions of Jennifer X
ISBN-10: *141969202X*

A Tortured Soul – The Unauthorized Biography of Nicholas Anderson
ISBN-10: *1419684337*

The Seduction of C.J. Cassidy
ISBN-10: *1439239967*

Jennifer, Katherine and C.J. donated recipies for this cookbook
whose proceeds help victims of domestice violence.
(Yeah Jennifer donated a recipe too, *what?*)
Please go to their website to buy a copy today!

"Remembering the Sabores of My Cocina"
**Supporting Alianza, the National Latino Alliance
For the Elimination of Domestic Violence**
To order go to: www.dvalianza.org

"The Tortured Soul Trilogy of Pain & Pleasure"

The Edited Works of Erotic Author C.J. Cassidy

ISBN-13: 978-1460934302
ISBN-10: 146093430X

To order additional copies
Go To CreateSpace.com/3565615

Or to contact C.J. Cassidy
http://www.myspace.com/duecexmachina
or
DueceXmachina@msn.com

Join us on FaceBook - Cee Jay Cassidy
Or
CJTorturedSoul @ Twitter

I'm through writing novels about the trials and tribulations of the women I know and love. It's heartbreaking and exhausting. I just don't have the strength anymore. I have enough on my plate just handling my relationship with Katherine and Jennifer. I will still however, lend moral support to any woman in need.

Suddenly there was a knock at the door.

"I'll get it!" I said into the house. I opened the door to find a beautiful, petite young lady standing there. She was about 26 years old and had soft, smooth mocha skin, a lot like Mandy. She was wearing simple eyeglasses like Katherine's. She had a lion's mane of hair that framed her beautiful face and had a broad smile that could make the sun shine during a thunderstorm. She was holding in her arms a notebook and a file folder filled with different papers and loose pages.

"Can I help you?" I asked.

She thrust her hand out to shake mine. She had the bubbly exuberance of a cheerleader.

"Hi! I'm Naughty... I'd like to get your help with my biography..."

(*FUCK ME*! Here we go again!)

Made in the USA
Lexington, KY
22 June 2012